# RESOLUTIONS,

## LAWS, AND ORDINANCES,

RELATING TO THE

PAY, HALF PAY, COMMUTATION OF HALF PAY, BOUNTY LANDS,
AND OTHER PROMISES MADE BY CONGRESS,

TO THE

## OFFICERS AND SOLDIERS OF THE REVOLUTION;

TO THE

SETTLEMENT OF THE ACCOUNTS BETWEEN THE UNITED
STATES AND THE SEVERAL STATES;

AND TO

## FUNDING THE REVOLUTIONARY DEBT.

Originally published: Washington, DC, 1838
Reprinted 1998 by Genealogical Publishing Co., Inc.
1001 N. Calvert St. / Baltimore, MD 21202
Library of Congress Catalogue Card Number 97-77442
International Standard Book Number 0-8063-1337-4
*Made in the United States of America*

The publisher gratefully acknowledges the
loan of the original of this book by the
Maryland State Law Library
Annapolis, Maryland

*This book was reproduced by the photo-offset process from
the original edition. A characteristic of the original, from which
the printer worked, was that the image was uneven and many
pages were discolored by age. Every effort has been made by
our printer to produce as fine a reprint of the original as possible.*

In compliance with the Resolution of the House of Representatives of the United States of April 11, 1836, which directs that " the Clerk of this House cause to be compiled, for the use of the House, in chronological order, and under appropriate heads, all the Resolves and Acts of Congress relating to the pay, half pay, commutation of half pay, bounty lands, and other promises made by Congress to the Officers and Soldiers of the revolutionary army; also, a synopsis of the provisions for funding the revolutionary debt of the United States, and of the several Acts in aid thereof; also, the Acts of the old and present Governments for the settlement of the accounts between the United States and the several States, and such other general information, to be ascertained from the archives of the Government, as may be useful in the settlement of revolutionary claims now pending," I have the honor to submit the following.

WALTER S. FRANKLIN,
*Clerk of the House of Representatives.*

# CONTENTS.

## CHAPTER IX.

## CHAPTER X.

## CHAPTER XI.

# RESOLUTIONS, LAWS, AND ORDINANCES

### RELATING TO

PROMISES MADE BY CONGRESS TO OFFICERS AND SOLDIERS OF THE REVOLU-
TION ; TO SETTLEMENT OF ACCOUNTS BETWEEN THE UNITED STATES
AND THE SEVERAL STATES; AND TO FUNDING THE REVOLUTIONARY
DEBT.

---

## CHAPTER I.

*Resolutions and Acts of the old and new Governments, relating to the
pay, depreciation of pay, half pay, and commutation in lieu of half
pay, promised to the Officers and Soldiers of the Revolution.*

[1775, June 16.]

*Resolved,* That two major generals be appointed for the American
army ;

That the pay of each of the major generals be one hundred and sixty-
six dollars per month ;

That when any of these act in a separate department, he be allowed,
for his pay and expenses, three hundred and thirty-two dollars per month;

That there be eight brigadier generals ;

That the pay of each of the brigadier generals be one hundred and
twenty-five dollars per month ;

That there be one adjutant general ;

That his pay be one hundred and twenty-five dollars per month ;

That there be one commissary general of stores and provisions ;

That his pay be eighty dollars per month ;

That there be one quartermaster general for the grand army, and one
deputy under him for the separate army ;

That the pay of the quartermaster general be eighty dollars per month,
and that of the deputy forty dollars per month ;

That there be one paymaster general, and a deputy under him, for the
army, in a separate department; that the pay, for the paymaster general
himself, be one hundred dollars per month ; and for the deputy paymaster,
under him, fifty dollars per month ;

That there be one chief engineer at the grand army, and that his pay
be sixty dollars per month ;

That two assistants be employed under him, and that the pay of each
of them be twenty dollars per month ;

That there be one chief engineer for the army, in a separate department, and two assistants under him ; that the pay of the chief engineer
be sixty dollars per month, and the pay of the assistants each twenty dollars per month ;

That there be three aids-de-camp, and that their pay be thirty-three dollars per month each;

That there be a secretary to the general, and that his pay be sixty dollars per month;

That there be a secretary to the major general, acting in a separate department, and that his pay be thirty-three dollars per month;

That there be a commissary of musters, and that his pay be forty dollars per month.

[1775, July 29.]

*Resolved,* That the pay of the commissary general of musters be forty dollars per month;

Deputy commissary general of stores and provisions, sixty dollars per month;

Deputy adjutant general, fifty dollars per month;

Deputy muster-master general, forty dollars per month;

Brigade major, thirty-three dollars per month;

Commissary of artillery, thirty dollars per month;

Judge advocate, twenty dollars per month;

Colonel, fifty dollars per month;

Lieutenant colonel, forty dollars per month;

Major, thirty-three dollars and one-third per month;

Captain, twenty dollars per month;

Lieutenant, thirteen dollars and one-third per month;

Ensign, ten dollars per month;

Sergeant, eight dollars per month;

Corporal, drummer, and fifer, each seven dollars and one-third per month;

Private, six dollars and two-thirds per month;

Adjutant, eighteen dollars and one-third per month;

Quartermaster, eighteen dollars and one-third per month;

Chaplain, twenty dollars per month;

That in the artillery, the pay of a captain be twenty-six dollars and two-thirds per month;

Captain lieutenant, twenty dollars per month;

Lieutenants, first and second, eighteen dollars and one-third per month;

Lieutenant fire-worker, thirteen dollars and one-third per month;

Sergeant, eight dollars and one-third per month;

Corporal, seven dollars and a half per month;

Bombardier, seven dollars per month;

Matross, six dollars and five-sixths of a dollar per month;

That the appointment of provost-marshal, wagon-master, and master-carpenter, be left to the commander-in-chief of the army, who is to fix their pay; having regard to the pay they receive in the ministerial army, and the proportion that the pay of the officers in said army bears to the pay of our officers.

[1776, July 5.]

*Resolved,* That a chaplain be appointed to each regiment in the continental army, and that their allowance be increased to thirty-three dollars and one-third of a dollar per month.

[1778, April 18.]
*Resolved,* That the pay of a brigadier of cavalry be one hundred and fifty-six dollars and a quarter per month.

NOTE.—Under subsequent organizations of the army, the pay of the officers of the *general staff* was, at various periods, increased or modified. Such changes, however, had no bearing on the ultimate promises of Congress, involving commutation pay and bounty lands, at the conclusion of the war; such pay and bounty being explicitly limited and regulated by the *lineal* rank of the officers to whom it was granted.

---

*Half pay for seven years to officers, and a gratuity of $80 to the non-commissioned officers and soldiers.*

[1778, May 15.]
*Resolved, unanimously,* That all military officers commissioned by Congress, who now are, or hereafter may be, in the service of these United States, and shall continue therein during the war, and not hold any office of profit under these States, or any of them, shall, after the conclusion of the war, be entitled to receive annually, for the term of seven years, if they live so long, one-half of the present pay of such officers : *Provided,* That no general officer of the cavalry, artillery, or infantry shall be entitled to receive more than the one-half part of the pay of a colonel of such corps respectively : *And provided,* That this resolution shall not extend to any officer in the service of the United States, unless he shall have taken an oath of allegiance to, and shall actually reside within, some one of the United States.

*Resolved, unanimously,* That every non-commissioned military officer and soldier who hath enlisted, or shall enlist, into the service of these States for and during the war, and shall continue therein to the end thereof, shall be entitled to receive the further reward of eighty dollars at the expiration of the war.

[1778, May 27.]
Monthly pay of the officers and soldiers of the continental lines, as established by the resolutions of Congress, fixing the arrangement of the American army on the 27th of May, 1778, which rate of pay (as it regarded *rank in the line of the army*) continued to the end of the war, and formed the basis of the settlements with the officers for their commutation of five years' full pay.

## I. INFANTRY.

| Commissioned. | Pay per month. | Commissioned. | Pay per month. |
|---|---|---|---|
| Colonels, - - | $75 | Sergeant majors, - | $10 |
| Lieutenant colonels, | 60 | Quartermaster sergeants, | 10 |
| Majors, - - | 50 | Sergeants, - - | 10 |
| Captains, - - | 40 | Drum majors, - | $9\frac{1}{2}$ |
| Captain lieutenants, | $26\frac{2}{3}$ | Fife majors, - | 9 |
| Lieutenants, - | $26\frac{2}{3}$ | Drummers and fifers, | $7\frac{1}{2}$ |
| Ensigns, - - | 20 | Corporals, - - | $7\frac{1}{3}$ |
| Surgeons, - - | 60 | Privates, - - | $6\frac{2}{3}$ |
| Surgeon's mates, - | 40 | | |

2

Paymasters, ⎫ taken ⎧ $20 ⎫
Adjutants, ⎬ from the ⎨ 13 ⎬ In addition to their pay as officers in the line.
Quartermasters, ⎭ line, ⎩ 13 ⎭

## II. ARTILLERY.

| Commissioned. | Pay per month. | Commissioned. | Pay per month. |
|---|---|---|---|
| Colonels, | $100 | Quartermaster sergeants, | $11\frac{23}{90}$ |
| Lieutenant colonels, | 75 | Drum majors, | $10\frac{38}{90}$ |
| Majors, | $62\frac{1}{2}$ | Fife majors, | $10\frac{38}{90}$ |
| Captains, | 50 | Sergeants, | 10 |
| Captain lieutenants, | $33\frac{1}{3}$ | Bombardiers, | 9 |
| First lieutenants, | $33\frac{1}{3}$ | Corporals, | 9 |
| Second lieutenants, | $33\frac{1}{3}$ | Gunners, | $8\frac{2}{3}$ |
| Surgeons, | 75 | Drummers and fifers, | $8\frac{2}{3}$ |
| Surgeons' mates, | 50 | Matrosses, | $8\frac{1}{3}$ |
| Sergeant major, | $11\frac{23}{90}$ | | |

Paymaster, ⎫ to be taken ⎧ $25 ⎫
Adjutant, ⎬ from the ⎨ 16 ⎬ In addition to their pay as officers in the line.
Quartermaster, ⎭ line. ⎩ 16 ⎭

## III. CAVALRY.

| | | | |
|---|---|---|---|
| Colonel, | $93\frac{3}{4}$ | Quartermaster sergeant, | $15 |
| Lieutenant colonel, | 75 | Sergeants, | 15 |
| Major, | 60 | Trumpet major, | 11 |
| Captain, | 50 | Trumpeters, | 10 |
| Lieutenant, | $33\frac{1}{3}$ | Corporals, | 10 |
| Cornet, | $26\frac{2}{3}$ | Dragoons, | $8\frac{1}{3}$ |
| Surgeons, | 60 | Saddler, | 10 |
| Surgeons' mates, | 40 | Farrier, | 10 |
| Riding master, | $33\frac{1}{3}$ | | |

Paymaster, ⎫ to be taken ⎧ $25 ⎫
Adjutant, ⎬ from the ⎨ 15 ⎬ In addition to their pay as officers in the line.
Quartermaster, ⎭ line. ⎩ 15 ⎭

## IV. PROVOST.

| | | | |
|---|---|---|---|
| Captain of provosts | $50 | Corporals, | $10 |
| Lieutenants, | $33\frac{1}{3}$ | Trumpeter, | 10 |
| Clerk, | $33\frac{1}{3}$ | Provosts or privates, | $8\frac{1}{3}$ |
| Sergeants, | 15 | Executioner, | 10 |

## ENGINEERS.

| | | | |
|---|---|---|---|
| Captains, | $50 | Corporals, | $9 |
| Lieutenants, | $33\frac{1}{3}$ | Privates, | $8\frac{1}{3}$ |
| Sergeants, | 10 | | |

Aid-de-camp, ⎫ $24 ⎫
Brigade quartermaster, ⎬ 24 ⎬ In addition to their pay as officers in the line.
Brigade major, ⎭ 15 ⎭

*One year's pay to supernumerary officers.*

[1778, November 24.]

Whereas, from the alteration of the establishment, and other causes, many valuable officers have been, and may be, omitted in the new arrangement as being supernumerary, who, from their conduct and services, are entitled to the honorable notice of Congress, and to a suitable provision until they can return to civil life with advantage :

*Resolved, therefore,* That Congress gratefully acknowledge the faithful services of such officers, and that all supernumerary officers be entitled to one year's pay of their commissions respectively, to be computed from the time such officers had leave of absence from the commander-in-chief on this account : and Congress do earnestly recommend to the several States to which such officers belong, to make such further provision for them as their respective circumstances may entitle them to.

[1779, May 22.]

*Resolved,* That all continental officers who are or may be exchanged, and not continued in the service, be, after such exchange, considered as supernumerary officers, and entitled to the pay provided by the resolution of Congress of the 24th November last.

---

*Half pay for seven years granted to officers, &c., extended to widows and orphans of those officers, &c.*

[1780, August 24.]

*Resolved,* That the resolution of the 15th day of May, 1778, granting half pay for seven years to the officers of the army who should continue in the service to the end of the war, be extended to the widows of those officers who have died, or shall hereafter die, in the service ; to commence from the time of such officers' death, and continue for the term of seven years : or if there be no widow, or in case of her death or intermarriage, the said half pay be given to the orphan children of the officer dying as aforesaid, if he shall have left any ; and that it be recommended to the Legislatures of the respective States to which such officers belong, to make provision for paying the same on account of the United States ; that the restricting clause in the resolution of May 15, 1778, granting half pay to the officers for seven years, expressed in these words, viz : " and not hold any office of profit under these States, or any of them," be, and is hereby, repealed.

---

*Pay and establishment of the officers of the hospital department and medical staff.*

[1780, September 30.]

*Resolved,* That the pay and establishment of the officers of the hospital department and medical staff be as follows :

Director, 150 dollars per month, two rations for himself, and one for his servant, per day, and forage for two horses.

Chief physicians and surgeons of the army and hospitals, each 140 do. lars per month, two rations per day, and forage for two horses.

Purveyor and apothecary, each 130 dollars per month.

Physicians and surgeons of the hospitals, each 120 dollars per month, one ration per day, and forage for one horse.

Assistant purveyors and apothecaries, each 75 dollars per month.

Regimental surgeons, each 65 dollars per month, one ration per day, and forage for one horse.

Surgeons' mates, in the hospitals, 50 dollars per month, one ration per day.

Surgeons' mates in the army, 45 dollars per month, one ration per day.

Steward for each hospital, 35 dollars per month, one ration per day.

Wardmaster for each hospital, 25 dollars per month, one ration per day.

---

*Half pay for seven years to supernumerary officers, under the reform of the army, to take effect on the 1st January, 1781.*

1789, October 3.]

Whereas, by the aforegoing arrangement, many deserving officers must become supernumerary, and it is proper that regard be had to them :

*Resolved*, That, from the time the reform of the army takes place, they be entitled to half pay for seven years, in specie, or other current money equivalent, and also grants of lands at the close of the war, agreeably to the resolution of the 16th September, 1776.

---

*Half pay for life to supernumerary officers, under the reform of the army, to take effect on the 1st January, 1781.*

[1780, October 21.]

*Resolved*, That the commander-in-chief and commanding officer in the Southern department direct the officers of each State to meet and agree upon the officers for the regiments to be raised by their respective States, from those who incline to continue in service, and where it cannot be done by agreement, to be determined by seniority, and make return of those who are to remain ; which is to be transmitted to Congress ; together with the names of the *officers reduced*, who are to be allowed *half pay for life*.

That the officers who shall continue in the service to the end of the war shall also be entitled to *half pay during life*, to commence from the time of their reduction.

[1780, November 28.]

Some doubts having arisen in the minds of the general officers, whether the resolution of the 21st October last, granting half pay for life to the officers who shall remain in service to the end of the war, was meant to extend to them :

*Resolved*, That the said half pay for life be extended to all major generals and brigadier generals who shall continue in service to the end of the war :

That the resolution of the 21st October was so meant and intended.

*Allowance during life in lieu of half pay to the officers of the hospital department and medical staff.*

[1781, January 17.]

Whereas, by the plan for conducting the hospital department, passed in Congress the 30th day of September last, no proper establishment is provided for the officers of the medical staff, after their dismission from public service, which, considering the custom of other nations, and the late provision made for the officers of the army, after the conclusion of the war, they appear to have a just claim to : for remedy whereof, and also for amending several parts of the above-mentioned plan,

*Resolved*, That all officers in the hospital department and medical staff hereinafter mentioned, who shall continue in service to the end of the war, or be reduced before that time as supernumeraries, shall be entitled to, and receive during life, in lieu of half pay, the following allowance, viz :

The director of the hospital equal to the half pay of a lieutenant colonel.

Chief physicians and surgeons of the army and hospital, and hospital physicians and surgeons, purveyor, apothecary, and regimental surgeons, each equal to the half pay of a captain.

---

*Half pay for life to chaplains.*

[1781, May 8.]

*Resolved*, That the commander-in-chief be, and he is hereby, authorized and directed to arrange the brigade chaplains of the several State lines serving with the army, and the commanding general of the Southern army, those of the line serving with that army ; so as to retain in service no more chaplains of each line than are equal to the number of brigades.

That every chaplain deemed and certified to the board of war to be supernumerary, be no longer continued in service, and be entitled to have their depreciation made good, and to the half pay of captains for life.

---

*Resolutions relating to depreciation of pay.*

[1780, April 10.]

*Resolved*, That when Congress shall be furnished with proper documents to liquidate the depreciation of the continental bills of credit, they will, as soon thereafter as the state of the public finances will admit, make good to the line of the army and the independent corps thereof the deficiency of their original pay, occasioned by such depreciation, and that the money and articles heretofore paid or furnished, or hereafter to be paid or furnished by Congress or the States, or any of them, as for pay, subsistence, or to compensate for deficiencies, shall be deemed as advanced on account, until such liquidation as aforesaid shall be adjusted ; it being the determination of Congress that all the troops serving in the continental army shall be placed on an equal footing: *Provided*, No person shall have any benefit of this resolution, except such as were engaged to serve during the war, or for three years, and are now in service, or shall hereafter engage during the war.

[1781, December 31.]

On report of the committee appointed to confer with the commander-in-chief, to whom was referred the report of the board of war, respecting a number of officers not belonging to the line of any particular State or separate corps of the army :

*Resolved,* That all officers of the line of the army, below the rank of brigadier general, who do not belong to the line of any particular State or separate corps of the army, and are entitled by acts of Congress to pay and subsistence, shall have the same, with the depreciation of their pay, made good to the first day of January, 1782.

*Resolved,* That the Secretary of War be, and he is hereby, directed to make returns to Congress, on or before the 20th day of January, 1782, of the names and rank of all the officers necessary to be retained in service, that are included in the preceding resolution.

*Resolved,* That all officers included in the foregoing description, and whose names shall not be inserted in the returns directed to be made in the preceding resolution, shall be considered as retiring from service on the 1st day of January, 1782: *Provided, always,* That nothing contained in these resolutions shall be construed so as to prevent or hinder any officer that shall retire as aforesaid, from enjoying all the emoluments that he may, upon retiring, be entitled to by any former acts of Congress.

*Resolved,* That it be recommended to the several States, respectively, to settle the depreciation of the pay of all the officers that are inhabitants of their respective States, and shall retire from service under the preceding resolutions, in the same manner as they settled with the officers of the line of their State, and charge the same to the United States; and that the depreciation of all the officers of the line of the army, not being inhabitants of the United States, nor belonging to the line of any State, be settled upon the same scale by which the settlement was made with the officers and privates of Colonel Hazen's regiment.

NOTE.—The several States, in compliance with the recommendation of Congress, made settlements with the officers and soldiers belonging to each of them, respectively, for the depreciation of their pay, commencing on the 1st January, 1777, and estimating in specie all sums of continental money by them received at different periods, agreeably to scales of depreciation made for the purpose, and granted certificates for the balances found due ; all of which was charged against the United States in the settlement of the accounts of the respective States with the United States.

---

*Commutation for five years' full pay in lieu of the half pay for life promised by the resolutions of the 3d and 21st October, 1780.*

[1783, March 22.]

On the report of a committee, together with a memorial of the officers of the army, Congress came to the following resolutions :

Whereas the officers of the several lines under the immediate command of his excellency General Washington, did, by their late memorial transmitted by their committee, represent to Congress that the half pay granted by sundry resolutions was regarded in an unfavorable light by the citizens of some of these States, who would prefer a compensation for a limited term of years, or by a sum in gross, to an establishment for life ; and did, on that account, solicit a commutation of their half pay for an equivalent in one of the two modes above mentioned, in order to remove all subject of dissatisfaction from the minds of their fellow-citizens : and whereas Congress are desirous as well of gratifying the reasonable expectations of the officers of the army as of removing all objections which may exist in any part of the United States to the principle of the half-pay establishment, for which the faith of the United States hath been pledged : persuaded that those objections can only arise from the nature of the compensation, not from any indisposition to compensate those whose services, sacrifices, and sufferings have so just a title to the approbation and rewards of their country : Therefore,

*Resolved*, That such officers as are now in service, and shall continue therein to the end of the war, shall be entitled to receive the amount of five years' full pay in money, or securities on interest, at six per cent. per annum, as Congress shall find most convenient, instead of the half pay promised for life by the resolution of the 21st day of October, 1780 ; the said securities to be such as shall be given to other creditors of the United States : *Provided*, It be at the option of the lines of the respective States, and not of officers individually in those lines, to accept or refuse the same : *And provided, also,* That their election shall be signified to Congress through the commander-in-chief, from the lines under his immediate command, within two months, and through the commanding officer of the Southern army from those under his command, within six months, from the date of this resolution : That the same commutation shall extend to the corps not belonging to the lines of particular States, and who are entitled to half pay for life as aforesaid ; the acceptance or refusal to be determined by corps, and to be signified in the same manner, and within the same time, as above mentioned : That all officers belonging to the hospital department, who are entitled to half pay by the resolution of the 17th day of January, 1781, may collectively agree to accept or refuse the aforesaid commutation, signifying the same, through the commander-in-chief, within six months from this time : That such officers as have retired at different periods, entitled to half pay for life, may collectively, in each State of which they are inhabitants, accept or refuse the same; their acceptance or refusal to be signified by agents authorized for that purpose, within six months from this period : That with respect to such retiring officers, the commutation, if accepted by them, shall be in lieu of whatever may be now due to them since the time of their retiring from service, as well as of what might hereafter become due ; and that so soon as their acceptance shall be signified, the Superintendent of Finance be, and he is hereby, directed to take measures for the settlement of their accounts accordingly, and to issue to them certificates bearing interest at six per cent : That all officers entitled to half pay for life not included in the preceding resolution, may also collectively agree to accept or refuse the aforesaid commutation, signifying the same within six months from this time.

[1783, May 16.]

*Resolved*, That the commutation in lieu of half pay, as well to chaplains as to the officers of the hospital department and medical staff, shall be calculated by what they are respectively entitled to, agreeably to the resolutions of the 17th of January and 8th of May, 1781.

[1784, January 26.]

*Resolved*, That half pay cannot be allowed to any officer, or to any class or denomination of officers, to whom it has not heretofore been expressly promised.

[1784, February 11.]

The committee to whom was referred a letter of 20th January last, from J. Pierce, paymaster general, respecting claims which have been made by certain officers to half pay and the commutation for half pay, report:

" That, by a resolve of November 24, 1778, it was provided that all deranged officers should be entitled to one year's pay; and it was further provided, that officers who had been prisoners with the enemy, and then were, or thereafter might be exchanged, should, if appointed by the authority of the State, be entitled to return into the service in the same rank they would have had if they had not been captured, under certain restrictions, and that they should receive half pay till the time of their entering again into the service. Under this act certain officers claim half pay to the end of the war, and the commutation for half pay from that period during life: on which the committee observe, that the half pay first mentioned was promised as a temporary support to such officers as should be reappointed by their respective States, and to none besides; and that all other continental officers who have been prisoners with the enemy, and deranged, are entitled to one year's pay, and nothing besides. That such was the intention of Congress, is explained by the subsequent acts of May 22, 1779, and May 26, 1781. There is no act under which those officers can claim the commutation for half pay. It is provided, by a resolve of the 28th June, 1782, 'that there shall be such additional pay and emoluments to the pay of captains and subalterns serving as aids-de-camp to major and brigadier generals, and to brigade majors, as shall make their pay and emoluments equal to the pay and emoluments of a major in the line of the army.' Under this resolution certain aids and brigade majors, who are captains or subalterns in the line, claim commutation equal to that of a major in the line. This claim appears, for sundry reasons, to be ill-founded. The offices which those gentlemen held out of the line were temporary, and the additional pay and emoluments were certainly promised to them while they continued to serve in those offices, and no longer. If they are supposed to found their claim to the commutation of a major, under the head of additional emoluments, their claim must be ill-founded; for it is clear, from the terms of the resolution, that pay and emoluments do not signify the same thing, but the commutation is the substitute for pay alone, or half pay, and not for rations nor any other emolument. On the whole, the committee are of opinion that the paymaster general, in settling the accounts of the army, in all claims which may be brought for half pay or commutation, should be determined by the act of the 26th January, 1784."

*Resolved*, That Congress agree to the said report.

[1785, March 8.]

*Resolved*, That the officers who retired under the resolve of the 31st December, 1781, are equally entitled to the half pay or commutation with those officers who retired under the resolves of the 3d and 21st October, 1780.

[1828, May 15.]

An Act for the relief of certain surviving officers and soldiers of the army of the Revolution.

Sec. 1. *Be it enacted by the Senate and House of Representatives of the United States of America in Congress assembled,* That each of the officers of the army of the Revolution in the continental line, who was entitled to half pay by the resolve of October twenty first, seventeen hundred and eighty, be authorized to receive, out of any money in the Treasury not otherwise appropriated, the amount of his full pay in said line, according to his rank in the line, to begin on the third day of March, one thousand eight hundred and twenty-six, and to continue during his natural life : *Provided,* That under this act no officer shall be entitled to receive a larger sum than the full pay of a captain in said line.

Sec. 2. *And be it further enacted,* That whenever any of said officers has received money of the United States as a pensioner, since the third day of March, one thousand eight hundred and twenty-six, aforesaid, the sum so received shall be deducted from what said officer would otherwise be entitled to under the first section of this act; and every pension to which said officer is now entitled shall cease after the passage of this act.

Sec. 3. *And be it further enacted,* That every surviving non-commissioned officer, musician, or private, in said army, who enlisted therein for and during the war, and continued in service until its termination, and thereby became entitled to receive a reward of eighty dollars, under a resolve of Congress passed May fifteenth, seventeen hundred and seventy-eight, shall be entitled to receive his full monthly pay in said service, out of any money in the Treasury not otherwise appropriated, to begin on the third day of March, one thousand eight hundred and twenty-six, and to continue during his natural life : *Provided,* That no non-commissioned officer, musician, or private, in said army, who is now on the pension list of the United States, shall be entitled to the benefits of this act.

Sec. 4. *And be it further enacted,* That the pay allowed by this act shall, under the direction of the Secretary of the Treasury, be paid to the officer or soldier entitled thereto, or to their authorized attorney, at such places and days as said Secretary may direct; and that no foreign officer shall be entitled to said pay, nor shall any officer or soldier receive the same, until he furnish to said Secretary satisfactory evidence that he is entitled to the same, in conformity to the provisions of this act; and the pay allowed by this act shall not, in any way, be transferable or liable to attachment, levy, or seizure, by any legal process whatever, but shall enure wholly to the personal benefit of the officer or soldier entitled to the same by this act.

Sec. 5. *And be it further enacted,* That so much of said pay as accrued by the provisions of this act before the third day of March, eighteen hundred and twenty-eight, shall be paid to the officers and soldiers entitled to the same, as soon as may be, in the manner and under the provisions before mentioned; and the pay which shall accrue after said day, shall be paid semi-annually, in like manner, and under the same provisions.

3

[1832, July 5.]

An Act to provide for liquidating and paying certain claims of the State of Virginia.

Sec. 1. *Be it enacted by the Senate and House of Representatives of the United States of America in Congress assembled,* That the proper accounting officers of the Treasury do liquidate and pay the accounts of the Commonwealth of Virginia against the United States, for payments to the officers commanding in the Virginia line in the war of the Revolution, on account of half pay for life promised the officers aforesaid by that Commonwealth, the sum of one hundred and thirty-nine thousand five hundred and forty-three dollars and sixty-six cents.

Sec. 2. *And be it further enacted,* That the Secretary of the Treasury be, and he is hereby required and directed, to pay to the State of Virginia the amount of the judgments which have been rendered against the said State, for and on account of the promise contained in an act passed by the General Assembly of the State of Virginia, in the month of May, anno Domini one thousand seven hundred and seventy-nine, and in favor of the officers or representatives of officers of the regiments and corps hereinafter recited, and not exceeding, in the whole, the sum of two hundred and forty-one thousand three hundred and forty five dollars, to wit:

*First.* To the officers, or their legal representatives, of the regiment commanded by the late Colonel George Gibson, the amount of the judgments which they have obtained, and which are now unsatisfied.

*Second.* To the officers, or their legal representatives, of the regiment denominated the second State regiment, commanded at times by Colonels Brent and Dabney, the amount of the judgments which they have obtained, and which are now unsatisfied.

*Third.* To the officers, or their legal representatives, of the regiments of Colonels Clark and Crockett, and Captain Rogers's troop of cavalry, who were employed in the Illinois service, the amount of the judgments which they have obtained, and which are now unsatisfied.

*Fourth.* To the officers, or their legal representatives, serving in the regiment of State artillery, commanded by the late Colonel Marshall, and those serving in the State garrison regiment, commanded by Colonel Muter, and serving in the State cavalry, commanded by Major Nelson, the amount of the judgments which they have obtained, and which are now unsatisfied.

*Fifth.* To the officers, or their legal representatives, who served in the navy of Virginia, during the war of the Revolution, the amount of the judgments which they have obtained, and which are now unsatisfied.

Sec. 3. *And be it further enacted,* That the Secretary of the Treasury be, and he is hereby, directed and required to adjust and settle those claims for half pay, of the officers of the aforesaid regiments and corps, which have not been paid or prosecuted to judgments, against the State of Virginia, and for which said State would be bound, on the principles of the half-pay cases already decided in the supreme court of appeals of said State; which several sums of money herein directed to be settled or paid shall be paid out of any money in the Treasury not otherwise appropriated by law.

[1835, March 3.]

By the fourth section of the act entitled " An act.to continue the office of Commissioner of Pensions," approved the 3d day of March, 1835, the

duties to be performed by the Secretary of the Treasury, under the provisions of the two last-recited acts, were transferred to, and made the duties
of, the Secretary of War, from and after the first day of June, eighteen
hundred and thirty-five.

## CHAPTER II.

*Resolutions, Ordinances, and Acts of the old and new Governments, providing Bounty Lands for the Officers and Soldiers of the Revolution.*

[1776, September 16.]

*Resolved*, That eigthy-eight battalions be enlisted as soon as possible, to serve during the present war; and that each State furnish their respective quotas in the following proportions, &c.

That Congress make provision for granting lands in the following proportions : to the officers and soldiers who shall so engage in the service, and continue therein until the close of the war, or until discharged by Congress, and to the representatives of such officers and soldiers as shall be slain by the enemy.   Such lands to be provided by the United States ; and whatever expense shall be necessary to procure such land, the said expense shall be paid and borne by the States, in the same proportion as the other expenses of the war, viz :

|  |  |  |
|---|---|---|
| To a colonel - - - | 500 | acres. |
| "  " lieutenant colonel - - | 450 | " |
| "  " major, - - - | 400 | " |
| "  " captain, - - - | 300 | " |
| "  " lieutenant, - - - | 200 | " |
| "  " ensign, - - - | 150 | " |
| each non-commissioned officer and soldier | 100 | " |

[1776, September 18.]

That the bounty and grants of land offered by Congress, by a resolution of the 16th instant, as an encouragement to the officers and soldiers to engage in the army of the United States during the war, shall extend to all who are or shall be enlisted for that term.

[1776, November 12.]

*Resolved*, That all non-commissioned officers and soldiers, who do not incline to engage their service during the continuance of the present war, and shall enlist to serve three years, unless sooner discharged by Congress, shall be entitled to and receive all such bounty and pay as are allowed to those who enlist during the continuance of the present war, except the 100 acres of land; which land is to be granted to those only who enlist without such limitation of time.

[1780, August 12.]

*Resolved*, That the provision for granting lands by the resolution of September 16, 1776, is hereby extended to the general officers, in the following proportion :

|  |  |  |
|---|---|---|
| To a major general, - - | 1,100 | acres. |
| "  " brigadier general, - - | 850 | " |

*Extract from the resolutions of Congress of this date, establishing the hospital department and medical staff.*

[1780, September 30.]

*Resolved*, That the several officers whose pay is established as above (except the stewards and ward-masters) shall, at the end of the war, be entitled to a certain provision of land, in the proportion following, viz :

The director to have the same as a brigadier general ;

Chief physician and purveyor the same as a colonel ;

Physicians and surgeons and apothecary, the same as a lieutenant colonel ;

Regimental surgeons, and assistants to the purveyor and apothecary, the same as a major ;

Hospital and regimental surgeons' mates, the same as a captain.

[1780, October 3.]

Congress, by their resolutions of this date, made a new arrangement of the army, to take effect on the 1st January following; and, on the ground that, by said arrangement, many deserving officers must become supernumerary, and it was proper that regard be hard to them, it was

*Resolved*, That, from the time the reform of the army takes place, they be entitled to grants of land at the close of the war, agreeably to the resolution of the 16th September, 1776.

---

*Ordinance of Congress for ascertaining the mode of disposing of the public lands in the Western Territory.*

[1785, May 20.]

Whereas Congress, by their resolutions of the 16th and 18th September, 1776, and 12th August, 1780, stipulated certain grants of lands to certain officers and soldiers of the late continental army ; and by their resolution of the 30th day of September, 1780, stipulated grants of land to certain officers in the hospital department and medical staff of the late continental army : for complying, therefore, with such engagements, *Be it ordained*, That the Secretary of War, from the returns in his office, or such other sufficient evidence as the nature of the case may admit, determine who are the objects of the above resolutions and engagements, and the quantity of land to which such persons, or their representatives, are respectively entitled ; and cause the townships, and fractional parts of townships, hereinbefore reserved for the use of the late continental army, to be drawn for in such manner as he shall deem expedient to answer the purpose of an impartial distribution.

---

*Supplementary ordinance of Congress.*

[1788, July 9.]

*Be it further ordained*, That the Secretary of War issue warrants for bounties of land to the several officers and soldiers of the late continental army, who may be entitled to such bounties, or to their respective assigns or legal representatives, certifying therein the rank or station of each officer, and the line, regiment, corps, and company in which the officer or soldier served.

1800, March 1.]

Sec. 5. *And be it further enacted,* That after the priority of location shall have been determined, and after the proprietors or holders of warrants for military services shall have designated the tracts by them respectively elected, it shall be the duty of the Secretary of the Treasury to designate, by lot, in the presence of the Secretary of War, fifty quarter townships, of the lands remaining unlocated; which quarter townships, together with the fractional parts of townships remaining unlocated, shall be reserved for satisfying warrants granted to individuals for their military services, in the manner hereafter provided.

Sec. 6. *And be it further enacted,* That the land in each of the quarter townships designated as aforesaid, and in such of the fractional parts of quarter townships as may then remain unlocated, shall be divided by the Secretary of the Treasury, upon the respective plats thereof, as returned by the Surveyor General, into as many lots, of one hundred acres each, as shall be equal, as nearly as may be, to the quantity such quarter township or fraction is stated to contain; each of which lots shall be included, where practicable, between parallel lines, one hundred and sixty perches in length, and one hundred perches in width, and shall be designated by progressive numbers upon the plat or survey of every such quarter township and fraction, respectively.

Sec. 7. *And be it further enacted,* That from and after the 16th day of March next, it shall be lawful for the holder of any warrant granted for military services, to locate, at any time before the first day of January, one thousand eight hundred and two, the number of one hundred acres expressed in such warrant, on any lot or lots from time to time remaining unlocated within the tracts reserved as aforesaid; and upon surrendering such warrant to the Treasury, the holder thereof shall be entitled to receive a patent, in the manner and upon the conditions heretofore prescribed by law; which patent shall, in every case, express the range, township, quarter township, or fraction, and number of the lot located as aforesaid: but no location shall be allowed, nor shall any patent be issued, for any lot or lots of one hundred acres, except in the name of the person originally entitled to such warrant, or the heir or heirs of the person so entitled; nor shall any land, so located and patented to a person originally entitled to such warrant, be considered as in trust for any purchaser, or be subject to any contract made before the date of such patent; and the title to lands acquired in consequence of patents issued as aforesaid, shall and may be alienated in pursuance of the laws which have been or shall be passed in the Territory of the United States northwest of the river Ohio, for regulating the transfer of real property, and not otherwise.

NOTE.—Prior to the year 1800, no locations of military land warrants granted by the United States could be made, unless such locations embraced an entire quarter township of 4,000 acres; consequently, no officer or soldier of the continental army could effect a location of the quantity of land embraced by the warrant he received for his services, unless he united with other officers and soldiers, or the holders of such warrants, and, together, surrendered to the Secretary of the Treasury such number thereof as would amount to the quantity of 4,000 acres. These pre-existing evils were remedied by the measures embraced in the act of Congress of the 1st March, 1800.

[1802, April 26.]

By the second section of the act of Congress of this date, it was made the duty of the Secretary of War to receive claims to lands for military services until the first day of January thereafter, and no longer.

NOTE.—Subsequent to the limitation fixed by the act of 1802, Congress, by successive acts, passed at intervals of from two to five years, continued to authorize the issue of military land warrants to the officers and soldiers of the continental lines whose claims for bounty lands remained unsatisfied ; the last of which acts was passed on the 27th January, 1835, and extended the time for such issues to the 1st day of January, 1840.

---

[1830, May 30.]

Act for the relief of certain officers and soldiers of the Virginia line and navy, and of the continental army of the revolutionary war.

*Be it enacted by the Senate and House of Representatives of the United States in Congress assembled,* That the officers and soldiers, sailors and marines, who were in the service of Virginia on her own State establishment during the revolutionary war, and who were entitled to military land bounties by the laws and resolutions of that State, their heirs and assigns, shall be, and they are hereby, authorized to surrender to the Secretary of the Treasury of the United States such of their warrants for the said land bounties as shall remain unsatisfied in whole or in part, and to receive certificates or scrip for the same, at any time before the first day of January, in the year one thousand eight hundred and thirty-five; which certificates or scrip shall be issued by the said Secretary, and signed by him, and countersigned by the Commissioner of the General Land Office, in the following manner, that is to say : There shall be a separate certificate or scrip for such sum as shall, at the time of issuing the same, be equal to the then minimum price of each quantity of eighty acres of land due by such warrant, and remaining unsatisfied at the time of such surrender ; and a like certificate or scrip for such sum as, at the time, shall be equal to the minimum price of the quantity that shall so remain unsatisfied of any such warrant, after such subdivisions of the amount into quantities of eighty acres ; and where any such warrant shall have been lost or mislaid by time or accident, it shall and may be lawful for the party desiring to surrender the same, to surrender an official copy thereof, certified under the seal of the land office of Virginia, with the affidavit of the party endorsed upon or accompanying the same, stating that such warrant has been lost or mislaid, and that the original hath not been sold or transferred, to the knowledge or belief of the party so surrendering, or his or her guardian.

Sec. 2. *And be it further enacted,* That it shall be the duty of the Commissioner of the General Land Office to request the Executive of Virginia to furnish him with a statement of all such warrants, within the purview of this act, as have already issued, showing the number and date of each warrant, and the quantity of acres granted by each ; and also a monthly statement of the same description, showing the number, date, and quantity of such warrants as shall hereafter be granted. And no warrant shall be taken to be within the provisions of this act, which shall hereafter be granted, unless the Executive of Virginia shall cause a certificate to be endorsed thereon, signed by some proper officer, stating that

4

the party to whom such warrant shall be so granted, his, her, or their ancestor or devisor, was entitled thereto by some law or resolution of the said State, in force at the time of the deed of cession by the State of Virginia to the United States.

Sec. 3. *And be it further enacted*, That, before the Secretary of the Treasury shall issue the scrip required by the provisions of this bill, the applicants shall produce to him the certificate of the register of the land office in Kentucky, and the certificate of the surveyor of the military lands of the Virginia line, that the warrant (when the original is presented,) or the copy (when the original has been lost or destroyed) has not been located, surveyed, or patented, in Kentucky, attested by the seal of his office.

Sec. 4. *And be it further enacted*, That the certificates or scrip to be issued by virtue of this act shall be receivable in payment of any lands hereafter to be purchased at private sale, after the same shall have been offered at public sale, and shall remain unsold at any of the land offices of the United States established, or to be established, in the States of Ohio, Indiana, and Illinois. And all such certificates or scrip as shall be issued by virtue of this act, shall be assignable by endorsements thereon, attested by two witnesses: *Provided*, That all certificates or scrip to be issued in virtue of any warrant hereafter to be granted, shall be issued to the party originally entitled thereto, or to his heir or heirs, devisee or devisees, as the case may be.

Sec. 5. *And be it further enacted*, That the provisions of this act shall be deemed and taken to extend to all such officers, soldiers, sailors, marines, chaplains, musicians, surgeons, and surgeons' mates, in the land or sea service of the State of Virginia during the revolutionary war, and, generally, to every person to whom the State had engaged to pay a land bounty for services in that war, of any description, by any law or resolution passed before, and in force at the date of the said deed of cession; except only such persons as are mentioned in, and provided for by, the reservation contained in the said deed of cession in favor of the officers and soldiers of the said State on continental establishment: *Provided*, That no scrip issued under the provisions of this act shall entitle the holder to enter or purchase any settled or occupied lands, without the written consent of such settlers or occupants as may be actually residing on said lands at the time the same may be entered or applied for: *And provided, also*, That the amount of land thus located shall not exceed two hundred and sixty thousand acres.

Sec. 6. *And be it further enacted*, That the provisions of the first and fourth sections of this act shall extend to, and embrace, owners of military land warrants issued by the United States in satisfaction of claims for bounty lands for services during the revolutionary war; and that the laws heretofore enacted, providing for the issuing said warrants, are hereby revived, and continued in force for two years.

Sec. 7. *And be it further enacted*, That the provisions of this act shall also be deemed and taken to extend to all the unsatisfied warrants of the Virginia army on continental establishment: *Provided*, That the quantity thereof shall not exceed fifty thousand acres, in addition to the two hundred and sixty thousand acres heretofore authorized to be located by their State line.

[1832, July 13.]

By the act of Congress of this date, the further quantity of three hundred thousand acres was appropriated, to be applied in the manner provided for by the aforesaid act of the 30th May, 1830.

[1833, March 2.]

By the act of Congress of this date, the further quantity of two hundred thousand acres of land was appropriated, to be applied in the manner provided for in the aforesaid acts of the 30th May, 1830, and 13th July, 1832.

[1835, March 3.]

By the act of Congress approved this date, six hundred and fifty thousand acres of land were appropriated, in addition to the quantity heretofore appropriated by the acts of May 30, 1830, July 13, 1832, and March 2, 1833, to be applied in the manner provided for in said acts.

---

[1835, January 27.]

Act to extend the time of issuing military land warrants to the officers and soldiers of the revolutionary army.

Sec. 1. *Be it enacted by the Senate and House of Representatives of the United States of America in Congress assembled,* That the time allowed for issuing military land warrants to the officers and soldiers of the revolutionary army shall be extended to the first day of January, eighteen hundred and forty.

## CHAPTER III.

*Resolutions, Ordinances, and Acts of the old and new Governments relating to the Settlement of the Accounts between the United States and the several States.*

[1787, May 7.]

An Ordinance for settling the accounts between the United States and individual States.

*Be it ordained by the United States in Congress assembled,* That five commissioners be appointed by the board of treasury, whose duty it shall be to go to the several States in the districts hereafter mentioned, for which they may be respectively appointed, for the purpose of stating the accounts of the States within those districts, against the United States.

That the States of New Hampshire, Massachusetts, Connecticut, and Rhode Island, form one district. That the States of New York and New Jersey form one district. That the States of Pennsylvania, Delaware, and Maryland, form one district. That the States of Virginia and North Carolina form one district. And that the States of South Carolina and Georgia form one district.

That it shall be the duty of the said commissioners respectively to receive of the States for which they are appointed, all their accounts and vouchers for payments made on account of bounties, pay, and depreciation of pay, to the late army of the United States; and for advances to the militia called out under the authority of the United States, and actually in their service; and to give descriptive acknowledgments thereof to the States from which they may be received; which accounts and vouchers shall be immediately forwarded to the commissioner of army accounts, whose duty it shall be to examine and pass such as are authorized by the resolves of Congress, and supported by proper vouchers; and to state such as may not fall under the above description, together with such remarks as may tend to elucidate the nature of these claims.

That it shall further be the duty of the said commissioners to receive in like manner the accounts and vouchers for money paid, and supplies furnished on the requisitions of Congress, made previously to October, 1781; and to forward the same to the office of the Comptroller of the Treasury.

That it shall also be the duty of the said commissioners to receive and examine all the claims of the States to which they are appointed, against the United States, for advances or disbursements by them made for the use of the late commissary, quartermaster, clothing, marine, and hospital departments, or under any other description whatsoever; to pass upon all such as are authorized by the resolves of Congress, and supported by proper vouchers, so far as it respects the evidence offered in support of the said claims; and to state such as are not thus warranted or supported, together with such remarks as may explain the nature of these accounts, and the reasons offered for the deficiency of vouchers.

*And be it further ordained by the authority aforesaid,* That on all the accounts aforesaid, interest shall be allowed at the rate of six per cent. per annum, agreeably to the resolves of Congress.

And whereas it is essential to the welfare of the confederacy, that the accounts of the several States should be speedily adjusted; that this adjustment should be effected on uniform principles; and that provision should be made for allowing such advances or disbursements as may have been made by the respective States for the use of the Union, although the same be not sanctioned by the resolves of Congress, or supported by regular vouchers :

*Be it therefore ordained,* That the several States be, and they are hereby, limited to the space of six months for exhibiting to the proper commissioner their claims against the United States, of whatever nature the same may be; and that such States as may neglect to exhibit the same within that period of time, after the commissioner has notified to the supreme Executive thereof that he is ready to proceed on the business of his commission, shall be precluded from any future allowance; but shall nevertheless stand chargeable with all advances of money or other articles which may have been made to them respectively by the United States, and with whatever balances may be yet due on their several quotas of the general requisitions.

*And be it further ordained,* That the said commissioners of districts shall, within twelve months after they enter on the duties of their several appointments, repair to the place where the United States in Congress may hold their sessions, with such accounts and vouchers as they may have in possession, and deliver the same to the Comptroller of the Treasury ; on which their commission shall terminate.

*Be it further ordained,* That a board, consisting of three commissioners, be appointed by the United States in Congress assembled, whose duty it shall be to receive from the Comptroller of the Treasury, and from the commissioner of army accounts, all the accounts and claims of the several States deposited in their respective offices, and to examine such of the said accounts as shall have been passed by the commissioners of the several districts, in order that the same may be finally adjusted on uniform and equitable principles, having reference to the settlement of accounts heretofore made by the commissioners of the different States : *Provided,* That such revision of the accounts above mentioned shall not in anywise affect the validity of the vouchers admitted by the commissioners of the respective districts.

*And be it further ordained,* That wherever it shall appear to the said board of commissioners that advances or disbursements, payments or supplies, of the description aforesaid, have been made by any of the States subsequent to the 18th of April, 1775, for articles or services for the use of the United States, that the said commissioners be, and they are hereby vested with full power and authority to make such allowance for the same as they shall think consistent with the principles of general equity, although such advances or disbursements may not be sanctioned by the resolves of Congress, or supported by regular vouchers, so as to enable the said commissioners to make a final adjustment of all the accounts subsisting between the United States and the several members thereof, agreeably to such quota as Congress shall hereafter determine.

*And be it further ordained,* That a determination of a majority of the aforesaid board of commissioners on the claims submitted to them shall be final and conclusive ; and that their commission shall continue in force for one year and a half from the time of their entering on the duties of their office, unless sooner revoked by Congress.

*And be it further ordained,* That the ordinance of the 13th of October, 1786, entitled "An ordinance for establishing a board to liquidate and settle all accounts between the United States and individual States," be, and it is hereby, repealed.

[1788, June 24.]

By a resolution of this date, the several States were allowed three months, in addition to the time limited by the aforegoing ordinance, for exhibiting to the district commissioners their respective accounts against the United States; and they were, at the same time, authorized to transmit to the accountant of the treasury, the commissioner of army accounts, and to the general board of commissioners to be appointed in pursuance of the ordinance aforesaid, such additional vouchers or other testimony as they might think necessary to support any claims by them exhibited to the respective officers aforesaid; provided the same be transmitted at least six months previous to the termination of the office of the general board, as fixed by the ordinance aforesaid.

[1788, October 10.]

By the resolve of this date, the board of commissioners appointed pursuant to the ordinance of the 7th May, 1787, were restrained from entering upon the business of their appointment, or finally determining any matter to them referred by the said ordinance, unless all three of the said commissioners shall be present.

---

An Act to provide more effectually for the settlement of the accounts between the United States and the individual States.

Sec. 1. *Be it enacted by the Senate and House of Representatives of the United States of America in Congress assembled,* That a board to consist of three commissioners be, and hereby is established, to settle the accounts between the United States and the individual States; and the determination of a majority of the said commissioners on the claims submitted to them shall be final and conclusive; and they shall have power to employ such number of clerks as they may find necessary.

Sec. 2. *And be it further enacted,* That the said commissioners shall, respectively, take an oath or affirmation before the Chief Justice of the United States, or one of the associate or district judges, that they will faithfully and impartially execute the duties of their office; and they shall, each of them, be entitled to receive at the rate of two thousand two hundred and fifty dollars per annum, payable quarter-yearly, at the Treasury of the United States, for their respective services.

Sec. 3. *And be it further enacted,* That it shall be the duty of the said commissioners to receive and examine all claims which shall be exhibited to them before the first day of July, one thousand seven hundred and ninety-one, and to determine on all such as shall have accrued for the general or particular defence during the war, and on the evidence thereof, according to the principles of general equity, (although such claims may not be sanctioned by the resolves of Congress, or supported by regular vouchers,) so as to provide for the final settlement of all accounts between the United States and the States individually; but no evidence of a claim heretofore admitted by a commissioner of the United States for any State or district shall be subject to such examination, nor shall the claim of any citizen be admitted as a charge against the United States in the account of any State, unless the same was allowed by such State before the twenty-fourth day of September, one thousand seven hundred and eighty-eight.

Sec. 4. *And be it further enacted,* That it shall be the duty of the said commissioners to examine and liquidate to specie value, on principles of equity, the credits and debits of the States already on the books of the Treasury, for bills of credit subsequent to the eighteenth of March, one thousand seven hundred and eighty.

Sec. 5. *And be it further enacted,* That the commissioners shall debit each State with all advances which have been or may be made to it by the United States, and with the interest thereon, to the last day of the year one thousand seven hundred and eighty-nine, and shall credit each State for its disbursements and advances on the principles contained in the third section of this act, with interest to the day aforesaid; and having struck the balance due to each State, shall find the aggregate of all the balances, which aggregate shall be apportioned between the States, agreeably to the rule hereinafter given; and the difference between such apportionments, and the respective balances, shall be carried, in a new account, to the debit or credit of the States respectively, as the case may be.

Sec. 6. *And be it further enacted,* That the rule for apportioning to the States the aggregate of the balances first mentioned, shall be the same that is prescribed by the constitution of the United States for the apportionment of representation and direct taxes, and according to the first enumeration which shall be made.

Sec. 7. *And be it further enacted,* That the States who shall have balances placed to their credit on the books of the Treasury of the United States, shall, within twelve months after the same shall have been so credited, be entitled to have the same funded upon the same terms with the other part of the domestic debt of the United States; but the balances so credited to any State shall not be transferable.

Sec. 8. *And be it further enacted,* That the clerks employed, or to be employed, by the said commissioners, shall receive like salaries as clerks employed in the Treasury Department.

Sec. 9. *And be it further enacted,* That the powers of the said commissioners shall continue until the first day of July, one thousand seven hundred and ninety-two, unless the business shall be sooner accomplished.

Approved August 5, 1790.

---

An Act to extend the time limited for settling the accounts of the United States with the individual States.

Sec. 1. *Be it enacted by the Senate and House of Representatives of the United States of America in Congress assembled,* That the powers of the board of commissioners, which, by an act passed in the second session of the first Congress, was established to settle the accounts between the United States and individual States, shall continue until the first day of July, one thousand seven hundred and ninety-three, unless the business shall be sooner accomplished.

Sec. 2. *And be it further enacted,* That the aforesaid act shall extend to the settlement of the accounts between the United States and the State of Vermont, and that until the first day of December next shall be allowed for the said State to exhibit its claims.

Sec. 3. *And be it further enacted,* That from and after the passing of this act, the pay of the principal clerk of the said board shall be the same as the pay of the principal clerk in the Auditor's office.

Approved January 23, 1792.

---

An Act in addition to, and alteration of, the act entitled "An act to extend the time limited for settling the accounts of the United States with the individual States."

*Be it enacted by the Senate and House of Representatives of the United States of America in Congress assembled,* That the second section of the act entitled " An act to extend the time limited for settling the accounts of the United States with the individual States," which extended the powers of the board of commissioners to the settlement of the accounts between the United States and the State of Vermont, be, and hereby is, repealed.

Sec. 2. *And be it further enacted,* That the board of commissioners established to settle the accounts between the United States and the individual States, in apportioning the aggregate of all the balances due to each State, between the States, agreeably to the act entitled " An act to provide more effectually for the settlement of the accounts between the United States and the individual States," shall have no regard to the State of Vermont.

Sec. 3. *And be it further enacted,* That, in the apportioning of the balances aforesaid, the State of Kentucky shall be deemed to be included in the State of Virginia, the admission of the said State of Kentucky as a member of the Union notwithstanding.

Approved February 27, 1793.

---

*Copy of the Commissioners' letter to the President of the United States.*

OFFICE OF ACCOUNTS, *June* 29, 1793.

SIR : We have the honor to submit to you the enclosed report upon the claims of the several States against the United States.

The difficulties we had to encounter, owing to the magnitude, intricacy, complexity, and variety of the claims, have been numerous. These, added to the loss of papers and other accidents, together with the peculiar nature of some of them, and the variety of paper which circulated during the war, have rendered it impracticable for us to follow with such minute precision the several charges, as might be expected in the settlement of the concerns of individuals.

We conceived that a speedy adjustment, having substantial justice for its basis, would best promote the end for which we were appointed ; we have therefore used our utmost endeavors to effect it, and we trust that the principles upon which we have proceeded, considered as a system, will in as great a degree produce the thing aimed at as could be done by any others ; at least we can with great truth declare that, in forming them, this was our intention and only view, and that they are the best our judgments could devise. We are therefore not without hope that our decision will meet the approbation of our fellow-citizens.

With all due deference, we are, sir,

Your obedient servants,<br>
WM. IRVINE,<br>
JOHN KEAN,<br>
WY. LANGDON.

---

### REPORT OF THE COMMISSIONERS.

#### OFFICE OF THE COMMISSIONERS OF ACCOUNTS,

*Philadelphia, June* 29, 1793.

The commissioners appointed to execute the several acts of Congress to provide more effectually for the settlement of the accounts between the United States and the individual States, report :

That they have maturely considered the claims of the several States against the United States, and the charges of the United States against the individual States.

That they have gone through the process prescribed in the 5th section of the act of Congress, passed the 5th day of August, 1790, the particulars whereof will be found in book A, lodged with the papers of this office in the Treasury Department, and find that there is due, including interest, to the 31st day of December, 1789,

*To the State of*—

NEW HAMPSHIRE, Seventy-five thousand and fifty-five dollars.

MASSACHUSETTS,- One million two hundred and forty-eight thousand eight hundred and one dollars.

RHODE ISLAND, - - Two hundred and ninety-nine thousand six hundred and eleven dollars.

CONNECTICUT, - - Six hundred and nineteen thousand one hundred and twenty-one dollars.

NEW JERSEY,- - - Forty-nine thousand and thirty dollars.

SOUTH CAROLINA, One million two hundred and five thousand nine hundred and seventy-eight dollars.

GEORGIA, - - - - Nineteen thousand nine hundred and eighty-eight dollars.

And that there is due, including interest to the 31st May, 1789,

*From the State of*—

NEW YORK, - - - Two millions seventy-four thousand eight hundred and forty-six dollars.

PENNSYLVANIA, - Seventy-six thousand seven hundred and nine dollars.

DELAWARE, - - - Six hundred and twelve thousand four hundred and twenty-eight dollars.

MARYLAND, - - - One hundred and fifty-one thousand six hundred and forty dollars.

VIRGINIA, - - - - One hundred thousand eight hundred and seventy-nine dollars.

NORTH CAROLINA, Five hundred and one thousand and eighty-two dollars.

Which several sums they, by virtue of the authority to them delegated, declare to be the final and conclusive balances due to and from the several States.

WM. IRVINE,
JOHN KEAN,
WOODBURY LANGDON.

---

*Final settlement of the State accounts by the board of commissioners appointed for that purpose, under the "Act to provide more effectually for the settlement of the accounts between the United States and the individual States,"*

DR.    *To sundry of accounts of the States respectively:*

For the following *credits* to the several States, founded upon the said report of the commissioners, and the minutes of their proceedings, in the words following:

At a meeting of the board, June 27, 1793, present William Irvine, John Kean, Woodbury Langdon, commissioners:

The board took into consideration the several claims of the States admitted by the examining clerks; also those which were suspended in order to make a final settlement and adjustment of the gross amount to be admitted to the credit of each State: whereupon, *Resolved*, That there be carried to the credit of the State of—

| | |
|---|---:|
| New Hampshire - - - - - | $4,278,015 02 |
| Massachusetts - - - - - | 17,964,613 03 |
| Rhode Island - - - - - | 3,782,974 46 |
| Connecticut - - - - - | 9,285,737 92 |
| New York - - - - - | 7,179,982 78 |
| New Jersey - - - - - | 5,342,770 52 |
| Pennsylvania - - - - - | 14,137,076 22 |
| Delaware - - - - - | 839,319 98 |
| Maryland - - - - - | 7,568,145 38 |
| Virginia - - - - - | 19,085,981 51 |
| North Carolina - - - - - | 10,427,586 13 |
| South Carolina - - - - - | 11,523,299 29 |
| Georgia - - - - - | 2,993,800 86 |
| | $114,409,303 10 |

Which several sums are in full of all claims made for the disbursements and advances of the said States, with the interest due thereon to the 31st December, 1789, and which were exhibited in conformity to the act of Congress of the 5th day of August, 1790.

DR.        *Sundry accounts of the States respectively,*

*To final settlement of the State accounts by the board of commissioners appointed for that purpose, under the "Act to provide more effectually for the settlement of accounts between the United States and individual States,"*

For the following *debits* to the several States, founded upon the said report of the commissioners, and the minutes of their proceedings of the 27th June, 1793, in the words following :

The board also took into consideration the advances made by the United States to the several States, which have been returned to them by the Treasury Department, and are charged in the books of the Treasury, the quartermaster's, commissary's, naval hospital, and clothing departments : whereupon, *Resolved,* That there be carried to the debits of the States of—

| | |
|---|---:|
| New Hampshire - - - - - | $1,082,954 02 |
| Massachusetts - - - - - | 6,258,880 03 |
| Rhode Island - - - - - | 1,977,608 46 |
| Connecticut - - - - - | 3,456,244 92 |
| New York - - - - - | 1,960,031 78 |
| New Jersey - - - - - | 1,343,321 52 |
| Pennsylvania - - - - - | 4,690,686 22 |
| Maryland - - - - - | 1,592,631 38 |
| Virginia - - - - - | 3,803,416 51 |
| North Carolina - - - - | 3,151,358 13 |
| South Carolina - - - - | 5,780,264 29 |
| Georgia - - - - - | 1,415,328 86 |
| | 36,742,625 10 |

Which several sums are in full of all advances made by the United States to the several States, with the interest due thereon to the 31st December, 1789, in conformity to the act of Congress passed the 5th day of August 1790, and for certificates of the several States, received on loan by the United States, in compliance with the acts of Congress of the 4th day of August, 1790, and of the 8th day of May, 1792.

*Sundry accounts of the States, respectively,*
DR.        *To final settlement of the State accounts, &c.*

For the following debits to the several States, founded upon the said report of the commissioners and their minutes aforesaid, viz :

The " board also took into consideration the return made by the Secretary of State, containing the enumeration of the inhabitants of the United States, and, by the rule prescribed by the constitution, declare the whole population of the United States, for the purpose of apportioning the aggregate of the balances by, is 3,530,393 souls ; and that the number in each State, by the same rule is"—

| | |
|---|---:|
| New Hampshire, - - - - - | 141,822 |
| Massachusetts, - - - - - | 475,327 |
| Rhode Island, - - - - - | 68,446 |
| Connecticut, - - - - - | 236,841 |
| New York, - - - - - | 331,590 |

| | | | | | | | |
|---|---|---|---|---|---|---|---|
| New Jersey, | - | - | - | - | - | - | 179,569 |
| Pennsylvania, | - | - | - | .. | - | - | 432,879 |
| Delaware, | - | - | - | - | - | - | 55,540 |
| Maryland, | - | - | - | - | - | - | 278,514 |
| Virginia, | - | - | - | - | - | - | 699,265 |
| North Carolina, | - | - | - | - | - | - | 353,523 |
| South Carolina, | - | - | - | - | - | - | 206,235 |
| Georgia, | - | - | - | - | - | - | 70,842 |

3,530,393

The whole amount of the advances, &c., made by the United States, being deducted from the gross admissions, leaves the aggregate of the balances ; which balances are ascertained by *debits* made upon the enumeration, and are as follow, and agree with the entries by said commissioners, viz :

| | | | | | | |
|---|---|---|---|---|---|---|
| New Hampshire, | - | - | - | - | - | $3,120,006 |
| Massachusetts, | - | - | - | - | - | 10,456,932 |
| Rhode Island, | - | - | - | - | - | 1,505,755 |
| Connecticut, | - | - | - | - | - | 5,210,372 |
| New York, | - | - | - | - | - | 7,294,797 |
| New Jersey, | - | - | - | - | - | 3,950,419 |
| Pennsylvania, | - | - | - | - | - | 9,523,099 |
| Delaware, | - | - | - | - | - | 1,221,849 |
| Maryland, | - | - | - | - | - | 6,127,154 |
| Virginia, | - | - | - | - | - | 15,383,444 |
| North Carolina, | - | - | - | - | - | 7,777,310 |
| South Carolina, | - | - | - | - | - | 4,537,057 |
| Georgia | - | - | - | - | - | 1,558,484 |

$77,666,678

*Sundry their old accounts,*
DR.                              *To sundry their new accounts :*

For the balances due from the United States to sundry of the States, upon the principles of the settlement made by the commissioners, viz :

" The whole amount of the advances, &c. made by the United States, being deducted from the gross admissions, leaves the aggregate of the balances ; which being apportioned among the States on the principles contained in the act of Congress ' to provide more effectually for the settlement of the accounts between the United States and the individual States,' and those apportionments being compared with the nett balances, leaves the amount due to or from a State, which are hereby declared to be as follows :"

| | | | | | | |
|---|---|---|---|---|---|---|
| New Hampshire, balance due | - | - | - | - | $75,055 |
| Massachusetts, | do | - | - | - | - | 1,248,801 |
| Rhode Island, | do | - | - | - | - | 299,611 |
| Connecticut, | do | - | - | - | - | 619,121 |
| New Jersey, | do | - | - | .. | - | · 49,030 |
| South Carolina, | do | - | - | - | - | 1,205,978 |
| Georgia, | do | - | - | - | - | 19,988 |

*Sundry their new accounts,*
Dᴿ. *To sundry their old accounts :*

For balances declared to be due to the United States by sundry of the States, by the commissioners appointed to settle the accounts of the United States with individual States as aforementioned :

| | |
|---|---:|
| New York - - - - - - - | $2,074,846 |
| Pennsylvania, - - - - - - | 76,709 |
| Delaware, - - - - - - | 612,428 |
| Maryland, - - - - - - | 151,640 |
| Virginia, - - - - - - | 100,879 |
| North Carolina, - - - - - - | 501,082 |

*Sundry State accounts,*
Dᴿ. *To interest on the unsubscribed balances of assumed debt:*

For twenty-nine thousand one hundred and fifty-seven dollars seventy-four cents, paid by the respective loan officers to several of the States, being for interest on the unsubscribed balances of the assumed debt arising on the first quarter of the year 1792, and which, by an endorsement by the commissioners for finally settling the accounts betwixt the United States and the individual States, " was received too late ; the entries and calculations being made, no alteration could have been made so as to have finished the business in due time:"

| | | |
|---|---:|---:|
| New Hampshire - - - - - | $527 | 07 |
| Connecticut, - - - - - - | 1,407 | 42 |
| Pennsylvania, - - - - - | 13,982 | 14 |
| Maryland, - - - - - - | 4,560 | 19 |
| Virginia, - - - - - - | 8,680 | 92 |
| | $29,157 | 74 |

Tʀᴇᴀsᴜʀʏ Dᴇᴘᴀʀᴛᴍᴇɴᴛ,
*Register's Office, June* 15, 1830.

I do hereby certify, that the foregoing report of the board of commissioners appointed to settle the accounts of the several States with the United States, is truly taken from the records of the revolutionary Government, (Journal, page 2601.)

T. L. SMITH, *Reg. Treas. U. S.*

*Abstract of the balances due to and from the several States on the adjustment of their accounts with the United States, by the general board of commissioners appointed for that purpose under the several acts of Congress for the final settlement of the State accounts, per their report of the 27th June, 1793.*

| States. | Sums allowed to the credit of the several States, with interest to the 1st January, 1790. | Advances made by the U.S. to the several States, together with the assumption of the State debts and interest to the 1st January, 1790. | Balance due to the several States. | Population of the United States, answering to rule prescribed in the constitution of the United States. | Proportion of the several States of $77,666,678, the aggregate amount of the balances. | Sums due to creditor States. | Sums due by debtor States. | Proportion of the several States' debts authorized to be funded by the 13th section of the act of 4th August, 1790. | Amount of debt funded by each State under the said section. |
|---|---|---|---|---|---|---|---|---|---|
| New Hampshire | $4,278,015 02 | $1,082,594 02 | $3,195,061 | $141,822 | $3,120,006 (c) | $75,055 | | $300,000 | $282,595 51 |
| Massachu-etts | 17,964,613 03 | 6,258,880 03 | 11,705,733 | 475,327 | 10,456,932 (c) | 1,248,801 | | 4,000,000 | 3,981,733 05 |
| Rhode Island | 3,782,974 46 | 1,977,608 46 | 1,805,366 | 68,446 | 1,505,755 (c) | 299,611 | | 200,000 | 200,000 00 |
| Connecticut | 9,285,737 92 | 3,456,244 92 | 5,829,493 | 236,841 | 5,210,372 (c) | 619,121 | | 1,600,000 | 1,600,000 00 |
| New York | 7,179,982 78 | 1,960,031 78 | 5,219,951 | 331,590 | 7,294,797 | | $2,074,846 | 1,200,000 | 1,183,716 69 |
| New Jersey | 5,342,770 52 | 1,343,321 52 | 3,999,449 | 179,569 | 3,950,419 c) | 49,030 | | 800,000 | 695,202 70 |
| Pennsylvania | 14,137,076 22 | 4,690,686 22 | 9,446,390 | 452,879 | 9,523,099 | | 76,709 | 2,200,000 | 777,983 48 |
| Delaware | 839,319 98 | 229,898 98 | 609,421 | 55,540 | 1,221,849 | | 612,428 | 200,000 | 59,162 65 |
| Maryland | 7,568,145 38 | 1,592,631 38 | 5,975,514 | 278,514 | 6,127,154 | | 151,640 | 800,000 | 517,491 08 |
| Virginia | 19,085,981 51 | 3,803,416 51 | 15,282,565 | 699,265 | 15,383,444 | | 100,879 | 3,500,000 | 2,934,443 29 |
| North Carolina | 10,427,586 13 | 3,151,358 13 | 7,276,228 | 353,523 | 7,777,310 | 1,205,978 (c) | | 2,400,000 | 1,793,803 85 |
| South Carolina | 11,523,299 29 | 5,78,264 29 | 5,743,035 | 206,235 | 4,537,057 (c) | | 501,082 | 4,000,000 | 3,999,651 71 |
| Georgia | 2,993,800 86 | 1,415,328 86 | 1,578,472 | 70,842 | 1,558,484 (c) | 19,988 | | 3,000,000 | 246,030 73 |
| | $114,409,303 10 | $36,742,625 10 | $77,666,678 | $3,530,393 | $77,666,678 | $3,517,584 | $3,517,584 | $21,500,000 | $18,271,814 74 |

TREASURY DEPARTMENT,
*Register's Office, February 9, 1831.*

T. L. SMITH, *Register.*

An Act making provision for the payment of the interest on the balances due to certain States, upon a final settlement of the accounts between the United States and the individual States.

Sec. 1. *Be it enacted by the Senate and House of Representatives of the United States of America in Congress assembled,* That interest upon the balances reported to be due to certain States, by the commissioners for settling accounts between the United States and individual States, be allowed, from the last day of December, one thousand seven hundred and eighty-nine, and to be computed to the last day of December, one thousand seven hundred and ninety-four, at the rate of four per centum per annum; and that the amount of such interest be placed to the credit of the State to which the same shall be found due upon the books of the Treasury of the United States, and shall bear an interest of three per centum per annum, from and after the said last day of December, one thousand seven hundred and ninety-four.

Sec. 2. *And be it further enacted,* That the interest on the said balances, reported by the said commissioners as aforesaid, which shall be funded agreeable to the terms of the act entitled "An act to provide more effectually for the settlement of the accounts between the United States and the individual States," together with the interest on the amount placed to the credit of any such State, for arrearages of interest on such balances, agreeable to the terms of this act, be paid quarter-yearly, after the said last day of December, one thousand seven hundred and ninety-four; that is to say: one-fourth part thereof on the last days of March, June, September, and December, respectively, in each year, at the offices of the commissioners of loans within such States as shall be entitled to receive the same; the first payment to be made on the last day of March, one thousand seven hundred and ninety-five: And for the payment of the said interest, so much of the duties arising, yearly, on imports and tonnage, from and after the last day of December, one thousand seven hundred and ninety-four, as may be necessary, and not heretofore otherwise appropriated, be, and the same is hereby, pledged and appropriated; and that the faith of the United States be, and the same is hereby, pledged to provide for any deficiency that may happen, by such additional and permanent funds, as may be necessary therefor.

Approved May 31, 1794.

---

An Act respecting balances reported against certain States, by the commissioners appointed to settle the accounts between the United States and the several States.

Sec. 1. *Be it enacted by the Senate and House of Representatives of the United States of America in Congress assembled,* That if any State, against which a balance was reported by the commissioners appointed to settle the accounts between the United States and the several States, shall, on or before the first day of April, one thousand eight hundred, by a legislative act, engage to pay into the treasury of the United States, within five years after passing such legislative act, or to expend, within the time last mentioned, in erecting, enlarging, or completing any fortifications for the defence of the United States, at such place or places, the jurisdiction whereof having been, previously to such expenditure, ceded by such State to the United States, with reservation that process, civil and criminal, issuing under authority of such State, may be served and executed therein, and according to such plan or plans as shall be approved by the President of the United States, a sum in money, or in stock of the United States, equal to the balance reported as aforesaid against such State, or to the sum assumed by the United States in the debt of such State, such payment or expenditure, when so made, shall be accepted by the United States as a full discharge of all demands on account of said balance ; and the President of the United States shall be, and hereby is authorized to cause credit to be given to such State on the books of the Treasury of the United States accordingly: *Provided, however,* That no more than one-third part of the whole payment or expenditure that may be made by any such State shall be made in three per cent. stock, nor more than one-third part of the remaining two-thirds shall be made in deferred stock: *And provided, also,* That any such State may obtain a full discharge, as aforesaid, by the payment or expenditure of a sum of money, sufficient, in the opinion of the Secretary of the Treasury, to purchase, at market price, the different species of stock, the payment or expenditure of which would be accepted as a full discharge as aforesaid.

Sec. 2. *Provided always, and be it further enacted,* That if any such State as aforesaid shall have expended, since the establishment of the present Government of the United States, any sum of money in fortifying any place since ceded by such State to the United States, or which may be so ceded within one year after the passing of this act, such expenditure, having been ascertained and proved to the satisfaction of the Secretary of the Treasury, shall be taken and allowed as part of the expenditure intended by this act.

Approved February 15, 1799.

---

### *Remarks on the Domestic Debts, Continental and State Certificates, &c.*

Immediately after the commencement of the revolutionary war, Congress agreed upon the measure of emitting a paper currency, on the faith of the United Colonies, to defray the accruing expenses : and as they could propose no other funds for the redemption of the money but taxes, and as some time must elapse before that could be brought into effective operation, therefore, in order to supply the treasury, and to anticipate the emissions of paper, they, on the 3d October, 1776, resolved that a loan office should be established in each State ; and for continental money or specie paid in, certificates were ordered to be given for the amount, promising payment of the principal at future periods, and that the interest should be paid annually, at the office where the money was lent. Loans were made accordingly, from time to time, to a large amount; and they were increased by the two emissions of continental money of May 20th, 1777, and April 11th, 1778, being called out of circulation in the year 1779; the holders of said bills having it at their election to give them on loan or to take others of like tenor.

There were certificates issued to quartermasters, commissaries, and other public officers, to be by them paid in lieu of money, for services performed and articles furnished; and also certificates to discharge the interest due upon loan-office certificates. And by a resolve of Congress of September 5th, 1780, certificates were given for the balances of accounts liquidated in specie value, under the direction of the Board of Treasury. The same kind were afterwards given to officers and soldiers in the army belonging to corps not considered as a part of either of the United States' quotas, for the depreciation upon their pay ; all of which came under the description of loan-office certificates.

Although it appears Congress were fully sensible of the depreciation of their money, from an early period, and labored under great difficulties on that account, it does not appear that they relinquished the idea of redeeming it agreeably to the nominal amount, until the 18th March, 1780; on which day a resolve was passed, that gold and silver, and the bills which, by said resolution, were ordered to be emitted, should be receivable in payment of the different States' quotas of taxes, at the rate of one Spanish milled dollar, in lieu of forty dollars of the bills then in circulation.

Having, at that period, (18th March, 1780,) fixed a rate of exchange, and as the decrease in value had been progressive for several years, it necessarily followed that they should look back, in order to do, at least, equal justice to all their creditors ; accordingly, on the 18th day of April, 1780, they declared that the holders of loan-office certificates should sustain no loss thereon, by any depreciation of the bills subsequent to the time of making the loan ; and on the 28th day of June, in the same year, it was resolved, that the principal of all loans that had been made should be finally discharged, by paying the full current value of the bills when loaned; and that the value thereof should be ascertained by computing a progressive rate of depreciation, commencing with the 1st day of September, 1777, and continuing to the 18th day of March, 1780, from period to period, assuming the depreciation at the several periods to be as follows, viz:

On the 1st day of March, 1778, one dollar and three-quarters of a dollar of the said bills for one Spanish milled dollar; on the 1st day of September, 1778, as four of the former for one of the latter; on the 1st day of March, 1779, as ten of the former for one of the latter; on the 1st day of September, 1779, as eighteen of the former for one of the latter; and on the 18th day of March, 1780, as forty of the former for one of the latter.

It was at the same time further resolved, that the principal of all certificates taken out since the 18th March, 1780, should be discharged at the rate of one Spanish milled dollar, or the current exchange thereof in other money at the time of payment, for forty dollars of the said bills of credit received on loan ; and that the principal of all certificates that should thereafter be taken out, until the further order of Congress, be discharged at the same rate, and in the same manner, as those that had been taken out since the 18th March, 1780; and that interest, at the rate of six per cent. per annum, be computed on the principal, ascertained as aforesaid, on all loan-office certificates, and the same be discharged annually.

Among the sufferings occasioned by a depreciated paper currency, and the insufficiency of the Treasury to answer the necessary demands during an eight years' war, those of the continental troops were far from being the least ; it being well known that, for a long period of faithful services, they received but an inconsiderable part of their stipends. And although the respective States had, in conformity with a recommendation of Congress, made settlements with their troops and given obligations for the sums found due for the depreciation of pay received in continental money, large arrearages were due at the conclusion of the war, and it was necessary to make a final settlement : therefore, on the 4th July, 1783, the Paymaster General was ordered to settle and finally adjust all accounts whatsoever between the United States and the officers and soldiers of the army, so as to include all and every demand, and to give certificates for the sums which might appear due on such settlement, in such manner and form as the superintendent of finance might direct.

The settlements were made with the regimental paymasters and an agent, and certificates were issued in the name of the person to whom granted, and the time from which they were to bear interest, and signed *John Pierce,* who was the paymaster general and commissioner of army accounts. These certificates, or the greater part of them, bear interest from the following periods: 1st August, 1780; 1st January, 1781; 1st January, 1782; the 1st January and 23d March, 1783, (which last was given to the officers who retired from the field on the different reforms of the army; and having been promised half pay for life at an early stage of the war, they agreed, together with the officers who continued in service, to commute the half pay for five years' full pay,) and the 4th and 15th November, 1783, which were given for the arrearages of pay due for that year, commutation to the officers, and a gratuity of eighty dollars to the non-commissioned officers and soldiers who engaged for and continued to serve to the end of the war.

The several States, in compliance with the recommendations of Congress, made settlements with the officers and soldiers belonging to each of them respectively, for the depreciation of their pay, commencing the 1st January, 1777, and estimating, in specie, all sums of continental money by them received at different periods, agreeably to scales of depreciation made for the purpose, and granted certificates for the balances found due.

Some of the States likewise granted certificates to their citizens for services in the militia, to troops called new levies, to ranging companies employed for the defence of the frontiers, to individuals for money lent and supplies furnished the State, and for claims due the creditors of persons whose estates had been confiscated. All of which debts, it is presumed, were, so far as they appeared to have been contracted for the common defence and general welfare, charged against the United States in the settlement of the general account.

These certificates, issued by the States, were mostly printed blanks, filled up in writing, and signed either by the comptrollers, treasurers, commissioners, or auditors of the different States, respectively, and the sums were always expressed in pounds; whereas, in all continental certificates, the sums were expressed in dollars, Congress having directed that mode of stating and keeping their accounts from the beginning.

## CHAPTER IV.

*Acts of Congress making provision for the Debt of the United States, for Funding the Domestic Debt thereof, and extending the time for receiving on loan the said domestic debt.*

### An Act making provision for the debt of the United States.

Whereas justice and the support of public credit require that provision should be made for fulfilling the engagements of the United States in respect to their foreign debt, and for funding their domestic debt upon equitable and satisfactory terms :

Sec. 1. *Be it enacted by the Senate and House of Representatives of the United States of America in Congress assembled,* That reserving, out of the moneys which have arisen since the last day of December last past, and which shall hereafter arise, from the duties on goods, wares, and merchandise imported into the United States, and on the tonnage of ships or vessels, the yearly sum of six hundred thousand dollars, or so much thereof as may be appropriated, from time to time, towards the support of the Government of the United States, and their common defence, the residue of the said moneys, or so much thereof as may be necessary, as the same shall be received in each year, next after the sum reserved as aforesaid, shall be, and is hereby, appropriated to the payment of the interest which shall from time to time become due on the loans heretofore made by the United States in foreign countries ; and also to the payment of interest on such further loans as may be obtained for discharging the arrears of interest thereupon, and the whole or any part of the principal thereof; to continue so appropriated until the said loans, as well those already made, as those which may be made in virtue of this act, shall be fully satisfied, pursuant to the contracts relating to the same, any law to the contrary notwithstanding : *And provided,* That nothing herein contained shall be construed to annul or alter any appropriation by law made prior to the passing of this act.

And as new loans are, and will be, necessary for the payment of the aforesaid arrears of interest, and the instalments of the principal of the said foreign debt, due and growing due, and may also be found expedient for effecting an entire alteration in the state of the same :

Sec. 2. *Be it further enacted,* That the President of the United States be, and he is hereby, authorized to cause to be borrowed, on behalf of the United States, a sum or sums, not exceeding in the whole twelve millions of dollars ; and that so much of this sum as may be necessary to the discharge of the said arrears and instalments, and (if it can be effected upon terms advantageous to the United States) to the paying off the whole of the said foreign debt, be appropriated solely to those purposes : And the President is, moreover, further authorized to cause to be made such other contracts respecting the said debt, as shall be found for the interest of the said States : *Provided, nevertheless,* That no engagement nor contract shall be entered into which shall preclude the United States

6

from reimbursing any sum or sums borrowed, within fifteen years after the same shall have been lent or advanced.

And whereas it is desirable to adapt the nature of the provision to be made for the domestic debt to the present circumstances of the United States, as far as it shall be found practicable, consistently with good faith and the rights of the creditors, which can only be done by a voluntary loan on their part:

Sec. 3. *Be it therefore further enacted,* That a loan, to the full amount of the said domestic debt, be, and the same is hereby, proposed ; and that books, for receiving subscriptions to the said loan, be opened at the Treasury of the United States, and by a commissioner to be appointed in each of the said States, on the first day of October next ; to continue open until the last day of September following, inclusively ; and that the sums which shall be subscribed thereto, be payable in certificates issued for the said debt according to their specie value, and computing the interest upon such as bear interest to the last day of December next, inclusively ; which said certificates shall be of these several descriptions, to wit :

Those issued by the Register of the Treasury.

Those issued by the commissioners of loans in the several States, including certificates given pursuant to the act of Congress of the 2d January, one thousand seven hundred and seventy-nine, for bills of credit of the several emissions of the twentieth of May, one thousand seven hundred and seventy-seven, and the eleventh of April, one thousand seven hundred and seventy-eight.

Those issued by the commissioners for the adjustment of the accounts of the quartermaster, commissary, hospital, clothing, and marine departments.

Those issued by the commissioners for the adjustment of accounts in the respective States.

Those issued by the late and present paymaster general, or commissioner of army accounts.

Those issued for the payment of interest, commonly called indents of interest.

And in the bills of credit, issued by the authority of the United States in Congress assembled, at the rate of one hundred dollars in the said bills for one dollar in specie.

Sec. 4. *And be it further enacted,* That for the whole, or any part, of any sum subscribed to the said loan, by any person or persons, or body politic, which shall be paid in the principal of the said domestic debt, the subscriber or subscribers shall be entitled to a certificate, purporting that the United States owe to the holder or holders thereof, his, her, or their assigns, a sum to be expressed therein, equal to two-thirds of the sum so paid, bearing an interest of six per centum per annum, payable quarter-yearly, and subject to redemption by payments not exceeding, in one year, on account both of principal and interest, the proportion of eight dollars upon a hundred of the sum mentioned in such certificate ; and to another certificate, purporting that the United States owe to the holder or holders thereof, his, her, or their assigns, a sum to be expressed therein, equal to the proportion of thirty-three dollars and one-third of a dollar upon a hundred of the sum so paid; which, after the year one thousand eight hundred, shall bear an interest of six per centum per annum, payable quarter-yearly, and subject to redemption by payments not exceeding, in one year, on account both of principal and interest, the proportion of eight dollars upon a hundred of the sum mentioned in such certificate: *Provided,* That it shall not be understood that the United States shall be bound or obliged to redeem in the proportion aforesaid; but it shall be understood only, that they have a right to do so.

Sec. 5. *And be it further enacted,* That for the whole, or any part, of any sum subscribed to the said loan by any person or persons, or body politic, which shall be paid in the interest of the said domestic debt, computed to the said last day of December next, or in the said certificates issued in payment of interest, commonly called indents of interest, the subscriber or subscribers shall be entitled to a certificate, purporting that the United States owe to the holder or holders thereof, his, her, or their assigns, a sum to be specified therein, equal to that by him, her, or them so paid, bearing an interest of three per centum per annum, payable quarter-yearly, and subject to redemption by payment of the sum specified therein, whenever provision shall be made by law for that purpose.

Sec. 6. *And be it further enacted,* That a commissioner be appointed for each State, to reside therein, whose duty it shall be to superintend the subscriptions to the said loan ; to open books for the same ; to receive the certificates which shall be presented in payment thereof; to liquidate the specie value of such of them as shall not have been before liquidated ; to issue the certificates above mentioned, in lieu thereof, according to the terms of each subscription ; to enter, in books to be by him kept for that purpose, credits to the respective subscribers to the said loan, for the sums to which they shall be respectively entitled ; to transfer the said credits upon the said books, from time to time, as shall be requisite ; to pay the interest thereupon as the same shall become due; and, generally, to observe and perform such directions and regulations as shall be prescribed to him by the Secretary of the Treasury, touching the execution of his office.

Sec. 7. *And be it further enacted,* That the stock which shall be created pursuant to this act, shall be transferable only on the books of the Treasury, or of the said commissioners respectively, upon which the credit for the same shall exist at the time of transfer, by the proprietor or proprietors of such stock, his, her, or their attorney : but it shall be lawful for the Secretary of the Treasury, by special warrant, under his hand and the seal of the Treasury, countersigned by the Comptroller and registered by the Register, at the request of the respective proprietors, to authorize the transfer of such stock from the books of the commissioner to those of another commissioner, or to those of the Treasury, and from those of the Treasury to those of a commissioner.

Sec. 8. *And be it further enacted,* That the interest upon the said stock, as the same shall become due, shall be payable quarter-yearly, that is to say : one fourth part thereof on the last day of March ; one other fourth part thereof on the last day of June ; one other fourth part thereof on the last day of September ; and the remaining fourth part thereof on the last day of December, in each year, beginning on the last day of March next ensuing and payment shall be made wheresoever the credit for the said stock shall exist at the time such interest shall become due, that is to say: at the Treasury, if the credit for the same shall then exist on the books of the Treasury, or at the office of the commissioner upon whose books such credit shall then exist. But if the interest for one quarter shall not be demanded before the expiration of a third quarter, the same shall be afterwards demandable only at the Treasury.

And, as it may happen that some of the creditors of the United States may not think fit to become subscribers to the said loan:

Sec. 9. *Be it further enacted*, That nothing in this act contained shall be construed in anywise to alter, abridge, or impair the rights of those creditors of the United States who shall not subscribe to the said loan, or the contracts upon which their respective claims are founded ; but the said contracts and rights shall remain in full force and virtue.

And that such creditors may not be excluded from a participation in the benefit hereby intended to the creditors of the United States in general, while the said proposed loan shall be depending, and until it shall appear, from the event thereof, what further or other arrangements may be necessary respecting the said domestic debt :

Sec. 10. *Be it, therefore, further enacted,* That such of the creditors of the United States as may not subscribe to the said loan, shall nevertheless receive, during the year one thousand seven hundred and ninety-one, a rate per centum on the respective amounts of their respective demands, including interest to the last day of December next, equal to the interest payable to subscribing creditors, to be paid at the same times, at the same places, and by the same persons, as is hereinbefore directed concerning the interest on the stock which may be created in virtue of the said proposed loan. But as some of the certificates now in circulation have not heretofore been liquidated to specie value, as most of them are greatly subject to counterfeit, and counterfeits have actually taken place in numerous instances; and as embarrassment and imposition might, for these reasons, attend the payment of interest on those certificates in their present form; it shall, therefore, be necessary, to entitle the said creditors to the benefit of the said payment, that those of them who do not possess certificates issued by the Register of the Treasury, for the registered debt, should produce, previous to the first day of June next, their respective certificates, either at the Treasury of the United States, or to some one of the commissioners to be appointed as aforesaid, to the end that the same may be cancelled, and other certificates issued in lieu thereof ; which new certificates shall specify the specie amount of those in exchange for which they are given, and shall be otherwise of the like tenor with those heretofore issued by the said Register of the Treasury for the said registered debt, and shall be transferable on the like principles with those directed to be issued on account of the subscriptions to the loan hereby proposed.

Sec. 11. *And be it further enacted,* That the commissioners who shall be appointed pursuant to this act shall, respectively, be entitled to the following yearly salaries, that is to say : The commissioner for the State of New Hampshire, six hundred and fifty dollars; the commissioner for the State of Massachusetts, fifteen hundred dollars; the commissioner for the State of Rhode Island and Providence Plantations, six hundred dollars; the commissioner for the State of Connecticut, one thousand dollars; the commissioner for the State of New York, fifteen hundred dollars; the commissioner for the State of New Jersey, seven hundred dollars; the commissioner for the State of Pennsylvania, fifteen hundred dollars; the commissioner for the State of Delaware, six hundred dollars ; the commissioner for the State of Maryland, one thousand dollars; the commissioner for the State of Virginia, fifteen hundred dollars; the commissioner for the State of North Carolina, one thousand dollars; the commissioner for the State of South Carolina, one thousand dollars; the commissioner for the State of Georgia, seven hundred dollars; which salaries shall be in full compensation for all services and expenses.

Sec. 12. *And be it further enacted,* That the said commissioners, before they enter upon the execution of their several offices, shall respectively take an oath or affirmation for the diligent and faithful execution of their trust, and shall also become bound, with one or more sureties, to the satisfaction of the Secretary of the Treasury, in a penalty not less [than] five thousand, nor more than ten thousand dollars, with condition for their good behaviour in their said offices, respectively.

And whereas a provision for the debts of the respective States by the United States would be greatly conducive to an orderly, economical, and effectual arrangement of the public finances :

Sec. 13. *Be it, therefore, further enacted,* That a loan be proposed, to the amount of twenty-one millions and five hundred thousand dollars, and that subscriptions to the said loan be received at the same times and places, and by the same persons, as in respect to the loan heretofore proposed concerning the domestic debt of the United States; and that the sums which shall be subscribed to the said loan shall be payable in the principal and interest of the certificates or notes which, prior to the first day of January last, were issued by the respective States, as acknowledgments or evidences of debts by them respectively owing, except certificates issued by the commissioners of army accounts, in the State of North Carolina, in the year one thousand seven hundred and eighty-six: *Provided,* That no greater sum shall be received in the certificates of any State than as follows; that is to say :

In those of New Hampshire, three hundred thousand dollars.

In those of Massachusetts, four million dollars.

In those of Rhode Island and Providence Plantations, two hundred thousand dollars.

In those of Connecticut, one million six hundred thousand dollars.

In those of New York, one million two hundred thousand dollars.

In those of New Jersey, eight hundred thousand dollars.

In those of Pennsylvania, two million two hundred thousand dollars.

In those of Delaware, two hundred thousand dollars.

In those of Maryland, eight hundred thousand dollars.

In those of Virginia, three million five hundred thousand dollars.

In those of North Carolina, two million four hundred thousand dollars.

In those of South Carolina, four million dollars.

In those of Georgia, three hundred thousand dollars.

*And provided,* That no such certificate shall be received which, from the tenor thereof, or from any public record, act, or document, shall appear, or can be ascertained, to have been issued for any purpose other than compensations and expenditures for services or supplies towards the prosecution of the late war, and the defence of the United States, or some part thereof, during the same.

Sec. 14. *Provided also, and be it further enacted,* That if the total amount of the sums which shall be subscribed to the said loan, in the debt of any State, within the time limited for receiving subscriptions thereto, shall exceed the sum by this act allowed to be subscribed within such State, the certificates and credits granted to the respective subscribers shall bear such proportion to the sums by them respectively subscribed as the total amount of the said sums shall bear to the whole sum so allowed to be subscribed in the debt of such State within the same. And every subscriber to the said loan shall, at the time of subscribing, deposite with the commissioner the certificates or notes to be loaned by him.

Sec. 15. *And be it further enacted,* That for two-thirds of any sum subscribed to the said loan, by any person or persons, or body politic, which shall be paid in the principal and interest of the certificates or notes issued as aforesaid by the respective States, the subscriber or subscribers shall be entitled to a certificate, purporting that the United States owe to the holder or holders thereof, or his, her, or their assigns, a sum to be expressed therein, equal to two-thirds of the aforesaid two-thirds, bearing an interest of six per centum per annum, payable quarter-yearly, and subject to redemption by payments not exceeding in one year, on account both of principal and interest, the proportion of eight dollars upon a hundred of the sum mentioned in such certificate; and to another certificate, purporting that the United States owe to the holder or holders thereof, his, her, or their assigns, a sum to be expressed therein, equal to the proportion of thirty-three dollars and one-third of a dollar upon a hundred, of the said two-thirds of such sum so subscribed, which, after the year one thousand eight hundred, shall bear an interest of six per centum per annum, payable quarter-yearly, and subject to redemption by payments not exceeding in one year, on account both of principal and interest, the proportion of eight dollars upon a hundred of the sum mentioned in such certificate; and that, for the remaining third of any sum so subscribed, the subscriber or subscribers shall be entitled to a certificate, purporting that the United States owe to the holder or holders thereof, his, her, or their assigns, a sum to be expressed therein, equal to the said remaining third, bearing an interest of three per cent. per annum, payable quarter-yearly, and subject to redemption by payment of the sum specified therein, whenever provision shall be made by law for that purpose.

Sec. 16. *And be it further enacted,* That the interest upon the certificates which shall be received in payment of the sums subscribed towards the said loan, shall be computed to the last day of the year one thousand seven hundred and ninety-one, inclusively; and the interest upon the stock which shall be created by virtue of the said loan, shall commence or begin to accrue on the first day of the year one thousand seven hundred and ninety-two, and shall be payable quarter-yearly, at the same time, and in like manner, as the interest on the stock to be created by virtue of the loan above proposed in the domestic debt of the United States.

Sec. 17. *And be it further enacted,* That if the whole sum allowed to be subscribed in the debt or certificates of any State, as aforesaid, shall not be subscribed within the time for that purpose limited, such State shall be entitled to receive, and shall receive, from the United States, an interest per centum per annum upon so much of the said sum as shall not have been so subscribed, equal to that which would have accrued on the deficiency, had the same been subscribed in trust for the non-subscribing creditors of such State, who are holders of certificates or notes issued on account of services or supplies towards the prosecution of the late war, and the defence of the United States, or of some part thereof, to be paid in like manner as the interest on the stock which may be created by virtue of the said loan, and to continue until there shall be a settlement of accounts between the United States and the individual States; and in case a balance shall then appear in favor of such State, until provision shall be made for the said balance.

But as certain States have, respectively, issued their own certificates, in exchange for those of the United States, whereby it might happen that interest might be twice payable on the same sums:

Sec. 18. *Be it further enacted*, That the payment of interest, whether to States or to individuals, in respect to the debt of any State by which such exchange shall have been made, shall be suspended, until it shall appear, to the satisfaction of the Secretary of the Treasury, that certificates issued for that purpose by such State have been re-exchanged or redeemed; or until those which shall not have been re-exchanged or redeemed shall be surrendered to the United States.

Sec. 19. *And be it further enacted*, That so much of the debt of each State as shall be subscribed to the said loan, and the moneys (if any) that shall be advanced to the same, pursuant to this act, shall be a charge against such State, in account with the United States.

Sec. 20. *And be it further enacted*, That the moneys arising under the revenue laws which have been, or during the present session of Congress may be, passed, or so much thereof as may be necessary, shall be, and are hereby, pledged and appropriated for the payment of the interest on the stock which shall be created by the loans aforesaid, pursuant to the provisions of this act; first paying that which shall arise on the stock created by virtue of the said first-mentioned loan, to continue so pledged and appropriated until the final redemption of the said stock, any law to the contrary notwithstanding; subject, nevertheless, to such reservations and priorities as may be requisite to satisfy the appropriations heretofore made, and which, during the present session of Congress, may be made by law, including the sums hereinbefore reserved and appropriated: And to the end that the said moneys may be inviolably applied in conformity to this act, and may never be diverted to any other purpose, an account shall be kept of the receipts and disposition thereof, separate and distinct from the product of any other duties, imposts, excises, and taxes whatsoever, except such as may be hereafter laid to make good any deficiency which may be found in the product thereof, towards satisfying the interest aforesaid.

Sec. 21. *And be it further enacted*, That the faith of the United States be, and the same is hereby, pledged to provide and appropriate hereafter such additional and permanent funds as may be requisite towards supplying any such deficiency, and making full provision for the payment of the interest which shall accrue on the stock to be created by virtue of the loans aforesaid, in conformity to the terms thereof, respectively, and according to the tenor of the certificates to be granted for the same pursuant to this act.

Sec. 22. *And be it further enacted*, That the proceeds of the sales which shall be made of lands in the Western Territory, now belonging, or that may hereafter belong, to the United States, shall be, and are hereby, appropriated towards sinking or discharging the debts, for the payment whereof the United States now are, or by virtue of this act may be, holden; and shall be applied solely to that use, until the said debts shall be fully satisfied.

Approved August 4, 1790.

NOTE.—To the preceding act, the act of May 8, 1792, is supplementary, and extends to the first day of March, 1793, the term for receiving on loan that part of the domestic debt of the United States which had not been subscribed pursuant to the provisions of the foregoing act. By act of March 2, 1793, the term is further extended until the last day of June, 1794 ; and still further extended, by act of May 30, 1794, until the last day of December, 1794. By act of January 28, 1795, until the 31st of December, 1795. By act of February 19, 1796, until the 31st of December, 1796. And the provisions of the act of the 19th of February, 1796, are continued in force, by the act of March 3, 1797, until the 31st of December, 1797. With regard to the transfer of stock, see the act of January 2d, 1795, which is revived and continued in force until the 4th day of March, 1799, by the act of the 6th of July, 1797. See, moreover, in relation to the public debt, the act of August 12, 1790. The fifth section of the act of March 2, 1799, apportions clerks and clerk-hire to the commissioners appointed in pursuance of the sixth section of the preceding act. By the second section of the act of April 7, 1798, the nett proceeds of certain lands are added to the fund for sinking the public debt.

---

An Act supplementary to the act making provision for the debt of the United States.

Sec 1. *Be it enacted by the Senate and House of Representatives of the United States of America in Congress assembled,* That the term for receiving on loan that part of the domestic debt of the United States which hath not been subscribed pursuant to the terms proposed in the act entitled "An act making provision for the debt of the United States," shall be, and it is hereby, extended, on the same terms as in and by the said act is provided, to the first day of March next; and books, for receiving such further subscriptions, shall be opened at the Treasury of the United States, and by the commissioner of loans in each of the said States, on the first day of June next, which shall continue open until the said first day of March next, inclusively; for which purpose said commissioners, respectively, are hereby invested with the like powers, and required to perform the like duties, as in and by the said act is directed.

Sec. 2. *And be it further enacted,* That such of the creditors of the United States as have not subscribed, and shall not subscribe, to the said loan, shall, nevertheless, receive a rate per centum on the amount of so much of their respective demands, as well for interest as principal, as on or before the first day of March shall be registered conformably to the directions of the said act, as shall be equal to the interest payable to the subscribing creditors, which shall be payable at the same times and places, and by the same persons, as in and by the said act is directed.

Sec. 3. *And be it further enacted,* That the term for receiving upon loan that part of the debts of the respective States which hath not been subscribed pursuant to the terms proposed in the act aforesaid, shall be, and it is hereby, enlarged, on the same terms as in and by the said act is provided, until the first day of March, one thousand seven hundred and ninety-three, inclusively; for which purpose books shall be opened at the Treasury of the United States, and by the commissioners of loans in each of the said States, on the first day of June next, which shall continue open until the first of March, one thousand seven hundred and ninety-three, inclusively; for which purposes the said commissioners are hereby invested with the like powers, and required to perform the like duties, as in and by the said act is directed.

Sec. 4. *Provided always, and be it further enacted,* That the commissioner of loans for North Carolina shall not be allowed to receive any certificate issued by Patrick Travers, commissioner of Cumberland county, or by the commissioners of army accounts at Warrenton.

Sec. 5. And whereas the United States are indebted to certain foreign officers on account of pay and services during the late war, the interest whereof, pursuant to the certificates granted to the said officers by virtue of a resolution of the United States in Congress assembled, is payable at the house of ———— Grand, banker, at Paris, and it is expedient to discharge the same : *Be it therefore enacted,* That the President of the United States be, and he hereby is, authorized to cause to be discharged the principal and interest of the said debt, out of any of the moneys which have been, or shall be, obtained on loan in virtue of the act aforesaid, and which shall not be necessary ultimately to fulfil the purposes for which the said moneys are, in and by the said act, authorized to be borrowed.

Sec. 6. *And be it further enacted,* That the President of the Senate, the Chief Justice, the Secretary of State, the Secretary of the Treasury, and the Attorney General, for the time being, shall be commissioners, who, or any three of whom, are hereby authorized, with the approbation of the President of the United States, to purchase the debt of the United States, at its market price, if not exceeding the par or true value thereof; for which purchase the interest on so much of the public debt as has already been, or may hereafter be, purchased for the United States, or as shall be paid into the Treasury, and so much of the moneys appropriated for the payment of the interest on the foreign and domestic debt, as shall exceed what may be sufficient for the payment of such interest to the creditors of the United States, shall be and are hereby, appropriated. And it shall be the duty of the said commissioners to render to the Legislature, within two months after the commencement of the first session thereof, in every year, a full and precise account of all such purchases made, and public debt redeemed, in pursuance of this act.

Sec. 7. And whereas it is expedient to establish a fund for the gradual reduction of the public debt : *Be it further enacted,* That the interest on so much of the debt of the United States as has been, or shall be, purchased or redeemed for or by the United States, or as shall be paid into the Treasury thereof in satisfaction of any debt or demand, and the surplus of any sum or sums appropriated for the payment of the interest upon the said debt, which shall remain after paying such interest, shall be, and hereby are, appropriated and pledged, firmly and inviolably, for and to the purchase and redemption of the said debt, to be applied, under the direction of the President of the Senate, the Chief Justice, the Secretary of State, the Secretary of the Treasury, and the Attorney General, for the time being, or any three of them, with the approbation of the President of the United States, for the time being, in manner following; that is to say: First, to the purchase of the several species of stock constituting the debt of the United States, at their respective market prices, not exceeding the par or true value thereof, and, as nearly as may be, in equal proportions, until the annual amount of the said funds, together with any other provisions which may be made by law, shall be equal to two per centum of the whole amount of the outstanding funded stock bearing a present interest of six per centum: Thenceforth, secondly, to the redemption of the said last-mentioned stock, according to the right for that purpose reserved to the United States, until the whole amount thereof shall have been redeemed: And lastly, after such redemption, to the purchase, at its market price, of any other stock, consisting of the debt of the United States, which may then remain unredeemed; and such purchase, as far as the fund shall at any time extend, shall be made within thirty days next after each day on which a quarterly payment of interest on the debt of the United States shall become due; and shall be made by a known agent, to be named by the said commissioners.

Sec. 8. *And be it further enacted*, That all future purchases of public debt, on account of the United States, shall be made at the lowest price at which the same can be obtained by open purchase, or by receiving sealed proposals, to be opened in the presence of the commissioners, or persons authorized by them to make purchases, and the persons making such proposals.

Sec. 9. *And be it further enacted*, That quarter-yearly accounts of the application of the said fund shall be rendered for settlement, as other public accounts, accompanied with returns of the sums of the said debt which shall have been, from time to time, purchased or redeemed; and full and exact report of the proceedings of the said commissioners, including a statement of the disbursements which shall have been made, and of the sums which shall have been purchased or redeemed, under their direction, and specifying dates, prices, parties, and places, shall be laid before Congress within the first fourteen days of each session which may ensue the present, during the execution of the said trust.

Approved May 8, 1792.

---

An Act for extending the time for receiving on loan that part of the domestic debt of the United States which may not be subscribed prior to the first day of March, one thousand seven hundred and ninety-three.

Sec. 1. *Be it enacted by the Senate and House of Representatives of the United States of America in Congress assembled*, That the term for receiving on loan that part of the domestic debt of the United States which shall not have been subscribed in pursuance of the act entitled "An act supplementary to the act making provision for the debt of the United States," be extended, from and after the first day of March, one thousand seven hundred and ninety-three, until the last day of June, one thousand seven hundred and ninety-four, inclusively, on the same terms and conditions as are contained in the act entitled "An act making provision for the debt of the United States:" *Provided*, That the books for receiving the said subscriptions shall be opened only at the Treasury of the United States.

Sec. 2. *And be it further enacted*, That such of the creditors of the United States as have not subscribed, and shall not subscribe, to the said loan, shall, nevertheless, receive, during the year one thousand seven hundred and ninety-three, a rate per centum on the amount of such of their demands as shall have been registered conformable to the directions contained in the said act, on or before the last day of June, one thousand seven hundred and ninety-four, equal to the interest which would be payable to them as subscribing creditors.

Approved March 2, 1793.

An Act further extending the time for receiving on loan the domestic debt of the United States.

Sec. 1. *Be it enacted by the Senate and House of Representatives of the United States of America in Congress assembled*, That the term for receiving on loan that part of the domestic debt of the United States which shall not have been subscribed in pursuance of the act entitled " An act for extending the time for receiving on loan that part of the domestic debt of the United States which may not be subscribed prior to the first day of March, one thousand seven hundred and ninety-three," be, and the same is hereby, further extended, from and after the last day of June ensuing, until the last day of December next, inclusively, on the same terms and conditions as are contained in the act entitled " An act making provision for the debt of the United States:" *Provided*, That the books for receiving the said subscriptions shall be opened only at the Treasury of the United States.

Sec. 2. *And be it further enacted*, That such of the creditors of the United States as have not subscribed, and shall not subscribe, to the said loan, shall, nevertheless, receive, during the year one thousand seven hundred and ninety-four, a rate per centum on the amount of such of their demands as have been registered, or as shall be registered at the Treasury, conformable to the directions in the act entitled " An act making provision for the debt of the United States," equal to the interest which would be payable to them as subscribing creditors.

Approved May 30, 1794.

----

An Act further extending the time for receiving on loan the domestic debt of the United States.

Sec. 1. *Be it enacted by the Senate and House of Representatives of the United States of America in Congress assembled*, That the term for receiving on loan that part of the domestic debt of the United States which has not been subscribed in pursuance of the provisions heretofore made by law for that purpose, be, and the same is hereby, further extended until the thirty-first day of December next, on the same terms and conditions as are contained in the act entitled " An act making provision for the debt of the United States :" *Provided*, That the books for receiving the said subscriptions shall be opened only at the Treasury of the United States.

Sec. 2. *And be it further enacted*, That such of the creditors of the United States as have not subscribed, and shall not subscribe, to the said loan, shall, nevertheless, receive, during the year one thousand seven hundred and ninety-five, a rate per centum on the amount of such of their demands as have been registered, or as shall be registered at the Treasury, conformable to the directions in the act entitled " An act making provision for the debt of the United States," equal to the interest which would be payable to them as subscribing creditors.

Approved January 28, 1795.

----

An Act further extending the time for receiving on loan the domestic debt of the United States.

Sec. 1. *Be it enacted by the Senate and House of Representatives of the United States of America in Congress assembled*, That the term for receiving on loan that part of the domestic debt of the United States which has not been subscribed, in pursuance of the provisions heretofore made by law for that purpose, be, and the same is hereby, further extended until the thirty-first day of December next, on the same terms and conditions as are contained in the act entitled "An act making provision for the debt of the United States:" *Provided*, That the books for receiving the said subscriptions shall be opened only at the Treasury of the United States.

Sec. 2. *And be it further enacted*, That it shall be lawful to reimburse so much of the principal of the debt or stock which may be subscribed pursuant to this act, as will make the reimbursement thereof equal, in proportion and degree, to that of the same stock subscribed antecedent to the present year; and the said reimbursement shall be made at the expiration of the quarter in which such debt or stock shall be subscribed, and pursuant to the rules and conditions prescribed by the act entitled "An act making further provision for the support of public credit, and for the redemption of the public debt."

Sec. 3. *And be it further enacted*, That such of the creditors of the United States as have not subscribed, and shall not subscribe, to the said loan, shall, nevertheless, receive, during the year one thousand seven hundred and ninety-six, a rate per centum on the amount of such of their demands as have been registered, or as shall be registered at the Treasury, conformably to the directions in the act entitled "An act making provision for the debt of the United States," equal to the interest which would be payable to them as subscribing creditors.

Approved February 19, 1796.

---

An Act extending the time for receiving on loan the domestic debt of the United States.

Sec. 1. *Be it enacted by the Senate and House of Representatives of the United States of America in Congress assembled*, That all the several provisions of the act entitled "An act further extending the time for receiving on loan the domestic debt of the United States," passed the nineteenth day of February, one thousand seven hundred and ninety-six, be, and they are hereby, continued in force until the thirty-first day of December next, and no longer: *Provided*, That nothing herein contained shall be construed to extend to any evidence of public debt which may be barred by any act of limitation.

Approved March 3, 1797.

---

An Act making provision for the redemption of the whole of the public debt of the United States.

Sec. 1. *Be it enacted, &c.*, That so much of the duties on merchandise and tonnage, as, together with the moneys other than surpluses of revenue, which now constitute the sinking fund, or shall accrue to it by virtue of any provisions heretofore made, and, together with the sums annually required to discharge the annual interest and charges accruing on the present debt of the United States, including temporary loans heretofore obtained, and also future loans which may be made for reimbursing or redeeming any instalments, or parts of the principal of the said debt, will amount to an annual sum of seven millions three hundred thousand dollars, be, and the same hereby is, yearly appropriated to the said fund; and the said sums are hereby declared to be vested in the commissioners of the sinking fund, in the same manner as the moneys heretofore appropriated to the said fund, to be applied by the said commissioners to the payment of interest and charges, and to the reimbursement or redemption of the principal of the public debt, and shall be and continue appropriated until the whole of the present debt of the United States, and the loans which may be made for reimbursing or redeeming any parts or instalments of the principal of the said debt, shall be reimbursed and redeemed: *Provided*, That after the whole of the said debt—the old six per cent. stock, the deferred stock, the seventeen hundred and ninety-six six per cent. stock, and three per cent. stock excepted—shall have been reimbursed or redeemed, any balance of the sums annually appropriated by this act, which may remain unexpended at the end of six months next succeeding the end of the calendar year to which such annual appropriation refers, shall be carried to the surplus fund, and cease to be vested, by virtue of this act, in the commissioners of the sinking fund; and the appropriation, so far as relates to such unexpended balance, shall cease and determine.

Sec. 2. *And be it further enacted*, That it shall be the duty of the Secretary of the Treasury, annually, and in each year, to cause to be paid to the commissioners of the sinking fund the said sum of seven millions three hundred thousand dollars, in such payments, and at such times in each year, as the situation of the treasury will permit: *Provided*, That all such payments as may be necessary to enable the said commissioners to discharge or reimburse any demands against the United States, on account of the principal or interest of the debt which shall be actually due in conformity to the engagements of the said States, shall be made at such time and times, in each year, as will enable the said commissioners faithfully and punctually to comply with such engagement.

Sec. 3. *And be it further enacted*, That all reimbursements of the capital or principal of the present debt of the United States, including future loans which may be made for reimbursing or redeeming any instalments, or parts of the same, and all payments on account of the interest and charges accruing upon the said debt, shall be made under the superintendence of the commissioners of the sinking fund. And it shall be the duty of the said commissioners to cause to be applied, and paid out of the said fund, yearly, and every year, at the Treasury of the United States, the several and respective sums following, to wit: first, such sum and sums as, by virtue of any act or acts, they have heretofore been directed to apply and to pay; secondly, such sum and sums as may be annually wanted to discharge the annual interest and charges accruing on any other part of the present debt of the United States, including the interest and charges which may accrue on future loans which may be made for reimbursing or redeeming any instalments, or parts of the principal of the said debt; thirdly, such sum and sums as may annually be required to discharge any instalment or part of the principal of the present debt of the United States, and of any future loans which may be made for reimbursing or discharging the same, which shall be actually due and demandable, and which shall not, by virtue of this or any other act, be renewed, or prolonged, or reimbursed out of the proceeds of a new loan; and, also, it shall be the duty of the said commissioners to cause to be applied the surplus of such fund as may at any time exist, after satisfying the purposes aforesaid, towards the further and final redemption, by payment or purchase, of the present debt of the United States, including loans for the reimbursement thereof, temporary loans heretofore obtained from the Bank of the United States, and those demands against the United States, under any treaty or convention with a foreign Power, for the payment of which the faith of the United States has been, or may hereafter be, pledged by Congress : *Provided, however*, That the whole or any part of such demands arising under a treaty or convention with a foreign Power, and of such temporary loans, may at any time be reimbursed, either out of the sinking fund, or, if the situation of the Treasury will permit, out of any other moneys which have been, or may hereafter be, appropriated to that purpose.

Sec. 4. *And be it further enacted*, That the commissioners of the sinking fund be, and they hereby are, empowered, with the approbation of the President of the United States, to borrow, on the credit of the United States, either in America or abroad, by obtaining a prolongation of former loans, or otherwise, the sums requisite for the payment of the instalments, or parts of the principal, of the Dutch debt, which become due in the years one thousand eight hundred and three, one thousand eight hundred and four, one thousand eight hundred and five, and one thousand eight hundred and six; and that a sum equivalent to that to be thus borrowed or reloaned, shall be laid out by the commissioners of the sinking fund in the purchase or redemption of such parts of the present debt of the United States, and other demands against them, as the commissioners of the sinking fund may lawfully pay, agreeably to the provisions hereinbefore made, and as the said commissioners shall, in their judgment, deem most expedient, so as to effect the payment annually of seven millions three hundred thousand dollars, towards the final discharge of the whole debt, agreeably to such provision: *Provided*, That the United States shall have a right to reimburse any loan thus made within six years after the date of the same, and that the rate of interest thereupon shall not exceed five per centum per annum, nor the charges thereupon the rate of five per centum on the capital borrowed: *And provided always*, That the power herein given shall not be construed to repeal, diminish, or affect the power given to the said commissioners by the tenth section of the act entitled " An act making further provision for the support of public credit, and for the redemption of the public debt," to borrow certain sums for the discharge of the instalments of the capital or principal of the public debt, in the manner and on the terms prescribed by the said section; nor the power given to them by an act entitled "An act making provision for the payment of certain debts of the United States," to borrow certain sums, and to sell the shares of the Bank of the United States, belonging to the United States, in the manner, on the terms, and for the purposes, authorized by the said act : *And provided further*, That nothing herein contained shall be construed to revive any act or part of an act authorizing the loan of money, and which hath heretofore expired.

Sec. 5. *And be it further enacted*, That, for the purpose of more effectually securing the reimbursement of the Dutch debt, the commissioners of the sinking fund may, and they are hereby, empowered, with the approbation of the President of the United States, to contract, either with the Bank of the United States, or with any other public institution, or with individuals, for the payment, in Holland, of the whole, or any part, of the principal of the said Dutch debt, and of the interest and charges accruing on the same, as the said demands become due, on such terms as the said commissioners shall think most advantageous to the United States; or to employ either the said bank, or any other public institution, or any individual or individuals, as agent or agents, for the purpose of purchasing bills of exchange, or any other kind of remittances, for the purpose of discharging the interest and principal of said debt, and to allow to such agent or agents a compensation not exceeding one-fourth of one per cent. on the remittances thus purchased or procured by them, under the direction of the said commissioners. And as much of the duties on tonnage and merchandise as may be necessary for that purpose, is hereby appropriated towards paying the extra allowance or commission resulting from such transaction or transactions, and also to pay any deficiency arising from any loss incurred upon any remittance purchased or procured under the direction of the said commissioners, for the purpose of discharging the principal and interest of the said debt.

Sec. 6. *And be further enacted,* That the commissioners of the sinking fund be, and they hereby are, empowered, with the approbation of the President of the United States, to employ, if they shall deem it necessary, an agent in Europe, for the purpose of transacting any business relative to the discharge of the Dutch debt, and to the loans authorized by this or any other act, for the purpose of discharging the same ; and also to allow him a compensation, not exceeding three thousand dollars a year, to be paid out of any moneys in the Treasury not otherwise appropriated.

Sec. 7. *And be it further enacted,* That nothing in this act contained shall be construed to repeal, alter, or affect any of the provisions of any former act, pledging the faith of the United States to the payment of the interest or principal of the public debt, and that all such payments shall continue to be made at the time heretofore prescribed by law ; and the surplus only of the appropriations made by this act, beyond the sums payable by virtue of the provisions of any former act, shall be applicable to the reimbursement, redemption, or purchase of the public debt in the manner provided by this act.

Sec. 8. *And be it further enacted,* That all the restrictions and regulations heretofore established by law for regulating the execution of the duties enjoined upon the commissioners of the sinking fund, shall apply to, and be in as full force for, the execution of the analogous duties enjoined by this act, as if they were herein particularly repeated and re-enacted : *Provided, however,* That the particular annual account of all sales of stock, of loans, and of payments by them made, shall hereafter be laid before Congress on the first week of February in each year ; and so much of any former act as directed such account to be laid before Congress within fourteen days after their meeting, is hereby repealed.

Approved, April 29, 1802.

---

An Act supplementary to the act entitled "An act making provision for the redemption of the whole of the public debt of the United States."

Whereas it is desirable to adapt the nature of the provision for the redemption of the public debt to the present circumstances of the United States, which can only be done by a voluntary subscription on the part of the creditors :

Sec. 1. *Be it enacted, &c.,* That a subscription to the full amount of the old six per cent. deferred, and three per cent. stocks, be, and the same is hereby, proposed; for which purpose books shall be opened at the Treasury of the United States, and by the several commissioners of loans, on the first day of July next, to continue open until the seventeenth day of March next following, inclusively, the fourteen last days of each quarter excepted, for such parts of the above-mentioned descriptions of stock as shall, on the day of subscription, stand on the books of the Treasury, and of the several commissioners of loans, respectively; which subscription shall be effected by a transfer to the United States, in the manner provided by law for such transfers, of the credit or credits standing on the said books, and by a surrender of the certificates of the stock subscribed.

Sec. 2. *And be it further enacted,* That, for the whole or any part of any sum which shall thus be subscribed, in old six per cent. or deferred stock, credits shall be entered to the respective subscribers, and the subcriber or subscribers shall be entitled to a certificate or certificates, purporting that the United States owe to the holder or holders thereof, his, her, or their assigns, a sum to be expressed therein, equal to the amount of principal of the stock thus subscribed, which shall remain unredeemed on the day of such subscription, bearing an interest of six per centum per annum, payable quarter-yearly, from the first day of the quarter during which such subscription shall have been made, transferable in the same manner as is provided by law for the transfers of the stock subscribed, and subject to redemption at the pleasure of the United States: *Provided,* That no single certificate shall be issued for an amount greater than ten thousand dollars: *And provided, further,* That no reimbursement shall be made except for the whole amount of any such new certificate, nor till after at least six months' previous public notice of such intended reimbursement.

Sec. 3. *And be it further enacted,* That for the whole or any part of any sum which shall thus be subscribed in three per cent. stock, credits shall likewise be entered to the respective subscribers; and the subscriber or subscribers shall be entitled to a certificate, purporting that the United States owe to the holder or holders thereof, his, her, or their assigns, a sum to be expressed therein, equal to sixty-five per centum of the amount of principal of the stock thus subscribed, bearing an interest of six per centum per annum, payable quarter-yearly, from the first day of the quarter during which such subscription shall have been made, and transferable, and subject to redemption, in the same manner, and under the same regulations and restrictions, as the stock created by the preceding section of this act: *Provided,* That no part of the stock thus created shall be reimbursable without the assent of the holder or holders of such stock, until after the whole of the eight per cent. and four and a half per cent. stocks, as well as all the six per cent. stock which may be created by virtue of the preceding section, shall have been redeemed.

Sec. 4. *And be it further enacted,* That the commissioners of the sinking fund shall be, and they are hereby, authorized to appoint an agent in London, and another in Amsterdam, whose duty it shall be to receive subscriptions and transfers, and to issue new certificates, in the manner, and at the times, above mentioned, and as the officers of the Treasury Department, or the commissioners of loans, might do : that is to say : the agent in London, in favor of such stockholders residing in the dominions of Great Britain in Europe, and the agent in Amsterdam, in favor of such stockholders residing in any other part of Europe, as may, respectively, become subscribers: *Provided,* That the certificates issued by the said agents shall bear interest only from the first day of the quarter next succeeding that in which the subscription shall have taken place; and that, in relation to subscriptions made in old six per cent. or deferred stocks, the sums expressed in such new certificates shall be equal to the amount of the principal of the old six per cent. or deferred stocks thus subscribed, which shall remain unredeemed, after payment of the dividend payable on such stock, on that day from which the interest on the new certificates shall commence. The foreign stockholders, thus subscribing with either of the said agents, shall be entitled to receive the dividend on the old six per cent. deferred, or three per cent. stock, subscribed by them, respectively, which shall be payable on that day, from which the interest on the new certificates shall commence. And it shall be the duty of the said agents, respectively, to transmit, before the end of each quarter, to the Register of the Treasury, and to the several commissioners of loans, respectively, triplicate abstracts of the certificates of stocks subscribed, and of the new certificates issued by them, during such quarter, in order that the proper credits may be entered on the books of the Treasury and of the commissioners of loans, as the case may be, to the holders of such new certificates. And the said agents, before they enter upon the execution of their several offices, shall, respectively, take an oath or affirmation for the diligent and faithful execution of their trust, and shall also become bound, with one or more sureties, to the satisfaction of the commissioners of the sinking fund, or of the Secretary of the Treasury, in the penal sum of twenty thousand dollars, with condition for their good behavior in their said offices.

Sec. 5. *And be it further enacted,* That the holders of old six per cent. deferred, or three per cent. stock, who may become subscribers, as aforesaid, either in the United States or in Europe, and who, on the first day of July next, and also on the day of the subscription, shall be resident in Europe, may, at their option, which must be made at the time of subscribing, receive the interest accruing on the stock created by virtue of the preceding sections of this act, either in the United States, as other creditors, or at London or Amsterdam; that is to say, the stockholders residing, at the times above mentioned, in the dominions of Great Britain in Europe, at London, and at the rate of four shillings and six pence sterling for each dollar; and the stockholders residing, at the times above mentioned, in any other part of Europe, at Amsterdam, and at the rate of two guilders and a half guilder, current money of Holland, for each dollar; in which last-mentioned option the condition shall be expressed in the new certificates to be issued, and the credit or credits to be given to the proprietors thereof shall be entered, and shall thereafter be transferable only on the books of the Treasury : *Provided, however,* That the interest thus payable in London and Amsterdam shall not be payable until the expiration of six calendar months from the day on which the same would be payable in the United States, and shall be subject to a deduction of one-half of one per cent. on the amount payable, for commission to the bankers paying the same : *And provided, also,* That every proprietor of such stock may, on surrendering his certificate, receive another to the same amount; the interest whereof shall be payable quarter-yearly in the United States, in the same manner as that accruing on the stock held by persons residing in the United States.

8

Sec. 6. *And be it further enacted,* That the same funds which heretofore have been, and now are, pledged by law for the payment of the interest, and for the redemption or reimbursement of the stock which may be subscribed by virtue of the provisions of this act, shall remain pledged for the payment of interest accruing on the stock created by reason of such subscription, and for the redemption or reimbursement of the principal of the same. It shall be the duty of the commissioners of the sinking fund to cause to be applied and paid out of the said fund, yearly and every year, such sum and sums as may be annually wanted to discharge the annual interest and charges accruing on the stock which may be created by virtue of this act. The said commissioners are hereby authorized to apply, from time to time, such sum and sums out of the said fund as they may think proper towards redeeming, by purchase or by reimbursement, in conformity with the provisions of this act, the principal of the said stock. And the annual sum of eight millions of dollars, vested by law in the said commissioners, shall be and continue appropriated to the payment of interest and redemption of the public debt, until the whole of the stock which may be created by the preceding sections of this act shall have been redeemed or reimbursed.

Sec. 7. *And be it further enacted,* That there shall be allowed to each of the agents to be appointed by virtue of this act, in addition to the necessary expenses incurred by them for printing, stationary, and postage, a sum of three thousand dollars, as a full compensation for their services. The said agents, and the commissioners of loans, shall also be allowed such additional sum as may be actually and necessarily expended for the clerk-hire requisite for carrying this act into effect. And for defraying the said compensations and allowances, and such other contingent charges as may be incurred for carrying this act into effect, a sum not exceeding sixteen thousand dollars, to be paid out of any moneys in the Treasury not otherwise appropriated, is hereby appropriated.

Sec. 8. *And be it further enacted,* That whensoever notice of reimbursement shall be given, as prescribed by the second and third sections of this act, the certificates intended to be reimbursed shall be designated therein. In every reimbursement, the preference shall be given to such holders of certificates as, previously to the said notice, shall have notified, in writing, to the Treasury Department, their wish to be reimbursed. If there should not be applications to the Treasury sufficient to require the payment of the whole sum to be applied to that purpose, the Secretary of the Treasury, after paying off all sums for the payment of which application shall have been made, shall determine, by lot, what other certificates shall be reimbursed, so as to make up the whole amount to be discharged : and in case the applications shall exceed the amount to be discharged, the Secretary of the Treasury shall proceed to determine, by lot, what applications shall be entitled to priority of payment.

Sec. 9. *And be it further enacted,* That the agents appointed by virtue of this act, and the several commissioners of loans, shall observe and perform such directions and regulations as shall be prescribed to them by the Secretary of the Treasury, touching the execution of this act.

Sec. 10. *And be it further enacted,* That nothing in this act contained shall be construed in anywise to alter, abridge, or impair the rights of those creditors of the United States who shall not subscribe to the loan created by virtue of this act.

Approved February 11, 1807.

An Act supplementary to the act entitled " An act making further provision for the support of public credit, and for the redemption of the public debt."

Sec. 1. *Be it enacted, &c.* That the powers vested in the commissioners of the sinking fund, by the tenth section of the act to which this act is a supplement, shall extend to all the cases of reimbursement of any instalments, or parts of the capital, or principal, of the public debt now existing, which may become payable according to law. And in every case in which a loan may be made accordingly, it shall be lawful for such loan to be made of the Bank of the United States, any thing in any act of Congress to the contrary notwithstanding.

Approved June 28, 1809.

## CHAPTER V.

*Acts of Congress providing for the Settlement of Claims which had been barred by limitations previously established, and for the settlement of such as had not been barred by any act of limitation, and had not been previously adjusted; also, limiting the time for presenting Claims for destroyed Certificates of certain descriptions, and reviving the laws and extending the time for paying Loan Office and Final Settlement Certificates, Indents of Interest, &c.*

[1792, March 23.]

An Act to provide for the settlement of the claims of widows and orphans barred by the limitations heretofore established.

*Be it enacted by the Senate and House of Representatives of the United States of America in Congress assembled,* That the operation of the resolutions of the late Congress of the United States, passed on the 2d day of November, 1785, and the 23d day of July, 1787, so far as they have barred, or may be construed to bar, the claims of the widow or orphans of any officer of the late army to the seven years' half pay of such officer, shall, from and after the passing this act, be suspended for and during the term of two years.

---

[1792, March 27.]

An Act providing for the settlement of the claims of persons, under particular circumstances, barred by the limitations heretofore established.

Sec. 1. *Be it enacted, &c.,* That the operation of the resolutions of the late Congress of the United States, passed on the 2d day of November, 1785, and the 23d day of July, 1787, so far as they have barred, or may be construed to bar, the claims of any officer, soldier, artificer, sailor, or marine, of the late army or navy of the United States, for personal services rendered to the United States in the military or naval departments, shall, from and after the passing of this act, be suspended for and during the term of two years; and that every such officer, soldier, artificer, sailor, and marine, having claims for services rendered to the United States in the military or naval departments, who shall exhibit the same for liquidation at the Treasury of the United States, at any time during the said term of two years, shall be entitled to an adjustment and allowance thereof, on the same principles as if the same had been exhibited within the term prescribed by the aforesaid resolutions of Congress: *Provided,* That nothing herein shall be construed to extend to claims for rations or subsistence money.

Sec. 2. *And be it further enacted,* That no balances hereafter to be certified as due from the United States, shall be registered in any other name than that of the original claimant, or of his heirs, executors, or administrators; and such balances shall be transferable only at the Treasury, by virtue of powers actually executed after such registry, expressing the sum to be transferred, and in pursuance of such general rules as have been or shall be prescribed for that purpose.

[1793, February 12.]

Act relative to claims against the United States, not barred by any act of limitation, and which have not been already adjusted.

*Be it enacted, &c.*, That all claims upon the United States for services or supplies, or for other cause, matter, or thing, furnished or done previous to the 4th day of March, 1789, whether founded upon certificates, or other written documents from public officers, or otherwise, which have not already been barred by any act of limitation, and which shall not be presented at the Treasury before the first day of May, 1794, shall forever after be barred and precluded from settlement or allowance : *Provided,* That nothing herein contained shall be construed to affect loan office certificates, certificates of final settlement, indents of interest, balances entered in the books of the Register of the Treasury, certificates issued by the Register of the Treasury, commonly called registered certificates, loans of money obtained in foreign countries, or certificates issued pursuant to the act entitled " An act making provision for the debt of the United States:" *And provided, further,* That nothing herein contained shall be construed to prohibit the proper officers of the Treasury from demanding an account or accounts to be rendered for any moneys heretofore advanced and not accounted for, or from admitting, under the usual forms and restrictions, credits for expenditures, equal to the sums which have been so advanced.

Sec. 2. *And be it further enacted,* That it shall be the duty of the Auditor of the Treasury to receive all such claims aforesaid, as have not been heretofore barred by any act of limitation, as shall be presented before the time aforesaid, with the certificates or other documents in support thereof, and to cause a record to be made of the names of the persons, and of the time when the said claims are presented ; which record shall be made in the presence of the person or persons presenting the same, and shall be the only evidence that the said claims were presented during the time limited by this act.

Sec. 3. *And be it further enacted,* That it shall be the duty of the accounting officers of the Treasury to make report to Congress upon all such of the said claims as shall not be allowed to be valid, according to the usual forms of the Treasury.

---

[1794, April 21.]

Act limiting the time for presenting claims for destroyed certificates of certain descriptions.

Sec. 1. *Be it enacted, &c.,* That all claims for the renewal of certificates of the unsubscribed debt of the United States, of the descriptions commonly called "loan office certificates," or " final settlements," which may have been accidentally destroyed, shall be forever barred and precluded from settlement or allowance, unless the same shall be presented at the Treasury on or before the first day of June, in the year one thousand seven hundred and ninety-five.

Sec. 2. *And be it further enacted,* That no claim shall be allowed for the renewal of loan office certificates destroyed before the fourth day of March, 1789, unless the destruction of the same was advertised, according to the resolution of Congress of the 10th day of May, 1780, or, before that time, was notified to the office from which the same was issued; nor shall c.aims be allowed for the renewal of loan office certificates destroyed on or after the said fourth day of March, 1789, nor of final settlement certificates destroyed at any time, unless the destruction of the same was so far made public as to be known to at least two credible witnesses soon after it happened, and shall have been, before the presentation of the claim, as hereinafter provided, advertised for at least six weeks successively, in some one of the newspapers of the State in which the destruction happened; and, also, in some one of the newspapers of the State in which the certificate issued, if that was another State; the advertisement or advertisements in such case expressing, with as much precision as possible, the number, date, and amount of the certificate alleged to have been destroyed, and the name of the person to whom the same was issued, together with the time when, the place where, and the means by which, the same was destroyed.

Sec. 3. *And be it further enacted,* That all claims for the renewal of destroyed certificates, of either of the descriptions aforesaid, not precluded by this act, shall be receivable, with the evidence in support of the same, by the Auditor of the Treasury, until the said first day of June, 1795, and shall, by the accounting officers of the Treasury, be duly examined; and if satisfactorily supported, the claimants shall be entitled to receive certificates of registered debt, equal to the specie value of the loan office or final settlement certificates so proved to have been destroyed.

---

[1795, March 3.]

Sec. 14. *And be it further enacted,* That all certificates commonly called loan office certificates, final settlements, indents of interest, which, at the time of passing this act, shall be outstanding, shall, on or before the first day of January, in the year 1797, be presented at the office of the Auditor of the Treasury of the United States, for the purpose of being exchanged for other certificates of equivalent value and tenor; or, at the option of the holders thereof, respectively, to be registered at the said office and returned; in which case, it shall be the duty of the said Auditor to cause some durable mark or marks to be set on each certificate, which shall ascertain and fix its identity, and whether genuine, or counterfeit, or forged; and every of the said certificates which shall not be presented at the said office within the said time, shall be forever after barred or precluded from settlement or allowance.

---

An Act respecting loan office and final settlement certificates, indents of interest, and the unfunded or registered debt, credited in the books of the Treasury.

Sec. 1. *Be it enacted by the Senate and House of Representatives of the United States of America in Congress assembled,* That so much of the act entitled "An act making further provision for the support of public credit, and for the redemption of the public debt," passed the third day of March, one thousand seven hundred and ninety-five, as bars from settlement or allowance certificates, commonly called loan office and final settlement certificates, and indents of interest, be, and the same is hereby, suspended for the term of one year from and after the time of the passing of this act; a notification of which temporary suspension of the act of limitation shall be published by the Secretary of the Treasury, for the information of the holders of the said certificates, in one or more of the public papers in each of the United States.

Sec. 2. *And be it further enacted,* That, on the liquidation and settlement of such of the said certificates, and indents of interest, as may be presented at the Treasury pursuant to this act, the creditors shall be allowed to receive certificates of funded three per cent. stock of the United States, equal to the said indents, and the arrearages of interest due on their said certificates prior to the first day of January, one thousand seven hundred and ninety-one.

Sec. 3. *And be it further enacted,* That the principal sums of the said loan office and final settlement certificates, with the interest thereon since the first day of January, one thousand seven hundred and ninety-one, shall and may be discharged, after liquidation at the Treasury, by the payment of interest and reimbursement of principal, equal to the sums which would have been payable thereon if the said certificates had been subscribed pursuant to the acts making provision for the debts of the United States contracted during the late war, and by the payment of other sums, equal to the market value of the remaining funded stock which would have been created by subscriptions as aforesaid; which market value shall be determined by the Comptroller of the Treasury.

Sec. 4. *And be it further enacted,* That the sum of twenty thousand dollars shall be, and hereby is, appropriated for the purposes aforesaid, to be paid out of any moneys in the Treasury not otherwise appropriated.

Sec. 5. *And be it further enacted,* That from and after the passing of this act, it shall not be lawful for the officers of the Treasury to issue, or cause to be issued, any certificates of registered or unfunded debt; and that, to satisfy such claims for services or supplies, furnished or done prior to the establishment of the present constitution of the United States, as shall be allowed according to law, and the course of settlement at the Treasury, there be appropriated a sum not exceeding twenty thousand dollars, to be paid out of any moneys in the Treasury not otherwise appropriated.

Sec. 6. *And be it further enacted,* That the commissioners of the sinking fund shall be, and they are hereby, required to reimburse, or cause to be reimbursed, the principal sums of the unfunded or registered debt of the United States credited on the books of the Treasury and commissioners of loans; and that they cause a notification to be published, informing the creditors generally of the said reimbursement, and that interest on the said debts will cease at the expiration of six months after the date of the said notification ; and that a sum, not exceeding ninety thousand dollars, be appropriated for the reimbursement of the debts aforesaid, out of any moneys in the Treasury not otherwise appropriated.

Sec. 7. *And be it further enacted,* That it shall be lawful for the creditors of the unfunded or registered debt, aforesaid, to receive certificates of funded three per cent. stock, equal to the arrearages of interest due to them, respectively, prior to the first day of January, one thousand seven hundred and ninety-one ; and, on the requisition of each or any of the said creditors, the proper officers of the Treasury are hereby required to issue, or cause to be issued, the said certificates of funded three per cent. stock, accordingly.

Approved June 12, 1798.

An Act to authorize the payment of certain certificates.

Sec. 1. *Be it enacted, &c.*, That so much of an act entitled "An act making further provision for the support of public credit, and for the redemption of the public debt," passed the third of March, one thousand seven hundred and ninety-five ; and so much of the act entitled "An act respecting loan office and final settlement certificates, indents of interest, and the unfunded and registered debt, credited on the books of the Treasury," passed the twelfth of June, one thousand seven hundred and ninety-eight, as bars from settlement or allowance certificates commonly called loan office and final settlement certificates, and indents of interest, be, and the same is hereby, suspended for the term of two years from and after the passing of this act ; a notification of which temporary suspension of the act of limitation shall be published by the Secretary of the Treasury, for the information of the holders of the said certificates, in one or more of the public papers in each of the United States.

Sec. 2. *And be it further enacted*, That all certificates, commonly called loan office certificates, countersigned by the loan officers of the States respectively, final settlement certificates, and indents of interest, which, at the time of passing this act, shall be outstanding, may be presented at the Treasury, and, upon the same being liquidated and adjusted, shall be paid to the respective holders of the same, with interest, at six per cent., from the date of the last payment of interest, as endorsed on said certificates.

Sec. 3. *And be it further enacted*, That, for carrying this act into effect, the sum of eighty thousand dollars be appropriated, out of any moneys in the Treasury of the United States not otherwise appropriated.

Approved, April 13, 1818.

---

An Act authorizing the payment of certain certificates.

Sec. 1. *Be it enacted, &c.*, That so much of an act entitled "An act making further provision for the support of public credit and for the redemption of the public debt," passed the third of March, one thousand seven hundred and ninety-five ; and so much of the act entitled "An act respecting loan office and final settlement certificates, indents of interest, and the unfunded and registered debt, credited on the books of the Treasury," passed the twelfth of June, one thousand seven hundred and ninety-eight, as bars from settlement or allowance certificates commonly called loan office and final settlement certificates, and indents of interest, be, and the same is hereby, suspended for the term of two years from and after the passing of this act, and from thence until the end of the next session of Congress ; a notification of which temporary suspension of the act of limitation shall be published by the Secretary of the Treasury, for the information of the holders of the said certificates, in one or more of the public papers in each of the United States.

Sec. 2. *And be it further enacted*, That all certificates, commonly called loan office certificates, countersigned by the loan officers of the States respectively, final settlement certificates, and indents of interest, which, at the time of passing this act, shall be outstanding, may be presented at the Treasury, and, upon the same being liquidated and adjusted, shall be paid to the respective holders of the same, with interest at six per cent. per annum, from the date of the last payment of interest, as endorsed on said certificates.

Sec. 3. *And be it further enacted*, That, for carrying this act into effect, the sum of fifteen thousand dollars be appropriated, out of any moneys in the Treasury of the United States not otherwise appropriated.

Approved May 7, 1822.

---

An Act to revive and continue in force " An act authorizing the payment of certain certificates," approved May 7, 1822.

Sec. 1. *Be it enacted, &c.*, That the " Act authorizing the payment of certain certificates," approved May 7, 1822, be, and the same is hereby, revived and continued in force for the term of four years from and after the passing of this act, and from thence to the end of the next session of Congress thereafter, a notification of which revival and continuance shall be published by the Secretary of the Treasury, for the information of the holders of the certificates, the payment of which is authorized by said act, in one or more of the public papers printed in each of the United States.

Sec. 2. *And be it further enacted*, That, for carrying this act into effect, the sum of forty thousand dollars be, and hereby is, appropriated, out of any money in the Treasury of the United States not otherwise appropriated.

Approved July 14, 1832.

## CHAPTER VI.

*Special Acts of Congress authorizing the Payment of Loan Office and Final Settlement Certificates, Indents of Interest, &c.*

### An act providing for the payment of the interest on a certificate due to General Kosciusko.

Sec. 1. *Be it enacted by the Senate and House of Representatives of the United States of America in Congress assembled,* That the Secretary of the Treasury be authorized and directed to pay to General Kosciusko, out of any moneys in the Treasury not otherwise appropriated, an interest, at the rate of six per centum per annum, on the sum of twelve thousand two hundred and eignty dollars and fifty-four cents, the amount of a certificate due to him from the United States, from the first day of January, one thousand seven hundred and ninety-three, to the thirty-first of December, one thousand seven hundred and ninety-seven.

Approved, January 23, 1798.

---

### An Act for the relief of John Dixon and John Murray.

Sec. 1. *Be it enacted, &c.,* That the Secretary of the Treasury be, and he hereby is, authorized to pay to John Dixon, out of any money in the Treasury not otherwise appropriated, the sum of three hundred and twenty-nine dollars and eighty-four cents, with six per centum per annum interest thereon, from the first of January, one thousand seven hundred and eighty-five, being the amount of a final settlement certificate, number five hundred and ninety-six, issued by Andrew Dunscomb, late commissioner of accounts for the State of Virginia, on the twenty-third of December, one thousand seven hundred and eighty-six, to Lucy Dixon, who transferred the same to John Dixon.

Sec. 2. *And be it further enacted,* That the accounting officers of the Treasury be, and they hereby are, authorized and directed to settle the account of John Murray, representative of Doctor Henry Murray, and that he be allowed the amount of three loan office certificates, number thirteen thousand nine hundred and seventy-five, for two hundred dollars; number thirteen thousand nine hundred and seventy-six, for two hundred dollars; number six thousand four hundred, for six hundred dollars; with interest from the twenty-ninth of March, one thousand seven hundred and eighty-two; issued in the name of Henry Murray, signed Francis Hopkinson, treasurer of loans, and countersigned Thomas Harwood; and that the amount due be paid to the said John Murray out of any money in the Treasury not otherwise appropriated.

Approved February 25, 1813.

An Act for the relief of the representatives of Samuel Lapsley, deceased.

Sec. 1. *Be it enacted, &c.*, That the accounting officers of the Treasury be, and they are hereby, authorized and directed to settle the account of John Lysle, and Margaret his wife, late Margaret Lapsley, widow and administratrix of Samuel Lapsley, deceased; and that she be allowed the amount of two final settlement certificates, No. 78446, for one thousand dollars, and No. 78447, for one thousand three hundred and sixty dollars, and interest from the twenty-second day of March, one thousand seven hundred and eighty-three, issued in the name of Samuel Lapsley, by the commissioner of army accounts, for the United States, on the first day of July, one thousand seven hundred and eighty-four; and that the amount due be paid out of any money in the Treasury not otherwise appropriated, to the said John Lysle, and Margaret his wife, administratrix as aforesaid, to be disposed of and distributed according to law.

Approved March 3, 1813.

––––––––

An act for the relief of Joseph Brevard.

Sec. 1. *Be it enacted, &c.*, That the accounting officers of the Treasury be, and they are hereby, authorized and directed to settle the account of Joseph Brevard, and that he be allowed the amount of a final settlement certificate, number ninety-one thousand nine hundred and fifteen, dated the first of February, one thousand seven hundred and eighty-five, for one hundred and eighty-three dollars and twenty-three ninetieths, and bearing interest from the first of January, one thousand seven hundred and eighty-three, and issued to the said Joseph Brevard by John Pierce, commissioner for settling accounts of the army; and that the amount due be paid, out of any money in the Treasury not otherwise appropriated, to the said Joseph Brevard.

Approved April 13, 1814.

––––––––

An Act for the relief of William Arnold.

Sec. 1. *Be it enacted, &c.*, That the accounting officers of the Treasury be, and they are hereby, authorized and directed to ascertain, agreeably to the provisions of the laws heretofore in existence on that subject, the amount due William Arnold, on a loan office certificate, numbered twelve hundred and sixty-seven, which issued from the loan office of Massachusetts, for six hundred dollars, on the twenty-fifth of October, one thousand seven hundred and seventy-seven, payable to Christopher Clarke, with interest thereon from the first of January, one thousand seven hundred and eighty-three, to which time the interest has been paid; and that the amount which shall be found to be due, be paid to the said William Arnold, out of any money in the Treasury not otherwise appropriated.

Approved February 2, 1815.

––––––––

An Act for the relief of Farrington Barkelow, administrator of Mary Rappleyea.

Sec. 1. *Be it enacted, &c.*, That the accounting officers of the Treasury be, and they are hereby, authorized and directed to ascertain, agreeably to the provisions of the laws heretofore in existence on that subject, the amount due Farrington Barkelow, administrator of the estate and effects of Mary Rappleyea, on two loan office certificates, issued to Mary Rappleyea, from the loan office of New Jersey, both dated the eighth of June, one thousand seven hundred and seventy-eight; the one numbered 1564, for six hundred dollars; the other, 294, for five hundred dollars, with such interest as still remains due thereon; and that the amount which shall be found to be due, be paid to the said Farrington Barkelow, as administrator, as aforesaid, to be distributed according to law.

Approved February 2, 1815.

---

### An Act for the relief of Aquila Giles.

Sec. 1. *Be it enacted, &c.,* That the proper accounting officers of the Treasury be, and they are hereby, authorized and directed to settle the claim of Aquila Giles, on account of a warrant issued by B. Lincoln, dated December twenty-eight, seventeen hundred and eighty-two, and attested by Joseph Carleton, expressing, on its face, to have issued for the balance of his pay as a major for that year, for five hundred dollars; and the amount which may be found due shall be paid to the said Aquila Giles, out of any moneys in the Treasury not otherwise appropriated: *Provided,* That any sum or sums of money with which he may stand charged on the books of the Treasury be first deducted out of the said amount.

Approved March 3, 1819.

---

### An Act for the relief of Thomas Leiper.

Sec. 1. *Be it enacted, &c.,* That there be paid to Thomas Leiper the specie value of four loan office certificates, numbered two thousand eight hundred and ninety-nine, two thousand nine hundred and four, two thousand nine hundred and five, and two thousand nine hundred and six, and issued by the commissioner of loans for the State of Pennsylvania, in the name of Thomas Leiper, on the twenty-seventh of February, seventeen hundred and seventy-nine, for one thousand dollars each; and also the specie value of two loan office certificates, numbered two thousand nine hundred and sixty, and two thousand nine hundred and sixty-one, issued by the commissioner of loans for the State of Pennsylvania, on the second of March, seventeen hundred and seventy-nine, for one thousand dollars each; which certificates appear to be outstanding on the books of the Treasury, with interest, at six per centum annually, out of any money in the Treasury not otherwise appropriated: *Provided,* That the said Thomas Leiper shall first execute and deliver to the Comptroller of the Treasury a bond of indemnity, in such sum and with such security as shall be satisfactory to the said Comptroller.

Approved May 15, 1820.

---

### An Act for the relief of John Crute.

Sec. 1. *Be it enacted, &c.,* That the proper accounting officers of the Treasury Department be, and they are hereby, authorized to audit and settle the claim of John Crute, on account of a certificate issued on the first of July, one thousand seven hundred and eighty-four, and numbered seventy-eight thousand four hundred and ninety-one, for two hundred and forty dollars, which certificate is alleged to have been accidentally destroyed, and appears, by the records of the Treasury, to be outstanding and unpaid; and to pay to the said John Crute the principal of the said certificate, and so much of the interest thereof as may remain due thereon: *Provided*, That the said John Crute execute and deliver to the Comptroller of the Treasury a bond of indemnity, in such sum, and with such security, as the said Comptroller may direct and approve ; the said moneys to be paid out of any money in the Treasury not otherwise appropriated.

Approved May 7, 1822.

---

An Act for the relief of the legal representatives of John Guthry, deceased.

Sec. 1. *Be it enacted, &c.*, That there be paid to the legal representatives of John Guthry, deceased, out of any money in the Treasury not otherwise appropriated, the sum of one hundred and twenty-three dollars and thirty cents, being the amount of a final settlement certificate, numbered seventy-eight thousand seven hundred and eighty-one, issued to the said John Guthry, and which certificate appears to be outstanding on the books of the Treasury, with interest at the rate of six per centum per annum from the first of January, one thousand seven hundred and eighty-eight: *Provided*, That the said legal representatives shall first execute and deliver to the Comptroller of the Treasury a bond of indemnity, in such sum, and with such security, as shall be satisfactory to the said Comptroller.

Approved May 7, 1822

---

An Act for the relief of the legal representative of James McClung, deceased.

Sec. 1. *Be it enacted, &c.*, That there shall be paid to the legal representative of James McClung, deceased, out of any money in the Treasury not otherwise appropriated, the sum of seventy-four dollars and sixty-two cents, being the amount of a final settlement certificate, numbered nine hundred and fifty-nine, issued to the said James McClung, and which certificate appears to be outstanding on the books of the Treasury, with interest, at the rate of six per centum per annum, from the first of January, one thousand seven hundred and eighty-eight: *Provided*, That the said legal representative shall first execute and deliver to the Comptroller of the Treasury a bond of indemnity, in such sum and with such security as shall be satisfactory to the said Comptroller.

Approved March 3, 1823.

---

An Act for the relief of Michael McKewen.

Sec. 1. *Be it enacted, &c.*, That the Attorney General of the United States be authorized and directed to cause satisfaction in full to be entered upon certain judgments of the United States against Michael McKewen, upon condition that the said Michael McKewen, or his legal representatives, execute a full release of all claims of the said Michael McKewen, for an assignment of an account of John Morris, a ward-master in the revolutionary war, for one hundred and seven dollars and forty-four ninetieths; and also for two final settlement certificates : the one of them numbered eighty-one thousand seven hundred and fifty-four, for eighty dollars, and the other of them numbered eighty-two thousand one hundred and fifty-four, for forty-three dollars and thirty-ninetieths, as well as for all other claims of the said Michael McKewen against the United States.

Approved March 3, 1825.

---

### An Act for the relief of John Crain.

Sec. 1. *Be it enacted, &c.*, That the accounting officers of the Treasury Department be, and they hereby are, authorized to audit and settle the claim of John Crain, on account of a certificate, number eight thousand three hundred and fourteen, issued in favor of James Swart, by John Pierce, and dated thirteenth of August, one thousand seven hundred and eighty-four, for one hundred dollars, which certificate has been lost, and appears to be outstanding and unpaid; and to pay to the said John Crain, or his legal representatives, the principal of the said certificate, and so much of the interest as appears to be due thereon, out of any money in the Treasury not otherwise appropriated: *Provided,* That the said John Crain, or his legal representatives, execute and deliver to the Comptroller of the Treasury a bond of indemnity, in such sum and with such security as the said Comptroller may approve.

Approved March 3, 1825.

---

### An Act for the relief of Bar. J. V. Valkenburgh.

Sec. 1. *Be it enacted, &c.*, That the proper accounting officers of the Treasury be, and they are hereby, authorized to pay to Bar. J. V. Valkenburgh, the sum of five hundred and ninety-seven dollars and twenty-four cents, being the amount of fourteen indents of interest, with interest thereon from the first of January, seventeen hundred and ninety-one, to the thirty-first of December, eighteen hundred and twenty-six ; which sum shall be paid out of any money in the Treasury not otherwise appropriated.

Approved March 3, 1827.

---

### An Act for the relief of the representatives of Patience Gordon, widow, deceased.

Sec. 1. *Be it enacted, &c.*, That there be paid to the legal representatives of Patience Gordon, deceased, the sum of one hundred and forty-five dollars and fifteen ninetieths, with interest at six per centum per annum, from the first of January, one thousand seven hundred and eighty-eight, it being the specie value of a certificate issued in the name of the said Patience Gordon, by the commissioner of loans for the State of New Jersey, bearing date April seventh, seventeen hundred and seventy-eight, number two thousand and twenty-seven, out of any moneys in the Treasury not otherwise appropriated : *Provided,* That the said legal representatives shall first execute and deliver to the First Comptroller of the Treasury a bond in such sum, and with such security, as the said Comptroller shall direct and approve, to indemnify the United States from and against the lawful claim of any other person or persons, for or on account of the said certificate.

Approved May 19, 1828.

---

An Act for the relief of Samuel Ward.

Sec. 1. *Be it enacted, &c.,* That the sum of one thousand and forty-seven dollars and fifty-two ninetieths be paid to Samuel Ward, surviving partner of the late firm of Samuel Ward and Brothers, out of any money in the Treasury not otherwise appropriated, being the principal sum due on a final settlement certificate, issued by Benjamin Walker to Abraham Whipple, Esq., dated the twenty-third day of October, one thousand seven hundred and eighty-six, number two hundred and eighty-one ; which certificate is alleged to have been lost or destroyed, and appears by the books of the Treasury to be outstanding and unpaid : *Provided,* That the said Samuel Ward shall first execute and deliver to the Comptroller of the Treasury a bond of indemnity in double the amount of the sum so to be paid, with such sufficient security as the said Comptroller shall direct and approve.

Approved May 24, 1828.

---

An Act for the relief of Archibald Bard and John Findley, executors of the last will and testament of Doctor Robert Johnson, deceased, and for the relief of John Scott, executor of Charles Yates, deceased.

Sec. 1. *Be it enacted, &c.,* That the proper accounting officers of the Treasury Department be authorized to audit and settle the claim of Archibald Bard and John Findley, executors of the last will and testament of Doctor Robert Johnson, deceased, on account of three several loan office certificates issued to and in the name of Doctor Isaac Foster, for the sum of four hundred dollars each, and numbered six thousand three hundred and thirty-one, six thousand three hundred and thirty-nine, and six thousand three hundred and forty ; and to ascertain the true specie value of the same, with interest at six per centum per annum thereon; (which certificates are alleged to have been lost or stolen, and appear by the books of the Treasury to be outstanding and unpaid ;) and that the amount so ascertained, as aforesaid, be paid to the said executors, or either of them, out of any money in the Treasury not otherwise appropriated : *Provided,* That the said executors shall first execute, and deliver to the Comptroller of the Treasury, a bond of indemnity in double the amount of the sum to be paid, with sufficient security, as the said Comptroller shall direct and approve.

Sec. 2. *And be it further enacted,* That the proper accounting officers of the Treasury Department be authorized to pay to John Scott, executor of Charles Yates, deceased, the specie value of a loan office certificate issued to, and in the name of Edward Watkins, for the sum of five hundred dollars, and numbered eight thousand four hundred and ninety-two.

Approved May 26, 1828.

---

### An Act for the relief of John Moffitt.

Sec. 1. *Be it enacted, &c.*, That the proper accounting officers of the Treasury Department be, and they are hereby, authorized and directed to settle and ascertain the value of a continental loan office certificate, number one hundred and four, issued in favor of John Moffitt, by the commissioner of loans of the State of South Carolina; and that the sum found to be due on said certificate (exclusive of interest) be paid to the said Moffitt out of any moneys in the Treasury not otherwise appropriated.

Approved May 28, 1830.

---

### An Act for the relief of the heirs and legal representatives of Joseph Falconer, deceased.

Sec. 1. *Be it enacted, &c.*, That the proper accounting officers of the Treasury Department be authorized to audit and settle the claim of Joseph Falconer, an officer of the Revolution, formerly of Philadelphia, deceased, on account of two several loan office certificates, issued April twenty-first, seventeen hundred and seventy-eight, to and in the name of John Cox; namely, one for the sum of one thousand dollars, and numbered thirty-five; and one for the sum of six hundred dollars, and numbered two thousand nine hundred and ninety-seven; and to ascertain the true specie value of the same, exclusive of interest; which certificates are alleged to have been lost, and appear by the books of the Treasury to be outstanding and unpaid: and that the amount so ascertained as aforesaid, be paid to the heirs or legal representatives of the said Joseph Falconer, or either of them, duly authorized and empowered to receive the same, out of any money in the Treasury not otherwise appropriated: *Provided*, That the person or persons receiving the amount aforesaid shall first execute and deliver to the Comptroller of the Treasury a bond of indemnity, in double the amount of the sum to be paid, with sufficient security, as the said Comptroller shall direct and approve.

Approved May 28, 1830.

---

### An Act for the relief of Samuel Ward.

Sec. 1. *Be it enacted, &c.*, That the Secretary of the Treasury be, and he is hereby, authorized and directed to pay to Samuel Ward, surviving partner of the late firm of Samuel Ward and Brothers, out of any money in the Treasury not otherwise appropriated, the legal interest due on a final settlement certificate, issued by Benjamin Walker to Abraham Whipple, Esq., dated twenty-third of October, seventeen hundred and eighty-six, number two hundred and eighty-one, the principal of which certificate has been paid to the said Samuel Ward, under a law passed the twenty-fourth of May, anno Domini eighteen hundred and twenty-eight: *Provided*,

That Samuel Ward shall first execute and deliver to the Comptroller of the Treasury a bond of indemnity in double the amount of the sum so to be paid, with such sufficient security as the said Comptroller shall direct and approve.

Approved May 31, 1830.

---

### An Act for the relief of Ann D. Baylor.

Sec. 1. *Be it enacted, &c.*, That the accounting officers of the Treasury be, and they hereby are, authorized, directed, and required to settle the account of Ann D. Baylor, widow of John Walker Baylor, Esq., deceased, who was only son and heir at law of Colonel George Baylor, late of the army of the United States in the revolutionary war, deceased, for all such loan office certificates as were issued from the loan office of the United States, in Virginia, in the name of the said George Baylor, payable to him, and now remain on the books of the Treasury outstanding and unpaid, and not transferred to any other person by him; and that they pay to her, the said Ann D. Baylor, as trustee for the heirs at law and distributees of the said John Walker Baylor, and to their sole use, the same amount of money which might have been received on said certificates had they been subscribed to the loan of the United States, under the act entitled "An act making provision for the debt of the United States," passed August fourth, seventeen hundred and ninety; making out said account, and settling and paying the same, in all respects, in manner and form, as if such subscription had then been made, and the dividends credited thereunto, according to the several provisions of said act, and the act passed April twenty-eight, seventeen hundred and ninety-six, in aid thereof, and the whole amount left uncalled for in the Treasury till the present time ; together with that part thereof which has been credited, with interest at three per cent. per annum ; and that the same be paid out of any money in the Treasury not otherwise appropriated.

Approved May 29, 1830.

---

### An Act for the relief of Benjamin Wells.

Sec. 1. *Be it enacted, &c.*, That the accounting officers of the Treasury be, and they hereby are, authorized, directed, and required to settle the accounts of Benjamin Wells, as deputy commissary of issues at the magazine at Monster mills, in Pennsylvania, under John Irvine, deputy commissary general of the army of the United States in said State, in the revolutionary war, and as deputy forage-master, under David Duncan, deputy quartermaster at the same magazine of the army aforesaid, in said war ; and that they credit to him the sum of five hundred and seventy-five dollars and four cents, as payable February ninth, one thousand seven hundred and seventy-nine, and three hundred and twenty-six dollars and sixty-seven cents, payable July twentieth, one thousand seven hundred and eighty, in the same manner, and with such interest, as if those sums, with their interest from the times respectively as aforesaid, had been subscribed to the loan of the United States proposed by an act entitled "An act making provision for the debt of the United States," passed August fourth, one thousand seven hundred and ninety, and such subscription had been made on the thirty-first of December, one thousand seven hundred and ninety ; and pay to him such sums so credited, together with the amount of principal which would have been paid or now remains due, under the provisions of said act ; and that the same be paid out of any money in the Treasury not otherwise appropriated.

Approved May 29, 1830.

---

An Act for the relief of the legal representatives of General Moses Hazen, deceased.

Sec. 1. *Be it enacted, &c.*, That the Secretary of the Treasury be, and he is hereby, authorized and directed to pay, out of any money in the Treasury not otherwise appropriated, to the legal representatives of the said Moses Hazen, the amount of interest due on the sum of thirteen thousand three hundred and eighty-six dollars and two-ninetieths of a dollar, a balance found to be due to the said Hazen, agreeably to a resolution of Congress of the twenty-fifth of April, A. D. seventeen hundred and eighty-one.

Approved March 3, 1831.

---

An Act for the relief of Richard G. Morris.

Sec. 1. *Be it enacted, &c.* That there be paid, out of any money in the Treasury not otherwise appropriated, to Richard G. Morris, the sum of five hundred and sixty-five dollars and fifty cents, the amount of two certificates issued by Timothy Pickering, Quartermaster General, numbered three thousand seven hundred and forty-four and three thousand seven hundred and forty-six, with such interest thereon from the first of September, seventeen hundred and eighty-one, (the medium time of payment,) as, together with the said principal, will amount to the sum that would have been payable on the said certificates if they had been subscribed to the loan created for funding the debts of the United States by the act of one thousand seven hundred and ninety ; which certificates were issued in the name of Henry Morris, and of whose estate the said Richard G. Morris is administrator : *Provided,* That the said Richard G. Morris shall first execute and deliver to the First Comptroller of the Treasury a bond, in such sum and with such security as the said Comptroller shall direct and approve, to indemnify the United States from and against the lawful claim of any other person or persons for or on account of the said certificates.

Approved May 19, 1832.

---

An Act for the relief of Ichabod Ward.

Sec. 1. *Be it enacted, &c.* That the proper accounting officers of the Treasury Department be, and they are hereby, authorized and required to pay to Ichabod Ward, of Connecticut, one certain certificate, given for interest due from the United States, signed by William Imlay, commissioner of the loan office of the State of Connecticut, numbered four thousand one hundred and seventy-four, for the sum of twenty dollars and forty-five-ninetieths, payable to James Shelden or bearer, and dated the twentieth of December, seventeen hundred and eighty-five, with three per centum interest per annum thereon from its date, out of any moneys in the Treasury not otherwise appropriated.

Approved June 15, 1832.

---

### An Act for the relief of Aaron Snow.

Sec. 1. *Be it enacted, &c.* That the proper accounting officers of the Treasury be, and they are hereby, authorized and directed to audit and settle the claim of Aaron Snow, a revolutionary soldier, on account of three several certificates issued to and in the name of the said Snow by John Pierce, late commissioner of army accounts, during the revolutionary war, namely: one numbered twenty-seven thousand and ninety-four, dated January first, seventeen hundred and eighty-four, for forty-four dollars and sixty-six-ninetieths ; and one numbered twenty-seven thousand three hundred and seventy-three, dated January twentieth, seventeen hundred and eighty-four, for eighty dollars; and one numbered thirty-one thousand three hundred and five, dated March first, seventeen hundred and eighty-four, for eighty-six dollars and sixty-ninetieths, which certificates appear, by the books of the Register of the Treasury, to be outstanding and unpaid ; and that the sums found to be due on said certificates, with interest thereon, be paid to the said Aaron Snow out of any moneys in the Treasury not otherwise appropriated : *Provided,* That the said Snow shall first execute and deliver to the Comptroller of the Treasury a bond of indemnity, in double the amount of the sum to be paid, with such sufficient security as the said Comptroller shall direct and approve.

Approved July 4, 1832.

---

### An Act for the relief of William P. Gibbs, executor of Benjamin Gibbs, deceased.

Sec. 1. *Be it enacted, &c.* That the proper accounting officers of the Treasury be, and they are hereby, directed and required to pay to William P. Gibbs, executor of Benjamin Gibbs, of Kentucky, deceased, the sum of twenty-five dollars and sixty-two-ninetieths, that being the true amount of a final settlement certificate held by said Gibbs, originally drawn in favor of David Johnson, dated twentieth of January, seventeen hundred and eighty-four, together with interest at six per cent. on said sum, from the first of January, seventeen hundred and eighty-three, up to the passage of this act; to be paid out of any money in the Treasury not otherwise appropriated.

Approved July 4, 1832.

---

### An Act for the relief of John Brickwood Taylor.

Sec. 1. *Be it enacted, &c.,* That there be paid, out of any money in the Treasury not otherwise appropriated, to John Brickwood Taylor, the specie value of a certificate issued by M. Hillegas, continental treasurer, numbered one thousand four hundred and fifty-two, with interest on the said specie value, at four per centum per annum, from the twelfth of June, one thousand seven hundred and seventy-seven ; which certificate was issued in the name of Stephen Ketchum, and of which the said John Brickwood Taylor is now owner : *Provided*, That the said John Brickwood Taylor shall first execute and deliver to the First Comptroller of the Treasury a bond, in such sum and with such security as the said Comptroller shall direct and approve, to indemnify the United States from and against the lawful claim of any other person or persons for or on account of the said certificate.

Approved 13th July, 1832.

---

### An Act for the relief of Gertrude Gates.

Sec. 1. *Be it enacted, &c.*, That there be paid out of any money in the Treasury not otherwise appropriated, to Gertrude Gates, the sum of twenty-seven dollars and fifty cents, being the amount of a final settlement certificate issued by William Barber, commissioner, numbered two thousand six hundred and sixty-two, with interest on said sum, at six per centum per annum, from the first of March, one thousand seven hundred and eighty ; which certificate was issued to Isaac Van Vrankin, and of which the said Gertrude Gates is now owner : also, the sum of five dollars and fifty-five cents, being the amount of another final settlement certificate, issued by William Barker, commissioner, numbered two thousand three hundred and forty-five, with interest on the said sum, at six per centum per annum, from the first of March, one thousand seven hundred and eighty ; which certificate was issued in the name of Jacob Clute, and of which the said Gertrude Gates is now owner : *Provided*, That the said Gertrude Gates shall first execute and deliver to the First Comptroller of the Treasury a bond, in such form and with such security as the said Comptroller shall direct and approve, to indemnify the United States from and against the lawful claim of any other person or persons for or on account of the said certificates.

Approved 14th July, 1832.

---

### An Act for the relief of John Peck.

Sec. 1. *Be it enacted, &c.*, That the proper accounting officers of the Treasury be, and they are hereby, authorized and required to liquidate and adjust the following final settlement certificates, namely : number sixty-two thousand five hundred and sixty-seven, dated May first, one thousand seven hundred and eighty-four, State of Pennsylvania, signed by John Pierce, commissioner, for eighty dollars, payable to Elijah Goodenough, or bearer, with interest at six per cent. from the first of January, one thousand seven hundred and eighty-three ; number thirteen thousand eight hundred and thirteen, dated January first, one thousand seven hundred and eighty-four, State of New York, signed by John Pierce, commissioner, for fifty-eight twenty-ninetieths dollars, payable to David Dunton, or bearer, with interest at six per cent. from the       day of January, one thousand seven hundred and eighty-two ; and number seventeen thousand nine hundred and eighty, dated January first, one thousand seven hundred and eighty-four, State of New York, signed by John Pierce, commissioner, for fifty-nine twenty-four-ninetieths dollars, payable to Hugh Paul, or bearer, with interest at six per cent. from the fourth of November, one thousand seven hundred and eighty-three ; and that there be paid out of any money in the Treasury not otherwise appropriated, to John Peck, the holder of the said several certificates, the amount thereof, with interest at six per centum from the first of January, one thousand seven hundred and eighty-eight, the date of the last payment of interest endorsed on the said several certificates.

Approved 14th July, 1832.

---

### An Act for the relief of Archibald Watt.

Sec. 1. *Be it enacted, &c.*, That the proper accounting officers of the Treasury do pay to Archibald Watt the specie value of three Treasury certificates, for six hundred dollars each, issued to Andrew Ross on the nineteenth of February, one thousand seven hundred and seventy-nine, payable to the said Ross, or bearer, and whereof the said Watt is holder, with such interest on the said specie value as would have become due thereon, had the same been subscribed to the loan created for funding the debts of the United States, by the acts of one thousand seven hundred and ninety, and that the same be paid out of any money in the Treasury not otherwise appropriated : *Provided*, He shall give a bond, to the satisfaction of the Secretary of the Treasury, in an amount to be determined by said Secretary ; conditioned that the said Archibald and his securities will refund the amount of money received under the provisions of this act, if any other person shall prove a legal title to the amount contained in said certificates, together with the interest on the sum so received.

Approved 27th February, 1833.

---

### An Act for the relief of John Bruce, administrator of Philip Bush, deceased.

Sec. 1. *Be it enacted, &c.*, That the proper accounting officers of the Treasury do settle the claim of John Bruce, administrator of Philip Bush, deceased, for a certain certificate issued on the third day of March, one thousand seven hundred and eighty, to the said Philip Bush, in his lifetime, by I. Brown, jr., for Archibald Steel, deputy quartermaster general, and payable on the thirty-first of March, one thousand seven hundred and eighty, for thirty-two thousand eight hundred and forty-two dollars and fifty-five-ninetieths, in continental emission ; and that the said settlement be made according to the rules of depreciation; and that the said claim be allowed and paid to the said John Bruce, as administrator of Philip Bush, deceased, under the principles of the funding system, in the same manner and in same amount as if the said Philip Bush had, on the thirty-first of December, one thousand seven hundred and ninety, subscribed to the loan made in payment of the debt of the United States; and that the sum so ascertained be paid to the said John Bruce, as administrator of Philip Bush, deceased, out of any money in the Treasury not otherwise appropriated.

Approved 2d March, 1833.

An Act for the relief of the legal representatives of Christian Ish, deceased.

Sec. 1. *Be it enacted, &c.*, That the Secretary of the Treasury be, and he is hereby, authorized and directed to pay to the legal representatives of Christian Ish, deceased, out of any money in the Treasury not otherwise appropriated, one hundred and forty-seven dollars and ten-ninetieths, together with such interest thereon as if a certificate for that amount had been funded under the act of August fourth, one thousand seven hundred and ninety, in full satisfaction of a certain certificate issued by George Ross, deputy quartermaster general, to the said Christian Ish, on the twenty-ninth of February, seventeen hundred and eighty.

Approved June 27, 1834.

---

An Act for the relief of the administrator of Michael Grate.

Sec. 1. *Be it enacted, &c.*, That the proper accounting officers of the Treasury be, and they are hereby, authorized and required to adjust and liquidate the value of two certificates issued from the loan office of New Jersey to Ogden and Curtis: the one numbered two thousand three hundred and forty-one, the other two thousand three hundred and fifty-three, both bearing date twenty-ninth March, seventeen hundred and seventy-nine, and each for the sum of five hundred dollars ; and also for another certificate, numbered one thousand three hundred and fifty-six, which issued from the loan office of Pennsylvania, to William Henderson, for one thousand dollars, dated January twelfth, seventeen hundred and seventy-nine ; and that the value, so adjusted, of said three certificates, together with interest thereon, at the rate of six per centum per annum, be paid out of any money in the Treasury not otherwise appropriated by law, to the administrators of Michael Grate, deceased : *Provided*, That, before payment is made as aforesaid, the said administrator shall give bond to the United States, to be approved of by the Secretary of the Treasury, for refunding the amount to be paid on either of said certificates, which may hereafter be presented for payment; or of all, if all should be presented.

Approved June 27, 1834.

---

An Act for the relief of Benjamin Jacobs; of Samuel Bayard, surviving executor of John Bayard, deceased; and of the executors of Joseph Falconer, deceased.

Sec. 1. *Be it enacted, &c.*, That the proper accounting officers of the Treasury Department be, and they are hereby, authorized and directed to settle the account of Benjamin Jacobs, for two loan-office certificates, amounting to seven hundred dollars, issued from the loan office in Connecticut in the name of said Benjamin Jacobs, viz: number nine thousand five hundred and forty-one, dated twenty-first of May, seventeen hundred and seventy-nine, for two hundred dollars ; and number six thousand one hundred and twenty-nine, dated April twenty-sixth, seventeen hundred and seventy-nine, for five hundred dollars; and to ascertain the true specie value thereof ; which certificates are alleged to have been lost, and appear by the books of the Treasury to be outstanding and unpaid : and that the amount so ascertained, with interest thereon, be paid to the said Benjamin

Jacobs, out of any money in the Treasury not otherwise appropriated, upon the said Benjamin Jacobs's executing and delivering to the Comptroller of the Treasury a bond of indemnity, in double the amount of the sum to be paid, with sufficient security, to be approved by the said Comptroller.

Sec. 2. *And be it further enacted,* That the proper accounting officers of the Treasury Department be, and they are hereby, authorized and directed to settle the claim of Samuel Bayard, surviving executor of John Bayard, deceased, for six certificates, issued on the twenty-second of February, seventeen hundred and seventy-seven, in the name of the said John Bayard, viz : numbers one hundred and fifty-one, one hundred and fifty-two, one hundred and fifty-five, one hundred and fifty-six, one hundred and fifty-seven, one hundred and fifty-eight, for three hundred dollars each, amounting to one thousand eight hundred dollars, and to ascertain the true specie value thereof ; which certificates are alleged to have been lost, and appear by the books of the Treasury to be still unsatisfied ; and that the amount so ascertained, with interest thereon from the first of January, seventeen hundred and eighty-eight, be paid to the said Samuel Bayard, surviving executor as aforesaid, out of any money in the Treasu y not otherwise appropriated, upon the execution and delivery of a bond of indemnity, from the said Samuel Bayard to the Comptroller of the Treasury, in double the amount of the sum to be paid, with sufficient security, to be approved of by the said Comptroller.

Sec. 3. *And be it further enacted,* That there be paid to the executors of Joseph Falconer, deceased, out of any money in the Treasury not otherwise appropriated, interest upon two loan-office certificates, number thirty-five, for one thousand dollars, of the value of four hundred and fifty-four dollars and thirty-seven ninetieths in specie, and number two thousand nine hundred and ninety-seven, for six hundred dollars, of the value of two hundred and seventy-two dollars and fifty-eight-ninetieths in specie ; to be computed from the first of January, seventeen hundred and eighty-eight, until the payment of the principal of those certificates, as directed by the act for the relief of the legal representatives of Joseph Falconer, approved twenty-eighth of May, eighteen hundred and thirty.

Approved June 28, 1834.

---

## An Act for the relief of the representatives of Samuel Gibbs.

Sec. 1. *Be it enacted, &c.,* That the proper accounting officers of the Treasury be, and they are hereby, authorized and required to liquidate and adjust the value of two certificates issued in May, seventeen hundred and seventy-nine, from the loan office of Pennsylvania, to Gilbert Palmer: one for three hundred dollars, numbered one hundred and thirty-eight, and the other for one thousand dollars, numbered two thousand three hundred and twenty-one ; and that the value so adjusted, together with interest thereon at the rate of six per centum per annum, be paid out of any money in the Treasury not otherwise appropriated by law, to the legal representatives of Samuel Gibbs, deceased : *Provided,* That, before payment is made as aforesaid, the said legal representatives shall give bond, to be approved of by the Secretary of the Treasury, for refunding the amount of either of the said certificates which may hereafter be presented for payment ; or of both, should both be so presented.

Approved June 28, 1834.

An Act for the relief of the legal representatives of Benjamin Bird and Grove Pomeroy.

Sec. 1. *Be it enacted, &c.*, That the accounting officers of the Treasury be, and they are hereby, authorized and directed to audit and settle the claim of the legal representatives of Benjamin Bird, on account of eight loan office certificates, issued at the loan office of the State of Massachusetts, in favor of Pierre Gomreye, and dated first of April, seventeen hundred and seventy-eight ; two of which were for the sum of two hundred dollars each, and numbered five thousand six hundred and eighty-one and five thousand six hundred and eighty-two ; three for the sum of four hundred dollars each, and numbered four thousand one hundred and twenty-eight, four thousand one hundred and twenty-nine, and four thousand one hundred and thirty ; and three for the sum of six hundred dollars each, and numbered four thousand and fourteen, four thousand and fifteen, and four thousand and sixteen ; which certificates appear on the books of the Treasury outstanding and unpaid. And also to audit and settle the claim of the legal representatives of Grove Pomeroy, on account of four final settlement certificates, one numbered twelve thousand two hundred and thirty-two, for two dollars and thirty-nine cents ; one numbered twelve thousand seven hundred and ninety-one, for seventy-five dollars and forty-nine cents ; one numbered thirteen thousand three hundred and twenty-three, for eighty dollars ; and one numbered thirteen thousand six hundred and ten, for eighty dollars, all dated the first of January, seventeen hundred and eighty-four ; the three first bearing interest from the first of January, seventeen hundred and eighty-three, and the latter from the fourth of November, seventeen hundred and eighty-three, and appearing outstanding and unpaid on tne books of the Treasury ; and the sum found due, together with the interest thereon, at six per centum per annum, be paid to the said representatives, out of any money in the Treasury not otherwise appropriated : *Provided*, That the legal representatives of the said Bird and of said Pomeroy, respectively, shall first deliver to the Comptroller of the Treasury, a bond in such sum and with such security as he shall approve, to indemnify the United States against all lawful claims for or on account of said certificates.

Approved June 28, 1834.

---

An Act for the relief of John Peck.

Sec. 1. *Be it enacted, &c.* That the Secretary of the Treasury is hereby authorized and directed to pay to John Peck, out of any money in the Treasury not otherwise appropriated, the interest which had accrued on three final settlement certificates set forth and described in the act of Congress for the relief of John Peck, approved July fourteenth, eighteen hundred and thirty-two, from the several periods at which interest had become due and payable thereon, to the first of January, seventeen hundred and eighty-eight.

Approved June 30, 1834.

---

An Act for the relief of William A. Duer, John Duer, and Beverly Robinson, trustees of the estate of Sarah Alexander, deceased.

Sec. 1. *Be it enacted, &c.* That the Secretary of the Treasury be, and he hereby is, authorized and directed to pay the sum of eighteen thousand

and fifty-one dollars and eighty-one cents, out of any money in the Treasury, to William A. Duer, John Duer, and Beverly Robinson, trustees of the estate of Sarah Alexander, deceased, who was the widow and devisee of Major General Lord Stirling, in full satisfaction and discharge of a certificate issued to the said Major General Lord Stirling by the State of New Jersey for the three-fourths part of the depreciation of his pay, bearing date the thirty-first of December, seventeen hundred and eighty-one, and amounting to the sum of sixteen hundred and two pounds four shillings and six pence three farthings, bearing interest at the rate of six per centum per annum, from the first of August, seventeen hundred and eighty; which said certificate shall be surrendered by them to the Secretary of the Treasury on receiving the payment thereof.

Approved, June 30, 1834.

# CHAPTER VII.

*Acts of Congress, and a Report of the Secretary of War, relating to Refugees from Canada and Nova Scotia during the Revolutionary War.*

An Act for the relief of the refugees from the British Provinces of Canada and Nova Scotia.

Sec. 1. *Be it enacted by the Senate and House of Representatives of the United States of America in Congress assembled,* That to satisfy the claims of certain persons claiming lands under the resolutions of Congress of the twenty-third of April, one thousand seven hundred and eighty-three, and the thirteenth of April, one thousand seven hundred and eighty-five, as refugees from the British Provinces of Canada and Nova Scotia, the Secretary of the Department of War be, and is hereby, authorized and directed to give notice, in one or more of the public papers of each of the States of Vermont, Massachusetts, New York, New Hampshire, and Pennsylvania, to all persons having claims under the said resolutions, to transmit to the War Office, within two years after the passing of this act, a just and true account of their claims to the bounty of Congress.

Sec. 2. *And be it further enacted,* That no other persons shall be entitled to the benefit of the provisions of the act than those of the following descriptions, or their widows and heirs, viz: First, those heads of families and single persons, not members of any such families, who were residents in one of the Provinces aforesaid prior to the fourth day of July, one thousand seven hundred and seventy-six, and who abandoned their settlements in consequence of having given aid to the United Colonies or States in the revolutionary war against Great Britain, or with intention to give such aid, and continued in the United States, or in their service, during the said war, and did not return to reside in the dominions of the King of Great Britain prior to the twenty-fifth of November, one thousand seven hundred and eighty-three. Secondly, the widows and heirs of all such persons as were actually residents, as aforesaid, who abandoned their settlements as aforesaid, and died within the United States, or in their service, during the said war ; and Thirdly, all persons who were members of families at the time of their coming into the United States, and who, during the war, entered into their service.

Sec. 3. *And be it further enacted,* That the proof of the several circumstances necessary to entitle the applicants to the benefits of this act, may be taken before a judge of the supreme or district court of the United States, or a judge of the supreme or superior court, or the first justice or first judge of the court of common pleas or county court, of any State.

Sec. 4. *And be it further enacted,* That, at the expiration of fifteen months from and after the passing of this act, and from time to time thereafter, it shall be the duty of the Secretary for the Department of War to lay such evidence of claims as he may have received before the Secretary and Comptroller of the Treasury, and with them proceed to examine the testimony, and give their judgment what quantity of land ought to be allowed to the individual claimants, in proportion to the degree of their respective services, sacrifices, and sufferings, in consequence of their attachment to the cause of the United States; allowing to those of the first class a quantity not exceeding one thousand acres ; and to the last class a quantity not exceeding one hundred ; making such intermediate classes as the resolutions aforesaid and distributive justice may, in their judgment, require; and make report thereof to Congress. And in case any such claimant shall have sustained such losses and sufferings, or performed such services for the United States, that he cannot justly be classed in any one general class, a separate report shall be made of his circumstances, together with the quantity of land that ought to be allowed him, having reference to the foregoing ratio : *Provided,* That, in considering what compensation ought to be made by virtue of this act, all grants, except military grants, which may have been made by the United States, or individual States, shall be considered at the just value thereof at the time the same were made, respectively, either in whole or in part, as the case may be, a satisfaction to those who may have received the same : *Provided also,* That no claim under this law shall be assignable until after report made to Congress as aforesaid, and until the said lands be granted to persons entitled to the benefit of this act.

Sec. 5. *Be it further enacted,* That all claims, in virtue of said resolutions of Congress, which shall not be exhibited as aforesaid, within the time by this act limited, shall forever thereafter be barred.

Approved April 7, 1798.

Note.—That part of the ordinance of May 20, 1785, which reserved three townships on lake Erie, for the use of the refugees, was never carried into effect, other lands having been appropriated in lieu thereof, by the preceding and other acts.

---

*Report on the report of the Secretary of War, the Secretary and Comptroller of the Treasury, on the subject of refugees from the British Provinces of Canada and Nova Scotia. Made the 9th of May, 1800.*

That 73 persons have presented claims as entitled to relief under the provisions of the act of April, 1798 ; that 18 claims have been disallowed ; 6 are suspended for want of sufficient proofs ; and 49 have been allowed.

In 4 special cases, the Secretaries and Comptroller recommended an allowance of 2,000 acres. The 45 other claimants have been arranged in five classes ; allowing to those of the first class, five in number, 1,000 acres each ; to those of the second class, fifteen in number, 750 acres each ; to those of the third class, fourteen in number, 500 acres each ; to those of the fourth class, ten in number, 250 acres each ; and to the only claimant of the fifth class, 100 acres—making altogether, and including the special cases, 33,500 acres. The six suspended cases, if allowed, would not increase the quantity of land to 40,000 acres.

The committee, considering that the whole amount of claims falls short of what was generally expected ; that all'the claimants are original holders ; that their losses or sufferings have been considerable ; that the greater number are now, and have been for many years, in indigent circumstances ; and that not only they have been thus reduced, on account of their having joined the American cause, but have waited twenty years for a compensation, recommend that there should be allowed, to those of the fourth class, half a section, or 320 acres, instead of 250 acres ; and to others in the same proportion ; which will make a difference of only 4,740 acres.

On the particular cases, the committee propose only two alterations:

The first relates to the case of L. F. Delesdernier, a Nova Scotia refugee, who is placed in the third class at the rate of 500 acres. The claim for his deceased brother John, who enlisted in the army of the United States, and served to the end of the war, and that of his father and mother, have been disallowed. The last is disallowed, because "it is not proved that they were *obliged* to leave Nova Scotia, nor that they came hither with intent to *aid* the United States." Although it was proper to have rejected the claim for want of that proof, yet as it appears that on account of their leaving Nova Scotia, during the war, and joining their son, they lost their property, and have ever since been supported by that son, (they being both past seventy, and the father having been deprived of his senses for a number of years,) this appeared to the committee a sufficient reason for raising the son, who was a meritorious and useful officer during the war, from the third to the second class.

The other case is that of the heirs of James Boyd, whose claim is considered by the Secretaries and Comptroller as one of the specific classes, and to whom they have allowed 2,000 acres. The Secretaries and Comptroller state that "James Boyd lost 50,000 acres of land, on which were some valuable improvements, on the *east* side of what is *now* known to be the river St. Croix." One of the heirs who attends to the business, considering the compensation as altogether inadequate, has requested that the claim should not be included amongst those now reported on, rather choosing that it should be referred, with the other suspended cases, to the next session of Congress, when there will be time to investigate its merits. The committee recommend a compliance with his request.

With those alterations, and adopting in every other respect the report of the Secretaries and Comptroller, the third section of the bill reported by the committee on the subject of the Nova Scotia and Canada refugees will stand as follows:

That the following persons be entitled, &c., to wit: Martha Walker, widow of Thomas Walker; Edgar and Seth Harding, respectively, 2,240 acres each.

Jonathan Eddy, Colonel James Livingston, Parker Clark, and John Allen, respectively, 1,280 acres each, and to the heirs of John Dodge 1,280 acres.

| | | |
|---|---|---|
| Thomas Faulkner, Edward Faulkner, David Gay, Martin Brooks, Lieut. Col. Bradford, Noah Miller, Joshua Lamb, Atwood Fales, John Starr, William How, Ebenezer Gardner, Lewis F. Delesdernier, John McGown, Jonas C. Minot, and P. Francis Cazeau, and to The heirs of Simeon Chester, respectively, | 960 acres each. | |
| Jacob Vander Heyden, John Livingston, James Crawford, Isaac Danks, Major B. Von Heer, Benjamin Thompson, Joseph Bindon, Joseph Levittre, Lieut. William Maxwell, John De Mercier, James Price, Seth Noble, and John Halsted, respectively, | | 640 acres each. |

| | | | |
|---|---|---|---|
| David Jenks, | | John Paskell, | |
| Ambrose Cole, | 320 | Edward Chinn, | 320 |
| Adam Johnson, | acres | Joseph Cone, and | acres |
| James Duggan, | each. | John Torrey, respectively, | each. |
| Daniel Earl, junr. | | | |

Samuel Fales, 160 acres.

Which several tracts of land shall, except the last, be located in half sections by the respective claimants.

----

An Act regulating the grants of land appropriated for the refugees from the British Provinces of Canada and Nova Scotia.

Sec. 1. *Be it enacted, &c.*, That the Surveyor General be, and he is hereby, directed to cause those fractional townships of the sixteenth, seventeenth, eighteenth, nineteenth, twentieth, twenty-first, and twenty-second ranges of townships, which join the southern boundary line of the military lands, to be subdivided into half sections, containing three hundred and twenty acres each, and to return a survey and description of the same to the Secretary of the Treasury, on or before the first Monday of December next ; and that the said lands be, and they are hereby, set apart and reserved for the purpose of satisfying the claims of persons entitled to lands under the act entitled " An act for the relief of the refugees from the British Provinces of Canada and Nova Scotia."

Sec. 2. *And be it further enacted,* That the Secretary of the Treasury shall, within thirty days after the survey of lands shall have been returned to him as aforesaid, proceed to determine, by lot, to be drawn in the presence of the Secretaries of State and of War, the priority of location of the persons entitled to lands as aforesaid. The persons thus entitled shall severally make their locations on the second Tuesday of January next, and the patents for the lands thus located shall be granted in the manner directed for military lands, without requiring any fee whatever.

Sec. 3. *And be it further enacted,* That the following persons, claiming lands under the above-mentioned act, shall, respectively, be entitled to the following quantities of land, that is to say : Martha Walker, widow of Thomas Walker, John Edgar, P. Francis Cazeau, John Allen, and Seth Harding, respectively, two thousand two hundred and forty acres each ; Jonathan Eddy, Colonel James Livingston, and Parker Clark, respectively, one thousand two hundred and eighty acres each ; and the heirs of John Dodge, one thousand two hundred and eighty acres ; Thomas Faulkner, Edward Faulkner, David Gay, Martin Brooks, Lieutenant Colonel Bradford, Noah Miller, Joshua Lamb, Atwood Fales, John Starr, William How, Ebenezer Gardner, Lewis F. Delesdernier, John McGown, and Jonas C. Minot, respectively, nine hundred and sixty acres each ; and the heirs of Simeon Chester, nine hundred and sixty acres ; Jacob Vander Heyden, John Livingston, James Crawford, Isaac Danks, Major B. Von Heer, Benjamin Thompson, Joseph Bindon, Joseph Levittre, Lieutenant William Maxwell, John de Mercier, James Price, Seth Noble, Martha Bogart, relict of Abraham Bogart and formerly relict of Daniel Tucker, and John Halsted, respectively, six hundred and forty acres each ; David Jenks, Ambrose Cole, James Cole, Adam Johnson, the widow and heirs of Colonel Jeremiah Duggan, Daniel Earl, junior, John Paskell, Edward Chinn, Joseph

Cone, and John Torrey, respectively, three hundred and twenty acres each ; Samuel Fales, one hundred and sixty acres ; which several tracts of land shall, except the last, be located in half sections by the respective claimants.

Approved February 18, 1801.

----

An Act in addition to the act entitled " An act regulating the grants of lands appropriated for the refugees from the British Provinces of Canada and Nova Scotia."

Sec. 1. *Be it enacted, &c.*, That Samuel Rogers, one of the claimants under the act entitled " An act for the relief of the refugees from the British Provinces of Canada and Nova Scotia," shall be entitled to two thousand two hundred and forty acres of land, to be located in the manner, and within the boundaries, of the tract designated by the act to which this act is a supplement, and shall receive a patent for the same, in the manner directed by the said last-mentioned act.

Approved March 3, 1803.

----

An Act to revive and continue in force an act entitled ",An act for the relief of the refugees from the British Provinces of Canada and Nova Scotia."

Sec. 1. *Be it enacted, &c.*, That the act entitled " An act for the relief of the refugees from the British Provinces of Canada and Nova Scotia," approved on the seventh of April, one thousand seven hundred and ninety-eight, shall be, and the same is hereby, revived and continued in force for the term of two years from the passage of this act, and no longer.

Approved March 16, 1804.

----

An Act further to provide for the refugees from the British Provinces of Canada and Nova Scotia, and for other purposes.

Sec. 1. *Be it enacted, &c.*, That all persons having claims under the resolutions of Congress passed the twenty-third day of April, one thousand seven hundred and eighty-three, and the thirteenth of April one thousand seven hundred and eighty-five, as refugees from the British Provinces of Canada and Nova Scotia, shall transmit to the War Office, within two years after the passing of this act, a just and true account of their claims to the bounty of Congress.

Sec. 2. *And be it further enacted,* That no other persons shall be entitled to the benefits of the provisions of this act than those of the following descriptions, or their widows and heirs, viz: First, those heads of families, and single persons not members of any such families, who were residents in one of the Provinces aforesaid prior to the fourth day of July, one thousand seven hundred and seventy-six, and who abandoned their settlements in consequence of having given aid to the United Colonies or States, in the revolutionary war against Great Britain, or with intention to give such aid, and continued in the United States, or in their service, during the said war, and did not return to reside in the dominions of the King of Great Britain prior to the twenty-fifth day of November, one thousand seven hundred and eighty-three. Secondly, the widows and heirs of all such persons as were actually residents as aforesaid, who abandoned their settlements as aforesaid, and died within the United States, or in their service, during the said war. And, thirdly, all persons who were members of families at the time of their coming into the United States, and who, during the war, entered into their service.

Sec. 3. *And be it further enacted,* That the proof of the several circumstances necessary to entitle the applicants to the benefits of this act, may be taken before a judge of the supreme or district court of the United States, or a judge of the supreme or superior court, or the first justice or first judge of the court of common pleas or county court of any State.

Sec. 4. *And be it further enacted,* That, at the expiration of fifteen months from and after the passing of this act, and from time to time thereafter, it shall be the duty of the Secretary for the Department of War to lay such evidence of claims as he may have received before the Secretary and Comptroller of the Treasury, and, with them, proceed to examine the testimony, and give their judgment what quantity of land ought to be allowed to the individual claimants in proportion to the degree of their respective services, sacrifices, and sufferings, in consequence of their attachment to the cause of the United States; allowing to those of the first class a quantity not exceeding one thousand acres, and to the last class a quantity not exceeding one hundred, making such intermediate classes as the resolutions aforesaid and distributive justice may, in their judgment, require, and make report thereof to Congress. And in case any such claimant shall have sustained such losses and sufferings, or performed such services for the United States, that he cannot justly be classed in any one general class, a separate report shall be made of his circumstances, together with the quantity of land that ought to be allowed him, having reference to the foregoing ratio: *Provided,* That, in considering what compensation ought to be made by virtue of this act, all grants, except military grants, which may have been made by the United States or individual States, shall be considered, at the just value thereof at the time the same were made respectively, either in whole or in part, as the case may be, as satisfaction to those who may have received the same: *Provided, also,* That no claim under this law shall be assignable until after report made to Congress as aforesaid, and until the said lands be granted to the persons entitled to the benefit of this act.

Sec. 5. *And be it further enacted,* That all claims in virtue of said resolution of Congress which shall not be exhibited, as aforesaid, within the time by this act limited, shall forever thereafter be barred: *Provided,* That no patent shall be issued to any person who may hereafter establish his claim under the said act, until he produce satisfactory evidence to the Secretary of the Treasury that he is at the time then being a resident within the United States.

Approved February 24, 1810.

--------

An Act making provision for certain persons claiming lands under the several acts for the relief of the refugees from the British Provinces of Canada and Nova Scotia.

Sec. 1. *Be it enacted, &c.,* That the following persons, claiming lands under the act entitled " An act to revive and continue in force an act entitled ' An act for the relief of the refugees from the British Provinces of

Canada and Nova Scotia,' " passed on the sixteenth day of March, one thousand eight hundred and four, shall respectively be entitled to the fol lowing lands; that is to say: Charlotte Hazen, widow of Moses Hazen; Chloe Shannan, wife of James Noble Shannan, and relict of Obadiah Ayer, deceased; the heirs of Elijah Ayer, and the heirs of Israel Ruland, respectively, nine hundred and sixty acres; Elijah Ayer, junior, and the heirs of Anthony Burk, respectively, three hundred and twenty acres. And that the following persons claiming lands under the act entitled " An act further to provide for the refugees from the British Provinces of Canada and Nova Scotia, and for other purposes," passed on the twenty-fourth day of February, one thousand eight hundred and ten, shall respectively be entitled to the following quantities of land; that is to say: the heirs of James Boyd, two thousand two hundred and forty acres; the heirs of Nathaniel Reynolds, the heirs of Edward Antill and Joshua Sprague, respectively, nine hundred and sixty acres: Robert Sharp, John Fulton, and John Morrison, each, six hundred and forty acres; James Sprague, David Dickey, John Taylor, and the heirs of Gilberts Seamans, deceased, respectively, three hundred and twenty acres: which several tracts of land shall be located within the boundaries of the fractional townships reserved and set apart for the purpose of satisfying the claims of the refugees from Canada and Nova Scotia; and the locations shall be made and patents granted, in the manner and on the conditions prescribed by former laws, except as to the time for making the locations; which locations shall be made on the day or days that the Secretary of the Treasury shall judge most convenient for the claimants, and shall designate for the purpose.

Approved April 23, 1812.

----

An Act for the relief of the heirs at law of Richard Livingston, a Canadian refugee, deceased.

Sec. 1. *Be it enacted, &c.*, That the provisions of the several acts of Congress in relation to refugees from Canada and Nova Scotia, be, and the same are hereby, extended to the heirs at law of Richard Livingston, deceased, a lieutenant colonel in the regiment commanded by Colonel James Livingston; and that the quantity of land which may be awarded by the officers of Government, designated in said several acts to settle and adjust similar claims, shall be located upon such lands belonging to the United States which have been offered at public sale, and subject to entry at private sale.

Approved June 27, 1834.

## CHAPTER VIII.

*Special Acts of Congress granting the seven years' Half Pay to Widows and Orphans of Revolutionary Officers who died or were killed whilst in service.*

An Act for the relief of certain widows, orphans, invalids, and other persons.

Sec. 1. *Be it enacted by the Senate and House of Representatives of the United States of America in Congress assembled,* That the Comptroller of the Treasury adjust the claims of the widows and orphans, respectively, as the case may be, of the late Colonel Owen Roberts, Captain William White, Lieutenant Colonel Bernard Elliott, Major Samuel Wise, Major Benjamin Huger, Lieutenant John Bush, and Major Charles Motte, deceased, all of whom were killed or died in the service of the United States, for the seven years' half pay stipulated by the resolve of Congress of the twenty-fourth day of August, one thousand seven hundred and eighty; and that the Register of the Treasury do issue his certificates accordingly.

Approved March 27, 1792.

---

An Act for the relief of the heirs of Doctor Samuel Kennedy.

Sec. 1. *Be it enacted, &c.,* That the proper accounting officers of the Treasury be, and they are hereby, required to settle and adjust the accounts of the heirs of Doctor Samuel Kennedy, and allow to them seven years' half pay for their father's services as surgeon in the revolutionary war, who died in the service on the 28th day of June, one thousand seven hundred and seventy-eight; to be paid out of any money in the Treasury not otherwise appropriated.

Approved May 25, 1832.

---

An Act for the relief of James Brownlee.

Sec. 1. *Be it enacted, &c.,* That the Secretary of the Treasury be, and he is hereby, authorized and directed to pay, out of any money in the Treasury not otherwise appropriated, to James Brownlee, sole heir of Alexander Brownlee, an ensign in the army of the Revolution, and slain in the battle of Guilford, the seven years' half pay to which his widow was entitled by a resolve of Congress, passed August twenty-fourth, one thousand seven hundred and eighty ; together with such interest thereon as would now be due if a certificate for the said seven years' half pay had been issued and subscribed under the principles of the funding act, and no payment made thereon.

Approved February 9, 1833.

12

An Act for the relief of the heirs of John Wilson, deceased.

Sec. 1. *Be it enacted, &c.*, That the Secretary of the Treasury be, and he is hereby, authorized and directed to pay, out of any money in the Treasury not otherwise appropriated, to the heirs of John Wilson, deceased, a lieutenant in the army of the Revolution, and slain in the battle of the Eutaw Springs, the seven years' half pay allowed by the resolution of Congress passed August twenty-fourth, one thousand seven hundred and eighty ; together with such interest thereon as would now be due if a certificate for said seven years' half pay had been issued and subscribed under the provisions of the funding act, and no payment made thereon.

Approved February 27, 1833.

---

An Act for the relief of Ann Mortimer Barron.

Sec. 1. *Be it enacted, &c.*, That the proper accounting officers of the Treasury be, and they are hereby, required to pay to Ann Mortimer Barron, only daughter and surviving heir of William Barron, an officer in the navy, killed in the service of the United States during the revolutionary war, the aggregate amount of the half pay of a first lieutenant of a frigate, for seven years, to be paid out of any money in the Treasury not otherwise appropriated : *Provided,* That the said Ann Mortimer Barron, before the payment thereof, do exhibit such proof to the Secretary of the Treasury as will satisfy him that she is the only daughter and heir of the said William Barron.

Approved June 30, 1834.

---

An Act for the relief of Margaret Riker.

Sec. 1. *Be it enacted, &c.*, That the Secretary of the Treasury be, and he is hereby, authorized and required to pay to Margaret Riker, the widow of Abraham Riker, a captain in the army of the Revolution, who died in service, on the seventh of May, seventeen hundred and seventy-eight, seven years' half pay of a captain of the second regiment of New York on continental establishment.

Approved June 30, 1834.

---

An Act for the relief of Francis and Judith Taylor.

Sec. 1. *Be it enacted, &c.*, That the Secretary of the Treasury be, and he is hereby, authorized and required to pay, out of any money in the Treasury not otherwise appropriated, to Francis and Judith Taylor, the latter being the child and sole representative of Henry Field, (formerly a lieutenant in the continental line of the revolutionary army, and who died while in the service,) a sum equal to the half pay of said Field as lieutenant for the term of seven years, in pursuance of the resolution of Congress of twenty-fourth of August, seventeen hundred and eighty.

Approved June 30, 1834.

An Act for the relief of the legal representatives of Lucy Bond, Hannah Douglass, Elizabeth Goodwin, and Margaret Leitch.

Sec. 1. *Be it enacted, &c.*, That there be paid, out of any money in the Treasury not otherwise appropriated, to the legal representatives of the late Lucy Bond, widow of the late William Bond, a colonel in the army of the Revolution, who died in service on the thirty-first of August, seventeen hundred and seventy-six; to the legal representatives of the late Hannah Douglas, widow of the late William Douglas, also a colonel in said army, who died in service on the twenty-seventh of March, seventeen hundred and seventy-seven; to the legal representatives of the late Margaret Leitch, widow of the late Major Andrew Leitch, a major in the army of the Revolution, who died in service the fifteenth of September, seventeen hundred and seventy-six ; and to the legal representatives of Elizabeth Goodwin, widow of the late Nathaniel Goodwin, a captain in the army of the Revolution, who died in service on the first of May, seventeen hundred and seventy-seven, the seven years' half pay of said officers, respectively, to which their widows and children were entitled by the resolution of Congress of twenty-fourth of August, seventeen hundred and eighty.

Approved June 30, 1834.

---

An Act for the relief of the legal representatives of John M. Gregory.

Sec. 1. *Be it enacted, &c.*, That the Secretary of the Treasury be, and he is hereby, authorized and directed to pay, out of any money in the Treasury not otherwise appropriated, to the legal representatives of John M. Gregory, sole heir of John Gregory, who was a lieutenant in the army of the Revolution, and slain in the service, the seven years' half pay allowed to the widows or orphan children of such officers as should die in the service, by a resolve of Congress passed August twenty-four, seventeen hundred and eighty.

Approved June 30, 1834.

---

An Act for the relief of the legal representatives of Francis Nash.

Sec. 1. *Be it enacted, &c.*, That the proper accounting officers of the Treasury Department be, and they hereby are, directed to ascertain and allow to the legal representatives of Francis Nash, late a brigadier general in the army of the Revolution, the amount of seven years' half pay, at a rate corresponding with the pay to which the said Nash was entitled at the time of his death; and that the said amount, when so ascertained, shall be paid to the said representatives, out of any money in the Treasury not otherwise appropriated.

Approved June 30, 1834.

---

An Act for the relief of Nancy Haggard, and for other purposes.

Sec. 1. *Be it enacted, &c.*, That the proper accounting officers of the Treasury be required to pay to Nancy Haggard, only daughter and surviving heir of William Grymes, who was a captain in the Virginia line on the continental establishment during the revolutionary war, and who died in the service of the United States during the said war, the aggregate amount of half pay of a captain of infantry for seven years, to be paid out of any money in the Treasury not otherwise appropriated: *Provided,* That the said Nancy Haggard, before the payment thereof, do exhibit such proof to the Secretary of the Treasury as will satisfy him that she is the only daughter and heir of said William Grymes.

Sec. 2. *And be it further enacted,* That the sum of money allowed to the representative of Robert Jouett, deceased, by the act passed at the present session of Congress, entitled " An act for the relief of the representatives of Robert Jouett, deceased," be paid out of any money in the Treasury not otherwise appropriated.

Approved July 2, 1836.

---

An Act for the relief of James Sutherland, and Rebecca his wife, formerly Rebecca Parkerson.

Sec. 1. *Be it enacted, &c.,* That the proper accounting officers shall ascertain the amount due to the said Rebecca, the only child of James Parkerson, who was a lieutenant in the continental line during the revolutionary war, and who died in the service, for the seven years' half pay of a lieutenant, promised by a resolution of the Congress of the United States; and, when ascertained, that they pay said sum to the said James Sutherland, and Rebecca his wife, in full compensation for said seven years' half pay, as promised by said resolution.

Sec. 2. *And be it further enacted,* That the sum found to be due be paid out of any money in the Treasury not otherwise appropriated.

Approved July 2, 1836.

---

An Act for the relief of the legal representatives of Joseph Hazlet and Jemima Mauro, surviving children of Colonel John Hazlet, of the State of Delaware, deceased.

Sec. 1. *Be it enacted, &c.,* That the proper accounting officers ascertain what will be the amount of seven years' half pay due to the children of the said Colonel John Hazlet, deceased.

Sec. 2. *And be it further enacted,* That said accounting officers do pay whatever sum may be found to be due to the legal representatives of Joseph Hazlet and of Jemima Mauro, the two surviving children of the said Colonel John Hazlet, deceased, out of any money in the Treasury not otherwise appropriated.

Approved July 2, 1836.

---

An Act for the relief of the heirs of James Moore.

Sec. 1. *Be it enacted, &c.,* That the proper accounting officers of the Treasury Department be, and they are hereby, directed to ascertain and allow to Mrs. Sarah Swan and Mrs. Mary Waters, the only surviving children of James Moore, late a brigadier general in the army of the Revolution, the amount of seven years' half pay, at a rate corresponding with the pay to which the said Moore was entitled at the time of his death; and that the said amount, when so ascertained, shall be paid to the said Sarah Swan and Mary Waters, out of any money in the Treasury not otherwise appropriated.

Approved July 2, 1836.

## CHAPTER IX.

*Special Acts of Congress allowing Claims for the Commutation of the Half Pay for Life.*

(Extract.)  An Act for the relief of certain widows, orphans, invalids, and other persons.

Sec. 4. *And be it further enacted,* That the Comptroller of the Treasury be, and he hereby is, required to adjust the accounts of Joseph Pannil, a lieutenant colonel in the service of the United States, as a deranged officer, upon the principles of the act of the late Congress of the third of October, 1780, and to allow him the usual commutation of the half pay for life of a lieutenant colonel; and that the Register of the Treasury be, and he hereby is, required to grant a certificate for the amount of the balance due to him.   That the said Comptroller adjust the account of Thomas McIntire, a captain in the service of the United States during the late war, and allow him the usual commutation of the half pay for life of a captain; and that the said Register grant a certificate for the amount thereof accordingly.

Approved March 27, 1792.

-----

An Act to authorize the settlement of the account of Lewis Dubois, for his services in the late army of the United States.

Sec. 1. *Be it enacted by the Senate and House of Representatives of the United States of America in Congress assembled,* That the Comptroller of the Treasury be, and he hereby is, required to adjust the accounts of Lewis Dubois, as a colonel deranged in the line of the late army of the United States, upon the principles of the act of the late Congress, of the third of October, one thousand seven hundred and eighty, and to allow him the usual commutation of half pay for life of a colonel; and that the Register of the Treasury be, and he hereby is, required to grant a certificate for the amount of the balance due to him.

Approved June 4, 1794.

-----

An Act for the relief of Philip Turner.

Sec. 1. *Be it enacted, &c.,* That the accounting officers of the Treasury be, and they hereby are, authorized and directed to liquidate and settle the account of Philip Turner, late hospital physician and surgeon, and that they allow him the commutation equal to the half pay of a captain, agreeably to a resolution of Congress passed on the seventeenth day of January, one thousand seven hundred and eighty-one : *Provided,* The said Philip Turner, on the receipt of the money directed to be paid him by this act, shall execute, in consideration thereof, a discharge to the United States of all demands whatsoever, and deposite the same in the office of the Register of the Treasury.

Approved April 22, 1808.

An Act for the relief of Anna Young, heiress and representative of Colonel John Durkee, deceased·

Sec. 1. *Be it enacted, &c.*, That the accounting officers of the Department of War be, and they are hereby, authorized and required to settle the account of Colonel John Durkee, deceased, and to allow Anna Young, his sole heiress and representative, his seven years' half pay, and interest thereon, to be paid out of any moneys in the Treasury not otherwise appropriated.

Approved July 1, 1812.

---

An Act for the relief of Elizabeth Hamilton.

Sec. 1. *Be it enacted, &c.*, That the proper accounting officers of the Treasury be, and they are hereby, required to settle the account of Elizabeth Hamilton, widow and representative of Alexander Hamilton, deceased, and to allow her five years' full pay for the services of her deceased husband, as a lieutenant colonel in the revolutionary war ; which five years' full pay is the commutation of his half pay for life ; to be paid out of any moneys in the Treasury not otherwise appropriated.

Approved April 29, 1816.

---

An Act for the relief of Alexander Garden.

Sec. 1. *Be it enacted, &c.*, That the proper accounting officers of the Treasury be, and they are hereby, required to settle the account of Alexander Garden, and to allow him five years' full pay as a lieutenant in the revolutionary war; which five years' full pay is the commutation of his half pay for life ; to be paid out of any money in the Treasury not otherwise appropriated.

Approved May 23, 1828.

---

An Act for the relief of Caleb Stark.

Sec. 1. *Be it enacted, &c.*, That the Secretary of the Treasury be authorized and directed to pay to Caleb Stark, out of any money in the Treasury not otherwise appropriated, the amount of his commutation for half pay as a lieutenant in the army of the United States on the continental establishment during the revolutionary war : *Provided*, That no interest shall be allowed on such commutation.

Sec. 2. *And be it further enacted*, That the Secretary of War issue to the said Caleb Stark a warrant for the land bounty to which he was entitled as a lieutenant in the said army.

Approved May 24, 1828.

---

An Act for the relief of Philip Slaughter.

Sec. 1. *Be it enacted, &c.*, That the proper accounting officers of the Treasury be, and they are hereby, required to settle and adjust the account of Philip Slaughter, and to allow him five years' full pay for his services as a captain in the revolutionary war, (without interest,) which five years' full pay is the commutation of his half pay for life; to be paid out of any money in the Treasury not otherwise appropriated: *Provided*, That the acceptance, by the said Slaughter, of the grant herein made, shall be in lieu of any claim he may have under the provisions of a bill passed at this session of Congress, entitled "An act for the relief of the surviving officers and soldiers of the Revolution."

Approved May 26, 1828.

---

### An Act for the relief of Mountjoy Bayly.

Sec. 1. *Be it enacted, &c.*, That the Secretary of War be directed to pay to Mountjoy Bayly his commutation of five years' full pay as a captain in the Maryland line, in the war of the Revolution: *Provided*, He shall satisfy the said Secretary that he was entitled to said commutation, and never received it from the United States.

Approved May 26, 1830.

---

### An Act for the relief of James Barnett.

Sec. 1. *Be it enacted, &c.*, That the proper accounting officers of the Treasury be, and they are hereby, required to settle the account of James Barnett, a lieutenant of infantry in the continental line in the revolutionary war, and to allow to him five years' full pay for his services in said war, as a lieutenant as aforesaid, it being the commutation for his half pay for life; and that it be paid out of any money in the Treasury not otherwise appropriated.

Approved May 28, 1830.

---

### An Act for the relief of Sarah Easton and Dorothy Storer, children and heirs at law of Lieutenant Colonel Robert Hanson Harrison, deceased.

Sec. 1. *Be it enacted, &c.*, That the accounting officers of the Treasury be, and they are hereby, directed and required to adjust and settle the account of Sarah Easton and Dorothy Storer, children and heirs at law of Lieutenant Colonel Robert Hanson Harrison, and pay to them five years' full pay, being the commutation for half pay for life, due to their said father in his lifetime, for services by him rendered to the United States in their army, during the revolutionary war, as a lieutenant colonel on the continental establishment; and that the same be paid out of any money in the Treasury not otherwise appropriated.

Sec. 2. *And be it further enacted*, That the Secretary of War be, and he is hereby, authorized, directed, and required to issue to said Sarah and Dorothy, and in their names, a land warrant for four hundred and fifty acres of military bounty land, as and for the lands to which the said Robert Hanson Harrison was, while in full life, entitled, for and on account of the services by him so as aforesaid rendered; and that the same may be located on any vacant or unlocated lands heretofore appropriated by Congress for said purposes.

Approved May 29, 1830.

An Act for the relief of William Price.

Sec. 1. *Be it enacted, &c.*, That the proper accounting officers of the Treasury be, and they are hereby, required to settle the account of William Price, and to allow him five years' full pay as a lieutenant in the revolutionary war, which five years' full pay is the commutation of his half pay for life; to be paid out of any money in the Treasury not otherwise appropriated.

Approved May 29, 1830.

---

An Act for the relief of Thomas Blackwell.

Sec. 1. *Be it enacted, &c.*, That the proper accounting officers of the Treasury be, and they hereby are, authorized and required to settle and adjust the account of Thomas Blackwell, a captain of the army of the Revolution, and allow to him five years' full pay, which five years' full pay is the commutation of his half pay for life; to be paid out of any money in the Treasury not otherwise appropriated.

Approved May 29, 1830.

---

An Act to repeal the proviso in the act for the relief of Philip Slaughter, passed twenty-sixth of May, eighteen hundred and twenty-eight.

Sec. 1. *Be it enacted, &c.*, That so much of the act for the relief of Philip Slaughter, passed twenty-sixth of May, eighteen hundred and twenty-eight, as provides "that the acceptance by the said Slaughter of the grant herein made shall be in lieu of any claim he may have under the provisions of a bill passed at this session of Congress, entitled ' An act for the relief of the surviving officers and soldiers of the Revolution,' " be, and the same is, hereby repealed.

Approved May 29, 1830.

---

An Act for the relief of the heirs of William Vawters.

Sec. 1. *Be it enacted, &c.*, That the proper accounting officers of the Treasury be, and they are hereby, required to settle and adjust the account of the heirs of William Vawters, and allow to them five years' full pay for their father's services as second lieutenant in the revolutionary war, with such interest thereon as the party would have been entitled to if a final settlement certificate had been issued for the amount of his commutation, and the same had been subscribed to the loan created by the act of one thousand seven hundred and ninety, providing for the funding of the debt of the United States; which five years' full pay is the commution of his half pay for life; to be paid out of any money in the Treasury not otherwise appropriated.

Approved May 25, 1832.

An Act for the relief of John Roberts, late major of infantry in the war of the Revolution.

Sec. 1. *Be it enacted, &c.*, That the proper accounting officers of the Treasury do settle and adjust the account of Major John Roberts, of the Virginia line on continental establishment, and allow him five years' full pay as major of infantry, in commutation of the half pay for life promised by the resolutions of Congress, with such interest thereon as the party would have been entitled to if a final settlement certificate had been issued for the amount of his commutation, and the same had been subscribed to the loan created by the act of one thousand seven hundred and ninety, providing for the funding of the debt of the United States ; and that the same be paid him out of any money in the Treasury not otherwise appropriated by law.

Approved May 25, 1832.

---

An Act for the relief of the legal representatives of Reginald alias Raynold Hillary.

Sec. 1. *Be it enacted, &c.*, That the proper accounting officers of the Treasury be, and they are hereby, directed and required to pay to Elizabeth Magruder, the legal representative of Reginald alias Raynold Hillary, five years' full pay, it being the commutation for half pay for life due to said Hillary in his lifetime, (for services rendered during the Revolution in the first regiment of Maryland troops,) and so much interest thereon as he would have been entitled to thereon by the principles of the " funding act," had a certificate issued for such commutation at the close of the war, and all dividends thereon were now remaining unpaid; to be paid out of any money in the Treasury not otherwise appropriated.

Approved May 25, 1832.

---

An Act for the relief of Ann D. Baylor.

Sec. 1. *Be it enacted, &c.*, That the Secretary of the Treasury be, and he is hereby, directed to pay Ann D. Baylor, as trustee for the heirs and distributees of John Walker Baylor, deceased, who was only son and heir at law of the late Colonel George Baylor, five years' full pay as a colonel of cavalry in the war of the Revolution, together with such interest as would have accrued on said five years' full pay, if a certificate for that amount had been issued by the United States on the fifteenth of November, seventeen hundred and eighty-three, and the said certificate, with its accruing interest, had been subscribed to the loan of the United States under the act entitled " An act making provision for the debt of the United States," passed August fourth, seventeen hundred and ninety ; making up the account, and settling and paying the same, in all respects, as if the same had been so subscribed, and was now outstanding and unpaid ; and that the same be paid to the said Ann D. Baylor, trustee as aforesaid, out of any money in the Treasury not otherwise appropriated by law.

Approved May 25, 1832.

An Act for the relief of the heirs and residuary legatees of William Carter, late of the State of Virginia, deceased.

Sec. 1. *Be it enacted, &c.*, That the proper accounting officers of the Treasury be, and they are hereby, required to settle and adjust the account of William Carter, (now deceased,) and to allow to his heirs or residuary legatees five years' full pay for his services as surgeon in the revolutionary war, which five years' full pay is the commutation of his half pay for life ; together with such interest as would have accrued on the said five years' full pay if a certificate for that amount had been issued by the United States and funded under the "act making provision for the debt of the United States," passed the fourth of August, one thousand seven hundred and ninety ; to be paid out of any money in the Treasury not otherwise appropriated.

Approved May 25, 1832.

----

An Act for the relief of Edmund Brooke.

Sec. 1. *Be it enacted, &c.*, That the proper accounting officers of the Treasury be, and they are hereby, authorized, empowered, and required to settle the account of Edmund Brooke, late a lieutenant in the army of the United States in the revolutionary war on continental establishment, and allow to him five years' full pay, that being the commutation for half pay for life due to him at the close of the war, in consideration of his services therein ; together with such interest as would have accrued on the said five years' full pay if a certificate for that amount had been issued by the United States on the fifteenth of November, seventeen hundred and eighty-three, and the said certificate, with its accruing interest, had been subscribed to the loan of the United States under the act entitled "An act making provision for the debt of the United States," passed August fourth, seventeen hundred and ninety ; making up the account, and settling and paying the same, in all respects as if the same had been so subscribed and was now outstanding and unpaid ; and that the same be paid to the said Edmund Brooke out of any money in the Treasury not otherwise appropriated by law.

Approved May 25, 1832.

----

An Act for the relief of the heirs and legal representatives of Dr. Samuel J. Axson, deceased.

Sec. 1. *Be it enacted, &c.*, That the proper accounting officers of the Treasury be, and they are hereby, authorized and directed to pay, out of any money in the Treasury not otherwise appropriated, to the heirs and legal representatives of Doctor Samuel J. Axson, five years' full pay as a surgeon in the revolutionary war; which five years' full pay is the commutation of half pay for life ; together with such interest thereon as would now be due if a certificate for such commutation had been issued at the close of the war, and subscribed under the principles of the funding act, and all dividends thereon were now remaining in the Treasury unpaid.

Approved June 15, 1832.

An Act for the relief of John Knight.

Sec. 1. *Be it enacted, &c.*, That the proper accounting officers of the Treasury be, and they are hereby, required to settle the account of John Knight, and to allow him five years' full pay as a surgeon's mate in the revolutionary war ; which five years' full pay is the commutation of his half pay for life; together with such interest thereon as would now be due if a certificate for such commutation had been issued and subscribed under the principles of the funding act, and no payments made thereon; to be paid out of any money in the Treasury not otherwise appropriated.

Approved June 15, 1832.

---

An Act for the relief of John J. Jacobs.

Sec. 1. *Be it enacted, &c.*, That the Secretary of the Treasury be authorized and directed to pay to John J. Jacobs, out of any money in the Treasury not otherwise appropriated, the amount of his commutation for half pay as a lieutenant in the army of the United States, on the continental establishment, during the revolutionary war, with such interest thereon as that the principal and interest will amount to the sum to which the said John J. Jacobs would have been entitled if a final settlement certificate had been issued for his said commutation, and the same had been by him subscribed to the loan created for funding the debt of the United States by the acts of seventeen hundred and ninety : *Provided,* That any sum found due by him to the United States be first deducted from the amount of said commutation.

Approved July 14, 1832.

---

An Act for the relief of the heirs of Thomas Davenport.

Sec. 1. *Be it enacted, &c.*, That the proper accounting officers of the Treasury be, and they are hereby, required to settle and adjust the account of the heirs of Thomas Davenport, and allow to them five years' full pay for his services as a captain in the revolutionary war, with such interest thereon as the party would have been entitled to if a final settlement certificate had been issued for the amount of his commutation, and the same had been subscribed to the loan created by the act of one thousand seven hundred and ninety, providing for the funding of the debt of the United States ; which five years' full pay is the commutation of his half pay for life ; to be paid out of any money in the Treasury not otherwise appropriated.

Approved July 14, 1832.

---

An Act for the relief of Sarah Easton and Dorothy Storer.

Sec. 1. *Be it enacted, &c.*, That the proper accounting officers of the Treasury be, and they are hereby, directed, in adjusting and settling the account of Sarah Easton and Dorothy Storer, for the commutation granted them as children and heirs at law of the late Colonel Robert Hanson Harrison, to allow and pay to them such sum, as interest, as would have accrued on such commutation, according to the regulations prescribed for funding and paying the domestic debt, had a certificate for such commutation been issued at the close of the war, and been in due time subscribed to said fund, and certificates of stock for the same regularly issued therefor, and all dividends thereon were now remaining in the Treasury unpaid; to be paid out of any money in the Treasury not otherwise appropriated.

Approved July 14, 1832.

---

An Act for the relief of the administrator of the late Colonel John Thornton, deceased.

Sec. 1. *Be it enacted, &c.*, That the proper accounting officers of the Treasury do settle, adjust, and pay over to his administrator, the account of the late Colonel John Thornton, deceased, for five years' full pay, in commutation of the half pay for life promised by the resolve of Congress to the officers of the continental line in the war of the Revolution, together with such interest thereon as would now be due if a certificate for such commutation had been issued and subscribed under the principles of the funding act, and no payment made thereon ; to be paid out of any money in the Treasury not otherwise appropriated. And the said administrator shall pay to the widow of the said Thornton one-fourth part of the money payable under this act, and the remainder he shall pay over, or distribute among the persons entitled thereto, according to the laws of the Commonwealth of Virginia.

Approved February 9, 1833.

---

An Act for the relief of John Thomas and Peter Foster.

Sec. 1. *Be it enacted, &c.*, That the proper accounting officers of the Treasury do settle the account of John Thomas, and allow him five years' full pay as a captain of infantry in the revolutionary army, in the Virginia line on continental establishment, with such interest thereon as would have been payable to the said John Thomas if a certificate had been given him for the amount of said commutation, and the same had by him been subscribed to the funded debt of the United States, under the act of one thousand seven hundred and ninety.

Sec. 2. *And be it further enacted*, That the same accounting officers do settle the account of Peter Foster, a lieutenant of infantry of the revolutionary army, of the Virginia line, and allow him five years' full pay as such lieutenant, with such interest thereon as is directed in the foregoing section to be allowed to John Thomas; and that the said several sums of money and interest be paid out of any money in the Treasury not otherwise appropriated.

Approved March 2, 1833.

---

An Act for the relief of the heirs of Doctor Isaac Ledyard, deceased.

Sec. 1. *Be it enacted, &c.*, That the proper accounting officers of the Treasury be, and they are hereby, directed and required to allow the heirs of Doctor Isaac Ledyard the five years' full pay of a surgeon, being the commutation of half pay for life of said Ledyard, as assistant purveyor of the hospital department of the revolutionary army, together with the interest thereon which would now be due had a certificate for that amount been issued by the United States, and subscribed under the "Act making provision for the debt of the United States," passed the fourth of August, one thousand seven hundred and ninety; and that the same be paid out of any money in the Treasury not otherwise appropriated.

Sec. 2. *And be it further enacted,* That the proper accounting officers of the Treasury Department be, and they are hereby, directed to revise the settlement of the account of Doctor Isaac Ledyard, assistant deputy director of the hospital department in the revolutionary army, made by Benjamin Walker, commissioner of accounts of the hospital, clothing, and marine department of said army, and to allow to the heirs of said Doctor Ledyard the compensation fixed by the resolution of Congress of February the sixth, one thousand seven hundred and seventy-eight, as specie, according to the report of the said Benjamin Walker, made to Congress on the fifteenth of September, one thousand seven hundred and eighty-six, which is of record in the report-book kept by said Walker, and filed in the office of the First Auditor of the Treasury; and that, on said settlement, if any balance is found due from the United States, the same be paid, with the interest now due, to the heirs of said Doctor Isaac Ledyard, as though a certificate had been regularly issued therefor at the time it was due, and the same had been subscribed to the loan created by the act of one thousand seven hundred and ninety, providing for the funding of the debt of the United States; and that the same be paid out of any money in the Treasury not otherwise appropriated.

Approved March 2, 1833.

---

An Act for the relief of Thomas Triplet.

Sec. 1. *Be it enacted, &c.,* That the proper accounting officers of the Treasury do settle the account of Thomas Triplet, (a captain of infantry in the revolutionary army,) and allow him five years' full pay as such captain, with such interest as would have become due thereon had a certificate for the same been duly issued, and afterwards, in due time, subscribed to the funded debt of the United States; and that the same be paid out of any money in the Treasury not otherwise appropriated.

Approved March 2, 1833.

---

An Act for the relief of the legal representatives of John Peter Waynan, deceased.

Sec. 1. *Be it enacted, &c.,* That the proper accounting officers of the Treasury be, and they are hereby, required to settle and adjust the account of John Peter Waynan, deceased, and to allow to his legal representatives five years' full pay as a lieutenant in the army of the Revolution, in commutation of the half pay for life promised by the resolves of Congress to the officers of the continental line in the war of the Revolution, together with such interest thereon as would now be due if a certificate for such commutation had been issued and subscribed under the principles of the funding act, and no payments made thereon; to be paid out of any money in the Treasury not otherwise appropriated.

Approved March 2, 1833.

An Act in aid of an act entitled "An act for the relief of James Barnett."

Sec. 1. *Be it enacted, &c.*, That the Secretary of the Treasury be, and he is hereby, authorized and required to pay to James Barnett such interest on his commutation provided for in "An act for the relief of said James Barnett," as he would have been entitled to receive if said commutation had been subscribed to the loan provided for by the several acts of Congress establishing the funding system, and the interest and principal had been paid under the several provisions of the said acts; and that the same be paid out of any money in the Treasury not otherwise appropriated.

Approved March 2, 1833.

----

An Act for the relief of James Gibbon and Sarah Price, widow of William Price, and Philip Slaughter.

Sec. 1. *Be it enacted, &c.*, That the proper accounting officers of the Treasury be, and they are hereby, authorized and required to settle and adjust the account of James Gibbon, a captain of the army of the Revolution, and allow to him five years' full pay, which five years' full pay is the commutation of his half pay for life ; with such interest thereon as would have been payable to the said James Gibbon if a certificate had been given him for the amount of said commutation, and the same had by him been subscribed to the funded debt of the United States, under the act of one thousand seven hundred and ninety ; to be paid out of any money in the Treasury not otherwise appropriated.

Sec. 2. *And be it further enacted*, That the proper accounting officers of the Treasury Department do also settle and adjust the account of William Price, late a lieutenant in the Virginia line on continental establishment, and pay to his widow, Sarah Price, whatever sum of money would have accrued and been payable to him as interest and dividends thereon, had he, the said Price, received a certificate for the amount of five years' full pay as a lieutenant of infantry, (according to the resolves of Congress of March, one thousand seven hundred and eighty-three,) and had subscribed the said certificate to the public debt, in conformity with the provisions of the acts of Congress of the fourth and fifth of August, one thousand seven hundred and ninety; which sum of money so found to be due as interest on dividends, and no more, shall be paid out of any money in the Treasury not otherwise appropriated.

Sec. 3. *And be it further enacted*, That the Secretary of the Treasury be authorized and directed to pay to Philip Slaughter, out of any money in the Treasury not otherwise appropriated, interest upon the commutation of half pay heretofore allowed him.

Approved March 2, 1833.

----

An Act for the relief of Ephraim Whitaker.

Sec. 1. *Be it enacted, &c.*, That the proper accounting officers of the Treasury be, and they are hereby, authorized and directed to pay, out of any money in the Treasury not otherwise appropriated, to Ephraim Whitaker, five years' full pay as a captain in the revolutionary war; which five years' full pay is the commutation of half pay for life.

Approved June 30, 1834.

An Act for the relief of the legal representatives of George Hurlbut, deceased.

Sec. 1. *Be it enacted, &c.*, That the proper accounting officers of the Treasury do settle the account of Captain George Hurlbut, a captain of the revolutionary army, in Colonel Sheldon's regiment of dragoons, of the continental line, and allow him five years' full pay of a captain of dragoons, as a commutation for the half pay for life which, by the resolve of seventeen hundred and eighty, Congress engaged to pay certain officers of the revolutionary army who should serve to the end of the war.

Sec. 2. *And be it further enacted,* That the sum so found due be paid to the legal representatives of the said George Hurlbut, out of any money in the Treasury not otherwise appropriated.

Approved June 30, 1834.

---

An Act for the relief of the legal representatives of Joseph Torrey, deceased.

Sec. 1. *Be it enacted, &c.*, That the proper accounting officers of the Treasury do settle the account of Joseph Torrey, a major of the revolutionary army, in Colonel Hazen's regiment of the revolutionary army, and allow him five years' full pay of a major, as a commutation for the half pay for life which, by the resolve of October twenty-one, seventeen hundred and eighty, Congress engaged to pay to the officers of the revolutionary army who should serve to the end of the war.

Sec. 2. *And be it further enacted,* That the sum so found due be paid to the legal representatives of the said Joseph Torrey, out of any money in the Treasury not otherwise appropriated.

Approved June 30, 1834.

---

An Act for the relief of the heirs and legal representatives of John Taylor, deceased.

Sec. 1. *Be it enacted, &c.*, That the proper accounting officers of the Treasury be, and they are hereby, authorized and directed to pay, out of any money in the Treasury not otherwise appropriated, to the heirs and legal representatives of John Taylor, deceased, five years' full pay as a lieutenant of infantry in the revolutionary war; which five years' full pay is the commutation of half pay for life.

Approved June 30, 1834.

---

An Act for the relief of the heirs and legal representatives of William Teas, deceased.

Sec. 1. *Be it enacted, &c.*, That the proper accounting officers of the Treasury be, and they are hereby, authorized and directed to pay, out of any money in the Treasury not otherwise appropriated, to the heirs and legal representatives of William Teas, deceased, five years' full pay as a cornet of horse in the revolutionary war ; which five years' full pay is the commutation of half pay for life.

Approved, June 30, 1834.

An Act for the relief of Thomas Minor.

Sec. 1. *Be it enacted, &c.*, That there be paid, out of any money in the Treasury not otherwise appropriated, to Thomas Minor, five years' full pay for the services of the said Minor as a captain in the war of the Revolution.

Approved June 30, 1834.

---

An Act for the relief of the legal representatives of Captain James Craine.

Sec. 1. *Be it enacted, &c.*, That the Secretary of the Treasury be, and he is hereby, directed, out of any money in the Treasury not otherwise appropriated by law, to pay to Edwin C. Brown and Maria Brown, (the latter being the only child and heir of Captain James Craine, deceased,) the amount of five years' full pay of a captain of infantry in the revolutionary army of the United States.

Approved June 30, 1834.

---

An Act for the relief of the legal representatives of Buller Claiborne, deceased.

Sec. 1. *Be it enacted, &c.*, That the proper accounting officers of the Treasury be, and they are hereby, required to settle the account of Buller Claiborne, deceased, and allow to his legal representatives five years' full pay as a captain in the service of the United States on continental establishment; which five years full pay is the commutation of his half pay for life; to be paid to the legal representatives of the said Buller Claiborne, deceased, out of any money in the Treasury not otherwise appropriated.

Approved June 30, 1834.

---

An Act for the relief of the legal representatives of Everard Meade, deceased:

Sec. 1. *Be it enacted, &c.*, That the proper accounting officers of the Treasury be, and they are hereby, required to settle the account of Everard Meade, deceased, and to allow his legal representatives five years' full pay as a captain in the Virginia regiment on continental establishment ; which five years' full pay is the commutation of his half pay for life ; to be paid to the said legal representatives of Everard Meade, deceased, out of any money in the Treasury not otherwise appropriated.

Approved June 30, 1834.

---

An Act for the relief of Lieutenant Robert Wilmot.

Sec. 1. *Be it enacted, &c.*, That the Secretary of the Treasury be, and he is hereby, authorized and required to pay to Robert Wilmot, a lieutenant in the army of the United States in the revolutionary war, on the continental establishment, five years' full pay, that being the commutation of the half pay for life promised by the resolves of Congress ; to be paid out of any money in the Treasury not otherwise appropriated.

Approved June 30, 1834.

An Act for the relief of the legal representatives of Enos Granniss, deceased.

Sec. 1. *Be it enacted, &c.*, That the proper accounting officers of the Treasury be, and they are hereby, required to settle and adjust the account of Enos Granniss, deceased, and to allow to his legal representatives five years' full pay as a lieutenant of the army of the Revolution, in commutation of the half pay for life promised by the resolves of Congress to the officers of the continental line who should continue in service to the close of the war, to be paid out of any money in the Treasury not otherwise appropriated.

Approved June 30, 1834.

------

An Act for the relief of John Emerson.

Sec. 1. *Be it enacted, &c.*, That the proper accounting officers of the Treasury be, and they are hereby, required to settle and adjust the account of John Emerson, and allow him five years' full pay as a lieutenant of infantry of the revolutionary army in the Virginia line on continental establishment; which five years' full pay is the commutation of his half pay for life; to be paid out of any money in the Treasury not otherwise appropriated.

Approved June 30, 1834.

------

An Act for the relief of the widow and heirs of Captain William Royall, deceased.

Sec. 1. *Be it enacted, &c.*, That the Secretary of War shall cause to be paid to Anne Royall, the widow, and to the heirs of the late William Royall, five years' full pay, as a captain from the State of Virginia, on the continental establishment, during the revolutionary war, in lieu of half pay for the life of said William.

Sec. 2. *And be it further enacted,* That the said amount of five years' full pay shall be paid to said widow and heirs, in such proportions as will conform to the laws of Virginia, for the distribution of the personal estate of persons dying intestate ; and that said payments be made out of any money in the Treasury not otherwise appropriated.

Approved June 30, 1834.

------

An Act for the relief of the heirs of Thomas Wallace, deceased.

Sec. 1. *Be it enacted, &c.*, That the proper accounting officers of the Treasury be, and they are hereby, required to settle the account of Thomas Wallace, deceased, and allow to his heirs five years' full pay, as a lieutenant in the eighth Virginia regiment on continental establishment ; which five years' full pay is the commutation of his half pay for life ; to be paid to the said heirs of Thomas Wallace, deceased, out of any money in the Treasury not otherwise appropriated.

Approved June 30, 1834.

14

An Act for the relief of the representatives of Robert Jouett, deceased.

Sec. 1. *Be it enacted, &c.*, That the proper accounting officers of the Treasury do settle the claim of James W. Bouldin, representative of Robert Jouett, deceased, a lieutenant of the Virginia line, on continental establishment in the revolutionary army, and to allow him five years' full pay of a lieutenant of infantry of said line.

Approved May 20, 1836.

———

[An Act for the relief of the legal representatives of Doctor Absalom Baird.

Sec. 1. *Be it enacted, &c.*, That the proper accounting officers of the Treasury be, and they are hereby, required to settle the account of Doctor Absalom Baird, deceased, as a surgeon in the regiment of artificers of the army of the United States, during the revolutionary war, and to allow his legal representatives compensation equal to five years' full pay of a captain of infantry in the service of the United States on continental establishment, without interest ; which five years' full pay is the commutation for his half pay for life; to be paid to the legal representatives of the said Absalom Baird, out of any money in the Treasury not otherwise appropriated.

Approved June 23, 1836.

———

An Act for the relief of the legal representatives of George Hurlbut, deceased.

Sec. 1. *Be it enacted, &c.*, That the proper accounting officers of the Treasury ascertain the amount that would have been payable on four final settlement certificates, issued twelfth of March, seventeen hundred and eighty-four, in the name of George Hurlbut, and afterwards recalled and cancelled, namely : number thirty-five thousand three hundred and thirty-six, for one thousand dollars ; number thirty-five thousand three hundred and thirty-seven, for one thousand dollars ; number thirty-five thousand three hundred and thirty-eight, for nine hundred and fifty dollars ; number thirty-five thousand three hundred and thirty-nine, for fifty dollars; making, together, three thousand dollars ; as if the said certificates had not been recalled and cancelled, but had been subscribed to the debt of the United States, under the act of August fourth, seventeen hundred and ninety; and that, after deducting from the amount so ascertained, the sum paid to the legal representatives of said George Hurlbut, under the act of June thirteenth, eighteen hundred and thirty-four, for their relief, the balance to be paid to the said legal representatives, out of any money in the Treasury not otherwise appropriated.

Approved July 2, 1836.

———

An Act for the relief of the legal representatives of Thornton Taylor, deceased.

Sec. 1. *Be it enacted, &c.*, That the proper accounting officers of the Treasury be, and they are hereby, required to settle the account of Thornton Taylor, deceased, and allow to his legal representatives five years' full pay as an ensign in the Virginia line on continental establishment, without interest ; which five years' full pay is the commutation of his half pay for life ; to be paid to the legal representatives of Thornton Taylor, deceased, out of any money in the Treasury not otherwise appropriated.

Approved July 2, 1836.

---

An Act for the relief of the legal representatives of Captain David Hopkins.

Sec. 1. *Be it enacted, &c.*, That the proper accounting officers ascertain the amount of five years' full pay of a captain serving to the end of the revolutionary war, on continental establishment, and pay the same, out of any money in the Treasury not otherwise appropriated, to the legal representatives of the late Captain David Hopkins, in full satisfaction of the commutation money promised by a resolution of the Congress of the United States.

Approved July 2, 1836.

## CHAPTER X.

*A Compend and Synopsis of the legislation of Congress on Revolutionary Claims, showing the cases in which Interest has been allowed, and in which it has not been allowed.*

Compiled from the Laws of the United States and the records of the Treasury.

---

### INTEREST ON REVOLUTIONARY CLAIMS.

By the laws or resolutions of the old Congress, *interest* was allowed on all claims, and to all creditors of the United States, from the time the payment became due. There are a great number of resolutions of Congress to this effect. Reference is, however, particularly made to that of the 3d June, 1784. See Journals old Congress, vol. 4, p. 443.

In respect to *commutation* of half pay, the resolution of Congress of 23d March, 1783, provides that the officers shall be entitled to receive, *at the end of the war*, their five years' full pay in lieu of half pay for life, in money, [that was specie,] or in securities *on interest*, as Congress should find most convenient. See Journals, vol. 4, p. 178.

Congress, in all cases, preferred issuing certificates on interest.

By the act for funding the debt of the United States, passed 4th August, 1790, (see Laws United States, vol. 2, p. 123,) *interest* was allowed on all certificates which might be subscribed to the funding system, and the *interest* became a part of the *principal,* and bore an *interest* from that time forward at 3 per cent.

By an act of Congress of March 23, 1792, (Laws United States, vol. 2, p. 259,) the statutes of limitation were removed for two years from the claims of widows and orphans to seven years' half pay. On all the claims settled at the Treasury under this removal, *interest* was allowed, commencing at seven years from the death of the officer ; although the law is silent about interest. See letter from the Register of the Treasury to the Hon. Mr. Marshall of the Committee on Revolutionary Claims.

By act of 27th March, 1792, (see Laws, vol. 2, p. 261,) the statutes of limitation were removed for two years from all claims for personal service, and the Treasury was directed to settle the same as though the claims had been exhibited and settled before the statutes of limitation went into operation ; and as all claims settled before the said statutes *bore interest,* of course those settled under this law also *bore interest,* and interest was paid accordingly at the Treasury.

By act of March 26, 1790, (Laws, vol. 2, p. 84,) *interest* is directed to be paid on certain small loans made by the Secretary of the Treasury.

By the act of August 11, 1790, certificates of registered debt, which bore *interest,* were directed to be issued for *arrears of invalid pensions.*

By an act of March 3, 1804, the invalid pensioners of South Carolina were transferred to the United States, and *certificates of registered debt, bearing interest,* were directed to issue for their *arrears of pension* from the time they were enrolled on the list of South Carolina ; that is, from the time of being wounded or discharged.

By act of 12th February, 1793, (Laws, vol. 2, p. 330,) certain claims are barred, if not presented by May 1, 1794 ; and those which should be presented, and were deemed valid, are to be settled as under former laws, all of which provide for the allowance of *interest.* Those claims not allowed are to be reported to Congress.

By an act of May 31, 1794, (Laws, vol. 2, p. 411,) *interest* is allowed on balances found due to individual States.

By act of April 13, 1818, (Laws, vol. 6, p. 286,) the statutes of limitation, barring the payment of loan office and other certificates of revolutionary debt, were suspended ; which suspension has been continued by subsequent acts to the end of the present session of Congress, (2d of the 24th) and these certificates are directed to be paid, when produced at the Treasury, with *six per cent. interest thereon.*

By act of 5th July, 1832, the half pay promised by Virginia to her officers of the revolutionary army, and which was assumed by the United States at the cession of the Northwestern Territory, was directed to be paid to those officers, or their representatives, *with interest upon each year's half pay,* from the time the same became due. See Laws United States, vol. 8, p. 654.

The claims of the following-named persons have been provided for by special acts of Congress ; upon which *interest* has been allowed, either by providing for the settlement of their claims according to former acts, by the issue of certificates of registered debt, (all of which bore interest,) or by specially directing the payment of interest :

Baron de Glaubeck, September 29, 1789, monthly pay, to be settled with as other foreign officers who received certificates bearing interest, which was payable in Paris, by Grand & Co. Vol. 2, p. 75.

Widow, &c., of Colonel Roberts, 7 years' half pay, March 27, 1792, vol. 2, p. 261.

Widow, &c., of Captain White, 7 years' half pay, March 27, 1792, vol. 2, p. 261.

Widow, &c., of Colonel Elliott, 7 years' half pay, March 27, 1792, vol. 2, p. 261.

Widow, &c., of Major Wise, 7 years' half pay, March 27, 1792, vol. 2, p. 261.

Widow, &c., of Major Huger, 7 years' half pay, March 27, 1792, vol. 2, p. 261.

Widow, &c., of Lieutenant Bush, 7 years' half pay, March 27, 1792, vol. 2, p. 261.

Widow, &c., of Major Motte, 7 years' half pay, March 27, 1792, vol. 2, p. 261.

The letter of the Register of the Treasury to Mr. Marshall expressly says *interest was paid* on these cases.

Captain Markley, commutation, August 11, 1790. Laws, vol. 2, p. 183.

Captain McIntire, commutation, March 27, 1792. Laws, vol. 2, p. 261.

Colonel Paunill, commutation, March 27, 1792. Laws, vol. 2, p. 261.

General De Haas, accounts, March 27, 1792. Laws, vol. 2, p. 261.

Doctor Debevere, accounts, March 27, 1792. Laws, vol. 2, p. 261.

Lieutenant King, accounts, March 27, 1792. Laws, vol. 2, p. 261.

Sailingmaster Sherman, accounts, March 27, 1792. Laws, vol. 2, p. 261. (See letter of the Register of the Treasury to Mr. Marshall.)

Lieutenant Brewster, money advanced, August 11, 1790. Laws, vol. 2, p. 183.

John Stevens, depreciation, August 11, 1790.  Laws, vol. 2, p. 183.

James Derry, accounts, August 11, 1790.  Laws, vol. 2, p. 183.

Benjamin Hardison, accounts, August 11, 1790.  Laws, vol. 2, p. 183.

Widow of General Lord Stirling, 7 years' half pay, August 11, 1790, vol. 2, p. 184.

Child of Colonel Laurens, 7 years' half pay, August 11, 1790, vol. 2, p. 184.

Oliver Pollock, commercial agent, December 23, 1791, vol. 2, p. 239.

Oliver Pollock, commercial agent, further allowance, March 3, 1807, vol. 4, p. 99.

General Nathaniel Greene, as surety of army contractor, April 27, 1792, vol. 2, p. 278.

Appropriation to pay General Greene, vol 2, p. 379.

Further allowance as surety of contractor, June 1, 1796, vol. 2, p. 572.

Col. Meigs, and ⎱ money advanced and repaid; this act was ⎱ vol. 2,
Col. Christ. Greene, ⎰ *special for the interest*, Jan. 14, 1793. ⎰ p. 327.

Appropriation to pay this interest, vol. 2, p. 374.

General St. Clair, pay, May 31, 1794, vol. 2, p. 411.

Colonel Dubois, commutation, June 4, 1794, vol. 2, p. 412.

Angus McLean, services and pay, February 27, 1795, vol. 2, p. 479.

General Kosciusko, *special for interest*, January 3, 1798, vol. 3, p. 25.

Moses White, pay as aid-de-camp, March 2, 1802, vol. 3, p. 543.

Widow, &c. of Thomas Flinn, guide, &c., pay, March 3, 1805, vol. 3, p. 664.

De Beaumarchais, supplies, April 18, 1806, vol. 4, p. 48.

Stephen Sayre, salary, March 3, 1807, vol. 4, p. 100.

Thomas Barclay, salary, &c., April 18, 1808, vol. 4. p. 165.

Moses Young, salary, &c., April 25, 1810, vol. 4, p. 264.

Colonel Durkee's daughter, 7 years' half pay, July 1, 1812, vol. 4, p. 461.

John Dixon, ⎱ loan office certificates, February 25, 1813, vol. 4, p. 504.
John Murray, ⎰

Samuel Lapsley, certificates, March 3, 1813, vol. 4, p. 537.

Joseph Brevard, certificate, April 13, 1814, vol. 4, p. 682.

Mary Rappleyea, certificates, February 2, 1815, vol. 4, p. 781.

William Arnold, certificate, February 2, 1815, vol. 4, p. 781.

Alexander Roxbury, certificate, April 26, 1816, vol. 6, p. 97.

John Holkar, certificates, April 29, 1816, vol. 6, p. 137.

John Thompson, *special for interest on advance*, April 14, 1818, vol. 6, p. 287.

Nicholas Vreeland, certificates, April 5, 1820, vol. 6, p. 468.

Samuel B. Beale, certificates, May 11, 1820, vol. 6, p. 510.

Thomas Leiper, certificates, May 15, 1820, vol. 6, p. 537.

John Guthrie, certificates, May 7, 1822, vol. 7, p. 63.

John Crute, certificates, May 7, 1822, vol. 7, p. 84.

James McClung, certificates, March 3, 1823, vol. 7, p. 195.

Walter S. Chandler, certificates, March 3, 1825, vol. 7, p. 371.

John Crain, certificates, March 3, 1825, vol. 7, p. 414.

George Baylor, ⎱
Le Roy Edwards, ⎰ balance on settlement, May 20, 1826, vol. 7, p. 507.
John Eustace, ⎰

B. J. Van Valkenburg, indents of interest, March 3, 1827, vol. 7, p. 599.

Charles Yates, executor, *special for interest*, May 29, 1830, vol. 8, p. 356.

Samuel Ward, *special for interest*, May 31, 1830, vol. 8, p. 386.

General Hazen's heirs, *special for interest*, March 3, 1831, vol. 8, p. 496.

J. and J. Pettigrew, property lost in Revolution, July 14, 1832, vol. 8, p. 702.

A. McKnight, property lost in Revolution, July 14, 1832, vol. 8, p. 702.

Colonel Laurens's heirs, salary, &c., July 14, 1832, vol. 8, p. 718.

William Price, commutation, *special for interest*, March 2, 1833, vol. 8, p. 860.

Philip Slaughter, commutation, *special for interest*, March 2, 1833, vol. 8, p. 861.

James Barnett, commutation, *special for interest*, March 2, 1833, vol. 8, p. 859.

Colonel Harrison's heirs, commutation, *special for interest*, July 14, 1832, vol. 8, p. 735.

Lieutenant Vawters, commutation, May 25, 1832, vol. 8, p. 562.

Major Roberts, commutation, May 25, 1832, vol. 8, p. 563.

Lieutenant Hillary, commutation, May 25, 1832, vol. 8, p. 564.

Doctor Carter, commutation, May 25, 1832, vol. 8, p. 564.

Colonel Baylor, commutation, May 25, 1832, vol. 8, p. 565.

Lieutenant Brooke, commutation, May 25, 1832, vol. 8, p. 565.

Doctor Axson, commutation, June 15, 1832, vol. 8, p. 592.

Doctor Knight, commutation, June 15, 1832, vol. 8, p. 593.

Lieutenant Jacobs, commutation, July 14, 1832, vol. 8, p. 722.

Captain Davenport, commutation, July 14, 1832, vol. 8, p. 724.

Colonel Thornton, commutation, February 9, 1833, vol. 8, p. 758.

Captain Thomas, commutation, March 2, 1833, vol. 8, p. 843.

Lieutenant Foster, commutation, March 2, 1833, vol. 8, p. 843.

Doctor Ledyard, commutation, March 2, 1833, vol. 8, p. 846.

Doctor Ledyard, balance of pay, March 2, 1833, vol. 8, p. 846.

Colonel John Ely, balance of pay, March 2, 1833, vol. 8, p. 847.

Captain Triplett, commutation, March 2, 1833, vol. 8, p. 849.

Lieutenant Wagnon, commutation, March 2, 1833, vol. 8, p. 857.

Captain Gibbon, commutation, March 2, 1833, vol. 8, p. 860.

Son of Alexander Brownlee, 7 years' half pay, Feb. 9, 1833, vol 8. p. 758.

Heirs of John Wilson, 7 years' half pay, Feb. 27, 1833, vol. 8, p. 774.

It ought to be remarked, that in both the two last-mentioned cases, Brownlee and Wilson, the bills were reported *without* interest. The House of Representatives amended the bills by *adding the interest ;* and they passed as amended.

Patience Gordon, certificates, May 19, 1828. Vol. 8, p. 60.

Robert Johnson, certificates, May 26, 1828. Vol. 8, p. 160.

A. D. Baylor, certificates, May 29, 1830. Vol. 8, p. 350.

Lucien Harper, certificates, March 2, 1831. Vol. 8, p. 434.

Richard G. Morris, certificates, May 19, 1832. Vol. 8, p. 557.

Ichabod Ward, certificates, June 15, 1832. Vol. 8, p. 594.

Aaron Snow, certificates, July 4, 1832. Vol. 8, p. 651.

Benjamin Gibbs, certificates, July 4, 1832. Vol. 8, p. 652.

John B. Taylor, certificates, July 13, 1832. Vol. 8, p. 679.

Gertrude Gates, certificates, July 14, 1832. Vol. 8, p. 728.

John Peck, certificates, July 14, 1832. Vol. 8, p. 734.

Archibald Watt, certificates, February 27, 1833. Vol. 8, p. 775.

Philip Bush, certificates, March 2, 1833.   Vol. 8, p. 842.

Dr. John Berrien, balance of account, June 19, 1834.   Sess. acts, p. 33.

Christian Ish, certificates, June 27, 1834.   Session acts, p. 49.

Michael Gratz, certificates, June 27, 1834.   Session acts, p. 64.

Walter Livingston, contracts, June 28, 1834.   Session acts, p. 78.

Benjamin Jacobs, certificates, June 28, 1834.   Session acts, p. 78.

Samuel Bayard, certificates, June 28, 1834.   Session acts, p. 78.

Joseph Falconer, certificates, *special for interest*, June 28, 1834.   Session acts, p. 78.

Samuel Gibbs, certificates, June 28, 1834.   Session acts, p. 81.

Benjamin Baird, certificates, June 28, 1834.   Session acts, p. 81.

Grove Pomeroy, certificates, June 28, 1834.   Session acts, p. 81.

John Peck, certificates, *special for interest*, June 30, 1834.   Sess. acts, p. 131.

Representatives of Gen. Lord Stirling, depreciation, June 30, 1834. Session acts, p. 138.

George Hurlbut, commutation certificates, *special for interest*, July 2, 1836.   Session acts, p. 213.

Widow of Alexander Hamilton, commutation, April 29, 1816.   Vol. 6, p. 128.

The act granting commutation to the heirs of Gen. Alexander Hamilton *is silent respecting interest.*   The claim for the interest, under the law, was referred to the Attorney General of the United States, who reported it was not necessary to specify the allowance of interest in an act for the payment of commutation, as the commutation act of March, 1783, itself, provided for the interest.   Under this decision, interest was paid Mrs. Hamilton.

Francis Cazeau, supplies, March 3, 1817.   Vol. 6, p. 220.

In this case the law says nothing about interest ; but upon an examination of the report, it is found that the *interest* is added to the principal, and, together, form the sum specified in the act.

Benjamin Wells, pay, May 29, 1830.   Vol. 8, p. 376.

Dr. Courts, pay, March 2, 1833.   Vol. 8, p. 845.

----

Acts have been passed by Congress, since the adoption of the present constitution, for the payment of revolutionary claims to the following-named persons, in which acts *nothing is said about interest;* but from the peculiar phraseology of several of the acts, it is believed that interest was allowed, viz :

Wilmington school-house, damages, April 13, 1792.   Vol. 2, pp. 272, 374.

Thomas Wishart, pay, February 22, 1793.   Vol. 2, p. 352.

Joseph Henderson, pay, February 22, 1793.   Vol. 2, p. 352.

General Lafayette, pay, March 27, 1794.   Vol. 2, p. 385.

Peter Covenhoven, curing his wounds, January 1, 1795.   Vol. 2, p. 454.

Samuel Prioleau, property destroyed, January 28, 1795.   Vol. 2, p. 461.

Benjamin Strother, expenses, February 19, 1796.   Vol. 2, p. 511.

Doctor Turner, commutation, April 22, 1808.   Vol. 4, p. 168.

General St. Clair, gratuity, May 1, 1810.   Vol. 4, p. 313.

William Dewees, property destroyed, April 11, 1818.   Vol. 6, p. 286.

M. Poirey, pay, February 24, 1819.   Vol. 6, p. 376.

M. de Vienne, pay, February 24, 1819.   Vol. 6, p. 377.
E. Stevens, Sands, &c., contracts, March 3, 1823.   Vol. 7, p. 200.
Lieutenant A. Garden, commutation, May 23, 1828.   Vol. 8, p. 79.
John Reynolds, balance of account, May 24, 1828.   Vol. 8, p. 152.
Lieutenant Caleb Stark, commutation, May 24, 1828.   Vol. 8, p. 153.
Benjamin Goodwin, rent, February 5, 1829.   Vol. 8, p. 183.
Benjamin Goodwin, rent, March 2, 1833.   Vol. 8, p. 851.
J. Foltz, pay, March 3, 1829.   Vol. 8, p. 231.
Captain Bayly, commutation, May 26, 1830.   Vol. 8, p. 323.
Captain Blackwell, commutation, May 29, 1830,   Vol. 8, p. 348.
John Campbell, pay, &c., March 2, 1833.   Vol. 8, p. 845.
Thomas Frothingham, property destroyed, March 2, 1833. Vol. 8, p. 852.
John Seyme, flour, May 23, 1834.   Session acts, p. 22.
Fred. Reymer, pay and supplies, June 28, 1834.   Session acts, p. 76.
Francis Nash, 7 years' half pay, June 30, 1834.   Session acts, p. 138.
Captain Wm. Royall, commutation, June 30, 1834.   Session acts, p. 149.

------

The following nineteen cases passed the House of Representatives at the first session, 24th Congress, *with interest.*  The Senate did not act upon the bills until the last two days of the session ; and as no rule had then been settled by the Senate, in respect to the allowance of interest, it was agreed, *pro forma,* that the interest should be stricken out of the bills, *without prejudice to the right of the parties,* each to be adjusted thereafter, either according to the merits of particular cases, or by a general rule, if any should be adopted :

John M. Gregory, 7 years' half pay, June 30, 1834.   Session acts, p. 140.
Lieutenant John Taylor, commutation, June 30, 1834.   Sess. acts, p. 141.
Cornet Teas, commutation, June 30, 1834.   Sess. acts, p. 141.
Major Torrey, commutation, June 30, 1834.   Sess. acts, p. 142.
M. Riker, 7 years' half pay, June 30, 1834.   Sess. acts, p. 142.
Lucy Bond,
Hannah Douglass,
Eliz. Goodwin,       } 7 years' half pay, June 30, 1834.   Sess. acts, p. 143.
Margaret Leitch,
Lieut. Thomas Wallace, 7 years' half pay, June 30, 1834. Sess. acts, p. 152.
James Bell, supplies and money, June 30, 1834.   Sess. acts, p. 155.
Lieut. Henry Field, 7 years' half pay, June 30, 1834. Sess. acts, p. 157.
Lieut. John Emerson, commutation, June 30, 1834.   Sess. acts, p. 158.
Lieut. Robert Wilmot, commutation, June 30, 1834.   Sess. acts, p. 159.
Lieut. Enos Granniss, commutation, June 30, 1834.   Sess. acts, p. 159.
Captain Buller Claiborne, commutation, June 30, 1834. Sess. acts, p. 160.
Captain Everard Meade, commutation, June 30, 1834.   Sess. acts, p. 160.
Ann M. Barron, 7 years' half pay, June 30, 1834.   Sess. acts, p. 161.
Captain James Craine, commutation, June 30, 1834.   Sess. acts, p. 162.

At the 2d session of the 23d Congress, the Senate decided that cases which had been presented in proper time, and had not been then allowed, ought to be entitled to interest ; and, on this principle, passed a bill to allow the interest on the claims of Hannah Douglass and Lucy Bond, and sent it to the House of Representatives, where it was not reached on the calendar. At the next session, that is, (the 1st session of the 24th Congress,) the Senate again passed a bill for the interest on the claims of Mrs. Douglass and Mrs. Bond. It was again reported favorably by the committee of the House. The bill was taken up in the House of Representatives on the last business day, but was not finally acted on.

On the same principle, also, at the 2d session of the 23d Congress, a bill was reported in the Senate for the interest on the claim of James Bell, but was not acted on. The bill was renewed at the last session, (the 2d of the 24th Congress,) passed the Senate, but was not finally acted on in the House.

At the last session of the 24th Congress, the following eight cases were passed upon without interest ; the allowance of the interest being left to await the decision now pending before the House of Representatives :

| | Sess. Acts, page |
|---|---|
| Nancy Haggard, seven years' half pay, July 2, 1836, - - - | 197 |
| Heirs of J. Moore, seven years' half pay, July 2, 1836, - - | 198 |
| Lieutenant Robert Jouett, commutation, May 20, 1836, - - | 56 |
| Doctor Baird, commutation, June 23, 1836, - - - - - | 105 |
| Heirs of Col. Hazlett, seven years' half pay, July 2, 1836, - - | 209 |
| Ensign Thornton Taylor, commutation, July 2, 1836, - - - | 215 |
| Heirs of Doctor Parkerson, seven years' half pay, July 2, 1836, - | 216 |
| Captain David Hopkins, commutation, July 2, 1836, - - - | 216 |

---

*Copy of a letter from the Register of the Treasury to the Hon. Thomas A. Marshall, showing the allowance of interest on claims paid under acts of 1792 and 1793, suspending the statutes of limitation, dated*

TREASURY DEPARTMENT,
*Register's Office, May* 9, 1834.

SIR : It appears from the records of this office, that certificates for the following sums were issued to the representatives of the officers mentioned in the 1st section of the act of March 27, 1792, viz :

To Colonel Owen Roberts, $4,200, at 6 per cent. per annum, from June 20, 1786.

To Captain William White, $1,679 99, at 6 per cent. per annum, from October 13, 1788.

To Lieutenant Colonel Bernard Elliott, $3,150, at 6 per cent. per annum, from October 28, 1785.

To Major Samuel Wise, $2,100, at 6 per cent. per annum, from October 9, 1786.

To Major Benjamin Huger, $2,100, at 6 per cent. per annum, from May 11, 1786.

To Lieutenant John Bush, $746 67, at 6 per cent. per annum, from October 10, 1786.

To Major Charles Motte, $2,100, at 6 per cent. per annum, from October 10, 1786.

It appears, also, that the certificates which were issued under the 1st section of the act of 23d March, 1792, to satisfy the claims of widows and orphans to the seven years' half pay of officers who lost their lives in the revolutionary war, *bore the same rate of interest,* (i. e. 6 per cent.,) commencing at different periods between 1781 and 1789.

The following sums were issued under the 4th section of the act of the 27th May, 1792, to Lieutenant Colonel Pannill and Captain McIntire, viz:

To Lieutenant Colonel Pannill, $3,600, on interest at 6 per cent. per annum, from March 22, 1783.

To Captain McIntire, $2,346 32, on interest at 6 per cent. per annum, from March 26, 1783.

I have the honor to be, &c.

T. L. SMITH.

Hon. Thomas A. Marshall.

————

*Extract from the report of the Register of the Treasury, also showing the allowance of interest on revolutionary claims, paid since the adoption of the present constitution, dated*

" Treasury Department,

" *Register's Office, April* 18, 1836.

" Sir : I have the honor, in compliance with your reference to this office of the resolution of the House of Representatives of the 11th inst., to report, that ' *all certificates of public debt,*' issued by the Register of the Treasury, by the commissioner of army accounts, and by the commissioners for settling the accounts of *individuals* in the several States, and in the quartermaster's, commissary's, marine, and clothing departments, for services rendered or supplies furnished during the war of the Revolution, or in fulfilment of promises contained in any ordinance or resolution of the old Congress, were on interest at six per cent. per annum from the termination of the service, or from the time the supplies were furnished."*

" The claims presented at the Treasury under the acts of the 23d and 27th March, 1792, were liquidated by issuing certificates of registered debt, *bearing interest.*"

————

*Copy of the opinion of the Attorney General of the United States in the case of the widow of Colonel Hamilton, showing that it is not necessary, in acts granting the commutation of half pay, in order to entitle to interest, that the allowance of interest should be specially mentioned in the act, as the interest is expressly allowed by the resolution of Congress of March 22d,* 1783.

The following case, stated by the Auditor, is submitted by the Secretary of the Treasury to the Attorney General for his opinion :

Alexander Hamilton was a lieutenant colonel in the army of the revolutionary war, but was understood to have retired from service towards the close of the year 1781 ; and in the month of November, 1782, took his seat in Congress as a member from the State of New York.

————

*As per resolution of the old Congress of the 3d of June, 1784. See old Journals, vol. 4, page 443.

Does the act for the relief of Elizabeth Hamilton, widow of Alexander Hamilton, passed on the 29th of April, 1816, place her on an equal footing with the officers entitled to commutation under the resolution of Congress of March, 1783; or, in other words, does the spirit and true meaning of the said act require that interest be allowed on the five years' full pay therein granted?

I think it does. I am given to understand that it has not been the practice in the accounting officers of the Treasury Department to allow interest upon an account directed to be settled or paid by an act of Congress, unless there be in the act itself special words to that effect. This rule, taken as a general one, it is not my part to controvert, nor is it supposed that the above opinion will imply any contradiction.

I ground it on the peculiar words of the act of April 29, 1816, which, taken in connexion with the resolution of March 22, 1783, appears to me, on full consideration, to enforce the construction, that it was the intention of Congress not merely to make an independent grant to Elizabeth Hamilton, but to place her upon a footing of equal advantage, in all respects, with the officers entitled to commutation under that resolution.

The consequence will be, that, as was the case with the officers themselves, (none of whom, it is believed, received the amount in money,) she too will be entitled to interest at six per cent., the rate specified in the resolution.

RICHARD RUSH, *A. G.*

WASHINGTON, *June* 29, 1816.

————

*Copy of a letter from the Register of the Treasury to the Hon. James Garland, showing the number of claims admitted and paid at the Treasury under the acts of March 27, 1792, and February 12, 1793, suspending the statute of limitation.* (These claims, it will be perceived by the letters of the Register of the Treasury, dated May 9, 1834, and April 18, 1836, were paid with six per cent. interest.)

TREASURY DEPARTMENT,
*Register's Office, January* 6, 1837.

SIR : Upon examining the records of this office, I can find no particular entries, without a more minute examination, of the cases admitted under the act of 23d March, 1792.*

The claims allowed under the acts of the 27th March, 1792, and 12th February, 1793, were in number 1,516.

I have the honor to be, &c.

MICH'L NOURSE, *for the Register.*

————

* The act suspending the statute of limitation against claims of widows to seven years' half-pay. See letter of Register of January 13, 1837, in explanation of this paragraph.

*Copy of a letter from the Register of the Treasury to the Hon. James Garland, showing the number of claims admitted and paid at the Treasury under the act of April 13, 1818, and the acts supplementary thereto, and which are now in force, suspending the statutes of limitation against loan office, final settlement, and other certificates.* (These acts provide for the payment of these certificates, with six per cent. interest.)

TREASURY DEPARTMENT,

*Register's Office, January* 13, 1837.

SIR : I have the honor to enclose a copy of the Attorney General's opinion in the case of Mrs. Hamilton.

The caption of the statement from which I ascertained the number of claims reported in my letter of the 6th instant, indicated that they had been adjusted under the acts of 27th March, 1792, and 12th February, 1793; but on referring to particular claims embraced in the statement, I find seventeen were for half pay [of widows and orphans]. These, of course, were included in the 1,516.

Under the act of 16th [13th] April, 1818, and the subsequent acts, in relation to the payment of loan office and other certificates, 116 claims have been adjusted.

I have the honor to be, &c.,

MICHAEL NOURSE.

Hon. JAMES GARLAND.

---

From these statements it will be found—

|  | Cases. |
|---|---|
| That, since the adoption of the present constitution, acts have been passed for the settlement of the claims of individuals, *by name,* on which, by the terms of the acts themselves, *interest has been allowed,* to the number of  -  -  -  -  - | 122 |

Of this number, thirteen were passed *specially for the allowance of interest after the principal had been paid, under former acts.*

That in two cases, (Brownlee and Wilson,) Congress *added interest* to bills which were reported without interest.

| That, under the acts of March 23, 1792, March 27, 1792, and February 12, 1793, suspending the statutes of limitation as to claims of widows and orphans, and claims for personal services of officers, &c., there were settled and paid at the Treasury, *with interest,* as per letter of the Register of the Treasury,  -  - | 1,516 |
| That, under the act of April 13th, 1818, and the acts supplementary thereto, (and now in force,) suspending the statutes of limitation so far as relates to loan office and to other certificates, (not lost or destroyed,) there have been admitted and paid at the Treasury, *with interest,* claims to the number of  -  -  - | 116 |
| Making of individual claims *paid with interest,*  -  -  - | 1,754 |

That, since the adoption of the constitution, claims have been paid under special acts, in which nothing is said about interest, to the number of 54. And of this number 19 *passed the House with interest,* which was struck out *pro forma* by the Senate, to be adjusted afterwards, upon some general rule ; and that 8 of the remaining cases have been passed subsequently, on the same principle ; that is, to await the general rule. So that it will be seen that 1,754 cases have been allowed *with interest,* and 54 *without interest ;* being upwards of *thirty-two cases allowed with interest to one case without interest.*

--------

### FUNDING SYSTEM.

Misapprehension prevails with respect to the computation of interest on the principles of the funding system. Some persons suppose that acts for the allowance of commutation, with interest on the principles of that system, would allow the interest up to the date of the act. It is not so. Under such an act, no more is allowed than would have been allowed if the officer had received his certificate of commutation on his leaving the army, and had subscribed the same under the funding act of the 4th August, 1790 ; and under such an act no more would be paid fifty years hence, than was paid when the certificate was finally redeemed by the extinguishment of the debt of the United States funded under the act of August 4, 1790.

In compiling this statement, the laws were examined page by page, from the first act of Congress, in March, 1789, to the close of the first session of the twenty-fourth Congress ; and it is believed that every act bearing on the question has been referred to.

## CHAPTER XI.

*Reports of Committees of Congress, of the Secretaries of the Treasury and War Departments, and of the Attorney General, relating to Claims for pay, arrears of pay, commutation of the half pay for life, seven years' half pay to Widows and Orphans of Revolutionary Officers, Loan Office and Final Settlement Certificates, Indents of Interest, Limitation Laws, &c.*

---

*Application of the officers of the regiment of artillery artificers for half pay or the commutation thereof.*

### February 3, 1835.

The committee to whom was referred a letter of 20th January last, from J. Pierce, paymaster general, respecting claims which have been made by certain officers to half pay and the commutation for half pay, report :

That, by a resolve of November 24, 1778, it was provided that all deranged officers should be entitled to one year's pay ; and it was further provided, that officers who had been prisoners with the enemy, and then were, or thereafter might be, exchanged, should, if appointed by the authority of the State, be entitled to return into the service in the same rank they would have had if they had not been captured, under certain restrictions, and that they should receive half pay till the time of their entering again into the service. Under this act certain officers claim half pay to the end of the war, and the commutation for half pay from that period during life : on which the committee observe, that the half pay first mentioned was promised as a temporary support to such officers as should be reappointed by their respective States, and to none besides ; and that all other continental officers who have been prisoners with the enemy, and deranged, are entitled to one year's pay, and nothing besides. That such was the intention of Congress is explained by the subsequent acts of May 22, 1779, and May 26, 1781. There is no act under which those officers can claim the commutation for half pay. It is provided, by a resolve of the 28th June, 1782, 'that there shall be such additional pay and emoluments to the pay of captains and subalterns serving as aids-de-camp to major and brigadier generals, and to brigade majors, as shall make their pay and emoluments equal to the pay and emoluments of a major in the line of the army.' Under this resolution certain aids and brigade majors, who are captains or subalterns in the line, claim commutation equal to that of a major in the line. This claim appears, for sundry reasons, to be ill-founded. The offices which those gentlemen held out of the line were temporary, and the additional pay and emoluments were certainly promised to them while they continued to serve in those offices, and no longer. If they are supposed to found their claim to the commutation of a major, under the head of additional emoluments, their claim must be ill-founded ; for it is clear, from the terms of the resolution, that pay and emoluments do not signify the same thing, but the commutation is the substitute for pay alone, or half pay, and not for rations nor any other emolument.    On the whole, the committee are of opinion that the paymaster general, in settling the accounts of the army, in all claims which may be brought for half pay or commutation, should be determined by the act of the 26th January, 1784.

*Resolved,* That Congress agree to the said report.

---

Communicated to the House of Representatives March 19, 1790.

WAR OFFICE, *March* 19, 1790.

The Secretary for the Department of War, to whom was referred the petition of Alexander Power and others, late officers of the regiment of artillery artificers, reports :

That the claim of the late officers of the regiment of artillery artificers for half pay, or the commutation thereof, granted to the officers of the late army, was several times submitted to the United States in Congress assembled, and received their decision on the 19th day of October, 1785.

That the principles whereon the said decision was founded will fully appear by the reports of the late commissioner of army accounts and a committee of Congress, both of which are herewith submitted, (Nos. 1 and 2.)

That the said decision being against the claim of the said officers of artillery artificers, the same was referred to the commissioner of army accounts to take order.

That the said decision appears to the Secretary of War to have been conformable to the several previous resolves of Congress relative to the object of half pay, and that the same ought to be final.

That the petitioners again brought forward their claim to Congress in the year 1788, which was referred to the subscriber, whose report is herewith submitted, (No. 3,) but which was never acted upon.

The Secretary of War embraces this occasion respectfully to observe, that it is of high importance to adhere generally to the decisions of the late Congress on the subjects of claims against the United States.

That he conceives no judgment of this nature should be reversed but on the most ample proof that the same was formed on a misrepresentation of facts ; but that, while such judgments are reversed with great caution, constructive judgments, made on previous resolves of Congress, ought to remain fully established.

That if a contrary conduct should be admitted, the accounts hitherto settled by the United States, and by the respective States, with individuals, would be liable to revision and unlimited confusion.

That when the abilities, integrity, and liberality of the former Congress be considered, it may be justly presumed that individuals experienced the fairest investigation of their claims, and that upright decisions were formed thereon.

That, with respect to the present petition, the Secretary of War is unable to perceive any new facts or circumstances of such a nature as to require a repeal of the former decision of Congress on the subject ; he therefore reports the following resolve :

*Resolved,* That the petition of the late officers of the artillery artificers for the commutation of the half pay cannot be granted, the United States in Congress assembled having decided against the same on the 19th of October, 1785.

All which is humbly submitted to the House of Representatives.

H. KNOX,

*Secretary of War.*

---

[Papers referred to in the foregoing report.]

No. 1.

NEW YORK, *August* 9, 1785.

The commissioner for settling the army accounts, to whom was referred the petition of John Jordan and Thomas Willey, late captains in the Pennsylvania corps of artillery artificers, begs leave to report :

That there are no existing resolutions of Congress, in his opinion, on which the petitioners can found a claim of the commutation in lieu of half pay for life ; and, therefore, if such a grant should be made, it will be necessary to adopt a new principle respecting the corps of artificers. The principles on which Captains Jordan and Willey appear to found their claim of commutation in lieu of half pay, are : 1st. That Congress have considered them in sundry resolutions as on the establishment of the army, and as part of the quota of the several States. 2d. That, on the 11th of February, 1778, they had granted them the same pay, clothing, and benefits as the artillery, and, on the 9th of February, 1780, were directed to be provided for, deemed and treated in the same manner as the several State lines. 3d. That on the 3d day of October, 1780, Congress directed the artificers to be formed into one corps, and promised to the supernumeraries half pay for seven years ; and on the 21st of the same month extended the half pay for life to the reduced officers and those who continued in service to the end of the war. As the former resolutions included the corps in express terms, it may be supposed it was intended to be comprehended in the latter. 4th. That they had been obliged to receive for their services the same kind of certificates with the military officers. Being subjected, therefore, to their disadvantages, it is no more than reasonable that they should also have their privileges.

It may be necessary to premise, that it appears to be the intention of Congress to retain the allowance of commutation as much as possible ; and, of course, where the clear intention of an act is not to be discovered in its words, the grant is not to be made by implication.

The commissioner, therefore, having founded his opinion on the following reasons, humbly submits the same to the consideration of Congress :

1st. That the assigning these corps as part of the State's quota was to determine the number of men who were to be furnished by each State, and to give their officers and men the advantages of the lines derived immediately from the States, but cannot be construed to extend to any demands the military officers, as such, may have upon the Union.

2d. That the resolution of February 11, 1778, and February 9, 1780, ought not to extend to this allowance, because the words "benefits or emoluments" appear reasonably to include the usual pay, subsistence, forage, and servants, of an officer only ; more especially as, at the time of passing these acts, the grant of half pay for life was not in existence ; and as the last-mentioned resolution has included the exceptions that had here-

16

before been made respecting the artificers, which undoubtedly refers to the special exception in the resolve of November 16, 1779.

3d. That the resolve of October 3, 1780, granting the seven years' half pay to the officers then deranged, having never been put into execution in respect to this corps, there can arise no question whether the officers are entitled to its benefits ; but that the one of the 21st of October should be construed as comprehending the corps is very doubtful, as Congress, in their first promise of half pay, confined it to military officers only, and having granted commissions to the artificers for the sole purpose of rank in their own corps, and to hold courts-martial ; and Congress have also expressly, in a resolution recommending this corps to their States, excepted the allowance of half pay ; and when Colonel Baldwin's corps was reduced in 1781, the officers retired without a promise of it, which would have been necessary to have entitled even the military to such allowance. It therefore appears to be the uniform intention of Congress, through their several acts before and after October, 1780, to exclude this corps from the half pay ; which furnishes sufficient foundation, with the nature of this promise, to conclude that the general term of " *the officer* " in the act of October 21, 1780, comprehends the military only.

4th. Whether it may be proper and reasonable to grant the commutation to these officers, in consideration of their being paid in the securities of the United States, or whether it will be just, in consideration that they are not entitled to the commutation, to pay them for the years 1782 and 1783, in specie, are questions that the commissioners cannot determine.

Resolves of Congress referred to in the foregoing :

A.—Resolve of February 11, and June 26, 1784.

B.—Resolve of February 11, 1784.

C.—Resolve of May 15, 1788.

D.—Resolve of February 11, 1788, and November 12, 1799.

E.—Resolve of November 11, 1779.

F.—Resolve of March 29, 1781.

### No. 2.

Copy of a report of a committee of Congress of the 19th October, 1785, sent to the commissioner of the army accounts to take order, it respecting the claims of Captains Jordon and Willey, and other officers of the corps of artificers, for commutation, of which committee Mr. Ellery was chairman.

The committee, consisting of Mr. Ellery, Mr. Gardner, and Mr. Williamson, to whom were referred the memorials of several officers of the late corps of artificers, praying that, in settling their accounts, they be allowed the commutation of half pay, as founded on justice, or on the acts of Congress, beg leave to report :

That the claims of those officers do not appear to be founded on the usage of nations, nor in equity ; they believe that half pay has been allowed to military officers, partly to a regard to the hardships and personal dangers to which they were exposed, but chiefly from a consideration that, by a long continuance in the military line, they may have lost those habits by which they had formerly been enabled to provide for themselves and families, which reasons do not apply so fully to the officers of artificers.

Your committee are of opinion that their sole rule on the occasion must be the acts of Congress respecting the officers in the corps of artificers, and they do not find any resolution by which they are entitled to half pay or commutation; on the contrary, they seem to be expressly cut off from any such claim.

The original act of Congress of May 15, 1778, by which half pay was promised for seven years, confines the same to military officers, which certainly did not include the artificers; and your committee are of opinion that in all subsequent acts which relate to the half pay, the same denomination of officers must be intended, unless where other officers are expressly mentioned. Surely the act of October 2, 1780, promising half pay to officers who might be deranged, never could be construed as giving pay to any class of officers who had no claim to half pay, had they continued in service to the end of the war. If any doubts could have arisen whether the artificers were intended in the promise of half pay, it must be fully removed by the act of the 16th November, 1779. It was then resolved, that it be recommended to the several States to allow the corps of artificers, established by Congress the 12th instant, all the benefits provided for officers in the line of their quotas of the continental battalions, except the half pay. After this pointed and express exclusion of those officers from the allowance of half pay, your committee are of opinion that nothing but a subsequent promise, equally pointed and express, can give them a title to the same. None such has been made; wherefore, they submit the following resolve:

That the officers of the late corps of artificers in the service of the United States are not entiled to half pay or the commutation of half pay.

The above is a true copy of an original referred to me by Congress, to take order.

JOHN PIERCE,
*Commissioner of Army Accounts.*

The Hon. the Secretary of War.

———

## No. 3.

War Office, *July* 30, 1788.

The Secretary for the Department of War, to whom was referred the memorial of Alexander Powers, attorney for a number of the officers of the late regiment of artillery artificers, claiming the commutation of the half pay granted to the late officers of the army of the United States, reports:

That the claim of the late officers of the regiment of artillery artificers for half pay, or a commutation thereof, has been several times submitted to Congress, and received their decision on the 19th October, 1785, as will more fully appear by the copy of a report of a committee of Congress, herewith submitted, which was referred to the Commissioner of Army Accounts to take order.

That this decision respecting artificers was conformable to the several resolves of Congress respecting the objects of the half pay.

But the memorialist assumes another principle, and asserts that he and his constituents were commissioned as artillery officers, disciplined as such and performed duty accordingly; that their services and promises were equal to other officers of artillery, and their reward ought to be the same. As this is an appeal to the justice of the sovereign for the performance of a public contract, it may be necessary to state the following circumstances, to show that it is unsupported by proper facts:

1st. The artificers were established as a part of the civil branch of the ordnance department, as will appear by the resolves of Congress of 11th February, 1778. The rank which was given to the officers was necessary for the government of the workmen, and the relative pay with the officers of artillery was the rule of pay to the officers of artificers; but no stipulation was then made, or at any subsequent period, that the officers of the artificers should have the same rewards as the officers of the army.

2d. The establishment of the battalions which form the corps of artillery, from time to time, will prove that the officers were not at any period considered as artillerists.

3d. The artificers did not, in any instance, act in the field as artillerists ; they were mostly stationed at the arsenal at Carlisle, and employed in making carriages of various kinds for the use of the artillery in the field. But there are two circumstances on which the memorialist and his constituents seem to place great confidence, viz : that their commissions expressed officers of "artillery and artificers," and that the surgeon of the regiment was allowed, by the resolve of Congress of the 5th May, 1782, all the emoluments heretofore allowed to reduced regimental surgeons. The manner of filling up the commissions must have been an error, as it was not authorized by any act of Congress.

It would appear, by the resolve of the 3d May, 1782, that Congress considered the surgeon differently circumstanced from the officers of the artificers, as the corps had been previously reduced by the resolve of Congress of the 29th March, 1781, and all the officers, except two, discharged without any specification of rewards.

On the whole, your Secretary is of opinion that it would be proper, in order to prevent further applications, for Congress to pass a resolution on the subject, as the report of the committee of the 19th October, 1785, has not been published. On this principle the following resolve is submitted:

*Resolved*, That the claim of the late officers of the artillery artificers for the commutation of the half pay granted to the late officers of the army of the United States, cannot be allowed.

---

### Claim of the Baron de Steuben.

Communicated to the House of Representatives, April 6, 1790.

Treasury Department, *March* 29, 1790.

The Secretary of the Treasury on the memorial of the Baron de Steuben, referred to him by an order of the House of Representatives of the 25th of September last, respectfully reports:

That it appears from the papers accompanying the said memorial, that the memorialist grounds his present claim on the United States upon a contract which he alleges to have been made with Congress at York, in the year 1777, previous to his joining the American army.

That the transaction respecting this alleged contract is stated by the memorialist in the following words : "At the arrival of the Baron de Steuben, in the year 1777, he was received by Congress with marks of distinction, and, the day after his arrival, was waited on by a committee of Congress, composed of Doctor Witherspoon, Mr. Henry of Maryland, and a third, whom at this time he cannot recollect. This committee demanded of the Baron the conditions on which he was inclined to serve the United States, and if he had made any stipulations with the commissioners in France. He replied, that he had made no agreement with them, nor was it his intention to accept of any rank or pay ; that he wished to join the army as a volunteer, and to render such services as the commander-in-chief should think him capable of, adding, that he had no other fortune than a revenue of about six hundred guineas per annum, arising from places and posts of honor in Germany, which he had relinquished to come to this country ; that, in consideration of this, he expected the United States would defray his necessary expenses while in their service ; that if, unhappily, this country should not succeed in establishing their independence, or if he should not succeed in his endeavors for their service, in either of those cases he should consider the United States as free from any obligations towards him ; but if, on the other hand, the United States should be happy enough to establish their freedom, and that he should be successful in his endeavors, in that case he should expect a full indemnification for the sacrifice he had made in coming over, and such marks of their generosity as the justice of the United States should dictate ; that if these terms were agreeable to Congress, he waited only their orders to join the army without delay. The committee were pleased to applaud the generosity of his propositions, in thus risking his fortune on that of the United States. The committee then left him, in order to make their report. The next day Congress gave him an entertainment ; after which the President, Mr. Laurens, told him it was the desire of Congress that he should join the army immediately, which he did."

That the evidence adduced by him in support of it consists principally of these documents, a certificate from John Witherspoon, dated November 1st, 1785, another from Elbridge Gerry, dated the 23d of November, 1785, and a third from William Duer, without date ; which several certificates are annexed to the statement above recited, and refer to it ; also two letters, one from Thomas McKean, dated 11th September, 1788, and another from Francis Lightfoot Lee, dated 25th of September, in the same year ; all which gentlemen were, at the time of the transaction, members of Congress, and three of them, viz : John Witherspoon, Francis Lightfoot Lee, and Thomas McKean, members of the committee mentioned in the said statement.

That the certificate from the said John Witherspoon is as follows :

PRINCETON, *November* 1, 1785.

I can recollect very distinctly that I was one of the committee who waited on Baron Steuben, on his arrival at Yorktown. He then could speak no English, and I believe I was the only member of the committee who could speak French, and was therefore obliged to be his interpreter to the other members, as well as to make the report to Congress. I am sensible that the above is a just and fair account of what passed on that occasion, and that we were all sensible that the Baron's proposals were honorable and generous ; and accordingly he was sent to General Washington, to receive his directions from him.

JOHN WITHERSPOON.

That the certificate from the said Elbridge Gerry is as follows :

New York, November 23, 1785.

The subscriber certifies that, having a seat in Congress at the time of the Baron de Steuben's arrival at Yorktown, he well remembers the facts herein stated, excepting what relates to the entertainment, which he doubts not was provided, and to the time of the Baron's arrival at that place, which was in the beginning of the year 1778. The subscriber further certifies that, in questions agitated in Congress while he has been a member, respecting the allowance that should be made in pursuance of the within stipulation, he has considered the claim of the Baron, for a full indemnification and compensation, as a claim of justice founded in the verbal contract of the parties.

E. GERRY.

That so much of the certificate of the said William Duer as relates to the fact, is as follows :

" I was a member of Congress and of the Board of War when the Baron de Steuben arrived at Yorktown, and though I was not present at that place when the Baron had his first interview with the committee of Congress, being absent for a few days, on a visit to Manheim, I perfectly remember that the account I received on my return to Yorktown, of the engagements entered into with the Baron Steuben, by the honorable Congress, was perfectly similar to that which the Baron had stated."

That the material part of the letter of the said Thomas McKean is as follows :

" My memory enables me to say that you came to Yorktown in the beginning of February, 1798; that Congress being informed of it, proceeded to name a committee (of which I was one) to wait upon you, learn the object of your visit, and to confer with you about entering into the service of the United States.

" They might have received further instructions, but I do not remember them. The committee (of which, Dr. Witherspoon was chairman) called upon you the next morning at your lodgings, when a conversation was had between the Doctor and you, in French, which he interpreted to his brethren ; part of what was then communicated was, that you came to America with a view to tender your services to Congress; that you had made no stipulations with their commissioners in France, and was desirous to join the army as a volunteer, and to act there in such situation as the commander-in-chief should think you best qualified to fill ; that you had held posts of honor and profit in the army of the King of Prussia, and afterwards, (I think,) of the Prince of Baden, which last you had relinquished in order to embark in the American cause, whose fortunes you were willing to partake ; that if it failed you asked nothing but a support, according to your condition, while you served, and if it succeeded and your services were approved, you would expect compensation for the sacrifices you had made, and the rewards commonly bestowed by a happy and grateful people, on faithful and successful servants. This, sir, is the amount of what I recollect."

That the material part of the letter of the said Francis Lightfoot Lee is as follows :

I was one of the committee appointed by Congress to wait upon you on your arrival at Yorktown, and understood French sufficiently to comprehend pretty fully all that you said to the committee.

" You informed them that you held considerable military rank in Europe, with posts and emoluments to the amount, I think, of five or six hundred guineas; that your great desire of being serviceable to the American cause had induced you to relinquish these, and offer your service to Congress; that you asked for neither rank nor pay, but expected your expenses in the army to be defrayed ; and if America should be successful in her contest, you depended upon the justice and generosity of Congress to make you amends for your losses, and reward your services; if unfortunate, you were willing to share her fortune. I do not recollect any particular stipulation for reimbursing the specific sum of money ; but it was, most certainly, well understood by the committee and Congress, that if our contest ended happily, and your services were approved, you would have a just claim to a very liberal compensation for what you had sacrificed, and for your services. Congress was very much pleased with your generous proposals when reported to them, as their consequent behavior to you sufficiently verified."

That, besides the foregoing document, there are two letters accompanying the said memorial, one from Horatio Gates, dated the 6th of December, 1785 ; the other from Richard Peters, dated the 30th October, 1785 ; the former of whom was President, and the latter member of the Board of War, at the time of the said transaction ; that the letter from the said Horatio Gates contains the following passage :

" When I was President of the Board of War, I very well remember your coming to Yorktown, and being most honorably received by Congress. A committee was immediately appointed to wait on you, and after they had conferred with you, you were invited to an elegant entertainment; and every mark of distinction was shown that could be shown to an officer of the first rank, into whose hands the inspection and discipline of the army was to be intrusted. With regard to pecuniary matters, I always understood they were to be settled upon the most liberal and generous plan, regard being had, not only to the high station you were to fill, but the sacrifice you had so generously made in coming to serve this country."

That the letter from the said Richard Peters contains the following passages :

BELMONT, *October* 30, 1785.

SIR : In answer to your inquiries respecting my recollection of what passed at Yorktown relative to your affairs, on your arrival at that place, I will state such circumstances as I became acquainted with. They are chiefly such as I understood from members of Congress, some of whom were appointed to assist the Commissioners of the Board of War, and to explain and communicate such matters as were necessary for our information in the business of our Department.

You were received by Congress with every mark of distinction their situation admitted, and had more particular attention paid to you than I had known given to any foreigner. Much pleasure was expressed at the arrival of a person of your military knowledge and experience, at a time when the want of discipline in our army, and the economy it produces, were severely felt and regretted. You were waited upon by a committee appointed for that purpose, from some of whom, as well as the other members of Congress, I was informed that you had conducted yourself, as to the manner in which you agreed to enter our service, with much generosity and disinterestedness, having made no terms either as to rank or pay; leaving it to Congress, after experience of your talents and usefulness as a volunteer in our service, to fix such as your merits and exertions entitled you to. Your having made no contract with our ministers in France was mentioned as a circumstance which prevented embarrassments, as some terms had been made with gentlemen, which did not meet the approbation of Congress. You agreed to take the risk of our affairs; if we were unsuccessful, you would of consequence be deprived of any means of compensation for the sacrifices you had made of a handsome revenue in Europe, and must have suffered the loss of military reputation generally attendant on unsuccessful service. But I always understood and believed that in case our cause issued happily, and your conduct was approved, Congress deemed it a matter of obligation on the United States, to indemnify you for the losses and expenses you had sustained, as well as to compensate you for services, in common with other officers. Precedents for such indemnification having been established even antecedent to experience in service, I never looked upon this as a claim upon the generosity, but a demand upon the justice of this country. And, although there was no written agreement to this purpose, there was clearly an implied contract. Your situation being fully stated, and your expectations explained, Congress desired you, through their President, to repair to camp and join the army; and the Board of War were directed to assist you for this purpose, in such matters as were requested."

That the following documents have been supposed to militate against the admission of the contract relied upon by the memorialist:

*First.* A letter from him to Congress, dated Portsmouth, December 6th, 1777, in the following terms:

Hon. Gentlemen: The honor of serving a respectable nation, engaged in the noble enterprise of defending its rights and liberty, is the only motive that brought me over to this continent. I ask neither riches nor titles; I am come here from the remotest end of Germany, at my own expense, and have given up an honorable and lucrative rank; I have made no condition with your deputies in France, nor shall I make any with you. My only ambition is to serve you as a volunteer, to desire the confidence of your general-in-chief, and to follow him in all his operations, as I have done during seven campaigns with the King of Prussia; two-and-twenty years passed at such a school seem to give me a right of thinking myself in the number of experienced officers; and if I am possessor of some talents in the art of war, they should be much dearer to me if I could employ them in the service of a republic such as I hope soon to see America. I should willingly purchase, at my whole blood's expense, the honor of seeing one day my name after those of the defenders of your liberty. Your gracious acceptance will be sufficient for me, and I ask no other favor than to be received among your officers. I dare hope you will agree with this my request, and that you will be so good as to send me your orders to Boston, where I shall expect them, and accordingly take convenient measures.

I have the honor to be, with respect, honorable gentlemen,
Your most obedient and very humble servant,
STEUBEN.

*Secondly.* A report on the files of Congress, of the committee which conferred with the memorialist at Yorktown, in these words:

The Baron Steuben, who was a lieutenant general and aid-de-camp to the King of Prussia, desires no rank; is willing to attend General Washington, and be subject to his orders; does not require or desire any command of a particular corps or division, but will serve occasionally, as directed by the general; expects to be of use in planning encampments, &c., and promoting the discipline of the army. He heard, before he left France, of the dissatisfaction of the Americans with the promotion of foreign officers; therefore, makes no terms, nor will he accept of any thing, but with general approbation, and particularly that of General Washington.

*Thirdly.* A letter from the momorialist to the President of Congress, dated in December, 1782, and containing this passage:

"My demands were these: To join the army as a volunteer; that I wished to be known to the commander-in-chief, and to leave it to the officers of the army, if my capacity entitled me to hold a commission in it; that the general would employ me in such a branch, where he thought my services most useful; that I was determined not to ask a favor or reward previous to having deserved it; that, however, I expected from the generosity of Congress that, in imitation of all European Powers, they would defray my expenses, although a volunteer, according to the rank which I held in Europe, as well for myself as my aids and servants.

That the Secretary, desirous of knowing what explanation of these documents the memorialist might have it in his power to give, did, on the 26th of January past, write to him a letter in the following words:

"Among the documents which relate to the circumstances of your entrance into the service of the United States, are a letter from you to Congress, dated at Portsmouth, the 6th of December, 1777, a report of the committee which conferred with you at Yorktown, and a letter from you to the President of Congress, dated in December, 1782. Enclosed you will find copies of the two first, and an extract from the last. As these may seem to militate against your claims, as founded in contract, I think it proper, before I report to the House of Representatives upon your memorial, to afford you an opportunity of making such remarks upon those documents as may appear to you advisable."

That to this letter the Secretary received an answer, dated the 27th of the same month, of which the following is a translation:

New York, *January* 27, 1790.

Sir : The letter which you did me the honor of addressing to me yesterday I have received, and am indebted to you for affording me an opportunity to elucidate the nature of my engagement with the United States.

From the information I received of the minister of France, that the preferment of foreigners to military employments had been a cause of discontent in the American army, I foresaw the necessity of pursuing measures different from those which had been adopted by my predecessors, in order to gain admission into your army.

Being sure of success in my enterprise, as soon as the commander-in-chief and the army should be convinced of the advantages of my military arrangements, there was but one difficulty to surmount, and, from the complexion of the times, that difficulty was of the greatest magnitude. It depended upon obtaining such a post in the army as would enable me to make use of the knowledge of my profession, and to render it beneficial to the interests of the United States, without exciting the dissatisfaction and jealousy of the officers of your army. Any conditions proposed by me, under the secircumstances, tending to ensure me a recompense proportional to my sacrifices and my services, would not have failed to render all negotiations abortive. But proposals to serve the United States as a volunteer, without rank or pay, could give no umbrage ; and surely the proposition was a generous one.

Suppose, however, I had added that, for the honor of serving the United States, I had resigned in my native country honorable and lucrative employments ; that I had come to America, at my own expense, for the purpose of fighting her battles ; and that, after she should have obtained her independence, I would decline all compensation for the services I had rendered : I would ask, sir, in what light would such a proposition have been received by so enlightened a body as the Congress of the United States ? To me it appears that common sense would have declared the author of·such a proposition to be either a lunatic or traitor. The former, for his coming from another part of the globe, to serve a nation unknown to him ; at the same time renouncing all his possessions for a cause to which he was an utter stranger, without having in view the gratification of ambition, or the advancement of interest. The latter, as it might appear that his making such generous proposals to introduce himself into your army was with the most dangerous views, for which he probably received compensation from the enemy.

In either of these aspects, would the person making similar propositions have been admissible ?

What measures, then, were necessary to be pursued to enable me to render those services to the United States which I had proposed to myself ?

Having made these observations, sir, I entreat you to read my letter to Congress, of January, 1778 ; badly translated as it is, it will be intelligible to you, as being one of those who are particularly informed of the critical situation of Congress and of the army at that period of the Revolution.

You will easily discover, sir, that this letter was dictated by no other motive than to facilitate my reception into your army. The effect has answered my conjectures and my desires. If, however, I should be charged with having made use of illicit stratagems to gain admission into the service of the United States, I am sure I have obtained my pardon of the army, and, I flatter myself, of the citizens of this republic in general. In consequence of this letter, I was directed by a resolution of Congress to join the army; nòtwithstanding which, I judged it necessary to proceed first to Yorktown, as well to pay my respects to that august body who presided over a nation whom I was going to serve, as to learn the advantage or disadvantage which might result to me from so hazardous an enterprise. At my arrival, the Congress did me the honor of appointing a committee to confer with me. If my first letter and the answer to it had been considered by them as a sufficient engagement, was there any occasion for this committee? Was there any necessity for this conferrence? All that passed in this conversation is sufficiently proved, and needs no further repetition.

If, on impartial examination of the subject, it should appear that my propositions to this committee were incompatible with my first letter to Congress, I confess that my judgment misleads me.

I represented to the gentlemen of that committee that I had not entered into any agreement with the American commissioners in France; that I would not insist upon making any at present, but would serve the United States as a volunteer, without rank or pay, on condition, notwithstanding, that my expenses in the army should be defrayed. I declared to them that I had no other fortune than a revenue of about six hundred louis-d'ors, arising from a post I held in my native country, which I was going to resign to serve the United States, being disposed to hazard the whole on the event; and that not until I had succeeded in my undertakings, and the United States had obtained their liberty by a satisfactory peace, would I ask an indemnification for my sacrifices and disbursements, and for such other marks of acknowledgment and generosity as in the justice of Congress should be deemed adequate to my services.

It appears that the committee reported to Congress I had made no conditions, and that I would not accept of any thing without general approbation, and particularly that of General Washington. Although I do not allow that report to be exact in its literal sense, yet I do not find it so extraordinary, that expectations founded upon the event of a revolution of this nature should be represented as making no stipulations. Besides, it seems probable that the politics of the times made it necessary to give such a complexion to the report as would remove all jealousy.

Permit me, sir, to suggest here a question: Why was not this report (like all other reports of committees) entered upon the journals of Congress? I doubt whether it would have been contradicted by me; but at least it would have afforded me an opportunity of taking precautions. I assure you, sir, upon my honor, that this report was never brought into view previous to the year 1788, and that I did not see it until General Washington had the goodness to send me a copy of it. But be this as it will, no person, sir, is better informed than yourself how difficult it was at that time to introduce a foreigner into your army, even without any condition whatever.

With regard to my second letter, of December, 1782, I confess I do not find in that any contradiction of the facts represented to have taken place in the conference at Yorktown.

In this letter I state that my desires were to join your army as a volunteer; that I did not ask any employ until the approbation of the commander-in-chief and the opinion of the army should assign me a place in which I could be useful; that I asked no compensation until it was merited; provided, however, that my expenses for my own person, as well as my suite, were defrayed by the United States, agreeably to the usage of European Powers. I perceive that it may be asked, why I did not at that time insist upon my contract? I answer, that it was my wish never to mention it, as it appeared to me more honorable to the United States, and more flattering to myself, to receive a recompense dictated rather by generosity than by conditions, and that it was with reluctance, and through urgent circumstances upon that stipulation, which was the basis of my engagement at Yorktown. But there is another reason why this contract was not mentioned in my letter immediately after the conclusion of the war.

The Congress were besieged by a crowd of foreign officers, who were as little satisfied as the national troops, which was a circumstance that probably induced some respectable persons, then members of Congress, (in whom I placed the greatest confidence,) to advise me to pass over in silence all that related to a former contract, and to rest my pretensions solely on the merit of my services, and the generosity of the United States. If my memory is faithful, yourself, sir, were of the number of those by whose opinion I was governed.

Once more I assure you, sir, that it is with regret I have recourse to that contract; but there remains no other resource to obtain that justice which is due to me.

These, sir, are all the explanations I can give you; if they are not sufficient, I submit to the consequences. All that I ask of you is, to accelerate the decision; no event can render my situation more unhappy: in fact, it is insupportable.

There must always remain one consolation: the truth of the facts stated in my memorial to Congress cannot be disputed, without raising a doubt of the veracity of some of the most worthy and respectable characters in the United States, several of whom have held, or now hold, the highest places in the Government of their country.

Having no secretary, you will please, sir, to excuse my addressing you in a language which is more familiar to me than the English.

I have the honor to be, &c.

———————,

————

The Secretary further reports:

That on the 5th of May, 1778, the memorialist was appointed by Congress inspector general, with the rank and pay of major general, to which was afterwards added a further allowance for the extra service and expense incident to the office of inspector general.

That there appears on the journals of Congress, a report of a committee of the 30th of December, 1782, stating:

1st. That the Baron de Steuben was possessed in Europe of respectable military rank, and different posts of honor and emolument, which he relinquished to come to America, and offer his services at a critical period of the war, and without any previous stipulations.

2d. That on his arrival, he actually engaged in the army in a very disinterested manner, and without compensations similar to those which had been made to several other foreign officers.

3d. That under singular difficulties and embarrassments in the department in which he had been employed, he has rendered very important and substantial services, by introducing into the army a regular formation and exact discipline, and by establishing a spirit of order and economy in the interior administration of the regiments; which, besides other advantages, have been productive of immense savings to the United States; that, in the commands in which he had been employed, he has, upon all occasions, conducted himself like a brave and experienced officer.

The committee are therefore of opinion, that the sacrifices and services of the Baron de Steuben, justly entitle him to the distinguished notice of Congress, and to a generous compensation, whenever the situation of public affairs will admit.

The committee further report that the Baron de Steuben has considerable arrearages of pay due to him from these States, on a liquidated account, and that, having exhausted his resources, it is now indispensable that a sum of money should be paid to him for his present support, and to enable him to take the field another campaign; and propose that the sum of two thousand four hundred dollars be paid to him for that purpose, and charged to his account aforesaid; whereupon, Congress resolved, That the foregoing proposal of the committee, be referred to the Superintendent of Finance, to take order.

That on the 15th of April, 1784, Congress did also resolve, That the thanks of the United States, in Congress assembled, be given to Baron Steuben, for the great zeal and abilities he has discovered in the discharge of the several duties of his office; that a gold-hilted sword be presented to him, as a mark of the high sense Congress entertain of his character and services; and that the Superintendent of Finance take order for procuring the same; that the proper officers proceed to the liquidation of moneys due from the United States to Major General Baron Steuben; that the Superintendent of Finance report to Congress his opinion of the most speedy and efficacious means of procuring and paying the same, either here or in Europe; that Baron Steuben be assured that Congress will adopt these, or such others as shall appear most proper and effectual for doing him that justice which the peculiarity of his case authorizes.

That on the 27th of September, 1785, Congress did further resolve, That, in full consideration of the Baron de Steuben's having relinquished different posts of honor and emolument in Europe, and rendered most essential services to the United States, he be allowed, and paid out of the Treasury of the United States, the sum of seven thousand dollars in addition to former grants; that the Baron de Steuben has received, at different times, sums equal to the amount of the pay and emoluments annexed to his station in the American army, to the commutation of a major general, and to the sum expressed in the resolution last recited.

A question arises whether the acceptance of these appointments, emoluments, and allowances, did not virtually supersede the antecedent contract relied on by the memorialist, admitting it to have existed.

To which he answered : " That it cannot be presumed that an individual, in accepting from a Government the emoluments annexed to a station to which he is appointed for the service of that Government, unsolicited by him, could renounce a prior and more beneficial contract.

" That the more natural presumption is, that Congress, by conferring those emoluments, meant to ascertain and limit the expenses they had stipulated to bear, and to support the respectability of the office they had thought proper to create.

" That, as a major general, he received the pay and other emoluments allowed to other major generals of the army ; as inspector general, he received an extra allowance, in consideration of extra trouble and expense.

" That the emoluments allowed to an officer in service can only be referred to the services he renders ; they can have nothing to do with an indemnity for revenues relinquished, and can never be deemed, by mere inference and implication, to extinguish a contract founded on that principle.

" That, with regard to the acceptance of the last grant, it was a matter of pure necessity, proceeding from a situation absolutely indigent; and that the reverse of a disposition to acquiesce in it has been uniformly manifested on his part."

Having stated the foregoing particulars, which are the most material that have come under the observation of the Secretary, relating to the claim of the memorialist, he proceeds to remark :

That the statement made by the memorialist of what passed in the conference at Yorktown, is authenticated by such strong, direct, and collateral evidence, as ought, in the opinion of the Secretary, to secure full credit to the existence of the fact. Waiving the regard due to the memorialist's own assertion, it is not supposable that, if his representation had been ill founded, it could have obtained the sanction of so many disinterested persons, agents in, or witnesses to, the transaction. That, notwithstanding this, it may be inferred, as well from the written report of the committee as from other circumstances, that the idea of a precise contract did not generally prevail. It is probable that, as the indemnity and reward for the sacrifices and services of the Baron were by him made to depend on the success of a national revolution, the mention of them was viewed rather as a suggestion of expectations than as a stipulation of terms. This might the more easily have happened, as it is presumable that the situation of affairs at the time must have disposed Congress to consider an officer who had had the opportunities of the memorialist as a valuable acquisition to the service, and to regard a compliance with the expectations intimated by him, in the event of success, as too much a matter of course to need a stipulation. That this view of the affair appears to the Secretary to afford a satisfactory solution of any difficulties which might result from seemingly discordant circumstances, and to place all the parts of the transaction in a simple and consistent light.

Upon the whole, therefore, as it cannot with propriety be questioned that a conversation of the kind stated by the Baron did take place at the conference at Yorktown ; as the services rendered by him to the United States are acknowledged to have been of a very signal and very meritorious nature ; as the expectations alleged to have been signified by him in the conference are all of them reasonable in themselves, being nothing more than that his necessary expenses while in the service of the United States should be defrayed by them ; and that in case they should establish their independence, and he should be successful in his endeavors to serve them, then he should receive an indemnification for the income he had relinquished in coming to this country, and to such marks of the generosity of the Government as its justice should dictate. The Secretary is of opinion that, whether the transaction relied upon by the Baron be deemed to have the force of a contract or not, it will be most consistent with the dignity and equity of the United States to admit it as the basis of a final adjustment of his claims.

Should this opinion appear well founded, it will remain to designate the rule by which the necessary expenses of the memorialist are to be adjusted. Taking it for granted that his actual expenses will not be deemed a proper one, there occurs to the Secretary no better criterion than the current allowances annexed to the stations he filled. This excludes the half pay or commutation. It is presumed that the current allowances to the officers of the American army in general were regulated wholly with a view to their present support, according to their respective situations, and the half pay granted as a future reward.

According to this principle, the Secretary has caused an account to be stated, which is hereunto annexed, in which the memorialist is credited with his emoluments as major general and inspector general, (exclusive of half pay or commutation,) and with an annuity of five hundred and eighty guineas, (being the amount of the income stated to have been relinquished by him,) from the time he left Europe to the last of December, 1789, with interest at six per cent. per annum ; and is charged with all the moneys, under whatever denomination, received by him from the United States, with interest at the like rate ; upon which statement there is a balance in his favor for seven thousand three hundred and ninety-six dollars and seventy-four ninetieths.

In addition to this, he would be entitled, for the remainder of his life, to the yearly sum of five hundred and eighty guineas, as a continuation of the indemnity for the income relinquished, and to such reward as the Government in its discretion should think fit to allow; for which purpose a moderate grant of land, if deemed expedient, would suffice.

The Secretary begs leave further to state that there is good ground to believe that the above-mentioned balance will be short of a sufficient sum to discharge the debts now owing by the memorialist, and contracted partly to enable him to come to this country, and partly for his subsistence here ; and, in the last place, to observe that the situation of the memorialist, who (being a foreigner) voluntarily came to offer his services to the United States in a critical and perilous moment, and who, from the circumstance of his having been a foreigner, is less likely to participate in the collateral rewards which in numerous instances await those who have distinguished themselves in the American Revolution, (while he cannot, like many other foreign officers, look for rewards elsewhere,) gives a peculiarity to his case which strengthens his other pretensions. That it appears unequivocally that his services have been of a nature peculiarly valuable and interesting to the American cause, and such as furnish weighty considerations, as well public as personal, for rescuing him from the indigence in which he is now involved, and from the still greater extremities with which he is threatened. A settlement on the principles suggested in this report will terminate all the claims of the memorialist on the United States in a manner equally satisfactory to him and honorable to them.

All which is humbly submitted.

ALEXANDER HAMILTON,
*Secretary of the Treasury.*

---

*Claims for expenses in Settling Accounts, Depreciation and Bounty Lands.*

Communicated to the House of Representatives, April 12, 1790.

TREASURY DEPARTMENT, *April* 10, 1790.

The Secretary of the Treasury, on the petition of William Finnie, referred to him by an order of the House of Representatives of the 25th of September last, respectfully reports:

That the relief sought by the petitioner relates to the following objects:

*First.* An allowance for expenses incident to his attendance at the seat of Government, for the settlement of his accounts.

*Secondly.* A compensation for a loss sustained on the sale of certificate issued to him for the balance which appeared due to him on that settlement.

*Thirdly.* Depreciation and pay, in the capacity of a commissary of military stores, from the 1st of January, 1777, to the 1st of January, 1781.

*Fourthly.* An allowance of land as a colonel of the army, in virtue of a commission from Congress, appointing him deputy quarter master general, with the rank of colonel.

That, as to the first article, the allowance claimed would, contrary to general usage, the reverse of which would be productive of considerable expense to the public, and would often (though not in the present instance) reward delinquency, by indemnifying individuals for delays occasioned in the settlement of their accounts, by their own mismanagement.

That, as to the second article, it is the common case of every person who has received a certificate for money owing to him from the public, and parted with it for less than its nominal value; and cannot therefore be discriminated by particular relief.

That, as to the third article, the facts are as follow:

### Extracts from the facts in the third article.

The memorialist, being deputy quartermaster general, was paid as such, but had exhibited a claim for pay, rations, and depreciation, as a commissary of military stores, which claim was rejected by the auditor on these grounds, as stated in substance by him: "That to support a claim on the principle of a compensation for extra service it ought to be shown that such service had been performed* after the period which payment had been made by the Board of War, that is, 1st of October, 1799."

That, as a claim to a stipend attached to an office, it was unadvisable, because contrary to a regulation of Congress prohibiting the enjoyment of the emoluments of two offices by one person. It further appears that, on a submission of the same claim to the Board of Treasury on the 25th of April, 1789, that board decided against it; from which the Secretary is of opinion that a revision of the matter would be inexpedient.

That, as to the 4th article, the claim is founded upon a commission from the President of Congress, dated the 28th of March, 1776, appointing the memorialist deputy quartermaster general in the southern department, with the rank of colonel; but it does not appear to be warranted either by the resolutions of Congress respecting bounties of lands to officers and soldiers, or by the practice upon those resolutions, nor does any circumstance occur to justify the allowance to the memorialist, without extending it to a number of other persons in a like situation.

That, upon the whole matter, though the misfortunes of the petitioner, added to the zeal manifested by him in the public service, appeared to the Secretary to entitle his case to as favorable a consideration as a due attention to general principles would permit, yet he has not been able to discover sufficient and unexceptionable ground upon which, in his opinion, any part of the prayer of the petitioner may with propriety be granted.

All of which is humbly submitted.

ALEXANDER HAMILTON,
*Secretary of the Treasury.*

---

The Secretary for the Department of War, to whom was referred the petition of Sarah Stirling, reports:

That the late Lord Stirling, deceased, husband of the petitioner, was a major general in the American army, and died while in actual service on the 14th day of January, 1783.

That the petitioner is entitled to an allowance of seven years' half pay of her late husband as a major general, and that this allowance is founded on the resolves of Congress of the 24th and 25th of August, 1780.

That it will appear, by the certificate of the treasurer of New Jersey, herewith annexed, No. 1, that the said seven years' half pay, or any thing in lieu thereof, has not been paid by the said State of New Jersey, of which Lord Stirling was a citizen.

That it will appear, by the certificate No. 2, that the petitioner preferred a petition to the late Congress on this subject, and that a report thereon was read the 28th of July, 1786, which was, that the petitioner should be recommended to the State of New Jersey for the benefit of the resolve of August 24th, 1780; but the said report does not appear to have been acted upon.

---

*[Whereas, it did not appear, in the case, that any extra service had been performed.

18

The petitioner being entitled to the provision established by the resolves of the 24th and 25th of August, 1780, the Secretary of War is of opinion that, therefore, it would be proper to make provision for paying to Sarah Stirling, the widow of the late Major General Stirling, the sum of six thousand nine hundred and seventy-two dollars, being the half pay of a major general in the late American army for the term of seven years.

The Secretary of War embraces the occasion of this report to submit to the House an estimate of the arrearages which are stated by the several States to be due to the widows and orphans. To this estimate it will be necessary to add such sums as Congress may authorize during the present session.

All which is humbly submitted to the House of Representatives.

H. KNOX,<br>
Secretary of War.

WAR DEPARTMENT, *July* 26, 1790.

---

*An estimate of the arrearages due to widows and orphans of officers of the late army of the United States.*

| | |
|---|---:|
| New Hampshire, | $276 33⅓ |
| Massachusetts, | none. |
| Rhode Island, | 2,310 00 |
| Connecticut, | none. |
| New York, | none. |
| New Jersey, | 995 17 |
| Pennsylvania, | no return received. |
| Delaware, | none. |
| Maryland, | 1,073 33⅓ |
| *North Carolina, | 15,960 00 |
| South Carolina, | no return received. |
| Virginia, | none. |
| Georgia, | no rerurn received. |

$20,614 83⅔

To this estimate it will be necessary to add such sums as Congress may authorize during the present session.

H. KNOX,<br>
Secretary of War.

WAR DEPARTMENT, *July* 26, 1790.

---

**Seven years' half pay to widows and children of officers who died in service.**

Communicated to the House of Representatives, February 15, 1791.

WAR OFFICE, *February* 14, 1791.

The Secretary for the Department of War, to whom were referred the petitions of Anne Roberts, and of the orphan children of the late Major Andrew Leitch, and of the late Captain William White, reports:

---

* North Carolina commenced payment in 1784.

That it appears, upon examination, that the late Owen Roberts was a colonel of the South Carolina continental regiment of artillery, and that he was mortally wounded in the service of his country on the 20th day of June, 1779.

That Andrew Leitch was a major of the first Virginia continental regiment, and that he was killed in the service of his country the 16th day of September, 1776.

That William White was a captain in the Massachusetts line, and that he was killed in the service of his country in October, 1781.

That, conformably to the resolve of Congress of the 24th of August, 1780, the widow of the late Colonel Owen Roberts was entitled to the half pay for seven years of a colonel of artillery.

That the orphan children of the late Major Andrew Leitch were entitled to the half pay of a major for seven years.

That the children of the late Captain William White, the widow having intermarried, were entitled to the half pay of a captain for seven years.

That, conformably to the said resolve, the widow and children aforesaid ought to have had the said half pay advanced to them, on behalf of the United States, by the States to which the aforesaid officers respectively belonged.

That it appears, from the returns and examinations of the accounts of the States of Virginia and Massachusetts, that the said half pay has not been advanced the orphans of the beforementioned deceased officers, Major Andrew Leitch, and Captain William White. That the accounts of South Carolina for the sums advanced the widows and orphans of that State have not yet been produced, but it is highly probable there will not be any charge for the object of the present petition. But it will be proper to take all due precautions on this subject, as hereafter mentioned.

That it is most probable, from the information received, that the non-payment of the said half pay has not been owing to any disinclination of the said States, but to the want of proper application.

On this statement the Secretary of War observes, that the only circumstance which is opposed to granting the prayers of the aforesaid petitions would be a rigid construction of the resolves of the late Congress, limiting the time for producing claims against the United States.

While the Secretary of War is deeply impressed with the importance of a firm adherence, generally, to the resolves of limitation, he is inclined to the opinion that the claims of the aforementioned widow and orphans cannot with justice be considered as involved in the beforementioned resolves of limitation.

The resolves of the 2d of November, 1785, and 23d July, 1787, relate to persons having unliquidated demands for military services, and for claims in the several staff departments and in the marine; that they were to produce their claims to the commissioners of the United States.

But the widows or orphans claiming pensions were, by the arrangement of Congress, to apply to the States to which the deceased officers belonged. Had the widow or orphan children of any officer, who died in the service, and who belonged to any individual State. applied to Congress in consequence of the aforesaid resolves, they would have been referred to the said State, in the same manner as before the said resolves were passed.

The resolve of the 11th of June, 1788, relates solely to the claims of invalids, and cannot, in any manner, be construed to comprehend the case of the widows and orphans. It is most probable that Congress considered any resolves upon this sort of claims unnecessary, as it was supposed that the widows and orphans entitled to pensions by the acts of Congress had received the same, annually, of the respective States. But it has appeared that there are a few existing, and probably but a few, well-founded claims of this nature.

Applying these general ideas to the claims of the petitioners, the Secretary of War is of opinion that the cause of justice and the dignity of the United States require that the prayers of the beforementioned petitioners should be granted; and that therefore it would be proper, by law, to direct and authorize the Comptroller of the Treasury to adjust the accounts of the widow of the late Colonel Owen Roberts, who was killed in the service of his country, for the amount of seven years' half pay of a colonel of artillery, upon the principles directed by the act entitled " An act for the relief of the persons therein mentioned or described," passed 11th of August, 1790; and that the Register of the Treasury issue his certificate for the amount accordingly: provided it shall be first made to appear that the State of South Carolina has not paid the said widow the pension to which she is entitled by the resolves of Congress.

That the Comptroller, in like manner, adjust the account of the orphan children of the late Major Andrew Leitch, who was killed in the service of his country, for the amount of seven years' half pay of a major of infantry; and that the Register of the Treasury issue his certificate accordingly.

That the said Comptroller adjust, in like manner, the account of the children of the late Captain William White, who was killed in the service of his country, for the amount of seven years' half pay of a captain; and that the Register of the Treasury issue his certificate accordingly.

All of which is humbly submitted to the House of Representatives.

H. KNOX,
*Secretary of War.*

---

WAR OFFICE, *February* 25, 1791.

The Secretary of War, on the petition of Simeon Thayer, reports:

That the petitioner was an officer of excellent reputation in the Rhode Island line.

That it appears, by the certificates and papers annexed, that the petitioner, on the 28th of June, 1778, lost his right eye by the effect of a cannon ball. That he is apprehensive that he shall also lose the sight of the other eye.

That, therefore, the petitioner prays that he may be at liberty to return his commutation certificates, and to be placed upon the pension list of the United States.

On this petition the Secretary of War remarks, that, could the merits of the petitioner as an officer, or the injury received, form a sufficient exception to a general rule, he ought to be placed on the invalid list at half pay. But the resolve of the 11th June, 1788, is opposed to this claim.

The Secretary of War, to whom were referred the petitions of the widows, or the children, or the representatives of the children, of the commissioned officers hereinafter named, who were killed or who died in the service of the United States during the late war, respectfully reports:

That having investigated the claims severally, and the evidence accompanying the same, as well as the evidence afforded by the public offices, the result is herein submitted:

*First.* That it appears that *William Bond*, deceased, was commissioned by Congress as the colonel of the 25th regiment of foot, on the 1st day of January, 1776, and that he died while in public service at Ticonderoga on the 31st day of August, of the same year.

That the petitioner, Lucy Bond, was left the widow of the deceased William Bond, with nine young children to support and educate, and that she still remains a widow.

That the said widow has not received any compensation for the seven years' half pay allowed in such cases by the United States.

*Second.* That it appears that *Wadleigh Noyes*, deceased, was a lieutenant in the 9th Massachusetts regiment, and that he was mortally wounded at Saratoga, the 7th October, 1777; of which wounds he died the 27th day of the same month and year.

That the widow of the deceased lieutenant having intermarried, the present petition is presented in behalf of her three children, had by the said Wadleigh Noyes, deceased.

That the said widow or children have not received any compensation for the seven years' half pay in such cases allowed by the United States.

*Third.* That it appears *Bernard Elliot*, deceased, was a lieutenant colonel of the South Carolina regiment of artillery on continental establishment, and that he died on the 25th of October, 1778, while in public service.

That no compensation has been made for the seven years' half pay in such cases allowed by the United States, either to the widow who has since married, or to the only son of the deceased, in whose behalf the petition is presented.

*Fourth.* That it appears the late *Samuel Wise*, deceased, was major of the 3d South Carolina regiment of infantry on continental establishment, and that he was killed while in public service at the lines of Savannah on the 9th day of October, 1779.

That no compensation has been made for the seven years' half pay.

That the petition states that Jane Ann Ball, the wife of the petitioner, Joseph Ball, is the only child of the deceased Major Samuel Wise; and from the register of her baptism, which is produced, it would appear that she was probably about the age of fourteen years at the time of her father's death; and that the petition further states that the widow of the said deceased is dead.

*Fifth.* That it appears that *Benjamin Huger*, deceased, was major of the 5th South Carolina regiment on continental establishment, and that he was killed in the service of the United States, while on duty before the lines of Charleston, on the 11th day of May, 1779, leaving a widow and three children.

That his said widow still remains such; and that she has not received any compensation for the seven years' half pay in such cases allowed by the United States.

*Sixth.* That it appears *John Bush*, deceased, was a lieutenant in the 2d South Carolina regiment on continental establishment, and that he was killed in the service of the United States, at the lines of Savannah, the 9th day of October, 1779.

That the petition states the deceased left three daughters, but it does not appear whether there was or is a widow ; and it appears that no compensation has been made for the seven years' half pay in such cases allowed by the United States.

*Seventh.* That it appears *Charles Motte*, deceased, was major of the 2d South Carolina regiment on continental establishment, and that he was killed in the public service at the lines of Savannah, on the 9th day of October, 1779.

That the petitioner states that there are two minor children, and that the widow of the deceased has since married.

That it appears no compensation has been made for the seven years' half pay in such cases allowed by the United States.

*Eighth.* That it appears that *Richard Shubrick* was a captain of the 2d South Carolina regiment on continental establishment, and that he died while in public service on the 8th day of November, 1777.

That the petitioner states the widow of the deceased to have since intermarried, and that the deceased left two daughters, who are now living.

That it appears no compensation has been made for the seven years' half pay in such cases allowed by the United States.

On due consideration, the Secretary of War is of opinion that each and every case hereinbefore recited was fully comprehended in the provision for the seven years' half pay to the widows or orphans of deceased officers, established by the act of Congress of the 24th of August, 1780.

But the lapse of time and other circumstances since the decease of the said officers may possibly occasion some objection to the propriety of Congress complying with the prayer of the said petitions at this period.

First, from the consideration that this subject was recommended to the several States, who it is presumed would have made due provision for their own citizens, more especially as the allowance was to be at the general expense of the United States. And, secondly, from the consideration that claims of this nature may be construed as involved in the general resolves of limitation relative to the services and supplies of the late war.

But it may be observed, with respect to the first objection, that it appears from unequivocal testimony, under the seal of the State of South Carolina, that the said State never in any instance made provision for the widows and orphans of officers who were killed or who died in the service during the late war.

Of the eight before-recited petitions, six of them are from the State of South Carolina ; the other two are from Massachusetts. The reasons given why the widow of the late Colonel Bond, and the children of the late Lieutenant Wadleigh Noyes, were not provided for by Massachusetts, are obscure and unsatisfactory.

The one, it seems from the evidence, because the colonel's commission was not produced at the time of application ; and the other, because the lieutenant's rank and death were not fully established. But whatever were the reasons which prevented the petitioners' receiving compensation from their State, the subscriber is of opinion that the widow of the said Colonel Bond, and the children of the said Wadleigh Noyes, are entitled to the benefit of the provision established by the resolves of the 24th of August, 1780.

How far the second objection is well founded, that is, whether claims of this nature are involved in the limitation acts, is submitted to Congress. The Secretary of War humbly offers it as his opinion, that the interest, dignity, and justice of the United States combine to oppose a rigid construction of the resolves of limitation, applying to the cases of widows and orphans, whose obscure and helpless situation prevented a proper application in due time. The reasons for this opinion are given at large in a report to the House of Representatives on the 14th of February last, on the case of sundry widows and orphans, to which, in order to prevent repetition, the subscriber humbly begs leave to refer.

But if any doubts should be entertained upon this subject, the act of Congress, passed the 11th of August, 1790, in favor of Frances Eleanor Laurens, the orphan daughter of the late Colonel John Laurens, who was killed while in the service of the United States, would seem to dissipate them ; for the circumstances of that case differ in no essential particular from the cases herein reported, belonging to the State of South Carolina. And the case of Sarah, the widow of the late Major General Stirling, provided for by the said act, is similarly circumstanced to the claim of the widow of Colonel Bond, and the children of the late Lieutenant Wadleigh Noyes.

If Congress, therefore, should please to grant the prayer of the beforementioned widows and children of the said officers, who were killed or who died in the service of the United States, it might be proper to direct that the Comptroller of the Treasury should adjust the claims for the seven years' half pay stipulated by the resolve of Congress of the 24th of August, 1780 ; and the Register of the Treasury issue his certificates accordingly to the widows or orphan children, as the cases respectively may be, of the late Colonel William Bond, Lieutenant Wadleigh Noyes, Lieutenant Colonel Bernard Elliot. of the artillery, Major Samuel Wise, Major Benjamin Huger, Lieutenant John Bush, Major Charles Motte, and Captain Richard Shubrick, deceased, all of whom were either killed or died in the service of the United States.

All which is humbly submitted to the House of Representatives.

H. KNOX,
*Secretary of War.*

WAR DEPARTMENT, *November 23,* 1791.

---

WAR DEPARTMENT, *January 22,* 1793.

The Secretary for the Department of War, to whom was referred the petition of Thomas Wishart, reports :

The petitioner states that, in November, 1776, he was appointed a lieutenant in the fifteenth regiment of the Virginia line, and that he served to the end of the war; that in consequence of the muster and pay-rolls of the Virginia line, subsequent to 1778, being destroyed in the town of Richmond, in the year 1780, by the British forces, he cannot obtain the settlement and payment of his accounts.

That he appears upon the pay-rolls, now in the late office of the commissioner of army accounts, for the years 1777 and 1778, and that his services in the southern department, particularly in the State of Virginia, are evidenced by certificates for the years 1779, 1780, and until April, 1781, when he was taken prisoner by the British troops, and continued in captivity until the surrender of Yorktown, in the month of October following.

In support of this petition the following certificates are produced:

1st. Of Colonel David Mason, the colonel of the fifteenth regiment, certifying the petitioner's being in service until the last of July, 1778, dated the 11th of January, 1787.

2d. Of Colonel James Innes, purporting that he understood the petitioner was kept in service until some time in the year 1779, dated 16th October, 1791.

3d. Of Colonel Josiah Parker, formerly of the Virginia line, stating his knowledge of the petitioner while with the northern army, and, also, in all the different invasions in Virginia, dated the 9th of December, 1791.

4th. Of Brigadier General Muhlenberg, who, in 1780, was senior continental officer: he certifies that he considered the petitioner as a continental officer, and employed him as such until April, 1781, when he was surprised and taken prisoner; and that this is stated, certified from vouchers in his hands, and his personal knowledge, having received a satisfactory account in what manner the petitioner had been employed during the time he had been in Virginia, dated the 2d of January, 1793. Several of the foregoing certificates testify that the petitioner was a valuable officer.

5th. A certificate of the auditor of Virginia, "that the petitioner has not received his pay and depreciation as an officer of the Virginia line on continental establishment," dated the

But the commissioner of army accounts produces the following objections to the claim of the petitioner:

" WAR DEPARTMENT,

*Accountant's Office, January* 9, 1793.

" SIR: Agreeably to your letter of yesterday, requesting *my objections* on your claim against the United States, for services done and performed as lieutenant in the late line of Virginia, I shall briefly state them; they are as follows, viz:

"1st. In the month of June, 1778, a partial arrangement of the army took place, at which time many officers became supernumerary, and, in September or October following, the arrangement of the Virginia line had taken effect.

"2d. The muster-rolls of a regiment have always been the guide to a settlement of army accounts. In the muster-rolls of the regiment to which you belonged, you have been left out from the 1st day of April, 1778.

" 3d. On the arrangement of the Virginia line, in 1781, under the acts of Congress of the 3d and 21st of October, 1780, you have not been mentioned, and

"4th. On the arrangement of the same line, in 1782, when all the officers of that line, who were considered in continental service, were called on to state their claims and rank to a board of officers appointed by the commanding officer to decide on them, it does not appear that any application on your part was made to the board ; neither does it appear that the board considered you as an officer of the line ; for, if they had, you would certainly have been mentioned on their minutes, as *one considered in service, retiring from it with the emoluments, or superseded for non-compliance with the general orders.*

" The certificates produced of your services, I grant, are given by respectable characters ; but, sir, they cannot, in my opinion, invalidate the foregoing objections. For it is well known that the State of Virginia, when she wanted officers to command either militia or levies, when not incorporated with continental troops, of choice employed those of the late army, who were supernumerary, or who had retired from service.

"On the whole, I am opinion that you must consider yourself a supernumerary officer, and that you are only entitled to the year's pay allowed under the act of Congress of the 24th November, 1778, and such nominal pay as may actually appear due, on a full investigation of the pay-rolls of the regiment to which you belonged.

" I am, sir, your obedient servant,<br>
" JOSEPH HOWELL.

" Mr. Thomas Wishart."

------

The arrangement of September 23, 1779, is made by Brigadiers General Woodford and Muhlenberg, and nine field officers of the Virginia line, and the petitioner's name does not appear to either of the regiments. The fifteen regiments of the Virginia line were reduced to eleven, in pursuance of the resolve of Congress of March 9, 1779.

As the petitioner's name does not appear upon the pay-rolls of the fifteenth regiment after the 15th of April, 1778, nor on the arrangement of the regiments of the establishment of 1779, it is incumbent on him to show how, and by what authority, he was connected with the Virginia line for part of 1778, and for the whole of the year 1779. The Virginia line marched from Morristown for South Carolina in the latter part of 1779, and Virginia was not invaded until the latter part of the year 1780.

Although the services of the petitioner, for part of the year 1778, and all 1779, do not appear substantiated by evidence, yet the certificate of Brigadier General Muhlenberg proves the petitioner in actual service, after the invasion of Virginia, in the latter part of the year 1780, and until April, 1781, when he was taken prisoner, and not released until the month of October of the same year.

19

It is difficult to perceive in what other capacity the petioner can be considered than as a deranged officer, under the acts of 1778 and 1779, unless the arrangements before recited, made at the time by responsible officers, be entirely disregarded.

Notwithstanding the petitioner is considered as a deranged officer of 1778 at this period, yet it is highly probable that he might have regarded himself as an officer of the line in the years 1778, 1779, 1780, and 1781 ; and it is evident, by the certificate, that he was regarded as such by Brigadier General Muhlenberg.

As the petitioner appears, by the evidence aforesaid, to have performed active services, as a continental officer, from the latter part of the year 1780, to April, 1781, when he was taken prisoner, and continued as such until the October following, he would seem to be equitably entitled to the pay of his grade for that time ; and also for such further time until his regiment was reformed, for which it shall appear he has not been paid.

But as it does not appear that he performed services after his release from captivity, and as his name does not appear upon any arrangement of the Virginia line subsequent to that time, it is presumed that he is not entitled to pay to any later period.

All of which is humbly submitted to the House of Representatives.

H. KNOX,

*Secretary of War.*

WAR DEPARTMENT,
    *January 22,* 1793.

---

Report on the report of the Secretary at War on the petition of Thomas Wishart, made the 25th of January, 1793 :

That Thomas Wishart is entitled to the pay of a lieutenant in the army of the United States, from the 15th of November, 1776, to the 15th of October, 1781 ; and that the Comptroller of the Treasury be authorized to settle and adjust the account of the said Thomas Wishart accordingly.

---

The Secretary for the Department of War, to whom was referred the petitions hereinafter enumerated, with instructions to examine the same, and report his opinion thereon, respectfully reports :

That Joanna Gardner states that she is the widow of the late Colonel Thomas Gardner, who was wounded in the battle of Charlestown, on the 17th day of June, 1775, and who died of his wounds on the 3d day of July following.

That she was left with three small children, and had to encounter many difficulties in bringing them up; that she has not received the relief provided by the resolution of Congress for the widows and children of officers who have died in the army since the month of August, 1775.

That she does not apprehend it was the intention of Congress to make any discrimination between the widows and children of officers who died in the service, on account of the time when such event took place. She therefore prays that the benefit of the aforesaid resolution of Congress may be extended to her and her children.

That Elizabeth McClary states that she is widow of the late Major Andrew McClary, of Colonel John Stack's regiment, who was killed by a cannon ball in the action of Bunker's Hill, on the 17th day of June, 1775.

That she did not know of the resolution of Congress, granting seven years' half pay to the widows of such officers as had lost their lives in the service, until after the time appointed for making application for said half pay had elapsed. She therefore prays for relief.

That Alpheus Moore, in behalf of himself and Willard Moore, orphan children of Willard Moore, late of Paxton, State of Massachusetts, and Mark Lincoln, of Leominster, in said State, and Elizabeth, his wife, late widow of the said Willard Moore, states that the said Willard Moore was a major in the regiment commanded by Colonel Doolittle, and was killed in the action of Bunker's Hill, on the 17th of June, 1775.

That they were, until very lately, ignorant of the provision made by Congress for the widows and orphans of officers who were killed in the service. He therefore prays that the seven years' half pay of a major may be granted to them.

That Sarah Parker states that she is the widow of the late Colonel Moses Parker, who was wounded and taken prisoner by the British troops in the action of Bunker's Hill, on the 17th of June, 1775, and who afterwards died of his wounds in Boston, in the month of July following. That she was left with a large family of young children, and has had to encounter many difficulties in supporting and bringing them up. That she has not received the relief provided by the resolution of Congress for the widows and children of officers who died in the service since the month of August, 1775. That she does not apprehend it was the intention of Congress to make any discrimination between the widows and children of officers who died in the service, on account of the time when they died. She therefore prays that the benefit of the said resolution of Congress may be extended to her and her children.

That Aaron Stratton, in behalf of, and as attorney to, Abiel Walker, of Chelmsford, State of Massachusetts, states that the said Abiel Walker is the widow of the late Captain Benjamin Walker, of Colonel Bridge's regiment, who was wounded in the action of Bunker's Hill, on the 17th of June, 1775, and died of his wounds in the month of August following.

That the said widow has not received any compensation of half pay, provided for by the resolution of Congress of the 24th day of August, 1780.

He therefore prays, in behalf of the said widow, that such provision may be made for her as the justice of her case demands.

That Josiah Harris, John Harris, Stephen Lee, and Polly Lee, state that they, the said Josiah and John Harris, and Polly Lee, are the sole surviving children of the late Lieutenant John Harris.

That their father was a first lieutenant in the second Connecticut regiment, and was killed in an action with the British troops at White Marsh, in the State of Pennsylvania, on the 7th of December, 1777.

That soon after the widow of the said Lieutenant Harris died, and left them young, without a friend to assist them, and wholly unacquainted with the method to be taken to obtain the relief intended for the orphan children of officers who died in the service, and they have not, to this time, received any benefit from the said provision; they therefore pray that they may receive seven years' half pay of a lieutenant.

That Margaret Ricker states that she is the widow of the late Captain Abraham Ricker, of the second New York regiment.

That the said Abraham Ricker died at Valley Forge, in the State of Pennsylvania, on the 7th day of May, 1778, while in the service of the United States, and left her with a young child to support.

That she had been driven by the enemy from Loud Island, the place of her residence.

She therefore prays that she may have such support and relief granted to her as her case requires.

The above-named persons are either the widows or children of officers who were killed or who died in the service of their country prior to the 15th of May, 1778. Several of them are widows of officers killed in the action at Bunker's Hill, in June, 1775. It may, by rigid principles, be questioned whether the regiments in action on that day were in continental service, and, therefore, whether, by any rule of construction, the officers then killed could be considered " as officers commissioned by Congress."

But if this was a doubt on the 17th of June, it was not so on the 27th day of June, the day General Washington arrived at Cambridge, and assumed the command of the army, and issued such orders as denominated, and to all intents and purposes made it a continental army, and the officers were commissioned accordingly.

Some of the States, in pursuance of the resolves of Congress of the 24th of August, 1780, did make provision for the widows of certain officers who were killed or who died before the 15th of May, 1778, as will appear by the list annexed.

And it will further appear, by the resolve of Congress of the 4th of May, 1785, that it was recommended to the State of Connecticut to pay to the widow of the late Brigadier General Wooster the seven years' half pay of a brigadier general, the amount whereof they are authorized to charge to the United States.

The precedents being thus established, both by particular States and by the United States, of extending the benefits of the resolve of the 24th of August, 1780, to periods prior to the 15th of May, 1778, it would seem proper, upon principles of consistency, that the petitioners should be equally benefited by the resolve of the 24th of August, as others similarly circumstanced, who shall have been provided for by individual States. But perhaps it may be thought proper to make a distinction between the widows of the officers killed at Bunker's Hill, and of those who, a few days afterwards, were " commissioned by Congress," which seems the characteristic description of those entitled to the seven years' half pay, by the resolve of the 15th of May.

If, however, it should be judged proper to extend the provision to any of the cases prior to the said 15th of May, 1778, it would seem incumbent on the character of the nation to provide for the widows of those gallant men who nobly sacrificed their lives, by which they eminently contributed to establish the cause and reputation of their country.

That Peter Covenhoven states that he entered the service in the month of August, 1777, as a sergeant of militia, and did duty near Fort Schuyler, on the Mohawk river. That, on the 6th of the same month, he was wounded, in an action with the enemy, with a musket ball, in his right knee, which wholly disabled and confined him, so that he was unable to walk for the space of two years and two months. That after this period he began to mend and acquire strength, and, at length, to do some easy service, which enabled him to subsist on a scanty maintenance. That in the month of February, 1787, his wound broke out, and grew worse, until the month of November, 1790, when, there being no longer any hope of preserving his limb, he submitted to an amputation, and has thereby become a needy cripple. That his physician's and surgeon's bills for the said first two years and two months amounted to twenty pounds, and upwards; that his boarding and maintenance, during the same period, amounted to fifty pounds, and upwards; that his board and maintenance, from the month of February, 1787, until December, 1789, amounted to seventy-five pounds; and that his physician's and surgeon's bill, for the amputation of his limb, and attendance afterwards, has amounted to sixty-four pounds; so that the actual expenses of his long and painful confinements have, in the whole, amounted to two hundred and nine pounds.

That he has received his half pay, being the monthly allowance of five dollars, from the time of his being wounded to the present time, part of which sum has been expended in the maintenance of a small family, and the residue has proved altogether inadequate to defray the expenses beforementioned. He therefore prays that he may be allowed, over and above the said half pay, such further sum as shall enable him to satisfy and pay the beforementioned expenses, and also that such further provision be made for his maintenance as the nature of his case requires.

Notwithstanding the petitioner's deplorable case, the expenses alleged to have arisen from curing his wounds during the war are precluded by the resolves of limitation. But the expenses incurred by his wounds breaking forth afresh in the year 1787, and thence continuing, to the misery of the petitioner until December, 1790, when he suffered the amputation of one of his thighs, seems, if the same shall be substantiated by the papers annexed, to be an irresistible claim upon the justice of the United States. The expenses of the surgeons and physicians amount to seventy-eight pounds and two shillings, equal to two hundred and eight dollars and twenty-six cents and one third of a cent; to this sum he adds, during the period from February, 1787, to December, 1790, the sum of two hundred dollars for his board and maintenance, alleging that five dollars per month during that period, being his pension from the United States, would not support his distressed family.

The first sum, arising from wounds received in the service of his country, seems a claim upon public justice, and the latter upon public humanity. The first appears to be an indispensable obligation, and the latter an act of liberality, which it may be expedient, or otherwise, to grant.

All which is humbly submitted.

H. KNOX,
*Secretary of War.*

War Department, *February* 21, 1793.

*Report on the petition of Ameliè, Adelaide, Melanie, and Silviè de Grasse, four daughters of the late Count de Grasse; made the 18th of February, 1795.*

That the memorialists, indulging the hopes of their being eventually repossessed of their considerable property near Port de Paix, in St. Domingo, request of Congress the loan of a sum of money; but although the committee suppose that, on the termination of the troubles of that colony, they may be in a condition to discharge the loan, they deem it unadvisable to grant it. But as the grateful sentiments universally entertained in the United States for the late Count de Grasse appeared to the committee to constitute a claim in favor of his daughters, who have taken refuge in our country, and are in a state of absolute want, to the sympathy, and if it could be done with propriety, to the generous assistance of the public, they thought it their duty to make more particular inquiry into the nature and circumstances of the services alluded to.

They find the most decisive evidence that the late Count de Grasse, being authorized to co-operate with the forces of the United States only during a limited period, and which would have proved too short for the successful prosecution of the siege of Yorktown, was prevailed upon by his zeal in our cause, and by the most urgent request of the American commander-in-chief, enforced by the Marquis de Lafayette in person, to remain with the fleet under his command in the Chesapeake, at his own risk and responsibility, until the surrender of Earl Cornwallis and the British army.

That had the Count de Grasse declined complying with the request of the commander in-chief of the forces of the United States, and retired with the powerful fleet under his command, as he was authorized to do by the letter of his orders, the brilliant attempt upon Yorktown would have been frustrated, with disgrace and aggravated injury to the American cause. That, considering the merit of the conduct of the Count de Grasse in this particular, as exclusively and perfectly personal, and as the event proved, decisive of the object of the war, (the independence of the United States,) if under the circumstances of the case the House should be of opinion that the interference of Congress for the relief of the memorialists would not only be a proper evidence of their grateful remembrance of the services before mentioned, but should, moreover, conceive that an allowance to them will be justified by such peculiar circumstances as will not afford a precedent to encourage embarrassing future applications, then the committee recommend as proper the following resolution:

*Resolved*, That, in consideration of the extraordinary services rendered the United States by the late Count de Grasse, in the year 1781, on the urgent request of the commander-in-chief of the American forces, beyond the time limited for his co-operation with the troops of the United States, there be allowed and paid to Ameliè, Adelaide, Melanie, and Silviè de Grasse, daughters of the late Count de Grasse, respectively, the sum of one thousand dollars.

*Claimants for arrears of pay or other emoluments in the army and navy of the Revolution.*

Communicated to the House of Representatives January 26, 1796.

Mr. Tracy, from the Committee of Claims, to whom was referred the following resolution, viz: " *Resolved*, That the proper officer be directed to lay before this House a list of all the officers and soldiers of the late army and navy of the United States who appear entitled to arrearages of pay or other emoluments for their services during the late war, upon the books of the United States together with a statement of the sums or emoluments which appear to be due to them, respectively," made the following report:

That there are two classes or descriptions of arrearages of pay and emoluments, which seem to be embraced by this resolution, viz:

1st. Balances entered in the books of the Register of the Treasury.

2d. Balances which may be found by searching the books and documents contained in the War office, Auditor's office, &c.

The first class contains continental or paper bills, final settlement certificates, &c., returned into the Treasury by paymasters and agents, and which had been delivered to them to pay over to the claimants, respectively, without such payment having been effected.

It is not an easy task to ascertain the sums and names of those to whom due, and is of no importance if done, as the claims of this description are not considered barred by any statute of limitations passed before February 12, 1793, and in that are specifically expressed.

The second class consists of two general divisions: first, army accounts; and, second, those of the navy; and these each into two subdivisions, viz: depreciation and pay, rations, clothing, bounties, and commutation of half pay. The books, papers, and documents, which contain the proper information for the discovery of names and balances, are very numerous; and such a list cannot be made with tolerable accuracy, without looking over the whole number of names to whom any sum has ever been due.

The books containing this information, together with the other necessary documents, can chiefly be found in the War office and Auditor's office; but no single view of these claims can be had; and the debt and credit is no where so situated, and balance struck in any one book, that, upon taking the name of a claimant, it can be ascertained whether or not he is a creditor; but a great variety of books and vouchers must necessarily be resorted to.

It is impossible to form an accurate idea of the length of time and quantum of labor necessary to effect such statements as are required by this resolution, without expending more time in the inquiry than the committee suppose this House would expect or justify. A statement made by the accountant in the War Office, and herewith laid before the House, (marked No. 1,) will furnish some idea of the difficulties attending such an attempt.

If the several statutes of limitation should not be suspended on obtaining the list contemplated by the resolution, the committee can discover no evil consequences resulting from an adoption of it, excepting the great expense of time necessarily consumed in forming such list; but, in this view of the subject, they can discern no benefits accruing from an adoption of it.

If a suspension of limitation is contemplated, the committee can discern no beneficial consequences resulting from an adoption of this resolution; but, on the contrary, many and very extensive evils, which must be obvious to every member of this House.

Contemplating this subject in every point of view the committee are capable of, they are of opinion that it would be improper for the House to adopt this resolution—

1st. Because it would require much expense of time and labor to comply with it; and,

2d. No benefits, but extensive evils, would result from the existence of such a list as the resolution describes.

All which is respectfully submitted to the House.

### No. 1.

#### DEPARTMENT OF WAR,
*Accountant's Office, January* 20, 1796.

In the year 1783 the army of the United States was disbanded, at which time the officers of the different regiments appointed agents to attend on the Commissioner of Army Accounts, to make a final settlement of the arrearages of pay due to the officers, non-commissioned officers, and privates, of the several regiments whose times of service had then expired; which was done, and the balance due each individual (excepting those who were by some reason or other left off of the muster-rolls, or returned dead or deserted) was settled by John Pierce, and final settlement certificates issued to the said agents, several of whom have settled their accounts, and returned the certificates, unissued, to the Executive of the State to whom they respectively belong: others have not made any settlement, nor accounted for the certificates placed in their hands. On a claim being made for arrearages of pay or depreciation claimed by an officer or soldier, the following process must be pursued before it can be ascertained whether any thing is due, viz:

1st. An investigation of the State settlements must take place, to ascertain if the State has not settled with the claimant, and charged the United States with the depreciation of his pay.

2d. The regimental settlements must also be examined, to find if the claimants have not been settled with, and the certificates placed in the hands of the agent.

3d. If he did not belong to the quota of any particular State, individual settlements might have been made with him in the commissioner's office for settling the accounts of the army, or at the Treasury of the United States. If no settlement has taken place, either by the State or United States, as above, it then will be necessary to examine the documents produced in support of the claim, with the muster and pay-rolls, to ascertain when his services commenced, and how long he continued in service, in order to find the balance due. In my opinion, it would be impossible to know who the claimants are, and what balances might be due to them, until they render their claims and the examination made as above; which, in every case, from the variety of documents to be examined, it would not take less than three days to each claim, and then the United States subject to great imposition by double payments, being very difficult to prove, in all cases, the settlements already made; and instances have already come to my knowledge where persons, for the same service, have been paid more than once by the United States.

WILLIAM SIMMONS, *Accountant.*

----

*Commutation.*

Communicated to the House of Representatives April 7, 1796.

MARCH 31, 1796.

The Attorney General of the United States, to whom was referred the memorial of Peter Perrit, late a captain in the Connecticut line of the continental army, most respectfully to the House of Representatives reports :

That the memorialist was a meritorious and unfortunate officer in the army of the United States, and was taken prisoner at Fort Washington, in November, 1776 ; from which time he remained in captivity till the 26th day of August, or 18th day of September, in the year 1778, when he was exchanged, holding the rank of captain in the Connecticut line upon continental establishment, to which he had been duly appointed in October, 1776 ; that, in the year 1777, while he was a prisoner, he was reappointed a captain in the Connecticut line ; and that, on the 9th day of December, in the year 1778, he applied for his place in the army, which was then occupied by another, and, therefore, could not be filled by himself ; and that, soon thereafter, he signified to the Governor of the said State his release, and desired to enter again into military service ; but that he was not reappointed, at any time after his exchange, to any military office on continental establishment, and that he never thereafter actually performed duty in the army of the United States.

That, on the 21st day of June, in the year 1779, the memorialist was appointed, under the authority of the State of Connecticut, a captain of a company in a regiment raised for the particular use of the State, in its controversy about boundary with the State of New York, for the space of one year, which commission he accepted ; and that he actually performed the duties and received the compensation of that office, but did not receive any civil office of profit during the late war.

That the memorialist did, on the 27th of March, 1784, receive the bounty of one year's pay, granted to the officers deranged, by virtue of the resolve of Congress of the 22d of May, 1779, which resolve is in these words :

" *Resolved,* That continental officers who are or may be exchanged, and not continued in the service, be, after such exchange, considered as supernumerary officers, and entitled to the pay provided by a resolution of Congress, of the 24th of November last."

That, on the 6th of May, 1784, upon his memorial, a resolve was passed, whereby, in addition to the pay to which he should be entitled under the resolves of the 24th of November, 1778, the 22d of May, 1779, and 26th of May, 1781, an allowance was made for so much as was

20

equal to the difference between the pay in sea service and in land service for the space of four months; and whereby also the depreciation of pay from the 16th of November, 1776, to the time of his return from captivity, was to be made up to him. At this time nothing is expressed either by Congress or the memorialist on his claim to half pay for life.

That, on the 8th day of February, 1793, the Secretary of War, to whom a petition of the memorialist, stating his claim upon the United States, had been referred, made a report, "that the petitioner had been settled with, conformably to the acts of the 24th of November, 1778, the 22d of May, 1779, the 26th of May, 1781, and the 11th of February, 1784."

That, in February, 1794, a memorial of the memorialist, stating the same claim as is now under consideration, was referred by the House of Representatives to the Secretary of War, who made his report against it on the 17th of March following, which was referred to a committee of the House, who reported thereon on the 21st of April following; and afterwards it was again, on the 6th of June, in the same year, referred to the Secretary of War, who again, viz. on the 24th of November, 1794, made his report thereon against the claim, which was approved by the Committee of Claims.

The Attorney General has considered all those proceedings, with every paper and document accompanying the memorial to him referred, and the several resolves of Congress to which any reference is made in support of the claim, or which appear to be connected with it, namely, of the 16th of September, 1776, 24th of November, 1778, 22d of May, 1779, 3d and 21st of October, 1780, 26th of May, 1781, 22d of March, 1783, 26th of January, 1784, 11th of February, 1784, 6th of May, 1784, and 2d of November, 1785, and the 13th article of the 14th section of the Rules of War; and it is his opinion that the memorialist was not taken into service after his exchange, and that the right of entering into service, if any he had, under the resolve of the 24th of November, 1778, was revoked or determined by the resolve of the 22d of May, 1779, when he became a supernumerary officer, and after which time he continued out of service; and, therefore, that he is not by law entitled to the benefits of the acts of 3d and 21st of October, 1780, and 22d of March, 1783, and that he has received all the money and emoluments from the United States which by law could be demanded.

All which is humbly submitted.

CHARLES LEE,
*Attorney General U. S.*

---

*Report on the memorial of the daughters of the late Count de Grasse, made the 27th December, 1797.*

That the sum heretofore granted by Congress to the petitioners seems to have been intended only as a temporary provision, until the events of the war should permit them to take possession of an estate in the island of St. Domingo; but that it was not considered as a permanent support, to which the amount was wholly inadequate.

The facts stated by the former committee of this House show that the most important services were rendered by the late Count de Grasse to the United States, from motives the most honorable, under the greatest responsibility, and at a risk the most hazardous that can be encountered by an officer of rank and reputation.

With the recollection of these services, and their extensive results, your committee conceive that it will consist neither with the honor nor justice of the United States to refuse an adequate provision for the orphan children of the man who rendered them. They therefore recommend the following resolution to the House:

*Resolved,* That in consideration of the important services rendered to the United States by the late Count de Grasse, provision ought to be made, by law, for the payment of —— dollars per annum, severally, during life, to Amelié, Adelaide, Melanie, and Silvié de Grasse, the daughters of the said Count de Grasse.

———

The Secretary of the Treasury, in obedience to the order of the House of Representatives of the 22d instant, respectfully submits the following report:

That the accounts of General Kosciusko, for services in the army during the late war, were settled at the Treasury in the year 1784, when a certificate was issued for the sum of twelve thousand two hundred and eighty dollars and forty-nine ninetieths, bearing interest at six per centum per annum, from the 1st of January, 1784.

In pursuance of a resolution of the late Congress, passed on the 3d of February, 1784, a stipulation was expressed in the certificates issued to the foreign officers who served in the United States, that the interest on their demands should be paid annually at Paris.

By the fifth section of the act entitled "An act supplementary to the act making provision for the debt of the United States," passed on the 8th day of May, 1792, moneys were granted to discharge the principal and interest of the debts due to the foreign officers as aforesaid. When this provision was made, it was supposed that all the officers had received their interest to the 1st day of January, 1789, as sufficient funds were known to have been remitted by the late Government.

It now appears from an examination of the accounts of Mr. Grand, the American banker at Paris, that no interest has been received by General Kosciusko for four years, namely, from 1785 to 1788, inclusive.

Sufficient funds to discharge the interest for the years 1789, 1790, 1791, and 1792, were, in the latter part of the year 1792, placed in Amsterdam, subject to the disposal of Mr. Morris, minister of the United States residing in Paris. It appears that a bill for the amount of this interest was, by direction of Mr. Morris, remitted to Mr. Pinckney, minister of the United States at London. Pursuant to the request of General Kosciusko, Mr. Pinckney directed the American bankers at Amsterdam to remit the amount to Leipsic or Dresden, according to the most favorable rate of exchange.

Whether the bankers at Amsterdam complied with the directions given by Mr. Pinckney, is not known. It is alleged by General Kosciusko, that the money has never been received by him; it must, therefore, remain subject to his disposal, at Amsterdam, Leipsic, or Dresden.

On the 17th of September, 1792, a notification was published by the Treasurer of the United States that provision had been made for discharging the *principal* debt due to foreign officers, at the Treasury, on the application of the creditors, at any time after the 15th of October, 1792; also, that provision had been made for the payment of *interest* at Paris, conformably to the stipulations expressed in the certificates. The creditors were also notified that the interest upon their respective demands would cease after the last day of December, 1792.

It is stated by General Kosciusko, that the certificate issued to him, which was of the description usually called registered debt, has been lost or destroyed.

Upon the foregoing facts, the Secretary respectfully reports:

1st. That the powers of the officers of the Treasury, founded on law and established usage, are competent to the payment of twelve thousand two hundred and eighty dollars and fifty-four cents, being the principal sum aforesaid; and to the payment of two thousand nine hundred and forty-seven dollars and thirty-three cents, being interest during the years 1785, 1786, 1787, and 1788, on receiving the bond of General Kosciusko to indemnify the United States against any claim on account of the certificate which has been destroyed or lost.

2d. It is not in the power of the Treasury to advance, at present, the amount of the interest supposed to have been remitted to Leipsic or Dresden; though for any sum which may hereafter be redrawn and credited to the United States at Amsterdam, payment will be immediately made.

3d. It is not in the power of the Treasury to take into consideration the circumstances which have prevented General Kosciusko from receiving payment of the principal sum due to him as aforesaid, or to allow interest thereon since the 1st of January, 1793.

All which is respectfully submitted by

OLIVER WOLCOTT,
*Secretary of the Treasury.*

Treasury Department,
*December* 28, 1797.

---

*Seven years' half pay.*

Communicated to the House of Representatives, February 7, 1797.

Mr. Dwight Foster, from the Committee of Claims, to whom was referred the petition of Anna Welsh, made the following report:

That the petitioner asks for an allowance; of the seven years' half pay promised to the widows and orphans of certain officers killed in the service of the United States during the late war.

It appears that Mrs. Welsh's husband was a captain of marines; that he served on the expedition to Penobscot, and was there slain. The resolutions of Congress, promising seven years' half pay to the widows of officers who fell in service, did not extend to officers of the navy.

The repeated decisions made by Congress against petitions of this nature forbid the expectation of an allowance; and the committee can discover no sufficient reason for making a discrimination between this and other similar cases heretofore considered.

The petitioner, as executrix of the last will and testament of her brother, George Hurlbut, deceased, further asks for an allowance of the commutation and land warrants, to which she apprehends she is entitled, on the principle that her brother continued in service till the end of the war. That gentleman was a captain in Sheldon's regiment of light dragoons; he was wounded by the enemy in the performance of his duty at Tarrytown, in the summer of 1781, and languished of his wounds until the 8th day of May, 1783, when he died. On this statement there is no doubt but a right to so much land as was promised to captains in the army has vested in the petitioner, and, on proof of the facts, she may now receive the warrants at the War Office, without aid from Congress.

With respect to the claim for commutation, some further attention will be requisite. By the act of Congress of the 21st of October, 1780, half pay for life was promised to the officers of the army who should continue in the service to the end of the war. This was afterwards, on the 22d of March, 1783, commuted for five years' full pay.

If Captain Hurlbut lived to the end of the war, he was entitled to commutation; and in his right the petitioner, as executrix of his will, and legatee, would be entitled; otherwise, not. The question then arising, is, when did the war end? or, in other words, was there an end of the war before the 8th of May, 1783, the day of Captain Hurlbut's death? On the solution of this question rests the claim of the petitioner for commutation, it being placed on the ground of contract only.

The provisional articles of peace between the United States and Great Britain were signed November 30, 1782; and the treaty between France and Great Britain, on which the efficacy of those articles was conditioned, upon the 20th of January, 1783. The first information Congress appears to have had of them was on the 24th of March, 1783, when the armed vessels, cruising under commissions from the United States, were recalled. On the 11th of April, 1783, a cessation of hostilities was ordered by proclamation of Congress.

On the 23d of April, Congress, by their resolution of that date, declared their opinion that " the time of the men engaged to serve during the war does not expire until the ratification of the definitive treaty of peace." By the acts of May 26, June 11, August 9, and September 26, 1783, Congress directed parts of the army to be furloughed; and by their proclamation on the 18th of October of the same year, they discharged absolutely, after the third day of November then ensuing, such part of the federal armies as had been furloughed by the several acts aforesaid.

On the 25th of November New York was evacuated by the British troops. The definitive treaty of peace was, in fact, signed on the 3d of September, 1783, but not received by Congress until about the middle of January, 1784. In the settlements made for pay, &c., by the commissioners of Congress, with the officers and men engaged to serve during the war, and furloughed as aforesaid the 3d day of November, (the day when the troops were discharged by proclamation,) has been regarded as the end of the war, and they have been settled with and paid to that day accordingly.

It appears, by the accounts of Colonel Sheldon's regiment, that certificates for Captain Hurlbut's commutation were, in fact, issued : but, on a further examination of the nature of the claim, it was thought that no act of Congress would justify the granting of commutation for any officer similarly circumstanced, and therefore the certificates were cancelled. Had the committee found no resolution of Congress which seemed to have determined the question when the war ended, they might have been induced to fix on a period antecedent to the death of Captain Hurlbut, and, consequently, have been of the opinion that the petitioner was entitled to relief. But as Congress seem to have fixed on a later period by their resolution of the 23d of April, and by continuing in service the troops engaged to serve during the war, and paying the officers and men till the 3d of November, 1783, as they were liable until that time to be again called into service, and, in case of disobedience, would have been subjected to the penalties of the rules and articles of war ; and as the House of Representatives, under the present Government, rejected a petition for commutation, founded on principles exactly similar to the present, by the administrator to the estate of Major Torrey, who died in September, 1783, the committee conceive they are not at liberty to contradict authority and precedent so respectable. They therefore report, that the prayer of the petition of the said Anna Welsh *ought not to be granted.*

---

Communicated to the House of Representatives, February 24, 1797.

The Committee of Claims, who were "instructed to inquire into and report on the expediency or inexpediency of designating certain claims against the United States, to be excepted from the operation of the acts of limitation," made the following report :

That, in obedience to the orders of the House, they have made all the inquiries which to them appear necessary; that they have attentively and deliberately considered the subject referred to them, and are of opinion that it would not be expedient to designate any species of claims against the United States, which are now affected by the acts of limitation, to be excepted from the operation of those acts.

In considering this subject, a review of the situation of the United States, as respected their finances, during the period when most of the demands originated, was requisite. It was also necessary to ascertain what measures had been adopted by Congress, both under the old and under the present Government, to bring all the demands against the States to a liquidation and settlement.

It will be recollected that, at the commencement of the war, the United States were destitute of money, and, during a long period of years afterwards, were obliged to rely principally on credit for carrying on all their important operations.

Having, at that time, no settled national government, a regular system for conducting public business, especially money transactions depending on credit, was not to be expected. Great numbers of individuals were necessarily invested with the powers of binding the public by their contracts. Almost every officer of the army, whether in the commissary's department or otherwise, in different stages of the war, had it in his power to contract debts legally or equitably binding upon the United States. We find Congress, at various times during the war, endeavoring to make arrangements which should prevent an undue use of the powers vested in individuals, and the dangerous consequences to which the Government was thereby necessarily exposed. The acts of the 5th of March, 1779, and of the 23d of August, 1780, were calculated to limit the public responsibility in such cases. After the peace, and under the old Government, periods were prescribed within which claims of certain descriptions, and, finally, all unliquidated claims, were to be exhibited for settlement, or to be forever thereafter barred.

It must be acknowledged by all, that during those periods, every provision which could rationally have been expected was made for the accommodation of individuals having claims against the public, to enable them to obtain proper settlements of their demands. The Journals of Congress, under the Confederation, will abundantly justify this remark.

Commissioners were appointed, with special or general powers, to settle the claims of individuals in all the departments; and, in every instance, the powers given were plenary and explicit. Sufficient time was given for every one to obtain information and pursue his remedy, and ample opportunity was given for all to substantiate their claims, or at least to present abstracts of them, which would have prevented their being foreclosed by the acts designed eventually to operate upon them. The cases cannot be numerous, in which the want of opportunity to bring forward claims can be justly pleaded as an excuse for the omission.

By the act of the 17th of March, 1785, all persons having unliquidated claims against the United States were required, within twelve months, to exhibit particular abstracts of such claims to some of the commissioners in the State in which they respectively resided, who were sent and empowered to settle accounts against the United States, under the penalty or condition that accounts not so presented should be thereafter settled only at the Treasury.

By another act of Congress of the same year, viz: November 2, 1785, all persons having claims for services performed in the military department were directed to exhibit the same for liquidation to the commissioners of army accounts, on or before the first day of August then ensuing. By that act it was expressly resolved that all claims under the description above mentioned, which might be exhibited after that period, should be forever thereafter precluded from adjustment and allowance.

And it was provided by the act of July 23, 1787, that all persons having unliquidated claims against the United States, pertaining to the late commissary's, quartermaster's, hospital, clothier's, or marine departments, should exhibit particular abstracts of such claims to the proper commissioner appointed to settle the accounts of those departments, within eight months from the date of the said act; and all persons having other unliquidated claims against the United States, were to exhibit particular abstracts thereof to the Comptroller of the Treasury of the United States, within one year from the date thereof; and all accounts not exhibited as aforesaid were to be precluded from settlement or allowance.

These regulations were adopted by Congress under the old Government. Great care was taken to have them extensively published, so that every individual who was interested might be informed of their existence and operation.

Under the present constitution there has not been wanting a disposition to relieve certain individuals whose claims were considered as peculiarly meritorious, which had been affected by the acts above recited.

With this view, in March, 1792, two several acts of Congress were passed, suspending for two years the operation of the resolutions of Congress of November 2, 1785, and July 27, 1787, so far as they had barred, or might be construed to bar, the claims of the widow or orphans of any officer of the late army to the seven years' half pay of such officer; or the claims of any officer, soldier, artificer, sailor, and marine, of the army of the United States, for personal services rendered to the United States in the military or naval departments.

In consequence of these suspensions, many claims were exhibited and allowed against the Government. There is reason to apprehend, in some instances, the public were defrauded for want of proper pre-existing checks and evidences of payments having been made. This suspension continued for the term of two years, which was till March, 1794. In the mean time, viz: on the 12th of February, 1793, the act "relative to claims against the United States, not barred by any act of limitation, and which had not been already adjusted," was passed by Congress, after a serious and attentive consideration of the subject.

By that law it was provided "that all claims upon the United States for services or supplies, or for other cause, matter, or thing, furnished or done previous to the 4th day of March, 1789, whether founded upon certificates or other written documents from public officers, or otherwise, which had not already been barred by any act of limitation, and which should not be presented at the Treasury before the 1st day of May, 1794, should forever after be barred and precluded from settlement or allowance." But this was not to be construed as affecting loan office certificates, certificates of final settlements, indents of interest, balances entered on the books of the Register of the Treasury, registered certificates, foreign loans, or certificates issued under the act making provision for the public debt of the United States.

One other act, passed the 3d day of March, 1795, provided that loan office certificates, final settlements, and indents of interest, then outstanding, should be presented at the office of the Auditor of the Treasury, on or before the 1st day of January, in the present year, 1797, or be forever after barred or precluded from settlement or allowance.

This summary contains a general view of the principal acts of limitation, by which claims against the public have been affected.

From an attentive consideration of them, and of the circumstances under which they were enacted, the committee are fully impressed with an opinion that it would not be expedient to suspend their operation.

Some remarks, extracted from a report heretofore made to Congress, are subjoined by the committee as pertinent to the subject.

It was essential to the public administration that the extent of just demands upon the Government should be, within a reasonable period, definitely ascertained. It was essential to public safety and to right, in relation to the whole community, that all unsettled claims should be made known within a time when there were yet means of proper investigation, and after which the public responsibility should terminate; and the possibility of charging the Government by collusive and fictitious contracts should be at an end.

The justice as well as policy of acts of limitation, under such circumstances, cannot be doubted.

The situation of no country ever presented a more clear necessity for, or a more competent justification of, precautions of that nature; and all the reasons for adopting them operate to recommend unusual caution in departing from them; with the additional force of this circumstance, that the subsequent lapse of time has increased the difficulties of a due examination.

The accounts of a considerable number of officers, who had it in their power to bind the public by their contracts, and who were intrusted with large sums of money for fulfilling their engagements, remain unsettled. Some of those persons are dead ; others have absconded. The business has been conducted by others with so little order as to put it out of their power to render a proper statement of their transactions : the books and papers of others, who had extensive trusts, have been destroyed, so as to preclude the possibility of settlement. Hence, it must appear that the Government would, in a great number of cases, be destitute of the means of repelling unfounded and even satisfied claims, for want of documents and vouchers ; which could only have resulted from a due settlement with those officers, and from the possession of their books and papers.

It might be inferred, without proof, (and it has appeared, in the course of business, at the Treasury,) that it was a practice with certain public officers, on obtaining supplies, to give receipts and certificates for them, and, when they made payments, either partially or totally, to take distinct receipts from the parties, without either endorsing the payments upon the original vouchers or requiring a surrender of them. Hence, it would often happen that parties could produce satisfactory vouchers of their having performed services and furnished supplies, for which, though satisfaction may have been made, the evidences of it would not be in the possession of the Government ; and hence, from relaxations of the limitation acts, there would be great danger that much more injustice would be done to the United States than justice to individuals.

The principles of self-defence, therefore, require and justify an adherence to those acts generally ; and there are not any particular species of claims which, in the view of the committee, ought to be exempted from their operation.

Those which have been most frequently referred to by some members of the House, are such claims as include the arrearages of pay and other emoluments to officers and soldiers of the late army, &c.

Pursuant to an order of the House, at the first session of the present Congress, a report was made to them, having special reference to this subject. It was considered in Committee of the Whole, and agreed to by the House on the 5th day of February, 1796. To that report, and the documents accompanying the same, the committee ask leave to refer the House, and respectfully submit the whole subject to their consideration.

The following are the report and documents above referred to:

Communicated to the House of Representatives January 26, 1796.

The Committee of Claims, to whom was referred the following resolution, viz: "*Resolved*, That the proper officer be directed to lay before this House a list of all the officers and soldiers of the late army and navy of the United States who appear entitled to arrearages of pay or other emoluments for their services during the late war, upon the books of the United States, together with a statement of the sums or emoluments which appear to be due to them, respectively," made the following report:

21

That there are two classes or descriptions of arrearages of pay and emoluments which seem to be embraced by this resolution, viz:

1st. Balances entered in the books of the Register of the Treasury.

2d. Balances which may be found by searching the books and documents contained in the War Office, Auditor's office, &c.

The first class contains continental or paper bills, final settlements, certificates, &c. returned into the Treasury by paymasters and agents, and which had been delivered to them to pay over to the claimants, respectively, without such payment having been effected.

It is not an easy task to ascertain the sums and names of those to whom due, and is of no importance if done, as the claims of this description are not considered barred by any statute of limitations passed before February 12th, 1793; and, in that, are specifically excepted.

The second class consists of two general divisions: first, army accounts; and second, those of the navy; and these, each, into two subdivisions, viz: depreciation and pay; rations, clothing, bounties, and commutation of half pay.

The books, papers, and documents which contain the proper information for the discovery of names and balances are very numerous; and such a list cannot be made with tolerable accuracy, without looking over the whole number of names to whom any sum has ever been due.

The books containing this information, together with the other necessary documents, can chiefly be found in the War Office and Auditor's office; but no single view of these claims can be had, and the debt and credit is nowhere so situated, and balance struck in any one book, that, upon taking the name of a claimant, it can be ascertained whether or not he is a creditor; but a great variety of books and vouchers must necessarily be resorted to.

It is impossible to form an accurate idea of the length of time and quantum of labor necessary to effect such statements as are required by this resolution, without expending more time in the inquiry than the committee suppose this House would expect or justify. A statement made by the Accountant in the War Office, and herewith laid before the House, (marked No. 1,) will furnish some idea of the difficulties attending such an attempt.

If the several statutes of limitation should not be suspended on obtaining the list contemplated by the resolution, the committee can discover no evil consequences resulting from an adoption of it, excepting the great expense of time necessarily consumed in forming such list; but, in this view of the subject, they can discern no benefits accruing from an adoption of it.

If a suspension of limitation is contemplated, the committee can discern no beneficial consequences resulting from an adoption of this resolution; but, on the contrary, many and very extensive evils, which must be obvious to every member of this House.

Contemplating this subject in every point of view the committee are capable of, they are of opinion that it would be improper for the House to adopt this resolution—

1st. Because it would require much expense of time and labor to comply with it; and,

2d. No benefits, but extensive evils, would result from the existence of such a list as the resolution describes.

All which is respectfully submitted to the House.

No. 1.

DEPARTMENT OF WAR,
*Accountant's Office, January* 20, 1796.

In the year 1783 the army of the United States was disbanded, at which time the officers of the different regiments appointed agents to attend on the commissioner of army accounts to make a final settlement of the arrearages of pay due the officers, non-commissioned officers, and privates of the several regiments whose terms of service had then expired, which was done ; and the balance due each individual (excepting those who were, by some reason or other, left off of the muster-rolls, or returned dead, or deserted,) was settled by John Pierce, and final settlement certificates issued to the said agents, several of whom have settled their accounts, and returned the certificates unissued to the Executive of the State to whom they respectively belong; others have not made any settlement, nor accounted for the certificates placed in their hands. On a claim being made for arrearages of pay or depreciation claimed by an officer or soldier, the following process must be pursued, before it can be ascertained whether any thing is due, viz :

1st. An investigation of the State settlements must take place, to ascertain if the State has not settled with the claimant, and charged the United States with the depreciation of his pay.

2d. The regimental settlements must also be examined, to find if the claimants have not been settled with, and the certificates placed in the hands of the agent.

3d. If he did not belong to the quota of any particular State, individual settlements might have been made with him in the commissioner's office for settling the accounts of the army, or at the Treasury of the United States ; if no settlement has taken place, either by the State or United States, as above, it then will be necessary to examine the documents produced in support of the claim, with the muster and pay-rolls, to ascertain when his services commenced, and how long he continued in service, in order to find the balance due. In my opinion, it would be impossible to know who the claimants are, and what balances might be due to them, until they render their claims, and the examination made as above ; which, in every case, from the variety of documents to be examined, it would not take less than three days to each claim, and then the United States subject to great imposition by double payments, being very difficult to prove in all cases the settlements already made ; and instances have already come to my knowledge where persons, for the same service, have been paid more than once by the United States.

WILLIAM SIMMONS, *Accountant.*

---

Report on the expediency of making further provision for the relief of the widow and orphan children of the late Colonel John Hardin, and for the orphan daughter of the late Major Alexander Trueman, made the 9th of April, 1800.

That it appears from the annexed papers, which the committee found on the file of the House, that both those officers, on undertaking a very hazardous service, received assurances that, in the event which afterwards happened, their families would be provided for by the Government of the United States; that, although the Government may not be absolutely bound to fulfil those engagements, and although the measure of its bounty is not fixed by them, the committee are of opinion that neither the honor nor interest of the Government should permit it wholly to violate such engagements, where the danger to be encountered justified their being entered into, or to make a provision inadequate to their objects.

That the committee are of opinion that the previous stipulation and the nature of the service in which Colonel Hardin and Major Trueman were engaged, should distinguish their cases from those of officers killed in ordinary military service. Little honor attending the most complete success in such enterprises, much smaller inducements exist for engaging in them than in those military risks which may produce great renown.

The committee are, therefore, of opinion that the United States ought to make a suitable provision for educating the sons of Colonel Hardin, and for the support of his daughters, and the daughter of Major Trueman, so long as they may remain unmarried; all of them, as the committee are informed, being destitute of the fortune necessary for those uses; and for this purpose beg leave to report a bill for the consideration of the House.

---

## No. 1.

WAR DEPARTMENT, *November* 26, 1792.

SIR : I have the honor to enclose you all the information in my power relative to the messengers who have fallen a sacrifice in bearing the messages of peace to the Indians.

Colonel Hardin has left a wife and five or six children ; Major Trueman has left three orphan children, two sons and a daughter; Mr. Gerard has left a widow at Columbia, in the Western Territory, and three or four children ; Mr. Freeman was a single man, of about 24 years of age, an inhabitant of Columbia, Western Territory.

I am, sir, with great respect,
Your most obedient servant,
HENRY KNOX,
*Secretary of War.*

---

## No. 2.

WAR DEPARTMENT, *November* 26, 1792.

Although nothing in writing was stipulated with Major Trueman, at his express desire, yet the subscriber assured him, in the name of the President of the United States, that if he should lose his life in the business of his mission, his children should be generously provided for by the public.

HENRY KNOX,
*Secretary of War.*

No. 3.

*Extract of a letter from Brigadier General Wilkinson to the Secretary of War, dated*

"FORT WASHINGTON, *April* 28, 1792.

"Immediately on the receipt of your letter of the 11th of February, I wrote to Colonel John Hardin, of Kentucky, making a request that he would undertake to convey a message to the hostile tribes; and it was to this gentleman I referred in my letter of the 27th of March.

"Colonel Hardin is a man of strong judgment; more conversant in the Indian modes and habits than any person I have ever seen; and, as a woodsman, is confessedly superior to the whole district of Kentucky. He is, withal, a man high in the public confidence, of spotless integrity, and invincible firmness.

I deem the aid and co-operation of such an agent, in the mission of Major Trueman, a matter of high moment, not only with relation to the negotiations impending, but with views to the clear, accurate, and extensive information he will be able to acquire of the country which may become the theatre of war. I shall, therefore, sir, venture to employ him in the business, in such manner as to avail the public of his judgment, knowledge, and experience, for which I am to allow him one guinea per day, during the time he is actually engaged; and it is stipulated between us, that, in case he should be murdered whilst in this service, I am to recommend his family to the bounteous consideration of Government."

Compared November 24, 1792.      JOHN STAGG, Jun.
*Chief Clerk War Department.*

———

*Report on the memorial and remonstrance of Moses Hazen. Made the 22d February, 1803.*

The memorialist complains that numerous errors have been committed by the accounting officers of the Government at different periods, in the adjustment of his accounts with the United States, and that he has suffered manifest injustice thereby. He prays that his accounts may be revised and re-examined. He also asks indemnification for the loss of his British half pay; and that his claim for the release of German prisoners may be considered and allowed.

The long and patient attention given by your committee to the representations of the agent of the memorialist, and to the examination of the numerous documents he has produced, has only served to convince them of the utter impropriety of interfering in the adjustment of accounts which come regularly before the officers appointed by law for that purpose. No legislative aid seems necessary to enable the Treasury Department to render ample justice to the memorialist. And, it is presumed, no want of disposition in this respect, can, with propriety, be ascribed to that Department. The accounts of the memorialist appear to have been in a course of examination from a period anterior to the existence of the present Government, down to the final decision made at the Treasury in June last.

Your committee, believing that every well-founded claim of the memorialist has been liquidated at the legal and proper board, and that legislative interference would, therefore, be highly inexpedient, are of opinion that the memorialist have leave to withdraw his memorial.

*Report on the petition of Moses White and Charlotte Hazen, executor and executrix of Moses Hazen, deceased. Made the 27th of February, 1804.*

The late Brigadier General Hazen was a lieutenant in the British army, in the half-pay establishment, at the time he entered into the service of the United States during the revolutionary war. On the 22d January, 1776, he was appointed colonel of the second Canadian regiment in the American service, and on the same day Congress passed the following resolution, to wit:

" *Resolved*, That the United States will indemnify Colonel Hazen for any loss of half pay he may sustain in consequence of his entering into their service."

The object of the present application is to obtain payment of the amount of half pay which accrued from the 25th December, 1781, the day on which the general's name was struck off the British establishment, until his death, which happened on the 4th February, 1803.

No measures seem to have been at any time adopted by the General Government to carry into effect the foregoing resolution, unless the provision made for the officers of the American army generally, of his rank and period of service, is to be considered in that light. But it is believed that, from a sound construction of the resolution, connected with a view of all the circumstances under which General Hazen entered into the service of the United States, it may be fairly presumed Congress intended for him some further provision than was contemplated for the other officers of the American army, who had not made a similar sacrifice.

It is certain the general, after the termination of the war, repeatedly claimed the allowance of his British half pay as the genuine intent of the indemnity promised him by Congress; and it also appears, by a letter from the Secretary of the Treasury, under date of the 15th July, 1795, that his claim was then recognised at that Department as being founded in principle, and as requiring only the evidence of its amount to entitle him, if not to immediate payment, at least to a credit on the books of the Treasury.

From an attentive consideration of the case, your committee are of opinion that the prayer of the petition is reasonable, and ought to be granted.

———

*Claims barred by the Statutes of Limitation, that ought to be paid.*

Communicated to the House of Representatives, January 6, 1807.

Mr. Stanton, from the committee appointed " to inquire whether any, and, if any, what description of claims against the United States are barred by the statutes of limitation, which in reason and justice ought to be provided for by law," made the following report:

That all claims for services rendered, and supplies furnished, or done, prior to the 4th of March, 1789, are barred by sundry resolutions of Congress passed in the years 1785 and 1787, and by laws of the United States passed 2d of February, 1793, and on the 3d of March, 1795, and on the 9th of July, 1798. Your committee are of opinion that justice and sound policy require that all just and equitable claims against the

United States, which are thus barred, should be fully paid and satisfied. We therefore recommend the following resolution :

*Resolved*, That all just and equitable claims against the United States, for services rendered and supplies furnished during the revolutionary war with Great Britain, and for loan office certificates, final settlement certificates, indents of interest, and balances credited on the books of the Treasury, which are now barred by any law of the United States, ought to be provided for by law.

---

Communicated to the House of Representatives, January 23, 1810.

The Committee of Claims, to whom was referred the petition of John Thomson, report :

That, from documents accompaning the said petition, and seeming upon the face of them to be correct and authentic, it appears that the petitioner was a captain in the revolutionary war, and belonged to a regiment commanded by Colonel Hazen, called " the Congress's own regiment."

That, after he had served as captain in the said regiment, with " honor and reputation," for about one year, he entered as a colonel into the service of Pennsylvania, to defend that State against the Indian incursions, having previously solicited and obtained from Major General Sullivan leave to retire from the American army, on account partly of his ill state of health, but principally because his proper rank had been withheld from him. That, in recruiting, and for the pay and subsistence of his company in the said congressional regiment, the petitioner expended considerable sums of money, which your committee are convinced have never been fully reimbursed to him ; and that from two accounts made out by Edward Chinn, paymaster to the regiment, (one during the war, and the other in the year 1788,) and from a letter written in 1809, by Mr. Nourse, the Register, it is manifest that the petitioner's account has never been finally adjusted.

The petitioner has exhibited an account showing a balance of two thousand six hundred and twenty-nine dollars and five cents in his favor, against the United States; which account, together with the vouchers supporting it, the committee have attentively investigated. Every item in the account is established to the entire satisfaction of the committee, except the charge of three hundred and forty-three dollars and thirteen cents, for the pay of the company in the month of August, 1777. The embarrassing and difficult situation of the regiment in relation to the enemy in that month, is offered by Captain Thomson as the cause of his not being able to produce a regular pay-roll in support of the charge or particular item alluded to. Let this item be stricken from the account, and then it appears that the United States are indebted to the indigent petitioner in the sum of two thousand two hundred and eighty-five dollars and ninety-two cents ; but, by the several resolves and statutes of limitation passed by Congress, his claim, in the eye of the law, is satisfied. The petitioner, however, alleges that, in his case, the principles of equity ought to control the rigor of the law ; because he endeavors to prove, and has indeed satisfied the committee, that the settlement of his account within the time limited by law was prevented by circumstances not within his power.

The letter of the Register, already referred to, and his certificate thereto subjoined, show that the petitioner attended in person, and also by Mr. Nourse, his agent, at the office of the commissioner of army accounts, in New York, for the purpose of getting his account settled; but that an adjustment of it did not take place in consequence of "some difficulty" arising out of the unsettled situation of the accounts of Lieutenant Colonel Antil, of the aforesaid regiment. To obviate this difficulty, the petitioner states that he made unremitting efforts for the liquidation of his account with Edward Chinn, the paymaster of the regiment; presuming that if he could succeed in this, his account would then be admitted by the agent of the United States. It appears, as well from the said letter of Mr. Nourse, as from the petitioner's representations, that his efforts were fruitless, and that Chinn not only refused or neglected to make a complete statement or settlement of the petitioner's account, but the petitioner moreover alleges that he was unable in due time to obtain from him such papers as were deemed indispensable for its adjustment. Chinn died; the statute of limitations began to operate; and here the subject rests.

In reporting in this, as in all other cases, the committee consider themselves bound by the law of the land. Could they indulge their feelings on the present occasion, they would not say to an old soldier, who has bravely fought the battles of his country, that his just claim is extinguished by the mere lapse of a given number of years, during which he had not the means of enforcing it. Not compassion alone for a poor soldier, but the mandates of justice, would impel them to speak a very different language. Conforming, however, to the positive limitations of Congress, they submit the following resolution:

*Resolved*, That the prayer of the petitioner ought not to be granted.

———

Communicated to the House of Representatives, March 14, 1810.

The Committee of Claims, to whom was referred the petition of Moses Young, report:

That the petitioner was engaged by Henry Laurens, Esq., as secretary of his embassy to Holland, at a salary of £500 sterling, as authorized by a resolution of Congress; that he embarked with Mr. Laurens on the said mission, was captured by the British, carried to England and imprisoned, effected his escape to France, where he aided in the execution of the public business in Dr. Franklin's office, and, upon the enlargement of Mr. Laurens in April, 1782, joined him in London and served as his secretary, and with Dr. Franklin until the 9th of July, 1782; at which period the objects of the mission of Mr. Laurens, having, in consequence of his capture and detention in England, been intrusted to Mr. Adams, the petitioner, with a view to save expense to the United States, with the approbation of Mr. Laurens, discontinued his services as secretary. In consequence of the failure in the mission of Mr. Laurens, in the object to which it was directed, that gentleman expressed a determination not to receive from Congress his salary as minister, and advised the petitioner to accept the one-half the salary to which he was entitled as secretary; to which recommendation the petitioner acceded: transmitted his account for services from the 18th October, 1779, up to the 5th February, 1782, (when his services were first accepted by Dr. Franklin,) at £250 sterling per annum, which account was so liquidated and settled at the Treasury of the United States, on the 21st of August, 1783. A reservation being made by Mr. Young, and by his agent, of his right of salary from the said 5th February, to the customary allowance for time and expenses of returning to the United States, and for interest. Mr. Laurens, however, having sustained losses by depreciation of continental money, afterwards felt himself justified in receiving from the Government the full amount of his salary; upon information of which fact the petitioner, having been subjected to an adverse fortune, conceived himself entitled, without question of his patriotism, to ask of the United States, in their state of prosperity, the satisfaction of a debt which at the period of their difficulties he had declined exacting; and did accordingly, on the 3d of May, 1787, present to the accountant of the Treasury a claim for the payment of the balance of his salary, and the allowance of three months' wages for time and expense in returning to the United States; which claim was by the accountant referred to the Board of Treasury on the 11th of August, 1788, and does not appear to have been by them acted upon. In December, 1792, Mr. Young presented a petition to Congress for the satisfaction of his claim, which was by the House of Representatives referred to the Secretary of the Treasury, who does not appear to have made report. The petitioner having resided abroad nearly eleven years, as secretary to one of the ministers of the United States at the Court of Spain, and as American consul at Madrid, the care of soliciting his claim has been intrusted to his agents in the United States, by whom it has several times, since December, 1792, been brought before Congress, submitted to the investigation of the Secretary of State, and of committees of both Houses, and has obtained on each reference the confirmation of the Secretary and committees of the justice and merits of the claim.

Your committee, taking into consideration the sacrifices, sufferings, and meritorious services of the petitioner, established by the certificate of the late Henry Laurens, Esq., and other respectable evidence, the patriotic consideration which prevented his claiming the whole salary due him, his subsequent disappointments, and long-continued claim for settlement since May, 1787, are of opinion that his claim is just.

It is a fact not disputed, that the petitioner presented an abstract of his claim to the proper officers of the Treasury on the 3d of May, 1787, which is established by the documents of the public officers and the account itself taken from the Treasury on the 12th of February, 1805, by the petitioner, and now before the House with his petition. The presentation of the claim at that time prevented the resolve of Congress from barring the claim. The resolve was adopted on the 23d of July, 1787, in the following words, viz:

"*Resolved*, That all persons having unliquidated claims against the United States, pertaining to the late commissary's, quartermaster's, hospital, clothier's, or marine departments, shall exhibit particular abstracts of such claims to the proper commissioner appointed to settle the accounts of those departments, within eight months from the date hereof; and all persons having other unliquidated claims against the United States shall exhibit a particular abstract thereof to the Comptroller of the Treasury of the United States, within one year from the date hereof. And all accounts, not exhibited as aforesaid, shall be precluded from settlement or allowance."

From the foregoing circumstances, your committee are of opinion that the said Moses Young has a just claim on the United States for the full amount of his salary, at the rate of £500 sterling per annum, from the 18th of October, 1779, to the 9th October, 1792, including the usual allowance of three months for returning to the·United States; and that after deducting the sum received from Dr. Franklin, and by his attorney, Joseph Nourse, the balance, with interest thereon, ought to be paid by the United States.

The committee ask leave to report a bill.

---

### Statutes of Limitation.

Communicated to the House of Representatives, December 21, 1811.

Mr. Gholson, from the Committee of Claims, in obedience to a resolution of the House, instructing them to inquire into the expediency of repealing or suspending the operation of the several acts of limitation, so far as they now operate to bar the payment of the following description of claims against the United States, to wit : 1st. Loan office certificates. 2d. Indents of interest on the public debt. 3d. Final settlement certificates. 4th. Commissioners' certificates. 5th. Army certificates. 6th. Credits given in lieu of army certificates cancelled. 7th. Credits for the pay of the army, for which no certificates were issued. 8th. Invalid pensions. 9th. Lost or destroyed certificates—made the following report :

That they have bestowed on the resolution that full consideration to which it was entitled. They felt, on the one hand, sincere solicitude to devise some just and adequate method of satisfying the claims in question, whilst, on the other, they were forcibly struck with the unavoidable scenes of speculation and fraud which would ensue the repeal or suspension of any of the acts of limitation, whereby those claims are barred. If the old soldier, his widow, or his orphan, were alone to be benefited by such suspension, your committee would not hesitate to recommend it. Past experience, however, hath evidently shown that similar legislative indulgences have inured almost exclusively to the advantage of the unprincipled speculator, and those who avail themselves of the ignorance and subsist upon the misfortunes of others. We have innumerable examples of the truth of this position, in the consequences that resulted, not only from the various suspensions of these acts which have hitherto taken place, but more especially from the adoption of the funding system. It is deemed unnecessary to enlarge upon the consequences; they are too well known. Although a communication received from the Treasury at a former session holds out an opinion that there are in the possession of that Department sufficient checks and guards to protect the United States from imposition and fraud in the payment of a certain part of those claims, the committee are differently impressed. They have seen a transcript from the books of the Treasury, published to the world, exhibiting the names of a certain class of claimants; and to suppose that a facility of this kind, thus offered to speculative artifice and management, would not be seized upon and used by the speculator, to impose upon Government, is to suppose a thing contrary to all experience. The committee feel themselves by no means able to draw a line of distinction between a just claim liquidated, and a just one unliquidated; and to attempt the invidious task of distinction in point of merit, where there can be no difference, and to open the statutes of limitation in order to relieve a part, or a few favorite classes of claims, does not comport, in the view of your committee, with any principle of fairness, or with that equal system of distributive justice, which ought to be dispensed towards all. When they take a retrospective view of the subject, and find that most of those statutes were first passed in the times and under the patriot counsels of the old Congress, and that the more general one, which took effect in 1794, was passed under the administration of General Washington, who was himself the chief of soldiers, as he was the chief of their patrons and friends in every station; but he was equally the friend of his country, and gave that act the sanction of his name, as founded, at least, in a policy of general justice and right, which the Government had been at length obliged to resort to and maintain in self-defence; that every Congress since has invariably adhered to the general policy of those laws; and, after the lapse of so many years, when the difficulty of doing justice has increased with the increase of time, and when a partial repeal would but tend to increase the discontent and dissatisfaction of every class of claimants which should remain unprovided for, the committee cannot, from any view they have been able to take of the subject, recommend the repeal or suspension of any of those statutes. They would therefore beg leave to submit the following resolution:

*Resolved*, That it is not expedient to repeal or suspend any of the acts of limitation, whereby the aforesaid descriptions of claims are barred.

---

## MARCH 4, 1812.

Read and committed to the Committee of the Whole House, on the report of the Committee of Claims on the petition of John Murray.

The Committee of Claims, to whom was referred the petition of John Dixon, report:

That, from documents exhibited by the petitioner, it appears he is the assignee of Lucy Dixon, his mother, of a certificate which was issued in her favor, by the commissioner for settling the accounts of the revolutionary war, in the State of Virginia, for the sum of $329 $\frac{84}{90}$, "payable with six per cent. from the 1st day of January, 1781," and dated the 23d of December, 1786. The original certificate is produced, and, by an endorsement on it, it appears the interest was paid to the 1st of January, 1785. A certificate of the Register of the Treasury is likewise exhibited, showing that Lucy Dixon stands a creditor on the records of that Department for the said certificate, which "remains unliquidated by the United States." As an apology (as it is presumed by the committee) for not presenting this claim at an earlier period, Lucy Dixon, in a petition formerly offered by herself, alleges that she, in the year 1793, left Virginia and went to the State of Georgia, where she remained until 1799, or 1800. That, on her return to her residence in Virginia, she, on looking over her papers, found the certificate in question, and likewise others, that were entirely destroyed. That she was ignorant, as well of the value of such certificates, as of the mode in which the law provided for their payment. That one of her sons took with him to the Mississippi Territory the said certificate, where he kept it, until a few years ago, when he returned to her, and she shortly afterwards presented her petition for the amount of it.

From the foregoing statement it would appear that there is no obstacle to the allowance of this claim but the statute of limitation. Your committee have recently very respectfully decided against the repeal of the law barring demands like the present.

It is for the House to determine on the course they will pursue on this subject.

The facts are faithfully detailed. Your committee, however, conforming to the rule by which it has been governed in similar cases, recommend the following resolution:

*Resolved*, That the prayer of the petitioner ought not to be granted.

---

### Seven years' Half Pay.

Communicated to the House of Representatives, March 30, 1812.

Mr. Gholson, from the Committee of Claims, to whom was referred the petition of Anna Young, daughter and sole heiress of Colonel John Durkee, deceased, made the following report:

That it appears the said Durkee commanded a regiment in the army of the United States, in the revolutionary war; that he was severely wounded, and that he died in the year 1782, in the military service. That, under the resolve of Congress of the 24th of August, 1780, the widow of the said Durkee became entitled to the seven years' half pay of a colonel, to which Durkee himself would have been entitled, had he lived and served to the end of the war. That the widow of the said Durkee is dead, and the petitioner is the sole claimant.

It seems that this claim was, at an early period, demanded of the Government; but that the allowance of it was withheld in consequence of a balance of $5,150, which appears, from the account of Colonel Durkee, to be due by him to the United States. It is supposed at the Department of War that this balance, in paper emissions, was appropriated by Colonel Durkee to his own use, in July, 1777, when paper money had become much depreciated. This sum should, therefore, be reduced by a scale of depreciation applicable to that period.

The committee are of opinion that the petitioner, on account of the services of her father, is entitled to his seven years' half pay as colonel, and interest thereon, after deducting therefrom the aforesaid balance, (reduced, as it should be, by the scale of depreciation,) which appears due by Colonel Durkee in his account with the United States. The committee therefore ask leave to report a bill for the petitioner's relief.

The Committee on Pensions and Revolutionary Claims, to whom was referred the petition of William Arnold, of East Greenwich, in the State of Rhode Island, report:

That the petitioner states that he was possessed of a loan office certificate, issued from the loan office in Massachusetts, payable to Christopher Clark, or bearer, for $600, and dated the 25th October, 1777. That, on the 27th December, 1787, his house was burnt, and with it this certificate, &c. He prays that another certificate of like value may be issued to him.

From the papers submitted to the committee, it appears that the house of the petitioner was destroyed by fire, as is stated in the petition. That the said certificate had been in the possession of the petitioner. That the fact of its destruction was made known to two witnesses soon after it happened; and that notice of said destruction was given in one of the public papers of Boston, and also in the Newport Herald. These advertisements were not inserted, however, until October, 1790, nearly three years after the destruction.

In December, 1790, the petitioner notified the commissioner of loans at Boston of the fact, and deposited with him the evidence thereof. That in November, 1791, he petitioned Congress on the subject, which was referred to the Secretary of the Treasury, who made his report in April, 1792. This report was referred to a committee, who reported thereon; but the report was not further acted on.

From the above facts it appears that the petitioner has complied with the requisites of the resolve of Congress of the 10th May, 1780, in every particular, except as to the time in which notice should have been given of the destruction.

It also appears, by a letter received from the Auditor of the Treasury, that this claim was presented and registered in his office on the 29th of May, 1795, which is within the time prescribed by the act of 21st April, 1794; and that the reason why it was not recognised and settled was, that the advertisement of the destruction of the certificate was too late to entitle the claimant to relief.

From the foregoing facts, the committee feel satisfied that the claim is a just one; and they find no *legal* objection to its being allowed, except that the provision of the resolve of 1780, relative to the notice of the destruction of the certificate, has not been complied with. They do not think this objection sufficient to bar the claim. It may not be proper on slight occasions to forego the provisions of a law founded in wisdom, and thereby give precedent to sanction claims supported neither by law nor equity; but when, to obtain justice, it is necessary to do so, the committee feel not only willing, but bound to do it. They therefore recommend the adoption of the following resolution:

*Resolved*, That the prayer of the petitioner ought to be granted.

TREASURY DEPARTMENT,

*Auditor's Office, October 28, 1814.*

SIR: In answer to your letter of the 27th inst., I have the honor to state that the claim of William Arnold, for the renewal of a loan office certificate of the *nominal* value of $600, under the act of the 21st April,

1794, was presented and registered at this office on the 29th of May, 1795; and that the papers in relation thereto (believed to be the same now offered in support of his petition) remained in my possession until the 5th of March, 1814, when they were withdrawn by Mr. Potter, of the House of Representatives. The objections to the admission of this claim at the Treasury, as noted on a general statement furnished the chairman of the Committee of Claims on the 8th of March, 1802, were in the following words: "The destruction appears to have taken place on the 27th December, 1787, but was not advertised until the month of October, 1790, which was too *late* to entitle the claimant to the benefit of the act." The petition and documents are herewith returned.

I have the honor to be,

With great respect, sir,

Your obedient humble servant,

R. HARRISON.

The Hon. JOHN J. CHAPPELL, *Chairman*
of the Committee on Pensions and Revolutionary Claims.

---

JANUARY 13, 1815.

The Committee on Pensions and Revolutionary Claims, to whom was referred the petition of Farrington Barkelow, administrator to Mary Rappelya, report:

That the petitioner states that the said Mary Rappelya was possessed of two loan office certificates; that her house was consumed by fire, and with it the said certificates. He prays that they may be renewed, or some other compensation made for them.

It appears that there were issued to the said Mary Rappelya two certificates from the loan office of New Jersey, one, No. 1564, dated June 8, 1778, for $600; the other, No. 294, dated the same day, for $500; and that the said certificates are still outstanding and unpaid. It also appears that she made known the fact of the destruction of the said certificates shortly after it happened, which was in March, 1787, but did not advertise it in the papers until February, 1792, near five years afterwards, which she has sworn was occasioned by her ignorance of its necessity. She petitioned Congress for redress in the case in February, 1795, and a favorable report was made thereon, but it was not finally acted on. She died in the year 1807, and in 1811 administration of her effects was committed to the petitioner.

From the foregoing facts it appears that the claim is a just one; but it is barred by the statute of limitation, it not appearing that the claim was presented at the Treasury on or before the 1st June, 1795, which is required by law. It also appears that the requisites of the resolve of 1780 have not been complied with so far as to advertise the destruction *immediately* after it happened. The committee feel satisfied, however, that as the destruction was advertised, and as a petition was presented to Congress, (and not to the Treasury,) before the limited time had expired, that there has been a compliance with the *spirit* although not with the *letter* of the laws. They are therefore of opinion that relief ought to be granted, and report a bill for that purpose.

### FEBRUARY 24, 1816.

The Committee on Pensions and Revolutionary Claims, to whom was referred the petition of Elizabeth Hamilton, respectfully report:

That it is stated by the petitioner that her late husband, Alexander Hamilton, was, as she is advised, justly entitled to five years' full pay (as commutation of half pay during life) of a lieutenant colonel, in which capacity he served in the regular army of the United States during the revolutionary war.

That her husband never received the said pay to which he was so entitled; that if he ever relinquished his claim to said pay, of which an apprehension is expressed by the petitioner, it was from the delicate motive of divesting himself of all interest upon the subject of making provision for the disbanded officers of the revolutionary army, who served during the war; in which important business he was called on to act, as a member of Congress, in the year 1782: and that the present situation of the family of her lamented husband renders it desirable that they should receive the remuneration to which he was justly entitled from his country. This remuneration, therefore, the petitioner respectfully solicits.

The committee are not aware of any public record or document, showing the time at which Colonel Hamilton resigned his commission in the army. From the uniform tenor of various letters of distinguished officers of the revolutionary army, addressed to the honorable Richard M. Johnson, as chairman of the Committee of Claims, in the year 1810, as well as from a brevet commission, dated the 28th day of October, 1783, by which Lieutenant Colonel Alexander Hamilton was promoted to the rank of colonel by brevet, in the army of the United States; the committee entertain the opinion that Colonel Hamilton served during the war; and that he never received either half pay during life, or full pay for five years in lieu thereof, as commutation, to which he was entitled by law.

Of any relinquishment of Colonel Hamilton to the claim now asked to be satisfied, the committee possess no knowledge, except that derived from the apprehension expressed in the petition, to which they have already adverted; and from a written document, signed A. H., importing to be a statement of the temporal concerns of Colonel Hamilton, in which allusion is made to a note by him signed, addressed to the Secretary of War, relinquishing the claim in question. The committee would further remark, that should a probability exist that Colonel Hamilton may have relinquished his said claim, and notwithstanding it is barred by the statute of limitation, nevertheless, as the services have been rendered to the country, by which its happiness and prosperity have been promoted, they are of opinion that to reject the claim, under the peculiar circumstances by which it is characterized, would not comport with that honorable sense of justice and magnanimous policy which ought ever to distinguish the legislative proceedings of a virtuous and enlightened nation.

They have therefore prepared a bill, granting the relief solicited in the premises.

The Committee on Pensions and Revolutionary Claims, to whom was referred the petition of John Guthry, have had the same under consideration, and report:

That the petitioner states that he was a soldier of the Revolution, and served in the army of the United States during the greater part of the struggle for independence ; that, in consideration of his military services, he obtained two final settlement certificates, one for eighty dollars, dated 2d August, 1784, the other for one hundred and twenty-three dollars and thirty cents, dated the 3d August, 1784 ; and on these certificates he drew, on the 29th day of December, 1788, three years' interest, to the amount of thirty-six dollars and fifty-ninetieths, as will appear from the certificate of James Hopkins, commissioner of loans for Virginia, dated October 19th, 1791, (and which is made, and is to be considered, as a part of this report,) through Zachariah Johnson, who, your committee presume was authorized to receive the interest accruing on said certificates ; that afterwards he became deranged, and in a fit of insanity he destroyed the certificates, as is presumed from the testimony of Isaac McClure, David McClure, and John Guthry, Jr., accompanying the petition. Your committee further report that it appears, from the certificate of Joseph Nourse, Register, dated at the Treasury Department, January 12th, 1821, that certificate No. 78,781, dated August 3d, 1784, issued to John Guthry, for one hundred and twenty-three dollars and thirty cents, bearing interest from the 1st January, 1788, remains outstanding and unpaid ; that the petitioner states he applied at the office of the Treasury for payment of his claim, under an act of Congress which took effect on the 13th of April, 1818, but was informed that the same could not then be adjusted, inasmuch as the certificates themselves were not produced. The circumstances attending and connected with the loss of the certificates, and it appearing that certificate No. 17,781, issued in the name of John Guthry, is outstanding and unpaid, have induced your committee to report a bill authorizing the payment of said certificate.

---

### Depreciation, Commutation, and Bounty Land.

The report of the Committee to whom was referred the petition of Edmund Brooke, made December 23d, 1817.

That the petitioner claims pay, depreciation of pay, commutation, and bounty lands, for his services in the Revolution, as first lieutenant in the first regiment of Virginia artillery, on the continental establishment. He states that he was appointed to that office in February, 1781, and that he continued in service " till the siege of Yorktown, when, being extremely ill, he was compelled to ask a furlough for a few weeks." The petitioner does not state that he ever afterwards joined the army, but that he held himself in readiness to obey any call that might be made on him. The committee are of opinion, from this statement of facts, that the acts of limitation would be amply sufficient to oppose to this claim ; but that the House may possess the same knowledge of facts with which they have acted upon the petition, they have determined to report in detail. This claim has often been before Congress, and has been reported against at several different sessions. The committee, before they proceed to an examination of its original merits, cannot but express their regret that the pertinacity of claimants has, in some measure, been encouraged by the apparent success of some supposed fortunate petitioners. The committee proceed to examine the several items of claims in the order in which they are presented, and have adopted the report of the Committee on Pensions and Revolutionary Claims, to whom this petition was referred at the third session of the eleventh Congress.

*1st. Pay.* In a certificate, dated March 17, 1798, signed " Aw. Dunscomb," late assistant commissioner of army accounts, Virginia, produced, as is supposed by the petitioner and referred to in his petition, are these words: " From an examination of the books in the office of the Auditor for the State of Virginia, it appears that Colonel Duval settled the account of Edmund Brooke, as a lieutenant of artillery, on the 5th day of March, 1784."

*2d. Depreciation of Pay.* By a resolve of Congress of the 10th of April, 1780, " the line of the army, and the independent corps thereof," were promised, when the public finance would admit, that the deficiency of their pay, occasioned by depreciation, should be made good ; but this provision is not applicable to any but such as were engaged during the war, or for three years, and were then in service. The petitioner does not come within the provisions of this resolution.

*3d. Commutation.* By a resolution of Congress of March 22, 1783, " all officers then in service, and who should continue therein to the end of the war, were entitled to receive the amount of five years' full pay, instead of the half pay for life" promised by the resolution of 21st of October, 1780. The latter resolution, from its obvious import, did not make provision for any officers except those then in service, or reduced. As the petitioner was not in service, or reduced, in October, 1780, he could never have been entitled to commutation, had he continued in service to the end of the war. It has long since been settled that the war ended when the troops were discharged, on the 3d November, 1783 ; and there is not sufficient proof that he continued in the service till that time.

*4th. Bounty.* This subject belongs to the Treasury Department; had it been the sole prayer of the petition, it is believed it would not have been referred to your committee.

The committee recommend to the House the adoption of the following resolution :

*Resolved,* That the prayer of the petitioner is entirely unfounded, and ought not to be granted.

---

## Military Service in the Revolution.

Communicated to the House of Representatives on the 30th of November, 1818.

Mr. Rhea, from the Committee on Pensions and Revolutionary Claims, to whom was referred the petition of John Staples, reported :

That it appears, from the petition and accompanying documents, that the petitioner enlisted and served in the army of the United States,

23

from the 1st of January, 1777, until the 1st of August, 1780 ; that for his said services he received certain certificates, but that the amount due him was drawn (as he states) without his knowledge or consent by the captain under whom he had served ; and he now prays Congress to take his case into consideration, and grant him relief.

The case of the petitioner was, in the year of 1794, referred to the Secretary of War, who made a report thereon, that " the certificates in question were issued by an officer under the authority of the State of Maryland, they being for depreciation of pay up to the 1st of August, 1780, when the petitioner was discharged. The amount of the certificates has probably been charged to the United States. It would appear, therefore, that if Captain Brown could not be compelled to refund the certificates, and if they were issued by the officer of Maryland without proper authority, the petitioner ought to make his application to that State for redress, instead of the United States. It would be attended with great difficulties for the United States to attempt to relieve the petitioner." The committee entirely concur with the report of the Secretary, and offer the following resolution :

*Resolved,* That the petitioner have leave to withdraw his petition and documents.

---

### Officers of the Revolution.

Communicated to the House of Representatives, December 7th, 1818.

Mr. Johnson, of Kentucky, from the committee to whom was referred the petition in behalf of sundry surviving officers of the revolutionary army, reported :

That, on the 21st of October, 1780, by resolution of Congress, it was provided that the officers who should continue in service to the end of the war should be entitled to half pay during life, to commence from the time of reduction. This stipulation emanated from a previous resolution of Congress, which promised seven years' half pay to the same class of officers, excepting those who might hold any office of profit under the United States, or any of the States.

By another resolution of Congress, in January, 1781, the stipulation was so extended as to embrace the hospital department and medical staff. In the beginning of the year 1783 a memorial was presented to Congress from a committee of the officers of the army under the immediate command of General Washington, proposing a relinquishment of the half pay for life, on condition that an equivalent should be provided, either by the payment of a gross snm, or by a full compensation for a limited time. This proposition, which originated with officers of the army, grew out of a conviction that the half pay for life was regarded by their fellow-citizens as savoring too much of the spirit of a privileged order, which rendered the measure unpopular with many of the community ; and the proposition on the part of the officers to relinquish the payment for life was, and ever will be, viewed as an act of the most distinguished prtriotism, in perfect accordance with that entire devotion to the country which is so strikingly manifested in all their sufferings, sacrifices, and services.

Congress, well apprized of the prevailing objection to the allowance for life, which had been adopted only from necessity, readily embraced the occasion of removing a measure objectionable in its principle, by a commutation of five years' full pay in lieu of the half pay for life, in a resolution of March 22, 1783, which provided that such officers as were then in service, and who should continue therein to the end of the war, should be entitled to receive the amount of five years' full pay in money, or securities on interest at six per cent. per annum, as Congress should find most convenient, instead of the half pay promised for life by the resolution of October 21st, 1780; the said securities to be such as should be given to other creditors of the United States: *provided*, it should be at the option of the lines of the respective States, and not of officers individually of those lines, to refuse or accept the same. The commutation was acceded to by the officers generally in the manner pointed out, and at the reduction of the army they received commutation certificates for the amount prescribed. The memorialists state a variety of facts, and present many considerations, to prove that by the commutation great injustice has been done to the officers originally entitled to half pay for life, and their object is to induce the Government to resume the original contract of half pay for life, upon certain terms therein expressed; and the memorial concludes with a specific prayer that an act may be passed directing the accounting officers of the Treasury to adjust the claim of each surviving officer of the revolutionary army of the United States, who, by the resolves of Congress, was entitled to half pay for life, calculating the amount of the principal of the arrearages from the time of his reduction, and deducting therefrom five years' full pay, and the balance of arrearages being thus ascertained, to issue a certificate, bearing an interest of six per centum per annum, to the officer, for the amount of said balance; and the officer to be thenceforth entitled to receive half pay, in half yearly payments, for and during the term of his natural life. The committee have endeavored to investigate the subject with all the candor and attention which its merits require; and, in any view, difficulties of no ordinary magnitude presented themselves.

When contemplating the eminent services and generous sacrifices of that illustrious band, the committee could not withhold a favorable report to the full extent of the prayer of the petitioners, could they be governed alone by feeling. The resources of the nation would never repay the debt of gratitude which is due to the patriots and sages of the Revolution, whose counsels and achievements so essentially contributed to the establishment of that freedom and independence from which so many blessings flow. Were the prayer of the petitioners asked as a gratuity only, new difficulties would arise; other classes of citizens equally meritorious, and much more numerous, whose sacrifices were not less extensive, would have equal claims, and merit equal attention. The whole revolutionary struggle was marked with public sacrifices and public devotion; every class of citizens endured with cheerfulness the privations and losses to which those trying times subjected them, and in the happiness and independence of the country which followed, every member of the community found his best reward; and however desirable it may be that every sacrifice in time of great public calamity may receive a pecuniary requital, the American Revolution demonstrates its impracticability, and necessity requires that the munificence of Government should have some limitation. Well aware of this view of the subject, the claim of the memorialists is predicated upon contract and legal obligation. In the light of justice, therefore, the committee have also considered this subject; and it is with feelings of extreme regret that they find themselves compelled in duty to differ in opinion with the memorialists in the prayer of the petition.

The resolution of Congress, under which the claim for the half pay was commuted, was proposed by the officers, and the commutation voluntarily accepted by them in the manner specified. The memorialists also urge their claim upon the supposition that the commutation was not an equivalent for the original stipulation; and more than five years' full pay was then equitably due. The committee, on this point, are of opinion that a just estimate was made by the parties when the commutation was agreed upon, under all the circumstances of the case, and ought not to be revived at this day; but if it were necessary to look for relief, by reviewing the comparative amount, it will be found that the interest of five years' full pay, at six per cent. per annum, is equal to three-fifths of the whole amount of half pay forever; for example, take the advance to a captain of five years' full pay, at forty dollars per month, $2,400, the annual interest on which would make the sum of $144, at six per cent.; and the whole amount of half pay would make a sum of $240 per annum. The advance of five years' full pay will also be found equal to the present worth of half pay for more than fifteen years. The committee cannot therefore discover such a great inadequacy in the amount stipulated. The resolution of March, 1783, provided that the five years' full pay should be in money, or securities on interest at six per cent. per annum, as Congress should find most convenient: the said securities being such as should be given to the other creditors of the United States.

Congress found it most convenient to pay in securities on interest, and, for this purpose, gave certificates conformably to the stipulation; the only evidence of debt in their power, and the same as were given to other creditors of the United States; the faith of the nation was pledged for the payment of these certificates, and the pledge was subsequently redeemed by the payment of the nominal amount, with interest, in gold and silver, or equivalents, in the hands of the officer or his assignee. If the officers could not command the money in hand for these certificates, neither could they have done so at that day, for their half pay, had there been no commutation; gold and silver were not within the reach of the Government at that period. This is suggested only to show that the mode of payment alone was changed, and that the commutation was granted as a fair equivalent.

Upon the view taken by the memorialists, the committee could not see any justice in confining the prayer of the petitioners to those only who still survive. To provide for those upon the principle of justice and legal obligation, and suffer the dead to be forgotten, would be but a partial remuneration; the heirs of the deceased would have equal claims upon the Government as the officer who survives. Again: the memorialists ask a resumption of the original contract; to which the same objections may be urged as in the year 1783. If then deemed objectionable, because not in accordance with the genius of our institutions, nor congenial with the sentiments of the American people, it may be equally so at this day. Upon the most extensive view which the committee have taken of this subject, they have found difficulties still thickening; and, to answer the prayer of the petition to its extent, would, in the opinion of the committee, go to establish a principle fraught with much evil. Conscious, at the same time, of the merits and worth of these distinguished heroes, whose devotion and deeds have given such glory and such happiness to our country; conscious of their patriotism and valor, which have imposed such lasting obligations upon the grateful remembrance of the nation, the committee could not reconcile to their feelings or duty an entire rejection of the memorial; and they have looked for a combination of the principle of equity, and of gratitude, on which might be rewarded, in some little degree, the labors and sufferings of the memorialists, without involving future difficulties, in the establishment of a dangerous precedent; this principle has been founded in the depreciation of the commutation certificates, and the losses sustained by the untimely sale of these certificates. It is a well-attested fact, that most of those certificates were sold at an amount of not more than from one-fifth to one-tenth of their nominal value. Gold and silver not being in the power of the Government, the pressing and immediate wants of the holders rendered it necessary for them to dispose of their certificates at any price; and, upon this view of the subject, the committee recommend the following resolution :

*Resolved*, That each officer of the revolutionary army, who was entitled to half pay for life under the several resolves of Congress upon that subject, and afterwards, on commutation thereof, received the amount of five years' full pay in certificates or securities of the United States, shall now be paid by the United States the nominal amount of such certificate or securities, without interest, deducting therefrom one-eigthth part of the said amount.

The question of relief for the surviving officers of the Revolution was finally determined by the passage of the act of Congress of May 15th, 1828, granting to those who were entitled to half pay for life, under the several resolves upon that subject, " full pay for life."

---

FEBRUARY 3, 1825.

The select committee appointed upon the petition of George Lewis, and to whom was referred, on the 22d of December, 1824, the petition of John Crain, report thereon :

That the petitioner represents that he was the owner of a final settlement certificate, No. 80,314, dated the 13th of August, 1784, for the sum of one hundred dollars, and was issued under a resolution of Congress of the 4th July, 1783.—(Journals of Congress, vol. 4, p. 237, Way's edition.) The petitioner further states that the interest due thereon was paid upon his order in the year 1787; that, shortly thereafter, the certificate, upon being returned to him, was destroyed, by being washed in the pocket of his waistcoat, of which the petitioner made oath at the time, before a magistrate of the State of Virginia.

It appears further to the committee, by a letter of the Register of the Treasury, marked A, and to which they refer, that, on the 13th of April, 1824, the certificate was outstanding and unpaid. They also refer to a report of the Third Auditor, marked C. The committee are satisfied that the petitioner has produced the best evidence in his power to prove his ownership of the certificate and its destruction. On these points they refer to the depositions of Hannah Battson, and of the petitioner, marked B.

Being satisfied that the petitioner was the owner of the certificate, that it has been destroyed and lost, and that it is recognised at the Treasury as a claim against the Government, they are of opinion that the same ought to be paid, and, for that purpose, ask leave to report a bill.

### A.

Treasury Department,

*Register's Office, April* 13, 1824.

Sir: I have the honor to communicate the information requested by your letter of the 12th instant, relative to a final settlement certificate, which was issued by John Pierce, late commissioner for adjusting the claims for services during the revolutionary war, stated to have been lost, and for the payment of which a petition has been presented to Congress by John Crain.

Permit me to premise that this certificate was issued in favor of James Swart, and payable to him or bearer; that, as it appears from the records of the Treasury to be yet outstanding, it would, upon presentation by the holder, be entitled to payment under the act of the 7th of May, 1822; but, from the circumstance of its having been lost, it cannot be paid without a special act of Congress, as in a similar case, per act of the 7th of May, 1822, entitled " An act for the relief of John Crute."

The resolution of the old Congress, under which John Pierce issued certificates for balances of pay, &c., due the continental army, bears date the 4th of July, 1783.—(Journal of Congress, vol. 8, page 289.)

By act of the 4th August, 1790, (Laws U. S. vol. 2, page 124,) and acts supplementary thereto, the certificate issued by John Pierce, together with the interest thereon, were authorized to be funded.

The acts of the 13th April, 1818, chap. 52, and 7th May, 1822, chap. 112, provided for payment of principal and interest, upon presentation of this description of certificates at the Treasury, within two years after the passage of each act.

The amount of certificates issued by John Pierce, late commissioner, and at the present time outstanding and unpaid, exclusive of interest, is $32,942 97. The certificates issued by him bore interest from the expiration of the period for which the claim was adjusted.

I have the honor to 'return the several papers connected with Mr. Crain's petition,

And to be, with great respect, sir,

Your obedient servant,

JOSEPH NOURSE.

The act of the 7th May, 1822, provides for the payment of outstanding certificates for two years from and after the passing the act, " and from thence until the end of the next session of Congress." This act appropriated $15,000, whereof there remains unapplied $12,527 30.
The Hon. PETER LITTLE.

C.

TREASURY DEPARTMENT,

*Third Auditor's Office, December 23, 1822.*

SIR: I have the honor to state, in reference to the petition and accompanying documents of John Crain, that it appears from the records of this office, that James Swart was a light dragoon, of Lee's legion, and served to the end of the war; and that he was entitled to bounty land. It further appears that, on the settlement of his account, 25th February, 1785, by J. Dunscomb, agent for distributing the final settlement certificates for the Virginia line, that two certificates of funded debt were issued to James Swart, viz:

No. 80,314, on interest from January, 1783, for $100 00.
  80,315,  do.  Nov. 15th, 1783, for $134 15.
The papers are returned.

With great respect,
Your obedient servant,
PETER HAGNER, *Auditor.*

The Hon. WM. H. CRAWFORD,
*Secretary of the Treasury.*

B.

I hereby certify that, some time after the close of the revolutionary war, I remember my brother James Swart, brought to my father's, where I then lived, two brood mares, which he stated he had got from Mr. John Crain, in a trade for his soldier's right; it being, as understood, his final claim on the Government.

Given under my hand, this 15th day of January, 1822.
HANNAH BATTSON.

*Loudoun County, ss.*

On this day the above certificate was qualified to before me, a justice of the peace for said county.

Given under my hand, this the 15th day of January, 1822.
LEVEN LUCKETT.

Some time in the year 1784, I purchased of James Swart two final settlement certificates: one for one hundred acres of land, the other for one hundred dollars, which were given him for his services in the revolutionary war. I gave to said Swart two brood mares for the certificates aforesaid; the last-mentioned one was No. 80,314, dated the 13th of August, 1784, for the sum of one hundred dollars. It was properly assigned by said Swart to me, and in the year 1787 the interest then due was paid to Colonel Powell; or his assigns, on my order. The certificate was returned to me. I put it into the pocket of another waistcoat, and it was washed to pieces, with other papers; when I found that to be the case, I made oath before Colonel Powell, a magistrate of Loudoun county, of the loss; and he applied to the Assembly of Virginia for a duplicate of the certificate, but failed in obtaining it; at the next sitting of the Assembly, as well as I can now remember, I sent a petition by Colonel Robert Randolph, one of our county members, praying payment of the amount, or a renewal of the certificate. He failed to get either; and stated, on his return, that it was the opinion of the Virginia Assembly, that the General Government had the settlement of all such claims. From the commencement of the Federal Government, as well as I can now recollect, I have been applying through various members of Congress for redress. Mr. Richard Bland Lee, Colonel Powell, Major Lewis, and Colonel Strother, have all had the management of this business heretofore, and Mr. Moore has now the management of it, who, I hope, will bring it to a close. I see not how the plea of limitation can apply to a case that has been so constantly pressed.

JOHN CRAIN.

*Loudoun County, ss.*

On this the 15th day of January, 1822, the above statement was sworn to before me, a justice of the peace for said county.

Given under my hand.

LEVEN LUCKETT.

---

JANUARY 26, 1826.

The Committee on Revolutionary Claims, to whom was referred the petition of Mrs. Ann D. Baylor, make the following report:

That Colonel George Baylor was entitled, at the close of the revolutionary war, to a sum of money from the United States, for his pay and emoluments. The Treasury Board, instituted for the purpose of settling those claims and demands, liquidated the pay account of said Colonel Baylor, and reported the sum of $354 17-90ths to be due to him for his *pay*, without noticing his subsistence or emoluments. In conformity with this settlement, the balance, so estimated to be due him, was deposited in the hands of John Hopkins, Esq., then commissioner of loans, on the part of the United States, for the State of Virginia; and it appears, from the testimony of said Hopkins, that Colonel Baylor never did receive or demand the funds so allotted him, and placed in the hands of said commissioner of loans, and, by consequence, it was returned to the Treasury of the United States. Apprehending that the debt might have been discharged through some other organ of the Government, and with the view to disencumber the subject of all uncertainty, the committee, through its chairman, communicated the petition and accompanying documents to the Secretary of the Treasury, with a request that he would impart all the information, within his Department, that might guide the committee to a rightful conclusion. His reply covered a letter from the Register of the Treasury, asserting that the debt due to Colonel Baylor is still outstanding and unpaid ; adding thereto very cogent reasons in favor of a provision by law for its payment.

Colonel George Baylor is since dead, leaving John Walker Baylor his only son and heir, as appears by the testimony of his mother. The said John Walker intermarried with the petitioner, and has since departed this life, leaving several infant children. The committee recommend a settlement of the account upon principles of equity and justice, and payment of whatever may be due to Mrs. A. D. Baylor, for the use of her infant children, now the heirs at law of Colonel George Baylor, and to this end report a bill.

TREASURY DEPARTMENT,

*Register's Office, January 20, 1826.*

SIR : I had the honor of your instructions, predicated on the letter of the chairman of the Committee of the House of Representatives of the United States on Revolutionary Claims, to the Treasury Department, with the petition and accompanying documents of Ann D. Baylor, relict of Colonel George Baylor, of the revolutionary army. The object of the committee, by their inquiry, being to ascertain from the records of the Treasury any evidence of the claim being outstanding and unpaid ; as also, whether any payments have been made at the Treasury, to persons named in a certain certificate list of moneys due and unpaid to officers and soldiers of the Virginia line on continental establishment, by John Hopkins, late commissioner of loans in the State of Virginia; which list was returned to the Treasury ; also, such other information as may more clearly develop the justness of the claim.

In compliance therewith I have the honor to state and certify that the sums exhibited in said list now remain outstanding and unpaid, to the amount of sixteen hundred and ninety-three dollars and seventy-ninetieths. Their non-payment by John Hopkins arose altogether from the parties not calling upon him for payment, as appears from his certificate, with the document.

The following reasons are submitted in favor of admitting this claim of Ann D. Baylor and the other persons named in the list.

1st. That they never received the drafts of the Board of Treasury on the receivers of taxes, which had been specifically issued in their favor.

2d. That those drafts were returned to the late Board of Treasury, who are debited with them in the books of the Treasury, thereby exonerating the persons in whose names they had been issued.

3d. That, on a careful examination of the Treasury records, it does not appear that Ann D. Baylor, or any of the persons named in the list, have received payment for the amount of their claims, but that they remain outstanding and unpaid.

I have the honor to be, sir,

With great respect,

Your obedient servant,

JOSEPH NOURSE, *Register.*

Hon. RICHARD RUSH, *Secretary of the Treasury.*

24

JANUARY 11, 1828.

The Committee on Revolutionary Claims, to which was referred the petition of Archibald Bard and John Findlay, executors of the last will and testament of Doctor Robert Johnston, deceased, has had the same under consideration, and begs leave to report:

The petitioners state that they are the executors of the last will and testament of the late Dr. Robert Johnston, of Franklin county, in Pennsylvania, who died some time in the month of November, 1808. That the said Robert Johnston, when on his death-bed, mentioned to the petitioners that he had moneys coming to him from some fund; but, as he could not articulate distinctly, he referred them to one of his brothers for further information; who, when called on, was not able to give any information about the business. That, some time in the month of February, 1825, the petitioners found among the papers of the said Dr. Johnston, in his own handwriting, the following entry, made in a small memorandum book, viz:

"Lost or stolen, 3 loan office certificates of $400 each, in the name of Doctor Isaac Foster, Nos. 6,331, 6,339, 6,340."

That the said certificates yet remain unpaid, as appears from the books of the Treasury Department. The petitioners pray that a law may be passed authorizing them to receive payment for said certificates, with the interest due thereon.

The memorandum book above mentioned accompanies the petition, and the entry of the loss of the certificates, and the description of them, is proved by the affidavit of Matthew St. Clair Clarke, Esq., to be in the proper handwriting of the said Dr. Robert Johnston. Mr. Clarke also swears to the good character of said Dr. Johnston for honesty and fair dealing; and that the petitioners themselves are men of irreproachable character, as far as regards integrity and moral honesty.

It also appears, from a certificate of the Register of the Treasury, of the 5th January, 1827, that, on the 26th September, 1778, there were issued to Isaac Foster fourteen loan office certificates, from No. 6,330 to No. 6,343, inclusive; and that all the said certificates have been paid, except the numbers 6,331, 6,339, 6,340, which appear to be still outstanding and unpaid. The certificates mentioned in the Register's certificate, and in the memorandum book above mentioned, your committee has no doubt are the same, inasmuch as they correspond in number and amount.

A resolution of Congress of the 10th May, 1780, which provides for the renewal of loan office certificates destroyed through accident, requires "that all certificates so destroyed be advertised immediately in the newspapers of the State where the accident happened; and if they have been taken out of a loan office of a different State, in the newspapers of such State also; and in every case where no newspapers are printed in a State, then, in one or more of those which circulate most generally therein: which advertisements shall be continued six weeks, and shall contain the numbers, dates, sums, and names, in which the certificates were taken out, and the time when, the place where, and the means by which, they were destroyed."

By the 2d section of the act of 21st April, 1794, the renewal of loan office certificates destroyed before the 4th March, 1789, was prohibited, unless the destruction of the same was advertised according to the directions of the resolution of Congress of the 10th May, 1780, or before that time was notified to the office from whence the same was issued; and it was provided that no claims for the renewal of loan office certificates destroyed on or after the 4th March, 1789, nor of final settlement certificates destroyed at any time, should be allowed, unless the destruction of the same was so far made public as to be made known to at least two credible witnesses soon after it happened, and shall have been advertised for at least six weeks, in some one of the newspapers published, &c. The 3d section limited the time in which application for the renewal of lost certificates might be made, to the 1st day of June, 1795.

There is no time mentioned in the memorandum made in the book, as to the loss of the certificates, when they were lost, nor is the memorandum itself dated; but, by reference to other entries which appear to have been made in said book about the same time, and which are evidently in the same handwriting, it will be found that memorandums of various descriptions were made in the years 1783, 1785, and 1786, from which it may be fairly inferred that the memorandum in question must have been made in some one of those years.

No evidence has been exhibited to show that the certificates were advertised by the decedent in his lifetime, according to the resolution and act of Congress. But the committee is of opinion that the entry of the loss of the certificates in the memorandum book of the deceased, having been proved to have been made in the handwriting of the deceased Dr. Robert Johnston, the numbers, sums, and name of the drawee, being mentioned in the memorandum made, and corresponding, in every particular, with those certified by the Register of the Treasury to be outstanding and unpaid, and the good character as well of the deceased as of his executors, the present claimants, as proved by the witness, Mr. Clarke, are circumstances so strong as to warrant the conclusion that the deceased Dr. Robert Johnston had been, in his lifetime, the owner of said certificates, and honestly and justly entitled to their value in specie.

Your committee would add that, in their opinion, the case acquires considerable strength from the circumstance that, from the 26th of September, 1778, up to the present time, the said certificates have never been presented at the Treasury of the United States for payment, or at any of the Departments for liquidation and settlement; from all which it is fair to presume that the said certificates have been lost or destroyed.

Your committee is of opinion that the statute of limitations ought not to be permitted to operate as a bar in any case, as between the Government and individuals, where the claim of the latter is supported by such evidence as satisfies the mind that it is founded in justice and equity. The committee is of opinion that the petitioners are entitled to relief, and report a bill.

The Committee on Revolutionary Claims, to which was referred the petition of Alexander Garden, report:

The petitioner states that, at the conclusion of the revolutionary war, he was perfectly independent in his circumstances, and did not apply for the commutation granted by Congress, in lieu of half pay to the officers. That unfortunate occurrences compel him, at this late hour, to solicit relief; that he served the country with zeal and fidelity; and, although it was not his good fortune to gain distinction, yet he obtained the favor of his brother officers, particularly Colonel Laurens, under whom he served as a volunteer, and General Greene, who, on the first vacancy in his military family, appointed him his aid-de-camp. Although the petitioner has not stated the rank he held in the line of the army, the evidence submitted with the petition shows, most satisfactorily, that he served as lieutenant in Lee's legion, and, shortly after the evacuation of Charleston, received the appointment of aid-de-camp from General Greene, in which capacity he served until the close of the war.

The committee think the petitioner is entitled to relief, and to that end report a bill.

---

The Committee on Revolutionary Claims, to which was referred the petition of Samuel Ward, has had the same, with the accompanying documents, under consideration, and submits the following report:

The petitioner represents that he, together with his brothers, John and Richard Ward, trading, in New York, under the firm of Samuel Ward & Brothers, and in Providence, Rhode Island, under the firm of John Ward & Co., purchased in Providence, about the month of June, 1788, of Abraham Whipple, Esquire, a final settlement certificate for one thousand and forty-seven dollars and fifty-two-ninetieths of a dollar, No. 281, dated October 23, 1786, issued by Benjamin Walker to Abraham Whipple, Esquire, and payable to bearer, with interest from the 23d July, 1780; that the said certificate was enclosed in a letter by John Ward & Co. addressed to Samuel Ward & Brothers, and put into the post office in Providence, but was never received by those to whom it was directed, whereby the said certificate was then, and has always been, lost to the petitioner and his said brothers; that, after the loss of the said certificate, notice was given thereof, and application made for its renewal; that John Ward died on the 18th September, 1823, and Richard Ward some time in 1807. The petitioner prays for a renewal of the certificate in his favor.

Accompanying the petition is the affidavit of John Ward, who swears that the certificate described in the petition was enclosed by him in a letter, and put into the post office at Providence, addressed to Samuel Ward & Brothers, his copartners in trade in New York, as a remittance, and that the letter with the enclosure was never received; that, as soon as he learned the certificate was not received, he advertised the loss o it in the Providence and New York papers, and had advertisements put up in every loan office in the United States; that, after the lapse of some time, he applied to Benjamin Bourne, Esquire, member of Congress from the State of Rhode Island, to assist him in obtaining a renewal of the certificate, who advised the deponent that it would be necessary to wait the operation of the act of limitation, and that, if the certificate was then outstanding, there could be no objection to its renewal; that, after the expiration of the time limited by the act for the renewal of certificates, he applied by letter to the Secretary of the Treasury for the renewal of the certificate in question, and was answered by the Comptroller that all such claims were barred in consequence of the limitation contained in the act of 21st April, 1794.

A newspaper, entitled "The Providence Gazette and Country Journal," of the 19th July, 1794, is exhibited with the petitioner's papers, containing the following notice:

### "FINAL SETTLEMENT NOTE LOST.

" Pursuant to an act of Congress, notice is hereby given, that, in June, 1788, a final settlement note, for one thousand and forty-seven dollars and fifty-two-ninetieths, was sent by John Ward & Co. to the post office in Providence, in a letter directed to Samuel Ward & Brothers, of New York, but miscarried, and has not been since found. The note (No. 281) was issued by Benjamin Walker to Abraham Whipple, dated October 23, 1786, and drew interest from July 23, 1780. Any person possessing information of the above is desired to communicate it to John Ward, at Providence, or to Samuel or Richard Ward, at New York.

" *Providence, June 13, 1794.*"

The affidavit of John Howland, taken on the 7th of November, 1823, proves that the above advertisement was continued to be published in the Providence Gazette and Country Journal, published by John Carter, in Providence, during the year 1794, from the 14th June until the 19th of July, in that year.

It appears from a certificate of Mr. Nourse, Register of the Treasury, dated 30th December, 1817, that the claim of Samuel Ward was presented at the Treasury by himself and brothers, under the act of 21st of April, 1794, but rejected for the want of evidence; and from the same paper it also appears that the certificate of Benjamin Walker to Abraham Whipple, No. 281, dated October 23, 1786, for $1,047\frac{52}{90}$ was upon the list of outstanding certificates unpaid at that time. And by another certificate, from the same officer, dated the 10th March, 1818, it appears that the said certificate is not subject to any depreciation, but was issued for the amount in specie value.

The resolution of Congress of the 10th May, 1780, requires that, in order that loan office certificates destroyed through accident may be renewed, all certificates so destroyed must be advertised immediately in the newspapers of the State where the accident happened. And the act of Congress of the 21st April, 1794, prohibits the renewal of certificates destroyed before the 4th March, 1789, unless the destruction of the same was advertised according to the resolution of Congress of the 10th May, 1780, or before that time was notified to the office from which the same issued; and provides, further, that no claims shall be allowed for the renewal of loan office certificates destroyed on or after the 4th day of March, 1789, nor of final settlement certificates destroyed at any time, unless the destruction of the same was so far made public as to be known to at least two credible witnesses soon after it happened, and shall have been advertised for at least six weeks in some one of the newspapers of the State in which the destruction happened, &c.; the advertisement expressing, with as much precision as possible, the number, date, and amount, of the certificate alleged to have been destroyed, and the name of the person to whom the same was issued, together with the time when, the place where, and the means by which, the same was destroyed. By the 3d section, the time for the renewal of such destroyed certificates is limited to the 1st day of June, 1795.

The foregoing is a summary of the petitioner's case, and it appears to your committee that the only questions for the determination of Congress are—

1st. Were Samuel Ward & Brothers possessed, in their own right, of the certificate in question, and, if so, was the same lost or destroyed through accident?

2d. Does the said certificate still remain upon the list of certificates outstanding and unpaid at the Treasury Department?

The committee is of opinion that, if the preceding questions must, from the facts of the case, be answered in the affirmative, the claimant ought to be paid the principal sum for which the certificate issued, although he has not complied with all the requisitions of the resolution of Congress of 10th May, 1780, and of the act of Congress of the 21st April, 1794. If he had complied with the terms of the resolution and act aforesaid, he could have obtained relief by an application to the proper Department, without a resort to Congress. The very reason why he applies to Congress is because he has been unable to satisfy the proper accounting officer that he had fully complied with all things required by law to enable him to procure a renewal of his certificate; and because the limitation contained in the act of 21st April, 1794, interposes a bar to such renewal. It would, in the opinion of your committee, be as dishonest in the Government of the United States to shield itself against the payment of a just debt under the statute of limitations, as it would for an individual to do so. The committee is not disposed to adopt the principle of the statute of limitations in any case where the claim is clearly shown to be founded in equity and justice, although the claim may have been of long standing, and the statute would interpose a bar to its payment or recovery.

In the case now under consideration, the certificate in question is alleged, and the allegation is sworn to by John Ward, one of the partners, to have been lost so long ago as the month of June, 1788, and, from that time to the present, it does not appear that the certificate was ever found, or that it was ever presented at the proper Department for liquidation and settlement, or that payment was ever demanded for it at the Treasury of the United States, by any individual other than the petitioner and his brothers, whilst the brothers were living, and the petitioner himself, since the death of his brothers. It does appear that application was made by the claimant and his brothers to the Comptroller of the Treasury, under the act of 21st April, 1794, for a renewal of the certificate, but without success, under an apprehension, on the part of the officer, of a deficiency of proof.

It is proved that the certificate was advertised in the months of June and July, 1794, by the then claimants, in a newspaper printed and published at Providence, Rhode Island, for six weeks successively; and it appears from the advertisement that a certificate, the description of which in the advertisement, as to number, date, amount, and names of the persons by and to whom issued, corresponds exactly with one now on the list of certificates in the Treasury Department, which is outstanding and unpaid. It would seem to your committee that the certificate in question must have been in the possession of the claimants, or they would not have had it in their power to have given so accurate a description of it as to make it correspond in every particular with that on the Treasury books.

The committee is of opinion that Samuel Ward & Brothers did possess the certificate in question in their own right, and that there is sufficient proof that the said certificate was lost or destroyed through accident; the lapse of time itself furnishes a strong presumption of the fact.

The certificates or letters of the Register of the Treasury admit that the certificate never was paid. The committee therefore think the petitioner is entitled to relief, and report a bill.

------

## FEBRUARY 11, 1828.

The committee to whom was referred the memorial in behalf of those of the surviving officers and soldiers of the army of the Revolution who continued in service until the close of the war, report :

That your committee have carefully examined the memorial, with the documents to which reference has therein been made. From these, the following facts have been selected, because they, in a more particular manner, are the grounds on which the petitioners rest their claim, both in behalf of themselves and of the surviving non-commissioned officers and soldiers who enlisted for the war, and continued in the service until the end of it. On the 15th of May, 1778, it was resolved by the Continental Congress, "that all military officers commissioned by Congress, who now are, or hereafter may be, in the service of the United States, and shall continue therein during the war, shall, after the conclusion thereof, be entitled to receive, annually, for seven years, if they live so long, the one-half of their present pay." And it was resolved at the same time, "that the non-commissioned officers and soldiers who had enlisted, or should enlist, for during the war, and shall continue to the end, shall then be entitled to receive a reward of eighty dollars." By the resolves of the 3d and 21st of October, 1780, and of the 17th of January, 1781, it was provided that the officers who should be reduced on the reform of the army, under the above resolve of the 3d of October, should receive half pay, from the time of their reduction, during life ; and that those of the line of the army, and the independent corps thereof, and of the hospital department and medical staff, who should continue in service until the end of the war, should receive the like half pay for the same period : provided, however, that the director of the hospital should receive the half pay of a lieutenant colonel, and that none of the other medical staff should receive more than the half pay of a captain.

At the definitive treaty of peace, signed on the 3d of September, 1783, such of those officers as had survived the war, and continued in the service until that time, became severally and individually vested with a complete right to the reward of half pay for the residue of their lives ; and each of such non-commissioned officers and soldiers who had so survived and continued, to a reward of eighty dollars. These promises were made, in consideration of such services to be performed. Those services were faithfully and successfully performed, and under every kind of difficulty, privation, and suffering. The reward was gallantly won at the point of the sword. It was the price of our independence, purchased with blood, and sanctioned by public faith. These solemn promises having been made on adequate considerations, it remains only for your committee to examine into the manner in which they have been performed.

*First.* In regard to the non-commissioned officers and soldiers, it appears that, after they had been discharged, and had gone to their respective homes, there was sent to each one of them, by regimental agents, a certificate that eighty dollars were due to him, and that this sum was payable to him or bearer, with interest, at six per cent. per annum, from the 4th of November, 1783. These certificates, as it was evidently intended from their transferable quality, were in general parted with at the market value, which was from one-fifth to one-tenth part of the nominal amount ; and were afterwards redeemed, under the funding system of the United States, in the hands of the ultimate holders. Owing to the low ebb of the public credit, this class of the army, lost their promised and expected extra reward, as much as if it had been refused or denied to them. Your committee, therefore, most respectfully submit, whether there ought not to be given to these aged survivors an indemnity for this loss : for, although the account was settled and closed with them, yet the condition of the nation then, and at this time, as well as the principles of equity, seem to call for opening it again, with regard to these men, and making to them some additional compensation.

*Second.* In regard to commissioned officers, Congress, by a resolve of the 22d of March, 1783, offered to those then in the service, as a substitute for this stipulated half pay, the amount of five years' full pay, in *money* or *securities*, bearing an interest of six per cent. per annum, at the option of Congress. These securities were to be such as should be given to the other creditors of the United States. In the same resolve there were offered to the officers entitled, who had retired from the service on the reform of the army, as such, substitute certificates to the like amount. To these offers were annexed two express conditions, viz : first, that they should be accepted or refused by lines and corps, and not individually ; and, second, that such acceptance or refusal should be signified to Congress by the commander-in-chief, as to the army under his immediate command, within two months ; and by the commanding officer of the southern army, as to those under his command, within six months from the date of the above resolve of 22d of March, 1783. At the time these offers were made, it is evident, from all the calculations on the probabilities of human life, that seven years' full pay, in advance, would have been somewhat less than an equivalent to the half pay for life, to the younger class of officers, who naturally are the present memorialists. And your committee are compelled to say that they have discovered no reason why the Government should have denied an individual right of refusing a disadvantageous offer, when the right was individual, and considering the Government under the obligation of an express solemn contract. Your committee do not perceive why it might not as well have annulled the original right, as to have enforced the memorialists to abide by the vote of others, who were interested, to put the value of the lives of all upon one equal footing. If, however, it should be considered by the House that an assent given in the manner prescribed by the resolve is binding upon each individual, then your committee beg leave further to observe that such assent, which is to work so much injury and injustice, ought to appear to have been given and signified strictly according to the conditions of the offer. In examining this part of the subject, your committee do not find any signification to Congress of any acceptance, other than a notice in the journals of a report made by the Secretary of War, on the 31st of October, 1783, and long after the officers had dispersed, that certain lines, from New Hampshire to Virginia, inclusive, had agreed to accept. This report itself is not to be found, but certain it is that no signification was made to Congress, either by the commander-in-chief, or the commanding officer of the southern army, or within the times prescribed in the offer; neither was there ever any resolve of Congress, specifying such assent, or declaring their option, whether to pay in money the amount offered, or to give securities for the same, on interest. If the offer had been complied with, according to its sense, your committee are of opinion that the loss of two years' full pay would have been submitted to, as a new sacrifice, with that patience and disinterestedness which were the distinguishing characteristics of an American officer. But, on a careful examination of this matter, your committee have been forced to the conclusion that the offer was not so complied with; which conclusion results from the following considerations, which are most respectfully submitted to the House: From the manner of calculating life annuities, which is by estimating, on the one hand, the purchase-money with compound interest, and, on the other, the probable duration of the life; from the pressing pecuniary necessities of the officers, and their want of capital to set up, with advantage, in some of the profitable pursuits of civil life, and from the absence of any specification in the resolve as to time, it is manifest that it was as well the common understanding of the parties, as the legal conclusion, that the offer was to be complied with in advance, or in anticipation of the growing annuities. After the peace, and after the officers had dispersed, a certificate was sent to each individual, indiscriminately, whether he had retired on the reform of the army, or had continued in the service, that an amount equal to five years' full pay was due to him, and that such amount, with interest, was payable to him or bearer. The certificates had no funds whereon to rest, and their market value was not equal to one year's pay; and it appears to your committee too much to say that the delivery of this almost valueless paper was a payment in money, according to the sense of the offer, or that these certificates were the securities intended thereby, either ac-

25

cording to the common understanding of the term, or the distinction expressly made in the resolve itself, between securities and certificates. And these certificates of the paymaster general, or of the commissioners for settling army accounts, were not securities to any creditor of the United States, until registered or funded, more than the other floating certificates of the quartermaster general, or the commissary general, which were issued and made payable, with interest, under express resolves of Congress, during the period of the war. Under these considerations, your committee, in the choice of the alternative, are obliged to say that, in their opinion, the delivery of these certificates, as well on general principles as on those which govern in courts of law or equity, did not annul the right to half pay, or exonerate the Government from the obligations of the original contract in this regard.

These certificates, about the 1st of January, 1791, were received in subscription by the Government, under the funding system of the United States, at a discount of about twenty per cent. But this transaction, in the opinion of your committee, does not vary the case, inasmuch as the payment was not made until the arrears on the growing annuities amounted to nearly an equal amount, which was altogether too late to be in compliance with the offer of a sum, in advance, for the half pay for life.

Under these views of the whole case, your committee are of opinion, according to the principles contained in the reports made to the House heretofore on this subject, which are hereunto annexed, that the memorialists are severally entitled to their half pay in future, and to an amount for arrears, under a liability to be charged with the nominal amount of the certificates delivered to them, respectively; but inasmuch as, by the protracted lives of these memorialists, there would now be an arrear of forty-four years, and as application for payment was not made until the year 1810, your committee have reason to believe that it would be satisfactory to the petitioners, and perhaps more consonant to the feelings of the House, not to carry back such accounts beyond that period; leaving them to be balanced, for all antecedent time, by the certificates which had been delivered. Your committee further beg leave to report, as their opinion, that it would be just to make a suitable annual allowance to the widow of each officer who, if living, would be entitled to the benefit of this act.

If, however, the House shall consider that the original right has been compromised, then there is another view of the subject which has forcibly pressed itself upon your committee, and is now respectfully presented to the House, namely : whether it is not due to national justice and honor, under a review of all the peculiar hardships attending the enforcement of this compromise, and the manner of executing it, on the part of the Government, that it it should now make good, in a degree at least, from what is absolutely gained to these aged memorialists, the part they actually lost thereby of that recompense of reward, the expectation of which had softened their hardships, lessened their privations, and animated their exertions in bringing the doubtful conflict to a successful issue.

Great nations are always just ; but, among private citizens, it would be deemed the height of dishonor and ingratitude to withhold, under the plea of a compromise, from an aged servant, an unpaid balance for hard and dangerous services, by which the very existence of the debtor had

been preserved from the violent assaults of his enemies, and the founda-
tions of his future fortunes laid and established.

To attain these ends, your committee have prepared a bill, with separate and different clauses to meet each particular object, which they beg
leave to report to the House, together with an estimate of the appropriation which may be necessary to carry each one into effect.

All which is respectfully submitted.

*Estimate of additional annual expenditure made by the provisions of the
bill to provide for surviving revolutionary officers, &c.*

If there be, as by the report of the Senate it appears, 230 officers now
alive, who served to the end of the war, under the resolution of Congress
dated October 20th, 1780, then it appears :

| | |
|---|---:|
| That the annual amount of the half pay of this number viz : 230, at an average of $15 per month, or $180 per annum, is | $41,400 00 |
| But it is believed that 60 of these officers are now on the pension roll, at $20 per month, or $240 per annum, amounting to the yearly sum of | 14,400 00 |
| If, therefore, this amount be deducted from the amount to be paid to the whole number of surviving officers, the additional per annum appropriation for these annuities will be | 37,000 00 |
| The number of widows now alive is probably 188. Their annuity, at one-third of the half pay, at the same average, will be $60 per annum, and for the whole 188 will be, per annum, | 11,280 00 |

At the close of the revolutionary war, the number of
commissioned officers, exclusive of foreigners, was 2,480.
Of these, it appears, 230 are now alive. At the close of the
same war, the number of non-commissioned officers, musicians, and privates, was 13,476. Of these there is, by the
same ratio of decrement, now alive, 1,180. It is found
that, of this description of the army, somewhat more than
two-thirds are on the pension roll. It is then probable
that, of this 1,180, not more than 394 remain unpensioned.

| | |
|---|---:|
| Annuities of $8 per month, or $96 per year, to each of these 394, will amount to | 37,824 00 |
| If the amount of arrears of half pay to each of the 230 be carried back to 1810, and no interest be allowed, it will amount to | 745,200 00 |
| Deduct from this amount the sum already received by 60 officers, on the pension roll, at $240 per annum, for 8 years, viz : | 119,200 00 |
| Then this sum | 626,000 00 |

In five per cent. stocks, will be the whole amount to be
provided.

| | |
|---|---:|
| The additional yearly expenditure will be— For annuities for officers, | 37,000 00 |

| | |
|---|---|
| For widows, - - - - - - | $11,280 00 |
| For soldiers who continued in service to the end of the war, - - - - - - - | 37,824 00 |
| For interest on $626,000, five per cent. stocks, - - | 31,300 00 |
| | $117,404 00 |

JANUARY 3, 1826.

The committee to whom were referred the memorials of the surviving officers of the army of the Revolution, report :

That delegates, in behalf of the surviving officers of the army of the Revolution, from the respective States of Rhode Island, New York, New Jersey, Pennsylvania, and South Carolina, convened at the city of Philadelphia, and agreed to present a respectful memorial once more to Congress, in hopes of obtaining from the nation that reward for their services and sacrifices which, in their opinion, is due, and which has been withheld for a period that is long and unreasonable, and until they have become far advanced in their old age, the youngest among them being within a year or two of seventy.

The memorialists refer to the general depreciation of the currency in which they received their pay, the paper of which being ultimately redeemed at one hundred for one. The certificates, also, of the commutation of the half pay for life, for five years' full pay, owing to no provision being made for the payment of interest or principal, soon depreciated to eight for one ; and even when the arrears of interest were funded, the certificates bore an interest only of three per cent., absorbing, thereby, at once, one-half their value.; and the payment of one-third of the principal, besides, was deferred for ten years, without interest.

The memorialists, after referring to the acts of Congress containing the stipulations concerning their pay, delicately decline to suggest any mode for the settlement of their demands, but leave the whole matter to the liberality and justice of Congress; impressed, however, with a belief that the general sentiments of their fellow-citizens would gladly approve of a generous proceeding, on the part of the Government, in favor of their stipulated reward.

In contrasting the darkness of the times in which the memorialists successfully fought the battles of their country with its present secure and eminently happy condition, all must feel friendly disposed to give to the claimants a patient hearing, and to be willing to decide on their case upon the fairest principles of equity.

The committee respectfully submit, in the first instance, whether the claims of the officers are not sustainable, on the footing of right, and due by the solemnity of a contract ; and, with this design, they will, in this place, bring into view the resolutions of Congress on the subject.

By a resolve of Congress of the 15th May, 1778, it is provided that all military officers who then were, or should thereafter be, in the service of the United States, and who should continue in the service during the war, and not hold any office of profit under the United States, or any of them, should, after the conclusion of the war, be entitled to receive, annually, for the term of seven years, if they should live so long, one-half of the then pay of such officers.

By a resolve of Congress of the 11th of August, 1779, it was provided that the half pay given by the aforesaid resolution of the 15th of May, 1778, should be extended to continue for life.

And by a resolution of the 21st of October, 1780, it was provided that the officers who should continue in service to the end of the war should be entitled to half pay during life, to commence from the time of their reduction.

By virtue of these resolves, a solemn contract between the Government and the officers was made ; it originated and was consummated by the free and unbiased will of the parties, without surprise or compulsion on either side. It has been most gallantly performed by the officers, and after a bloody conflict of eight years ; and when the liberties and independence of their country were secured, following the example of the celebrated Roman, they returned with cheerfulness to their private citizenship.

It seems to the committee that the performance of a contract, on such an occasion, and especially one which has produced such boundless consequences, ought to be observed, on the part of the Government, with the most profound sanctity ; and that nothing but the free expression of the will of both parties, unaffected by necessitous circumstances, ought to be allowed to abrogate or rescind it. But, as it appears to the committee, it is manifest that the resolve of the 22d of March, 1783, which commuted the half pay for life for five years' full pay, grew out of the impoverished state of the Treasury ; for, had the finances of the country been in a good condition, it is inconceivable that Congress would have proposed a change so disadvantageous to the officers, to whom the country, independent of the discharge of its contract with them, owed such a large debt of gratitude. And, on the other hand, it cannot be believed that the officers would have given any assent to the commutation, either by lines or corps, or individually, if the most urgent necessity had not deprived them of any other alternative.

The acceptance, too, by lines and corps, deprived many individual officers of the right of choice, and placed the young and the aged on terms disproportionate with the original stipulation.

The subsequent acceptance of the commutation certificates ought not to be considered as altogether impairing the rights of the officers, as they were then entirely in the power of the Government, and could do nothing which presented better prospects for themselves. The whole transactions, as it appears to the committee, were of a similar character, and were indisputably governed by the inability of the Government and the immediate wants of the officers ; and as severe as the departure from the original contract must have appeared to the officers at the time, they did not then foresee the extent of their misfortunes ; for, as no fund was pledged for the payment of the principal or interest of the commutation certificates, instead of receiving good money, in punctual payments, as expected, the credit of the country became so low that nothing of the interest was paid, and the certificates rapidly decreased in value, while the necessities of the officers continued to increase. They had suddenly been transferred from the habits of war to civil society, and could not successfully engage all at once in the ordinary pursuits of life ; and it is as notorious as it was unavoidable, that most of the officers were com- pelled to part with their certificates at the lowest stage of depreciation of eight for one ; and, in this manner, without incurring any blame on themselves, the half pay for life was reduced to a little more than half pay for a single year. From hence it plainly appears that the conside- ration to be performed, on the part of the Government, failed, in a certain degree, and totally deprived the officers of the chance of deriving any benefit from the future credit of the country.

The reward for life arose from the natural effusion of justice which the times indicated ; but, in consequence of these unhappy occurrences, it has disappeared, and nothing has been preserved for the officers to enjoy but a consciousness of their own merits and the consequent unex- ampled prosperity of their country.

The performance of contracts, morally or politically speaking, is equally sacred ; and when the power of decision resides exclusively in the bosom of one of the parties, it should be exceedingly cautious that justice is done to the other. Let it be imagined that the claim of the officers of the army of the Revolution could be submitted to the people or to a court and jury possessing legal and equitable jurisdiction, the committee verily believe that their demand, in some shape, could not be resisted.

If even an individual, in the midst of his misfortunes, should, by a fair understanding, disengage himself from his creditors without discharg- ing the entire debts, it could not be applauded as any remarkable instance of benevolence or honesty if he should afterwards pay the remainder to relieve the sufferings of the aged and meritorious, as soon as affluence and good fortune had rendered his own condition flourishing beyond ex- ample.

Although the case between the Government and the officers of the continental army resembles the above in some respects, yet, in other essential particulars, it is a much stronger case, as the claims of the officers are founded on a contract, which, in the opinion of the commit- tee, under all the circumstances, has not been fairly rescinded, and, if it has, there cannot possibly exist a doubt that the commutation contract has not been fulfilled : for, if the officers had been able to have held their certificates to the period in which they were funded, they would not have received their interest according to their contract ; and, besides, the arrears of the interest were then funded at three 'per cent., which was a clear infringement of the contract, as the arrears ought to have been paid before, instead of being reduced to one-half of their value. The payment, likewise, of the one-third of the principal, was deferred for ten years without interest, which is again a departure from the con- tract. But the weighty and most important circumstance of all, that the inability of the Government to perform its contract inevitably obliged the officers to part with their certificates at the reduced prices of eight for one, presents an argument in equity sufficiently powerful to satisfy Congress that a claim of some description, in favor of the officers, does in good faith exist.

The results of the Revolution, which have transcended anticipation, are now every where seen and admired. They invited our national guest to revisit each State in the Union, to witness, in person, the unrivalled prosperity and political glory which have been achieved by the war of the Revolution. Among the vicissitudes of the life of this illustrious and extraordinary man, it would be a felicitous incident if his reappearance here, after the lapse of near half a century, should have so excited the feelings of the nation, and occasioned such a recurrence to the trying times of the Revolution, as to be serviceable to his companions in arms in the evening of their days.

Under all the circumstances of this highly interesting case, it appears to the committee that one of two modes ought to be adopted for the final settlement of the claim of the memorialists, as reasonable, and becoming the faith and dignity of the nation. *First*, by the terms proposed by a former memorial, that is to say, of deducting from the arrears of the half pay, computed from the cessation of hostilities to the present time, the full nominal amount of the commutation certificates, and paying the surviving officers the balance, and henceforward, during the remainder of their lives, paying to them the half pay stipulated by the resolve of 1780.

Or, *secondly*, that Congress should proceed upon the equitable circumstances of the case, and pay such a specific sum rateably among the officers, according to their rank and the resolves of Congress, as may appear reasonable and just.

The first has, in substance, been twice reported to the House of Representatives, and not sustained. The committee, therefore, paying a due respect to these decisions, have unanimously agreed to recommend the latter mode, and to confine its provisions to the comforts of the living, and make its acceptance a final discharge of all claims on the part of the surviving officers of the army of the Revolution; and, in conformity with these views on the subject, the committee have herewith reported a bill appropriating the sum of —— dollars for the purposes aforesaid. The committee have also annexed to this report the report of 1810, and the report of 1819, and several extracts of letters from General Washington.

It is but a rational conclusion, that it is the last time that the military officers of the Revolution, in a body, will ask of Congress the favor to consume any of its time concerning them; if their prayer be granted, they will have no inducement, and if it be not, it will be hopeless to make any more solicitations: indeed, they have now not much time to spare; their approaching dissolution is near at hand; a little while longer, and the earthly scene between them and their country will be closed forever.

### Extracts of letters from General Washington.

" That, in the critical and perilous moment when the last-mentioned communication was made, there was the utmost danger that a dissolution of the army would have taken place, unless measures similar to those recommended had been adopted, will not admit of a doubt."

" That the adoption of the resolution granting half pay for life has been attended with all the happy consequences I had foretold, so far as respected the good of the service, let the astonishing contrast between the state of the army at this instant and at the former period, determine; and that the establishment of funds, and the security for the payment of all just demands of the army, will be the most certain means of preserving the national faith, and the future tranquillity of this extensive continent, is my decided opinion. By the preceding remarks, it will be readily imagined that, instead of retracting or reprehending, from further experience and reflection, the *mode* so strenuously urged in the enclosures, I am more and more confirmed in the sentiment, (and, if in the wrong, suffer me to please myself with the grateful delusion;) for if, besides the simple payment of wages, a further compensation is not due to the sufferings and sacrifices of the officers, then have I been mistaken indeed. If the whole army have not merited whatever a grateful people can bestow, then have I been beguiled by prejudice, and built opinion on the basis of error. If this country should not, in the event, perform every thing which has been requested by the late memorials to Congress, then shall my belief become vain, and the hope which has been excited void of foundation; and if (as has been suggested for the purpose of inflaming their passions) the officers of the army are to be the only sufferers by this Revolution; if, in retiring from the field, they are to grow old in poverty, wretchedness, and contempt; if they are to wade through the vile mire of dependency, and owe the miserable remnant of that life to charity, which has, hitherto, been spent in honor, then I shall have realized a tale which will imbitter every moment of my future life. But I am under no such apprehensions; a country rescued by their arms from impending ruin will never leave unpaid the debt of gratitude."

In a letter from General Washington to Congress, dated March 18, 1783, he says: " I am pleading the cause of an army which has done and suffered more than any other army ever did, in defence of the rights and liberties of human nature." And, in a letter to the Governors of the different States, he says: " The provision of half pay for life, as promised by the resolves of Congress, was a reasonable compensation, offered by Congress at a time when they had nothing else to give to the officers of the army, *for services then to be performed :* was the price of their blood, and of your independence ; and, as a debt of honor, it can never be cancelled until it be fairly discharged."

After the conclusion of the war, said (by Congress, in one of its addresses to the people of these United States,) to be " unparalleled in the annals of mankind," (and in every leaf of its history the pains of its army are registered,) and after the army had been disbanded, in November, 1783, certificates, bearing an interest of six per cent. per annum, were issued ; but, as no provision, for want of ability of means, had been made by Congress for their redemption, they remained, of course, almost valueless, for any of the purposes on account of which they had been agreed by the officers to be received in lieu of their half pay.

*Report of the select committee to whom was referred, on the* 10th *December,* 1819, *the memorial of the officers of the revolutionary army, accompanying a bill for their relief.*

The committee to whom was referred the memorial of the surviving officers of the army of the Revolution, praying for an equitable adjustment of their claim of half pay for life, have agreed to submit the following report :

The memorialists represent that, by the resolve of the 21st of October, 1780, Congress stipulated that half pay for life should be allowed to the officers of the revolutionary army who should continue in service till the end of the war ; that they did continue in service till the end of the war, and therefore became entitled to the benefit of the contract thus entered into with them by their country :. That this contract has not been fulfilled, and they are now entitled to ask its fulfilment.

They further represent that the commutation offered and received under the resolve of the 22d of March, 1783, ought not to be considered as cancelling the obligation of the Government, or impairing the claims of the officers, because it was itself an acknowledgment, by the Government, of its incapacity, at that time, to fulfil the contract ; because it was offered, not to individuals, but to lines and corps, for their acceptance, which gave an undue influence to officers of age and rank, who were likely to be gainers by the arrangement, and did not afford a full opportunity to the younger officers, of inferior grade, who were chiefly interested in retaining the half pay for life ; and excluded altogether from a voice in the decision many meritorious officers, whose lines had been broken up by the casualties of war ; because, also, it was offered to men whose necessities obliged them to accept what they could obtain for the immediate supply of their wants ; and, finally, because the commutation was not, as it ought to have been, and was intended to be, an equivalent for the half pay for life.

Referring to a report made to the House in the month of February, 1810, a copy of which accompanies the present report, and contains, at length, the several resolves of Congress, and the principal facts and arguments having relation to the claim, the committee proceed respectfully to submit their views of the nature of the case, and of the obligations on the part of Government thence arising.

It is not necessary to remind the House either of the merit or the value of the services rendered by the memorialists to their country. History has already consecrated the one, and the other is sufficiently attested, in a manner that must appeal to the best feelings of every citizen of the United States, by the rapid growth and eminently happy condition of that country for which they devoted the most valuable portion of their lives ; for which they took up their swords, and for which, too, with no less patriotism, they laid them down, when her liberty and independence had been effectually secured. If, in behalf of this interesting remnant of the officers of the Revolution, of all that remains to us to cherish of the gallant and illustrious band who have done so much for us, an appeal were made to the national sense of gratitude, we presume, respectfully, to say, that it could scarcely be resisted. It would then be recollected that these survivors are precisely the men who have made the greatest sacrifices for their country, as, from the time that has since elapsed, it will be seen that most of them must have spent in her service that very portion of life when, according to the order of nature, the habits are formed, and the acquirements made, which, in a great measure, determine its future fortune and character ; and that, while they were thus generously preparing for the nation an abundant harvest of political and social happiness, they gave up the only opportunity, for themselves, of becoming qualified for any occupation which, in time of peace, could assure to them the means even of a comfortable subsistence. If accidental good fortune, or distinguished capacity, or the good feelings of their fellow-citizens, displayed in selecting them for public offices of profit, have placed some of them above the reach of want, it is nevertheless believed that there are many who have little to console them in the decline of life but the recollection of the share they have contributed in laying the foundation of their country's independence. To all such, how welcome and how gladdening would be the substantial manifestation of that country's gratitude ! A provision for their few remaining years would alleviate the sufferings of age ; and the veteran of the Revolution would feel continually, and be quickened and animated by the feeling, that the time he had devoted to the public service was not, to himself, altogether waste and unprofitable ; that his exertions and his sufferings were not wholly overlooked ; but, by a natural and honorable return, that country, whose infancy he had aided by his sword to guard, now, in the day of her strength and her prosperity, extended her hand to sooth and support the weakness of his declining years.

It is not, however, upon grounds like these that the memorialists rest their application. They claim upon the footing of right, maintaining, your committee respectfully submit, with great force, that what they ask for is due to them by contract. In the examination of this claim, it appears to the committee that, towards men whose merits are so unquestionable, the Government ought to be guided by principles of liberal justice, having regard to all the circumstances, giving them *all* their due weight, and, even where there might be some doubt upon the application of the rules that govern between man and man, to incline in favor of the memorialists. With this explanation, the committee beg leave to state that they consider the resolve of the 21st October, 1780, as a contract between the Government and the officers, voluntarily and freely entered into at a time when both parties were at liberty in regard to the subject of it ; and stipulating, as the consideration on the part of the officers, their future services until the end of the war, whatever might be its duration. It is not to be questioned that the stipulated service was rendered, nor that it was eminently useful. But it deserves to be remembered, in connexion with all which subsequently occurred, that, after the officer had rendered the service, he had no further reliance but upon the faith and ability of the Government. This was his condition when the resolve of the 22d March, 1783, was adopted. The preliminaries of peace had been signed, the army was about to be disbanded, and he to be thrown into society, there to seek his livelihood by civil pursuits, for which the tenor of his preceding life was calculated only to disqualify him. Had he, under the pressure of circumstances so urgent, and growing out of his previous services, assented to the commutation, his country could scarcely deem it a voluntary assent, but rather a submission to an uncontrollable and' instant necessity, which admitted of no deliberation or delay. But there is another reason why this assent ought not to be considered as binding. The contract of 1780 was with the individual officers, and it is not strictly reconcileable with justice that it should be varied, rescinded, or released, as to any one of them, without his own individual consent. The commutation, except as to certain retired officers, was offered, not to the individuals, but to lines and corps, thereby subjecting the individual, as to his own particular rights, to the decision of others, and with respect to the younger and inferior officers, exposing them to be governed by the overruling influence of superior rank and years, to which they were habitually accustomed to submit.

The committee are aware that it may be urged, (and between individuals it might be decisively urged,) that the subsequent acceptance of the commutation certificate, of itself, amounted to an assent. If the officer had been left free to make his choice, and, having made it, the Government had given him what he freely consented to receive, the argument would not have been without some force. But he was not so free. The resolve of Congress, an act of the Government and a law, left him no choice, except to abide by the decision of the lines and corps of the army, or wait, whatever might be his wants, till a more fortunate period should enable him to approach that body, not with a power to enforce his rights, but only to sue for it in the language of solicitation. It may be remarked, though somewhat out of order, that this is substantially the course which these memorialists are now pursuing. They have waited till their country is able to do them justice, and they now petition for their right, offering to relinquish all they have received.

But it is also true, and furnishes an additional answer to the objection, that the Government was not able to comply with the terms of the resolve of 1783. It could not pay in money, and it did not pay in what was equivalent to money. The commutation certificate was then, and for some time after, worth not more than one-eighth, perhaps even less, of its nominal value. When, at the distance of eight years afterwards, the funding system was established, it is notorious that, generally speaking, the certificates no longer remained in the hands of the officers. The restoration of the public credit came too late for men whose necessities were so imperious ; and thus the half pay for life, which had been solemnly stipulated, and most meritoriously earned, dwindled in the hands of the officers, without any fault of theirs, to scarcely more than half pay for a single year.

Under this view of the case, it seems to your committee just and reasonable, and becoming the faith of the nation, to execute the contract originally made, upon the terms proposed by the memorialists : that is to say, of deducting from the arrears of the half pay, computed from the cessation of hostilities to the present time, the full nominal amount of the commutation certificate, and paying to the surviving officers the balance ; and, henceforward, during the remainder of their lives, paying to them the half pay stipulated by the resolve of 1780. For the arrears, the memorialists are willing to receive stock, bearing an interest.

In order to define and limit, with as much precision as possible, the extent of the demand which will thus be created upon the Treasury, your committee have thought it right to assume, as a basis, the number of surviving officers, and the aggregate of claim, which are stated by the memorialists themselves; and they recommend, respectfully, that any provision which may be made be limited accordingly, so as not to exceed that sum.

In conformity with these suggestions, the committee herewith report a bill.

*Report of a committee of the House of Representatives, February,* 1810.

The committee to whom were referred the petitions of sundry surviving officers of the late revolutionary army, in behalf of themselves and others, report:

That, by a resolution of Congress of the 15th of May, 1778, all military officers who then were, or should thereafter be, in the service of the United States, and who should continue in service during the war, and not hold any office of profit under the United States, or any of them, should, after the conclusion of the war, be entitled to receive, annually, for the term of seven years, if they should live so long, one-half of the then pay of such officers; provided, that no general officer of the cavalry, artillery, or infantry, should be entitled to receive more than the one-half part of the pay of a colonel of such corps, respectively; and provided that the said resolution should not extend to any officer in the service of the United States, unless he should have taken an oath of allegiance, and should actually reside within some one of the United States.

That, by a resolution of Congress of the 11th August, 1779, it was resolved that the half pay provided by the aforesaid resolution of the 15th May, 1778, should be extended to continue for life.

That, by a resolution of Congress of the 21st of October, 1780, it was provided that the officers who should continue in the service to the end of the war should be entitled to half pay during life, to commence from the time of their reduction.

That, by a resolution of Congress of the 17th January, 1781, all officers in the hospital department and medical staff, thereinafter mentioned, who should continue in service until the end of the war, or be reduced before that time as supernumeraries, should be entitled to receive, during life, in lieu of half pay, the following allowances, viz: the director of the hospital, equal to the half pay of a lieutenant colonel; chief physicians and surgeons, purveyor, apothecary, and regimental surgeons, each, equal to the half pay of a captain.

That, by a resolution of Congress of the 22d of March, 1783, it was provided that such officers as were then in service, and should continue therein until the end of the war, should be entitled to receive the amount of five years' full pay in *money,* or securities on interest at six per cent. per annum, as Congress should find most convenient, instead of the half pay promised for life by the resolution of the 21st October, 1780; the said securities being such as should be given to the other creditors of the United States; provided it should be at the option of the lines of the respective States, and not of officers individually in those lines, to accept or refuse the same; provided, also, that their election should be signified to Congress through the commander-in-chief, from the lines under his immediate command, within two months, and through the commanding officer of the southern army, from those under his command, within six months from the date of the resolution.

That the same commutation shall extend to the corps not belonging to the lines of any particular State, and who were entitled to half pay, as aforesaid ; the acceptance or refusal to be determined by corps, and to be signified in the same manner, and within the same time, as above-mentioned. That all officers belonging to the hospital department, who were entitled to half pay by the resolution of the 17th January, 1781, might, collectively, agree to accept or refuse the aforesaid commutations ; signifying the same, through the commander-in-chief, within six months. That such officers as had retired at different periods, entitled to half pay for life, might collectively, in each State of which they are inhabitants, accept or refuse the same ; their acceptance or refusal to be signified by agents ( authorized for that purpose ) within six months. That, with respect to such retiring officers, the commutation, if accepted by them, should be in lieu of whatever might be then due to them, since the time of their retiring from service, as well as what might hereafter become due ; and that, so soon as their acceptance should be signified, the Superintendent of Finance should be, and he was thereby, authorized to take measures for the settlement of their accounts accordingly, and to issue to them certificates, bearing interest at 6 per cent. That all officers entitled to half pay for life, not included in the preceding resolution, might, also, collectively, agree to accept or refuse the aforesaid commutation ; signifying the same within six months from the passage of said resolution.

The petitioners state, and the fact is of too general a notoriety to be disputed, that, although they confidently expected, at the time they were compelled, from imperious necessity, to accept the sum in gross, in lieu of half pay for life, that it would be paid to them in reality, and not by a fresh promise, without any sufficient guarantee for its due performance; yet they were compelled to receive *certificates,* which, for want of any specific provision for the payment of them, or the interest accruing on them, were immediately depreciated to five for one, and, by degrees, to ten for one, in exchange for money. They therefore pray that half pay for life, to commence from the time of the reduction of the army, may be granted to them, according to the solemn stipulations entered into with them by Congress, by the resolutions before referred to ; deducting therefrom the five years' full pay received by them, in depreciated paper, by way of commutation.

It is well known to your committee, and to the whole nation, that the far greater part of the officers were compelled, by hard necessity, to dispose of their commutation certificates, at prices infinitely below their nominal amount. That this did not proceed from want of patriotism, of which they had before given proof most unequivocal, or of want of confidence in their Government; but that, after having spent the vigor of their manhood in the service of their country, they returned to the walks of civil life, ( many of them maimed, and scarcely able to halt along,) ignorant of what was passing, or likely to pass, in the councils of their country. The griping hand of poverty bore hard upon them ; and, unacquainted, as they necessarily were, with civil affairs, they fell an easy prey to the wiles of the artful and insidious speculator, who was lying in wait to fatten upon their hard earnings. Under circumstances like these, it would have been strange, indeed, if they had kept their certificates in their pockets. No: the thing was impracticable : go they must, for whatever they would bring, and be the consequences whatever they might.

Upon the whole, the committee are of opinion the contract entered into by Congress with the officers of the late revolutionary army, for giving them half pay for life, has not been substantially complied with by our Government: they therefore recommend the following resolution :

*Resolved*, That the prayer of the petitioners is reasonable, and ought to be granted.

---

## MAY 8, 1826.

The Committee on Military Pensions, to which was recommitted the bill and amendments, entitled " An act for the relief of the surviving officers of the army of the Revolution," report :

Those who served during the revolutionary war, at different periods thereof, and for whom no provision has been made by law, may be divided into two classes. The first comprehends the officers of the army who, under the resolution of Congress of October 21st, 1780, continued in service until the army was disbanded, October 18th, 1783, after the establishment of the independence of the United States. Their number is known to have been, at that time, 2,480. The average age of these officers was, when they left the service, thirty years; and, since that period, more than forty-two years have elapsed.

The decrement of human life, founded on the expectation of it, derived from observation and experience, in several different countries similar to our own, is such, that, upon a fair calculation, not more than 400, of the 2,480, are now alive; and those at the average age of 72 years and upwards. At this advanced age, they ask from their country for some additional compensation. 1st. They ask for this aid now, because they are now unable to aid themselves. At 72, most men are beyond the power to labor, or the hope of acquisition by any kind of business. 2d. They served their country when, without that service, its independence and the establishment of republican Government in this hemisphere must have been lost. 3d. They were promised their pay monthly ; and, after the war, annuities for life, equal to half that amount. 4th. Congress were without funds; continental money had ceased to be of any value; and the army was unpaid from that time till the close of the war. 5th. The States were dissatisfied with the half pay establishment, and they offered to surrender their annuities to the United States for an equivalent. 6th. Congress resolved, March 23d, 1783, to give them five years' full pay, in cash or securities, as an equivalent for, and in lieu of, their annuities. 7th. In place of cash, Congress was obliged, from the total insolvency of the old confederation, to give them commutation certificates, signed by the paymaster general, and payable to them or bearer. These, from inability to pay in the maker, and to wait in the holder, were thrown into the market for cash, and soon fell to 12½ cents on the dollar. 8th. No provision was or could be made by Congress for payment or funding of these certificates, till after the adoption of the constitution, when, by the law on that subject, they were again commuted, by giving the holders a three per cent. stock for the interest in arrear; a six per cent. stock for two-thirds of the principal; and a deferred stock, bearing no interest till the expiration of ten years, for the other third. 9th. Upon a fair calculation of the probabilities of life, the half pay annuities of these officers, then thirty years old, were, October 18th, 1783, worth 14.08 years' purchase. It is seen that they received for them but ten years' purchase; that is, five years' full pay. It is also seen that, under this funding system, they so received this, that each captain sustained a loss, in interest, of $2,436 34. By the report from the Treasury Department, it appears that each of these annuitants, being a captain, and now alive, would, as half pay, have received $10,080. By commutation he received a certificate for $2,400, by which this officer has lost, and the Government saved, $7,680. These two sums are $7,680 by the commutation, and $2,426 34 by the funding; making a total of $10,106 34 saved by the nation, and lost by each individual of these officers now alive. It must be allowed that, to these officers, at thirty years old, the expectation of life could not have been over thirty-two years, and may be said not to have exceeded twenty-eight. A captain, then, being entitled to half pay, or $240 per annum, for twenty-five years, would receive $6,720; but, by the commutation, he did receive $2,400. The difference is $4,320. To this add the loss of interest, by the manner of funding, $2,426 34, and then it appears the nation did save, and the officers did lose, $6,746 34. By the last statement it therefore appears that 2,480 officers have lost, and the nation have saved, $16,730,923 20; and it appears, by the first statement, that the same officers have lost, and the nation have saved, $25,063,733 20. The committee do not feel themselves called upon to offer any opinion on the nature of the contract originally made by Congress with this very meritorious class of men, nor upon the manner in which, as it appears, the same was fulfilled. At the close of the war, the nation was comparatively small, about 3,000,000. The public debt was heavy, and the then United States had no funds and no revenue. Under these circumstances the Government, though obliged to pay in gold and silver, to the full amount, their foreign creditors, was nevertheless enabled to settle at least this part of their domestic responsibilities on terms very favorable to the economy of the country. The people are now multiplied to more than ten millions; they are rich, free, and prosperous, and the revenue is large, abundant, and increasing. Any remuneration hitherto proposed to be given to these men is less than a disme to each individual of the nation; and if formed into a stock and left to some future generation for payment, will, when that generation choose to do it, enable them to recall the memory of those gallant men whose labors and dangers, under God, secured to them their freedom, independence, and prosperity. The committee therefore feel themselves fully justified in reporting that the survivors aforesaid of this first class of those who served during the war of the Revolution ought to be provided for by law; and, considering all the foregoing facts, they do believe that the justice, honor, and magnanimity of the nation would not be satisfied, unless Congress appropriate for that object the sum of $1,000,000. For this purpose they have proposed the first and second sentences as part of an amendment to the bill herewith reported as amended. Although the resolution aforesaid does not in terms refer to them, the question of a provision for the widows of the non-survivors of the officers aforesaid; yet because the House did, when the case of the surviving officers aforesaid was under consideration, strongly express an opinion in favor of making such provision, the committee therefore further report that the number of such widows to be provided for can be estimated only by a calculation of probabilities. At the close of the war each officer being thirty years old was, probably, a married man. It may be assumed as a fact, that men marry at a later age than women; and if these officers, at the close of the war, were, on an average, thirty years old, it is not improbable that their wives were twenty-six. Of two thousand four hundred and eighty wives, at that period and of that age, calculating agreeably to the established rules of the probability of human life, according to the annual decrement thereof, there may be now alive of that number seven hundred and forty-three. Of this number it is probable that four hundred are now wives of four hundred husbands, who, it has been found, are probably alive; because it is more probable that a wife at twenty-six will live forty-two years, than that a husband at thirty will live the same number of years. The probable number of these widows is, then, three hundred and forty-three. These are now at an advanced age, and not likely to be in any condition of great affluence. If we call to mind the character and conduct of our countrywomen in that war, we shall not forget with what alacrity they sent their sons and husbands to the defence of their country. Domestic affection gave place to a patriotism worthy of the best nations, in the best ages of the world. It must not be forgotten that while these officers were without pay in the army, and compelled to exhaust their property to support themselves in the field, their wives at home endured all the inconvenience of a very small and inadequate provision. Gallant men need not be told of the anxieties of a soldier's wife for the fate of her husband; for although women despise a coward, they nevertheless think with inexpressible anguish on the perils of the brave in the day of battle. It is the opinion of the committee that a provision for these widows should be made by law; and that it ought to be made by way of annuity, rather than a gross sum paid off at once; they therefore recommend raising a fund for paying annuities to those who now are or hereafter may be widows of those officers of the army who continued in service till the end of the revolutionary war or died after the 21st of October, A. D. 1780. This fund may be raised by deducting from the one million appropriated to a provision for said officers the sum of $200,000. These annuities will be a charge upon this fund, and the interest of the balance will be annually a credit to be added to it, until the whole shall be exhausted. In this way this fund may provide annuities of $100 to each of these venerable matrons for the remainder of their lives. With a view to the establishment of such a fund, the committee have prepared the proviso to the 1st section of the amendment of the bill aforesaid, herewith reported. The second class of those who served at different periods during the war comprehends all officers and men in the land and naval service for nine months or upwards at one time, other than the officers aforesaid, and who were of the continental establishment or regular troops not of the line. It is estimated at the War Department that the number of these now alive is not more than 18,500. Of these, 500 were regular troops not of the line and served from one to three years. On the continental establishment, 1,500 served nine months and upwards; 2,000 served one year and upwards; 3,000 served two years and upwards; and 11,500 served three years and upwards. If we subtract from this number 12,985, now on the pension roll, 5,515 will remain, for whom no provision has been made by the United States.

These constitute the remnant of that army which achieved the independence of our country. Their age is the same, or nearly the same, as that of those of the first class aforesaid. Though some of them are possessed of some property, yet none of them are known to be affluent. A public pecuniary testimonial of national gratitude to them would be highly honorable to the United States, and every way acceptable to these men. The severity and perilous nature of their service cannot be forgotten. Their rations, clothing, and camp provisions, were at all times scant, often interrupted, and not unfrequently wholly wanting. Their pay was always low, and being made to them in a depreciating medium, finally became of little value. This depreciation was promised to be made up to them, but it was made up in a medium equally depreciated. At the close of the war the sufferings of the country were too great to consider their condition; the prosperity of it now is fully equal to that consideration.

The committee therefore report that this last description of persons, being of the number of those who served during the war of the Revolution, ought to be provided for by law, and that for this purpose the sum of $1,200,000 ought to be distributed among them in stocks, bearing an interest of five per cent., according to their grade and term of service, in manner as is provided by the 3d and 4th sections of the amendment to said bill, herewith reported. For reasons which, among others, induced the committee to recommend a provision for the surviving widows of the officers who served to the close of the revolutionary war as aforesaid, they also recommend a provision for the surviving widows of this class of those who served in that war. Assuming the same data and making the same calculation as was made in the first case, their number probably is 4,729. The committee recommend providing for them by way of annuities, and that a fund be raised for that purpose. This fund cannot be less than $800,000; so that, by charging such annuities to this fund, and giving credit for interest on the balance annually, it might afford to such widows annuities of $30 each, and the whole amount not be exhausted until the expiration of eight years, or, as it may be, not until all or nearly all the annuities had fallen into said fund. For this purpose the committee have prepared the 5th section of the amendment to the bill aforesaid, herewith reported.

The Committee on Revolutionary Claims, who were instructed, by a resolution of the House of Representatives of the 17th December last, to inquire into the propriety of remunerating Captain Philip Slaughter for his services in the continental army during the war of the Revolution, have duly considered the subject referred to them, and report:

That, from the facts submitted to the committee, it appears that, in the month of June or July, 1776, the claimant was appointed a lieutenant in Captain Long's company, in the 11th Virginia regiment on continental establishment, commanded by Colonel Daniel Morgan; that he was afterwards appointed a captain in the same regiment; that he faithfully served through the northern campaigns of 1777, 1778, and 1779; that, in the two latter years, he acted both as captain and paymaster; and, in the year 1779, he performed the additional duty of regimental clothier; that, soon after the campaign of 1779, he returned to his home in Virginia, on furlough, got married, remained at his residence in Virginia, and did not afterwards join the army; that, in the month of November or December, 1779, a portion of the officers of the Virginia line were ordered to the South; Captain Slaughter, deeming it inconvenient for him, circumstanced as he then was, to perform a southern campaign, and supposing it likely that he would receive orders to join the southern army, authorized his friend, the present Chief Justice Marshall, who was an officer in the same regiment, to resign his commission for him in case he (Slaughter) should receive such orders. Judge Marshall, however, says, the impression on his mind is very strong that he did not give in Slaughter's resignation, and that impression is strengthened, he says, by the fact that Captain Slaughter was not ordered to the South, the order being confined to the elder officers.

It appears, by statements from the Pension and Bounty Land Offices, that Captain Slaughter, on the 1st of April, 1783, received a certificate for £563 15s. 2d., the balance of his full pay as captain and paymaster, agreeably to an act of the Virginia Assembly, passed in November, 1781; and that he also received four thousand acres of land from the State of Virginia. He now asks his commutation of five years' full pay, in lieu of half pay for life.

Your committee are of opinion that Captain Slaughter did, virtually, continue in the service of the United States until the end of the revolutionary war; that he was a meritorious officer, and, from the character given him by highly respectable witnesses, entitled to receive from the Government all the emoluments to which officers of his grade were, under the resolves of Congress, entitled. They therefore report a bill in his favor.

[*Annexed to the foregoing report.*]

WAR DEPARTMENT,

*Pension Office, February* 4, 1828.

I certify that, in a book kept in the Pension Office, containing a list of officers of the Virginia line on continental establishment, who have received certificates for the balance of their full pay, agreeably to an act of the Virginia Assembly, passed November, 1781, the name of Philip Slaughter, a captain, appears thereon, and opposite to his name the words " captain and paymaster" appear. And it appears, also, that the certificate for £563 15s. 2d. was delivered to himself on the 1st of April, 1783.

J. L. EDWARDS.

Treasury Department,

*Register's Office, February* 1, 1828.

I certify that, after a minute examination of the register of certificates issued for pay, and commutation of five years' full pay, to the officers of the revolutionary army, in lieu of half pay for life, the name of Captain Philip Slaughter, of the Virginia line, hath not been discovered, either for his pay or his commutation.

JOSEPH NOURSE,<br>*Register.*

Treasury Ddpartment,

*Register's Office, February* 1, 1828.

Sir : I have the honor to enclose an extract in relation to the sum paid Captain Philip Slaughter by the State of Virginia; but I have been, without effect, examining the register of certificates issued by the United States for the pay, and commutation of five years' full pay, in lieu of half pay for life. The name of that officer cannot be discovered, either for the payment of his pay or commutation.

I am, with great respect,<br>Sir, your most obedient servant,

JOSEPH NOURSE,<br>*Register.*

Hon. John S. Barbour.

*A list of the officers of the Virginia line on continental establishment, who have received certificates for the balance of their full pay, agreeable to an act of Assembly, passed November session,* 1781.

Philip Slaughter, captain and paymaster, 1st April, 1783, . . . . . . . £563 15s. 2d.

Treasury Department,

*Register's Office, February* 1, 1828.

I certify that the foregoing is a true copy from the records preserved in this office, of the names of officers on the continental establishment, who belonged to the Virginia line, by which it appears that Captain Philip Slaughter, who belonged to that line of the revolutionary army, did on the 1st of April, 1788, receive of the State of Virginia the sum of five hundred and sixty-three pounds fifteen shillings and two pence, specie, under an act of said State passed in November session, 1781.

JOSEPH NOURSE,<br>*Register.*

*Washington, February 7*, 1828.

SIR : Upon examination, I do not find that Captain Philip Slaughter, of the Virginia line on continental establishment, in the revolutionary war, was returned as having served to the end of the war; he is therefore not entitled to bounty land of the United States. Upon looking over a list of such officers to whom Virginia gave land, as having served long enough to entitle them, I find that Captain Philip Slaughter received 4,000 acres, which was the quantity of land to which a captain was entitled for any service of three years, and not more than six years, under the grants of the States.

Yours, &c.

ROBERT TAYLOR.

The Hon. JONATHAN HUNT.

*Chief Justice Marshall's Certificate.*

Captain Philip Slaughter was appointed a lieutenant in Captain Long's company in June or July, 1776. The regiment was to be commanded by Colonel Stevenson, and to be raised partly in Maryland and partly in Virginia. A part of the regiment commanded by Lieutenant Colonel Rawlings was captured in Fort Washington, after which, the companies raised in Maryland were attached to some regiment of that State, and the Virginia companies were attached to the 11th Virginia regiment, commanded by Colonel Daniel Morgan. Captain Long's company was in that regiment. I served in the same regiment, and was long and intimately acquainted with Lieutenant afterwards Captain Slaughter. He served through the campaigns of 1777, 1778, and 1779. I always thought him a good officer, who performed his duty faithfully, and believe that the officers generally entertained the same opinion of him. In the years 1778 and 1779 he acted as captain and paymaster; and I think that, in 1779, he performed the additional duty of regimental clothier. He performed every duty which devolved on him to the entire satisfaction of the regiment, and was generally esteemed.

J. MARSHALL.

SOLDIER'S RETREAT, *January* 22, 1828.

MY DEAR FRIEND: I feel extremely mortified at the delay which has attended your letter to me; my son was at the post office in Waynesborough on yesterday, when it was handed to him, which I observe bears date 25th ultimo. I am the more concerned at this delay in obtaining the evidence of your services in the war of the Revolution, fearing it may come to hand too late in the support of your claim, set forth in your petition to Congress, which would be to me matter of real unfeigned regret; and, under such adverse circumstances, can only hope my certificate may yet reach you in time to assist in effecting the object. Beside, I feel distressed lest my not answering your letter promptly might have induced you to doubt that affectionate feeling for you which never has abated one moment since our first acquaintance. I subjoin the certificate required.

No one can regret more than I do the pecuniary embarrassment under which you are laboring; and the more especially, as it has been incurred by your friendly liberality to others. Would to God it were in my power to relieve you.

Be so good as to present my most respectful compliments to Mrs. Slaughter and your children. Tell her my sister Heth yet lives, and often talks about her. My son joins me in respects, &c.

With all the sincerity of affection,<br>Your very true friend,<br>RO. PORTERFIELD.

Capt. SLAUGHTER.

*General Porterfield's Certificate.*

AUGUSTA COUNTY, VIRGINIA.

I hereby certify, that Captain Philip Slaughter, of the county of Culpeper, Virginia, was an officer in the war of the Revolution; that he belonged to and served as a lieutenant in the 11th Virginia regiment on continental establishment, during the campaign of 1777; and in said regiment, as captain and paymaster, the campaign of 1778; and as captain, paymaster, and clothier, for the regiment, in the campaign of 1779, with the main army, under the command of General Washington, in the States of New York, New Jersey, and Pennsylvania; that he performed the various and complicated duties pertaining to the aforesaid offices with ability, promptitude, and integrity, to the entire satisfaction of all concerned, never availing himself of the additional regimental appointments as a shield to the performance of the duties incumbent on an officer of the line; and especially, at all times when a battle was in prospect; fighting at the battles of Brandywine, Germantown, &c.

Having been an officer in the 11th Virginia regiment, and having served with Captain Slaughter the whole three years, as above, the foregoing circumstances are stated from my personal knowledge, and a perfect recollection of the facts.

Given under my hand, this 22d day of January, 1828.

RO. PORTERFIELD.

I, David Jameson, of the county of Culpeper, in the State of Virginia, aged 75 years, do hereby certify that my brother, John Jameson, enlisted a company of minutemen in the year 1775, and that Philip Slaughter, then a youth, was one of his soldiers, and marched with said company, in fall 1775, to Williamsburg; that, in the spring 1776, my brother, John Jameson, raised a company of horse, and that the said Philip Slaughter enlisted as a soldier in said troop; that, in July, 1776, the said Philip Slaughter was appointed, by the committee of safety of the county of Culpeper, a lieutenant in Captain Gabriel Long's company of riflemen, which said company marched, in the fall of 1776, to join the northern army under General Washington; that I was deputy clerk of the said county of Culpeper during the revolutionary war, and well remember that said Slaughter continued in the American army several years.

Given under my hand, this 27th day of December, 1827.

D. JAMESON.

Attest: Jeremiah Strother.

I, John Williams, of the county of Culpeper, and State of Virginia, aged 75 years, do hereby certify that, in the fall of 1775, I commanded a company of minutemen, who marched, that fall, to Williamsburg, in company with several companies of minutemen, raised in the counties of Fauquier, Orange, and Culpeper; that I well remember that Philip Slaughter was a soldier (then a youth) in Captain John Jameson's company of minutemen, and marched with us to Williamsburg; that, in 1776, he, the said Philip Slaughter, left school and enlisted, a common soldier, in Captain John Jameson's troop of horse; that, before Captain Jameson's company was completed, the said Philip Slaughter was appointed, by the committee of safety of the county of Culpeper, a second lieutenant in Captain Gabriel Long's company of riflemen; that they raised the company, and marched, that fall, to join the main army under General Washington, to the North; that, in September, 1777, a few days after the battle of Brandywine, I arrived at camp, and there saw the said Philip Slaughter, and other officers, collecting the dispersed soldiers, who informed me how much their regiment had suffered in the action of Brandywine; that I was a near neighbor to the said Philip Slaughter's father, and am well assured that the said Slaughter was absent from home, with the American army, for several years.

Given under my hand, this 26th day of December, 1827.

J. WILLIAMS.

Witness: Isaac H. Williams.

THE UNITED STATES OF AMERICA IN. CONGRESS ASSEMBLED.

No. 50.—*To Philip Slaughter, Esq., Greeting:*

We, reposing especial trust and confidence in your patriotism, valor, conduct, and fidelity, do, by these presents, constitute and appoint you to be a captain in the seventh Virginia regiment, in the army of the United States, to take rank as such from the 1st day of November, 1778. You are therefore carefully and diligently to discharge the duty of a captain, by doing and performing all manner of things thereunto belonging. And we do strictly charge and require all officers and soldiers under your command to be obedient to your orders as captain; and you are to observe and follow such orders and directions, from time to time, as you shall receive from this or a future Congress of the United States, or committee of Congress for that purpose appointed, a committee of the States, or commander-in chief, for the time being, of the army of the United States, or any other your superior officer, according to the rules and discipline of war, in pursuance of the trust reposed in you. This commission to continue in force until revoked by this or a future Congress, the committee of Congress before mentioned, or a committee of the States.

Witness, His Excellency SAMUEL HUNTINGTON, Esq., President of the Congress of the United States of America, at Philadelphia, the 23d day of November, 1779, and in the fourth year of our independence.

SAM. HUNTINGTON, *President.*

Entered in the War Office, and examined by the Board.

Attest: BEN. STODDERT,
*Secretary of the Board of War.*

---

FEBRUARY 22, 1828.

The Committee on Revolutionary Claims, to whom was referred the petition of Joshua Foltz, have had the same under consideration, and report:

The petitioner states that, on the 27th of February, 1779, he enlisted as a soldier in the service of the United States, for eighteen months; that he served in the company commanded by Captain Wayles, in Colonel Beaufort's regiment, in General Scott's brigade, at Williamsburg and Petersburg, until the 26th day of December, 1779, when the petitioner was, at the request of Colonel Elliott, A. D. Q. General, and by the orders of Colonel Beaufort and General Scott, directed to take charge of a wagon and team belonging to Colonel Elliott, then in the service of the United States. That he continued in the capacity of wagoner in the public service until the 27th of October, 1780, when he was discharged by General Muhlenburg, at the Bowling Green, in Virginia. That, during the time he served as a soldier, he received his pay, but for the time he served as a wagoner he received no pay. The petitioner further states that, at the time he was discharged, Colonel Elliott, or his assistant, gave him a certificate for one hundred and eighteen pounds five shillings and four pence, continental money; that, several years after, he gave the certificate to a Mr. Williams, who informed the petitioner that he placed it in the hands of Alexander White, then a member of Congress, to receive the money; that White died; that the petitioner has not been able to get the certificate, and has not received any part of the sum due; and prays relief.

The petitioner, in support of his claim, exhibits the following paper, purporting to be a discharge:

" Petersburg, *October* 27, 1780.

" The bearer hereof, Joshua Foltz, an eighteen months' soldier, having faithfully served his time, is hereby discharged.

(Signed)            P. MUHLENBURG, *B. G.*"

Likewise, the deposition of two witnesses, stating the fact of the petitioner's enlistment, for eighteen months, as a soldier in the revolutionary army. The deposition of another witness states that the petitioner had, exclusive of his discharge from General Muhlenburg, as a soldier, a certificate for wages due him, as a wagoner, in the service of the United States, in Colonel Aylett's department, for driving a team in the public service about ten months, commencing about the 26th December, 1779, for the sum of £118 5s. 4d.; that the petitioner sent the certificate with the witness to Richmond for settlement, about the year 1789; that the office for settling such claims, he found, had been discontinued, and returned the certificate to the petitioner, from whom he afterwards learned that the certificate was placed in the hands of a Mr. William C. Williams, to use his exertions to have the same settled. The witness states that the petitioner has lived in his neighborhood since the war; that he has written several letters for him in relation to his claim, and expresses his belief that the claim has never been paid.

Another deposition states that, upwards of twenty years ago, the deponent saw in the possession of the petitioner a discharge for a tour of duty performed during the revolutionary war; and that the same was delivered to William C. Williams, for the purpose of applying for the amount due; and afterwards heard Williams inform the petitioner that he had delivered his papers to Alexander White, then a member of Congress, to procure what was due. From the evidence accompanying the petition, it appears that the petitioner, although a very illiterate man, and living remote from the place where accounts of this description were settled, adopted the true means in his power to obtain the amount due to him by the Government, in the appointment of agents, from time to time. The committee are satisfied that the services were performed, and that no compensation has been received; and think the petitioner is entitled to relief, and to that end report a bill.

--------

Marsh 28, 1828.

*The Committee on Revolutionary Claims, to which was referred a bill from the Senate entitled " An act for the relief of the legal representatives of General Moses Hazen, deceased," have had the same, and the evidence on which it is predicated, under consideration, and beg leave to report :*

That, on the 22d day of January, 1776, Moses Hazen was appointed a colonel in the army of the United States ; and, on the same day, Congress resolved, " That the United Colonies will indemnify Colonel Hazen for any loss of half pay he may sustain in consequence of his entering into their service." By a letter, under date of the 22d August, 1825, addressed by Robert Lukin, chief clerk in the War Office, at London, to Thomas Aspinwall, American consul at that place, duly authenticated, it appears that Moses Hazen was a lieutenant upon half pay, of the 44th regiment of foot, at the rate of two shillings and four pence per diem; and that he was struck off the establishment of half pay, from the 25th December, 1781, in consequence of his having served in arms against the British forces in North America.

A paper purporting to contain extracts of a letter, dated the 4th of December, 1789, from Mr. Knox, then Secretary of War, to Brigadier General Hazen, (which paper is attested by Moses White, the petitioner, to be a copy,) has been exhibited with the petitioner's documents; from which it appears that said Hazen's claim to indemnity for the loss of his half pay as aforesaid was considered by Mr. Knox to be valid ; but it seems that General Hazen had not then exhibited any evidence of the loss of his said half pay, inasmuch as the Secretary of War, in his letter above mentioned, advises him that, in order to make good his claim to indemnity from the United States, it would be necessary for him to establish, 1st, that he was entitled to half pay from the British Government, and the rate thereof; and, 2d, that he was deprived of the said half pay in consequence of his having entered the American service.

There is also a paper among the documents, purporting to be a copy of a memorandum made by John Pierce, Esq., commissioner of army accounts, (which paper is also authenticated by the attestation of Moses White, the petitioner,) from which it would seem that General Hazen's claim for indemnity for his loss of half pay above mentioned, was presented to the said commissioner, and rejected, " because it was not ascertained what General Hazen's loss had been in consequence of his relinquishing his British lieutenant's half pay."

It does not appear that any evidence of this part of the petitioner's claim, showing the amount, value, and loss of the half pay aforesaid, whereby the account could have been liquidated and settled, was ever exhibited at the proper department of this Government, at any period prior to the fall of the year 1825, although notice was given to General Hazen, in his lifetime, so long ago as the 4th of December, 1789, by the then Secretary of War, that such evidence would be required.

Your committee are of opinion, therefore, that the reason why the indemnity for the loss of the half pay aforesaid was not made to the said Hazen in his lifetime, or to his executor and representative since his death, was, not that the Government was unable or unwilling to satisfy and discharge the demand, but that the parties claiming from time to time neglected and refused to produce the evidence necessary to a just and equitable liquidation and settlement of the claim.

The committee, therefore, recommend that the first section of the Senate's bill be so amended, as to prohibit the allowance of interest on the amount of loss for the half pay aforesaid.

Your committee beg leave further to report, that, by reference to the Journals of Congress of 1781, it appears that, on the 25th of April of that year, Congress ordered that the Board of Treasury place to the credit of Colonel Moses Hazen the sum of $13,386$\frac{2}{90}$, specie, being the principal and interest of the money due to him to the first day of May, 1781 ; and that the same bear interest at six per cent. per annum, &c.

It appears that General Hazen's account, in reference to this sum of $13,386$\frac{2}{90}$, so placed to his credit as aforesaid, was settled by the Auditor of the Treasury on the 11th of January, 1799, exhibiting a balance in favor of General Hazen of $8,683 88, at that date ; that afterwards, to wit, on the 30th June, 1802, the said account was submitted to the Comptroller of the Treasury for his supervision and correction, who rejected the allowance of interest, and states the principles by which he was governed, in the following words :

"It is difficult to do justice in this case. On the one hand, General Hazen ought not to be charged with the new emissions at par ; on the other, it is not reasonable to subject the United States to such an accumulation of interest. If depreciation be allowed, General Hazen will have no reason to complain if interest on the balance should be refused. This appears to me to be more conformable to the principles of equity, and to the usage of the Treasury, than any other mode of adjustment that can now be devised. Before the date of the act of June 12th, 1798, balances which originated under the former Government, if to be paid in specie, were uniformly ascertained without interest ; if to be paid by issuing certificates, interest thereon was allowed. That act precluded the issuing of certificates ; in consequence of which, all balances liquidated since, for any matter or thing prior to the 4th March, 1789, have been paid in specie, without interest. This claim being of that description, I do hereby admit and certify it, for the sum of four thousand two hundred dollars, without interest, in pursuance of the 5th section of the act above referred to.

"JOHN STEELE, *Comptroller.*"

Thus, it appears, that the sum of money on which interest is now claimed, was settled, and accounted for, and adjusted, on principles adopted by the accounting officers of the Treasury, under the then existing laws, and the usages and practice arising under those laws, so long ago as the 30th of June, 1802 ; and that the account of General Hazen, thus settled and adjusted, was settled and adjusted on precisely the same principles on which the accounts of other individuals, similarly circumstanced, were settled by the Government, and none other.

Your committee have examined a paper, purporting to be a copy of a petition presented to Congress by Moses White and Charlotte Hazen, executor and executrix of the last will and testament of Moses Hazen, deceased, in the year 1804, in which no mention whatever is made of the claim for arrearages of interest: so that this claim of interest, alleged to be due and unpaid at this time, on the said sum of $13,386$\frac{2}{90}$, would seem to have been an afterthought altogether : for, if the petitioner has a claim on the Government for that interest now, the petitioners had a claim for a portion of the same interest then ; and your committee do not believe that the petitioners would have omitted to ask for so important an item in their claim, in 1804, had they then believed it to exist.

Your committee would remark, that, however Congress might be disposed to extend its munificence to General Hazen, as a meritorious officer of the Revolution, were he now living, or to his children, had he died leaving issue, they can see no good reason why Congress should, at the expiration of twenty-six years and upwards, unravel and unsettle an account, which, after so great a lapse of time, the committee is bound to believe was settled according to law, and upon principles which governed in all similar cases, in favor of an individual whose claim can only rest for allowance on principles of strict justice.

It is proper to observe, in addition to what has already been advanced, that General Hazen, after he entered the American army, was promoted, on the 29th of June, 1781, to the rank of brigadier general by brevet ; that, in the settlement of his accounts, he was allowed the sum of $4,500, his commutation in full for half pay for life; and that, after his death, Congress, by act of the 23d of January, 1805, granted to Charlotte Hazen, widow and relict of Brigadier General Moses Hazen, deceased, for her support, the annual sum of two hundred dollars, during her life, to commence on the 4th February, 1803 ; and, by act of 23d April, 1812, Congress made further provision for the said Charlotte Hazen, by granting to her nine hundred and sixty acres of land. Taking into consideration, therefore, all the circumstances connected with this claim, your committee do not hesitate to declare it as their decided opinion, that the Government of the United States has long since cancelled every obligation it may, at any time, heretofore, have been under to General Moses Hazen, except the indemnity promised for loss of half pay as hereinbefore mentioned ; that the representative of said Hazen has no just claim against the United States for arrearages of interest, as alleged by him in his petition ; and that the bill from the Senate for the relief of said representative ought to be further amended by striking out the second section thereof, which allows the interest aforesaid.

------

JANUARY 18, 1830.

*The Committee on Revolutionary Claims, who were instructed by a resolution of the House of Representatives, of the 15th of December last, to inquire into the expediency of allowing John Moffitt, a colonel in the militia of South Carolina, in the revolutionary war, payment for a continental loan office certificate, for the sum of three thousand and fifty-four dollars, deposited in the loan office in Charleston, in conformity to a resolution of Congress passed the 2d of July, 1779, have duly considered the same, and report :*

That, by a letter of the 19th January, 1827, addressed by the Register of the Treasury to the Secretary of that Department, it appears that the certificate in question is genuine ; but that, in consequence of Colonel Moffitt's not having presented his certificate, either under the old Government or during the period prescribed by the present Government for funding the revolutionary debt, no relief can now be afforded him, but by an act of Congress in his favor.

On the part of the claimant, it is alleged that he presented his certificate to the commissioner of loans for settlement, who could not adjust the same for want of funds ; that he repeatedly, afterwards, applied to the State Legislature for relief, but without success ; to which circumstances are ascribed the delay in presenting his claim to Congress.

Your committee are of opinion that the claim is just, and ought not to be barred by the statute of limitations : they, therefore, ask leave to report a bill for the relief of the claimant.

*The Committee on Revolutionary Claims, to whom was referred the petition of George Concklin and William Warner, of the city of New York, (executors of Joseph Falconer, of said city, lately deceased,) and of Rebecca Williams, of Newcastle, in the State of Delaware, report:*

That the petition and papers in this case were referred to the Committee on Revolutionary Claims of the last Congress, who, on the 24th day of January, 1829, made a report thereon, stating all the material facts in this case. That your committee, having deliberately examined the said report, and all the papers and evidence referred to them, and duly considered the same, concur with that committee in the opinion expressed by them in that report, and ask that the same may be taken and considered as part of this report. Your committee, therefore, ask leave to report a bill for the relief of the petitioners.

---

*The Committee on Revolutionary Claims, to which was referred the petition of George Concklin and William Warner, of the city of New York, (executors of Joseph Falconer, of said city, lately deceased,) and of Rebecca Williams, of Newcastle, in the State of Delaware, report:*

That the petitioners state that the said Joseph Falconer, deceased, and Rebecca Williams, are children of Joseph Falconer, formerly of Philadelphia, who was an officer in the service of the United States, in the war of the Revolution ; and for services rendered during said war, he received two several loan office certificates, namely, one for the sum of one thousand dollars, and one for the sum of six hundred dollars, both dated (as the petitioners supposed) on the 21st of April, 1780, and issued to and in the name of *James Cox.* That, in the year 1784, the said Joseph Falconer, of Philadelphia, advertised said certificates as having been lost ; and the same remain on the books of the Treasury as unpaid, bearing an interest of six per cent.; the principal and interest amounting, on the 21st of October, 1828, to the sum of $2,798 34 ; which sum said petitioners ask to be paid them.

It appears, by the official certificate of the Register of the Treasury, that two loan office certificates were issued by Thomas Smith, loan officer of the State of Pennsylvania, which, by the records of the Treasury, are outstanding and unpaid, and which your committee (notwithstanding the mistakes made by the petitioners in regard to date and the name of the payee) have no doubt are the certificates referred to in the petition, namely, one numbered 35, issued April 21, 1778, to John Cox or bearer, for one thousand dollars, and of the specie value of $454\frac{37}{90}$; and one of same date, numbered 2997, payable to said John Cox or bearer, for six hundred dollars, and of the specie value of $272\frac{58}{90}$.

It also appears, by a record made in the office of the Register of the Treasury, that, on the 8th of April, 1820, Joseph Falconer, by a letter dated at New York, entered a caveat against any person, other than himself, deriving any benefit from said outstanding and unpaid certificates.

Your committee, however, find no satisfactory testimony to establish the fact, that Joseph Falconer, of New York, and Rebecca Williams, of Newcastle, in the State of Delaware, are the only heirs of Joseph Falconer, formerly of Philadelphia; or that George Concklin and William Warner are legal representatives of such heirs, and entitled to receive the amount of said loan office certificates ; but believing that they remain unpaid and outstanding, and belong to the heirs or legal representatives of said Joseph Falconer, a revolutionary officer, formerly of Philadelphia, therefore report a bill for their relief.

---

JANUARY 26, 1830.

*The Committee on Revolutionary Claims, to which was referred the petition of James Barnett, an officer of the revolutionary war, report:*

That it is stated in this petition, and the statement is proved by the evidence in this case, that the petitioner was an officer in that war from 1776 to the close of it.   He was, a part of the time, in the recruiting service; but most of it, actively engaged in the several distinguished campaigns, both at the North and the South.   In the battles of Trenton, Princeton, Germantown, and Monmouth, he was engaged with the enemy ; and afterwards was with General Lafayette, in Virginia, in all the arduous services against Cornwallis.   He held the commission of lieutenant, and performed the duties of that office till the close of the war.   Immediately after that event he removed to Kentucky, and has never received his half pay, or the commutation therefor awarded by Congress; and he now prays that this may be granted to him.   In support of this claim, the petitioner presents the depositions of two witnesses, who swear to their knowledge of the truth of most of the facts stated by him.   His commission from Congress accompanies the papers, together with a certificate that he has not received the commutation, and another that he has received the benefit of the law of May, 1828, made for the relief of such officers and soldiers as served till the close of the war.

Wherefore, the committee conceive that the petitioner is entitled to receive the relief prayed for.

*Resolved,* That the same be granted, and that a bill for the relief of James Barnett be reported to the House.

---

JANUARY 26, 1830.

*The Committee on Military Pensions, to whom were referred the petition and documents of John H. Wendal, report :*

That petitioner states he enlisted, on the first day of March, 1776, in the continental service, as a captain in one of the New York regiments, and continued in such service until the fifth day of April, 1781, when ill health compelled him to resign, and he was honorably discharged.   That his claim for services has been adjudged by the Secretary of War not to be within the act of Congress of the 15th of May, 1828.   The committee, however, believing that, having served so long, and being compelled to leave the service at so late a period, Captain Wendal would have been embraced in the general provisions of that act, if his case had been then known to Congress, report a bill for his relief. His services seem to be substantially but not accurately proved, by Wilhelmus Richerman and Nicholas Van Rensselaer, of the State of New York. These witnesses both further state, that they always understood, and believe, that Captain Wendal's resignation took place on account of his ill health, and inability to serve in consequence of it. Being assured of the good standing and character of Captain Wendal, the committee believe themselves justified in making a favorable report.

----

JANUARY 29, 1830.

*The Committee on Revolutionary Claims, to which was referred the petition of Thomas Blackwell, have had the same under consideration, and report:*

The petitioner claims that, by his services as a captain in the army of the Revolution, to the end of the war, he became entitled to half pay for life ; that he has never received it, or the commutation therefor ; that he is poor, and prays relief.

No commission or discharge has been presented to the committee in proof of the office or service of the petitioner ; nor was his name on the general list of officers returned as having served to the end of the war of the Revolution ; but, by sundry certificates accompanying the petition, from the Departments having charge of documents relating thereto, it does appear that, in the years 1777 and 1778, he was discharging the duties of a captain, in the Virginia line ; that, in May, 1783, there was a settlement with him for his services as a captain in that line ; that he received one warrant for bounty lands for three years' service, and afterwards another for his seventh and eighth years' service in the war. It also, on the list of officers, called a miscellaneous list, made out by the Secretary of War, subsequent to the general return for bounty lands, appears that the name of Thomas Blackwell is found ; and that the certificates then adduced to establish his claim to bounty lands, stated explicitly his services to the end of the war ; and it may now be added, that the Secretary of the Treasury has decided that the petitioner is entitled to the benefits of the act of the 15th of May, 1828, which, of course, depended on proof of service to the end of the war : from all which, there can remain no reasonable doubt that the petitioner, at the close of the war, became entitled to half pay or the commutation ; and that he had not received it as late as 1793, is inferrible from the fact that he then established his claim to a warrant for bounty, by certificates of his service, when proof of his having received half pay, or commutation, or the production of the certificate for it, would have been convenient and sufficient evidence. It also appears that, after a careful examination, no registry of any certificate issued to the petitioner, for either half pay or commutation, has been discovered.

The committee are, therefore, satisfied of the truth of the facts on which the petitioner rests his claim, and no doubt is suggested of the propriety of granting the relief prayed for, except what arises from the fact, that he is entitled to, and receiving, the benefits of the act of 15th of May, 1828, giving him full pay for life. It will be recollected that this act includes, and extends its benefits to, all the officers of the Revolution embraced in the resolve of October 21, 1780, promising half pay for life. It will also be recollected, and is matter of record, that nearly all the officers embraced in this resolve have, long ago, by taking and funding their certificates, or otherwise, received their pay ; some, however, actually realizing from it more, and some less. It is also now well known, that by the settled construction of the act of 1828, all those who, before the passage of it, had thus received their pay, are regularly admitted to its benefits, without returning or accounting for whatever they did receive; and if the result of these payments had been equally beneficial to all, it is evident that the only proposition which could do equal justice to all would be to allow that, as the payment of the claim, under the resolve of 1780, does not preclude the benefits of the act of 1828, the benefits of the act of 1828 should not preclude payment under the resolve. And the committee do not perceive any sufficient reason in these cases for making a distinction, which shall give to this act a different operation upon those seeking payment from what, by its terms and construction, it is allowed to have on those who have already recovered it, which would be the effect of rejecting this claim. The committee are aware that equal justice can never be done in these cases ; but they believe that, to finish the payments to those few (if any more) who remain unpaid, will be the nearest approach that can be made, under present circumstances, to equality, consistency, and humanity ; and therefore report a bill.

---

JANUARY 29, 1830.

*The Committee on Revolutionary Claims, to which was referred the petition of Sarah Easton and Dorothy Storer, report :*

That the petitioners, children and heirs at law of Robert H. Harrison, Esq., deceased, pray that Congress would grant to them the commutation of half pay and bounty lands due to their father in virtue of his services as a lieutenant colonel in the army of the United States in the revolutionary war, which he never received. It appears by the resolution of the Continental Congress, that Robert Hanson Harrison, the father of the petitioners, was, on the 5th of June, 1776, being then one of the aids-de-camp of the commander-in-chief, made a lieutenant colonel in said army. He held his commission, and continued in that rank, until the close of the war. From October, 1775, when he entered the service as aid-de-camp, as aforesaid, he continued in the service, actively and arduously employed, either in the immediate duties of his station, or as principal secretary to General Washington, until 1781, when, being reduced by the laborious duties of the service, he was compelled to leave the army on furlough. He was not, after this time, able to join it again, by reason of his enfeebled health ; but held himself ready at all times to do so, whenever his state of health would permit. The following testimonials are incorporated into this report, and made a part of it, because they do, better than any language which can be used by the committee, express the character of Colonel Harrison, the nature of the service he performed, and the estimation in which he was held by the most distinguished officers of the army. It is also submitted that these testimonials, though not under oath, furnish to the House satisfactory evidence of the truth of those facts which are contained in them :

MORRISTOWN, *January* 9, 1777.

MY DEAR HARRISON : I often intended, but before I had it in my power forgot, to ask you whether your brother-in-law, Major Johnson, would not, in your opinion, make a good aid-de-camp to me. I know it is a question that will involve you in some difficulty, but I beg you will not consider the connexion between you in answering of it. I have heard that Major Johnson is a man of education ; I believe him to be a man of sense : these are two very necessary qualifications ; but how is his temper ? As to military knowledge, I do not expect to find gentlemen much skilled in it : if they can write a good letter, write quick, are methodical and diligent, it is all I expect to find in my aids. Do not, therefore, if Major Johnson possesses these qualities, and a good disposition, withhold (from false modesty) your recommendation ; because, in that case, you will do him injustice and me a disservice.

If you think Mr. Johnson will suit me as well as any other, I should prefer him ; and, therefore, beg that he may be sent hither immediately, as Webb only waits the arrival of another aid to set out for Connecticut.

I am, ever, your affectionate friend and obedient servant,

GEORGE WASHINGTON.

MORRISTOWN, *January* 10, 1777.

MY DEAR SIR : Enclosed are unsealed letters for Baylor and Major Clough ; let every thing be put in motion agreeably to them as speedily as possible, and Clough or Stark, or both, set off as speedily as possible for Virginia.

If Grayson accepts the offer of a regiment, he should set out immediately to raise it ; in doing which, he will, I expect, derive great assistance from Levin Powell, if he inclines to serve as lieutenant colonel; the other officers, under the reserve of a negative, I leave to themselves to name. Young Ross I shall put into Gist's regiment.

Let me have a copy of the instructions given to Sheldon ; and if you could let me know exactly how the matter stands with respect to the exchange of prisoners, I should be glad to be furnished with it as soon as possible, as I am blamed, it seems, for not facilitating that matter more. Take the most speedy and effectual measures to communicate the releasements that have come out, in order that the several officers concerned may be under no doubt or embarrassment with respect to the part they are to act.

The enclosed came to me from Richard Henry Lee, Esq. I send it, that, if Grayson thinks proper to make use of Captain Kendall, he may. Colonel Lee gives a good character of him. I shall add no more at present, than that I am, most sincerely, yours,

GEORGE WASHINGTON.

P. S. Send me a copy of the resolution of Congress relative to General Lee. I hear they are about to try him as a deserter.

MORRISTOWN, *January* 20, 1777.

MY DEAR SIR : Mr. Johnson (who is now become a member of my family) delivered me your letter of the 18th last night. I beg you to consult, and, in my name, advise and direct such measures as shall appear most effectual to stop the progress of the small-pox. When I recall to mind the unhappy situation of our Northern army last year, I shudder at the consequences of this disorder, if some vigorous steps are not taken to stop the spreading of it. Vigorous measures must be adopted (however disagreeable and inconvenient to individuals) to remove the infected and infection before we feel too sensibly the effect.

I wish to Heaven the expected reinforcements were joined. (Under the rose I say it,) my situation, with respect to numbers, is more distressing than it has ever been yet ; and at a time when the enemy are assembling their force from all quarters, no doubt with a view either to route this army, or to remove towards Philadelphia, as I cannot suppose them so much uninformed of our strength as to believe they are acting upon a defensive plan at this hour.

I am exceeding glad to hear you are getting better of your complaints. I would not wish you to come out too soon ; that may only occasion a relapse, which may add length of time to your confinement.

Be so good as to forward the enclosed to Captain Hamilton.

Most affectionately, I am yours,

GEORGE WASHINGTON.

P. S. Doctor Cochran will set out to-morrow for Newtown, and will assist you in the matters before mentioned, relative to the small-pox people.

MOUNT VERNON, *November* 18, 1781.

DEAR SIR : A few days previous to my leaving the camp before York, I was favored with your letter of —— ultimo. Thinking I should see you on my return, I postponed acknowledging the receipt of it, till now I despair of that pleasure, being on the eve of my departure for Philadelphia, without making any stay on the road, except one day at Annapolis, if the Governor should be there.

I desired Doctor Draper, who came to this place with me on Tuesday last, and proposed being at Port Tobacco next day, to let you know I should stay a few days at home, and should be glad to see you ; he possibly did not go there, or you might be attending the courts.

I thank you for your kind congratulations on the capituation of Cornwallis. It is an interesting event, and may be productive of much good, if properly improved ; but if it should be the means of relaxation, and sink us into supineness and security, it had better not have happened. Great Britain, for some time past, has been encouraged by the impolicy of our conduct to continue the war ; and should there be an interference of European politics in her favor, peace may be further removed from us than we expect ; while one thing we are sure of, and that is, that the only certain way to obtain peace is to be prepared for war. Policy, interest, economy, all unite to stimulate the States to fill the continental battalions, and provide the means of supporting them. I hope the present favorable moment for doing it will not be neglected.

Mr. Custis's death has given much distress in this family. I congratulate you on your late change, and am, dear sir, your most obedient and affectionate servant,

GEORGE WASHINGTON.

Robert Hanson Harrison, Esq.

Certificate of Services.—No. 300.

*To Lieutenant Colonel Robert Hanson Harrison.*

I certify that Robert Hanson Harrison, Esquire, lieutenant colonel in the continental army, entered the service in the month of October, 1775, as one of my aids-de-camp, and in May following became my secretary, the duties of which offices he discharged with conspicuous abilities ; that his whole conduct, during all the interesting periods of war, has been marked by the strictest integrity, and the most attentive and faithful services, while by personal bravery he has been distinguished on several occasions.

Given at headquarters, this 25th day of March, 1781.

New York, *September* 28, 1789.

Dear Sir : It would be unnecessary to remark to you, that the administration of justice is the strongest cement of good government, did it not follow, as a consequence, that the first organization of the Federal judiciary is essential to the happiness of our country, and to the stability of our political system.

Under this impression, it has been the invariable object of my anxious solicitude, to select the fittest characters to expound the laws and dispense justice. To tell you that this sentiment has ruled me in your nomination to a seat on the Supreme bench of the United States, would be but to repeat opinions with which you are already well acquainted; opinions which meet a just coincidence in the public mind.

Your friends and your fellow-citizens, anxious for the respect of the court to which you are appointed, will be happy to learn your acceptance, and no one among them will be more so than myself.

As soon as the acts, which are necessary accompaniments of the appointments, can be got ready, you will receive official notice of the latter. This letter is only to be considered as an early communication of my sentiments on this occasion, and as a testimony of the sincere esteem and regard with which I am your most obedient and affectionate humble servant,

GEORGE WASHINGTON.

The Hon. Robert H. Harrison.

New York, *November* 25, 1789.

My dear Sir : Since my return from my tour through the Eastern States, I have received your two letters, dated the 27th of last month, together with the commission which had been sent to you as a Judge of the Supreme Court of the United States.

I find that one of the reasons which induced you to decline the appointment rests on an idea that the judicial act will remain unaltered. But in respect to that circumstance, I may suggest to you, that such a change in the system is contemplated, and deemed expedient, by many in as well as out of Congress, as would permit you to pay as much attention to your private affairs as your present station does.

As the first court will not sit until the first Monday in February, I have thought proper to return your commission, not for the sake of urging you to accept it, contrary to your interest or convenience, but with a view of giving you a further opportunity of informing yourself of the nature and probability of the change alluded to. This you would be able to do, with the less risk of mistake, if you should find it convenient to pass some time here, when a considerable number of members of both Houses of Congress shall have assembled ; and this might be done before it would become indispensable to fill the place offered to you. If, on the other hand, your determination is absolutely fixed, you can, without much trouble, send back the commission under cover.

Knowing, as you do, the candid part which I wish to act on all occasions, you will, I am persuaded, do me the justice to attribute my conduct in this particular instance to the proper motives, when I assure you that I would not have written this letter if I had imagined it would produce any new embarrassments. On the contrary, you may rest assured that I shall be perfectly satisfied with whatever determination may be consonant to your best judgment, and most agreeable to yourself.

I am, dear sir, with sentiments of real esteem and regard, your most obedient and affectionate servant,

GEORGE WASHINGTON.

P. S. As it may be satisfactory to you to know the determination of the other associate judges of the Supreme Court, I have the pleasure to inform you that all of them have accepted their appointments.

BLADENSBURG, *January* 21, 1790.

MY DEAR SIR : I left home on the 14th instant, with a view of making a journey to New York, and, after being several days detained at Alexandria by indisposition, came thus far on the way. I now, unhappily, find myself in such a situation as not to be able to proceed farther. From this unfortunate event, and the apprehension that my indisposition may continue, I pray you to consider that I cannot accept the appointment of associate judge, with which I have been honored. What I do, my dear sir, is the result of the most painful and distressing necessity.

I entreat that you will receive the warmest returns of my gratitude for the distinguished proofs I have had of your flattering and invaluable esteem and confidence, and that you will believe that I am, and shall always remain, with the most affectionate attachment, my dear sir,

Your most obedient and obliged friend and servant,

ROBERT H. HARRISON.

(Endorsed "Private.")

The PRESIDENT *of the United States.*

Mr. Harrison lived to return home, and died in March following.

My happy intimacy at headquarters, during the revolutionary war, and a mutual friendship with Colonel R. H. Harrison, have enabled me to witness his high virtues, distinguished abilities, important services, as well as the very great share he had in the confidence, affection, and gratitude of General Washington.

While I had lived in, and during my ensuing intercourse with, the military family of which I am proud to have ever been considered as a member, I have seen Colonel Harrison intrusted with every secret, consulted in every emergency, employed on opportunities where patriotism and talents were most required ; and although, at the time of the colonel's retreat, I was employed on a separate command in Virginia, I may attest that his brother soldiers regarded him as an officer on furlough, ready to reassume his post in case his health would allow it. So far, at least, goes my general recollection, and the remembrance of General Washington's own expressions, that, if I had the honor of a seat in Congress, I should not hesitate to give a favorable vote on that subject.

And, in case there is an application made before the State Legislature, in behalf of Colonel Harrison's children, I wish it may not appear too presuming from a survivor of the headquarters of those early times, to say that a mark of satisfaction to the memory of their excellent father, gratifying, as it cannot fail to be, to the actual veterans of the revolutionary army, would not have been less gratefully applauded by those who are departed, namely, by our venerated commander-in-chief.

LAFAYETTE.

The services rendered by the late Colonel Robert H. Harrison, in our revolutionary war, were of that distinguished character, as to be known to the whole army, to the Congress who conducted the affairs of the Revolution, and, in general, to the American people. In the commencement of the war, being a neighbor of General Washington's, and well known to him, he was invited by the general to join him as aid-de-camp and principal secretary, and he served in that station with as pure and unsullied a fame as any person ever enjoyed. In all the actions in which General Washington commanded, Colonel Harrison was present, near the person of the general, and exposed with him to equal danger. He assisted, as I have always understood, in the councils of war, where his opinions were highly respected. He was the faithful depositary of the secret counsels of the General, of the confidential communications to him from Congress, of the military movements that were intended to be made, and of all those secret counsels, on the preservation of which the success of the army, and of the Revolution itself, depended ; and he was a most virtuous, able, and active agent, in promoting every measure that was decided on.

In the most gloomy periods of the Revolution, he was firm, persevering, and undaunted. I particularly remember that, in the ever-memorable retreat through Jersey, his example, in aid of that of the illustrious commander-in-chief, cheered the drooping spirits of others, and animated them to action. No person was more brave than Colonel Harrison, none more faithful ; and, I say with confidence, that few, very few, rendered more important services to their country. Had he sought promotion in the army, there can be no doubt that he might easily have obtained it ; but he had no such ambition. To be eminently useful in the station which he held, was the sole object of his heart. It is impossible to look back to this eventful period, and especially to the great achievements of the army, in which he sustained so distinguished and useful a part, by the various, important, and complicated duties he had to perform, without being deeply impressed with a sense of his rare merit, and acknowledging, with gratitude, his very important services. He did not leave the army until the liberties of his country were secured ; nor then, till his constitution had received a severe shock. No sooner, however, was an opportunity afforded to the late commander-in-chief, than he seized it, to bestow on him a new and strong proof of his confidence and attachment, as well as of his high respect for his merit. On the adoption of the present constitution of the United States, when General Washington was called to the head of the Government, he appointed Colonel Harrison a judge of the Supreme Court of the United States. His constitution, however, was too far exhausted to permit him to enter on the duties of that office. He set out to undertake them, but did not survive the effort.

I certify these facts, from a personal knowledge of them in their most important circumstances, having served myself, in our revolutionary war, three campaigns—those of 1776, 1777, and 1778 ; in the first as a lieutenant in the third Virginia regiment, and in the two last as aid-de-camp to Major General Lord Stirling ; and they were afterwards known to me, in common with other citizens who enjoyed public trusts, by which they became acquainted with public affairs. The documents, however, of the late army, and of the Congress, will sufficiently prove the facts. Of the recompense which Colonel Harrison received for his important services, I can say little : I have no doubt, however, that he received nothing more than his pay by the month, depreciated as it was when received. He was among the most diffident and modest of men, and the last to set up a pretension, or to make any claim for his services.

Given under my hand, at Washington, this ——.

JAS. MONROE.

The two following certificates are, in like manner, made a part of this report, to show that Colonel Harrison never resigned his office in the army, nor received the commutation due to him in virtue of his services, and by the laws in such cases provided by the continental Congress :

TREASURY DEPARTMENT,<br>
*Register's Office, December* 24, 1822.

I certify that, having carefully examined the records of the Treasury, in relation to the commutation to the officers and soldiers of the revolutionary army, it is ascertained that Colonel Robert Hanson Harrison, secretary and aid-de-camp to his excellency General Washington, did not receive commutation for five years' full pay.

JOSEPH NOURSE, *Register.*

WAR DEPARTMENT,
*January* 15, 1823.

I certify that the records of this office do not furnish any information relative to the resignation of Colonel Robert H. Harrison, who was aid-de-camp and secretary to General Washington during the revolutionary war.

C. VANDEVENTER,
*Chief Clerk War Department.*

Whereupon the committee resolve that the prayer of the petition of Sarah Easton and Dorothy Storer be granted, and that a bill for that purpose be herewith reported to the House.

---

FEBRUARY 9, 1830.

*The Committee on Revolutionary Claims, to which was referred the petition of Aaron Snow, report :*

That said Snow has furnished your committee with satisfactory evidence from the Treasury Department, that three several certificates were issued in his favor by John Pierce, late commissioner of army accounts, for military services rendered by said Snow during the revolutionary war, namely : one numbered 27094, dated January 1, 1784, for $44\frac{66}{90}$; and one numbered 27373, dated January 20, 1784, for $80 ; and one numbered 31305, dated March 1, 1784, for $86\frac{60}{90}$ ; and that said certificates remain outstanding and unpaid on the books of the Treasury. It being thus made to appear that said Snow has never received the amount due him upon these certificates, the committee herewith report a bill for his relief.

---

FEBRUARY 26, 1830.

*The Committee on Revolutionary Claims, to whom was referred the memorial of Philip Slaughter, report :*

A former Committee on Revolutionary Claims were instructed, by a resolution of the House of the 17th December, 1827, "to inquire into the propriety of remunerating Captain Philip Slaughter for his services in the continental army, during the war of the Revolution;" who reported, among other matters, that "Captain Slaughter did, virtually, continue in the service of the United States until the end of the revolutionary war ; that he was a meritorious officer, and, from the character given him by highly respectable witnesses, entitled to receive from the Government all the emoluments to which officers of his grade were, under the resolves of Congress, entitled ;" and the committee therewith reported a bill in his favor, allowing him five years' full pay, without interest, which was the commutation of his half pay for life. Had this bill, as reported by said committee, been passed, it would have entitled Captain Slaughter to the benefit of the act of Congress of the 15th May, 1828, entitled "An act for the relief of certain surviving officers and soldiers of the army of the Revolution ;" but, on its passage through the House, the said bill was *amended*, by inserting the following *proviso: " Provided*, That the acceptance by the said Slaughter of the grant herein made shall be in lieu of any claim he may have, under the provisions of a bill passed at this session of Congress, entitled ' An act for the relief of the surviving officers and soldiers of the Revolution.' The said Slaughter did, after the passage of said act, accept the grant therein made to him ; and now he comes and prays that the subject may be reconsidered by Congress, and alleges that he accepted the said grant, "to release securities from distressing embarrassments, in the full persuasion that the rigor and hardship of the *exclusion* of which he complains would be released, in a spirit of justice, by the representatives of the people."

Your committee, on full examination of the subject, do most entirely concur in the report of the former committee, above referred to, and ask that the same may be considered as a part of this report ; and, with great deference to the decision of a former Congress, they cannot persuade themselves out of the belief that Captain Slaughter ought not to be deprived of the benefit of the aforesaid act of the 15th May, 1828 ; and they very respectfully submit whether Captain Slaughter ought not to be restored to an equality with other meritorious officers of the army of the Revolution. Believing that he ought, the committee report a bill, repealling the *proviso* above cited.

MARCH 22, 1830.

*The Committee on Revolutionary Claims, to whom was referred the petition of Ichabod Ward, report :*

That the petitioner presents and asks pay for a certain certificate or indent of interest, which is in the words following :

" Number 4174.
"According to the resolution of the United States in Congress assembled, passed the twenty-eighth day of April, 1784, I do certify that there is due to James Sheldon, or bearer, twenty dollars and forty-five-ninetieths, for interest. Given at the loan office of the State of Connecticut, this 20th day of December, 1785." And signed,
"WM. IMLAY, *C. L. O.*"

Which certificate is proved by the certificate of the Register of the Treasury to be genuine, and outstanding against the United States.

Since the term limited for presenting these certificates expired, Congress has, in some cases, authorized their payment with six per cent. interest; but as the provisions for funding them confined their interest to three per cent., the committee report a bill in this case allowing three per cent. only.

*The Committee on Revolutionary Claims, to which the petition of Ann D. Baylor was referred, report :*

That she sets forth therein that she is the widow of John Walker Baylor, deceased, the only son and heir at law of Col. George Baylor, late of the United States army in the revolutionary war, deceased; that the said Col. Baylor, in his lifetime, held, and was the sole owner of, certain certificates, issued from the loan office of the United States in Virginia to him, the said George Baylor, or bearer, which have never been paid; and that said certificates are now, of right, the property of the children of her, the said Ann, and John Walker Baylor, aforesaid, deceased.

It appears by a certificate from the Register of the Treasury, dated February 2, 1830, that certificates were issued from the loan office aforesaid to said Col. Baylor, of the following tenor and dates, to wit : March 31, 1778, No. 3358 to 3363, inclusive, for $300 each, and equal in specie to $149$\frac{72}{90}$ each; and from No. 3366 to 3379, inclusive, for $300 each, equal in specie to $149$\frac{72}{90}$ each; and from No. 525 to No. 528, inclusive, for $500 each, and equal in specie to $249$\frac{61}{90}$ each ; and amounting, in the whole, in specie, to $3,994$\frac{64}{90}$ ; and that these certificates remain outstanding and unpaid by the United States. It is, moreover, stated by the petitioner, and the fact is well known and admitted, that the said Col. Baylor, worn out by hard and perilous service during the whole war, did, at the close of it, leave the country on a sea voyage, and in the year 1783 died, in the island of Barbadoes, leaving the said John, afterwards the husband of the petitioner, then an infant of very tender age. It appears by the last will and testament of the said Col. Baylor, that he bequeathed these certificates thereby, and directed the interest thereof to be expended in educating his said son, and such other child (his wife being pregnant) as might be born to him afterwards. Though his last will and testament was received by his executors from Barbadoes, yet these certificates, believed to have been there with him, have never been found.

No other reason than what may be suggested by these facts is offered to the committee to account for the delay in calling for the amount of this claim before this time. Be that as it may, no reason can be given why the United States should not now pay the same.

The question of interest offers some difficulty. . It may be said, that if the principal were due March 31, 1778, then the interest is now due from that time to the present; and that the United States having, during all that time, paid interest quarterly on loans to a great amount, cannot now, with any justice, refuse to pay this sum, with simple interest, from that to the present time. To this it may be replied, that ever since the establishment of the funding system, except a few years during the last war, the United States, although owing large amounts on loans, yet at all times had in the Treasury money, not otherwise appropriated, in amount sufficient to pay this demand, or so much thereof as would have been due thereon, according to the terms of that system, had these certificates been subscribed to the loan proposed thereby, for making provision for the domestic debt of the United States. It is, therefore, considered by the committee, that the same justice will be extended to this claimant as has been to others, the creditors of the United States, if she be permitted to subscribe to said loan as under date of December 31, 1790, when the first subscription was made. Whereupon it is

*Resolved*, That the accounting officers of the Treasury ought to account with the petitioner on the principles aforesaid, crediting her with interest and dividends of the principal of said certificates, in the same manner as if the same had been subscribed and paid into the loan as aforesaid, but allowing no interest on any dividends after the same were payable ; and that a bill for her relief accordingly be reported to the House.

---

FEBRUARY 26, 1830.

*The Committee on Revolutionary Claims, to which was referred the claim of Benjamin Wells, report :*

1st. That the claimant states in his petition that he served in the office of deputy commissary of issues at Montser mill, in Pennsylvania, in the army of the United States, during the revolutionary war, under John Irvin, deputy commissary general, from the 4th day of March until the 31st day of December in the year 1778, and furnished a laborer in that service for the United States during that time ; and that he received therefor from said Irvin £164 5s. on the 9th of January, 1799, in continental paper money ; and that, otherwise, he has not been compensated therefor. In proof of these allegations, the claimant produces a letter of John Burrall, stating that the amount of £164 5s., continental money, was, by the said John Irvin, deputy commissary general, charged as paid to the said Wells, for the services done and furnished as aforesaid, in the continental money account of the said Irvin against the United States, and by them allowed to him.

2d. The claimant further states in his petition aforesaid, that he was afterwards employed by the said Irvin to sell the damaged provisions then in said magazine, and that he performed that service for the United States ; but that therefor, and for the expenses by him incurred therein, by advertising and in going to Pittsfield, and settling with said Irvin, and paying the money over unto him, he has never received any compensation. It appears by the letter aforesaid of J. Burrall, that the said Irvin did not charge the United States for any amount paid to the claimant for these last services and expenses ; for no allowance does appear to have been made to him on that account. The time of doing these services, though not precisely stated, appears to have been after the first services were performed, and the £164 5s. received by the claimant. He offers, in proof, a receipt for the sum of £3 4s. 3d., signed by J. Johnston, for David Duncan, dated February 10, 1799, and purporting to have been given by him for his board, while settling his accounts as deputy commissary of issues with the commissioners. No other evidence of this part of his allegation is offered by the claimant.

3d. The claimant states that, afterwards, David Duncan, deputy quartermaster at the said magazine, employed him as issuing foragemaster, for the term of seven months, to wit: from the 20th November, 1779, to the 29th of June, 1780. These services are satisfactorily proved by a certificate of the settlement of his account therefor at the Treasury Department, in due form, and signed by Joseph Nourse, Register. Herein the claimant alleges that he suffered injury and loss by the manner of settling his account. It appears that he was allowed $80 per month wages, and $10 per month for subsistence, during the seven months, and, in the whole, amounting to $630. It further appears, also, that this sum was reduced by applying to it a supposed scale of depreciation, at the rate of $24 of the account for one dollar made in payment of it; and that he was allowed and paid but $26 25 for the whole.

4th. The claimant further alleges that he furnished William Harrison, issuing foragemaster, with corn; and to others, beef, flour, and bacon, for the use of the United States, for which he received certificates, which he was compelled to sell at a discount. Further, he alleges that certain other certificates, by him delivered to Barnard Webb, as he believed a clerk in the Auditor's Office, were lost, and he has received no benefit from them.

On these allegations, the committee further report, that, though the facts contained in the fourth are, by papers presented to them by the claimant, rendered probable, and may be true, yet, for the last certificates, the United States cannot be held accountable without more full and distinct proof of their contents, and the reasons why the said Webb has not restored them. For the certificates sold at a discount by the claimant, the United States are not now accountable, in any part of them, to him; because they have already accounted, or are liable to account, for the whole, to whomsoever he may have transferred them.

Concerning the claims for services and expenditures in the second allegation mentioned, neither the one nor the other is specified with regard to the amount or value; nor are they so supported by evidence as that the committee can recommend the allowance of them.

The claim contained in the fourth allegation is supported by satisfactory proof; and the amount of services rendered by the claimant, as deputy foragemaster under the orders of Duncan, together with the gross error made at the Treasury Department in settling therefor, is fully proved. The petitioner has doubtless made an error in stating the time when those services terminated. By the account produced from the Treasury, which he acknowledges to be correct, they ended on the 20th of June, 1780. A much greater mistake was made by that Department, in ascertaining the money value, in Spanish dollars, of those services. It must have been known to all the officers of that Department that Congress had, on the 28th of June, 1780, resolved that continental money was, on the 10th of March of that year, at 40 for 1 in silver. It was, from that date, out of circulation; and when these services terminated, on the 20th of June, there was no such currency as continental paper money. The accounting officers should have settled with the claimant at the value set by Congress on such services when the currency was gold and silver, or continental money before it had depreciated.

On the 24th of May, 1776, Congress resolved that the wages of issuing commissaries should be $40 per month, and 4 rations. On the 18th of September, of the same year, they resolved that the money value of a ration should be $\frac{8}{90}$ of a dollar, or 8 pence Pennsylvania currency, equal to 8.8 cents. The rations for each month of 30 days equalled $10 56; the monthly pay of the claimant should therefore have been $50 56, and the amount for the seven months, $353 92. He received $26 25 when his account was settled; and whenever that was, (and by the Register's certificate it appears to have been before March 26th, 1800,) the balance due to him then was $326 67.

Should it be said, in justification of the Treasury Department, that Congress, by a resolution of May 11, 1779, established the pay of deputy foragemaster at $80 per month, and $10 for subsistence, it is a full answer to say that Congress also resolved, on the 29th of February, 1780, " That all grants to the army, in addition to pay or rations made since January, 1777, were made (except for extra services) in consideration of enhanced prices of the necessaries of life, by the depreciation of the currency, and ought to be so considered in making up original contracts." These resolutions, therefore, do no more than show that the wages and rations of the army were not in reality altered by them ; and that all payments made under the nominal increase of either were to be charged and accounted for according to the value, in Spanish dollars, of the continental money in which they were made, and at the time of making them. The claimant's services were not to be estimated by the value of continental money at any time while he was rendering them, but by the value of money when the price of such services was established by Congress. The scale of depreciation was established to ascertain the hard money value of payments in continental money made by the United States, and was therefore to be applied to such payments made to the army, and not to the services rendered by the army. No payment had been made to the claimant, and so no use could be made of the scale of depreciation relative to his claim.

Had the claimant used due diligence in calling on the United States to rectify this error, he might have realized the whole amount of interest on the balance which thereby would have been found due to him ; but as he has delayed it so long, the committee do not feel warranted in allowing to him, at this time, the whole amount thereof.

The allegations stating the first claim of the petitioner are for nine months and twenty-seven days' services at the magazine aforesaid, as deputy commissary of issues, under John Irvin, deputy commissary general of Pennsylvania ; and are so supported that the committee cannot fairly question that they were rendered in manner as stated. It appears by the letter of John Burrall, shown as evidence by the claimant, that John Irvin, deputy commissary general as aforesaid, charged in his account to the United States, £164 5s., paid to the claimant in continental money, on the 9th of January, 1799, on account of those services rendered and furnished by him. It does not appear, and the committee have no reason to suspect, that the claimant ever received, otherwise than as above stated, any compensation whatever. This sum must have been paid on account, and not in full. It was paid and charged as £164 5s., in a currency of account, reckoning 7s. 6d. to the dollar, and amounted to $438. The services of the claimant, without any allowance for those of the laborer furnished, amounted, by the price, according to the resolution of May 24th, 1776, to $454, and, according to that of May 11, 1779, to $891 ; but adding those services in the first instance, the amount is $630 20 ; and, in the second, $971 33. For a still stronger reason, this was not a payment in full. It was made in continental money, January 9, 1779. At that time this money was so depreciated, that it appears by the resolve aforesaid, it was, on the 1st of March following, ten for one. It could not, therefore, when paid to the claimant, have been better than eight for one. The amount paid was $438, and was, at that rate, worth $54 75 in hard money. It should have been stated, that the wages of a day laborer at a magazine of issues were settled by the resolution aforesaid of May 24, 1776, at 2*s*. 8*d*. per day, and one ration. This, allowing 7*s*. 6*d*. to the dollar, and the money price of the ration at $\frac{8}{90}$ of a dollar, amounts to $13 20 per month ; and the amount for the whole term being added, makes the sum before stated equal to $630 20. If, from this, the specie value aforesaid of the continental money paid to him be deducted, the balance due to him, January 9, 1779, was $575 45.

It is believed that, had this account been brought forward at any time before the establishment of the funding system, it would have been adjusted on the principles aforesaid, and interest would have been allowed thereon up to December 31, 1790 ; and, therefore, such interest as was allowed on all outstanding debts against the United States, subscribed or not subscribed to the loan at that time proposed.

These two items in the claimant's account ought to be allowed and paid. The first results from a gross error made at the Treasury ; and, had the second been offered then, it may be presumed that a like error would have been made in that. That these errors have never been corrected, is, in part, owing to the delay of the claimant, and therefore the United States ought not, at this time, to place him on a better footing, in respect to interest, than other creditors whose claims were subscribed to the loan aforesaid. Had the claimant received the quartermaster's certificates at the termination of his services, they would have been payable, as all others were, in one month from and after their date ; and, if not then paid, would have drawn interest at six per cent. until paid. This one would have been dated January 9th, 1779, for $575 45, payable February 9th, 1799 ; the other, June 20th, 1780, for $326 67, payable July 20th, 1780 ; and each on interest after those dates.

The claimant should be settled with for these sums on the principles of the funding system. He should be credited with interest on the two sums aforesaid, from the time at which they were payable up to December 31st, 1790, at six per cent., and with interest on that amount from December 31st, 1790, to the present time, at three per cent., in the same manner as if indents of interest had been issued to him therefor, and the same subscribed and paid in for stocks to the loan aforesaid. On the principal he should be credited with interest, and a yearly amount on such principal, in like manner as if the same had been subscribed and paid in to said loan, and stocks been issued to him therefor; and this amount should be, in all respects, so stated and paid that the claimant shall receive so much only in amount as he would had he received his dividends quarterly, when they would have become due at the Treasury, or at any loan office in any of the several States.

Whereupon, the committee resolve that the claimant ought to receive the amount aforesaid of his claim, and no more, and in manner as aforesaid, and not otherwise ; and that a bill therefor be reported to the House.

----

### FEBRUARY 27, 1830.

*The Committee on Revolutionary Claims, to which was referred the petition of Samuel Ward, report :*

That said petitioner states that, heretofore, to wit, before the establishment of the funding system of the United States, he was the owner of a loan office certificate, issued by Benjamin Walker to Abraham Whipple, Esq., dated October 23, 1786, for $1,047$\frac{42}{90}$, und numbered 281, whereon interest was due from July 23, 1780 ; and that the said certificate was by him, before the establishment of said system, casually lost, and is undoubtedly destroyed ; that Congress, by a law for that purpose, passed May 24, 1828, directed the principal sum of said certificate to be paid to him, but without the payment of interest thereon : whereupon, he prays that this Congress would grant to him the same relief, by the payment of interest on said certificate, which has been extended to many others—a reference to whose cases (being many in number) is made by the petitioner. The facts alleged in this case are placed beyond doubt; and the existence, date, tenor, amount, ownership, and loss of it, together with the payment of the principal only, and that the whole interest is now due and unpaid, cannot be questioned by any reasonable man. The committee is not aware of any case other than this, in which the principal has been allowed and paid on such outstanding certificates, without, at the same time, paying the whole amount of interest. It is impossible to imagine any sound principle by which a principal sum of money, at all times due, with annually accruing interest at six per cent., can be adjudged to be payable, unless, at the same time, it should be adjudged that interest, at some rate, and to some amount, is also payable. While the committee are convinced that paying *no* interest in such case is a denial of justice to the claimant, they cannot doubt that paying *full* interest would be doing injustice to the United States.

Although the United States have at all times been in debt on loans to a large amount, and yearly have paid a great weight of interest on such loans, yet such have been their fiscal arrangements that, at all times, except a very few years during the last war, claims of this kind might have been liquidated and paid from moneys in the Treasury " not otherwise appropriated." Had this claim been presented at the Treasury at any time before December, 1797, it might have been registered, and a new certificate issued, and interest equal to the amount paid to other creditors received ; or it might have been subscribed to the loan of the United States, and placed on a footing of equality with all other claims on them. This statement is not made in mere mockery of the claimant, when it is known that he had lost his certificate, and could, therefore, make no such application. Although, in this case, the character of the claimant is such as to preclude all suspicion that the certificate had been transferred, and not lost, yet some general rule, applicable to all cases of loss, must govern the United States. Bonds given forty years ago, to refund the money if such certificates should reappear regularly transferred to the then claimant, might, when that event took place, be of little value. Nothing could effectually save harmless the United States but that length of time which induces a violent and conclusive presumption of loss. Whether this be ten, twenty, thirty, or forty years, it is needless, in the present case, to ascertain ; because the loss of the claimant happened more than the longest of these periods before the present time.

While this time is running to create this violent and conclusive presumption of loss in favor of claimants who could not otherwise conclusively prove such loss, shall the United States, which, at all times, were ready to pay such claims in manner as all other creditors were paid, suffer by having an interest account run up against them to several times the amount of the principal ? Had not the loss happened, this certificate would, in all probability, have been funded, and paid as all other funded certificates of debt have been paid. Shall the United States be placed in a worse condition by this loss, which, as it is the peculiar misfortune of the claimant, ought not to induce injury to the United States? Especially should it not be so, because at all times, as before stated, they were compelled by fiscal arrangement to keep in the Treasury a yearly sum to meet contingencies, a part of which were certificates like this, known to be outstanding, and which might yearly be called for at the Treasury, in some cases without, but in almost all with, the intervention of Congress.

What interest, then, ought this claimant to receive ? The cases quoted by him are in point, but they must have been allowed and passed without a due regard to the principles on which the United States funded and paid the whole domestic debt. If those were just when established, then is it unjust at this time to place those creditors who omitted, either from loss or neglect, to present their certificates, in a better condition than those who did present them. The justice of that system rests on one fact, to wit, that, though it diminished the whole sum due, from the nominal amount to about four-fifths thereof, yet it increased, by a better security for payment, the market value from one-eighth of that nominal amount to a price nearly one-fifth thereof above par. Those who subscribed, and those who did not subscribe, to the loan under this system, were kept on a footing of equality nearly as long as the subscription was kept open. The cases cited by the claimant are a departure from the principles of the funding system, and so far anomalous; and therefore afford no principle to govern this committee in this or similar cases. The claimant is, in this case, entitled to receive the same amount from the United States which he would have received had he not lost his certificate, but subscribed the amount of it to the loan of December 31, 1790, and received his certificates of stock under the provisions of the act of August 4, 1790, entitled "An act making provision for the debt of the United States," and the other acts made in aid thereof.

---

### DECEMBER 15, 1830.

*The Committee of Claims, to which was referred the petition of Moses White, executor of the will of Gen. Moses Hazen, deceased, report :*

That the petitioner represents that General Moses Hazen was appointed a colonel in the army of the United States, on the 22d day of January, A. D. 1776; that he was then entitled to the half pay of a lieutenant during life from the British Government; and that, in consideration of his acceptance of said appointment, Congress, by a resolution of that date, promised to indemnify him for any loss of said half pay which he might sustain in consequence of his entering into the service of the United States.

The petitioner further states that the British Government, on the 25th day of December, A. D. 1781, adjudged and declared that the half pay of the said Moses Hazen was forfeited, in consequence of his having served in arms against the British forces in North America.

The petitioner further represents, that, on the 26th day of April, A. D. 1781, Congress ordered that the Board of Treasury should place to the credit of Colonel Moses Hazen the sum of $13,386$\frac{2}{90}$, in specie, being the principal and interest of money due to him from the 1st day of May, A. D. 1781; and that the same bear an interest at the rate of six per cent., from the said 1st day of May till paid.

The petitioner further states that this debt accrued from said Hazen's disbursements for the army of the United States in Canada, (where the paper money of the United States was not current,) in specie, and in his own personal obligations.

The petitioner further represents, that, in 1781, the necessities of said Hazen compelled him to receive from the Treasury seven thousand dollars in a depreciated paper, called new emission money, at a rate above its then actual value; and that, in A. D.. 1789, he received from the Treasury the further sum of six thousand three hundred and eighty-six dollars and two cents, in a paper security, called a certificate, which was then of less value than the specie which had been expressly promised to him.

The petitioner further represents, that, upon said Hazen's application at the Treasury Department, in A. D. 1799, for the adjustment and payment of the balance of said debt then due, the Auditor reported that there was then due to said Hazen the sum of eight thousand six hundred and eighty-three dollars eighty-eight cents, as principal, and interest thereon, agreeably to the resolution of Congress of April 26th, A. D. 1781; and that the Comptroller, on the 30th day of June, A. D. 1802, passed upon this report, and decided that interest ought not to be allowed on said debt; which interest, although expressly promised by Congress, has never been paid.

The petitioner further represents, that he has never been fully indemnified for the loss of said Hazen's half pay; and respectfully requests that the balance due on said claims, assured by the express promise and plighted faith of Congress, may be paid to him, as the legal representative of the said Moses Hazen.

The committee further report, that, by a recurrence to the journal of the proceedings of Congress on the 22d day of January, A. D. 1776, and on the 26th day of April, A. D. 1781, and by the evidence laid before them by the petitioner, they find that all the material facts alleged by said petitioner in support of said claims are satisfactorily established.

The committee further report, that the petitioner made application to Congress for payment of said claims at the first session of the twentieth Congress; and that a bill making provision for their payment passed the Senate, and came before the House of Representatives at a late period in their session, where it was amended by expunging the provision which it contained for the payment of interest on said sum of thirteen thousand three hundred and eighty-six dollars and two-ninetieths of a dollar, and by adding to said bill a proviso, "that no interest should be allowed on the amount due for loss of half pay;" which amendments were concurred in by the Senate, and the said bill became a law on the 26th of May, A. D. 1828.

The committee further report, that they are aware that it has not been the practice of this Government to pay interest upon the claims of its creditors, where interest had not been promised; but they believe that it has never failed to pay interest on claims where the payment of interest had been expressly stipulated.

The committee consider the resolutions of Congress of the 22d of January, A. D. 1776, and 26th of April, A. D. 1781, as express stipulations to pay interest on the claims to which they refer; and they cannot discover any ground, consistent with good faith, on which the payment of the interest on the amount of these claims can be refused. They therefore report, herewith, a bill for the relief of the petitioner.

---

*Petition of Moses White, as executor of Moses Hazen, deceased, praying for the fulfilment of a contract made with Congress by said Hazen.*

*To the honorable the Senate and House of Representatives of the United States in Congress assembled:*

The petition of Moses White, executor and representative of Moses Hazen, a brigadier general in the revolutionary army, humbly sheweth:

That, in the last Congress, a bill was passed in the honorable Senate, granting relief to the representatives of the late Moses Hazen, a brigadier general in the revolutionary army, for the loss of his British half pay, agreeably to the resolution of Congress of the 22d January, 1776, and also for the claim for the interest due on the order of Congress of the 25th April, 1781, placing to his credit on the books of the Treasury the sum of $13,386\frac{2}{90}$, specie, bearing an interest at six per cent. per annum, until paid.

This bill was introduced into the House of Representatives, and referred to the Committee on Revolutionary Claims, who made several amendments to said bill, refusing the allowance of any interest on the loss of said half pay, and rejecting the interest due on the order of Congress of the 25th April, 1781, altogether; and the committee assign their reasons for so doing; which reasons, your petitioner believes, upon a full investigation of all the documents and proceedings had in the case, will be found insufficient to debar him of his just right to the interest due on both claims.

The committee, in their said report, after reciting the resolution of Congress of the 22d January, 1776, "that the United States will indemnify Colonel Moses Hazen for any loss of half pay he may sustain in consequence of his entering into their service," and the evidence adduced from the half-pay office in London in support of said claim, which the committee seem to consider as conclusive evidence in support of said claim; the report goes on to state, however, that "a paper purporting to contain extracts of a letter dated the 4th December, 1789, from Mr. Knox, then Secretary of War, to Brigadier General Hazen, (which paper is attested by Moses White, the petitioner, to be a copy,) has been exhibited with the petitioner's documents; from which it appears that said Hazen's claim to indemnity for his loss of his half pay as aforesaid, was considered by Mr. Knox to be valid; but it seems that General

Hazen had not then exhibited any evidence of the loss of his half pay, inasmuch as the Secretary of War, in his letter above mentioned, advises him that, in order to make good his claim to indemnity from the United States, it would be necessary for him to establish, 1st, that he was entitled to half pay from the British Government, and the rate thereof; and, 2d, that he was deprived of said half pay in consequence of his having entered the American service."

The extracts mentioned by the committee were made to prove a different fact. If the committee had examined the original letter of General Knox, which was filed with your petitioner's other documents in the case before the Senate, they might have seen, in the last clause of said letter, that General Knox had undertaken himself to procure such evidence as he described as necessary to make said claim good. He says that a British officer (General Munsal) was then with him, bound direct to London, who had kindly promised to procure such certificate from the pay office there, and forward the same to him. Such a certificate was received by General Knox the next year, bearing date February 17, 1790. General Hazen was furnished with a copy of said certificate, and no reasonable doubt can be entertained but that General Knox filed the original in the proper Department of the Government: this appears to be corroborated by the letter of Oliver Wolcott, Esq., Secretary of the Treasury, dated the 15th July, 1795, in answer to General Hazen's application to the Government for a settlement of said claim for loss of his half pay, and referred to by the Committee of Claims of the House, in their report of February, 1804, wherein he tacitly admits that he was possessed of the evidence; for he says in said letter, that "the said claim for loss of half pay then only waited for provision to be made by Congress, to be adjusted:" he does not intimate the want of further evidence.

The committee of the House further report, that "there is also a paper amongst the documents, purporting to be a copy of a memorandum made by John Pierce, Esq., commissioner of army accounts, (which paper is also authenticated by the attestation of Moses White, the petitioner,) from which it would seem that General Hazen's claim for indemnity for his loss of half pay above mentioned was presented to the said commissioner, and rejected, because it was not ascertained what General Hazen's loss had been in consequence of his relinquishing his British lieutenant's half pay. It does not appear that any evidence of this part of the petitioner's claim, showing the amount, value, and loss of the half pay aforesaid, whereby the account could have been liquidated and settled, was ever exhibited at the proper Department of this Government, at any period prior to the fall of the year 1825, although notice was given to General Hazen, in his lifetime, so long ago as the 4th December, 1789, by the then Secretary of War, that such evidence would be required."

" Your committee are of opinion, therefore, that the reason why the indemnity for the loss of the half pay aforesaid was not made to the said Hazen in his lifetime, or to his executor and representative since his death, was, not that the Government was unable or unwilling to satisfy and discharge the demand, but that the parties claiming from time to time neglected and refused to produce the evidence necessary to a just and equitable liquidation and settlement of the claim." " The committee, therefore, recommend that the first section of the Senate's bill be so amended, as to prohibit the allowance of interest on the amount of loss for the half pay aforesaid."

The misunderstanding between Mr. Pierce and General Hazen, on this item of his claim, arose in consequence of their construing differently the resolution of Congress of the 22d January, 1776, and in the evidence necessary to support it. General Hazen contended, that he understood the committee of Congress who conferred with him, on his appointment of a colonel in their service, to agree that the Government of the United States would put itself in the place of Great Britain, and pay him his annuity of half pay in the same manner as he was entitled to receive it from that Government; and that the British Army Register, in which his name, rank, and pay were mentioned, was the best evidence in the case. Mr. Pierce, however, was of a different opinion; and this item of claim, with some others disallowed by Mr. Pierce, by a resolution of Congress, April 26, 1785, were removed from the commissioner of army accounts, and referred to the Board of Treasury, to examine and report thereon.

But the Board of Treasury made no report; and the first that was heard from this claim afterwards, was the letter of General Knox of the 4th December, 1789, in which he gives the Government's construction of the resolution of the 22d January, 1776, and undertakes to procure the necessary evidence to establish it; but he states further, in his said letter, that the money cannot be obtained till Congress shall make provision for its payment.

For the neglect of the Board of Treasury to report, most surely General Hazen will not be held responsible for the delay up to the date of General Knox's letter. General Hazen patiently awaited the arrival of the evidence, reasonably expecting when it did arrive the Treasury Department would set about a settlement of the claim; but learning from the Department that it waited for provision to be made by Congress before it could be settled, in February, 1793, General Hazen addressed a memorial to Congress, and, among other things, asks for a settlement of the said claim for the loss of his half pay, (a copy of which was with his documents before the Senate.) After waiting a reasonable time, and finding nothing to have been done toward any settlement of his said claim, in the summer of 1795 General Hazen addressed a letter to the President of the United States, complaining that he could obtain no money from the Treasury Department of what was admitted to be due him; that his loss of the British half pay remained unsettled; and that the balance due on the order of Congress of the 25th April, 1781, was withheld, &c. This letter was answered by Mr. Wolcott, the Secretary of the Treasury, which has been above mentioned, dated the 15th July, 1795, in which he mentions the dissatisfaction of General Hazen to the settlement made by the Treasury Department of his general account current, and adds, that his claim for loss of half pay then only waited provision to be made by Congress to be adjusted.

It did not occur to your petitioner that any positive evidence of a certificate from the pay office in London would have been required to substantiate this claim, since the documents in the case furnish circumstantial evidence tantamount to positive proof.

The first certificate obtained by General Knox may probably be in the

Treasury Department still; the second was left with his application in 1805, with other vouchers, and, he understands, cannot be found; he has now some further evidence in the case to offer.

In January, 1803, General Hazen, in a memorial to Congress, again asks for a settlement of this claim, and also for a revision of his account current, &c. The report of the Committee of Claims, to whom it was referred, stated that, in the opinion of the committee, the Treasury Department were competent to correct any errors existing in his accounts, and to settle all just claims against the Government. (Said report was, with his other documents, before the Senate.) In this condition were the accounts of General Hazen at the time of his decease, February 3d, 1803.

The report of the Committee of Claims last mentioned on General Hazen's last memorial, will show that he was dissatisfied with the settlement that had been made of his accounts by the Treasury Department in 1790. The said committee gave it as their opinion that the Treasury Department are competent to correct any errors that may be found to exist in said accounts, &c.

The settlement of General Hazen's estate being likely to devolve upon your petitioner, in the latter part of the year 1803, having a favorable opportunity, he sent to London for another certificate from the pay office, of the like import to the one obtained by General Knox, and received it; and in 1804, having accepted the trust of executor, he, with Mrs. Hazen, (who was appointed executrix, but who afterwards declined the trust,) petitioned Congress, praying that provision might be made for the settling the said claim of half pay. It was referred to the Committee of Claims—the same committee who had, the year previous, made a report on General Hazen's last memorial, and who, after a full investigation of the subject, and being satisfied with the evidence before them, reported that the prayer of the petitioners was reasonable, and ought to be granted. A bill was accordingly ordered to be brought into the House of Representatives, making provision for settling and paying both principal and interest of said claim of loss of half pay. After a lengthy discussion, the said bill passed the House, and was sent to the Senate, but at so late a period of the session that there was not time to take it up.

Here, then, it will appear that ample evidence was produced by General Hazen's representative, so early as 1804, to satisfy a Committee of Claims and the House of Representatives of the validity and justice of said claim.

He also applied to the Treasury Department, to know if a revision of the settlement of General Hazen's accounts could be had, and when.

In 1805, this subject came again before the House, went through the committee, who reported a similar bill to the last, which, after another discussion, passed with an amendment, moved by a member, who wished the avails should be given to Mrs. Hazen, to her own use. It was sent to the Senate, and there negatived, because its avails had been diverted from the proper and legal course.

It thus appears, in 1805, the Committee of Claims and the House of Representatives were fully satisfied with the evidence and vouchers produced in support of said claim for loss of half pay, and passed a bill granting a full indemnity. Copies of the reports of the Committee of Claims of 1804 and 1805 were with his documents before the Senate; all which afford circumstantial evidence sufficient to satisfy any one, and remove all doubt of its having been produced.

In 1806-7, he again petitioned Congress for the said claim of half pay : in the House it was referred to the Committee of Claims; which was the last he ever heard of it.

His friends in the House represented to him that the funds in the Treasury were low, and advised him to wait a more favorable opportunity to push the claim ; which advice he took, being exhausted in patience and funds. Embargo and non-intercourse laws followed, together with the late war. He was willing his claims should lie as a loan to the Government till better times ; if he had possessed thousands, he would have taken a pride in contributing liberally to so just and necessary a war.

In 1819, understanding the Treasury was in a flourishing condition, your petitioner renewed his application to Congress for the said claim of General Hazen's loss of half pay. His petition was referred in the House to the Committee on Revolutionary Claims. He relied on the evidence and vouchers that were left with his application in 1806-7, supposed to be on file in the office of the Committee of Claims, to support the claim ; but these being mislaid, or not to be found, the committee proceeded to make up a report without them, which, of course, was unfavorable.

In 1822 he again applied to Congress, by petition, for said claim, and also for the interest due and withheld by the Comptroller June 30th, 1802, on the order of Congress of April 25th, 1781, praying for leave to file a bill in equity and law before the honorable supreme judicial court of the United States for both claims, promising to abide their decision. This petition was referred by the House to the same committee as the last ; but the committee made no report.

In 1824 he sent on another like petition, which was referred by the House to the same committee as the last, and it was treated with the same silence.

He then withdrew his papers from the committee of the House, sent to London for a new certificate, and procured the best vouchers in his power; and, in the fall of 1825, presented a memorial to Congress, praying for the fulfilment of the resolution of Congress of the 22d January, 1776; and, also, for the interest due on his Canada disbursements, agreeably to the order of Congress of the 25th of April, 1781. The honorable Senate, after a full investigation of the evidence and documents in the case, passed a bill making provision for the settlement and payment of both claims; but, in the House, the Committee of Claims reported a non-concurrence of the bill : here, then, there was no pretence of the want of evidence, but it does not appear that the Government were ready and willing to discharge them.

In 1827 the subject came again before the Senate, and a similar bill to the last mentioned was passed ; but, in the House, the committee reported an amendment that went to reject both claims, except a small portion of the indemnity for the loss of the said half pay.

Your petitioner cannot forbear here to remark, that, in the proceedings had on this case by Congress, there appears something extremely anomalous. Formerly, in 1804 and 1805, provision was made by bills in the House of Representatives, at two different sessions, providing for a full indemnity for the loss of the said half pay, which failed in the Senate ;

and, recently, provision has been made by bills in the Senate, at two different sessions, for indemnifying both of said claims, that have failed in the House.   He is fully persuaded that nothing is wanting but a thorough investigation of the documents and evidence in the case, to lead both Houses to an agreement in the justice of a full indemnity in both claims.

The said Committee of Claims of the House, in the last Congress further report : "that, by a reference to the journals of Congress of 1781, it appears that, on the 25th April of that year, Congress ordered that the Board of Treasury place to the credit of Colonel Moses Hazen the sum of $13,386$\frac{2}{90}$, specie, being the principal and interest of the money due to him to the first day of May, 1781 ; and that the same bear an interest at six per cent. per annum," &c.   " It appears that General Hazen's account, in reference to this sum of $13,386$\frac{2}{90}$, so placed to his credit as aforesaid, was settled by the Auditor of the Treasury on the 11th of January, 1799, exhibiting a balance in favor of General Hazen of $8,683 88, at that date; that, afterwards, to wit, on the 30th June, 1802, the said account was submitted to the Comptroller of the Treasury, for his supervision and correction, who rejects the allowance of interest, and states the principles by which he was governed, in the following words :

' It is difficult to do [perfect] justice in this case : on the one hand, General Hazen ought not to be charged with the new emissions at par ; on the other, it is not reasonable to subject the United States to such an accumulation of interest.   If depreciation be allowed, General Hazen will have no reason to complain if interest on the balance should be refused.   This appears to me to be more conformable to the principles of equity, and to the usages of the Treasury, than any other mode of adjustment that can now be devised.   Before the date of the act of June 12, 1798, balances which originated in the former Government, if to be paid in specie, were uniformly ascertained without interest; if to be paid by issuing certificates, interest thereon was allowed.   That act precluded the issuing of certificates, in consequence of which all balances liquidated since, for any matter or thing prior to the 4th of March, 1789, have been paid in specie without interest.   This claim being of that description, I do hereby admit and certify it for the sum of four thousand two hundred dollars, without interest, in pursuance of the 5th section of the act above referred to.

JOHN STEELE, *Comptroller.*'

" Thus it appears that the sum of money on which interest is now claimed, was settled and accounted for, and adjusted on principles adopted by the accounting officers of the Treasury, under the then existing laws, and the usages and practice arising under those laws, so long ago as the 30th June, 1802 ; and that the account of General Hazen, thus settled and adjusted, was settled and adjusted on precisely the same principles on which the accounts of other individuals, similarly circumstanced, were settled by the Government, and none other."

Your petitioner will beg leave to remark, that, if there were any " individuals similarly circumstanced," that gave up their interest for the sake of obtaining their principal, they had a right so to do ; and they had an equal right to give up their principal also : but this will not authorize the Comptroller to compel others to do likewise.   That there was any law in existence, at the time, to authorize the Comptroller to withhold interest " on similar claims," in violation of a solemn contract made by

Congress with an individual, without better reasons than any offered by the Comptroller, he does not and cannot believe : after diligent search, he has never been able to find any.

The above order of April 25, 1781, arose as follows : General Hazen, being charged by Congress with important trusts in Canada, and the continental paper currency being of no use there, was under the necessity of making advances in specie, or giving his personal obligations for the United States, in various exigencies of the public service, particularly in recruiting his regiment, and providing supplies for the army on its retreat from that country. His account of these disbursements having been liquidated and settled by the competent authority, and a report on the subject having been made by the Board of Treasury, April 25, 1781, Congress confirmed the settlement, and passed the following order for payment of the balance, with interest, viz :

" *Ordered,* That the Board of Treasury place to the credit of Colonel Moses Hazen the sum of thirteen thousand three hundred and eighty-six dollars and two-ninetieths of a dollar, specie, being the principal and interest of the money due to him to the 1st of May, 1781 ; and that the same bear interest at the rate of six per cent. per annum, from the first day of May next aforesaid, until paid."

Nothing could be clearer than the obligation of the United States, pursuant to this order, to pay the debt in specie, and also to pay interest upon it until paid. But the specie was not to be obtained, and General Hazen's necessities obliged him soon afterward to take $7,000 of the debt in " bills of the new emission," at the rate of two dollars and a half for one in specie, their agreed value at the time, though, when he received a part of them, they were current in the market at three for one.

He was also under the necessity of accepting a certificate, of even date with the order of Congress establishing this debt, and worth at the time from 2*s.* 6*d.* to 3*s.* on the pound, but which has been liquidated as equal to specie.

Gen. Hazen made frequent and urgent applications for the balance due to him on this order of Congress; but it was not till January 11, 1799, that the Auditor of the Treasury adjusted the payments that had been made on it, and ascertained the balance remaining due. Liquidating the bills of new emissions at two and a half for one in specie, and the certificate for $6,386 the same as specie, the Auditor reported that the balance then due to Gen. Hazen was $8,683 88 ; that is, $4,200 principal, and $4,483 88 interest, calculated to January 10, 1799.

Though, as is manifest, the Auditor has liquidated these payments altogether in favor of the United States, yet no part of this balance could then be obtained for Gen. Hazen, nor could the Comptroller of the Treasury be induced to certify upon the Auditor's report, alleging, as his excuse for deferring it, the pressure of public business. He continued to defer it for nearly four years, during all which time Gen. Hazen was in distress from want of the money thus wrongfully withheld.

On the 30th June, and when about to retire from office, the Comptroller turned his attention to the subject, being probably in too great haste to examine into the case ; for he manifestly overlooked or disregarded the order of April 25, 1781, and also misapplied a law of the United States, as well as " the usage of the Treasury," to justify his disallowance of the interest found by the Auditor, and specially engaged to be paid by that order. And so he certifies upon the Auditor's report only for the sum of $4,200, rejecting the whole amount of interest found due, being $4,483 88, "in pursuance," as he adds, "of the 5th section of the act of June 12th, 1798;" thus confounding General Hazen's specie debt with the class of unsettled accounts to which that section refers, and overlooking another section of the act, which expressly provides for the payment of debts like General Hazen's, "credited on the books of the Treasury," with interest.

General Hazen's original claim, as already stated, arose from his specie disbursements in Canada, and was liquidated and settled by the former Government; and his vouchers were given up when the order of Congress was passed establishing it as a *specie* debt, with *interest* until paid. Nothing remained to be liquidated but the payments that had been made towards the discharge of this debt; and this the Auditor had done in a manner the most favorable to the United States, cancelling with the certificate $6,386, an equal amount of the original debt, and liquidating the remaining sum, $7,000, received in bills of the new emissions, at their highest value, and calculating interest only on $4,200, the balance of principal found to have been due June 23, 1781, when the new emissions were received. There could have been no difficulty, therefore, in doing full justice, at least to the United States, if the Comptroller had at once certified for the whole balance, principal and interest, found to be due by the Auditor's report; or if, when he did certify upon the report, he had added to that balance the interest which had accrued during the three or four years that he had most unreasonably withheld the money from Gen. Hazen. But, if it was "difficult to do perfect justice in this case," it could not have been necessary to do such palpable injustice to Gen. Hazen as the Comptroller manifestly has done, even upon his own principles; for he states that General Hazen ought not to be charged with the new emissions at par. How he ought to be charged, he does not state; but he doubtless considered that the rate of $2\frac{1}{2}$ for 1 in specie, as agreed upon at the time, and noted in the books of the Treasury, was the highest rate at which they ought to be charged; this being higher than the actual market value when they were received. Liquidating them at this rate, the Auditor had reduced the balance of the principal of the debt to its lowest point, allowing General Hazen no more than he would have been entitled to, June 23, 1781, when the new emissions were received, had it been then paid to him in specie; or than he would have been entitled to at any time, had the order of April 25, 1781, instead of expressly engaging that the debt should "bear an interest at six per cent. per annum until paid," expressly provided otherwise.

Yet the Comptroller, in consideration of allowing this balance of principal, to which General Hazen was so strictly entitled, deprives him of a greater sum of interest due, to which he was equally entitled. Thus, in fulfilling the engagement of the United States as to payment in *specie*, he wholly violates their engagement, not less explicit and binding, to pay the *interest*.

The order of Congress of April 25, 1781, binds the United States as fully to the payment of *interest*, and until the principal sum is paid, as it does to the payment of the principal sum in *specie*. If the Comptroller could annul the order in part, why not in the whole? If, by a dash of his pen, he could strike off the interest found to be due, why not the principal also? Both depend upon the same rules of right and justice. By virtue of this order of Congress, General Hazen had a vested right of property, as well in the interest as in the principal of this debt, of which no power could divest him—certainly no power in any officer of the Government.

It is manifest, therefore, that General Hazen ought to have received all the interest which the Auditor reported to be due to him; and that the Comptroller, either through inattention to the order of Congress, or from mistaken views of the subject, committed a gross error in striking off this amount of interest from the Auditor's report: consequently, justice requires that the sum of $4,483 88, the amount so struck off, should be now paid, with interest from January 11, 1799, when it was found to be due, as liquidated by the Auditor, and when it ought to have been paid to General Hazen.

Thus, by referring to the Auditor's report of January 11, 1799, and to the act of June 12, 1798, it will fully appear that the Comptroller's certificate of June 30, 1802, was done without any authority.

The Auditor had adjusted the claim according to the usage of the Treasury Department. The law of June 12, 1798, enjoins it upon the Department to pay all such balances standing on the books of the Treasury bearing interest, as General Hazen's does, both principal and interest, up to January, 1800.

Upon balances upon which interest was never promised, it was the practice to pay the principal in specie, without interest. The balance of General Hazen's account current, of near $4,000, was in this situation, and was paid after his death, without interest, after twenty years' standing. However contrary this course might have been to the principles of equity and justice, the Government, as yet, has never heard any complaint from your petitioner on that head. He has ever been willing to conform to the usage of the Government, when that usage was uniform and impartial; but the doings of the Comptroller will be found, he is in the full belief, partial, contrary to the usage of the Treasury Department, in the face of law, and in violation of a solemn contract between the United States and General Hazen. The same principles which governed the Comptroller in this case, if he had been uniform and impartial, would have led him to withhold the interest on loan-office certificates, and others that were given for specie upon settlements made "prior to the act of March 4, 1789." They bore no higher authority, nor had higher security pledged for the allowance of interest, than the one given to General Hazen by Charles Thomson, Secretary of Congress, April 25, 1781.

By referring to the journals of the old Congress, it will appear that, on the 7th June, 1785, General Hazen's claim to the immediate payment of money was referred to the Board of Treasury to report. At this time, the obligations which he had entered into, making a part of his disbursements in Canada, which constituted a part of this debt, came upon him, but he could obtain no money; nor did the Board of Treasury make any report. And this claim remained in the fiscal department of the Government, unanswered, until January 10, 1799, when the Auditor reported upon it; then the Comptroller detained it near four years longer, before he turned his attention to it and certified upon it. Is it reasonable or just that General Hazen should be made to suffer for the unreasonable accumulation of interest?

In March, 1790, General Hazen petitioned Congress again for the money; his petition was referred to the Secretary of the Treasury, Mr. Hamilton. It appears that, on the organization of the Government under the constitution of the United States, all the accounts and papers of General Hazen, which had been from time to time referred to the Board of Treasury, went into the Treasury Department under the new Government; and it appears Mr. Hamilton, in looking up General Hazen's claims, had recourse to the late Mr. Pierce's office, on the files of which was found a statement of General Hazen's account current. It will be borne in mind that Congress, on the 26th of April, 1785, removed his accounts from Mr. Pierce, and referred them to the Board of Treasury to report; but the account current found on Mr. Pierce's files bore no signature of Mr. Pierce, nor the sanction of the Board of Treasury, but was certified by one of the clerks in said office to contain all General Hazen's claims against the United States, and that every thing had been allowed him that the laws would justify, *or even equity and good conscience required.* This stated account current was sanctioned by all the heads of the several departments of the Treasury, and by Mr. Hamilton himself, as will appear by his report of the 9th of August, 1790, (with his documents,) as a final settlement of all General Hazen's claims against the United States.

Against this pretended settlement General Hazen objected and protested : 1st, because his accounts had been taken out of Mr. Pierce's hands by Congress, and referred to the Board of Treasury to examine and report, and that said board did not report ; and Mr. Pierce, who had prejudged them, could not be supposed to be an impartial judge ; 2d, because a claim of a Mr. Chinn, to whom he owed nothing, had been admitted in said account against him by said clerk, which had been previously settled by General Hazen himself, and had been rejected by Mr. Pierce ; 3d, because the said account current contained great and manifest errors : but General Hazen could not obtain any redress, nor any money.

The report of Mr. Hamilton will show he could not even obtain any part of the small balance that was admitted to be his due ; and thus the Department insisted that the said adjustment of the said account current should be a final settlement of all his claims.

But General Hazen as constantly remonstrated against it, and petitioned Congress that a revision of said accounts might take place. This course continued for nearly ten years, when, in 1799, the Auditor discovered the error in one item of said account current of no less sum than $8,683 88, and General Hazen contended that there were many others equally notorious ; but he was never able to obtain a revision of said accounts.

From the foregoing statement, it will appear that no blame ought to attach to General Hazen for the long delay, and, of course, the accumulation of interest that accrued upon the balance of the order of Congress of the 25th April, 1781. He asked for this money the 7th June, 1785, as stated above. Why was it not then paid, and the accumulation of interest stopped? He asked for it again in March, 1790 ; but it seems then to have escaped the penetrating ken of the whole Treasury Department, from Mr. Howell, the successor of Mr. Pierce, the then Auditor, the Comptroller, and up to the Secretary himself, as may be seen by their several reports in the Treasury Department, notwithstanding the charge of the 25th April, 1781, occupied a prominent place in said account current. Hence General Hazen will stand justified with the Government and the world for his dissatisfaction and " wilful obstinacy," in his objection and opposition to that pretended settlement of his public accounts.

32

The Committee of Claims of the House for 1828, in their report, make mention of an application to Congress by your petitioner and Mrs. Charlotte Hazen, in 1804, " in which no mention whatever is made of the claim for arrearages of interest ; so that this claim of interest, alleged to be due and unpaid at this time, on the said sum of $13,386$\frac{2}{90}$, would seem to have been an afterthought altogether ; for if the petitioner has a claim on the Government for that interest now, the petitioners had a claim for a portion of said interest then ; and your committee do not believe that the petitioners would have omitted to ask for so important an item in their claim in 1807, had they then believed it to exist."

" Your committee would remark, that, however Congress might be disposed to extend its munificence to General Hazen, as a meritorious officer of the Revolution, were he now living, or to his children, had he died leaving issue, they can see no good reason why Congress should, at the expiration of twenty six years and upwards, unravel and unsettle an account, which, after so great a lapse of time, the committee are bound to believe, was settled according to law, upon principles which governed in all similar cases, in favor of an individual whose claim can only rest for allowance on principles of strict justice."

There were good reasons for not asking for the said interest on the said sum of $13,386$\frac{2}{90}$ in 1804, at the same time with the loss of half pay ; besides, he knows of no law or usage which obliges an executor to know *instanter* every item of claims his testator might have had against the Government. If any claim is subsequently discovered to exist, and to be just, he cannot believe the mere delay would in any manner destroy or lessen its validity. The committee, however, may rest assured this claim was not then, and never has been, forgotten.

The true reason why it was not asked for in the same petition with the loss of half pay, in 1804, was, that there were two distinct claims ; that of half pay, resting on a special contract of Congress with General Hazen, and had been long waiting for special provision to be made by Congress, to be settled by the Treasury Department ; that for interest due on the order of Congress of the 25th of April, 1781, was connected with General Hazen's account current, and was then waiting a different issue.

The committee consider this item of interest on the order of the 25th April, 1781, an important item of the claim, which, indeed, it is—an all-important claim to an individual, although but as a drop in the bucket to the United States; yet they seem willing to sacrifice the individual's right, rather than unravel and unsettle an old settled account, to remedy a wrong or to correct an error.

The committee seem to consider the doings of the Comptroller, like the laws of the Medes and Persians, unalterable : they seem not to perceive that even the Auditor's report of the 11th January, 1799, was but a correction of an error, which had been standing nearly ten years on General Hazen's pretended settlement of his account current : hence, no blame ought to attach to him for the accumulation of interest to that time, and from thence to the 30th June, 1802.

Your petitioner has always understood that time cannot sanctify a wrong nor justify an error; nor does he know of any law closing the door of equity and justice against him. Had the committee fully investigated all the documents accompanying his memorial, and the law of the 12th June, 1798, he cannot have a doubt but that they would have been satisfied of the justice of the claim; and that there had been no unreasonable neglect or want of due diligence on the part of General Hazen in his lifetime, or on that of his executor since his death, to obtain the said claim.

Within twenty years, the justice of the settlement by the Comptroller had been questioned both by General Hazen and his executor, as may be seen by the report of the Committee of Claims of 1803, (a copy of which was with his documents,) and his petition of 1822; the greater part of the time was during the embarrassed state of the Treasury.

Although your petitioner served his country in the revolutionary war from beginning to end, and lost his health therein, which he has never since entirely recovered; and although he spent a great deal of his time with General Hazen, during his long and helpless sickness; he has never asked for any munificence from Congress, nor has he expected any favor, more than a fair and equitable settlement of his claims. He has asked only for his rights, founded upon the very best security—the solemn promise of Congress; the good faith of the United States being pledged for its fulfilment. All that he has ever asked from Congress is "strict justice"—such justice as would be enforced by a court of law.

The said committee further report, "It is proper to observe, in addition to what has already been advanced, that General Hazen, after he entered the American army, was promoted, on the 29th of June, 1791, to the rank of a brigadier general by brevet; that, in the settlement of his accounts, he was allowed the sum of $4,500, his commutation in full for half pay for life. After his death, Congress, by act of January 23, 1805, granted to Charlotte Hazen, widow and relict of Brigadier General Moses Hazen, deceased, for her support, the annual sum of two hundred dollars during her life, to commence on the 4th February, 1803; and by an act of 23d April, 1812, Congress made further provision for the said Charlotte Hazen, by granting to her nine hundred and sixty acres of land," &c. The said committee conclude their report in the following manner, viz:

"Taking into consideration, therefore, all the circumstances connected with this claim, your committee do not hesitate to declare it as their decided opinion, that the Government of the United States has long since cancelled every obligation it may at any time heretofore have been under to General Moses Hazen, except the indemnity promised for loss of half pay, as hereinbefore mentioned; that the representative of said Hazen has no just claim against the United States for arrearages of interest, as alleged by him in his petition; and that the bill from the Senate for the relief of said representative ought to be further amended by striking out the second section thereof, which allows the interest aforesaid."

Your petitioner could not conceive what object the committee had in mentioning the promotion of General Hazen to the honorary rank of brigadier general by brevet, and his receiving a colonel's commutation of $4,500, which was given him for his revolutionary services. His commutation was the same in amount as was given to every other officer of the grade of colonel in the army, for services rendered, and which became his private property, as much so as any other private property he possessed: he had earned it, and had paid for it with his services in full.  The general's promotion to the honorary rank of brevet general, the committee do not estimate at its value ; it would be difficult to do it : this was also given him for his services in the revolutionary army, and not from pecuniary considerations ; and he would have been equally entitled to receive both this and the commutation, if the resolution of the 22d January, 1776, and the order of 25th April, 1781, had never existed.

The provision made for Mrs. Hazen was made to her upon her private application to Congress, (a copy of which was with his documents,) as a Canadian refugee, under the acts providing for the losses of the Canadian and Nova Scotia refugees, and has no connexion whatever with the claims in question.

It was not looked for that the committee would resort to General Hazen's private property for funds to offset against his public claims : it is believed to be a new thought altogether, to discharge the public contracts with the private property of the creditor ; but the committee, after mentioning the brevet promotion of General Hazen, and receiving his commutation, &c., " do not hesitate to declare, as their decided opinion, that the Government of the United States has long since cancelled every obligation it may at any time heretofore have been under to General Moses Hazen, except the indemnity promised for the loss of half pay," of which they allow the principal only, rejecting all the interest.

The committee have not shown, through the whole of their lengthy report, that the value of a cent has ever been paid to General Hazen, or to his executor, towards the indemnity promised General Hazen, nor for the interest due upon the order of the 25th April, 1781, which equally secured the payment of interest as it did that of principal, except what was paid him out of his own private property.  To this mode of paying these claims your petitioner cannot accede, but feels himself bound to protest against as being unreasonable, improper, and unjust ; and he humbly conceives that the said obligations of the 22d January, 1776, and the order of the 25th April, 1781, remain unsatisfied in part, and uncancelled.

The committee of 1828, in their report, refuse the allowance of interest on the claim for the loss of half pay, because it did not appear to them that the requisite evidence to establish said claim had ever been exhibited to the proper Department of the Government, to enable it to settle said claim, until the fall of 1825.  The documents in the case before the Senate furnished strong circumstantial evidence of the fact of such evidence having been produced.  General Knox's letter, of the 4th December, 1789, and the reports of the Committees of Claims for 1804 and 1805, before mentioned, were before the Senate.  It could hardly be supposed, by any one, that the House of Representatives should, at two different sessions, have deliberately passed bills for indemnifying said claim, both principal and interest, without having all the requisite evidence before them, necessary to establish the justice of the said claim.  Some further evidence is now offered in confirmation that such evidence was before them.

In conclusion, your petitioner, having answered the objections made by the Committee of Claims to his claims, (he hopes, in a satisfactory manner;) and believing that Congress will not deliberately violate their own contracts, he considers it to be his duty, and feels a confidence in coming before Congress, and asking for that indemnity which the resolution of the 22d January, 1776, promised; and also for the fulfilment of the order of Congress of the 25th April, 1781, according to the intentions and understanding of the parties at the time they were entered into. Therefore,

Your petitioner prays that provision may be made to indemnify the loss of General Hazen's half pay, by allowing interest on the several payments from the time they became due; and also for the interest due on the order of Congress of the 25th April, 1781, which was withheld by the Comptroller, June 30, 1802, and interest on the same from and after it was so wrongfully withheld.

And your petitioner prays.

MOSES WHITE.

Lancaster, N. H., *December* 7, 1829.

Treasury Department,

No. 10295.                  *Auditor's Office, January* 11, 1799.

I have examined and adjusted an account between the United States and Brigadier General Moses Hazen, and find that he is entitled to the following credits :

By this sum, passed to his credit on the books of the Treasury, pursuant to a resolution of Congress of the 25th April, 1781, payable in specie, and to bear interest, at 6 per cent. per annum, from the 1st May, 1781, per certificate of the Register herewith,  -    -    -    -    -   $13,386 02

By interest account, for interest due in consequence of this credit, calculated at 6 per cent. per annum, to the 10th January, 1799, per statement,  -    -    -    -   4,483 88

$17,869 90

I also find that he stands chargeable for the following sums on said account, viz :

To amount paid him on the 23d June, 1781, in warrants on the loan offices of Pennsylvania and New Hampshire, for 7,000 dollars, in bills of new emissions, already at his debit, but subject to liquidation, pursuant to the report of Joseph Hardy, accountant of the Treasury, dated March 30th, 1789, and which sum is now liquidated at 2½ for 1, being the estimated value at the period of payment,  -  $2,800 00

To amount of a certificate, issued in his favor by the Register of the Treasury, on the 29th May, 1789, bearing interest from the 1st May, 1781, being in part payment of the sum at his credit, per statement of said Register, herewith,  -  6,386 02

Leaving a balance of eight thousand six hundred and eighty three dollars eighty-eight cents, due from the United States unto the said Moses Hazen,  -    -    -  8,683 88

$17,869 90

As appears from the statement and vouchers herewith transmitted for the decision of the Comptroller of the Treasury thereon.

R. HARRISON, *Auditor.*

To JOHN STEELE, Esq.,
*Comptroller of the Treasury.*

TREASURY DEPARTMENT,
*Comptroller's Office, June 30, 1802.*

It is difficult to do perfect justice in this case. On the one hand, General Hazen ought not to be charged with the new emissions at par; on the other, it is not reasonable to subject the United States to such an accumulation of interest. If depreciation be allowed, General Hazen will have no reason to complain if interest on the balance should be refused. This appears to me to be more conformable to the principles of equity, and to the usage of the Treasury, than any other mode of adjustment that can now be devised. Before the date of the act of June 12, 1798, balances which originated under the former Government, if to be paid in specie, were uniformly ascertained without interest; if to be paid by issuing certificates, interest thereon was allowed. That act precluded the issuing of certificates; in consequence of which, all balances liquidated since, for any matter or thing prior to the 4th March, 1789, have been paid in specie, without interest. This claim being of that description, I do hereby admit and certify it for the sum of four thousand two hundred dollars, without interest, in pursuance of the 5th section of the act above referred to.

JOHN STEELE, *Comptroller.*

TREASURY DEPARTMENT,
*Register's Office, December 26, 1804.*

I do hereby certify that the above is a true copy of the original filed in this office.

JOSEPH NOURSE, *Register.*

TREASURY DEPARTMENT,
*Register's Office, March 30, 1826.*

I do certify that not any variation hath taken place in relation to the document to which my certificate, above affixed, was given the 26th December, 1804; and that, as it then stood, so it now stands on record in the books of this office.

JOSEPH NOURSE, *Register.*

———

DECEMBER 21, 1831.

*The Committee on Revolutionary Claims, to which was referred the petition of John H. Wendell, report:*

That they have reviewed the case of the petitioner, and concur in the report made upon it by the Committee on Revolutionary Claims of the second session of the last Congress; to which report reference may be had. Believing him to be entitled to the relief he asks, they have directed a bill to be reported.

DECEMBER 23, 1831.

*The Committee on Revolutionary Claims, to which was referred the petition of the heirs and legal representatives of Doctor Samuel Kennedy, report:*

That a bill for the relief of the petitioners, No. 413, was reported by this commitee at the first session of the twenty-first Congress, accompanied by a report, in the principles of which report this committee entirely concur, and incorporate it herewith, and accompany it with a bill for their relief, similar to that which formerly received the assent of the committee.

APRIL 9, 1830.

*The Committee on Revolutionary Claims, to which was referred the petition of the heirs of Doctor Samuel Kennedy, report:*

The petitioners state that the said Samual Kennedy joined the revolutionary army in the year 1776, as surgeon, in Colonel Anthony Wayne's regiment; that he continued in the service until some time in 1778, when he died at the military hospital at the Yellow Springs, in Chester county, in the State of Pennsylvania. They allege that he never received any pay for his services, and now claim it, together with bounty land.

Accompanying their petition are a number of letters written by Doctor Kennedy to his wife, from various military posts; and, from the statements of Doctor Cutting of this city, and of Joseph Anderson, Comptroller of the Treasury, the committee are satisfied that Doctor Kennedy performed the services as stated in the petition, and that he was a valuable and meritorious officer.

There is, however, no evidence before the committee respecting his pay, nor can any be found on the records in the Departments; and it can hardly be presumed that Doctor Kennedy served for a period of two years without receiving any pay; and, although a part may have been due him, the committee can fix upon no data from which to make out a calculation, or arrive at any certainty respecting it. They are, therefore, of opinion that it is inexpedient to allow this part of the claim. They are also of opinion that they are not entitled to bounty land, as there is no law of Congress allowing bounty land, except to such officers and soldiers only who engaged to serve for and during the war; and there is no evidence before the committee that Doctor Kennedy was among that number.

By a resolve of Congress of the 23d of May, 1778, half pay for seven years was granted to the widows or heirs of officers who were slain in battle, or died in the service. This does not appear to have been drawn; and the committee believe them to be entitled to it, and therefore report a bill for this purpose.

DECEMBER 23, 1831.

*The Committee on Revolutionary Claims, to which was referred the petition of the heirs of William Vawters, report:*

That the case of the petitioners was presented to Congress at the 1st session of the 21st Congress, referred to the then Committee on Revolutionary Claims, who made a report thereon, accompanied by a bill for the relief of the petitioners; in which report your committee concur, and beg leave to report a bill.

MARCH 19, 1830.

*The Committee on Revolutionary Claims, to whom was referred the petition of the heirs of William Vawters, (late of the State of Kentucky, deceased,) make the following report:*

That the said William Vawters enlisted as a soldier, in the year 1777, in the 1st Virginia regiment, commanded by Colonel George Gibson, (said regiment being on State establishment;) and continued in the service of the State until the battle of Germantown, at which battle the 9th Virginia regiment, on continental establishment, was captured by the enemy; in consequence of which, the State of Virginia, by an act of her Legislature, passed in December, 1779, transferred the aforesaid regiment from the State to the continental establishment, in lieu of the 9th regiment which had been captured as aforesaid.

It also appears, from the documents and evidence before your committee, that the said Vawters, while in the service, was promoted first to an ensign, and subsequently to lieutenant, which office he held when deranged out of service, and made a supernumerary, by an arrangement of the army, pursuant to two resolutions of Congress, passed on the 3d and 21st of October, 1780; and continued a supernumerary, subject at all times to the call of his country, to the close of the war; and, considering this case to come within the provisions of the resolution of October 21st, 1780, which allows to all officers deranged by that arrangement half pay for life, do herewith report a bill.

DECEMBER 23, 1831.

*The Committee on Revolutionary Claims, to which was referred the petition of Major John Roberts, report:*

That the case of the petitioner has heretofore been presented to Congress; and, at the second session of the twenty-first Congress, the Committee on Revolutionary Claims made a report thereon, hereto annexed, which is fully concurred in by your committee, and adopted. That committee also reported a bill for the relief of the petitioner, which is likewise approved by this committee, and they report the same bill.

DECEMBER 21, 1830.

*The Committee on Revolutionary Claims, to which was referred the petition of Major John Roberts, report:*

That the said John Roberts entered the army of the Revolution early in the war; that he was appointed a captain in the Virginia line on continental establishment prior to January, 1779 ; that, in the month of March of that year, he was commissioned a major of infantry, in the said line ; that evidence is produced that he continued to do duty as a major in actual service so late as September, 1781 ; that he was subject to the orders of Col. James Wood, of the Virginia continental line, in that last-named month and year, and discharged various duties in relation to the Saratoga prisoners under the orders of said Colonel Wood, who subscribed himself his colonel commandant.   It appears by the certificate of Mr. Edwards, of the Pension Office, that Colonel Wood was of the continental line from the State of Virginia.   The petitioner states, that late in 1781 he was without command, and endeavored to find service by travelling to the Southern States, which effort proved abortive, and that he had no command afterwards until the close of the war.   He further states, on oath, that, after the discharge of his troops, he was without command ; that he never did resign his commission ; and that he was at all times willing again to enter the service, if required so to do; but that he never was so required.

J. L. Edwards, Esq., clerk of the Pension Office, certifies that the name of John Roberts appears in the list of continental officers of the Virginia line on continental establishment, as a major ; and that he received, on the 8th November, 1783, a certificate of balance of pay, amounting to £404 1s. 10d. Virginia currency; and that, on the 24th June, 1786, a further certificate was received by him, through General James Wood, for £78.   The resolve of Congress of October 21, 1780, promised half pay for life to all officers who should remain in service to the close of the war, or who should be supernumerary and willing to enter service again, if required so to do ; and the resolution of that body of March, 1783, commuted the half pay for life by five years' full pay in lieu thereof, to all persons entitled under the resolves of October, 1780 ; and your committee, believing that John Roberts, a major of infantry of the Virginia line on continental establishment, is clearly within the said resolutions, and entitled to the benefit thereof, report a bill in his favor.

---

DECEMBER 28, 1831.

*The Committee on Revolutionary Claims, to which was referred the petition of Sarah Easton and Dorothy Storer, report:*

That the case was minutely examined, and an able report submitted thereon by the Committee on Revolutionary Claims of the second session of the twenty-first Congress, which report your committee now concur in, and ask that the same may be taken and considered as part of this report.   In conformity thereto, a bill is herewith submitted for the relief of the petitioners.

*The Committee on Revolutionary Claims, to whom was referred the petition of Ann D. Baylor, submit the following report:*

That the petition and documents relating to this case were referred to the Committee on Revolutionary Claims of the first session of the 19th Congress, and favorably reported on; that they were again referred to the same committee of the second session of the last Congress, which committee also presented a favorable report, together with a bill for the relief of the petitioner. In these reports your committee, after having again examined the evidence, now concur, and accordingly submit a bill.

---

*The Committee on Revolutionary Claims, to whom was referred the application of Benjamin Gibbs, beg leave to report:*

That, at the last session of Congress, when this case was referred to the Committee on Revolutionary Claims, a favorable report was made thereon, to which this committee refer, and adopt as their own.

*The Committee on Revolutionary Claims, to which was referred the petition of Benjamin Gibbs, submitted the following report:*

It appears, in this case, that the petitioner was the innocent purchaser of a final settlement certificate, dated " State of New York, January 20, 1784," and signed by " John Pierce, commissioner," purporting to be for " four hundred" dollars, payable, with interest, at six per cent. from the first day of January, 1783, to David Johnson, or bearer; that the petitioner sold the same to one David Rice, and said Rice to one Simmes; that it was presented at the Treasury Department, and there pronounced to be a counterfeit or altered certificate, having been originally issued for twenty-five dollars and sixty-two-ninetieths, instead of four hundred dollars; that the petitioner, after a protracted lawsuit with Rice, was obliged to take back said certificate; and that Berry, of whom he purchased, was insolvent, and that he has lost the whole amount: whereupon, the petitioner prays that he may be paid the amount for which said certificate originally issued, and the interest thereon, the same never having been paid by the Government; which prayer the committee consider reasonable, and that it ought to be granted; and report a bill for that purpose.

---

*The Committee on Revolutionary Claims, to which was referred the petition of Thomas Triplett, report:*

That the petitioner claims commutation, in lieu of half pay for life, as a captain in the revolutionary army, who served to the close thereof. The facts that the petitioner was such officer, and did serve to the close of the revolutionary war, are fully proven by the evidence certified by the Secretary of the Treasury, whereon the petitioner obtained the benefit of the act of 1828 : and it appears by the letter of Peter Hagner, (Third Auditor,) that the petitioner has never received the half pay, or commutation in lieu thereof, due to him. Your committee therefore report a bill for his relief.

---

JANUARY 3, 1832.

*The Committee on Revolutionary Claims, to whom was referred the resolution of this House, instructing the committee " to inquire into the expediency of paying to Elizabeth Magruder the commutation pay which was due to her father, Reynold Hillary, as an officer in the revolutionary war," beg leave to report :*

That, at the last session of Congress, this case was referred to this committee, and a favorable report made thereon, which is adopted, and a bill reported for the relief of said Elizabeth Magruder.

FEBRUARY 24, 1831.

*The Committee on Revolutionary Claims, to whom was referred the resolution instructing the committee " to inquire into the expediency of paying to Elizabeth Magruder the commutation pay which was due to her father, Reynold Hillary, as an officer in the revolutionary war," have had the same under consideration, and report as followeth :*

It appears from the deposition of Captain Joseph Cross, whose testimony is entitled to the fullest confidence, who was also in the service, and well acquainted with the said Lieutenant Hillary and his service, that the said Hillary entered the army of the Revolution in the year 1776, and obtained a commission, in the year 1777, as a lieutenant in the company commanded by Captain Joseph Gray, of the first regiment of infantry of Maryland troops, on the continental establishment, and served to the close of the war ; and died on his way home, returning from his service at the South. Certificates from the pay-rolls for pay and depreciation confirm this statement of his rank and service, by showing that he received pay accordingly. The same is further confirmed by the fact that bounty land for such service has been allowed at the War Department.

A certificate further shows that it appears from the pay-rolls that the commutation due to Lieutenant Hillary has not been paid.

The committee have therefore reported a bill, allowing the commutation to his said heir, with such interest as has been received by others, through the provisions made for funding and paying the domestic debt.

*The Committee on Revolutionary Claims, to which was referred the
petition of John Thomas, report :*

That the petitioner claims commutation in lieu of half pay for life, (as
a captain of infantry in the revolutionary war,) under the resolves of Congress of 1780 and 1783.  It appears, by the certificate of the Secretary of
the Treasury, that the petitioner is now in the receipt of the compensation given by the act of 1828 to certain officers and soldiers of the revolutionary army, which compensation depends on the petitioner's having had
a right to the commutation now claimed by him ; and it also appears, by
the certificate of the Third Auditor, that the petitioner has received no
part of the half pay, or commutation in lieu thereof, due to him under the
said resolves of Congress.  Your committee, therefore, report a bill for
his relief.

JANUARY 4, 1832.

*The  Committee on Revolutionary Claims, to which was referred the
petition of Peter Foster, lieutenant of infantry in the revolutionary
war, report :*

That the petitioner claims the commutation of five years' full pay, in lieu
of half pay for life, as lieutenant of infantry, under the resolves of Congress of 1780 and 1783.  It appears by the certificate of the Secretary of
the Treasury that the petitioner receives the compensation given by the
act of 1828 to certain surviving officers and soldiers of the revolutionary
war, which compensation depends on the petitioner's having had a right
to the commutation now claimed ; and it appears by the certificate of Peter Hagner, (Third Auditor,) that the petitioner has received no part of the
said half pay, or commutation in lieu thereof.  Your committee, therefore,
report a bill for his relief.

JANUARY 6, 1832.

*The Committee on Revolutionary Claims, to whom has been referred the
petition of Jane Thornton, report :*

That, at the last session of Congress, a report was made by this committee on the said petition, to which the committee refer and adopt it as
their own.

FEBRUARY 2, 1831.

*The Committee on Revolutionary Claims, to whom was referred the petition of Jane Thornton, report :*

The petitioner states that her late husband, Colonel John Thornton,
entered the army of the Revolution as a captain in the third Virginia regiment, commanded by Colonel Hugh Mercer, on the 22d of February
,

1776, and served as such until the 20th of March, 1777, when he was promoted to the rank of major in one of the sixteen additional regiments, commanded by Colonel Thruston; and shortly after, in the same year, was promoted to the rank of lieutenant colonel; that he was in actual service more than three years, and never resigned his commission during the war; that the commissions and other papers, showing more fully the military services of Colonel Thornton, were intrusted, some years ago, to Philip R. Thompson, then a member of the Virginia Legislature, and were presented by him to that body, which decided that, as Colonel Thornton was an officer of the continental, and not the State troops, the application for his bounty land and half pay should be made to the General Government: those papers were unfortunately mislaid or lost by Mr. Thompson, and have never been recovered; that Colonel Thornton never received the bounty land to which he was entitled; and the petitioner prays that those lands may be granted to her, and such emoluments as other officers, similarly situated, were entitled to receive. The loss of the original papers has compelled the petitioner to resort to secondary evidence. That loss is shown by the deposition of Isaac Wurston, and a letter addressed to Colonel Thornton by Philip R. Thompson. A letter from James Monroe, late President of the United States, shows that Colonel Thornton held the rank of captain in the third Virginia regiment, as stated in the petition, and was distinguished for his gallantry and good conduct. The deposition of Colonel Abraham Maury shows that, after the battles of Trenton and Princeton, in which Colonel Thornton was engaged, he was appointed by General Washington a lieutenant colonel in one of the sixteen additional regiments raised by order of Congress. Colonel Thornton, in a petition addressed by him to the Virginia Legislature, states, that in March, 1777, he was appointed major in Colonel Thruston's regiment, and soon afterwards was promoted to the rank of lieutenant colonel in the same; that in that station he was active in endeavoring to raise the said regiment, and continued his exertions in that line until the summer of 1778, after which he was not called into service, as the regiment was never entirely completed, and there was no command for him; but that he was, nevertheless, at all times ready to perform services when his country demanded them. This statement, the committee think, is sustained by several letters addressed to Colonel Thornton in the years 1777 and 1778, showing that he was then in service. That Colonel Thornton continued to be a continental officer in 1781, and was ready to perform services when required, the committee think is shown by the depositions of Captain Moore, Reuben Rosson, and Thomas Vaughan. They state that, in 1781, during the invasion of Virginia by Lord Cornwallis, the command of a Virginia regiment of militia was, by the order of the Marquis Lafayette, given to Colonel Thornton, as a continental officer. The depositions of Colonel Abraham Maury, of Thomas Walden, and of the petitioner, are also exhibited to show that Colonel Thornton did not resign his commission, but that, in consolidating the regiments, he became a supernumerary officer, in which capacity he remained until the termination of the war. The committee believe, from the evidence in this case, that Colonel Thornton was entitled to the benefit of the resolutions of Congress of October 21st 1780, and of March 22d, 1783; that this claim was asserted by him in his lifetime, but never received ; and that the commutation of five years' full pay is now due to his legal representatives.

A bill is therefore reported.

---

*The Committee on Revolutionary Claims, to which was referred the petition of James Brownlee, report:*

The petitioner states that he is the only heir of his mother, who was the widow of Alexander Brownlee, an ensign of the army of the Revolution, slain in the battle of Guilford, and prays to be paid the seven years' half pay to which his mother was entitled by a resolve of Congress passed May 23, 1778.

It appears, from evidence satisfactory to the committee, that Alexander Brownlee did hold the commission of an ensign in the continental establishment ; that he was a meritorious officer ; that he was slain, as stated, in the battle of Guilford ; that the half pay to which his widow was entitled has never been drawn ; and that the petitioner is the sole heir. A bill is therefore reported for his relief.

---

*The Committee on Revolutionary Claims, to whom was referred the petition of John Bruce, administrator of Philip Bush, deceased, report :*

That this case was, at a former session, referred to this committee, and a report, imbodying all the facts, made thereon. To that report the committee refer ; and they concur in the decision then made, that the petitioner is entitled to relief.

The true ground upon which all limitation acts rest, is the prevention of fraud in setting up State demands, which, from lapse of time, may be fairly presumed to have been satisfied. When a claim is clearly proved to have been originally just, and never to have been adjusted or discharged, the moral obligation still exists, and the debtor cannot conscientiously avail himself of the protection of an act of limitation. The committee are satisfied of the original justice of this claim, and of its non-payment. A bill is, therefore, reported.

---

*In the case of John Bruce, administrator of Philip Bush, deceased, the Committee on Revolutionary Claims, to which the same was referred, report:*

That it is alleged in the petition setting out this claim, that the said Philip Bush, while in full life, to wit, on the 3d day of March, 1780, did, in consideration of provisions furnished by him before that time, for the use of the army of the United States in the revolutionary war, receive from J. Brown, jr., for Archibald Steel, then deputy quartermaster general, a certificate, whereby it appeared that the United States owed the said Philip $32,842$\frac{55}{90}$, in old continental emission; that afterwards, to wit, in the year 1785, said Philip sent said certificate, by the hands of George Slough, of the county of Lancaster, to the said Steel, for payment, he being then believed by the said Philip to be at Lancaster, in said county; that said Slough, not finding Archibald Steel at Lancaster enclosed said certificate in a letter directed to said Philip Bush, and committed the same to the care of one John McMinn, to be by him conveyed to said Philip at Winchester; and that neither the letter nor the certificate ever reached him, but the same was and is wholly lost.

The existence of this certificate is proved by a certificate from the Auditor's office of the United States, showing that it was issued at the time, for the amount, by the person, and to the said Philip, as alleged; and that it was payable March 31, 1780. It is proved by the deposition of George Slough, that he received said certificate, carried it to Lancaster, enclosed it in a letter, and delivered it to McMinn—all as alleged. Philip Bush has made oath to all the alleged facts; and also that he never received it again, and did verily believe it to have been lost. The character of Philip Bush for integrity is well sustained. On the whole, the existence, date, amount, time of payment, maker, and payee, of this certificate, are all proved beyond all doubt. The proof of its loss, when the time elapsed since that event is alleged to have happened, and the total want of all inducements to conceal it if in existence, are considered, leave no reason to question the fact.

The non-payment of this certificate is proved in the same unquestionable manner; not only by a continual claim encountered by no indicated suspicion of payment, but also made certain by certificates from all the loan offices in the United States, and from the Treasury thereof, that no payment of the same has been made at either of them; and from the latter, that it is now outstanding and unpaid.

It is respectfully submitted, that the many limitation laws, both of the United States and the Continental Congress, do not create any reasonable objections, much less legal bar, to the payment of this claim. These were made from the pressure of the times, and can find no justification in equity when that pressure is removed. It is believed that a nation cannot, with more justice than an individual can, abrogate and nullify its own contract. It has the power to refuse payment, by a law for that purpose enacted; but the debt will remain, and justice will not cease to demand its discharge. Length of time may raise a presumption in favor of an individual, or a nation, that a claim made against either, is without consideration, or has been discharged. If, in a state of nature it could not be just in one party, without the consent of the other, to rescind a contract, it may fairly be questioned whether any number of men can, by mere association under any form of government, acquire the right to rescind, at their own mere will, any contract to which they are a party. Could it have been intended by the people of the United States, when, by the constitution, they negatived a power in either of the several States to impair the obligation of contracts, that they, by any implication, conferred that power on the Congress of the United States?

These principles do not impugn the right of the nation to prescribe the time of payment, or the rate of interest, when these are unsettled by the contract. Neither does it take from it the right to stop all interest, if, at the time prescribed for payment, it is ready to pay, and the creditor refuses or is not ready to receive his money. Equally just is it for a nation to propose a new contract in discharge of a former one, either in a different amount, at a different rate of interest, or with other terms of payment and pledges for security.

On some or all these principles, the justice of the funding system is sustained. It proposed a voluntary loan, with new terms and conditions, together with better security for the payment of the whole domestic debt of the United States. It is fairly presumable that the present claimant, and all those who had, like him, before the establishment of that system, lost their certificates, would have willingly given up their claims in exchange for equal amounts of stocks, under the provisions of that system. The United States would not have been secure at that time in making such exchanges, because many claims might then have been made, under a pretence of loss, when certificates had been *bona fide* sold and transferred. The United States could never be safe in doing this, until, by length of time, the presumption that such certificates are lost is violent and conclusive. While this time is running, to create this presumption in favor of such claimants, the United States ought not to be placed in a worse condition thereby, because they were originally ready to comply with the terms of the loan under the funding system. The loss of the evidence of his debt was the loss of the claimant; and if, when the time arrives when the United States may with safety rely on the presumption of such loss, they are willing to place him in a condition equally just with that of other creditors, he may regret his loss, but he cannot require the nation to sustain the effects of it. It is therefore

*Resolved by the committee,* That the claimant, administrator as aforesaid of the said Philip Bush, recover and receive the amount of his said claim according to the rules of depreciation; and that the same be allowed and paid to him under the principles of the funding system, in the same manner, and to the same amount, as if he had, on the 31st of December, 1790, subscribed to the loan made in payment of the debt of the United States; and that a bill for his relief be reported accordingly to the House.

---

JANUARY 10, 1832.

*The Committee on Revolutionary Claims, to which was referred the petition of Archibald Watt, of the city of New York, report:*

That the petitioner is holder of three certificates, for six hundred dollars each, issued from the Treasury of the United States, payable to Andrew Bass, or bearer, and dated the 19th day of February, 1779. These certificates were issued for so much money received at the Treasury; and it appears by the certificate of the Register of the Treasury, that the said certificates remain due and unpaid. Your committee, therefore, report a bill, directing the payment of their specie value, with such interest as the holder would have received had he subscribed the same to the funded debt of the United States, under the act of 1790.

The Committee on Revolutionary Claims, to whom was referred the petition of the heirs of John Wilson, deceased, report:

This case has been heretofore submitted to the committee, and a favorable report made thereon, which is hereto annexed. This committee concur in the opinion there expressed, that the petitioner is entitled to relief, and report a bill.

## March 27, 1830.

The Committee on Revolutionary Claims, to whom was referred the petition of Lieutenant John Wilson's heirs, have had the same under consideration, and beg leave to report:

That the said John Wilson entered into the service of his country, as a private soldier in the Virginia line on continental establishment, in the year 1776. Soon after joining the service he was appointed an ensign, and subsequently a lieutenant. That he continued in the service up to the year 1781, when, on the 8th of September of that year, at the battle of Eutaw Springs, he was killed, leaving two infant children, whose names were, in the year 1787, placed on the pension roll of the State of Virginia, at the rate of £20 per annum; but being removed from that State, in the autumn of the same year, to the State of Kentucky, and being very young, they were not able, and did not avail themselves of the bounty of their country, and in the opinion of your committee never did receive any part of said pension.

By a resolution of the 24th August, 1780, half pay for seven years was granted to the widows and children of those who might die in the service or be slain in battle; and your committee, believing this case falls within the strict letter and spirit of said resolution, report a bill for their relief.

---

## January 18, 1832.

The Committee on Revolutionary Claims, to whom was referred the petition of the legal representatives of John Peter Wagnon, report:

That the petitioners claim commutation, in lieu of half pay for life, due to John Peter Wagnon, a lieutenant of the Georgia line on the continental establishment, under the resolves of Congress of 1780 and 1782. It appears by the certificate of the Secretary of the Treasury that the said Wagnon did, during his lifetime, receive the compensation given by the act of 1828, to certain surviving officers and soldiers of the revolutionary war; which compensation depends on having a right to the commutation now claimed. And it further appears, by a letter of the Third Auditor of the Treasury, that there is no record of any part of the said half pay, or commutation in lieu thereof, having been paid. The committee therefore report a bill for the relief of his legal representatives.

The Committee on Revolutionary Claims, to whom was referred the petition of Edmund Brooke, report:

The petitioner sets forth in his petition that he was appointed and commissioned a lieutenant of artillery, in the first Virginia regiment in the continental establishment, and served until the siege of Yorktown, when he was taken sick, and left the service on furlough, to recover his health; and, while absent therefrom, the remnant of his regiment, being two full companies only, was ordered South, and joined General Greene's army in South Carolina, and continued there to the close of the war; during which time the petitioner held his commission and was subject to orders. In the reduced state of his regiment, his services were not needed; and he was of course never ordered to resume his station and command in the line of the army. He now claims for the balance of his pay, depreciation of pay, and commutation.

The claim has been before Congress for many years. The committee see no equitable claim, on the part of the petitioner, to pay or depreciation of pay; but they think he is entitled to commutation. He held his commission and was subject to orders to the close of the war. He received from the State of Virginia the pay to which he was entitled from the State in the continental line, and the bounty in land, as having served to the close of the war. And he has at the Treasury Department been found entitled to, and admitted to, the benefit of the act of May 15, 1828, and consequently the committee think was entitled, under the resolve of October 21, 1780, to half pay. The ground upon which this claim has been resisted is, that the name of the petitioner was not to be found upon the last pay-roll of his regiment, nor in the Treasury or War Department, as having served to the close of the war; but the evidence of the fact and manner of his service, combined with his recent admission to the benefit of the act aforesaid, leaves no doubt with the committee that he is justly entitled to the commutation he claims; for which they report a bill.

The Committee on Revolutionary Claims, to which was referred the petition of M. L. Jones, agent of the representatives of Dr. Samuel J. Axson, report:

The petitioner is the duly authorized agent of the heirs and legal representatives of Dr. Samuel J. Axson. He states that the said S. J. Axson served as a surgeon in the army of the Revolution on continental establishment, to the close of the war, and prays that the five years' full pay promised by the resolves of Congress to such officers as should continue in the service to the close of the war may be granted.

Charles Cotesworth Pinckney, late colonel of the first continental regiment of South Carolina, and late major general in the armies of the United States, testifies: "As my surgeon, Dr. Henry Collins Flagg, was appointed apothecary general to the military hospital for the southern department, I appointed Dr. Samuel J. Axson surgeon to the first continental regiment of South Carolina, and had him regularly commissioned, and

Dr. Axson conducted himself as surgeon with zeal and ability to the end of the war."

J. C. Calhoun states, as Secretary of War, in a letter addressed, in reference to this case, to Hon. A. Jackson, of the United States Senate, under date of January 20, 1824, "the evidence of a major general, or even a field officer, is always considered sufficient proof of the service of any officer."

It appears by a certificate from the Bounty Land Office, that Samuel J. Axson " was entitled to the rank of surgeon," and that land warrants, as such, have been issued in his favor.

By a reference to the resolves of Congress of October 21, 1780, and January 17, 1781, it will be seen that surgeons were entitled to half pay during life ; and that, by the resolve of March 21, 1783, they became entitled to receive five years' full pay instead of the half pay promised for life.

It appears, also, to the satisfaction of the committee, by statements made from the Third Auditor's office, that neither Dr. Samuel J. Axson, nor his representatives, received the five years' full pay promised as above.

It being therefore established, to the satisfaction of the committee, that Dr. Samuel J. Axson served as a surgeon on the continental establishment of the Revolution to the end of the war ; that he was entitled to five years' full pay, and that it has not been paid him or his heirs ; a bill is reported granting such five years' full pay, with the usual allowance of interest in such cases.

---

DECEMBER 17, 1833.

The Committee on Revolutionary Claims, to which was referred the petition of Thomas Minor, report :

The petitioner states that he entered the army of the United States during the early part of the revolutionary struggle, as a lieutenant, and afterwards became a captain of the Virginia line on continental establishment, in which rank he served in that establishment to the end of the war. He therefore claims the benefit of the resolves of Congress of October, 1780, and March, 1783, giving as a reason why his rights, although well known, were left unasserted, that the poverty of the country, and his own good circumstances for many years after the Revolution, held him back ; but thinks, as the country is now able to give, and has given to others, that his just claims also should be satisfied.

The evidence of his having served on continental establishment to the end of the war is satisfactory to the committee. He appears to have commanded a company until the reduction or remodelling of the army under the resolves of October 3 and 21, 1780, when the enlistment of his men having expired, he was left without a command. At the siege of Yorktown he was, however, again in service, as an aid to General Stevens, and continued in the service to the actual termination of the contest. These facts are sustained by the depositions of William Jackson, William Long, James Bullock, Richard Peacock, and others, engaged in the revolutionary contest, and who were personally acquainted with the petitioner, and knew his services to the end of the war of their own personal knowledge. In addition to this evidence, he is found to have been admitted to the benefits of the act of May 15, 1828, the admission to which depends upon his having served in the continental line to the end of the war.

The committee have therefore no doubt of his being entitled to commutation of half pay for life; and, as this appears never to have been paid, a bill is reported for his relief.

---

DECEMBER 17, 1833.

The Committee on Revolutionary Claims, to which was referred the petition of Francis and Judith Taylor, having considered the same, report:

That the petitioners state that Henry Field, the father of Judith Taylor, entered at a very early period into the revolutionary army, as a lieutenant in the continental line; that while in the service, about the close of the year 1777, or the beginning of 1778, he died, leaving the said Judith and her sister Elizabeth, both infants, and his only children; and that previous to his death, his wife, their mother, had died. They also state that, about the year 1795, the said Elizabeth departed this life, unmarried and childless, leaving the said Judith, who about that time intermarried with the petitioner, Francis Taylor, the sole heir and representative of Lieutenant Field. The object of the petition is to obtain the seven years' half pay, the promise of which was, by the resolution of Congress of 24th of August, 1780, extended to the widows, or, if no widow, to the children of such officers as had died, or might thereafter die, in the service; no part of which has been, they allege, in any manner received by them or the said Elizabeth.

All these statements are sufficiently proven by the depositions and other papers accompanying the petition. The claim was first brought before Congress in 1804; and the committee, satisfied that there was at least as good reason for the delay in presenting as there has been for the delay in allowing it, feel no hesitation in reporting a bill granting the amount of the seven years' half pay, with such interest as would have accrued thereon if it had been regularly funded under the act of 1790.

They therefore present the accompanying bill.

---

DECEMBER 19, 1833.

The Committee on Revolutionary Claims, to which was referred the petition of Starling Claiborne, report:

The petitioner is the son and administrator of Buller Claiborne, deceased. He states that his father was an officer of the Revolution, and served to the end of the war in the Virginia line on continental establishment; that he held the rank of captain or of brigade major, or of both; that neither he as administrator, nor the heirs of the said Buller Claiborne, have ever, at any time, received, either in whole or in part, the commutation pay from the Federal Government to which their father was justly entitled, according to the various resolutions of Congress on that subject. He asks that a law may be passed granting this commutation.

It appears, from the evidence submitted to the committee, that the principal facts alleged by the petitioner are amply sustained. Joseph Jones, John Crawford, Henry Tatum, and others, testify that Buller Claiborne entered the army in the Virginia line on continental establishment in the year 1775, as a lieutenant; that he was promoted to a captaincy; that he became an aid to General Lincoln; and that they believed him to have served to the end of the war. Captain George Blake Moore certifies that he knew him at Springfield and at Valley Forge; that he was brigade major, and he thinks served to the end of the war. Robert Rives, senior, declares that he entered the service at the commencement of the war, and continued during the war, and he believes on continental establishment. General Robert Porterfield testifies that he knew Buller Claiborne as an officer of the revolutionary army; that he acted as a brigade major, and served to the end of the war. The auditor of Virginia states that his name appears as a captain in the Virginia continental line, on a list of such officers in his office, and the register of the Virginia land office, that Buller Claiborne was entitled to, and that his heirs received, the proportion of land allowed to a captain of the Virginia continental line, for eight years' service.

The committee, believing the proof sufficient that Buller Claiborne served as an officer of the Revolution on continental establishment, with the rank of a captain, acting occasionally as a brigade major, to the end of the war, report a bill giving the commutation of half pay asked for to his legal representatives, it not having been heretofore paid, as would appear from a certificate of the Third Auditor of the Treasury.

---

### DECEMBER 20, 1833.

The Committee on Revolutionary Claims, to which was referred the petition of the residuary legatees of Major Everard Meade, deceased, report:

That a bill was reported for the relief of the petitioners, in the House of Representatives, at the first session of the twenty-second Congress, which was not definitively acted on. The committee have examined the report made on the 7th of July, 1832, and, concurring therewith, adopt it as a part of this report, and report a bill in all particulars similar to that heretofore reported.

### JULY 7, 1832.

The Committee on Revolutionary Claims, to which was referred the petition of the residuary legatees of Major Everard Meade, deceased, report:

The petitioners represent that their father, the late Major Everard Meade, early in the revolutionary war, entered into the continental service, in the Virginia line, as a captain; that he was afterwards promoted to the rank of major in the said service; that he continued therein to the end of the war ; that he never received half pay for life, or commutation in lieu thereof ; and they pray that the five years' full pay due to their father, with such interest thereon as may be deemed reasonable, may be granted to them. The Second Auditor states that it appears from the general account books of the revolutionary army, on file in his office, that Everard Meade, stated to be an aid-de-camp, was in service in the early part of the war, but that those books do not show how or when he left the service. That the records of the Virginia line do not show that he received the commutation, or that he was returned as entitled thereto. In a petition presented by the widow of Major Meade to the Virginia Legislature, a more minute and detailed account is given of his rank in the army, and of his services during the war, than in the petition of the residuary legatees. It is there stated that he entered into the continental army as a captain in the 2d regiment of infantry, in the spring of 1775 ; in which regiment he continued until 1777, when he was appointed an aid-de-camp to Major General Lincoln. That he served as aid, with the rank of major, until the fall of Charleston, early in 1780. That he was afterwards a colonel in a legion authorized to be raised by the State of Virginia, to be commanded by Brigadier General Alexander Spotswood. That, owing to the difficulty of enlisting men, the legion never was filled ; but that the officers thereof were held in readiness to take command of draughted militia when required. That her late husband did actually command a regiment in 1780, 1781, and 1782. That he claimed the rank of major at the end of the war, under a belief that, as the legion never was filled, the officers thereof could not claim their rank in it. Several letters and documents are produced to support this statement. Among them are two letters from Major General Steuben, one dated 21st of April, 1781, addressed to Everard Meade, Esq., colonel in General Spotswood's legion ; the other June 21st, the year omitted, but doubtless in the same year as the former one, but without any designation of rank. Also two letters from H. Baylies, addressed to Colonel Everard Meade, one dated November 6, 1781, the other February 3, 1782. From these letters, as well as one from General Lincoln to Major Meade, dated August, 1782, it appears that the latter was engaged in military duties in the year 1781, and that much reliance was placed on his zeal and capacity by Major General Steuben. General Charles Scott, in a letter addressed to Colonel Everard Meade, dated 30th December, 1783, enclosing a certificate for the highest rank which Major Meade claimed, charges him with neglect to himself in not asking more, and that he must have been entitled to a higher rank than a majority at the time of his leaving the service.

The register of the land office in Virginia certifies that a military land bounty warrant for 5,333⅓ acres, bearing date February 20, 1784, issued to Everard Meade, as a major of the continental line, for three years' service. It appears by an official certificate from the auditor's office of Virginia, that on the 30th of October, 1783, a certificate issued to Everard Meade, major of infantry, for £594, agreeably to an act of Assembly of that State, passed November session, 1781, which provided that the whole pay and subsistence of the officers and soldiers of the Virginia line in continental service should be made equal to specie from the first of January, 1777, to the last of December, 1781. That Everard Meade became a supernumerary officer is shown by the certificate of George W. Munford, keeper of the rolls of Virginia, stating that it appears in a list of resigned and supernumerary officers of the Virginia continental and State troops, filed in his office, that Captain Everard Meade is enrolled as a supernumerary officer; and that his name does not appear in the column containing such officers as resigned.

The committee believe that Everard Meade was entitled, as a supernumerary officer, to claim the benefit of the resolution of Congress of March 22d, 1783, of five years' full pay as a captain, in lieu of half pay for life. A bill for the relief of his legal representatives is reported accordingly.

---

### December 20, 1833.

The Committee on Revolutionary Claims, to which was referred the petition of the heirs of Thomas Wallace, deceased, report:

That they have examined the documents upon which the claim is founded, and also the report upon the same subject, made at the last Congress, which report they make a part of this, and submit a bill based upon the principles contained therein.

The petitioners allege that their father, Thomas Wallace, was a lieutenant in the Virginia line on continental establishment; that he continued in the service of the United States until the end of the revolutionary war, and they ask the commutation of five years' full pay. The commission of Thomas Wallace, as a lieutenant in the 8th Virginia regiment, in the army of the United States, is produced as evidence in support of this claim. It is dated on the 23d day of November, 1779, signed by Samuel Huntington, President of Congress, and countersigned by Benjamin Stoddert, Secretary of the Board of War. In 1781, Lieutenant Wallace was ordered to take command of a company belonging to his regiment, then equipped, and under marching orders to the southern army, as appears by a letter dated 19th November of that year, addressed to him as a lieutenant in the 8th Virginia regiment, by Christian Febiger, colonel commandant. On the 28th day of March, 1807, a patent for 366⅔ acres in the Virginia military reservation, was granted by the United States to Thomas Wallace, in consideration of military services performed by him as lieutenant, for three years, to the United States, in the Virginia line on continental establishment.

The records in the Third Auditor's office do not show that Lieutenant Thomas Wallace served to the end of the war, when he entered or left the service, nor that he received commutation, or was entitled thereto, though his name appears in the account books of the army. Yet, notwithstanding this deficiency of record evidence, the committee think that the presumption is very strong that Lieutenant Wallace continued in service until the end of the war; the patent for his bounty land recognises him as a lieutenant for three years, and that fact must have been satisfactorily established before the issuing of the land warrant. Three years from the date of his commission will bring the time of his service to November, 1782, at which period the war was virtually at an end. A bill for the relief of his heirs is therefore reported.

DECEMBER 20, 1833.

The Committee on Revolutionary Claims, to which was referred the petition of Ann Mortimer Barron, report :

This case has repeatedly been before Congress ; a favorable report was made thereon in the 21st and 22d Congresses, and a bill reported for the relief of the petitioner. The bill has, however, owing to a pressure of business, never been reached. This circumstance alone seems to have prevented a favorable action upon it. Upon reviewing the case, the committee concur in a former report, which is hereto annexed, and direct a bill to be again reported.

JANUARY 7, 1831.

The Committee on Revolutionary Claims, to which was referred the petition of Ann Mortimer Barron, of the borough of Norfolk, in the State of Virginia, make the following report :

The petitioner states that she is the only daughter and surviving heir of William Barron, a native of Virginia, who was killed in the service of his country during the revolutionary war, while acting as first lieutenant of the frigate Boston ; that he volunteered to perform the duties of the station to assist his friend, Captain Tucker, in conveying safely to France the late John Adams, Esquire ; and that, at the time of his death, the frigate was on her voyage thither from the United States. The petitioner adds, that she has heretofore enjoyed the advantage of generous friends, of whom many are now dead, and, from the natural course of events, she cannot long calculate upon the assistance of others ; and she has therefore yielded ( though with reluctance ) to the necessity of stating that, unless some recompense be made for her early and irreparable loss, the remainder of her life may be such as no nation would in justice permit.

To corroborate the principal facts set forth, the petitioner has produced the certificate, on oath, of Captain Tucker, who commanded the Boston on the melancholy occasion of her parent's death. Captain Tucker swears that William Barron was ordered on board the frigate in the month of January, 1778, and served faithfully and bravely as his first lieutenant until the 14th day of March ensuing, when he received a wound which caused his death in twelve days thereafter; "we being then," he says, "on our voyage to France, for the purpose of conveying the late Hon. John Adams, as minister plenipotentiary, with the treaty of alliance between this country and France." In a letter accompanying this certificate, Captain Tucker expresses the highest respect for the memory of Mr. Barron, "whose unfortunate and untimely death was deeply lamented by every soul on board the Boston."

The committee are of opinion that this is a strong case, and that it falls within the principle of the resolution of Congress, adopted on the 24th day of August, 1780. The third clause of that resolution is in these words :

"That the resolution of the 15th day of May, 1778, granting half pay for seven years to the officers of the army who should continue in service to the end of the war, be extended to the widows of those officers who have died, or shall hereafter die, in the service, to commence from the time of such officer's death, and continue for the term of seven years; or, if there be no widow, or in case of her death or intermarriage, the said half pay be given to the orphan children of the officer dying as aforesaid, if he shall have left any; and that it be recommended to the Legislatures of the respective States to which such officers belong, to make provision for paying the same on account of the United States."

The committee are aware that, in this clause, no allusion in terms is made to officers of *the navy;* but it should be remembered that, as a distinct and an efficient arm of the national defence, the navy was not fully recognised by Congress during the revolutionary war, and that the Department itself was not organized until April, 1798.  It may with reason, then, be inferred that individuals engaged in the naval as well as the land service, at that period, were included by Government under one general military head, or that the word *navy,* in the resolution of August, 1780, was accidentally omitted.  It could not have been the intention of Congress to make an unfair and invidious distinction between the widows and orphans of those brave men who fell in defence of their country's rights.  Later experience favors this construction; for, to say nothing of the act of January, 1813, which expressly provides for the widows and children of officers of the navy or marines, killed or dying of wounds received in the line of their duty, the pension laws of 1792, 1803, 1806, and 1818, apply alike to the soldier and the sailor.

The committee, therefore, are of opinion that the half pay of a first lieutenant of a frigate for seven years ought to be allowed to the petitioner, and have, accordingly, directed a bill to be reported for that purpose.

---

## DECEMBER 23, 1833.

The Committee on Revolutionary Claims having, under the order of the House, considered the propriety of paying to the administrators of Michael Gratz, deceased, the amount of their loan office certificates, alleged to have belonged to the said Michael, and to have been lost by him, report:

The petition alleges that, in 1779, Michael Gratz was the owner of three continental loan office certificates, two of them, Nos. 2,341 and 2,353, dated March 29, 1799, in favor of Ogden and Curtis, for five hundred dollars each, value in specie forty-five dollars sixty-four cents, and the third, No. 1,356, dated January 12, 1779, in favor of William Henderson, for one thousand dollars, value in specie one hundred and twenty-seven dollars forty-five cents, issued from the Pennsylvania loan office.  The certificate of the Register of the Treasury shows that these certificates are outstanding and unpaid, and there is no evidence of the payment of any interest upon either of them since their date.  There is filed with the petition a letter of Michael Gratz, bearing date Williamsburg, June 3, 1779, and purporting to enclose to his correspondent, to be expended for the use of Gratz, at some of the West India ports, these loan office certificates, corresponding in number and amount, and name of the party, with those described in the petition and in the Register's certificate. This letter is proven to be in the proper handwriting of Michael Gratz, and the committee see no reason to doubt that it was written at the time it bears date. It is difficult not to believe that the three certificates therein named were then the property of Gratz; the fact that no other person has ever produced them, or claimed the right of receiving their value, leads strongly to the inference that they were still the property of Gratz when lost or destroyed, and, consequently, that he or his representatives are entitled to their value. In the absence of every fact calculated to weaken this inference, the committee adopt it as the true one. They are the more ready to act upon it, because, before making payment, provision will be made for refunding the money in case the certificates should ever be presented. With these views they report a bill for the relief of the administrators of Michael Gratz.

---

### DECEMBER 23, 1833.

The Committee on Revolutionary Claims, to which was referred the petition of the heirs of Richard Livingston, deceased, report:

That this case has been thrice favorably reported on: on the 24th of February, 1832, the 9th of February, 1830, and the 15th of February, 1827. Your committee concur in all the said reports. The last named, but first in order of the time; states the facts of the case, and is adopted. Your committee therefore report a bill in conformity with the said report.

### FEBRUARY 24, 1832.

The Committee on Revolutionary Claims, to which was referred the petition of Richard Livingston and Stephen Livingston, heirs of Richard Livingston, deceased, report:

That the committee concur with the reports heretofore made in this case on the 15th February, 1827, and on the 9th February, 1830; to which they refer, and ask that they may be taken as a part of this report. A bill is accordingly reported.

### FEBRUARY 9, 1830.

The Committee on Revolutionary Claims, to which was referred the petition of Richard Livingston and Stephen Livingston, heirs of Richard Livingston, deceased, with the documents and papers accompanying the same, have had the same under consideration, and report:

That they have examined the documents and evidence referred to them, and have also examined a report made on the petition in this case by the Committee on Revolutionary Claims, on the 15th February, in the year 1827, in which report all the material facts presented in this case are stated, and concur with that committee in the opinion expressed by them in their said report, and ask that the same may be taken and considered as a part of this report; and further ask leave to submit a bill for the relief of the heirs of the said Richard Livingston, deceased.

The Committee on Revolutionary Claims, to which was referred the petition of Richard Livingston and Stephen Livingston, respectfully report:

That the petitioners set forth that their father, Richard Livingston, before and at the commencement of the American Revolution, was a quartermaster in the service of the King of Great Britain, and a resident in Montreal; that, when the American army retreated from Canada, the said Richard Livingston removed therefrom, with his family, into the State of New York, and was soon after appointed a lieutenant colonel in a regiment commanded by Colonel James Livingston, of the American army, and served therein until the year 1781; that the said Richard Livingston resided in the State of New York until the year 1786, when he died, leaving the petitioners infants; that the petitioners are the only children and heirs at law of the said Richard Livingston, who, they are advised, was entitled to lands as a Canada refugee. The petitioners represent that they have been ignorant of their rights, and have, therefore, heretofore neglected to apply for said lands, and pray that they may be granted.

Accompanying the petition is the affidavit of Colonel James Livingston, who fully proves all the allegations of the petitioners which are material to the claim. Colonel Livingston, who commanded the regiment in which the father of the petitioners served, states in his affidavit that the said Richard Livingston remained attached to his regiment until the year 1781, when several regiments were reduced; that the said Richard Livingston, at the time of his death, left several children, all of whom were infants, and all of whom, except the petitioners, are dead, without issue.

Upon this statement of facts, the committee are clearly of opinion that the petitioners are entitled to the relief they ask, and that the obligation imposed upon the Government by the early resolutions of Congress in favor of the Canada refugees, and since ratified by repeated acts of legislation, cannot, in justice or propriety, be overlooked or disregarded. The only objection to their claim, in the opinion of the committee, arises from the late period at which it was preferred; but that is removed by the fact that Richard Livingston died shortly after the war, and while the petitioners were minors, without the knowledge of their rights, and without capacity to enforce them.

The committee therefore ask leave to report a bill.

---

DECEMBER 23, 1833.

The Committee on Revolutionary Claims, to which was referred the petition of Ephraim Whitaker, report:

The petitioner claims the commutation of five years' full pay in lieu of half pay for life, under the resolves of Congress of 1780 and 1783.

It appears that he served from the early part of the revolutionary war, on continental establishment, as a sergeant and sergeant major, until after the battle of Monmouth, when he was appointed brigade forage master, with the rank of a captain, in which situation he continued to the close of the war.

After an examination of his case by Congress, he was considered as entitled to the compensation ordered under the act of May 15, 1828, and an act passed giving him the full benefit thereof. If he was entitled to the compensation given under the act of 1828, (and the committee do not question it,) he must also be entitled to the commutation of half pay for life, as the one necessarily depends on the other; the condition of both being, an officer's having served on continental establishment to the close of the war.

A case perfectly similar was decided at the first session of the last Congress—the case of John J. Jacobs. By an act approved May 29, 1830, the benefits of the act of May 15, 1828, were extended to Ephraim Whitaker and John J. Jacobs; and by an act approved July 14, 1832, the Secretary of the Treasury is directed to pay to John J. Jacobs the amount of his commutation of half pay, with such interest as would have accrued if a certificate for the same had been funded.

The committee, believing the petitioner entitled to the same measure of justice that others have received, report a bill in his favor.

---

DECEMBER 23, 1833.

The Committee on Revolutionary Claims, having had under consideration the petition of the heirs of Captain James Craine, report thereon:

That the petitioners, Edwin C. and Maria Brown, state that they are the sole representatives, the said Maria being the only child of James Craine, who, they say, was a captain in the Virginia continental line of the revolutionary army, and served to the close of the war. They pray for the commutation of five years' full pay, with interest.

It appears from the statements of several witnesses that James Craine entered the army as a private in 1775; that he was afterwards commissioned as a lieutenant, and then as a captain, in the Virginia continental line. One witness states, with certainty, that he was in service at the siege of Yorktown; another that, " to the best of his recollection, he continued in the service during the war, and he is certain he never resigned." In addition to this, the petitioners exhibit a certificate from the register of the land office of Virginia, showing that land warrants had issued from that office on account of the services of Captain James Craine, of the Virginia continental line, for two years and three months' service above six years. They also exhibit the certificate of the auditor of Virginia, showing that, on the 12th December, 1783, a certificate issued to James Craine, as captain of infantry, for pay for services up to 31st December, 1781, and a certificate from the Bounty Land Office of the United States, showing that a land warrant for 300 acres of land (the quantity promised by the resolution of 16th September, 1776, to a captain who should engage and continue in service during the war) had issued from that office in the name of Maria Brown, sole heir of James Craine, deceased, a captain in the Virginia line. From all these evidences, the committee think it sufficiently appears that Captain Craine served to the end of the war; that he was therefore embraced in the resolution of Congress granting half pay for life, and afterwards offering five years' full pay in lieu thereof; and that the petitioners, as his sole representatives, are entitled to the same, with such interest as would have accrued thereon if a certificate had issued at the proper time, and been subscribed as stock under the act of August, 1790; they therefore report a bill for that purpose.

<hr style="width:15%">

## December 23, 1833.

The Committee on Revolutionary Claims, to which was referred the memorial of the legal representatives of Captain George Hurlbut, deceased, report:

That this claim was presented to Congress in the year 1797, when a report was made, which, with the evidence now adduced, shows that George Hurlbut, deceased, was a captain of dragoons in Colonel Sheldon's regiment of the Connecticut continental line; that he was a meritorious officer; that in the year 1781, at the request of General Washington, he engaged in the hazardous enterprise of swimming to a transport, laden with supplies for the army, which had been set on fire by rockets thrown by the enemy from the opposite shore; he performed the task, and, unaided, extinguished the flames. In attempting to regain the shore in the same manner, he received a gun-shot wound from the enemy, of which he languished until the 8th day of May, 1783, never having resigned his commission.

On these facts his devisee, Ann Welsh, claimed the commutation of five years' full pay, which she deemed her right, under the resolutions of Congress of 1780, and of March, 1783. The committee to which that case was referred, in deference to a supposed previous declaration of Congress, and against their own opinion, decided that the said Captain George Hurlbut did not live to the end of the war, within the meaning of the contract resulting from the resolution of 1780, but they at the same time decided that the petitioner was entitled to the land promised to those who should serve to the end of the war, by the resolution of 1776; and that, upon proof of the facts, a warrant would issue without the action of Congress; and accordingly a warrant was issued upon the exhibition of the said proofs to the proper Department. The committee close their said report with a resolution that the petition be rejected. The House reversed this resolution, and directed a bill to be reported granting the commutation prayed. A bill was accordingly brought in; but it was afterwards so amended as to provide for all such cases, and in that shape finally rejected.

Your committee will enter into no elaborate argument on the question at what time the war of the Revolution actually ended; perhaps this question might properly receive different answers, according to the circumstances in allusion to which it should be propounded. The provisional articles of the treaty of peace were made between the United States and England the 30th of November, 1782. The peace between France and England, on the conclusion of which the provisional articles were made to depend, was concluded in January, 1783. The definitive treaty of peace with Great Britain was made on the 3d day of September,

1783. Information of the latter fact was officially communicated to Congress on the 13th December, 1783, though it is believed the treaty had been received some time before, but could not be communicated to Congress because of the want of a quorum. The definitive treaty was not formally ratified by Congress till 14th January, 1784. Congress had notice of the provisional articles of November 30, 1782, in January following; and in March, 1783, that body received information of the treaty between France and England. On the 16th day of April, of the same year, a cessation of hostilities was declared, though the army was not finally and entirely disbanded until the proclamation of October, which directed the disbanding of the remainder of the army on the 3d of November following, to which last day the accounts for pay of the troops were extended.

From a careful review of all these facts, your committee are of opinion that, as a precautionary measure, Congress might well have justified keeping the troops imbodied whose services had been engaged " during the war," until 14th January, 1784, at which time Congress finally ratified the treaty of peace, which, as to the United States, had been concluded so long ago as the 30th of November, 1782. The Congress might have insisted on keeping the troops imbodied, because the hostilities had ceased ; whether that which had been done would finally prove to have been the end of the war depended on the subsequent ratification. But your committee are of opinion that the said subsequeut final ratification did prove that the war was, in point of fact, at an end, at least as early as the 16th of April, 1783. The ratification in 1783 introduced no new relation between the parties, but simply confirmed the state of things agreed on the preceding November, and which, by an actual cessation of hostilities, had in fact existed from the said 16th day of April. Your committee therefore think that Captain Hurlbut did live and serve to the end of the war ; that he literally performed his part of the contract on which his right to half pay for life depended. Your committee are equally clear that the said Captain Hurlbut, under the act of March, 1783, was entitled to the commutation of five years' full pay, in lieu of the half pay for life ; for, although he died shortly after that act, the adoption thereof by the whole of the officers of the continental line constitutes the same a contract between the Government and the said officers, and in fact, as your committee believe, a gainful one on the part of the Government, as the pension list and the claim of the officers of the Virginia line established against that State, and subsequently assumed by Congress, will fully prove.

Your committee therefore beg leave to report a bill directing the payment of the said commutation, with such interest as has been heretofore allowed in such cases, to the legal representatives of the said George Hurlbut, deceased.

---

### December 23, 1833.

The Committee on Revolutionary Claims, to which was referred the petition of Robert Wilmott, report :

The petitioner states that he entered the service of the United States in the year 1776, as a lieutenant in the Maryland State artillery ; that, in the following year, he was transferred to Harrison's Virginia regiment of artillery in the continental establishment, and remained therein to the close of the war and the disbanding of the army; that he never applied for or received the five years' full pay promised by the resolves of Congress of October, 1780, and March, 1783; having, for many years after the Revolution, enjoyed good health, with a sufficiency, and not wishing to submit his claims while in such a situation, or while the finances of his country were in any way embarrassed; that he is now aged, infirm, and a cripple, unable for years to walk without crutches, and in want of pecuniary assistance.

Under these cirumstances, he prays that the five years' full pay, in lieu of half pay for life, promised by the resolves of Congress, may be granted him.

The statement of the petitioner is fully verified in all its parts by a number of respectable witnesses. There can be no doubt that he was a lieutenant on continental establishment, and that he served to the end of the war. Besides having been admitted to the benefits of the act of May 15, 1828, at the Treasury Department, Dr. Richard Pendell, Captain William Meredith, Lieutenant William B. Wallace, of the revolutionary army, and Harrison's regiment, as also John Wilmott, and Zebulon Heddington, with others, testify upon oath that they know him to have served on the continental establishment to the close of the war.

As there is no evidence in the records of the Third Auditor's office to show that the petitioner ever received the commutation he now asks for, and as the committee believe him justly entitled to it, they accordingly report a bill for his relief.

---

### December 27, 1833.

The Committee on Revolutionary Claims, to which was referred the petition of John M. Taylor, administrator, with the will annexed, of John Taylor, a lieutenant in the army of the Revolution, report:

That the petitioner is the son and administrator, with the will annexed, of John Taylor. He states that his father was an officer of the Virginia continental line, in the regiment commanded by Colonel Francis Taylor, and served from the commencement of the war to the spring of the year 1781, when he became a supernumerary lieutenant, and continued such to the close of the war. He claims, as the administrator of his father, the commutation of half pay for life promised by the resolves of Congress to such officers as should continue in the service to the end of the war, or become supernumerary after the resolves of 1780.

The statements of the petitioner, as to the services of his father, are fully verified by the testimony of Major John Roberts, who served in the same regiment, became a supernumerary at the same time, and has received his commutation of half pay.

In addition, Governor Floyd, of Virginia, testifies that "the heirs of John Taylor are allowed land bounty for his services as a lieutenant in the continental line to the end of the war." James E. Heath, of the auditor's office of Virginia, testifies that, on the 8th day of July, 1783, a certificate for the balance of full pay issued to John Taylor, a lieutenant of infantry of the Virginia line on continental establishment. By a resolution of Congress, passed September 16, 1776, lieutenants serving to the end of the war became entitled to 200 acres of bounty land. A warrant for this quantity has been issued by the United States to the administrator of Lieutenant John Taylor, as appears from a certificate dated at the War Department, Bounty Land Office, and signed "William Gordon, first clerk."

The committee, believing that Lieutenant John Taylor was clearly within and entitled to the benefit of the resolves of 1780, allowing half pay for life to such officers as should serve to the close of the war, or become supernumerary, and of March, 1783, commuting the half pay for life, by five years' full pay in lieu thereof, and not having received the same, accordingly report a bill in favor of his heirs.

---

## DECEMBER 30, 1833.

The Committee on Revolutionary Claims, to which was referred the petition of Charles Drish, legal representative of Christian Ish, deceased, report:

The subject embraced in this petition was brought before the 21st and 22d Congresses, a favorable report made thereon, and a bill submitted to the House. The committee herewith again report the same bill; and, in explanation of the grounds on which the petitioner's claim rests, would respectfully refer to the annexed report, made by the Committee on Revolutionary Claims on the 2d February, 1831; which report, upon a re-examination of the case, is fully concurred in.

*The Committee on Revolutionary Claims, to which was referred the petition of Charles Drish, report:*

The petitioner, as the legal representative of Christian Ish, deceased, claims payment of a certificate issued by George Ross, deputy quartermaster general, to Christian Ish, for $5,432. The certificate is dated on the 29th day of February, 1780, at Lancaster, in the State of Pennsylvania. Jacob Wolfly, in a deposition made by him on the 13th of April, 1812, says that, twenty years previous, or more, he had the care of a United States certificate in favor of Christian Ish, which had been liquidated, settled, and signed by George Ross, of the borough of Lancaster, Pennsylvania—he, the said Ross, then being in commission for making such settlements; that this certificate was given to Christian Ish, for smith-work and other services rendered to the United States. Its amount was more than $4,000, but that he, the deponent, did not recollect the exact sum. That he sent the certificate to Congress by Andrew Gregg, though he cannot recollect that the said Gregg was then a member of Congress, or a private citizen. About two years after the delivery of the certificate to Gregg, it was sent back to the deponent, who transmitted it to the widow and heirs of Christian Ish, then residing in Virginia. The character of the deponent, Jacob Wolfly, for veracity and integrity, as fully sustained by the certificates of General Joseph Heister, Robert Harris, and C. Spayd. The committee are satisfied of the genuineness of the certificate, and that it is the one spoken of by Jacob Wolfly in his deposition.

Although it was not presented to the commissioner appointed under the resolution of the 8th of May, 1786, yet, having been given for services rendered to the United States, and the heir being then a minor, the committee are of opinion that the non-presentment, or the lapse of time, ought not, under the circumstances shown by the evidence, to prevent the allowance and payment of the claim. A bill is therefore reported for one hundred and forty seven dollars and ten-ninetieths, being the value of the said certificate, according to the scale of depreciation established under a resolution of Congress of the 28th June, 1780.

<hr>

### December 31, 1833.

The Committee on Revolutionary Claims, to which was referred the petition of Frederick Raymer, report:

The petitioner states that in the year 1777 he resided on and cultivated a farm near the city of Albany, in the State of New York; that in the summer of that year he was pressed into the service of the American army, with his team of two horses and wagon, by the order of General Glover, commanding a brigade of continental troops; that he continued in the service ten days, and was then permitted to return home on account of sickness, leaving, however, his team in the service; that neither horses, wagon, nor harness, were ever returned to him, or any compensation received for them. He also states that he suffered many other losses and privations, being driven from his farm, his house plundered, two of his horses carried off and sold to the British by a party of tories, his crops destroyed, and himself detained as a prisoner for several months; also, that he served at different times, about four months, on the lines, often in cases of great emergency, invariably defraying his own expenses, and receiving no compensation for his services.

These statements are proved to be correct by evidence perfectly satisfactory to the committee. His integrity, patriotism, and warm attachment to the American cause, during the Revolution, are fully testified to by respectable witnesses. He is now aged, infirm, and in reduced circumstances.

It appears to the committee that the petitioner is justly entitled to receive compensation for the property taken for the service of the Government by its authorized agents. They therefore report a bill for his relief. It is the bill which was passed at the 2d session of the last Congress, but was not reached in the Senate.

<hr>

### January 2, 1834.

The Committee on Revolutionary Claims, to which was referred the petition of Charles Perrow, administrator of William Teas, deceased, report:

That the petitioner prays for the commutation of five years' full pay, in

36

lieu of half pay for life, promised by the resolves of Congress of October[?] 1780, and March, 1783, to such officers of the revolutionary army as should continue in the service to the close of the war; and to which William Teas became entitled by such service.

It appears, from the testimony submitted to the committee, that said Teas served as a cornet in Colonel William Washington's corps of horse, on continental establishment, to the close of the war.

Hezekiah Hargrove, a soldier of the Revolution, who served in the southern campaigns, testifies that he became acquainted with Teas during the Guilford expedition, and knew him to be attached to Washington's corps of horse; that he was severely wounded, and served to the close of the war.

Joseph Royal, of the 9th Maryland regiment on continental establishment, testifies that he saw Teas do duty as a cornet in Washington's corps at the battle of the Cowpens, (January 17, 1781,) and at the battle of the Eutaw Springs, (September 8, 1781.)

Other testimony establishes the good character and veracity of Teas, who often declared that he had thus served and continued in the service to the close of the war; and that, although he had claims on the Government, he would not urge them, from feelings of patriotism.

The committee, believing that Teas was fully entitled to the benefit of the resolves of Congress of 1780 and 1783, report a bill for the relief of his heirs and legal representatives.

------

### JANUARY 3, 1834.

The Committee on Revolutionary Claims, which was instructed to inquire into the propriety of allowing and paying to the legal representatives of Benjamin Bird and of Grove Pomeroy certain loan office certificates and final settlement certificates, which have been lost or destroyed, report:

That it very satisfactorily appears, from documents and affidavits filed in the cases, respectively, that not many days previous to the 20th day of February, 1779, Grove Pomeroy, the ancestor, was in possession of four final settlement certificates, issued in his favor, and numbered 12,232, 12,791, 13,323, and 13,610, respectively, and for the sums of $2 39, $75 49, $80, and $80, all dated the 1st day of January, 1784, the three first bearing interest from the 1st day of January, 1783, and the latter from November 4, 1783; that, on the said 20th day of January, 1779, the said Pomeroy's dwelling-house was burned, with most of its contents. It also appears that about the 1st of April, 1778, Benjamin Bird had assigned to him the following loan office certificates, issued from the loan office in Massachusetts, in favor of Pierre Gourrege, dated the 1st day of April, 1778, and numbered 5,681, 5,682, 4,128, 4,129, 4,130, 2,014, 2,015, and 2,016, the two first for $200 each, the three next for $400 each, and the three last for $600 each, which it is alleged were lost with his pocket-book on the 27th day of April, 1778. It is shown by satisfactory evidence that the said Pomeroy, after the burning of his dwelling-house, made the necessary advertisement, preparatory to an application for the renewal of his said certificates, according to the provisions of a resolve of Congress of 10th May, 1780, and that the said Bird duly advertised the loss of his said certificates, and gave notice thereof in person to the commissioner of loans in Massachusetts, from whom they issued. It appears also that repeated applications have been made by the said Pomeroy and Bird, and their representatives since, and that all said certificates appear on the books of the Treasury to this time unpaid. The committee are of opinion that these facts are all the proof that can be expected in such cases, and, with the precaution of a bond of indemnity usual in such cases, report a bill for relief.

----

### January 2, 1834.

The Committee on Revolutionary Claims, to which was referred the petition of the legal representatives of Enos Granniss, report:

That this claim was favorably reported on the 27th February, 1833; that report, with the evidence, has been re-examined; and your committee, concurring entirely with that report, adopt it, and report a bill in all respects the same as the one then reported.

### February 27, 1833.

The Committee on Revolutionary Claims, to which was referred the petition of the heirs and legal representatives of Enos Granniss, report:

It appears, from the testimony submitted to the committee in this case, that Enos Granniss enlisted in Captain Pendleton's company of artificers, September 13, 1777, for and during the war; that on the 12th of November, 1779, he was promoted to the rank of lieutenant, and that he continued to serve in that capacity until the end of the war. He received bounty land for that grade, to which bounty land those only were entitled who continued in the service to the close of the war.

Not having received the commutation of half pay for life promised by the resolves of Congress of October, 1780, and March, 1782, to such as should serve to the end of the war, it is now claimed by his heirs and legal representatives. The committee, believing them justly entitled to this commutation, report a bill for their relief.

----

### January 3, 1834.

The Committee on Revolutionary Claims, to which was referred the petition of the heirs and legal representatives of John M. Gregory, report:

The petitioners state that their father, John M. Gregory, was the only son and heir at law of John Gregory, a lieutenant in the sixth Virginia regiment on continental establishment; that their grandfather, the said John Gregory, was killed in the service; and that neither they nor their father, John M. Gregory, ever received the seven years' half pay allowed to the heirs of officers who died in the service, by the resolution of Congress, passed August 24, 1780, extending the resolution of May 15, 1778, to the widows of those officers who died in the service; or, in case of their death or intermarriage, to the orphan children of the officer dying as aforesaid. They pray that this half pay may now be granted to them.

It appears, from evidence perfectly satisfactory to the committee, that John Gregory did serve as a lieutenant in the Virginia line on continental establishment, that he was killed in the service, and that his heirs have never received the seven years' half pay allowed by the resolve of Congress above mentioned. A bill is therefore reported for their relief.

----

JANUARY 7, 1834.

The Committee on Revolutionary Claims, to which was referred the memorial of Edward P. Torrey, on behalf of himself and the other heirs and representatives of Joseph Torrey, deceased, report:

That it appears from a report of the Secretary of War, made to the House of Representatives on the 4th day of November, 1791, that Joseph Torrey entered the army, as an officer, in the very commencement of the revolutionary war, and served with high reputation until his death, which took place on the last of the month of September, 1783, at which time he was a major of Hazen's regiment, commonly called " *Congress' own regiment.* " This report of the Secretary of War speaks in high terms of commendation of the services and character of Major Torrey.

In the adjustment of his accounts with the public, by his brother and executor, the commutation of half pay was refused, on the ground that Major Torrey did not live to " the end of the war ;" and it is for this commutation that the present application is made.

The half pay stipulated by the resolution of the 21st October, 1780, is promised to " *the officers who shall continue in service to the end of the war.*" If, then, Major Torrey served to the end of the war, himself or his representatives became entitled, as matter of right, to the commutation of that half pay, as provided in the resolution of Congress of the 23d March, 1783.

This case is nearly allied to the case of Captain Hurlbut, on which the committee have already favorably reported. The only difference is this, that Major Torrey lived several months after Captain Hurlbut died. The committee might content itself by a bare reference to the report in the case of Captain Hurlbut, as containing the reasons for a favorable decision in this; they will, however, again recapitulate them.

The provisional articles of peace between the United States and Great Britain were signed on the 30th of November, 1782. Major Torrey was living and in service at that time. The peace between France and Great Britain (on the conclusion of which the efficacy of the provisional articles was made to depend) was concluded on the 20th of January, 1783. Major Torrey was living and in service on that day. On the 24th of March, 1783, the armed vessels of the United States, cruising against Great Britain, were recalled ; and the reason given therefor by Congress is, that information had been received "*announcing a general peace.*" Major Torrey was living on this day, and in service. On the 11th of April, 1783, Congress declared that all hostilities by land and water should cease from that day, on the express ground that *a general peace had been concluded* between Great Britain and France, Great Britain and Spain, and *Great Britain and the United States.* Major Torrey was living and in service on this day. The *last seal* was put to the war, and it was declared *in due form* to be at an end, by the final conclusion of the definitive treaty of peace, which was on the 3d day of September, 1783. Major Torrey was living and in service on that day. He did not die until the last of September of that year, and the treaty was signed on the 3d.

Congress, by the proclamation of the 18th day of October, 1783, ordered the army to be finally disbanded on the 3d of November following; and the accounting officers of the Government, in the settlement of commutation, *assumed, without authority of Congress*, that day as "the end of the war," and refused commutation to all who were not in service on the 3d November, 1783. It is clear that Congress considered the war as ended before the 3d November, 1783, as on the 23d of April, 1783, a resolution was passed declaring that, *in the opinion of Congress*, the time of the troops enlisted for the war did not end till the *final ratification* of a treaty of peace, yet leaving it discretionary with General Washington to discharge men so enlisted, or not, as he should see fit. That *final ratification* did not take place, on the part of Congress itself, till the 14th of January, 1784; and if any day has been specifically fixed by Congress as "*the end of the war*," it is the 14th January, 1784; yet Congress, in October preceding, ordered the army to be disbanded on the 3d November following. It is then clear that Congress never absolutely *fixed* a day as "the end of the war." The offer of half pay for life (and afterwards commuted for five years' full pay) on condition of serving to the end of the war, being distinct from ordinary pay, and in the nature of bounty, might not, on a strict or ordinary construction of the terms, depend absolutely, as seems to have been assumed, on the disbanding of a part or the whole of the army; for that might (and did in this case, as is well understood) depend on considerations of policy and convenience; while the amenability of officers, under military duties and discipline, might and should depend (as also their ordinary pay, of course,) on the orders under which they found themselves acting, till the final and formal disbanding of the army; and even if this were not so, the stipulation in question, in a civil point of view, might be truly fulfilled, while military obligation was differently construed, or even disregarded.

From a careful review of all these facts, it would seem to the committee that, so far as the United States was concerned, the war ended on the 30th November, 1782, when the provisional articles were concluded, or on the 20th January, 1783, when the treaty between France and Great Britain was signed; on the conclusion of which, those articles were to assume all the sanctions of a formal treaty. If, however, it were doubtful whether either of those days could be legally taken as the end of the war, there can be none that Congress considered the war as ended on the 11th April, 1783, when it issued its proclamation for a cessation of all hostilities, on the ground that a *general peace had been concluded* between Great Britain and France, Great Britain and Spain, and *Great*

*Britain and the United States.* But even if the last day be taken which can be as the end of the war, that is, the 3d of September, 1783, when the treaty of peace was finally concluded, Major Torrey was entitled to his commutation, as he lived after that day. The resolution of Congress of the 16th of September, 1776, granting land bounties, confines the grant to officers and soldiers " who shall continue in service to the close of the war." In the execution of this resolution, it has always been held, and so decided and acted upon, that if an officer or soldier lived until the 11th of April, 1783, when the proclamation for ceasing hostilities was issued, he was entitled to land.

Under every view of the facts which the committee can take, they think that Major Torrey did live and serve to the end of the war; that he literally performed his part of the contract on which a right to half pay for life depended.

Your committee are equally clear that Major Torrey became entitled to the commutation of that half pay under the resolution of 23d March, 1783, as he lived long after that period, and was consequently a party to the contract between the officers of the army and the United States which commuted the half pay for life into five years' full pay.

Your committee therefore report a bill for the payment of his commutation to his heirs and legal representatives.

---

### January 7, 1834.

The Committee on Revolutionary Claims, to which was referred the petition of John Emerson, report:

The petitioner states that he entered the service of the United States in the early part of the war, as a lieutenant of infantry, in the 13th Virginia regiment on continental establishment, commanded by Colonel William Russel, and continued in the service to the close of the revolutionary war. He therefore deems himself entitled to, and claims, the five years' full pay allowed by the resolve of Congress of March 22, 1783, in lieu of the half pay for life promised by the resolve of October, 1780.

It appears by a certificate issued from the Treasury Department, and dated August 3, 1829, that the petitioner has been admitted to the benefits of the act of May, 1828, giving compensation to certain officers and soldiers of the revolutionary army, which compensation depends upon having served to the close of the war, and therefore having a right to the commutation of half pay now claimed. Knowing the strictness with which revolutionary claims are examined into by that Department, the committee cannot doubt his having served as stated, and being, therefore, entitled to what he claims. His commission is upon file in the War Department. There is also the deposition of Charles Thuxman, who declares that he served to the close of the war in Russel's regiment. There is no evidence in the records of the Third Auditor's office of his having received the commutation, or any part of it.

The committee, believing him to have continued in the service to the end of the war, and entitled to the five years' full pay in lieu of half pay for life, in accordance with the resolves of Congress, report a bill for its payment, with the usual interest heretofore allowed in such cases.

The Committee on Revolutionary Claims, to which was referred the petition of Margaret Riker, (by resolution,) report:

The petitioner alleges that she is the widow of an officer who died in service in the army of the Revolution, and entitled to his half pay for seven years, according to the resolution on that subject, and prays for the same.

A report of the Secretary of War, (General Knox,) in 1793, and sundry depositions accompanying the petition, agree in establishing the fact that Abraham Riker was a captain (a highly meritorious officer) in the second New York regiment on continental establishment, and that he died of excessive exertion and fatigue in service, at Valley Forge, on the 7th day of May, 1778. The affidavits referred to fully prove that the petitioner is the widow of the said Captain Riker.

These facts, very satisfactorily established, bring her case, unequivocally, within the letter and spirit of the resolution referred to, and the practice of the Government in relation to these claims.

The petitioner further states, after recounting many losses and misfortunes following the loss of her said husband, that her only daughter and child, and the only child of her said husband, is deceased; and that she is now in the ninety-third year of her age, wholly blind and helpless, and dependant on her friends for support.

The committee, with cheerfulness, report a bill.

---

The Committee on Revolutionary Claims, which was directed to inquire into the propriety of allowing and paying to the heirs and legal representatives of Colonel William Bond, Colonel William Douglass, and Captain Nathaniel Goodwin, respectively, the seven years' half pay promised by the resolution of Congress of the 24th of August, 1780, to the widows and children of officers who may have died or been killed in the service of the United States in the revolutionary war, report:

That it appears from original documents, reports of the Secretary of War, copies of public records, and other satisfactory evidence filed in these cases, respectively, that William Bond was a colonel in the Massachusetts line of the continental army, and died in service at Ticonderoga, in the State of New York, on the 31st day of August, 1776; that William Douglass was a colonel in the Connecticut line of the continental army, and died while recruiting his regiment in the State of Connecticut, on the 27th day of May, 1777; and that Nathaniel Goodwin was a captain in the Connecticut line of the continental army, and died in service at the hospital in Litchfield, in Connecticut, on the 1st day of May, 1777. It appears that, in each of these cases, the deceased left a widow and children; that the said widows are now all deceased, having survived their said husbands more than seven years, and continued unmarried till their deaths. Petitions, in each of these cases, were early presented to Congress, and, in some of them, to the State Legislatures, and have been favorably received, and reported thereon; but, from various delays incident to prosecution and legislation, final action and redress appear never to have been obtained. The committee therefore report a bill for the relief of their representatives.

------

JANUARY 9, 1834.

The Committee on Revolutionary Claims, to which was referred the petitions of Benjamin Jacobs, of Samuel Bayard, surviving executor of John Bayard, deceased, and of the executors of Joseph Falconer, deceased, report:

The petitioner, Benjamin Jacobs, asks payment of two loan office certificates issued to him from the loan office in Connecticut, and which he alleges were stolen from him on the 27th day of October, 1783. It appears from the certificate of Thaddeus Betts, formerly deputy receiver of loans in Connecticut, and from the certificate of the Register of the Treasury of the United States, that two certificates were issued from the loan office in Connecticut in favor of Benjamin Jacobs, one, No. 9,541, dated 21st May, 1779, for $200; the other, No. 6,129, dated 26th April, 1779, for $500; and the latter officer certifies that the same are outstanding and unpaid. It further appears that the petitioner, on the 29th of October, 1783, caused an advertisement to be inserted in a newspaper published in the city of New York, stating that on the 27th of that month he had lost a pocket-book, containing (among other things) two continental certificates, payable to Benjamin Jacobs, and offering a reward for their return. The committee are satisfied that the petitioner is entitled to the payment of those certificates at their specie value, with interest thereon, on his giving security to indemnify the Treasury against any claim which may be set up by the holder of such certificates.

The petitioner, Samuel Bayard, states that, in the month of February, 1777, six certificates, numbered 151, 152, 155, 156, 157, and 158, each for $300, and amounting together to the sum of $1,800, were issued from the loan office of the United States to his testator, Colonel John Bayard, and that the said certificates are mislaid or lost. Colonel John Bayard died in 1807, and the surrogate of Somerset county, in the State of New Jersey, certifies that the petitioner is the surviving executor of the will of the said John Bayard. It appears, from the records in the office of the Register of the Treasury, that certificates Nos. 151, 152, 155, 156, 157, and 158, dated February 22, 1777, of $300 each, amounting to $1,800, were issued in the name of John Bayard, and are still unsatisfied. The committee believe the petitioner is entitled to the payment of those certificates at their specie value, with interest thereon, on giving security to indemnify the Treasury against the claims of any holder thereof.

A favorable report was made at the last session of Congress on the petition of the executors of Joseph Falconer, which this committee refer to and adopt. A bill is therefore reported for the relief of the several petitioners.

JANUARY 22, 1833.

The Committee on Revolutionary Claims, to which was referred the petition of the heirs and representatives of Joseph Falconer, having had the same under consideration, report :

That the petitioners pray that interest may be paid to them on two loan office certificates, the principal of which was directed to be paid by an act for the relief of the legal representatives of Joseph Falconer, approved the 28th May, 1830.

The committee is satisfied that interest is due on the certificates. They have found some difficulty, however, in determining the period at which it should be considered as commencing, in consequence of the loss of the original certificates. They have considered it safest, in conformity with the opinion of the late Register of the Treasury, to allow the interest from the 1st day of January, 1788, and for that purpose report a bill.

JANUARY 10, 1834.

The Committee on Revolutionary Claims having, according to the order of the House, had under consideration the propriety of paying to the heirs of Samuel Gibbs, deceased, the amount of two loan office certificates, alleged to have been lost, report :

The original petition of Samuel Gibbs states that two certificates issued from the loan office of Pennsylvania to Gilbert Palmer, of the State of New York, one, No. 2,321, for $1,000, the other, No. 138, for $300; that they were put into his hands by Gilbert Palmer, (his uncle,) for the purpose of having them funded, but were accidentally lost before an opportunity occurred of funding them ; that he gave his obligation to said Gilbert Palmer for seventy-six pounds, in consideration of said certificates, and that he has paid the same. He prays the payment of the certificates to himself.

The Register of the Treasury certifies that the two above-described loan office certificates, issued to Gilbert Palmer, remain outstanding and unpaid, and that the interest thereon cannot have been paid since the 31st day of December, 1787. The committee are satisfied, from the evidence exhibited, that these certificates were delivered by Palmer to Gibbs, for the purpose of receiving the interest, and having them liquidated; that they were lost by Gibbs, and that he compensated Palmer for their loss, and became entitled to their proceeds. Under these circumstances, the committee are of opinion that the representatives of Samuel Gibbs are entitled to the payment of the two certificates, with interest from the 1st day of January, 1788, and report a bill accordingly.

MARCH 5, 1834.

The Committee on Revolutionary Claims, to whom was referred the memorial of William A. Duer, John Duer, and Beverley Robinson, trus-

37

tees of the estate of Sarah Alexander, deceased, who was the widow of Major General Lord Stirling, praying payment of a certificate issued to that officer by the State of New Jersey, in December, 1781, on account of the depreciation of his pay, and that the same may be paid either in money or in lands at the Government price, as may best comport with the convenience of Government, report:

That they have inquired into the facts and circumstances of the case, and find that, on the 12th of August, 1780, Congress passed a resolution, "that the general officers be informed that Congress have, at no time, been unmindful of the military virtues which have distinguished the army of the United States through the course of this war, &c. That it has been recommended to the several States to make compensation to the officers and soldiers, to them respectively belonging, for the depreciation of their pay; and that Congress will take speedy measures for liquidating and paying what is due on that account to the officers and soldiers who do not belong to the quota of any State."

That, on the 28th September, 1781, another resolution was passed by Congress, "that it be, and hereby is, recommended to the several States of which the general officers of the army are inhabitants, to settle with them for the depreciation of their pay, on the principles adopted in settlements with the officers of their respective lines."

That Lord Stirling was an inhabitant of the State of New Jersey, and that, in pursuance of the above resolution, the said State, on the 31st December, 1781, adjusted with him the amount of the depreciation to which he was entitled, and issued to him two certificates, one for £534 1s. 6¼d., for the one-fourth, and the other for £1,602 4s. 6¾d. for the remaining three-fourths of such depreciation. That the first-mentioned certificate was payable at a short day, and was paid by the State of New Jersey to Lord Stirling, in cash, on the — day of February, 1782, with interest from the 1st of August, 1780. That the other certificate was made payable in three years from the 1st of January, 1781, and has never been paid. It is in the following words:

"No. 1,025.

"The State of New Jersey is indebted unto Major General Lord Stirling in the sum of sixteen hundred and two pounds four shillings and six pence and three farthings, being the three-fourth parts of the sum allowed for the depreciation of his pay; which said sum shall be paid unto Major General Lord Stirling, or his lawful representatives, in specie, or the value thereof, within three years from the 1st day of January, one thousand seven hundred and eighty-one, bearing an interest of six per centum per annum from the 1st day of August last.

"Witness my hand, this 31st day of December, one thousand seven hundred and eighty-one.

"JOHN STEVENS, Jr., *Treasurer.*
"JAMES EWING, *Auditor.*"

"The interest on the above to commence on the 1st of August, 1780.
"JOHN STEVENS, Jr."

That Lord Stirling died in January, 1783; that, shortly before his death, he gave the certificate in question to his widow; that she applied to the treasurer of the State of New Jersey for payment in 1785, and was refused, on the ground that there was a bond and mortgage on the files of the treasury office that had been executed by Lord Stirling to Stephen Skinner, a former treasurer of the colony of New Jersey, in the year 1767, on which there appeared to be a balance due beyond the amount of the said certificate.

That it does not appear that the widow made any other application for payment of this certificate until the year 1802, when she petitioned to the Legislature of New Jersey for payment, which was refused on the same ground. That she died in 1804, having first made a will, appointing the late Judge Brockholst Livingston and Matthew Clarkson her executors and trustees, upon certain trusts therein mentioned.

That, in the year 1806, Judge Livingston presented a petition to the Legislature of the State of New Jersey, which was referred to a committee of the House of Assembly. That the pecuniary transactions between the State of New Jersey and Lord Stirling were inquired into by that committee, and the following facts made to appear:

That Lord Stirling's estate being encumbered by mortgages to a very considerable extent at the beginning of the Revolution, some of which mortgages being held by persons within the lines of the enemy, and others by persons who had been attainted in the State of New Jersey, whereby such debts became the property of that State, a law was passed by the State of New Jersey, at the request of Lord Stirling, in the year 1779, vesting all his estate in trustees, to be sold by them for the payment of his debts. That, by the terms of this law, the trustees were empowered to sell and convey, free from encumbrances; and they were directed to advertise in the most public manner for all creditors to come in and receive their debts. That the trustees were also specially directed to pay all debts due from Lord Stirling to persons against whom inquisitions had been taken, to the commissioners of forfeitures of the county where such inquisitions should be taken. That, in execution of their trust, the trustees sold a large portion of Lord Stirling's estate; received a large sum of money therefor; paid a number of debts, and, amongst others, a large sum of money to the commissioners of forfeitures of the county of Hunterdon; and, on the 18th December, 1780, reported their proceedings to the Legislature of New Jersey: "That they had disposed of certain parts of said estate, sufficient in their estimation to pay off the debts of the said William, Earl of Stirling; that they then had in hand a large sum of money arising from such sale; that *there were no demands before them unsatisfied;* and praying directions for their government in the said business." It does not appear that the Legislature of New Jersey made any order upon the said report.

It appears that the purchase-money on these sales was paid in paper money, which, at that period, was a legal tender in the payment of debts within the State of New Jersey. That in *June,* 1781, the Legislature of New Jersey repealed the *tender act,* as it was termed, by which the said paper currency was declared to be no longer a legal tender.

Thus, by the operation of the act intended for Lord Stirling's benefit, the greater part of his real estate was conveyed away, and, by the operation of the act repealing the tender act, the proceeds thereof were rendered of no value.

In tracing a history of the bonds and mortgages of 1767, it appears that, in the year 1772, a judgment was rendered on the bond against Lord Stirling, and that an execution was issued on it in that year. That, in the year 1775, the mortgaged premises were sold by the sheriff of the county of Hunterdon under that execution, and that the said premises did not, on such sale, produce half the amount of the debt.

It also appears from a statement in the handwriting of John Mehelm, the surviving trustee, drawn up by him in 1806, that the said debt was considered by him as extinguished by the sacrifice of property caused by the said sheriff's sale.

That it also appears, by such statements, that the said John Mehelm offered to pay the fund in his hands to the treasurer of New Jersey, and that he refused to receive it; and, further, that the said fund finally depreciated to nothing, excepting a small amount that had been received in loan office certificates, amounting to about nine hundred pounds.

That upon the question submitted by the committee to the Legislature of the State of New Jersey on the said petition of the said Brockholst Livingston, "shall the prayer of the petitioner be granted?" it was decided in the negative.

That another application was made by Judge Livingston to the Legislature of New Jersey, in the year 1811, which was also rejected upon the ground that the facts of the case had been fully investigated and decided upon in 1806.

That it does not appear whether the State of New Jersey ever charged the amount of the certificate in question in her account with the United States, or not; but your committee do not think it material whether she did or not, for if the United States admitted the charge when the State had no right to make it, they did it in their own wrong, and the holders of the *only voucher* for such charge are not to be prejudiced by the admission.

That, upon a full consideration of all these facts, your committee are of opinion—

1. That the debt for which this certificate was given was originally a debt of the United States.

2. That the same has never been paid, nor in any manner satisfied.

3. That your committee cannot consider it a *payment*, to attempt to set off against the certifiate the aforesaid debt, even supposing the said debt to have been an existing valid debt at that time; but,

4. That the said debt was, in the opinion of your committee, cancelled in equity, by the course of transactions between the State and Lord Stirling, viz:

1. The sacrifice of the mortgaged premises at the sheriff's sale in 1775, on the execution issued in 1772, which was probably done, without order, by some subordinate officer;

2. The State having at their disposal *in December*, 1780, the fund created by the joint act of the Legislature and Lord Stirling, for the payment of his debts;

3. The repeal of the tender act, in June, 1781, by which the value of that fund was destroyed;

4. No claim of such a debt having been advanced by the State when the certificates were issued in December, 1781; nor,

5. In February, 1782, when one of the certificates was actually paid.

That, whatever may have been the strict legal rights of the State of New Jersey, your committee are of opinion that, considering the signal services of Lord Stirling, and the peculiar circumstances of the case, the prayer of the petitioner ought to be granted.

Your committee further report, that it appears from documents exhibited by the memorialists, that they have been substituted the trustees of the estate of the said Sarah Alexander, in the place of the said Brockholst Livingston and Matthew Clarkson, both now deceased. Your committee report a bill authorizing and directing the Secretary of the Treasury to issue scrip to the amount of                to the said William A. Duer, John Duer, and Beverley Robinson, trustees of the said Sarah Alexander, deceased, receivable in payment for public lands at any of the land offices for the sale of public lands of the United States, in full satisfaction and discharge of the said certificate, which is to be surrendered up by them to the Secretary of the Treasury on receiving such scrip.

Trenton, February 15, 1834.

Dear Sir : Agreeably to your request, I have examined all the books and papers in the treasurer's office in relation to the depreciation pay of individuals assumed by the United States' Government, and paid to the State of New Jersey, and have entirely failed of success in reaching the object you wish. There are no papers nor accounts of any kind or description relating to that subject in the office. I have also made, and caused to be made, a search for the same information in the office of the secretary, but have also failed of success. There are, however, in the secretary's office, two books containing charges against the United States for military services from 1775 up to 1785, amounting to a very large sum, (say several millions of dollars.) In them I do not find any thing charged as having been paid or due to Lord Stirling ; and there is nothing to show that any of those claims were ever assumed or settled by the General Government.

I have been informed that James Ewing was the auditor of accounts in this State, through whose hands most of the accounts in which the State had an interest passed ; and it is very probable that the papers relating to the settlement between the State and General Government were lodged with and filed by him ; it appears probable that duplicates, as well of the particulars settled and accounted for, as the general statement, were preserved and filed by both parties ; as Mr. Ewing was very particular in preserving all papers coming into his hands, it may be that some satisfaction can be obtained from his files. The present James Ewing, in whose care all the papers of his grandfather are, has been absent from town all the week past, attending the Burlington court. As soon as he returns, I will cause a search to be made.

I do not consider my certificate necessary, as no trace of the information wanted can be found. You shall hear from me by Monday's mail.

Yours, &c.<br>CHARLES PARKER.

James Parker, Esq.

TREASURY DEPARTMENT,

*Register's Office, February* 25, 1834.

SIR: I have the honor, in compliance with your reference to this office of Mr. Shepley's letter of the 22d inst., to state that the reports rendered to this Department by the commissioners who settled the accounts between the United States and the several States do not exhibit the items, nor do they refer to any abstracts or vouchers upon which the credits were given to the States; that the vouchers and papers which accompanied their reports, when received by this office, were without any marks or endorsements designating which had or which had not been allowed; and that, from this circumstance, no satisfactory information on that point, could be obtained were they now in existence. They were, however, lost by the burning of the Treasury building in 1814.

With respect to the certificate issued by the State of New Jersey for the depreciation of pay to Lord Stirling, I take leave to remark that, had the State taken it up prior to the 28th of September, 1788, and charged it in their account with the United States, it would have come under the class of claims authorized to be allowed by the 3d section of the act of 5th of August, 1790.

I have the honor to be, sir,

Your obedient servant,

T. L. SMITH.

Hon. R. B. TANEY, *Secretary of the Treasury.*

Mr. Shepley's letter is enclosed.

---

APRIL 25, 1834.

The Committee on Revolutionary Claims have had under consideration the petition of Elizabeth Roane, which was referred to them, and submit the following report:

The petitioner represents that William Royall was a captain from the State of Virginia on continental establishment, during the revolutionary war; that he continued in service until the close of said war, and thus became entitled to half pay during his life, or, in lieu thereof, to five years' full pay; that said William is now dead, and that she is his heir, and entitled to the half pay or commutation to which he, if living, would have been entitled.

The proof produced by the petitioner and the widow of said William shows that the said William was allowed, by the State of Virginia, four thousand four hundred and eighty-nine acres of land, for seven years and four months' services, as a captain on continental establishment during the war; that said William died in the year 1815; several witnesses state that said William was a captain in the service during the war, and they believe that he served until the close of the war; and one witness states, positively, that said William did continue in ervice till the war terminated. The committee have not been able to find any evidence from the records, which show the services of said William, but it is in evidence that the records are, in many instances, defective, and do not contain the names of officers who were without doubt in the service.

The committee are of opinion that, after the lapse of so much time, parol testimony is to be received with great caution, to establish claims of this description; but think that, in some instances, such testimony must be relied upon, or great injustice will be done to individuals. In this case the verbal testimony supported by the evidence of the allowance of land for seven years and four months' service, renders it reasonably certain that the services of Captain Royall were actually continued until the end of the war; and that he was, therefore, entitled to the commutation of five years' full pay, or to half pay for life.

The committee, therefore, report a bill, allowing the widow and heir said five years' full pay. They do not allow any interest thereon, because the committee do not believe interest ought to be allowed in any such case, unless application had been made in due time, and the evidence furnished to the Government that the officer was entitled to receive the principal.

---

JANUARY 5, 1836.

The Committee on Revolutionary Claims, to which was referred the petition of Thomas H. Baird, report:

That a bill was reported for the relief of the petitioner, on the 2d of March, 1835, accompanied by a report, to which the committee refer, and make it a part of this report. This committee concur with the former committee, and report a bill accordingly.

MARCH 2, 1835.

The Committee on Revolutionary Claims, to which the petition of Thomas H. Baird was referred, report:

That the petitioner states that, in the early part of the year 1776, his father, Absalom Baird, was appointed a mate in the general hospital of the continental army, and continued to serve in that capacity until the spring of 1780, when he was transferred to the corps of artificers, under Colonel J. Baldwin, in the capacity of surgeon, and continued to serve in such corps, and as surgeon, until it was dissolved, and, in part, discharged by Congress, on the 29th of March 1781, when he became a retiring officer. It appears by the journals of Congress, that, on the 12th of November, 1779, it was resolved that the eleven companies of artificers, raised by the quartermaster general, be re-formed, and incorporated and arranged in such manner as the commander-in-chief shall deem proper; and that the officers and men of said corps be considered as part of the quotas of the eighty battalions, as apportioned on the several States to which they respectively belong. On the 16th of the same month, it was resolved, that it be recommended to the several States to allow the corps of artificers established by Congress all the benefits provided for officers and soldiers in the line of their quotas of the continental battalions, except the half pay. The half pay here referred to was granted for seven years; by the resolution of the 15th May, 1778, and by the subsequent resolution of August 11, 1779, was extended to continue for life. In the reorganization of the army, on the 3d October 1780, a regiment of artificers was retained, to consist of eight companies, and each company to consist of sixty non-commissioned officers and privates. On the 29th March, 1781, the regiment of artificers commanded by Colonel Baldwin was dissolved. The resolution of January 17, 1781, granted half pay for life to the officers in the hospital department and medical staff, who should continue in service to the end of the war, or be reduced before that time as supernumeraries. Dr. Absalom Baird was, in the opinion of the committee, entitled to claim the benefit of this provision. He was an officer of the medical staff at the passage of this resolution, in a regiment on continental establishment, which regiment was subsequently reduced by Congress. The exclusion of the officers of the corps of artificers from the benefit of half pay, by the resolution of the 16th November, 1779, is not contained in the resolutions of 21st October, 1780, and of January 17, 1781. Colonel Baldwin, who commanded this regiment, and other officers belonging to it, were allowed the same emoluments received by officers of the line who retired under the resolutions of Congress of the 3d and 21st of October, 1780. No reason can exist for a distinction between those officers and the surgeon of the same regiment, as Congress, by the resolution of 17th January, 1781, extended the benefit of half pay to officers in the hospital department and medical staff. The committee therefore report a bill for the relief of the heirs of Dr. Baird.

---

## JANUARY 12, 1836.

The Committee on Revolutionary Claims, to which was referred the petition of Mrs. Nancy Haggart, heir of William Grymes, deceased, report :

This case was examined at the second session of the twenty-third Congress, and a favorable report made thereon, accompanied by a bill for the relief of the petitioner. The bill was, however, not reached, and remained unacted on.

The committee, in reviewing the case, find no cause for a change of opinion. They adopt the former report, and ask that it may be made a part of this report. A bill is accordingly again reported.

The Committee on Revolutionary Claims, to which was referred the petition of Mrs. Nancy Haggart, only child of William Grymes, deceased, report :

The petitioner states that she is the only child of the late Major William Grymes; that her father entered the service of the United States at an early period of the revolutionary war ; that he served in the Virginia line on continental establishment as a captain ; that he died in the service shortly after the battle of Germantown, having before been promoted to the rank of major.

As the only child and heir of Major Grymes, her mother having died in her widowhood, in the year 1789, she claims the seven years half pay promised to the widow or orphan children of such officers as should die in the service, by the resolves of Congress, passed May 15, 1778, and August 24, 1780.

It has been established to the satisfaction of the committee, by sufficient evidence, that William Grymes was a captain in the 15th Virginia regiment on continental establishment; that he died in the service, August 1, 1777, and that he left a widow, now deceased, and an only child, the petitioner. It also appears, from the records in the Third Auditor's office, and those in the office of the Register of the Treasury, also from the records of tne auditor's office of the State of Virginia, that neither the seven years' half pay, nor any part of it, has been paid to the widow or child of said Grymes. The committee, believing it justly due, report a bill for its payment, Having, however, not found sufficient evidence that Mr. Grymes was promoted to the rank of major before his death, it is made according to the rank of a captain only.

---

FEBRUARY 8, 1836.

The Committee on Revolutionary Claims, to which was referred the petition of Woodford Taylor, administrator of Thornton Taylor, deceased, report:

That the petitioner states that his intestate, Thornton Taylor, was an ensign of the Virginia line on continental establishment, in the army of the Revolution, and continued in service as such till the end of the war; that is, that he was either engaged in actual service during the whole war, or was, towards the close of it, a supernumerary. And he therefore claims the commutation of five years' full pay, in lieu of the half pay for life, of an ensign.

The committee being satisfied, by the proof adduced by the petitioner, of the truth of the facts alleged in his petition, report a bill giving him the relief prayed in his petition.

---

FEBRUARY 8, 1836.

The Committee on Revolutionary Claims, to which was referred the claim of James and Rebecca Sutherland, of the State of North Carolina, submit the following report:

It appears to the committee, from very satisfactory evidence, that James Parkerson, of North Carolina, was a lieutenant in the continental line, and died in the service during the revolutionary war; and, consequently, that his widow or children became entitled to seven years' half pay of a lieutenant. It further appears that the said Rebecca is the only child of the said James Parkerson; and it is proved to a reasonable certainty that the wife of said Parkerson has been dead for many years; but whether before or after the death of her husband does not appear.

38

The committee are of opinion that the said James and Rebecca Sutherland are well entitled to the seven years' half pay claimed by them; and therefore report a bill for their relief.

---

## FEBRUARY 8, 1836.

The Committee on Revolutionary Claims, to which were referred the petition and papers of Sarah Hopkins, have had the same under consideration, and submit the following report:

It appears that David Hopkins, of South Corolina, entered the service of the United States during the revolutionary war, and was a captain in the continental line from that State to the battle at the Fish Dam, in the year 1780, after which he was promoted to the rank of colonel, and commanded the third regiment in the continental line to the end of the war, and that neither he nor his representatives have received the half pay for life or the commutation promised in lieu thereof.

The above facts the committee believe are satisfactorily established by the depositions of Robert Cowley, Philip Pearson, William Vaughan, Joseph McJunkin, and sundry papers of ancient date which are filed with the petition. They therefore report a bill for the relief of the legal representatives of the deceased.

---

## MARCH 22, 1836.

The Committee on Revolutiouary Claims, to which was referred the memorial of the representatives of Colonel John Hazlet for the half pay to which he was entitled, have had the same under consideration, and respectfully submit the following report :

That it appears the said John Hazlet was a colonel, and commanded the Delaware regiment on continental establishment from January, 1776, to the 3d day of January, 1777, when he was killed in the battle at Princeton. At the time of his death he left a widow and five children; that his widow survived him but a very short time. The names of his children were John, Mary, Ann, Joseph, and Jemima, three of whom, to wit : John, Mary, and Ann, have also departed this life, leaving no children. Joseph married, and is now dead, leaving no children—Ann, John, Joseph, and Jemima—and of these, Joseph died in the year 1813, without issue.

Jemima, the daughter of Colonel Hazlet, married George Monro, and died in the year 1821, leaving five children, namely, Lydia, now married to E. W. Gilbert ; Mary Ann, married to Thomas J. Boyd ; Margaretta, married to William Darrach; George Monro, and Susan E. Monro ; and the said George Monro last named is dead without issue.

The committee are of opinion that, upon the death of Colonel Hazlet's widow, his children then living were entitled to the seven years' half pay promised to the widows and children of such officers as had died or might thereafter die in the service of the United States, and that upon their death their next of kin became entitled to the respective proportions of this debt, under the statutes of distribution.

It does not appear that this debt, or any part of it, has ever been paid: therefore the committee report a bill for the relief of the petitioners.

---

The Committee on Revolutionary Claims, to which was referred the petition of Elizabeth Hunt, report:

That the petitioner, as the sole heir of Captain William Hendricks, of the Pennsylvania line on continental establishment, claims the seven years' half pay and bounty lands given by the resolves of Congress to the representatives of officers slain in battle. Captain Hendricks was one of the gallant band who performed the extraordinary march from the Kennebec river, in the depth of winter, through the wilderness, to the walls of Quebec, and was slain in the unsuccessful attempt to storm that fortress, at the side of the much lamented Montgomery. Captain Hendricks lives in history, and will ever be considered as one of the first martyrs in the cause of American freedom. His memory must ever be dear to his countrymen as one of those heroes who bled and died for his country's good. Others have had honors and remards, but Captain Hendricks's family have never received any mark of gratitude or bounty of the Government.

The petitioner, the niece of Captain Hendricks, cannot receive the seven years' half pay prayed for, as the resolution of Congress limits it to the widow and children of the deceased officer. But the grant of lands is not so restricted; and the committee think she is, as the representative of Captain Hendricks, entitled to the three hundred acres allowed by the Congress of the Revolution to captains serving in the continental establishment. A bill is accordingly reported.

---

The Committee on Revolutionary Claims, to which was referred the petition of Levin K. Adams, John B. Bowers, Peter Adams, and John Adams, praying for the renewal of certain land warrants, report:

That the petitioners state that they are the heirs of the late Lieutenant Colonel Peter Adams and Lieutenant William Adams, of the Maryland line, and Captain Nathan Adams, of the Delaware line, of the army of the Revolution; that they have never received any benefit from three land warrants, issued from the Bounty Land office at Washington city, 15th December, 1807, said warrants having been placed in the hands of the honorable Samuel White, of the State of Delaware, for the purpose of having them located; and he dying shortly after receiving them, the warrants were not to be found among his papers. The petitioners therefore pray that an act may be passed authorizing the renewal of the said lost warrants, to wit: warrants Nos. 371, 372, and 373, issued as above mentioned for services performed by the said Peter, Nathan, and William

Adams, in the revolutionary war. The Commissioner of the General Land Office having stated that the warrants aforesaid have not been surrendered or satisfied, the committee report a bill according to the prayer of the petitioners.

----

### December 22, 1837.

The Committee on Revolutionary Claims, to which was referred the petition of Rebecca Sampson and Harriet Fisher, report:

That the Committee on Revolutionary Claims, at the 1st session of the 23d Congress, made a favorable report on the said petition; that the same not being finally acted upon by that Congress, was re-examined by the Committee on Revolutionary Claims at the 1st session of the 24th Congress, and the report of the former committee was adopted. No final disposition of the case having been made by that Congress, the committee, on a new examination of the matter of the petition, have come to the same conclusions of the two former committees, and therefore adopt their reports, which are as follows :

" That it appears, at the 1st session of the 23d Congress, the Committee on Revolutionary Claims made a favorable report on the said petition, which is as follows:

" That the petitioners represent that Crocker Sampson, late of Kingston, Massachusetts, deceased, was a lieutenant in the Massachusetts line of the revolutionary army; and that, during his life, he was the holder and owner of a military bounty land warrant, No. 1,915, for 200 acres of land, and that said warrant has been lost by accident; that the petitioners, together with Lucy Sampson and Rebecca Crocker, (wife of Zenas Crocker,) are the legal heirs of said Crocker Sampson. The petitioners pray that a duplicate warrant may issue for said 200 acres of land.

" It appears that a warrant, as described in the petition, did issue to said Crocker Sampson; and the committee are satisfied, from the evidence in the case, viz : the affidavit of the said Rebecca Sampson, and the certificate of T. P. Beal, Esq., that the same warrant has been lost or destroyed by accident."

" The committee, therefore, report a bill in conformity to the prayer of the petitioner."

" The committee, on re-examination of the case, have come to the same conclusion, and therefore report a bill."

The committee, therefore, report a bill.

----

### December 22, 1837.

The Committee on Revolutionary Claims, to which the petition of Levi Chadwick was referred, report :

It appears that on the 4th day of December, 1818, warrant No. 716, for one hundred acres, issued from the Bounty Land Office, in the name of Levi Chadwich, alias Shadwick, a soldier in the New Jersey continental

line.  No location has been made on this warrant, nor has it been surrendered at the General Land Office for the purpose of obtaining either a
patent or scrip; and, from the testimony, it appears to have been lost.
The petitioner, who is shown to be the person to whom the original warrant issued, prays that a duplicate warrant may be issued to him; and
the committee report a bill accordingly.

--------

DECEMBER 22, 1837.

The Committee on Revolutionary Claims, to which was referred the
case of William Vawter's heirs, report:

This case has heretofore received the conderation of the Committee on
Revolutionary Claims, and a report at length made thereupon on the 26th
January, 1835, by Mr. Marshall.  Your committee adopt the views con-
tained in the said report, and, in conformity thereto, report a bill.

JANUARY 26, 1835.

The Committee on Revolutionary Claims, to which was referred the
case of William Vawter's heirs, report:

That, on the 25th of May, 1832, an act was approved allowing five
years' full pay to the heirs of William Vawter, for their father's services
in the revolutionary war, with interest thereon, according to the funding
act of August, 1790; which five years' full pay is declared to be commutation of his half pay for life.  On the 5th of July, 1832, the act entitled " An act for liquidating and paying certain claims of the State of
Virginia," became a law.  This act provides, among other things, that
the Secretary of the Treasury shall pay to the officers of certain regiments of the Virginia line, named in the act, " those claims for half pay
which have not been paid or prosecuted to judgment against the State of
Virginia, and for which said State would be bound on the principles of
the half-pay cases already decided by the court of appeals of said State."
Among the regiments named in the act, and to which the provision just
cited relates, is that commanded by Colonel George Gibson ; and the
main principle of the half-pay cases decided by the court of appeals of
Virginia was, that the officers of the Virginia State line who served to
the close of the revolutionary war, or who, becoming supernumerary by
the reduction of any of the State-line regiments, &c., did not refuse to re-
enter the service if required so to do, were entitled to half pay for life, under the Virginia act of May, 1779.  The provision of the act of 5th July,
1832, above recited, is an assumption by the United States of the liability of Virginia, thus defined, to pay to the officers of the regiments
named in the act their half pay for life.

William Vawter was a lieutenant in the regiment commanded by
Colonel George Gibson, and was one of the officers of that regiment who
had brought himself within the principle by which, according to the decision of the court of appeals of Virginia, he was entitled to half pay for
life.  (See Reports of the House, 1st session 22d Congress, No. 191,
page 53.)  The claim of William Vawter to half pay for life, having
never been paid or prosecuted to judgment against the State of Virginia,

is clearly one of those which the Secretary of the Treasury is directed to pay by the act of July 5, 1832. Accordingly, after the passage of that act, his heirs, alleging that the five years' full pay, with interest, allowed to them in the name of commutation by the special act in their favor of the 25th of May, 1832, was not equal to the half pay for the life of their father, payable under the act of the 5th July, applied at the Treasury for payment of the difference under the provisions of the latter act. This application was refused, upon the ground that the Committee on Revolutionary Claims had, in December, 1831, reported that William Vawter was embraced in the resolution of Congress of the 21st October, 1780, promising half pay for life to certain officers, and was, therefore, entitled to commutation ; and that a bill, allowing commutation, &c. to his heirs, had passed, &c.

TREASURY DEPARTMENT,

December 10, 1832.

SIR : In answer to your letter, I have the honor to inform you that the State of Virginia passed an act in 1779, giving half pay to their military officers, both State and Continental, who should become supernumerary, or serve until the close of the war, unless they should refuse to rejoin the army, if supernumerary, and required so to do, or " Congress do not make some tantamount provision for them." On the 21st October, 1780, Congress passed a resolve allowing half pay for life to the officers of the continental line who should serve to the end of the war, or become supernumerary. It appears, by the report of the 23d December, 1831, of the Committee on Revolutionary Clasms of the House of Reprentatives, that William Vawter was a lieutenant of Colonel George Gibson's regiment of the Virginia line on continental establishment, and so continued until the resolves of the 3d and 21st October, 1780, made him a supernumerary, and that, as such, he was entitled to the provisions of the resolve of Congress of the 21st October, 1780. The committee, therefore, reported a bill for his relief, which passed, giving him commutation, with interest. This placed him on a footing with other Virginia continental officers, who, if Congress had not made provision for them by the resolve of the 21st October, 1780, would have been entitled to half pay for life from Virginia. Under these circumstances, it is not conceived that Mr. Vawter has any claim on the United States.

I am, sir, very respectfully, your obedient servant,

LOUIS McLANE,<br>Secretary of the Treasury.

The Hon. R. M. JOHNSON, H. of Reps.

It is evident that the belief that Vawter was embraced by the resolution of 21st October, 1780, led to the allowance of commutation to his heirs, and to their exclusion from the provision of the act of the 5th July, 1832. The basis of the report, and of the allowance of commutation, is the fact that the 9th Virginia continental regiment, having been captured at Germantown, Gibson's regiment, acknowedged to have been originally a State regiment, commanded by State officers, was, by an act of the Virginia Legislature, substituted in the place of the captured regiment until the latter should be exchanged ; and that it did, in fact, serve for some period, not exactly known, with the continental army, out of the

State of Virginia. The report goes on to state, that Vawter had served with this regiment until, by the arrangement of the army, at the close of the year 1780, he was deranged ; and, from these facts, concludes that he was embraced in the resolution of the 21st October, 1780. The facts here stated certainly present very strong ground for the conclusion to which the committee came, and for the allowance of commutation. They were of the most persuasive force, when the alternative seemed to be, that if Vawter's case did not come within the resolution of the 21st October, 1780, his services were to go unremunerated. But the evidence already referred to (contained in report 191, 1st sess. 22d Cong.) was not only not before the Committee on Revolutionary Claims when the facts of this case were first investigated, and the report made thereon, but its existence was scarcely known, even in Virginia. The discovery of that evidence forced upon Virginia the full acknowledgment of her liability, under the act of May, 1779, to pay to the officers of her State regiments the half pay for life promised in that act. This evidence proves that, notwithstanding the facts stated with respect to Gibson's regiment, it was, at the close of the war, regarded as a State regiment, whose officers were entitled to the provision of the act of May 1779, and were not embraced by the resolve of October, 1780. The subsequent application of Virginia to the United States (in 1831) to assume the performance of her promise of half pay for life to the officers of this and other regiments, and the express assumption of the United States, by the act of 5th July, 1832, to pay the half pay for life to the officers of this regiment, as due to them under the act of May, 1779, show conclusively the opinion of both Governments as to the character of the regiment, and determine finally the rights of its officers. If they were entitled to the half pay for life from Virginia, they were not entitled to half pay for life, or commutation, under the resolves of Congress; and if embraced by the resolve of Congress of October, 1780, they were thereby deprived of all claim to half pay for life from Virginia. In affiring their right to the half pay from Virginia, the public acts referred to decide, finally, that they were not embraced by the resolve of 21st October, 1780.

The case of Vawter cannot be distinguished from that of the other officers of his regiment, either as regards the application of the resolve of Congress, or the effect of the decision implied in the act of July 5, 1832. If, because he was an officer of a regiment which had been substitued in the place of a continental regiment, he is to be considered as one to whom the resolve of October, 1780, offers half pay for life, for the same reason that offer must be considered as extending to all the officers of the same regiment. If the fact that he was reduced or deranged at the end of the year 1780 demonstrates that he was embraced by the resolution, or of itself brings him within it, the fact that the others were retained had the same effect as to them ; for the resolution provides as well for the officers who should be retained, as for those who should be reduced. The act of 5th July, 1832, asserting the right of the officers of Gibson's regiment to half pay for life from Virginia, denies their right to the half pay under the resolves of Congress, and to the five years' full pay, into which it was commuted. It makes no discrimination between the officers of that regiment, who had brought themselves within the decision of the court of appeals, but deems all such entitled to half pay from Virginia, and provides for the payment of all arrearages to them.

It is unquestionable that, but for the allowance of commutation by the act of 25th May, 1832, Vawter's heirs would have received the full amount of their father's half pay for life, under the act of 5th July. What, then, is, and ought to be, the effect of the former act? Does it preclude Vawter's heirs from the benefit of the latter?

The act of 25th May was passed upon the supposition, and impliedly asserts the fact, that the officers of Gibson's regiment were embraced in the resolve of 21st October, 1780. The act of 25th May, so far as it relates to that regiment, rests upon, and impliedly asserts, the fact that its officers were not embraced in that resolution. If the fact assumed in the first act be true, then neither Vawter nor the other officers of Gibson's regiment were entitled to the half pay for life from Virginia, which the last act directs to be paid. If the fact assumed in the last act be true, then Vawter was not entitled to the commutation allowed to his heirs by the first; and he and all other officers of Gibson's regiment, whose services brought them within the principle of the cases decided by the court of appeals of Virginia, were entitled to half pay for life from that State, and were properly provided for by the act of 5th July. Comparing these two acts, in every point of view; considering the source of the application for each; the nature of the evidence on which each was based; the amount of money involved in each; and the degree of consideration given to each, by both Houses of Congress, the committee are of opinion that, as to all matters of fact and principle involved in each, the act of 5th July must be allowed superior weight and authority. They are, moreover, of the opinion that the evidence in support of the right of the officers of Gibson's regiment, as settled by the act of 5th July, is, itself, entitled to great weight. It follows that, when the act of 25th May passed, allowing commutation to Vawter's heirs, they had no claim whatever against the United States, either for commutation or for half pay, but had a claim against the State of Virginia for half pay during the life of their father; which claim against the State of Virginia was afterwards assumed by the United States, by the act of 5th July.

There is no ground to suppose that, in applying for commutation, or in allowing it, either party intended to deceive the other; on the contrary, the facts, as then believed, justified both the application and the allowance. The question, then, is, whether the payment by the United States to Vawter's heirs of a sum supposed to be due from the former to the latter, when, in fact, nothing was due between them, shall be held to be a full satisfaction of a greater sum actually due from Virginia to Vawter's heirs, and of which the payment was afterwards assumed by the United States? In the opinion of the committee, this question can only be answered in the negative.

It is a known fact, that in cases in which Virginia, shrinking from the full discharge of her promise, had authorized partial payments, (for instance, five years' full pay,) with the express declaration that they were to be taken as a full discharge of half pay for life, and the payments were made and received under this declaration, they have yet been considered at the Treasury of the United States as (what they in reality were) mere partial payments; and the residue of the half pay for life has been paid, under the provisions of the act of 5th July. But if a partial payment by Virginia, the real debtor, made and received under an express declaration on her part that it is to be taken as full satisfaction of the whole demand,

# 305

cannot, in that elevated sense of moral right which characterizes this Government, be considered as extinguishing the residue of a just debt; upon what principle can the United States, after having assumed to pay to the officers of Gibson's regiment the entire amount of the half pay for life promised by Virginia, and remaining unpaid, claim that a previous payment to one of those officers (to whom they then owed nothing) of a sum less than that which, by the assumption, is now found to be due to him, shall be considered as a full satisfaction of this greater sum justly due? The committee do not find authority for this position in any principle compatible either with justise or the character of the Government, and think it would better comport with both to consider the payment made under a mistaken liability, and in a mistaken name of commutation, as so much paid towards the real claim of half pay for life, rather than to rest upon the full discharge of the mistaken claim as a full satisfaction of a greater one which is real. Upon the whole, the committee do not find, in the passage of the act for the benefit of Vawter's heirs, and the payment under it, a reasonable ground for excluding them from the benefit of the act of the 5th July, 1832, which has been, or may be, received by all the other officers of Gibson's regiment. They therefore report a bill authorizing the payment to the heirs of William Vawter of so much of the half pay for the life of their father as remains unpaid, after crediting the sum already paid under the said act of 25th May, 1832.

---

DECEMBER 22, 1837.

The Committee on Revolutionary Claims, to which was referred the memorial of Colonel Francis Vigo, report:

That this claim was presented at the last Congress, and was investigated by the committee. They refer to their report of the last session, and make it a part of the present report, together with additional evidence and documents. Heretofore it was the opinion of the committee that the justice of this claim had been evinced; and its non-payment was admitted by the commissioner of Virginia. But the next question presented for the consideration of the committee, was, whether it was ever settled by the United States with Virginia, either in the particular account of the latter rendered in 1788, or in the aggregate amount of disbursements and advances credited to Virginia in her settlement with the United States in 1793. These were the only settlements, between the United States and Virginia, in which the claim of the memorialist could have been embraced as forming part of the account current of Virginia against the Government of the Union. For, if it should appear that the bill of exchange drawn by General Clarke, in favor of the memorialist, on Pollock, the commercial agent of Virginia at New Orleans, and "protested for want of funds," was embraced in either of those settlements, as a charge on the part of Virginia against the United States for "disbursements and advances," or otherwise in the "particular account" of that State, as settled in 1788, or in the aggregate amount of her account for "disbursements and advances" as settled with the United States in 1793, it is clear the United States are exonerated from the payment of the same, and the memorialist must look to Virginia, who has received the money, and who alone would be liable to him. It is to be regretted that the accounts between the State of Virginia and the United States, for "expenses incurred and advances made" by the former in the Illinois campaign of 1778 and '79, are not to be found in the office of the Treasurer of the United States, or in the offices of the Auditor and Treasurer of Virginia, where, if they existed at all, they would probably be found. There is no trace either of the settlement of 1788, or that of 1793, between Virginia and the United States, to be found among the public archives, either at Richmond or at Washington. (See documents C, D, H, certificate of Mr. Hagner and of the Auditor and Treasurer of Virginia.) Could they have been produced, all doubt in this case would have been removed.

In the absence of any positive proof, the committee have been obliged to resort to secondary evidence. They believe, from all that has been taken in support of the memorial of the claimant; from the memorial itself, sworn to by Colonel Vigo, sustained by the high character he possesses for honor and integrity, as testified by gentlemen of the first respectability in the West; as well as from the certificate of Mr. Smith, (the commissioner of revolutionary claims on the part of Virginia,) in whose possession and custody the original accounts current of Clarke and Pollock, as settled with Virginia, now are, (see document No. 3;) that the presumption is great, and the inference clear, that in no settlement between the United States and Virginia, was the bill of the petitioner for $8,616 ever made an item in the account of the latter against the former for "expenses incurred or disbursements made," in the Illinois campaign of 1778 and '79. What are the facts, as shown in the memorial, and in the documents and proofs accompanying it?

The bill of exchange, mentioned in the memorial of the claimant, was drawn in his favor by General Clarke on Pollock, the commercial agent of Virginia, at New Orleans, in 1778. It was to be paid in specie. It was for supplies actually furnished by the memorialist to the "Illinois regiment" then in the service of Virginia, and under the command of Clarke. The bill was "protested for the want of funds," as is sworn to by the memorialist, Vigo. In the year 1788, (the year when the first settlement took place between the United States and Virginia, "for expenses incurred in the Illinois campaign,") Vigo was in possession of the bill, and presented the same again to Pollock for settlement, at Carlisle, Pennsylvania, "who advised Vigo to keep it, as it would be paid some time or other." (See deposition of Pierre Menard.) It further appears, that after Pollock's refusal to pay it when presented the second time, Vigo retained it, and kept possession of it until December, 1799, six years after the settlement between the United States and Virginia, as finally made. That it was then (December, 1799,) unpaid and unsatisfied in the hands of the payee, (Vigo,) and was by him delivered to Judge Burnett, of Cincinnati, for collection; from which time the bill has been lost. In addition to which, the committee have the certificate of Mr. Smith, the commissioner of Virginia, (in whose possession and custody the original accounts current of Clarke and Pollock, as settled with Virginia, now are) that in neither of these accounts, as settled with Virginia, in their final settlement with that State, "for expenses incurred and advances made" in the "Illinois campaign" is this bill of exchange charged as an item, although the other bills mentioned by Vigo, in his memorial, as having been sold at a discount, are. (See certificate, doc. 3.)

From these facts, and on this proof, in the absence of positive testimony, the presumption is great, and the inference almost irresistible, that neither in the settlement between the United States and Virginia, in 1788, nor in that of 1793, nor at any other time, was the bill of the memorialist, for $8,616, ever made an item in the account of Virginia against the United States, and credited by the latter. That it could not be, the reasons are plain.

In the first place, the commissioners of the United States would not, (nor by law, could not,) in a settlement with Virginia or any other State, pay an account rendered without the proper vouchers accompanying each item, and showing the expenditures and disbursements actually made. Secondly, " the bill of exchange" mentioned in the memorial of Vigo as drawn by General Clarke on Pollock, the commercial agent of Virginia, could not have been produced as a voucher in the settlement between the United States and Virginia, because it was neither included in the account current of Clarke, the drawer, or Pollock, the drawee of the bill, as finally settled between them and Virginia. The committee can imagine no other settlement or document that would be allowed to form the basis of the account of Virginia against the United States for " disbursements and expenditures" in the Illinois campaign. General Clarke, or Mr. Pollock, if this bill had been paid by either, would have taken it up, and charged Virginia with its payment, producing the bill as evidence of such payment. Thirdly, it could not have been an item in the accounts of Virginia, as settled in 1788 or 1793 with the United States ; because six years after the last settlement, the bill was in possession of Vigo, the payee, unpaid, and " protested for want of funds."

Under all these circumstances, with this strong state of facts in favor of the memorialist, and in the absence of positive proof as to the items of the accounts settled between Virginia and the United States in 1788 and 1793, in consequence of the destruction of those accounts, the committee cannot entertain a reasonable doubt that the amount of said bill and interest is due to Colonel Vigo, and should long since, in good faith, have been paid him. Why it has not been paid, is apparent from the memorial, and from the certificate of Mr. Smith, the commissioner on the part of Virginia. It was not until 1833 that Virginia took any steps to " adjust and settle" these old but *bona-fide* and honest claims. (See resolution A.) It was not until March, 1834, that an act of the Virginia Legislature was passed, authorizing " the investigation and adjustment" of these claims by a commissioner. (See act, doc. B.) It was in vain for the claimant to apply to Congress until this was done. Upon presenting his claim, he was told he must have his account " investigated and adjusted" by Virginia, before the United States could recognise its validity.

It was in vain that he applied to Virginia ; until the passage of the act alluded to, there was no relief there. It is more than probable, but for the mass of papers connected with the affairs and accounts of the " Illinois campaign," accidentally discovered in the attic story of the Capitol at Richmond in 1833, (see Mr. Smith's letter,) " and which threw much light on these ancient but meritorious demands against the Commonwealth," that neither Virginia nor the United States would have been disposed to take them into serious consideration. The committee feel no wish to extol the services of the memorialist, the question with them being purely as to the pecuniary obligation of the Government. It appears, however, from the history of the country, and the documents presented, but for the services and advances of Vigo and others, the campaign of 1778–'9 in Illinois might have had a termination less glorious to the American arms than that which secured at that day, to the confederacy, the Mississippi, instead of the Ohio river, for a boundary in the West. From the country thus acquired and thus ceded by Virginia, the national treasary has probably received five millions of dollars the last year. For expenses incurred in the conquest of it, the United States, by compact, solemn and irrevocable, are bound to Virginia, and, in this case, directly to the claimant himself; because his claim has been "settled and adjusted" by the legal and duly authorized agent of Virginia for this purpose, and because justice to the parties, as well as the proper observance and fulfilment of engagements on the part of the United States, would seem to require a payment to the claimant in the first instance, without forcing him to proceed to judgment against Virginia for an acknowledged debt, for which the United States are ultimately liable.

The committee therefore report a bill.

---

### No. 2.

#### February 24, 1825.

The Committee on Revolutionary Claims, to which was referred the memorial of Colonel Francis Vigo, report:

That the petitioner presents an account against the State of Virginia, settled, adjusted, and certified by the lawfully authorized commissioner of that State, as will appear by document marked A.

This claim is founded on bills of exchange, alleged to have been drawn by General George R. Clarke, commissioned and acting under the authority of said State; which bills were drawn upon her commercial agent, Oliver Pollock, intended to be in payment of supplies furnished the troops in her service in the year 1778, usually denominated "the Illinois regiment."

The important and hazardous campaign of General Clarke, his successful attacks on the then British posts of Kaskaskia and Vincennes, and the military ocupation of those posts by the forces of Virginia under his command, are notorious historical facts.

The American commissioners, in the treaty of peace of 1783, insisted that the boundaries of the United States should be settled and acknowledged to include the country northwest of the river Ohio, and between the river Mississippi and the lakes; on the ground that the British posts were conquered, and the possession of that country maintained by and for the State of Virginia as above mentioned.

By the resolve of the Congress of the 10th of October, 1780, the Confederation engaged "that the necessary and reasonable expenses which any particular State shall have incurred, since the commencement of the present war, in subduing any British posts, or in maintaining forts and garrisons within and for the defence, or in acquiring any part of the territory that may be ceded or relinquished to the United States, shall be reimbursed."

The Northwest territory was relinquished by the State of Virginia in 1784. Connected with the cession of this territory, the resolve of Congress of 10th October, 1780, constituted a subsisting engagement on the part of the United States with Virginia, to reimburse the necessary expenses that State had incurred in subduing the British posts, and in maintaining the jurisdiction and possession of Virginia within and over the ceded territory.

This obligation on the Government of the Union has been expressly recognised by Congress. It was recited in the deed of cession by Virginia as one of the terms and conditions of the cession, which the United States agreed to fulfil in acquiring the territory. The same understanding and condition were expressed in every act, both of Congress and of the State of Virginia, connected with the transfer of the territory to the United States.

The first section of the sixth article of the constitution of the United States provides that "all debts contracted, and engagements entered into, before the adoption of this constitution, shall be as valid against the United States under this constitution as under the confederation."

This claim is for a subsisting debt against Virginia, having been incurred in subduing the British posts, and in maintaining the title of Virginia to the territory ceded to the United States.

Since Virginia acknowledges the debt, and certifies that it has never been paid, the obligation, in good faith, devolves upon the United States to pay it. The privity of contract exists between the State of Virginia and the holder of the bills of exchange. This debt was created by the necessary and lawful act of General George R. Clarke, in drawing at Kaskaskia upon the agent of Virginia at New Orleans, for supplies and subsistence for the troops of Virginia under his command, engaged in the conquest and maintenance of the Northwest territory.

The commissioner of the State of Virginia having settled, adjusted, and acknowledged this debt, the State would be bound to pay it; but then the obligation would rest upon the United States to reimburse Virginia. Ought the United States to insist upon the State to pay the debt first? An observance and fulfilment of the engagement of the United States to pay the debt cannot, in good faith, require circuity and delay; because the United States have long since received the cession of a territory of immense value, upon which the promise was binding, and which was the consideration for which the confederation engaged and contracted to pay the necessary and reasonable expenses of its acquisition and defence.

Is this claim a part of the reasonable and necessary expenses of Virginia, in the conquest of the British posts and the occupation of the Northwest territory? In answer to this question affirmatively, it does not appear necessary to go beyond the authority of General Clark to draw the bills of exchange. That he acted in fidelity to Virginia, and within the powers of his commission, cannot be questioned. With regard to the economy of the campaign, and the reasonableness of its expenses, it must be admitted as worthy of admiration, that, under the very embarrassing circumstances attending it, so much should have been accomplished with so little expense.

Is the claim just? and where is the proper place to examine this question? Where there is the most evidence on the subject—among the archives of Virginia. The campaign originated in her councils. The memorialist made his advances to her. There was no privity of contract subsisting between him and the Congress of the confederation. Few documents exist here upon the subject of that campaign. Accordingly, Virginia appointed John H. Smith, Esq., on the 11th of March, 1834, a commissioner to investigate claims for supplies furnished in that campaign, with authority to adjust the same. The State of Virginia, through that commissioner, has adjusted the claim of Colonel Vigo, and, to all intents and purposes, now stands bound for the payment of it, as adjusted. (See doc. A.) What credit ought to be given to this adjustment? If not conclusive, it could hardly be denied but that it would be testimony of the highest order in favor of the claim—the testimony of Virginia against her own interest; for if the United States do not pay the claim, Virginia would be bound for it. The committee have examined the evidence referred to in the report of the commissioner, and think the facts found in his report amply supported by the evidence.

Does justice require that the United States should grant the interest allowed by the commissioner of Virginia, on the debt due from her to the memorialist? Advances made during the Revolution have been considered as so much advanced on loan, to be repaid with interest. The rule that Governments should pay no interest, unless on loans, ought not to be applied to advances made to revolutionary Governments, when the presumption of their being always ready to pay is rebutted by facts. Secretary Hamilton's report of January 14, 1790, recognised in effect, and the law of August 4, 1790, was evidently passed upon, *this principle;* or rather an *exception* to that general rule, that Governments pay no interest.

This act, creating the funding system, allowed interest of six per cent. per annum on all debts of the United States up to 1791, as well to nonsubscribers as subscribers to the funding system. The subscribing to the fund was deemed a privilege. Subscribers had the interest that had accrued up to 1791 funded, and drawing interest of three per cent. per annum, payable quarterly, besides receiving interest of six per cent. upon the principal.

But as the contract of the memorialist was made with Virginia, whose rate of interest was five per cent. per annum, it is thought best to let it be regulated by her laws, as the contract must have been entered into with a full knowledge of them. It should not be urged that, because the memorialist was not fortunate enough to become a subscriber to this funding system, (thereby sustaining a loss of some thousands of dollars, accruing to the benefit of the United States by his not receiving his interest quarterly upon the principal of his claim, and the interest that had accrued up to December 31, 1790,) he shall receive *no interest at all*, not even the five per cent. allowed by Virginia, and that, too, in derogation of the law of 1790, allowing interest upon all debts of the Government.

In addition to these general principles, it appears the claim of Francis Vigo was liquidated by a bill of exchange, payable at New Orleans; that he would have been entitled to the interest under the law of that place, to wit, ten per cent., and damages of protest, if the claim had originated against an individual instead of a State. It does not appear, either, that he has slumbered on his rights for this long period of time. His failing to importune the Government more repeatedly than he has done, is attributed to his liberality to the Government at the time its pecuniary affairs were embarrassed, and when his own circumstances were prosperous. Reasonable diligence appears to have been used by him, considering the great distance he lived from the seats of Government of Virginia and the United States, and the difficulty of communication at the time, and long after the origin of his claim; having presented his drafts to the agent of the State, upon whom they were drawn, not many months after their ex-execution, when the said agent protested them, for the want of funds in hand belonging to the State. Again: four or five years after this, it appears he disposed of some of the bills at a discount of about eighty per cent. About the year 1788, '89, the memorialist met said agent of the State, who regretted that he had been under the necessity of protesting said bills for the want of proper funds, and advised him to keep this claim on the State; that she would pay him "some time or other." About the year 1802, when the affairs of the memorialist had become embarrassed, he states that he put the claim he now prosecutes in the hands of Jacob Burnett and Arthur St. Clair, esquires, for collection. In addition to the testimony by which these facts appear to be established, his acquaintances of forty years (men of great respectability) say that they always understood that he had a very large claim on the State of Virginia.

His services and aid appear to have been sought, at different periods, by officers and agents of Virginia and of the United States, and to have been highly appreciated and generally acknowledged. He obtained and communicated to General Clarke, at the risk of his life and fortune, the important information by which that officer was enabled to surprise and capture the British forces at Port St. Vincent, far superior in numbers and the munitions of war. In many other respects his services have been greatly beneficial to the United States, proceeding from honorable and patriotic motives, with little or no regard to pecuniary reward.

Although the justice of this claim has been evinced, and its non-payment admitted by the commissioner of Virginia, still the committee are of opinion that there are not sufficient reasons to authorize them to report a bill for the relief of the claimant. Under the compact between the United States and Virginia, by which the latter was to be reimbursed for the expenses of that campaign, &c., the committee find that a board of commissioners was organized in pursuance of the following resolution:

"In Congress, *April* 13, 1785.

"*Resolved,* That, agreeably to the act of cession from the State of Virginia, a commissioner be appointed, who, jointly with the commissioner on the part of the said State, shall be authorized to appoint a third; and that they, or a major part of them, shall be empowered to adjust and liquidate the accounts of the said State against the United States, for the necessary and reasonable expenses incurred by that State in subduing any British post, or maintaining any forts within and for the defence, or in acquiring any part, of the territory ceded by the said State to the United States, conformably to the resolve of Congress of the 10th of October, 1780."

On the 8th April, 1831, the General Assembly of Virginia required the Governor thereof "to appoint some competent person as commissioner, for and on behalf of this Commonwealth, whose duty it shall be to prepare the testimony and documents touching the claims of Virginia upon the United States, on account of moneys paid, or for which Virginia may be liable, to the officers and soldiers of her State line during the Revolution," &c. In this act no mention is made of the liabilities of Virginia on account of supplies furnished the troops under General Clarke. The commissioner so appointed, in his memorial, admits that the special accounts for the expenses of these troops were, "after much difficulty, at length adjusted, it is believed, about the year 1788, when the United States agreed to allow Virginia the amount of what had been then *disbursed* to the troops employed in the reduction and defence of this territory." (Vide Rep. No. 191, H. R., 1st session, 22d Congress.) Although the half-pay claims of the officers of those troops are insisted upon, so far as Virginia has become legally liable, in consequence of former judgments obtained, or may become so, on the principles of those judgments; yet it is not urged that there is a class of claims against her like the one under consideration. It does not appear, from the documents accompanying said memorial, that there were outstanding obligations against her of this description, after the settlement of her accounts with the United States, under the compact in relation to the territy, in 1788. Whether this settlement comprehended all the actual disbursements, as well as the then known liabilities of Virginia, arising from the conquest and defence of the territory, is the material question at issue. The committee do not feel at liberty to doubt that bills of exchange to a large amount were drawn by General Clarke, in favor of various individuals, on the commercial agent of Virginia. It appears equally probable that a full account of the same was rendered to the State of Virginia, anterior to 1788, by General Clarke; otherwise, her actual *disbursements* could not have been known and credited to her by the United States in the settlement with that State in 1788. But as this settlement was embraced in the final settlement between the several States and the United States, which was made on the 29th of June, 1793, under the acts of August 4th and 5th, 1790, the committee consider it pertinent to refer thereto, in order to elucidate the material points in the case, which are important to the Treasury, to the rights of the claimant, and to the interest of Virginia. The act of 4th August, 1790, "makes provision for the debt of the United States." It proposed a loan; and that the "sums which shall be subscribed to the said loan shall be payable in the principal and interest of the certificates or notes which, prior to the 1st of January last, were issued by the respective States as acknowledgments or evidences of debts by them, respectively, owing." "*And provided,* That no such certificate shall be received, which, from the tenor thereof, or from any public record, act, or document, shall appear, or can be ascertained, to have been issued for any purpose other than compensations and expenditures for services or supplies towards the prosecution of the late war and the defence of the United States, or some part thereof, during the same." The commissioners appointed under the act of August 5, 1790, were required "to receive and examine all claims which shall be exhibited to them before the 1st day of July, 1791, and to determine on all such as shall have accrued for the general or particular defence during the war, and on the evidence thereof, according to the principles of general equity, (although such claims may not be sanctioned by the resolves of Congress, or supported by regular vouchers,) so as to provide for the final settlement of all accounts between the United States and the States individually; but no evidence of a claim, heretofore admitted by a commissioner of the United States, for any State or district, shall be subject to such examination; nor shall the claim of any citizen be admitted as a charge against the United States, in the account of any State, unless the same was allowed by such State before the 24th September, 1788." Said commissioners were to "debit each State with all advances which have been or may be made to it by the United States," "and shall credit each State for its disbursements and advances, on the principles contained in the 3d section of this act," which is above recited. Now, it does not appear, from any evidence before the committee, whether the bill of exchange drawn in favor of Francis Vigo, by General Clarke, on the commercial agent of Virginia, and which was protested "for want of funds," was comprehended in the particular account of said State settled in 1788, or in her aggregate amount of "disbursements and advances," which was credited on the 29th June, 1793.

The committee do not insist that the United States are exonerated by lapse of time from any obligation to admit claims of this character; but they regard it, in the absence of testimony, as inducing a presumption that they were credited to the State of Virginia in 1788 or 1793, inasmuch as the obligation of Virginia to pay them must have been known, as her right to demand payment from the United States was then acknowledged to exist.

The committee, therefore, move to be discharged from the further consideration of the subject.

---

A.

OFFICE OF THE COMMISSIONER OF REVOLUTIONARY CLAIMS
FOR THE STATE OF VIRGINIA,

*Richmond, December* 16, 1835.

I have examined the claim of Francis Vigo, of Vincennes, and State of Indiana, for supplies furnished to the Illinois regiment in the fall of the year 1778, to the amount of eight thousand six hundred and sixteen dollars, evidenced by a set of bills of exchange drawn by George R. Clarke on Oliver Pollock, at New Orleans, for the said sum of $8,616, (which said bills have been lost or mislaid,) and which the said Vigo alleges remain unpaid to this day. I have examined, also, every public document within my reach, which I believed would give information respecting the transactions in which the claims of individuals against the State of Virginia for supplies furnished to the Illinois regiment originated, and especially respecting the claim of Colonel Vigo. In this examination and investigation I have ascertained the following facts, to wit:

1st. That Francis Vigo was "the Spanish merchant," as he has been called by way of honorable distinction, who was renowned for his integrity, liberality, and benevolence, as well as for his firm friendship for, and disinterested and efficient support of, Virginia in the war of the Revolution.

2d. That, being the subject of a foreign Power, he warmly espoused the cause of the colonies against the mother country, and made large sacrifices in supporting the western troops of Virginia.

3d. That bills of exchange were drawn by General Clarke, in the year

1778, upon Oliver Pollock, at New Orleans, in favor of Francis Vigo, for upwards of $10,000, for supplies furnished by him to the Illinois regiment in that year; that these bills were protested by Mr. Pollock (who was the agent of the State) for the "want of funds;" that some of them were sold by Mr. Vigo, and afterwards paid by Virginia; that one, amounting to $298, was paid by the said Pollock to the said Vigo; that the bill for $8,616 was one of them which was not parted with by Mr. Vigo, but remained in his possession (that is to say, the second of the set remained in his possession—the set consisting of Nos. 1 and 2; and the first having been lost) until he suffered with a long and severe illness, commencing in 1802, and continuing for several years; that, during this illness, he handed over the said bill for $8,616 to Judge Jacob Burnett, of Ohio, to obtain something, if possible, from Virginia upon it. (See statements of Francis Vigo, Pierre Menard, and Jacob Burnett, all on oath; and, also, as proof of the credit which should be given to the statements of the said Vigo, see the affidavits of John Badollet and Nathaniel Ewing, and statement of General Harrison, and letters from Generals Wayne, Clarke, and Knox, &c.)

4th. That the said bill of $8,616 was drawn for supplies actually furnished to the Illinois regiment, under the command of General G. R. Clarke, by said Francis Vigo. (See the memorial of Francis Vigo, which has been sworn to, and the affidavits of Pierre Menard and J. Badollet.)

5th. That this set of bills of exchange (both first and second) have been lost. (See here, also, Francis Vigo's statement on oath, and the affidavits of Jacob Burnett and Nathaniel Ewing.)

6th. That the said amount of $8,616 remains at this day unsatisfied, and due to the said Francis Vigo. (See said Vigo's statement on oath, Pierre Menard's affidavit, and the affidavits of John Badollet and N. Ewing; also, certificates of the Auditor and Treasurer of Virginia.)

7th. That all General Clarke's bills on Pollock, at New Orleans, were for specie. (See General Clarke's certificate, Journal of the House of Delegates, May session, 1783, page 73.)

8th. That the smaller bills, which were drawn in the latter part of the year 1778, by General Clarke, upon Oliver Pollock, in favor of Francis Vigo, and which he says in his memorial were parted with by him, and afterwards paid by Virginia, are proved, by the Illinois documents and papers now in my possession, to have been paid by Virginia. But these documents and papers furnish no proof whatever of the payment of the said larger bill of $8,616, the amount of which is now claimed by Francis Vigo.

In conformity with the foregoing facts, I have adjusted the claim. It gives me pleasure to be able to make a favorable adjustment, and to ascertain the sum of money due from the State of Virginia to a man who has rendered the most important services to his adopted country, and who (if his neighbors, who are amongst the most distinguished men in the part of the United States in which he resides, are to be believed) is one of the most upright and honorable of men.

*The State of Virginia to Francis Vigo,*     Dr.

1778. To advances made to General Clarke, for the use of
the Illinois regiment, under the command of the
said Clarke,     -     -     -     -     -     $8,616 00
To interest on the same, at 5 per cent. per annum,
from March 20, 1779, to January 10, 1835,     -     24,038 85

Total, -     -     -     - $32,654 85

After having made a satisfactory examination of the evidences touching
this claim, I have adjusted it according to the above statement, and have
found a sum of money due to the said Francis Vigo, of principal and interest, amounting to thirty-two thousand six hundred and fifty-four dollars and eighty-five cents.

JOHN H. SMITH,
*Commissioner, &c.*

### B.

*To John H. Smith, Esq., appointed by the State of Virginia to ascer-
tain and liquidate the claims of the individuals who had furnished
supplies and made advances to the troops of Colonel George Rogers
Clarke, in what was called the "Illinois campaign," in the year
1778:*

The memorial of the undersigned Francis Vigo, of the town of Vincennes,
county of Knox, and State of Indiana, respectfully represents:

That he was, in the year 1778, residing in the town of St. Louis, now
State of Missouri, then a Spanish post, doing business as a merchant and
Indian trader, and having considerable influence and property; that, in
the summer of that year, Colonel George Rogers Clarke arrived at Kaskaskia, with the troops under his command, on what was called the "Illinois campaign;" that the undersigned, being well acquainted with the
French inhabitants of that section, with whom he had large dealings for
the supply of the Spanish troops, and on his own account, and being
friendly disposed to the object of Colonel Clarke's visit and expedition to
that quarter, and feeling a warm interest in the success of the American
arms in the contest in which they were then engaged, although the subject
of another Government, waited on Colonel Clarke, soon after his arrival
at Cahokia, to which place he had sent Major Bowman to take possession of, organize the militia, and establish a civil government, and voluntarily tendered him such aid as he could furnish in supplying his troops,
then greatly in need of provisions, clothing, and ammunition; that his
offer was gratefully accepted by Colonel Clarke, and his aid and assistance
required; that, in pursuance of the request of Colonel Clarke, and from a
sincere disposition to aid him in the cause of his country, he requested the
inhabitants, who were well acquainted with this deponent, to furnish Colonel Clarke with whatever he needed, and to look to him for the pay—

they being Frenchmen, and unacquainted with Colonel Clarke, and having no knowledge of his means of payment, or his ability to make it, and unwilling to furnish supplies for the troops under Colonel Clarke's command, unless on the guaranty of this deponent.

Your memorialist agreed to become paymaster to many of them for all supplies they furnished said troops, and did pay them for all furnished, besides furnishing himself a large amount out of his own stores, on the order of Colonel Clarke; that said troops were destitute of all necessaries and materials of war; and your memorialist believes the expedition must have been abandoned, and the troops dismissed, had he not stepped forward and generously and patriotically (he makes the declaration in no vain boast) supplied Colonel Clarke and his troops with the articles which were needed, amounting, in all, to nearly *twelve thousand dollars*, and which sum he actually advanced or paid for the benefit of Colonel Clarke and the troops under his command. Your memorialist would further remark, that, in payment of the amount due your memorialist, Colonel Clarke drew in favor of your memorialist the following bills of exchange, as nearly as he can recollect; the exact dates of which are not recollected by your memorialist, but all drawn at Kaskaskia during the year 1778, by Colonel Clarke, on Oliver Pollock, Esq., agent of the State of Virginia, then at New Orleans, and being solely for advances made and supplies furnished the troops under his command, to wit : one for $298, paid by Pollock from goods shipped from New Orleans to Colonel Clarke, and received by your memorialist; one for $921; one for $1,452=$2,373; both of which last-mentioned drafts having been presented to said Pollock for payment, and the same having been refused for the " want of funds" on the part of Virginia in his hands, were retained by your memorialist until July, 1780, when, believing that nothing could be obtained on them from the State of Virginia, he disposed of them, while sick and unable to attend to business, in consequence of his long confinement, for the sum of $575, to one Saucier, who informed deponent that, unless that sum was received, he would get nothing; although your memorialist has lately understood the same has been settled by the State of Virginia. But said sum of $575 was all ever realized by your memorialist for both of said drafts, amounting, as aforesaid, to the sum of $2,373.

Your memorialist would represent that, in addition to the drafts aforesaid, Colonel Clarke, in payment of what was due him for advances made and supplies furnished some time in the year 1778, according to the best recollection and belief of this deponent, gave your memorialist a draft upon the said Oliver Pollock, as agent of Virginia, for the sum of $8,516, in specie, or its equivalent, directed to him at New Orleans ; that, some time in February, 1779, this deponent went to New Orleans with said draft drawn on said Oliver Pollock, as agent of the State of Virginia, for the sum last mentioned, but the same was protested by said Pollock for "want of funds;" that there were two sets of said drafts, (first and second,) both for the same sum, drawn by Colonel Clarke on said Pollock; that, on the return of this deponent to St. Louis, then a Spanish post, and where he resided, he was advised by the commandant of the place (his friend) to send one of them to Spain, as, perhaps, the Spanish Government might pay it for the honor of the State of Virginia, or perhaps it could be disposed of there ; that he delivered it to the commandant for that purpose, (who was then acting as Governor of Louisiana, and through whose influence he hoped something might be got,) and was informed by him that the same was sent to Spain; but your memorialist never has heard of the same, nor does he believe it ever was paid, but supposes the same to have been lost, never having heard of it; that the second draft or bill (of the same tenor and date as the first) given by Colonel Clarke to this deponent for the same sum, to wit, the sum of $8,616, and drawn on Pollock at New Orleans, was, after the refusal of Pollock to pay it, for "want of funds, kept by this deponent until some time in the year 1788, when deponent, on his way to Philadelphia, met said Pollock in Carlisle, Pennsylvania, and presented the same to him again for payment; but said Pollock again refused payment, but requested deponent "not to part with said draft, as the State of Virginia would, some time or other, pay it, with interest;" saying, further, "that he had no funds of Virginia in his hands with which to pay it, although it was due, and should long since have been paid;" that this deponent kept said draft until about the year 1802, when said deponent was sick, and continued so for a number of years, confined to his bed; that, during that time, his papers became very much deranged, and many were destroyed, lost, or mislaid; among others, the draft above alluded to, (being the second of the bills drawn by Colonel Clarke on Pollock for the sum of $8,616, and which had been protested by said Pollock;) that deponent's recollection is, that said draft or bill was, during this deponent's sickness, as aforesaid, in the year last aforesaid, handed over to the honorable Jacob Burnett, of Cincinnati, Ohio, to obtain something, if possible, for your memorialist from the State of Virginia on his claim aforesaid; but is informed, by letter from Jacob Burnett, that he has hunted all his papers, and can find no such draft or bill, and, if delivered by this deponent to him, (Burnett,) the same has been either lost or mislaid.

This deponent further states, that for all advances made by him at that period, amounting to nearly $12,000 in specie, or its equivalent, he has never received but the aforesaid sum of $575, (the proceeds of the two drafts, one for $921, the other for $1,462, and sold at the discount before mentioned, and the said draft of $298,) either from the United States, the State of Virginia, or any other person; that he is now in his 88th year; that his fortune and his life have been perilled in the service of his adopted country; that your memorialist has not asked nor received any compensation for *his own services,* though he is warranted in saying, and the history of the times will prove it, that but for his own personal services, at great risk and hazard to himself, Colonel Clarke never would have been enabled to have surprised Hamilton and the garrison at Vincennes. It was only through and by the information communicated by the undersigned, that Colonel Clarke succeeded in surprising that fort, and capturing the troops under Colonel Hamilton's command, with about ten thousand pounds sterling of goods : the whole of which, by means of the undersigned, became the property of the captors.

The services of the *"Spanish merchant"* have been mentioned in the history of those times; (vide Marshall's Life of Washington, vol. 3, page 566; Colonel Clarke's letter to Mr. Jefferson, then Governor of Virginia, Jefferson's Memoirs, 1st vol., 453;) but for those services the undersigned never has asked a compensation from his Government. The acknowledgment that they were rendered to his country, is to him a sufficient reward. For advances made, and for money expended, he believes he has a *legal* and *equitable* claim upon those for whom the first was made, and the last expended: it is all he asks; and he believes the great, the patriotic, and magnanimous State of Virginia, will not deny his claim. During her minority, while a colony, and before she was advanced in her career of wealth and prosperity, the undersigned delayed pressing his just claims. To call for vouchers after fifty years, and during so many vicissitudes of human affairs as the undersigned has passed in a long and eventful life, is, and would be, a perfect denial of justice. What he has received, pitiful as the allowance has been, he has candidly and fairly acknowledged. What is still due—the draft for $8,616—he as fairly claims. Not a dollar of it has been paid; and your memorialist would respectfully submit to your own justice and magnanimity, whether his declining years should not be made comfortable by the repayment of this sum advanced, with the usual interest granted in such cases, when, without your memorialist's aid, the troops of Virginia could not have been supported, or the State hardly obtained a dollar on her own faith and credit.

All which is respectfully submitted.

VIGO.

STATE OF INDIANA, *Knox county, ss.*

Personally appeared before me, Colonel Francis Vigo, a citizen of the county of Knox, well known to me for many years as a gentleman of high character for truth and veracity, and who, being sworn, deposeth and saith the matters and things contained in the foregoing memorial are just and true, to the best of his knowledge and belief; and that said Vigo is in the full possession of the faculties of his mind; and that full faith and credit is due, and would be given, to any statement made by him.

In testimony, I have hereunto set my hand and seal, as a justice of the peace, duly commissioned and qualified, for said State and county, this 7th day of December, 1834.

JOHN COLLINS, *J. P. K. C.* [SEAL.]

STATE OF INDIANA, *Knox county, ss.*

In testimony that the above-written John Collins was a magistrate, authorized to administer oaths, take acknowledgments, &c., in the State of Indiana, and county of Knox, aforesaid, at the above date, and that his name then subscribed appears to me to be his usual signature, I, Alexander Dunlap Scott, clerk of the Knox circuit court of said State of Indiana, have hereto affixed my seal of office, and subscribed my name and quality, at Vincennes, this 11th day of December, A. D. 1834.

[L. S.] A. D. SCOTT.

*Statement of Colonel Pierre Menard, of Kaskaskia, Illinois, in relation to a claim of Colonel Francis Vigo, on the State of Virginia, for supplies, &c. furnished " the Illinois regiment" during the revolutionary war.*

Colonel Menard states that he has been acquainted with Colonel Francis Vigo ever since the year A. D. 1787, and was intimately acquainted with his business for a considerable time, about the commencement of his acquaintance with him; that he had been informed by Colonel Vigo, and has always understood, that he (Colonel Vigo) had made large advances to the " Illinois regiment," under the command of Colonel George Rogers Clarke, during the revolutionary war, a few years before his acquaintance with him, and for which he had received no pay, or at least but a very small part; that the amount, however, had been liquidated by Colonel George Rogers Clarke, and drafts given by him on Oliver Pollock, agent of the State of Virginia, in Colonel Vigo's favor. The amount of all the drafts, Colonel Menard states, from the recollection of the impression made on his mind about the year 1788, must have exceeded $10,000.

Colonel Menard further states, that somewhere about the year A. D. 1788, he was present at an interview in Carlisle, Pennsylvania, between Colonel Vigo and said Pollock, when Colonel Vigo presented the said drafts to said Pollock; upon which Mr. Pollock observed he was " very sorry he had been under the necessity of protesting them, for the want of funds;" that he recollects of no objection being made on account of their genuineness, or on account of the authority of Colonel George Rogers Clarke to draw them; but, on the contrary, Mr. Pollock advised Colonel Vigo to keep the drafts, as they would be paid some time or other.

PIERRE MENARD.

State of Indiana, *Knox county, sct :*

Be it remembered, that on this sixth day of November, A. D. 1834, the abovenamed Colonel Pierre Menard, of Kaskaskia, to me personally known, came before me, a justice of the peace in and for the county aforesaid, and made oath, according to the best of his knowledge and belief, to the truth and correctness of the foregoing statement.

Given under my hand and seal, this 6th day of November, A. D. 1834.

[L. S.]          JOHN COLLINS,
*Justice Peace, Knox county.*

State of Indiana, *Knox county, sct :*

In testimony that the aforewritten John Collins was a magistrate, authorized to administer oaths, take acknowledgments, &c. in the said county of Knox and State of Indiana, at the date of the preceding attestation, and that his name there subscribed appears to be his usual signature, I, Alexander Dunlap Scott, clerk of the Knox circuit court of said State of Indiana, have hereto affixed my seal of office, and subscribed my name and quality, this 12th day of December, A. D. 1834.

[L. S.]          A. D. SCOTT.

---

*Statement of John Badollet, Esq., register of the land office of the United States at Vincennes, Indiana, relative to the claim of Colonel Francis Vigo on the State of Virginia, for supplies furnished General George Rogers Clarke, and the troops under his command, in his " Illinois campaign," during the revolutionary war.*

Mr. Badollet states that he has been intimately acquainted with Colonel Francis Vigo for about thirty years. That he has always had the greatest confidence in him in all respects, and particularly as a man of the most scrupulous regard for truth, disinterestedness, and honor.

Further, that he has always understood from Colonel Vigo, and those of his friends that knew him at the time of General George Rogers Clarke's campaign in Illinois, about the year 1779, that he had rendered very great service to General Clarke, and the cause in which he was engaged, by giving him important information, obtained at a great personal and pecuniary risk, as well as in procuring, at his own expense, supplies to support the troops under said Clarke's command, to a large amount, and that he has never received but very little compensation therefor; and that he believes the State of Virginia and the United States not only owe Colonel Vigo a very great debt of gratitude, but are under great pecuniary obligations to him, that in justice ought speedily to be discharged.

Further, Mr. Badollet states that, from the very intimate knowledge he has of the character of Colonel Vigo, and of his high sense of honor, if the alternative were presented him of either receiving a large pecuniary recompense for the services and pecuniary aid he has rendered the American cause, or simply receiving a public acknowledgment of them by the Government, though very poor, he believes Colonel Vigo would not hesitate a moment in choosing the latter.

JOHN BADOLLET.

State of Indiana, *Knox county, sct :*

Personally appeared before me, a justice of the peace for said county, John Badollet, Esq., to me personally known, and made affirmation to the truth and correctness of the foregoing statement, according to the best of his knowledge and belief.

Given under my hand and seal this 21st day of November, A. D. 1834.

[L. S.]                                SAMUEL HILL,
*Justice Peace, Knox county.*

State of Indiana, *Knox county, sct :*

In testimony that the above-written Samuel Hill was a magistrate authorized to administer oaths, take acknowledgments, &c. in the said county of Knox and State of Indiana, at the above date, and that his name there subscribed appears to be his usual signature, I, Alexander Dunlap Scott, clerk of the Knox circuit court of said State of Indiana, have hereto affixed my seal of office, and subscribed my name and quality, at Vincennes, this 12th day of December, A. D. 1834.

[L. S.]                                        A. D. SCOTT.

--------

*Affidavit of Judge Burnett, in relation to Colonel Vigo's claim on Virginia.*

In the summer of 1798, James Abbott, of Detroit, gave a power of attorney to Arthur St. Clair and myself to collect or secure a debt due from Colonel F. Vigo, of Post Vincennes, to the Miami Company. In December, 1799, we went to Vincennes, and obtained from Colonel Vigo a mortgage on several tracts of land, for the security of the debt. While we were at Col. Vigo's, he handed me a draft in his favor, drawn by General George Rogers Clarke on the Commonwealth of Virginia, or her agent, for several thousand dollars—I think about eight thousand. The object for which the draft was shown to us, I do not distinctly recollect ; but I believe it was to ascertain whether we could not aid him in collecting the money. There is an impression on my mind that he gave us the draft for that purpose; but I have searched diligently among my papers, without being able to find it, or any memorandum relating to it. I remember, however, that Colonel Vigo had the draft in his possession in the year 1799, and that some conversation was had on the subject of our taking it. If the paper came into my hands, it has been lost or mislaid.

I have known the general character of Colonel Vigo since the year 1796, and believe him to be as honorable and high-minded a man as any other in the Western country.

J. BURNETT.

State of Ohio, *Cincinnati, ss.*

Personally came before me, mayor of said city, J. Burnett, and made oath that the foregoing statement is true.

Given under my hand and seal of said city, this 23d December, 1834.

[L. s.] SAM. W. DAVIS, *Mayor.*

---

*Affidavit of N. Ewing relative to Colonel Vigo's claim.*

Personally appeared before me the subscriber, a justice of the peace duly commissioned and qualified for the county of Knox and State of Indiana, Nathaniel Ewing, Esq., of said county, aged 62 years, who being sworn, deposeth and saith: That he came to the town of Vincennes, then "Post Vincennes," in the year 1790 or 1791, from which period he dates his first acquaintance with Colonel Francis Vigo, then a resident of said post, and known as the "Spanish merchant." That this deponent was every year at Vincennes, off and on, until the year 1804 or 1805, when he was appointed, by the Government, commissioner to examine land titles; and from that period until the present time has been a constant resident of said place; during all which time he has been well acquainted with said Vigo, and, for the most part, a neighbor, living on an adjoining plantation, and well acquainted with his affairs, business, habits, and dealings. That said Vigo is known to the deponent as a man of the strictest integrity and honor. That he is an uneducated man, but of a remarkably clear mind, and a memory retentive beyond that of any man ever known to the deponent. That Colonel Vigo, during the years 1798, 1799, 1800, 1801, 1802, and until the year 1803, was closely confined by a protracted illness, and most of the time to his bed. That during said period he was unable to do any business; and deponent believes, from his own knowledge of him and his affairs at that period, that his (Colonel Vigo's) papers became deranged and out of order, as was the case with his personal affairs, not being able to attend to them. That Colonel Vigo, from his general habits and want of education, rather trusted through life to the integrity and honor of others, than to any written memorandum of the transaction in which he was engaged, or the affairs about which he was dealing.

That the deponent has always understood, ever since he first came to Vincennes, from Colonel Vigo and others, that a large sum of money was due him from the State of Virginia, which was unpaid, being due for advances made by Colonel Vigo to the troops under Colonel George R. Clarke, in the "Illinois campaign" in 1778; and that, from all he has understood from Colonel Vigo and others, on his first arrival in the coun-

41

try, and since, he has no doubt such was the fact. That Colonel Vigo, in consequence of not having been paid these claims, and in consequence of the losses sustained, and partly growing out of the circumstances alluded to, has become greatly embarrassed, though once wealthy.

That this deponent would place the utmost reliance in any statement made by Colonel Vigo; and the fullest faith and credit is due to his declarations in relation to his own affairs, or those of others in relation to which he might be called on to state his recollection; and whether under oath or on honor, those who know him, or can have known him, would believe him in every particular.

And further this deponent saith not.

NATH. EWING.

Sworn to and subscribed before me this 3d December, 1834.

SAM. HILL,<br>*Justice of the Peace for Knox co., Indiana.*

STATE OF INDIANA, *Knox county, sct.*

In testimony that the aforewritten Samuel Hill was a magistrate, authorized to administer oaths, take acknowledgments, &c., in the said county of Knox, and State of Indiana, at the date of the preceding affidavit, and that his name there subscribed appears to me to be his usual signature, I, Alexander Dunlap Scott, clerk of the Knox circuit court, have hereto affixed my seal of office, and subscribed my name and quality at Vincennes, this 12th day of December, A. D. 1834.

[L. S.]
A. D. SCOTT.

---

*General Wm. H. Harrison's statement in relation to Colonel Vigo's claim.*

I have been acquainted with Colonel Francis Vigo, of Vincennes, for thirty-nine years, and during the thirteen years I was the Governor of Indiana I lived in the same town with him, and upon terms of the most intimate friendship.

I have often heard him speak of the draft which had been given to him by General Clarke, for supplies furnished for his army, and that it had never been paid. The old gentleman was always of the opinion that he had put it into the hands of Jacob Burnett and Arthur St. Clair, esquires, who had been employed by a mercantile house at Detroit to settle a large debt due by him to them. I applied some time since to Judge Burnett, on behalf of Colonel Vigo, and an accurate search was made among his papers, but the draft was not found. The judge, however, well recollects that Colonel Vigo had such a draft, and it was possible it might have been given to him or to Mr. St. Clair. The latter gentleman has been dead for some years; several successive administrations have been granted on his estate, and his papers much scattered. I have, indeed, been unable to find the person who has the custody of that portion of them amongst which the missing paper would probably be found.

With respect to the credibility of Colonel Vigo's statement, I solemnly declare I believe him utterly incapable of making a misrepresentation of the facts, however great may be his interest in the matter; and I am also confident that there are more respectable persons in Indiana who would become guarantees of his integrity than could be induced to lay under a similar responsibility for any other person. His whole life, as long as his circumstances were prosperous, was spent in acts of kindness and benevolence to individuals; and his public spirit and attachment to the institutions of our country are proverbial.

W. H. HARRISON.

CINCINNATI, *December* 22, 1834.

---

LOCUST GROVE, NEAR LOUISVILLE,<br>
August 1, 1811.

DEAR SIR: A letter from a man who has always occupied a distinguished place in my affection and esteem, must ensure the warmest and most cordial reception; an affection, the result not so much of being associates in the placid stream of tranquillity, and the benign sunshine of peace, as companions amidst the din of war, and those struggles where the indefatigable exertion of every muscle and nerve was demanded. But it may be enough to remark, that while the one is the effect of your uniformly discreet and irreproachable conduct in the intricate path of civil and domestic life, the other is wrought by a strong sense of that gratitude due from your adopted country, having myself both witnessed and experienced the signal advantages flowing to our common country from your inestimable conduct, and, what is more enhancing to such services, having rendered them at a time when the cloud on which our fate hung assumed the most menacing aspect.

When I contemplate the glowing affection with which your letter is fraught, and only the revival of such you in past times—ah! better times, troublous as they were—were wont to evince for me, I am so filled with correspondent feelings that I am at a loss for words to express them. How happy would I be could those sentiments of entreaty to a trustful Providence, in the conclusive part of your letter, for a serene and happy evening, be realized! But that Providence, submitting as I do with manly patience to his decrees, has long since denied me that boon. He has cut asunder the life's tenderest string.

With sentiments of the warmest regard, I remain,<br>
GEORGE R. CLARKE.

---

Additional memorial of F. Vigo.

The additional memorial of Francis Vigo further represents, in addition to the facts set forth before, in the memorial to which this is a supplement, (and the statement is made at his request,) that, some time in December, 1778, this memorialist, then being in Kaskaskia, now Illinois, where Colonel George R. Clarke then was, the said Clarke received a communication from Captain Helms, then commanding at Vincennes a company of Virginia troops, that he was destitute of provisions and ammunition, and requested deponent to go to Vincennes for the purpose of furnishing said

Helms's company with provisions and ammunition, said Vigo being well acquainted with the French inhabitants at said post.   That, in pursuance of said request, he left Kaskaskia for Vincennes, on the 18th December, 1778, and when about six miles from Vincennes, on the Embarras river, on the 24th of December, 1778, was taken prisoner by a party of Indians, commanded by an English officer; the garrison at Vincennes having been captured by Hamilton and the English forces a short time before, and Captain Helms being a prisoner; that the Indians took from him a valuable horse, deponent's arms, saddlebags, and clothing, valued at $500, including some paper money ; that, when taken prisoner, he was carried to Vincennes, and found Hamilton in possession of the post; that he was released by Hamilton, on condition "that he would do nothing to injure the British cause during his journey home ;" that he agreed to this, and departed.   During the time of his stay at Vincennes, he ascertained accurately the situation of the garrison ; and, "after his return home" to St. Louis, immediately went to Kaskaskia, and gave Clarke the information by which he captured Vincennes.   That he was taken prisoner in company with Mr. Renau ; that he never received a cent for the losses occasioned by his capture while in the service of Virginia, nor ever asked for any.

VIGO.

Sworn and subscribed to by the deponent, Colonel Francis Vigo, at Vincennes, this 21st November, 1834, before the subscriber, a justice of the peace, duly commissioned and qualified, for said county of Knox, and State of Indiana.

SAM. HILL, *J. P.*   [seal.]

State of Indiana, *Knox county, sct.* :

In testimony that the above-written Samuel Hill was a magistrate, authorized to administer oaths, take acknowledgments, &c., in said county of Knox, and State of Indiana, at the above date, and that his name there subscribed appears to me to be his usual signature, I, Alexander Dunlap Scott, clerk of the Knox circuit court of said State of Indiana, have hereto affixed my seal of office, and subscribed my name and quality, at Vincennes, this 12th day of December, A. D. 1834.

[l. s.] A. D. SCOTT.

------

*Letters from the Secretary of War to Francis Vigo.*

War Department, *July* 20, 1790.

Sir :   Major Doughty has, in expressive words, given an account of the services which you have rendered him, and of the zeal you have manifested for the United States in the difficult business which had been committed to his care.   Your conduct therein, sir, has attracted the attention of the President, and I am directed by him to tender to you his acknowledgments therefor.   It is with the greatest pleasure, sir, that I discharge that duty, being well informed that the essential services you have rendered to Major Doughty were the consequence of your zeal for the public welfare.   You have also instanced it in your proceedings towards Major

Hamtramck, and the troops under his command, as I have been informed by General Harmar.

I have the honor to be your most humble and obedient servant,

H. KNOX,
*Secretary of the War Department.*

Mr. FRANCIS VIGO.

WAR DEPARTMENT, *December* 30, 1790.

SIR: As you have already received, by the special order of the President of the United States, a commission to trade with the Chickasaws and Choctaws, and as the United States have received complete [satisfaction] of your integrity and devotion to their interests, I intrust to your care two talks for the aforesaid Chickasaws and Choctaws, signed by the President of the United States. You will be pleased to deliver both talks to each of those two nations.

You will seize every convenient opportunity to impress upon the minds of the aforesaid Chickasaws and Choctaws the adherence of the United States to the treaty of Hopewell; that the United States do not want their lands; that if anybody endeavors to inspire them with different sentiments, they must consider such persons in no other light than that of their enemies, and the enemies of the United States. You will please to make a discreet use of this letter, and to communicate it only to Governor St. Clair, Brigadier General Harmar, and to such other persons in whom you can place a full confidence.

I am, sir, respectfully, your most obedient servant,

H. KNOX,
*Secretary of the War Department.*

Mr. FRANCIS VIGO.

---

*Letter from General A. Wayne to F. Vigo.*

HEADQUARTERS, GREENVILLE, *May* 27, 1794.

SIR: From the uniform character you support, of being a gentleman of integrity and influence, and a steady and firm friend of the United States, and perfectly acquainted with all the trading people passing between Post Vincennes and Detroit, as well as from St. Louis and Cahokia to that place, will it be practicable for you to procure one or two trusty people, either Frenchmen or Indians, to go as far as Roche de Bout, in order to discover the number and designs of the enemy, and particularly what number of British troops are there, and whether they have built any fort or fortification at that place?

Whatever sum of money it may cost to obtain this important intelligence shall be paid to your order upon sight, from $100 to $300 or $400. Perhaps some resident at Roche de Bout, or at Grand Glaize, might be prevailed upon to send the necessary information from time to time.

Would it be practicable to bribe or purchase the Spanish express, from St. Louis to Detroit, to deliver his despatches to Captain Pasteur? This is a delicate business, and requires address and secrecy.

Pray let me hear from you as soon as convenient, and depend upon the best services I can render you upon all occasions.

Interim, I am your most humble servant,

ANT'Y WAYNE.

Major VIGO.

*Letter from F. Vigo to General Wayne.*

VINCENNES, *June* 24, 1794.

SIR: The man who went from this place on the 11th instant, and undertook to perform the first request of your letter of the 27th May last, returned on the 22d instant. He was accompanied by an Indian chief, under the pretence [of being,] and who was actually, hired to go to the Pottawatamies for prisoners. They went within seven or eight miles of the Wea town, which is about two hundred miles from this place by water, where they met with some Indians they were acquainted with, who turned them back. The particulars Captain Pasteur will inform your excellency by this opportunity. You may rest assured I will use my best endeavors to get further information by some other route, in conjunction with Captain Pasteur.

The galleys that arrived at New Madrid on the 27th of April last, stopped at the Chickasaw bluffs, where they delivered a quantity of goods to that nation of Indians, in payment for that * * spot, in order to build a garrison. The Chickasaws received for this place $500 cash, and fifty pieces of stroud, assorted; the whole amounting to $8,000. This information comes by an inhabitant of this town, who was at New Madrid when the galleys arrived, and left that place on the 17th of May last. They offered him very high wages to go to the Chickasaw bluffs, as an artificer to assist in building a garrison there. It was at the same time published and read in the fort, where a number of the Chickasaws were daily expected.

I have the honor to be, with the greatest respect and esteem, your excellency's most obliged, humble servant,

VIGO.

Major General WAYNE.

---

*Letter from General Wayne to Francis Vigo.*

HEADQUARTERS, GREENVILLE, *July* 5, 1794.

SIR: I have to acknowledge the receipt of your letter of the 24th ultimo, and thank you for the measures you have already taken, and mean to pursue, in order to gain intelligence.

The conduct of the Spaniards, in attempting to establish a post at the Chickasaw bluffs, so far within the acknowledged boundaries of the United States, is a very extraordinary conduct, and an aggression of the highest nature. I therefore wish, if possible, that the express, as mentioned in my letter of the 27th of May, could be obtained, either directly or indirectly, because it might be a means of throwing light upon a subject which is at present rather dark and mysterious.

It would appear from that part of the information from No. 1, which mentions that the British, or Simcoe, told the Indians, " You have fought by yourselves a long time ; now I am come to help you—take courage ! you go before, surround the garrison, and I will follow you with the cannon ; after that, I will show you what I will do with them ;" that the credulous savages, to the amount of at least 1,500 warriors, surrounded and attempted to carry Fort Recovery, by a *coup de main*, on the 30th of

June ; but were repulsed by that gallant garrison, and compelled to re-treat with disgrace and slaughter from the very same field where they were proudly victorious on the 4th of November, 1791.

Captain Pasteur will give you the particulars. Mr. Simcoe has actually fortified at St. Roche de Bout. It is more than probable I shall shortly reconnoitre that place.

Interim, I am, with respect and esteem, your most obedient, humble servant,

ANT'Y WAYNE.

Major Francis Vigo.

---

Letter from General Wayne to F. Vigo.

Headquarters, Miami Villages,<br>September 29, 1794.

Sir : I have to acknowledge the receipt of your letter of the 6th ultimo, by Mr. Evans, which met me at Grand Glaize, where I have established a strong post, and have another at great forwardness at this place.

You will, probably, before this reaches you, have heard of the brilliant success of the army under my command, in a general action on the 20th ultimo, on the banks of the Miamia, at the foot of the rapids, against the combined force of the hostile Indians and militia of Detroit.

Captain Pasteur is instructed to communicate the contents of my letter to him of this date, to you, which will give you the particulars.

By the best information, the force of the enemy amounted to 2,000 men, who were beaten and totally routed by less than half that number. The front line only of our army was engaged, who charged the Indians with such impetuosity, and drove them with such velocity, as prevented the second line and main body to arrive in time to participate in the action ; the savages being driven at the point of the bayonet near three miles in the course of one hour, through a thick bushy wood, when they abandoned themselves to flight, leaving the ground strewed with their dead bodies, intermixed with Canadians and other white men painted and dressed like savages.

I wish your agents may succeed in obtaining the despatches, &c., which may eventually lead to important discoveries.

Interim, I am your most obedient, humble servant,

ANT'Y WAYNE.

Major Vigo.

---

License from General Wayne to Colonel Vigo to trade with different posts.

Francis Vigo is hereby permitted intercourse with the posts of Forts Wayne, Knox, and Massac, and any which may be established on the Wabash river ; and has liberty to trade with the same, conformably to the rules thereof.

Given under my hand and seal, at headquarters, Greenville, August 18, 1795.

ANT'Y WAYNE.

*William Henry Harrison, Governor of the Indiana Territory, superintendent of Indian affairs, and commissioner plenipotentiary for treating with the Indian tribes—to all who shall see these presents :*

Know ye, that the bearer hereof, Colonel Francis Vigo, has been sent by me on a mission to the Indian tribes, the Pottawatamies, Eel Rivers, and Miamies; and all officers in the service of the United States are hereby required to furnish him with every necessary assistance; and he is hereby authorized to demand from any military post he may pass, such articles of provisions, either for his own use or that of the Indians, as he may think proper to take.

Given under my hand and seal, at Vincennes, 26th of May, 1805.

[SEAL.]

RICHMOND, VA., January 14, 1835.

SIR : You will confer a favor on the undersigned by causing an examination to be made in your office, to ascertain whether there is any evidence of the payment of a bill of exchange for $8,616, drawn by Colonel George R. Clarke, in the fall of 1778, in favor of Francis Vigo, on Oliver Pollock, Esq. at New Orleans, and acquaint the undersigned of the result.

Very respectfully, yours, &c.

AB. T. ELLIS,<br>
Att'y for Col. Francis Vigo.

To the TREASURER OF VIRGINIA.

TREASURY OFFICE, January 15, 1835.

I have not been able to find any entry on the books of this office, showing the payment of the claim within mentioned to Francis Vigo.

I do not intend to be understood as saying that the said claim has not been paid ; because many entries on the books are made to persons presenting the claim, instead of the person who rendered the service ; and because of the absence of the vouchers upon which those claims were founded.

L. BURFOOT,<br>
Treasurer of the Commonwealth.

STATEMENT.

Draft drawn on Oliver Pollock, agent of Virginia, by Colonel George R. Clarke, in favor of Francis Vigo, for $8,616, the latter part of the year 1778.

Bill of exchange on the Treasurer of Virginia, drawn by Lieutenant Colonel John Montgomery, April 8, 1780, in favor of Captain John Williams, and assigned to Mr. Renau, April 12, 1780 : amount $182, in *specie.*

Also, a bill of exchange from the same, in favor of the same, and assigned to the same, $12½.

AUDITOR'S OFFICE, *January* 12, 1835.

I have caused a search to be made, to ascertain whether the bills and drafts above mentioned were paid through this office, but can find no direct evidence of such payment. There is evidence of various payments to Oliver Pollock, to wit : £1,000, £2,637 10*s.*, and £307 10*s.* 10*d.* entered in a journal, commencing on the 1st of June, 1786 ; but whether they have any connexion with the bills and drafts above mentioned, I am not enabled to determine.

I do not consider the absence of positive proof in this office as affording any just presumption in favor of these claims against the Commonwealth.

JAMES E. HEATH,
*Auditor of Virginia.*

---

AUDITOR'S OFFICE, *January* 15, 1835.

SIR : In answer to your note of the 14th instant, I beg leave to state that the expression in my certificate respecting Vigo's claim, that there was no *direct* evidence of the claim having been paid, was not intended to convey the idea that I had discovered evidence of any kind, *direct* or *indirect,* of such payment. I intended to be understood, however, as meaning that Vigo's claim might have been paid, and yet this office furnish no evidence of the fact. It is impossible, at this late day, to understand, with precise accuracy, how the financial transactions of the revolutionary period were conducted. As a general proposition, it may, I think, be safely affirmed, that but little system or regularity was observed ; but if the fact were otherwise, the objection still remains that the books and records of this office which contain the transactions of the period referred to, are necessarily imperfect. Hence I have certified it as my opinion that the absence of proof of payment here ought not to raise any just presumption in favor of the claim.

I am, very respectfully, yours,
JAMES E. HEATH, *Auditor.*

---

OFFICE OF THE COMM'R OF REV'Y CLAIMS OF THE
STATE OF VIRGINIA,

*Richmond, Va., January* 20, 1835.

I do hereby certify that the foregoing pages contain true copies of papers which have been filed with me, in support of the claim of Francis Vigo against the State of Virginia, for supplies furnished to the Illinois regiment, under the command of General George R. Clarke, in the year 1778. The originals are now on file in my office.

Given under my hand :

JOHN H. SMITH, *Commissioner, &c.*

---

### C.

WASHINGTON CITY, *February* 12, 1835.

DEAR SIR : My father, a trader in the Illinois country at the time General George R. Clarke conquered it in 1778, has frequently told me that

General Clarke was unprovided with means or credit to maintain his troops, and that he and others entered warmly into the support of his troops, and made advances to him (General Clarke) upon the credit of Virginia, and prevailed upon all the inhabitants to furnish provisions and other necessaries to the troops under Clarke and his officers. My father and others received bills of exchange drawn by General Clarke and other officers, on Mr. Pollock, and on the Treasurer of Virginia. After my father had exhausted his fortune and credit, some time between the years 1780 and 1784, he went to New Orleans, and from thence took passage for Havana, and there embarked, in company with Mr. Pollock, and, I believe, Mr. Tardiveaux or Mr. Poiduser, (one of the two,) on board of a ship bound to Europe, which landed them on Baldhead island, on the coast of North Carolina, from whence they proceeded to Richmond. He took that route as the most safe, as all the Western country was then a wilderness, infested by hostile savages. A journey at that day, and for many years thereafter, was attended with imminent risk; indeed, it was rarely, if ever, undertaken from the shores of the Mississippi but in cara-vans composed of armed men. My father was engaged two or three years in efforts to procure payment of his demands, and, but for the Pres-ton family and Colonel Monroe, who befriended him and advised him to persevere, he would have returned home in despair, a ruined man. At last, through that influence, he procured a tardy settlement of his claims, and received a small part in money, the balance in negroes, tobacco, and lands; the two first at a high price, and the latter was not considered as being of any value, and were consequently not looked after. When he (my father) returned to the Illinois, (the familiar name of all the country now divided into Illinois and Missouri,) and reported the discouragements he had met with, the other creditors lost heart; and when we consider the character, ignorance, and subsequent want of confidence consequent on the difficulties reported to exist, is it to be wondered at that these claim-ants lost every hope of being eventually paid, and abandoned, as hopeless, their further prosecution?

It is proper to remark, that I do not make the foregoing statement upon my own knowledge, not being then in existence. I am, however, not the less confident of its accuracy; and I have no doubt that claims to a very large amount would have been asserted in due time, if a belief had not fastened itself on the minds of those people that it was fruitless; and I am also well convinced that, from the same cause, evidence of debts to a very large amount has been lost.

At the time of General Clarke's conquest, the population of the Illinois was small, cultivation very imperfect, and no greater supplies raised than were necessary for the immediate support of the inhabitants; and when an accession of their numbers took place, the price became exceedingly high. In 1780 or 1781, the scarcity of bread became so great, that none but the wealthiest could indulge in its use, and that, too, moderately. To that circumstance St. Louis owes its nickname of *Pain Court*,[*] by which it is known by all the old inhabitants to this day.

I believe the foregoing furnishes all the traditionary knowledge I pos-sess of the points you have questioned me about.

I am, with respect, your obedient servant,

Judge Pope.                                 C. GRATIOT.

[*] Short bread.

## No. 3.—A.

Resolution requiring the Governor to employ a competent person to examine certain revolutionary documents. [Agreed to by both Houses, February 21, 1833.]

*Resolved by the General Assembly,* That the Governor of this Commonwealth be, and he is hereby, required to employ some competent person to examine the revolutionary documents, &c., in the several offices of this Government, and the papers, &c., recently discovered in the attic story of the capitol, and to report to the Executive of this State a list of the names of all such persons as may be entitled to unsatisfied claims on Virginia for bounty land, on account of service rendered in the war of the Revolution, and such other information touching revolutionary service as may be deemed important; and that the Governor be, and he is hereby, required to take such steps as in his judgment may be best calculated to communicate the information thus derived to the parties interested, and to preserve their rights effectually from abuse or imposition.

STATE OF VIRGINIA, ⎱ *to wit:*
  *City of Richmond,* ⎰

I, George W. Munford, Clerk of the House of Delegates, and keeper of the rolls of Virginia, do hereby certify and make known, that the foregoing is a true copy of a resolution of the General Assembly of Virginia, adopted February 21, 1833. Given under my hand, this sixteenth day of January, 1836.

GEORGE W. MUNFORD,
*Clerk of the House of Del., and Keeper of the Rolls of Va.*

---

## B.

An act to provide for the appointment of a commissioner to examine and report upon claims for unsatisfied military land bounties, and for other purposes. [Passed March 11, 1834.]

*Be it enacted by the General Assembly,* That John H. Smith, be, and he is hereby, appointed and constituted a commissioner, whose duty it shall be to continue the examination directed under a resolution of the General Assembly of the 21st day of February, 1833, touching the revolutionary documents of this Commonwealth; and he shall lay before the Governor any information he may discover, as to any unsatisfied revolutionary claims of this Commonwealth on the Government of the United States. It shall, moreover, be the duty of the said commissioner to examine all claims for military land bounties, not heretofore decided on, which may arise under any existing laws or resolutions of the General Assembly, and report the facts relating to the same, together with any remarks which he may deem pertinent and proper, to the Governor of this Commonwealth, whose decisions thereupon shall be final: *Provided,* That warrants for such land bounties shall be issued as heretofore by the register of the land office, on the authority of the Governor. The said commissioner shall have authority to employ an assistant or clerk, whensoever, in the opinion of the Governor, it shall be necessary;

which assistant or clerk shall receive such compensation as the Governor shall deem proper, not exceeding the sum of fifty dollars per month. And the said commissioner shall receive, as compensation for his services aforesaid, such sum as the Governor shall deem proper, not exceeding twelve hundred dollars per annum, or at that rate for a shorter period.

*Be it further enacted,* That the said commissioner shall investigate and adjust the claims against the State of Virginia, for supplies, in money or otherwise, made to the Illinois regiment, under the command of George Rogers Clarke, whether acknowledged by the said Clarke, or Lieutenant Colonel John Montgomery.

*Be it further enacted,* That the sum of two hundred and twenty-five dollars be, and the same is hereby, appropriated, to refund expenses incurred by John H. Smith, who has acted as commissioner to examine revolutionary claims, under a resolution adopted at the last session of the General Assembly.

This act shall be in force from and after its passage.

Sᴛᴀᴛᴇ ᴏғ Vɪʀɢɪɴɪᴀ, } *to wit:*
   *City of Richmond,* }

I, George W. Munford, Clerk of the House of Delegates, and keeper of the rolls of Virginia, do hereby certify and make known, that the foregoing is a true copy of an act of the Legislature of Virginia, passed March 11, 1834. Given under my hand the eighteenth day of January, 1836.

GEORGE W. MUNFORD,
*Clerk of the House of Del., and Keeper of the Rolls of Va.*

---

Rɪᴄʜᴍᴏɴᴅ, *February* 7, 1836.

Dᴇᴀʀ Sɪʀ: In reply to your notes of January 29th and February 4th, I can only say, that having never seen the items embraced in the settlement of the accounts of the Illinois or Northwestern expedition, or any detailed statement of those accounts, it was altogether impossible that I could have known, or intended to state in my memorial to Congress on the subject of the half-pay claims of the State of Virginia, that the claims of Colonel Vigo, or any other specific claims, were included in that settlement: I only know that there was a settlement under the terms of the cession, but I am ignorant of the particular items included in that settlement.

With much respect, I am your obedient servant,
THOMAS W. GILMER.

Jᴏʜɴ Lᴀᴡ, Esq., *Washington City.*

---

C.

Vɪʀɢɪɴɪᴀ Tʀᴇᴀsᴜʀʏ Oғғɪᴄᴇ, *June* 25, 1835.

Sɪʀ: I have not been able, after a tedious examination, to find an entry on the books of this office showing the payment of a "bill of exchange for $8,616, drawn by General (then Colonel) George Rogers

Clarke, on Oliver Pollock, the agent of Virginia, at New Orleans, in favor of Francis Vigo." I do not intend to be understood as saying that this claim has not been paid; because many of the entries on the books are made to persons presenting the claim, instead of the person who rendered the service; and because of the absence of the vouchers upon which those claims were founded.

I can find no statement in this office of a settlement between Virginia and the United States.

L BURFOOT,
*Treasurer of the Commonwealth.*

To J. G. MOSBY, Esq.

---

RICHMOND, *January* 15, 1836.

DEAR SIR: You will much oblige me by furnishing me, as early as possible, with an official statement from your office, in answer to the following interrogatory, to wit:

Whether, from any documents in your office, it will appear "that a bill of exchange, for the sum of $8,616, or any similar sum, drawn some time in the year 1778, by Colonel George R. Clarke, on Oliver Pollock, Esq., the agent of Virginia at New Orleans, in favor of Francis Vigo, and which bill was 'protested for want of funds,' was comprehended in the particular account of the State of Virginia against the United States, as settled in 1788, or in the aggregate account of 'disbursements and advances' credited said State in her settlement with the United States on the 29th June, 1793," or in any settlement between the United States and Virginia.

With sentiments of respect, I have the honor to be, yours, &c.,

JOHN LAW.

LAWSON BURFOOT, Esq.,
*Treasurer of the State of Virginia.*

---

### D.

I do hereby certify, that, after due examination made, no evidence has been found in this office of any payment made by the State of Virginia to Francis Vigo, on account of a draft drawn by George Rogers Clarke on Oliver Pollock, in favor of said Vigo, or on any other account. I do not consider, however, that the absence of any such evidence, or the inability to find it, is sufficient to establish, positively, that no such payment was made; inasmuch as the books and records, especially of so ancient a date as 1778, when the draft is supposed to have been drawn, are either imperfect or have not been preserved. I further certify, that although there was undoubtedly a settlement between Virginia and the United States, on account of expenses incurred by the former in the revolutionary war, the evidence of such settlement is not to be found among the books and records of the Auditor's office, and consequently there is no proof that I have been enabled to find of any moneys having been paid over to the State of Virginia by the United States, on account of the draft above referred to.

Given under my hand at the Auditor's office, Richmond, this 30th day of June, 1835.

JAMES E. HEATH,
*Auditor of Virginia.*

E.

*Extract from the Journal of the House of Delegates, of Saturday, June 21, 1783.*

Attached to the report of the committee to which was referred the petition of Simon Nathan, and referred to by the committee, is the following certificate:

"I hereby certify, that the above table of depreciation made out by Colonel Todd is just, as far as I can recollect; and all bills which were drawn by me on New Orleans, were passed at the rate of a hard dollar for every one named in the bill, and all which were drawn on the Governor or Treasurer of Virginia were for paper dollars, and understood to be at such rate of depreciation as prevailed at the time and place of drawing; the *drafts* in *livres* were at five livres to a dollar, to be paid in silver if on New Orleans, or in depreciated dollars as above, if drawn on Virginia.

G. R. CLARKE.

A copy: Archibald Blair."

Virginia,  ⎫
City of Richmond,  ⎬  *to wit:*

I, George W. Munford, Clerk of the House of Delegates and keeper of the rolls of Virginia, do hereby certify and make known, that the foregoing is a true copy of a certificate imbodied in a report of a committee, extracted from the Journal of the House of Delegates, of Saturday, June 21st, seventeen hundred and eighty-three.

Given under my hand this 23d of June, 1835.

GEORGE W. MUNFORD,<br>
C. H. D. and keeper of the rolls of Virginia.

---

F.

*Extract from the Journal of the House of Delegates, Saturday June 28, 1783.*

"Mr. Nicholas reported, from the committee to which the petition of Francis Besserton was committed, that the committee had, according to order, had the same under their consideration, and had agreed to a report, and come to several resolutions thereupon, which he read in his place, and afterwards delivered in at the Clerk's table; where the same was again twice read, and agreed to by the House as followeth:

It appears that there is due to the said Francis Besserton £5,024 10s. 6d. specie.

*Resolved,* That it is the opinion of this committee that the treasurer ought to be directed to pay to the said Francis Besserton the sum of three hundred dollars for his present relief; and that the auditors ought to issue their warrants for the balance, with an allowance of two years' interest, at the rate of five per centum per annum, to be paid out of such funds as shall be hereafter established for the payment of debts of a similar kind.

*Resolved,* That it is the opinion [of the committee] that the bill of exchange No. 9, and the certified account No. 5, ought to be returned to the petitioner.

VIRGINIA, } *to wit:*
*City of Richmond,* }

I, George W. Munford, Clerk of the House of Delegates and keeper of the rolls of the Commonwealth of Virginia, do hereby certify and make known, that the foregoing is a true copy of a part of the Journal of the House of Delegates of Virginia, of Saturday, June the twenty-eighth, seventeen hundred and eighty-three.

Given under my hand, this 23d June, 1835.

GEORGE W. MUNFORD,
*C. H. D. and Keeper of the Rolls of Virginia.*

---

### G.

*Extract from the Journal of the House of Delegates of Monday, 22d December, 1783.*

" *Resolved,* That the two-tenths of the revenue arising from the tax on free male titheables, and all taxable property included in the revenue law, which, by the appropriation act of the last session, was directed to be reserved in the treasury, subject to the future direction of the General Assembly, shall be applied as follows :

" For payments of the claim of Charlos Gratiot, amounting to £1,463 14*s.* 6*d.*, with interest from the first day of January, 1783 ; for the claim of the said Gratiot, attorney for Godfroy Linetot, amounting to £1,076 5*s.*, with interest from the 30th of June, 1783 ; for the claim of the said Gratiot, attorney for Nicholas Janis and Vital Beauvois, amounting to £525 18*s.*, with interest from the said 30th June, 1783 ; for the claim of Francis Bosseron, amounting, on his own account, to £1,039 16*s.*, and on account of Bosseron & Co. for £3,894 16*s.* 6*d.*, with interest on both sums from the 28th of June, 1781 ; for the claim of Philip Legrass for £582 18*s.*, with interest from the said 28th June, 1781 ; and for the claim of Francis Carbonneau for £861 18*s.*, with interest from the said 28th day of June, 1781, after payments shall be made (out of the said two-tenths) of the sum of two thousand pounds to Thomas Bentley, agreeable to a resolution of the present session of Assembly ; and that where warrants for the same have not already issued, the auditors do issue their warrants for the same accordingly.

" And the said resolution being read a second time, was, on the question put thereupon, agreed to by the House."

VIRGINIA, } *to wit:*
*City of Richmond,* }

I, George W. Munford, Clerk of the House of Delegates and keeper of the rolls of the Commonwealth of Virginia, do hereby certify and make known, that the foregoing is a true copy of a part of the Journal of the House of Delegates of Virginia, of Monday, the twenty-second of December, seventeen hundred and eighty-three.

Given under my hand this 23d of June, 1835.

GEORGE W. MUNFORD,
*C. H. D. and Keeper of the Rolls of Virginia.*

## H.

TREASURY DEPARTMENT,
*Third Auditor's Office, June 26,* 1835.

SIR: Your letter of the 19th instant, to the Secretary of the Treasury, has this day been referred to this office, and, in reply to the inquiries therein made, I have to state that there are no existing accounts which will furnish the information you call for. The expenses of the Illinois regiment, defrayed by the State of Virginia, would, it is presumed, appear in the accounts of that State against the United States, which have been destroyed.

Very respectfully,
PETER HAGNER, *Auditor.*

HENRY A. WISE,
*Accomac Court-house, Eastern shore, Va.*

---

### No. 1.

RICHMOND, *January* 21, 1836.

DEAR SIR: Will you have the goodness to inform me under what circumstances a mass of papers "throwing much light" on the subject "of claims for supplies" furnished in the "Illinois campaign of 1778–'9," were found in the "attic story of the Capitol, in 1833, and what has been the subsequent action of the "Virginia Legislature" since that time, and subsequent to Mr. Gilmer's appointment in 1831. Any information you can give me on this subject will confer a great favor.

With sentiments of respect, your obedient humble servant,
JOHN LAW.

JOHN H. SMITH, Esq.,
*Commissioner of Revolutionary Claims.*

---

### No. 2.

RICHMOND, *January* 28, 1836.

DEAR SIR: In answer to your interrogatory contained in your note dated 21st January, 1836, I have to say: That in the year 1833 there was a large mass of papers connected with the "Illinois campaign" under Colonel Clarke, in the year 1778–'9, found in the attic story of the Capitol, where they had lain unnoticed and unknown for many years. By a resolution of the General Assembly, I was appointed "Commissioner of Revolutionary Claims," and took said papers into my care and custody, where they have been ever since, except when in possession of the auditor of public accounts. The act of the Legislature, a certified copy of which you have, will show the action of the Legislature in relation to those claims. I have every reason to believe that the resolution and act of the Virginia Legislature would not have passed, had not those papers been discovered. They were found subsequent to Mr. Gilmer's appointment as agent on the part of the State.

Very respectfully, yours, &c.
JOHN H. SMITH.

No. 3.

I hereby certify that among the papers connected with the "Illinois campaign" of 1778–'9, under the command of Colonel George R. Clarke, found in the attic story of the capitol in 1833, and which papers are now in my possession and custody, and, ever since their discovery as aforesaid, have been in my custody and possession, as "commissioner of revolutionary claims," and in the custody of the auditor of public accounts, &c., I find the account current Colonel George R. Clarke, as commander of said expedition, as settled with Virginia, for "expenses incurred, and disbursements made," in that campaign: as well also as the "original account current" of Oliver Pollock, the agent of Virginia at New Orleans, as settled by him with the State of Virginia, "for bills drawn, disbursements made, and moneys advanced," by said Pollock, on account of Virginia, in relation to the "Illinois campaign," and on other accounts; and that neither in the account of Colonel Clarke, nor Mr. Pollock, as settled with Virginia, is there any credit allowed, or charge made, either by Colonel Clarke or Mr. Pollock, for a bill of exchange drawn in 1778, by said Clarke, on Pollock, as the agent of Virginia, at New Orleans, for $8,616, in favor of Francis Vigo; but that the other bills mentioned in the said Vigo's memorial to Congress, to wit: one for $298, one for $921, and one for $1,442, are mentioned in both the accounts of Clarke and Pollock as settled by them with the State of Virginia, and credited said Pollock on the settlement with the State.

                                 JOHN H. SMITH, *Commissioner, &c.*

JANUARY 29, 1836.

---

DECEMBER 22, 1837.

The Committee on Revolutionary Claims, to which was referred, a second time, the petition of Robert Pollard, administrator of Philip Quarles, with additional documents, report:

That since their report of the 19th of January, additional evidence has been adduced from the auditor's office of the State of Virginia, showing more at large how the alleged mistake occurred. The amount of Mr. Heath's (the auditor general's) statement, is this:

| | |
|---|---:|
| That judgment was rendered for half pay from 6th of February, 1781, to 22d of February, 1804, 23 years and 16 days, which, at $160 per year, amounted to  -  -  - | $3,686 66 |
| In being ascertained, after judgment, that his half pay had been received by him up to 1st of February, 1783, to wit, 2 years, it should be deducted  -  -  -  -  - | 320 00 |
| And that the true balance due is  -  -  -  - | $3,366 66 |
| But in the estimates prepared by the auditor, by some error in calculation, Quarles's judgment was carried out for  - | 3,020 00 |
| | $346 66 |

The auditor admits that various errors were committed in making out the several amounts due upon the judgments obtained in the court of Virginia, &c. Upon this statement of the case, and upon the further evidence showing how the alleged mistake occurred, which was deficient in the proof furnished before, on which the former report was predicated, the committee have concluded to report a bill for the $346 66, but no interest.

### DECEMBER 22, 1837.

Upon a re-examination of the claim of the legal representatives of Major Tarlton Woodson, deceased, the Committee on Revolutionary Claims adopt the accompanying report, made at a former session, and report a bill for their relief.

### APRIL 6, 1836.

The Committee on Revolutionary Claims, to which was referred the petition of Charles Woodson, executor of Major Charles Woodson, report:

That the petitioner prays the passage of a law directing to be paid to him the sum of $250 66, the balance appearing to be due to Major Tarlton Woodson, on an account rendered by the commissioner of army accounts, on the 10th February, 1791.

It appears, that at the period when Major Woodson's account was stated by the commissioner, all such claims received the action of the officers of the Treasury, before any balance found due was paid.

The certificates of the Third Auditor, and of the Register of the Treasury, show that this account was not paid subsequent to the 10th February, 1791. That it was not paid at that time, and previous, the reason is obvious, and appears from the records.

The claim of Major Woodson was considered as barred by the statute of limitation of the 2d November, 1785. The committee, therefore, report a bill for the relief of his legal representatives.

### TREASURY DEPARTMENT,
#### *Register's Office, January 26, 1836.*

SIR: The claim of Major Tarlton Woodson, adjusted by the acting commissioner of army accounts, on the 10th February, 1791, and which, in consequence of its not having been presented within the period limited by the resolution of Congress of the 2d November, 1785, was not at that time paid, does not appear, from the records of this office, to have been liquidated under any subsequent act of Congress.

I have the honor to be, sir, your obedient servant,

T. L. SMITH.

Hon. GEO. L. KINNARD.

### DECEMBER 22, 1837.

The Committee on Revolutionary Claims, to which was referred the memorial of John Turner, of Norwich, in the State of Connecticut, son of Doctor Philip Turner, deceased, on behalf of himself and the other heirs at law of the said Doctor Philip Turner, report:

That it appears from the documents that Doctor Philip Turner was an hospital physician and surgeon in the revolutionary army, and that at the close of the war he demanded his five years' full pay, as the commutation of half pay for life, to which he conceived himself entitled. It also appears that the officer appointed to settle the accounts of the hospital and medical departments differed with Doctor Turner as to his right to commutation, and refused to make him the allowance. Doctor Turner made repeated attempts to get the officer to reverse his dedision, but without success. He at length appealed to Congress, and Congress differed from the commissioner of the hospital department, reversed his decision, and passed an act allowing Doctor Turner his commutation, on the 22d April, 1808. Nothing was said in the act respecting the interest, and the Treasury officers refused to allow the interest : and it is for the allowance of this interest that the present petition is presented.

It is a uniform principle with the committee, in claims for commutation, to allow interest in cases where the principal was demanded in due time, and the party had been kept out of his just rights by the act of the officer of the Government. Such, by the decision of Congress itself, appears to have been the fact in this case ; as Congress allowed the claim in 1808, and it is abundantly proved by the original papers that it was demanded as long ago as 1783, the very earliest period at which it could be demanded.

This petition was before the committee at the last Congress, and was favorably reported on. That report your committee now refer to, and pray may be taken as part of this report. The bill which accompanied that report passed the House of Representatives on the 15th February, 1834, and was not finally acted upon by the Senate.

The committee think, according to established principles, the petitioners are fairly entitled to their interest ; for the payment of which, they herewith report a bill.

---

DECEMBER 22, 1837.

The Committee on Revolutionary Claims, to which was referred the memorial of Samuel Richards, of the city of Philadelphia, executor of William T. Smith, late of said city, deceased, report :

That it appears that, in the revolutionary war, William T. Smith was a merchant, and resided in the island of St. Eustacia, and shipped to the United States large quantities of coarse woollens, of which the country and the public service stood in great need at that time ; the proceeds of which goods he loaned to the United States, and received loan-office certificates therefore. Among these certificates were sixteen issued from the loan offices in South Carolina and Georgia, of the numbers, dates, and amounts given in a schedule which accompanies the memorial; which sixteen certificates, it appears, were lost or mislaid by the said William T. Smith in the year 1790. In 1794, Mr. Smith applied to the loan offices in South Carolina and Georgia, and ascertained that no one had offered the certificates to be funded; and it was found that they had not been. In 1798, Mr. Smith, through Mr. Fitzsimmons, a member of Congress from the city of Philadelphia, applied at the Treasury for relief, which he could not obtain, as Congress alone were competent to grant relief in the case of lost certificates. Accordingly, in 1804, Mr. Smith presented his petition to Congress, and, no action being had upon it, it was renewed at the succeeding session. Mr. Smith died in the year 1805, and his petition, with the original papers, have remained on the files of the House of Representatives from that time; which fact, the executor states, was unknown to him till a short time ago, when he immediately revived the claim on behalf of the estate of his testator.

It appears by the certificate of the Register of the Treasury of the United States, dated on the 15th day of December, 1836, and which accompanies this report, that these certificates (being the same mentioned in the list which accompanied the memorial of Mr. Smith, presented to Congress in his lifetime) are still outstanding and unpaid; which fact being clearly established to the satisfaction of the committee, they are of opinion the specie value of the certificates, amounting, according to the certificate of the Treasury, to eight hundred and eleven dollars, ought to be paid to the legal representative of William T. Smith, with the interest due thereon; for which purpose the committee herewith report a bill.

*Loan-office certificates.*

| No. | Date. | Loan office. | To whom payable. | Nominal amount. | Specie value. |
|---|---|---|---|---|---|
| 6895 | Dec. 1, 1778 | Georgia | Samuel Jack | $300 | $51 74 |
| 6896 | do. | do. | do. | 300 | 51 74 |
| 6897 | do. | do. | do. | 300 | 51 74 |
| 6898 | do. | do. | do. | 300 | 51 74 |
| 6899 | do. | do. | do. | 300 | 51 74 |
| 6900 | do. | do. | do. | 300 | 51 74 |
| 6901 | do. | do. | do. | 300 | 51 74 |
| 6902 | do. | do. | do. | 300 | 51 74 |
| 9175 | Dec. 20, 1778 | do. | Robert W. Jones | 200 | 28 58 |
| 9285 | do. | do. | John Glenn | 200 | 28 58 |
| 9287 | do. | do. | do. | 200 | 28 58 |
| 9288 | do. | do. | do. | 200 | 28 58 |
| 9293 | do. | do. | do. | 200 | 28 58 |
| 9294 | do. | do. | do. | 200 | 28 58 |
| 312 | Nov. 12, 1779 | S. Carolina | Wm. Smith and Joseph Darrell | 5,000 | 208 05 |
| 158 | do. | do. | do. | 400 | 16 58 |

TREASURY DEPARTMENT,
*Register's Office, December* 15, 1836.

This is to certify that it appears, from the books of this office, that the loan-office certificates mentioned and described in the above list are still outstanding and unpaid.

T. L. SMITH, *Register.*

---

DECEMBER 22, 1837.

The Committee on Revolutionary Claims, to which the petition of Samuel Young was referred, report:

That this case was examined by this committee, and a favorable report made thereon, on the 31st of January, 1835, which is hereto annexed, and made part of this report. The case has been re-examined by the committee; and, concurring in the opinion heretofore expressed, a bill is reported for the relief of the heirs and legal representatives of Joseph Young, deceased.

The Committee on Revolutionary Claims, to which the petition of Samuel Young, report :

That the petitioner, as one of the heirs of Joseph Young, deceased, asks compensation for the destruction of the house, barn, and out-houses of his father, by the enemy, during the revolutionary war. It appears from the testimony, that the house of Joseph Young, situate in Westchester county, in the State of New York, and near the lines, was occupied from the autumn of 1776, to February, 1780, by American troops, and as a place of deposite for military stores. In 1778, a detachment stationed there, commanded by Captain Williams, was attacked and defeated by the enemy. Captain Williams and several of his men, together with Joseph Young, were taken prisoners. After obtaining possession of the house, the barn was burnt down by the enemy. In February, 1780, Colonel Thompson, then commanding at that post, was attacked by a superior force, and, after a severe contest, in which fifty of his command were killed or wounded, was compelled to surrender. The house and out-houses were burnt by the British after the surrender. This case has been heretofore investigated by this committee. An unfavorable report was made in 1826, and a similar one in 1828. The impolicy of opening the treasury to claims of this description, after so great a lapse of time, is urged in both those reports. A reference is also made to the resolution of Congress of June 3, 1784, that the subject of making compensation to citizens of the United States for damages done by the enemy, or by the wanton and unauthorized acts of the American army, should be submitted to the States, and such relief granted, at their own expense, as they should think requisite ; and if it should afterwards appear reasonable that the United States should make an allowance to any particular State who might be burdened much beyond others, Congress should determine such allowance. The inference is drawn, that, if this claim had been well founded, it would have been presented to and allowed by the State of New York. The certificate of the comptroller of the State of New York shows that no allowance has been made by that State to Joseph Young or his representatives. By the act of Congress of August 10, 1790, no claim of any citizen could be admitted as a charge against the United States, in the account of any State, unless the same was allowed by the State before the 24th of September, 1788. A period of little more than four years was allowed to Joseph Young to make his application to the State of New York. He was made prisoner in 1778; released, after a year's captivity, with a broken constitution, and died in 1789. Colonel Burr certifies, that, in 1793, he, then being a Senator of the United States from the State of New York, received a letter from the petitioner, requesting his attention to this claim ; but Colonel Burr is unable to state what disposition was made of the subject. The failure to present this claim within the period limited, seems to be accounted for by the situation of the country, and the peculiar circumstances of the case. The question now presented is, whether the United States ought not to compensate a citizen for the loss of his propriety, exposed to peculiar danger by the act of the Government. One of the witnesses, Isaac Webbers, states that General McDougal's object in occupying the house, &c.,

of Joseph Young with a body of American troops, was to check plundering parties of the refugees, and to serve as a rallying point for the militia of the neighborhood, and that he promised remuneration to Joseph Young for any loss which he might sustain in consequence. Without undertaking to determine how far this promise was obligatory on the United States, the long-continued occupation of this house, &c., as a military post, and its subsequent destruction in consequence of such occupation, furnish a strong claim on the liberality of the United States for remuneration. The destruction of these buildings was not one of those wanton outrages for which Governments cannot be responsible; they were destroyed in consequence of being occupied as a military post, when other buildings in the neighborhood were uninjured. This occupation was not casual and temporary—it was maintained for four years; and though during this period the American troops were compelled, by the superior force of the enemy, to abandon this post in two instances, it was again reoccupied, and held until its complete destruction.

The allowance of this claim cannot furnish a precedent for other claims for destruction of property by the enemy, unless they present equally strong grounds for relief. The danger of such a precedent, whatever it may be, has been already incurred, for relief has been granted by Congress in similar cases. The committee therefore report a bill in favor of the heirs of Joseph Young, deceased. The value of the buildings destroyed is estimated at from four to five thousand dollars. The lowest estimate, four thousand dollars, made by Colonel Burr, does not include the barn. The committee have taken the sum of four thousand three hundred and twenty dollars, the estimate of the petitioner, as the full value of the buildings destroyed. The committee have made no allowance for the furniture, grain, &c., destroyed with the buildings, as the amount and value of that property are shown only by the testimony of the petitioner.

The petitioner also claims compensation for his services as a guide to the continental troops on the lines for five months, and also for sixty days' services on the lines. The evidence is not considered by the committee sufficient to sustain the claim for payment for those services. The committee are not aware of any obstacle to the presentment and settlement of this claim at the proper time.

NOTE.—The committee, upon the evidence being re-examined, think that $3,100 only should be allowed for the property destroyed.

---

### DECEMBER 22, 1837.

The Committee on Revolutionary Claims, to which the petition of the heirs and devisees of Col. Willis Reddick, deceased, was referred, report:

That this case was referred to this committee, and a favorable report made thereon, on the 17th April, 1834, which is hereto annexed, and made part of this report. The committee have again examined this case, and, concurring in the opinion before expressed, report a bill for the relief of the petitioners.

The Committee on Revolutionary Claims, to which was referred the pe
tition of the heirs and devisees of Colonel Willis Reddick, decesed, report :
The petitioners state that in the spring of 1779, a detachment of British
troops marched from Norfolk, in the State of Virginia, towards Suffolk, in
Nansemond county, where a quantity of public property, consisting of
about one thousand barrels of pork, and a considerable quantity of beef,
were stored, with the intention, as was supposed, of taking possession of or
destroying that property. Colonel Willis Reddick was then colonel commandant of the militia of Nansemond county, and, to secure this property,
consented that it should be removed from Suffolk to his dwelling-house
and premises. The enemy, having discovered the removal of the property,
proceeded to the residence of Colonel Reddick, and set fire to his dwelling,
barn, and outhouses, in which the said public property was stored, and
destroyed not only the public property and the buildings, but his furniture,
corn, bacon, &c. The petitioner asks compensation for the loss thus sustained. There is no direct evidence to show why this public property was
deposited in the house and outhouses of Col. Reddick ; but the fact of its
being so deposited, and the destruction by the enemy of the dwelling-house,
barn, and outhouses, of Col. Reddick, together with his furniture and
other personal property, is fully established by the testimony of Zaccheus
Lupiter, Henry Skinner, Christian Williamson, William Faulke, Wm.
Writer, and Henry Harrison. These witnesses concur in the opinion that
the destruction of Col. Reddick's property was in consequence of the public stores being deposited in his dwelling-house, and other buildings ; and
they assign a satisfactory reason for this opinion—that no other private
property was destroyed by the enemy in this incursion. They estimate
the loss of Colonel Reddick at from eight to ten thousand dollars; his
dwelling-house is represented to have been one of the best in the county.
The committee are satisfied that the dwelling-house and other buildings
of Col. Reddick were destroyed by the enemy, in consequence of having
been made the depository of the public stores. The Auditor of the State
of Virginia has certified that, on an examination of the books and papers
in his office, he can find no entry or other evidence that compensation has
been made to Col. W. Reddick for this destruction of his property by the
enemy, or that any claim has been presented for compensation. That
Col. Reddick believed he had a just claim to compensation for the loss he
had sustained, is apparent from the following clause in his will, dated
April 10, 1781, and proved on the 8th of April, 1782 : " Whereas I have
reason to judge that the General Assembly of this State will think it just that
a proper allowance should be made me for the damage I have sustained
in the burning and destroying of my houses by the British forces ; in such
case, I give whatever the said allowance may be (if any) unto my son
Willis and his heirs forever." The committee are aware of the objections to claims of this description, arising from the great lapse of time,
and from the impolicy of establishing a precedent which may bring forward many similar claims still outstanding and unsettled. The question
of policy has been settled by Congress, in the case of the widow and
heirs of William Dewees. In 1817, compensation was made to them for
buildings and other property destroyed by the enemy at Valley Forge, in
1777. That case, according to the report of the committee, differs from

the present one in these particulars : the claim was exhibited to the Board
of Treasury within the period limited by the acts of Congress, and the
buildings of Mr. Dewees were occupied by the public as a deposite for
military stores, contrary to the wishes and remonstrances of the owner.
In this case no such early application was made, owing, probably, to the
death of Col. Reddick. But the statute of limitations is not interposed as
a bar to other revolutionary claims, and the committee know no reason why claims of this description should be distinguished from all others.
That this public property was stored in Col. Reddick's house and other
buildings with his assent, as is stated in the petition, does not, in the
opinion of the committee, affect the claim to compensation for the loss
sustained in consequence of such occupation. From the description of
that part of the country, it appears that Col. Reddick's house was not near
any public road, nor visible from any part of a private road which passed
through that neighborhood ; it was, therefore, naturally selected as a place
of greater security for the public property than the town of Suffolk. If,
as the petition states, Col. Reddick had the command in that district, it was
his duty to take all the measures in his power to secure the public property ; but if the occupation of his buildings cannot be considered as an
official act, his willingness to encounter the hazard to promote the public
interest was an act of patriotism which ought not to operate to his prejudice. From this view of the subject, the committee consider that a just
compensation for the loss sustained should be made to the representatives
of Colonel Reddick. In fixing the amount of that compensation, they
have taken the lowest estimate of the witnesses, without interest, which,
in their opinion, should not be allowed upon any unsettled and unliquidated claims.

And they report a bill accordingly.

---

DECEMBER 22, 1837.

The Committee on Revolutionary Claims, to which were referred the
petition of the heirs of Nathaniel Tracy, deceased, and the resolution instructing said committee to inquire into the expediency of allowing to
the heirs or legal representatives of Thomas Gordon, deceased, a sum of
money due him for services rendered during the revolutionary war,
report :

That, on the 7th of February, 1778, two certificates, No. 5167 for
$122 29, and No. 1240 for $611 57, both specie value, and with interest,
together amounting to the sum of $733 86, were issued from the loan
office of the United States to Nathaniel Tracy, deceased, late of Newbury-
port, Massachusetts. Those certificates have been lost, but they remain
on the books of the Treasury unsatisfied, as appears by the certificate of
the Secretary of the Treasury. The committee, therefore, report a bill for
their payment.

A certificate was issued on the 29th of July, 1782, by Timothy Pickering, quartermaster general, countersigned by Samuel Postlethwait, assistant deputy quartermaster, stating that there was due from the United
States to Mr. Thomas Gordon $19$\frac{18}{90}$, for nine days' hire of a four-horse
team, and thirteen and a half loads of wood, with interest at the rate of

six per cent. per annum, from the 5th day of April, 1781. The Register of the Treasury states that there are no records in his office by which the said certificate can be ascertained to be genuine, although it bears all the evidence on the face of it of its being so. Certificates of the same character were authorized to be liquidated by Jonathan Burrell, appointed a commissioner under the resolve of Congress of the 8th of May, 1786, and the certificates issued by Mr. Burrell were fundable under the 3d section of the act of 4th August, 1790. Had this certificate been liquidated, of which there is no record, it would have been cancelled.

The committee, being satisfied that the certificate is genuine and unpaid, report a bill for its payment.

---

### December 22, 1837.

The Committee on Revolutionary Claims, to which was referred the petition of the heirs of Peter Helphenston, deceased, report :

The petitioners, heirs of Peter Helphenston, deceased, ask for the seven years' half pay promised by the resolve of Congress, passed August 24, 1780, to the widow or orphans of those officers who died in the service of the United States.

They represent that their ancestor entered the service at the commencement of the Revolution, and continued therein until his death ; and that neither they nor his widow ever received the half pay promised under the above resolve.

In support of the above allegations, the following testimony has been submitted : 1st. A certificate from Generals Muhlenberg and Wood, of the continental line of the army, in which it is stated that Helphenston was appointed major of the 8th Virginia regiment (Muhlenberg's) in December, 1775, and joined in April, 1776 ; that he continued in active service in South Carolina until after the battle at Sullivan's island, when, having contracted a painful disease, he was furloughed, with the approbation of General Lee, until his health should be re-established ; that he never rejoined his regiment, but died at Winchester, Virginia ; that he never resigned ; and that the vacancy caused in the regiment by his death was not filled until that event became known.

2d. A commission from the committee of safety of Virginia, dated March, 1776, of major.

3d. A certificate from the Register of the Treasury, showing that Peter Helphenston appears, from a list of Virginia continental officers, to have been a major.

4th. The affidavits of Henry Butler, Margaret Cooley, and John Smith, showing that Peter Helphenston was a major in the continental line of the Revolution, and returned home sick, and never recovered.

5th. A certificate from the Commissioner of the General Land Office, showing that the representatives of Major Peter Helphenston, of the Virginia continental line, received bounty land as such from that State.

6th. A letter from the Third Auditor, stating that it appears, from "a list of payments made by the State of Virginia, on account of seven years' half pay granted to the widows and children of officers dying in the service," furnished by the Auditor of Virginia, that "Catharine Helphenston, widow of Major Peter Helphenston, a continental officer who died in the service," was allowed £40 for her present relief, and a pension of £20 per annum, for five years, by a resolution of the Assembly, passed November 27, 1782, all of which she received. The last payment was made June 12, 1787."

7th. A certificate from Frederick county court, stating that it was proved to the satisfaction of that court that Peter Helphenston was a major in the Virginia continental line, and died in that county whilst on furlough, from a disease contracted during active service; that he left a widow, who is since dead, and several children and grandchildren, named, who are the heirs at law of Major Peter Helphenston.

From this evidence, the committee are satisfied that Peter Helphenston was a major in the 8th Virginia regiment on continental establishment; that he died in service; and that his heirs are in consequence entitled to seven years' half pay, promised under such circumstances. A bill is, therefore, reported for the relief of the petitioners; but as a portion of the amount has already been paid by the State of Virginia, there is a proviso added, deducting that amount.

---

### December 22, 1837.

The Committee on Revolutionary Claims, to which was referred the petition of the legal representatives of Wadleigh Noyes, report:

The petitioners are the children of Wadleigh Noyes, an officer of the continental line of the army of the Revolution, slain by the enemy whilst in the service, and, as such, claim the seven years' half pay promised by the resolution of Congress of August 24, 1780, in these words: "That the resolution of the 15th of May, 1778, granting half pay for seven years to the officers of the army who should continue in the service to the end of the war, be extended to the widows of those officers who have died, or shall hereafter die, in the service, to commence from the time of such officer's death, and to continue for the term of seven years; or if there be no widow, or in case of her death or intermarriage, the said half pay to be given to the orphan children of the officer dying, as aforesaid, if he he shall have left any."

The evidence submitted satisfactorily proves that Wadleigh Noyes was a lieutenant in Wesson's regiment of the Massachusetts continental line, and that he was slain by the enemy on the 27th day of October, 1777, at or near Stillwater, in the State of New York. The committee are satisfied that he left a widow and several children; that the widow is now deceased, and that the seven years' half pay claimed has never been paid, either by the United States or the State of Massachusetts, to the widow or orphan children of said Lieutenant Noyes. For this fact the committee rely upon a statement made by the Third Auditor of the Treasury, in a letter addressed to their chairman. A bill is therefore reported for the relief of the petitioners.

The Committee on Revolutionary Claims, to which was referred the petition of the heirs of James Conway, deceased, report:

The petitioners are the heirs at law of James Conway, deceased, late a lieutenant in the continental line of the army of the Revolution. They claim, as such, the seven years' half pay allowed by the resolution of August 24, 1780, to the widows or orphan children of such officers "as have died, or may hereafter die in the service."

It appears from records on file in the Third Auditor's office, that James Conway was a lieutenant of the 6th Virginia regiment on continental establishment, and that he died in the service. The same fact is testified to by several credible witnesses on oath, who also depose that he left, at the time of his death, a widow and four children. The committee are satisfied that the seven years' half pay, to which the widow or children of Lieut. Conway became entitled by reason of his dying in the service of his country, has never been paid to either of them. The widow being deceased, a bill is reported for the relief of the children, heirs of Lieut. Conway.

---

DECEMBER 22, 1837.

The Committee on Revolutionary Claims, to which the case of the heirs of Lieutenant Colonel Henry Irwin, deceased, was referred, report:

That it appears from the certificate of William Hill, Secretary of State of North Carolina, that the muster-rolls of the continental line of that State, in the revolutionary war, show that Henry Irwin, lieutenant colonel of the 5th regiment, was commissioned on the 15th of April, 1776, and killed on the 4th day of October, 1777. The following entry is found in the journal of the Continental Congress of May 7, 1776: "The convention of North Carolina having recommended sundry gentlemen for field officers of the sixth battalion, raised in that colony, Congress proceeded to a choice, and the following gentlemen were elected: (among others,) Henry Irwin, Esquire, lieutenant colonel of the 5th battalion." Colonel Irwin was killed at the battle of Germantown, leaving a widow and five children. On the 13th of April, 1810, his children and heirs obtained the bounty land promised by Congress in the resolution of 16th September, 1776. The committee are satisfied, from these facts, that the children of Colonel Irwin (his widow being dead) are entitled to the seven years' half pay promised by Congress to the widows and orphan children of officers dying in the service; and report a bill accordingly.

---

DECEMBER 22, 1837.

The Committee on Revolutionary Claims, to which was referred the petition of the heirs of Lieutenant Colonel Richard Campbell, report:

Lieutenant Colonel Campbell was a highly meritorious and brave officer of the army of the Revolution. He entered into the Virginia continental line at an early period of the war, and continued in the service until the battle at the Eutaw springs, when he was slain gallantly leading the Virginia brigade, in a charge upon the British line. His gallant conduct and death is a matter of history. Marshall thus speaks of it, vol. 4, page 551 : "Colonel Williams and Lieutenant Colonel Campbell were ordered to charge with trailed arms. These orders were executed with the most determined courage, under a tremendous fire of artillery and musketry." "Among the slain was Lieutenant Colonel Campbell, who fell while leading the Virginia brigade to that bold and decisive charge which broke the British line. He just lived long enough to hear that the enemy were retreating, and his last breath was employed in expressing the joy that event had given him. The death of this gallant officer was deplored by General Greene in terms which evinced a high respect for his memory."

His heirs claim the benefit of the resolve of August 24, 1780, granting seven years' half pay to the widows and orphan children of officers dying in the service. It appears, however, that the State of Virginia paid to the widow of Colonel Campbell, of this half pay, three years three months and twenty-five days, so much having been due to her up to the time of her intermarriage ; at which time the balance vested in, and became payable to, her children, according to the tenor of the resolution of August 24, 1780. This balance appearing unpaid, and the children of Colonel Campbell being undoubtedly entitled to it, a bill is accordingly reported for their relief.

---

## December 22, 1837.

The Committee on Revolutionary Claims, to which was referred the petition of the heirs of John Chilton, deceased, report :

The petitioners are the only children and heirs at law of Captain John Chilton, deceased, who, they say, was killed in the battle of Brandywine, and as such ask the seven years' half pay promised by the resolution of August 24, 1780, to the widow, or, in case of her death or intermarriage, to the orphan children, of those officers who have died, or shall hereafter die in the service.

It appears, from the evidence submitted to the committee, that John Chilton was a captain in the third regiment Virginia continental line, and was slain in the battle at Brandywine, on the 11th of September, 1779; that he left at his death no widow, but several orphan children, who are the petitioners in this case. It appears, also, that the heirs of Captain Chilton have received the bounty land from the United States to which officers slain by the enemy were entitled, and also the land to which they had claim from the State of Virginia.

The committee, believing the claim fully established, and having satisfied themselves that it has never been paid, either by the United States or the State of Virginia, report a bill for the relief of the petitioners.

DECEMBER 22, 1837.

The Committee on Revolutionary Claims, to which was referred the petition of the heirs of Joshua Fanning, report:

The petitioners are the surviving children of Mary Fanning Hibbs, who was the only child of Lieutenant Joshua Fanning. They state that their ancestor was one of three brothers, who, with their father, entered the naval service of the United States, and perished in the revolutionary contest: the father on board a British prison-ship ; the one brother in the Trumbull frigate ; the other as an officer of a tender to the Randolph ; and the last, whose immediate descendants they are, in the unfortunate Randolph. The mother, unable to bear up under the loss of her husband and all her children, shortly after their fate was ascertained, died also, of a broken heart. The wife of Lieutenant Joshua Fanning survived the lamentable fate of her husband but two years, and left their mother, an infant of four years, who was reared and sustained by the kindness and compassion of pitying friends and relatives. Having never in any way experienced the bounty of their country, they now ask what they deem justly due them, and what others, similarly situated, have never been refused. They ask the seven years' half pay to which the widow or orphan children of officers who died in the service became entitled under the resolution of August 25, 1780.

In examining the evidence submitted, the committee find the above allegations confirmed, and the following circumstances substantiated : Joshua Fanning entered the naval service of the United States at an early period of the revolutionary war, and, after serving in different vessels, became a lieutenant in the Randolph frigate, Captain Biddle, as early as 1776. He continued with that continental vessel, and sailed in her from Charleston on her last cruise, in which, on the 9th of March, 1778, in an engagement with the British man-of-war Yarmouth, off Barbadoes, she was blown up ; the whole of her officers, with a crew of 350 men, perishing. The fate of the Randolph, with her officers and crew, is a matter of historical record, and cannot be doubted. That Joshua Fanning sailed in her as a lieutenant, is rendered certain by the testimony of several respectable witnesses. Charles Biddle, brother to the captain of the Randolph, states that he was at Charleston shortly before the Randolph sailed on her last cruise; and "at that time I remember that Lieutenant Fanning was an officer on board of her. I have always understood that he sailed in the Randolph, and was lost in her." Richard Fordham, master carpenter of the Randolph, and left at Charleston to superintend the building of some boats, when she sailed on her last cruise, testifies, "that in the capacity of master carpenter he well knew Lieutenant Fanning, who, to his certain knowledge, then actually sailed on board said vessel as an officer, and was undoubtedly blown up with said ship." There can be no doubt that Lieutenant Fanning perished on board the Randolph. The committee are also satisfied from the evidence that he left a widow, who shortly afterwards died, leaving an orphan child of four years; that the petitioners are the lawful heirs ; and that they have never received what they now claim, nor any portion of it.

The case appears to be a strong one, and has been before Congress since 1807, without receiving any action, owing, not to want of merit, but an unfortunate combination of circumstances and delays. The committee have no doubt that it falls within the principle of the resolution of

Congress adopted August 24, 1780, whereby seven years' half pay was granted to the widow, or, in case of her death or intermarriage, to the orphan children of such officers as have died, or shall hereafter die, in the service of the United States.

The committee are aware that in this clause no allusion is made in terms to the officers of the navy, but they cannot believe that they were intended to be excluded. It must be remembered that, as a distinct arm of the national defence, the navy was not recognised by Congress during the revolutionary war, and that the Navy Department itself was not organized until April, 1798. It may, therefore, be reasonably inferred that individuals engaged in the naval as well as the land service at that period were included by Government under one general military head, and that the word *navy*, in the resolution of August, 1780, was not deemed necessary. It could never have been the intention of Congress to make an unfair and invidious distinction between the widows and orphans of those brave men who fell in defence of their country's rights. Later experience favors this construction, for, to say nothing of the act of January, 1813, which expressly provides for the widows and children of officers of the navy or marines killed or dying of wounds in the line of their duty, the pension laws of 1792, 1803, 1806, 1818, and 1832, apply alike to the soldier and sailor. Congress has indeed recognised the construction given by the committee, through the passage of an act for the relief of Ann Mortimer Barron, (approved June 30, 1834,) who was the orphan child of Lieutenant William Barron, killed in the service during the revolutionary war, while acting as lieutenant of the frigate Boston.

The committee are of the opinion that the half pay of a first lieutenant of a frigate for seven years ought to be allowed to the petitioners, and have accordingly reported a bill for that purpose.

---

## December 22, 1837.

The Committee on Revolutionary Claims, to which was referred the petition of the heirs of William B. Bunting, have had the same under their consideration, and report :

That the petitioners represent that William B. Bunting, their ancestor, was an ensign in the ninth Virginia regiment of the army of the Revolution on continental establishment, and that he died while engaged as such officer in that service ; and pray Congress to allow them the seven years' half-pay promised by the resolution of the 24th of August, 1780, to the widows and orphan children of those officers who had died, or should hereafter die, in that service.

In support of the claim, the following evidence has been adduced :

1st. The affidavit of Samuel Waples; which states that the affiant was a lieutenant in the Virginia continental line, in the revolutionary war; that William B. Bunting was commissioned as an ensign in Captain John Cropper's company of the ninth Virginia regiment, in the latter part of 1775 or first of 1776 ; that said Bunting marched with the said regiment to the North in December, 1776, and died at the hospital in Philadelphia in 1777 or 1778, as he was informed by the soldiers then in the hospital ; and of which fact he has not the slightest doubt.

2d. The certificate of John Cropper, jun., formerly lieutenant colonel commandant of the eleventh Virginia regiment, (this certificate is extracted from the records of the Executive Department of Virginia,) which exhibits a list of the names of sundry officers and soldiers of the Virginia line, who served in the army of the United States to the end of the revolutionary war, in which list is found the name of " ensign William B. Bunting," with this remark connected: " No warrant—died in the army."

And 3d. An extract from the records of the same department of the State of Virginia ; which, together with the extract above referred to, is certified by William H. Richardson, the Secretary of that Commonwealth.

This latter extract exhibits a list of names, among which is " Ensign William B. Bunting's R.," (the letter R evidently stands for representatives;) at the bottom of which list is this remark : " Allowed, June 15, 1807."

The committee are satisfied that the latter list of names was intended to designate those whose right to bounty land from Virginia had been favorably passed on.

In addition to the foregoing evidence, the committee, in reply to a call for information in regard to the case, have received a letter from the Third Auditor, by which it appears that William B. Bunting was appointed a lieutenant in the Virginia line, on the 31st of August, 1776, and that he died on the 1st of April, 1777 ; and that there is nothing on the files of his office going to show that the widow of William B. Bunting, or any other person, ever received the seven years' half pay due on account of his death in the service. The committee, therefore, think the evidence fully establishes the facts that William B. Bunting was first an ensign, and afterwards a lieutenant, in the continental line of the army of the Revolution, and that he died in the service whilst he was a lieutenant ; and as nothing appears to raise the presumption that the seven years' half pay due in such cases has been paid, the committee report a bill in favor of William Core, Edward Core, and Margaret Core, who are, by the circuit superior court of law and chancery for the county of Accomac, in the State of Virginia, certified to be the grandchildren and only heirs of the said William B. Bunting.

---

DECEMBER 22, 1837.

The Committee on Revolutionary Claims, to which was referred the petition of Frederick Knowlton and the other children, heirs of Col. Thomas Knowlton, deceased, report :

That Thomas Knowlton, the father of the petitioners, entered the service of the United States in the war of the Revolution, in 1775 ; was soon after appointed a major in the 20th regiment, commonly called Durkee's regiment ; and that, on the 10th day of August, 1776, he was appointed by Congress a lieutenant colonel of the same regiment, and was killed in service on the 16th day of September, 1776, on the commencement of the battle at Harlem heights, much regretted on account of his valor and virtue. These facts are fully proved by extracts from the returns in the Departments, the journals of the Continental Congress, and affidavits filed with the petition. It is also proved that Colonel Knowlton left a widow and eight children, and that his widow died in 1808 : wherefore, the petitioners, his children, pray for the seven years' half-pay promised in such cases by the resolution of Congress of 24th of August, 1780. On these facts the committee report a bill for their relief.

---

## DECEMBER 22, 1837.

The Committee on Revolutionary Claims having again considered the claim of the legal representatives of Captain James Purvis, deceased, adopt the report heretofore made in this case, and offer a bill for their relief.

## MARCH 1, 1837.

The Committee on Revolutionary Claims, to which was referred the petition of the legal representatives of James Purvis, deceased, report :

That it appears from the evidence, that James Purvis entered the service of his country in the 1st Virginia regiment, in September, 1775 ; was afterwards appointed an ensign, in which capacity he served until February, 1778, when he resigned ; that in the month of January, 1779, he was appointed a lieutenant in the regiment raised to guard the convention prisoners ; was promoted captain on the 8th of October of the same year, and became supernumerary on the disbandment of the regiment ; and that he never received commutation. The facts of the service are shown by his petition to the Legislature of Virginia, for bounty land, in 1784 ; the report of the committee of the House of Delegates of Virginia ; the certificate of Colonel Francis Taylor, the colonel of the regiment of guards ; and the certificate of James E. Heath, Esq., auditor of Virginia. The regiment to which Captain Purvis belonged has been repeatedly recognised as belonging to the continental line. The committee are of opinion that Captain Purvis was entitled to commutation, and report a bill in favor of his legal representatives.

---

## DECEMBER 22, 1837.

The Committee on Revolutionary Claims, to which was referred the petition of Henrietta Barnes, report :

This case was reported on by the Committee on Revolutionary Claims during the last session, to which report reference is now made. The committee still think the claim should be allowed, and to that end report a bill.

## JANUARY 19, 1836.

The Committee on Revolutionary Claims, to which was referred the petition of Henrietta Barnes, report :

That a favorable report was made from the committee on this case in 1832, accompanied by a bill allowing to the legal representatives of Captain Lathrop Allen the commutation of five years' full pay in lieu of half pay for life, for his services as captain on continental establishment. It appears, from the testimony, that Lathrop Allen entered into the service of the United States in May, 1775 ; that he was a sergeant in Captain Baldwin's company, in a regiment commanded by G. Van Schaick, and served as such in the expedition against Canada, until the expiration of his enlistment; that in December, 1775, at Montreal, in Canada, he was appointed a lieutenant in the company of Captain Roswell Beebe. In February, 1776, he received from the committee of Congress the appointment of a captain in a regiment commanded by Colonel Samuel Elmore ; and afterwards received a commission as captain, dated April 15, 1776. The regiment was raised for one year, and in April, 1777, the men so enlisted were discharged at Albany. Captain Allen, in a deposition made on the 6th November, 1818, states that, on the dissolution of his regiment, and not being appointed in the new regiments raising to serve for three years, or during the war, he applied to General Gates, then commanding at Albany, to know whether he was discharged from the service ; who replied in the negative, and that, as his commission was during the pleasure of Congress, it was probable that he would soon be appointed to his rank in another corps. Captain Allen continued afterwards in the service, and was engaged in the battle of Bennington, and at Saratoga, in the capture of General Burgoyne. In the aforesaid deposition, after relating his services previous to his application to General Gates, he states, "in this view, and holding himself ready, he was variously employed by General Gates in sundry services, and by other continental officers, and particularly under General Stark, at the battle of Bennington, and under General Gates, at the capture of Burgoyne : in all, he thinks, he was in the continental service about three years, if not more." The question is here raised, whether this statement should be considered a material and fatal discrepance with the depositions of other credible witnesses, who testify that Captain Lathrop Allen continued in service till the end of the war. This part of the deposition of Captain Allen seems to refer to the actual service performed after Colonel Elmore's regiment was disbanded, which it was necessary to state in specific terms, to enable him to obtain a pension under the act of March 18, 1818. His service as captain in Elmore's regiment was previously stated in precise terms, and his expression above quoted is not necessarily construed to include all his services from the beginning. The infirmity of Captain Allen at the time of making said declaration, (being sixty-six years of age,) is proven by the affidavit of Moses Younglove, who knew Captain Lathrop Allen in Elmore's regiment, and was surgeon's mate. When the object of this declaration, and the probability of an inadvertence of the person who drew it up, are considered, it cannot be viewed as derogating from the weight to be attached to the testimony of Abigail Allen, (the widow of Captain Allen,) or of Lieutenant Archibald Jackson, who states positively that Captain Allen continued in the service, in his rank as captain, until the close of the revolutionary war in 1783, which is corroborated by the statements of Oliver Parrish and John Folerd, both soldiers of the Revolution. It is not probable that Captain Allen held an inferior rank to that designated in his commission, which continued in force after Colonel Elmore's regiment was disbanded.

The committee believe that Captain Allen was entitled to be considered as a supernumerary officer, and, as such, to the commutation granted by the resolution of March 22, 1783. A bill is therefore reported for the relief of his legal representatives.

---

DECEMBER 22, 1837.

The Committee on Revolutionary Claims, who were, by a resolution of the House, instructed to inquire into the expediency of paying to the heirs of Lieutenant Timothy Feely, deceased, five years' full pay, in lieu of half pay for life, for his services in the war of the Revolution, report:

That the rolls of the army of the revolutionary war, on file in the War Department, show that Timothy Feely was appointed an ensign in the eleventh Virginia regiment, on the 10th of December, 1776, and that he was afterwards, on the 6th of November, 1777, appointed a lieutenant in the seventh Virginia regiment; and as a lieutenant his name is borne on the rolls of the last-mentioned regiment up to November, 1779; after this period his name does not appear upon any of these records; and, if no other evidence were produced, the inference would be clear that he retired from the service at this time, either as a supernumerary or resigning officer. But this inference is repelled by the production of a copy of his pay certificate, which, in 1783, issued to him under the act of the Virginia Legislature, passed at the November session, 1781, and which shows that he was paid for his services, as a lieutenant in the Virginia continental line, up to the 31st of December, 1781. From this evidence the committee think it clear that Timothy Feely was in the continental service until the 31st of December, 1781, and, if so, he was clearly entitled to his commutation, unless he forfeited it by resigning his commission, or by being expelled the service, of which there is no ground of suspicion whatever.

The committee report a bill allowing *commutation* to his legal representatives.

---

DECEMBER 22, 1837.

The Committee on Revolutionary Claims, to which was referred the petition of the heirs of Charles Snead, report:

The petitioners ask for the commutation of half pay for life, to which they assert their ancestor became entitled under the resolves of Congress of October 21, 1780, and March 22, 1783.

In support of this claim, evidence is produced which convinced the committee that Charles Snead was a captain in the 8th Virginia regiment on continental establishment; that he served from the commencement of the war until the spring of 1781, when he became a supernumerary by the reorganization of the army ordered under the resolve of October, 1780, giving half pay for life to such as should then become supernumeraries, as well as to those who should serve to the close of the war. Among other evidence, the committee find a certificate from the Auditor of Virginia, showing that Charles Snead's heirs received bounty land from that State for seven years' service in the Virginia continental line of the army. Also, a certificate from the same officer, stating that he received a certificate of the balance of his full pay under the act of Assembly of that State, passed November session, 1781, which was given for services prior to the 1st of January, 1782, to wit: As lieutenant from 1st January, 1777, to 4th July, 1778, and as captain from 4th July, 1778, to 31st December, 1781. Also, an extract from the Chesterfield arrangement of the Virginia continental line, made under the resolve of October 22, 1780, certified by the Auditor of Virginia, from which it appears that Captain Charles Snead became a supernumerary by the arrangement then and there made.

The committee, being satisfied that the case of Captain Snead is clearly brought under the resolves of October, 1780, and March, 1783, and also that the amount claimed has never been paid to himself or his heirs, report a bill.

---

## December 22, 1837.

The Committee on Revolutionary Claims, to which was referred the petition of the heirs of William Hooker Smith, report:

It appears, from the testimony in this case, that William Hooker Smith was appointed a surgeon's mate, in the Pennsylvania line, on continental establishment, at an early period of the revolutionary contest, and continued in service to the end of the war. It further appears, from the depositions of Thomas Williams, George P. Ranson, Rufus Bennet, Elisha Blackman, and General William Ross, that, from July 3, 1778, until the close of the war, Doctor Smith acted as surgeon at the post of Wilkesbarre, Wyoming valley, and that he was the only officer of the medical staff attached to that post during that period. The garrison consisted of two companies of regulars, and the militia of the valley. These facts sustain, in the opinion of the committee, the claim of the petitioners to commutation on account of the services of said Dr. Smith; and a bill is accordingly reported. A favorable report, accompanied by a bill, was made on this case at the 1st session 24th Congress, but not reached.

---

## December 22, 1837.

The Committee on Revolutionary Claims, to which was referred the petition of John McDowel, report:

The petitioner claims the commutation of half pay for life as a lieutenant of infantry in the Virginia line on continental establishment, under the resolves of Congress of October, 1780, and March, 1783.

It appears from the certificate of the Secretary of the Treasury, that the petitioner has been admitted by that Department to the benefits of the act of 1828, giving compensation to certain officers and soldiers of the revolutionary war; which compensation depends upon having served in the continental line to the close of the war—precisely the condition upon which half pay for life, and the commutation thereof, had been promised under the resolves of the Congress of the Revolution.

Colonel Bowman, of the 8th Virginia regiment, testifies that he was well acquainted with John McDowel, and "knows him to have been a lieutenant in the Virginia line ;" and, also, that he "did serve to the end of the revolutionary war, and would have gotten his commutation certificates if he had applied for them." Colonel Buford, of the 11th Virginia regiment, testifies that he knew Lieutenant McDowel in the year 1778, when he was serving in the Northern army in the Virginia line, and continued to do so until the year 1780, when he was ordered to, and did, join his own regiment, in Carolina ; that, in 1781, he (Buford) returned to Virginia, sick, and left McDowel in service, and did not see him until November, 1781, after the surrender of Cornwallis, and that the said McDowel was then belonging to the army ; that he never heard of his resigning his commission ; that he (Buford) had received his commutation certificates ; that he considered Lieutenant McDowel's situation as similar to his own, and knows that McDowel could have obtained his certificates, also, had he applied for them. Colonel Mathews, of the 3d Virginia regiment, certifies that John McDowel served in the 8th Virginia regiment, from January 1, 1777, to February 16, 1781, and that he was neither cashiered nor superseded.

The committee are satisfied that the petitioner is entitled to the commutation he asks, having served as directed by the resolves of Congress, and never having received it or any part of it. The bill reported for his relief at a former session of Congress, and which remained unacted on, is therefore again reported.

---

### DECEMBER 22, 1837.

The Committee on Revolutionary Claims, to which was referred the petition of the legal representatives of John Winston, deceased, report :

That this case was favorably reported on, with a bill for the relief of the petitioners, as well in the 22d as also in the 23d Congress. The last report is annexed as part of this. In addition to the statement and evidence found in that report, the committee have been put in possession of the deposition of Captain Thomas Price, a highly respectable witness, who swears that Winston served in the Northern army under Washington, and adds: "Whether Captain Winston remained to the end of the war, I cannot (my memory being much impaired by age) positively say ; but this I know, that he was at the siege of York, in the fall of 1781, because I saw him there ; and from this fact I must infer he served through the war."

### FEBRUARY 19, 1835.

The Committee on Revolutionary Claims, to which was referred the petition of the heirs and legal representatives of John Winston, report :

That this case was before the last Congress, and favorably reported on, with a bill for the relief of the petitioners; which, however, was not reached.

The petitioners, as the heirs of John Winston, late a captain in the Virginia line on continental establishment, state that their father entered the army of the Revolution as a captain, in the year 1776, and, immediately enlisting a company, joined General Washington while retreating through New Jersey; that he was engaged in the battles of Trenton, Princeton,

Brandywine, Germantown, White Plains, Monmouth, and other actions fought in the North; that he never returned to visit his family until the year 1781, when he came with the army to the siege of Yorktown, and continued in the service to the close of the war; that he died shortly after the peace, without having received the commutation of his half pay, which they now claim as his heirs and legal representatives.

The committee, upon reviewing the case, believe the above statement to be substantially correct.

Colonel John Nicholas, of the revolutionary army, testifies that he knew Winston; that he served with him in Muhlenberg's brigade; that he was in the principal battles of the North; that he did not return to Virginia " until the autumn of 1781, when he came with Washington's army to the siege of Yorktown, where he served."

Major William Duval certifies that he was well acquainted with Captain Winston, and believes him to have continued in the service to the end of the war; as he could not have returned to his father's family, with whom he was intimate, without his knowledge.

By a certificate from the War Department, it appears that John Winston settled for his pay as a captain of infantry in the Virginia line on continental establishment, on the 5th of March, 1783, agreeably to an act of the Virginia Legislature, passed November, 1781, and was paid as a captain from January 1, 1777, to February 13, 1781.

By another certificate from the Virginia land office, it appears that he received, on the 21st of May, 1783, a warrant for the usual quantity of land allowed a captain of the Virginia line on continental establishment, for military services from December 6, 1776, to February 13, 1781; and by a statement of the Third Auditor, it appears that there is nothing on record in that office to show that he had received his commutation, or any part of it.

From this evidence, the committee conclude either that Captain Winston became a supernumerary under the resolves of October, 1780, by which the Virginia line was reorganized on the 13th of February, 1781, or that he served to the close of the war; either of which would entitle him to commutation. It is probable that he became a supernumerary under the resolves of 1780, and, as such, acted at the siege of York, and occasionally afterwards to the close of the war. A bill is therefore again reported for the relief of his heirs and legal representatives.

---

DECEMBER 22, 1837.

The Committee on Revolutionary Claims, to which was referred the petition of the legal representatives of Colonel George Gibson, deceased, report:

Colonel Gibson was a brave and meritorious officer. He entered the service of his country at the commencement of the Revolution; enlisted a hundred men at Pittsburg, then under the jurisdiction of Virginia; marched to Williamsburg, and was commissioned a captain in the Virginia line. Powder and lead becoming scarce, the Government of Virginia selected him as a person well qualified to conduct a secret negotiation with the Spanish Government for a supply. He was successful in procuring it not only for the State of Virginia, but engaged a resident merchant of eminence (Oliver Pollock) to ship large quantities to the States in Spanish vessels. On his return he was offered a pecuniary recompense or promotion, and accepted the latter. He was accordingly appointed colonel of the first Virginia regiment.

With this regiment he continued, and was in all the severe engagements in the North, subsequent to the battle of Germantown, until 1781, when the regiment, being nearly annihilated, was ordered to the South to recruit. He then became a supernumerary, but was shortly afterwards ordered to march the prisoners taken with Cornwallis to York, in Pennsylvania, and they remained under his charge until sent to England.

Colonel Gibson's services did not, however, close with the revolutionary war. In 1790 he was appointed by General Washington a colonel of one of the regiments recruiting for General St. Clair's army, and was ordered to the West to assist in the campaign against the Northwest Indians. He fell on the fatal 4th of November, 1791, sustaining the character for bravery and coolness which had ever distinguished him.

Colonel Gibson's regiment was originally a State regiment. About the 1st of June, 1777, it was ordered to the North, and joined General Washington two days after the battle of Germantown, (*vide* Washington's Letters, vol. 2, p. 180,) and was placed on continental establishment, in lieu of Mathews's regiment, which was taken by the enemy in that battle, by an act of the Virginia Legislature, in these words : " *Be it enacted*, That the battalion on commonwealth establishment, under the command of Colonel George Gibson, and now in the continental service, be continued in the said service, instead of the 9th Virginia regiment, made prisoners in the battle of Germantown." This act was never repealed. Colonel Mathews's regiment never resumed its place in the line, and Gibson's remained until 1781, when it was ordered home to recruit.

In addition to this proof of the character of the regiment, it is proper to state that the War Department decided, on the 12th of January, 1830, " that the regiment commanded by Colonel George Gibson was a continental regiment from October, 1777." The Treasury Department also so decided. In consequence of which, the benefit of the act of May 15, 1828, applicable only to the continental line, was extended to a number of individuals belonging to this regiment. Congress itself has viewed the regiment as continental, having passed an act allowing to the heirs of an officer belonging to that regiment " five years' full pay, with such interest as would have accrued if a certificate had issued, and been funded, under the act of 1790." ( *Vide* act for the relief of William Vawter's heirs, approved May 25, 1832.)

By an act of the State of Virginia of May, 1779, officers of the continental and State line of Virginia were placed upon an equal footing in regard to the bounty of the State, (half pay for life,) and directed to look for recompense to the State, " provided Congress did not make some tantamount provision for them." For the State line Congress did nothing ; but for the continental line it made tantamount provision.

Owing, in some measure, to Gibson's regiment having been both State and continental, its officers received neither half pay from Virginia nor commutation from the United States. In applying to the State, they were referred to the United States ; and in applying to the United States, they were referred to the State.

By the act of July 5, 1832, the claims of the Virginia State line were directed to be liquidated and paid by that State. In that act the regiment of Colonel Gibson was included, and his legal representatives received a certain amount, but not equal to the commutation paid to other officers of the same grade on continental establishment, nor in proportion to what had been paid to subalterns of the same regiment, for whose relief acts had been passed by Congress. The most important question in the whole case seems to be, whether the regiment really belonged to the continental line' proper. That such was the case the committee have no doubt, and they believe that its colonel should be placed upon an equally favorable footing with his subalterns. They think justice should be evenhanded, and that the petitioners are entitled to the same measure that others have received. A bill is accordingly reported for their relief.

DECEMBER 22, 1837.

The Committee on Revolutionary Claims, to which was referred the petition of John Clark, report:

The petitioner states that he enlisted in the Virginia continental line of the Revolution, in October, 1775, under Captain Burgess Ball, for two years ; that he served as a sergeant during the whole term of his enlistment, and was discharged at White Marsh, Pennsylvania ; that he immediately re-enlisted in Colson's company of the 5th Virginia regiment, commanded by Colonel Parker, for three years, and acted as sergeant-major of the regiment until the army went into winter-quarters at Valley Forge, when he was appointed an ensign ; which situation he resigned on being appointed a cornet in Ash's company of cavalry, of the North Carolina line ; that, subsequently, the troop was ordered to Pittsburg and Beaver creek, where he remained until the latter end of 1780, when, owing to the expiration of enlistments and other causes, the troop was ordered to North Carolina to recruit; that on the way from Beaver to Halifax, (owing to sickness,) he received a furlough and permission to return to Virginia, with orders to join again in March following ; that he did rejoin the army, and remained with it until after the capture of Cornwallis, at York, when a return of illness caused him to receive another furlough, with orders to hold himself in readiness to return, whenever called for.

The petitioner further states that he preserved his commission and furlough for a long period of time, but that they were finally lost ; that he did not apply for his commutation after the close of the war, (because the certificates were considered of little or no valne,) until the claim had been barred by an act of limitation; that he has received from the State of Virginia the quantity of land allowed a cornet of horse, for services during the war; that, in consequence, he deems himself entitled to the commutation of half pay for life granted to others similarly situated, and prays for the passage of an act accordingly.

These statements of Clark are made upon oath before a magistrate, who certifies that he is a man of unspotted character, to whom the fullest credit is due. A certificate, signed by twenty-five citizens of Virginia, is added, to the same effect, and to whose respectability and credibility a magistrate certifies.

Clark's statement is sustained by *Richard Shackelford,* who deposes that it is correct to his own personal knowledge; that they both entered the service about the same time, and served together; and that Clark was considered an active, brave, and meritorious officer. He says, "both of us served in the continental service to the close of the war, except the time Mr. Clark has stated he was on furlough." *Carter Croxton, sen.,* deposes that Clark's statement "contains minutely and substantially the truth ; that, to his knowledge, he enlisted twice, as stated; that he was appointed a cornet in the cavalry, and served in that capacity to the end of the war, except the time he was on furlough." He adds, " Mr. Clark and myself were in service at the same time." The credibility of both these witnesses is certified by a magistrate. The Auditor of Virginia certifies that he received land bounty as a cornet of cavalry in the continental line, for services during the war.

The committee, believing the claim sustained and unpaid, report a bill for the relief of the petitioner.

---

## December 22, 1837.

Upon a re-examination of the petition of the legal representatives of Doctor Charles Taylor, deceased, the Committee on Revolutionary Claims adopt the accompanying report made at a former session, and offer a bill for their relief.

## April 12, 1836.

The Committee on Revolutionary Claims, to which was referred the petition of the heirs of Dr. Charles Taylor, report :

That it is proved, by the papers submitted to the committee, that Charles Taylor was surgeon's mate of the second regiment of the Virginia line on continental establishment, before July, 1776, and until the regiment of guards, commanded by Colonel Francis Taylor, was raised in October, 1779, when he was appointed a surgeon in that regiment, which station he held until the regiment was disbanded in 1781.

Your committee are of opinion that commutation should be granted, and have brought in a bill accordingly.

---

## December 22, 1837.

The Committee on Revolutionary Claims, to which was referred the petition of Richard De Treville, Ellis De Treville, Caroline De Treville, Elizabeth De Treville, Harriet De Treville, and Samuel Lawrence, report :

That the Committee on Revolutionary Claims, at the first session of the twenty-fourth Congress, made a favorable report on the petition, accompanied by a bill for relief; that the committee, on a re-examination of the case, adopt the report of the former committee, which is as follows :

" The petitioners state that their grandfather, John De Treville, was a captain of artillery in the regular continental army, and served therein until the end of the war of the Revolution : that they have been informed, and believe, that Captain John De Treville, in his lifetime, never received any pay for his services as such officer, nor the commutation to which officers who had served till the close of the war are entitled.

" The petitioners further state, that Captain John De Treville died in the year 1790, and left surviving him only two children, namely, Robert De Treville, who is the father of the petitioners, Richard De Treville, Caroline De Treville, Elizabeth De Treville, Harriet De Treville, and Ellis De Treville ; and Harriet De Treville, who is the mother of the petitioner, Samuel Lawrence ; both of whom died about the year 1817 : which facts are proved by the affidavit of Mary Mackie. The petitioners allege that the children of the said Captain John De Treville never presented any claim, or received any compensation for the revolutionary services of their father.

" It appears on a register on file in the Pension Office, that John De Treville was a captain in the fourth regiment of the South Carolina continental line.

" Accompanying the petition is an original order issued by Brigadier General William Moultrie, in the words and figures following, to wit :

' May 11, 1779.

'Sir : Upon the receipt of this, you are to spike up all the cannon at Fort Johnston, if time will admit, throw them into the river, set fire to the fort at several places, leave the powder in it that it may blow up, and make the best of your way to this place.

I am yours,

WILLIAM MOULTRIE, Brig. Gen.

' To Captain De Treville, or the
Commanding officer at Fort Johnston.'

" It is proved by the affidavit of Daniel Stevens, that John De Treville was a captain in the continental army of the United States, in a regiment of artillery ; that he was a brave and efficient officer, and continued in the continental service to the end of the war. Mary Mackie also testifies that John De Treville was an officer in the continental army, and continued and remained an officer therein until the end of the war of the Revolution.

" The committee being satisfied that Captain John De Treville, deceased, was entitled to the benefit of the resolutions of Congress granting commutation for five years' full pay to such officers on continental establishment as should serve to the close of the revolutionary war, in lieu of half pay for life, have, therefore, reported a bill for the relief of his heirs at law."

The committee therefore report a bill for the relief of the legal representatives of Captain John De Treville, deceased.

46

The Committee on Revolutionary Claims, to which was referred the petition of Lucy Marks, report:

That this case was examined, and a favorable report made thereon, accompanied by a bill for the relief of the heirs and legal representatives of Captain John Marks, deceased, named in the said petition, at the first session of the twenty-fourth Congress ; that the committee having examined this case, adopt the former report, which is annexed, and report a bill for relief.

"It appears from the certificate of the Third Auditor of the Treasury, that John Marks, deceased, late husband of the petitioner, was a captain of the 14th, and afterwards of the 10th Virginia regiment on continental establishment, and in that capacity he is borne on the revolutionary rolls of the last mentioned regiment up to November, 1779.

"It also appears from a certificate of the auditor of public accounts of Virginia, under date of the 15th day of December, 1834, that, from a list in his office of such officers and soldiers of the Virginia continental line, during the revolutionary war, as settled their accounts and received certificates for the balance of their full pay, according to the act of Assembly, passed the November session, 1781, a certificate issued on the 9th day of April, 1783, in the name of John Marks, as captain, for £787 11s. 4d.; which certificate appears to have been delivered to himself, and was given for services prior to the 1st January, 1782, to wit : pay as captain from 1st January, 1777, to 15th February, 1781.

"It further appears from the certificate of the register on the land office of Virginia, that a warrant for 4,000 acres of land issued to Captain John Marks, the 3d September, 1782, he having served in the Virginia continental line more than three years, and being entitled to the proportion of land allowed to officers who have served that term.

"It is proved by the certificate of Robert Porterfield, late a captain in the Virginia continental line, that the said Captain John Marks served till the end of the war of the Revolution. He certifies that he was personally acquainted with Captain John Marks, who was in the Virginia continental line in the war of the Revolution, early in the year one thousand seven hundred and seventy-seven, and that he did serve through the war ; that he married the widow of William Lewis after the close of the war, and removed to the State of Georgia, where he died : the widow of the said John Marks returned to Virginia, and lives in the county of Albemarle. The said certificate bears date the 28th day of May, 1834.

"The committee are unanimously of the opinion that the documentary and other evidence accompanying the petition establishes, satisfactorily, that the said John Marks, deceased, served as captain of the Virginia line of continental troops in the war of the Revolution, from the year 1777, until the close of the war ; and that he would be entitled, under the resolution of Congress of the 22d of March, 1783, to commutation of five years' full pay, in lieu of half pay for life. A bill is therefore reported by the committee for the relief of the heirs and legal representatives of the said John Marks, deceased."

DECEMBER 22, 1837.

The Committee on Revolutionary Claims have examined the petition of Robert Taylor, on behalf of himself and others, as distributors and heirs of the late Francis Taylor, deceased, and the evidence in support thereof, and now report:

That Colonel Francis Taylor commanded the regiment raised to guard the convention prisoners, (as they were called,) and in that capacity served, as it satisfactorily appears to the committee, until June 17, 1781. The regiment he commanded was disbanded upon the removal of the prisoners from Winchester, Virginia, where they had been kept; and by the discharge of the troops, Colonel Taylor became supernumerary, for it does not appear that he ever resigned. He had been an officer of inferior grade before his appointment to command the regiment of guards. The regiment he commanded has been repeatedly recognised as belonging to the continental line. The committee are of opinion that Colonel Taylor was entitled to commutation, and report a bill in favor of his legal representatives.

---

DECEMBER 22, 1837.

The Committee on Revolutionary Claims, to which was referred the petition of Samuel Jones, report:

Samuel Jones, son, and representing himself as sole heir of Captain Samuel Jones of the revolutionary army, petitions for commutation.

It appears, from a letter from the Third Auditor, that there were two individuals named Samuel Jones, each with the rank of lieutenant, in the army of the Revolution. One of them, who acted as paymaster in the 15th Virginia regiment, was dismissed from service on the 6th June, 1778; the other likewise acted as paymaster, but in the 11th Virginia regiment; and of this Samuel Jones, the Auditor says the records of his office furnish no evidence of his service subsequent to November, 1779. From this it may be inferred that the records show that he served up to that period; consequently, there must have been a Samuel Jones different from the one dismissed in June, 1778. It appears, from an account settled by the State of Virginia, that an individual named Samuel Jones was paid as lieutenant and paymaster from early in 1777, to January, 1780; and from January, 1780, up to the 1st of February, 1781, he was paid as captain. This document, certified by the Auditor of the State of Virginia, justifies the belief that Samuel Jones was promoted to the rank of captain, and continued in service after 1779, subsequent to which period the Auditor states that his name does not appear on the records of his office. The late Chief Justice Marshall certifies that he knew Captain Jones, boarded with him in Richmond in 1782, and does not recollect to have ever heard of his resignation. The Chief Justice also states facts in relation to the expiration of the term of service of the soldiers of the Virginia line, in the fall of 1779, and the raising of new recruits, which render it very probable that Captain Jones became a supernumerary. There is other evidence conducing to show that he never resigned, and the committee have come to the conclusion that he remained a supernumerary to the end of the war. He died in 1784, before the petitioner, as he states, was born. The delay is satisfactorily accounted for. The committee report a bill for the relief of Captain Jones's legal representatives.

---

## December 22, 1837.

The Committee on Revolutionary Claims, to which the petition of James Witherell was referred, report :

That the petitioner claims commutation as an ensign in the Massachusetts continental line during the war of the Revolution.

The petitioner was appointed an ensign in the 11th regiment, commanded by Colonel Tupper, on the 26th of September, 1780, having served as a non-commissioned officer in the continental line previous to that appointment. By the affidavit of Josiah Abbott, who was an ensign in the Massachusetts line, it appears that in the autumn of 1781 he became acquainted with the petitioner, then an ensign in the same line ; and he states that the petitioner was in service so late as the 16th of May, 1783. He refers in his affidavit to a journal kept by him during that period, and which enables him to speak with greater confidence as to the continuance of Ensign Witherell in the service. The petitioner, in his declaration made on the 10th of March, 1830, for the benefits of the act of the 15th of May, 1828, states that he served to the end of the war ; and it appears by the certificate of the Commissioner of Pensions that he has been admitted to the benefits of the act of 1828.

The evidence in this case is, in the opinion of the committee, sufficient to establish the claim of the petitioner to commutation, and they report a bill accordingly.

---

## December 22, 1837.

The Committee on Revolutionary Claims, to which the subject was referred, made the following report:

The petitioner, as sole heir of John Baptiste Ashe, claims commutation for the services of his ancestor as a major in the continental line of the revolutionary army.

It appears that John Baptiste Ashe was commissioned by John Jay, president of the Congress of the Revolution, in 1779, as major of the first North Carolina regiment, to take rank as such from the 26th day of January, 1777. This fact is proved by the original commission. From other papers, it seems that J. B. Ashe entered the service in April, 1776, with the rank of captain, and that before the end of the war he was promoted to the rank of lieutenant colonel. But it does not appear that he ever obtained a commission as lieutenant colonel.

It is proved by two witnesses that he served during the war. The committee are therefore of opinion that the said John Baptiste Ashe was entitled to commutation. They report a bill in favor of his legal representatives, believing that the executor or administrator is entitled to the money, and not the heir.

DECEMBER 22, 1837.

The Committee on Revolutionary Claims, to whom the subject was referred, make the following report:

The service of Captain Jordan in the continental line to the close of the war, is fully proved. He was commissioned as a captain lieutenant in the artillery artificers, in 1779, and at the termination of the war held the commission of captain in the same regiment, which regiment formed part of the quota of the State of Pennsylvania in the army of the United States. He received land from the United States for his services to the close of the war, and was admitted to the benefits of the act of the 15th of May, 1828, which he could not have been, unless, in the opinion of the Secretary of the Treasury, his services had been such as would have entitled him to commutation. It is certified by the Third Auditor that he received pay to the 1st of January, 1783, but did not receive commutation.

By the printed Journals of Congress, it appears that on the 18th of September, 1777, a memorial from Colonel Flower, with a list of the corps of artillery artificers, having been presented to Congress, it was resolved that commissions be granted to the officers, agreeably to their respective ranks.

On the 15th of May, 1778, Congress promised half pay for seven years to "all military officers commissioned by Congress, who now are or hereafter may be in the service of the United States, and continue therein during the war."

On the 15th of March, 1779, Congress resolved "that all officers, non-commissioned officers, and soldiers, now belonging to the corps of light dragoons, and artillery and infantry, and the corps of *artillery artificers*, commissioned and enlisted since the 16th of September, 1776, for three years, or during the war, or which shall hereafter be so commissioned and enlisted, not being part of the 88 battalions originally apportioned to the States, shall be considered as parts of the quotas of the several States to which they did or shall respectively belong when so commissioned or enlisted," &c.

On the 17th of August, 1779, Congress, " recommended to the several States that have not already adopted measures for that purpose, to make such further provisions for the officers, and for the soldiers enlisted for the war, to them respectively belonging, who shall continue in service till the establishment of peace, as shall be adequate compensation for the many dangers, losses, and hardships they have suffered and been exposed to in the course of the present contest, either by granting to their officers half pay for life, and proper rewards to the soldiers, or in such other manner as may appear most expedient to the Legislatures of the several States."

So far, there is nothing to raise a doubt whether the *officers of the artillery artificers* are entitled to half pay, or such other provision as might be made by the United States; they were commissioned by order of Congress, as other officers; they were declared to be parts of the quotas of the several States to which they belonged when commissioned; and, as officers belonging to the several States, they are included in the recommendation of Congress for half pay for life.

But doubts have been suggested, in consequence of a report made by a committee of Congress in 1786, expressing the opinion that officers in the late corps of artificers are not entitled to half pay. Those doubts, however, will be removed by a brief examination of the grounds of the opinion expressed in the report.

These are, first, " that half pay was granted to military officers chiefly from a consideration that, by a long continuance in the military line, they may have lost those habits by which they formerly had been enabled to provide for themselves or families; which reasons do not apply so fully to the officers of artificers."

Now, it will be seen, by referring to the resolve of 17th of August, 1779, quoted above, that the consideration put forward in the report was an imaginary one ; Congress themselves having declared the object of granting half pay to officers to be, to' make " an adequate compensation for the dangers, losses, and hardships they have suffered and been exposed to in the course of the present contest." If further proof were wanting to show the error of the report in this particular, it would be found in the fact that half pay was also granted not only to surgeons, but to chaplains, who certainly could not have lost in the army the habits by which they had before been enabled to support themselves.

The second objection of the report, is, that the resolve of the 15th of May, 1778, " confines the half pay to *military officers*, which certainly did not include the artificers." The resolutions which have been already quoted show that the officers of artillery artificers were military officers, whether that term be construed according to its ordinary or its professional acceptation. But it is evident, from various other resolves of Congress, that the limited and restricted interpretation of the term given in the report was not according to the intention of Congress. Among those is the resolve of 24th of August, 1780, extending to widows of officers dying in service the half pay provided by the resolve of 15th of May, 1778, which it describes as "granting half pay for seven years to the *officers of the army.*" The resolve of August, 1779, just quoted, recommends that provision, by half pay or otherwise, be made by the States to " *the officers* to them respectively belonging," and provision for the widows of such of " *their officers*" as may die in the service. There are, also, the memorable resolves of October, 1780, reorganizing the army ; the words of which are, " that the *officers* who continue in service to the end of the war, shall also be entitled to half pay during life." And the resolve of the 22d of March, 1783, by which commutation was offered, uses the terms " *officers of the several lines*," and " *officers of the army,*" and declares " that such *officers* as are now in the service, and shall continue to the end of the war, shall be entitled to receive the five years' full pay in money, or securities on interest, at 6 per cent., instead of the half pay promised for life by the resolution of the 21st of October, 1780."

From all this it is clear, that in these promises of allowances the terms " military officers," " officers of the army," " officers of the several lines," and " officers," must be taken as synonymous ; or, if not, that Congress must have intended by the resolve of 1780, granting half pay for life, and of 1783, granting commutation, to enlarge the class to whom those allowances were to be made. And it is to be borne in mind that it is under the resolves of 1780 and 1783 that the claim of Captain Jordan, as an officer, serving in the continental line to the end of the war, is made ; consequently, any objection derived from the restricted interpretation given in the report to the term " military officer," in the resolve of 1778, would be wholly inapplicable to his case.

The third objection to the report is, that "the corps of artificers" is expressly excluded from half pay by a resolve of Congress of the 16th of November, 1779. It is easy to show that this resolve does not apply to the artillery artificers, but to a different corps, and therefore does not apply to the claim of Captain Jordan. The resolve quoted in the report is in the following words: "That it is recommended to the several States to allow the corps of artificers established by Congress on the 12th instant, all the benefits provided for officers and soldiers in the line of their quotas of the continental battalions, except the half pay." This resolve, it will be seen, relates to a particular corps of artificers, viz: that established by Congress on the 12th of November, 1779, which corps was established by the following resolve:

"*Resolved*, That the eleven companies of artificers raised by the quartermaster general be re-formed and incorporated and arranged in such manner as the commander-in-chief shall deem proper; that when such arrangement shall have been made, the same be transmitted to the board of war, to the intent the officers may receive their commissions, which shall entitle them to rank only in their respective corps, and enable them to hold regimental courts martial in cases that concern their own corps only, and are usually cognizable by the regimental courts martial of the line."

It is, therefore, to the artificers raised by the quartermaster general, and arranged into a corps by the resolve of November 12, 1779, and *to that only*, that this special exception applies. It has no reference, direct or indirect, to the regiment of artillery artificers, which, as has been already shown, had existed as an organized corps since 1777, had been declared to be a part of the continental line, and had been promised half pay for seven years.

That these were different corps, is well known to all who are familiar with the organization of the army of the Revolution. The fact is evident by various passages in the printed Journals; and the very resolution quoted in the report to show the exclusion of the corps of artificers established November 12, 1779, from half pay, shows the existence, at that time, of the artillery artificers as a different corps. That resolve, after fixing the pay of the commanding officer of the "corps of artificers," adds, "that the allowance of pay, subsistence, and clothing of the other officers and men of the said artificers, be the same as that of the 'artillery artificers' under the command of Colonel B. Flower."

Whether any of the artificers raised by the quartermaster general were afterwards incorporated with the artillery artificers in the regiment of artificers which, by the reorganization of the army in October, 1780, was made part of the quota of Pennsylvania, does not appear. But, if any were so incorporated, the exception of half pay in the resolve of November 16, 1779, would not exclude them from half pay. That resolve was merely a recommendation to the States, and could not, by any rule of construction, nullify a resolve subsequently adopted by Congress expressly promising half pay to the regiment of artificers, as part of the Pennsylvania line in the regular army of the United States.

It is also to be observed, that among the individual officers reported to Congress on the 31st of October, 1783, by the Secretary of War, as having "agreed to accept the commutation of five years' full pay, in lieu of half pay for life," were Patton's and Pendleton's artificers, and Major Bruin, of the artificers. It is not to be supposed that those officers would have been included in such a report, as, belonging to the artificers, they had been expressly excluded from half pay.

More time has, perhaps, been bestowed on answering the objections of the report, than they deserve; for, after all, the claim of Captain Jordan, as an officer of the artillery artificers, serving to the end of the war, rests upon promises contained in the resolves of Congress, plain, explicit, and positive, neither to be misunderstood nor to be set aside.

On the 3d of October, 1780, Congress determined upon a new arrangement or reform of the army, and resolved " that the *regular army* of the United States, from and after the 1st of January next, consist of four regiments of cavalry or light dragoons; four regiments of artillery; forty-nine regiments of infantry, exclusive of Colonel Hazen's regiment, hereafter mentioned; *one regiment of artificers.*" By the same resolve the strength of each regiment was prescribed, and, among others, " the regiment of artificers." The resolve also assigns to each State the quota to be furnished by it; that of Pennsylvania being " six regiments of infantry, one of artillery, one of cavalry, and one of *artificers.*" It likewise directs " that the States shall select from the line of the army a proper number of officers to command the several regiments to them respectively assigned." It further directs " that the regiments of cavalry, artillery, and of *artificers,* as they now stand, be considered as belonging to the States respectively to which they are assigned;" and the resolve concludes as follows: " And whereas, by the foregoing arrangement, many deserving officers must become supernumerary, and it is proper that regard be had to them, *Resolved,* That from the time the reform in the army takes place, they be entitled to half pay for seven years," &c.

On the 21st of October Congress completed the arrangement of the army, and by a resolve of that date, directed, among other things, the manner in which the officers who were to be reduced, and those who were to be continued in service, should be selected, and determined that " the officers reduced are to be allowed half pay for life;" and that " the officers who shall continue in service to the end of the war shall also be entitled to half pay during life."

From the foregoing it is evident, 1st, That the regiment of artificers formed part of the regular army of the United States, as established by the resolves of October, 1780, and part of the quota of that army assigned to the State of Pennsylvania; 2d, That the promise of half pay for life was made to all the officers of that army who were reduced under those resolves, or should continue to the end of the war; and it follows conclusively that the officers of the regiment of artificers were entitled equally with any other officers.

This conclusion is too irresistible to need support or corroboration from any circumstance; but the consideration naturally suggests itself, that it is altogether improbable that Congress would have required, or Pennsylvania consented, that a part of the quota of that State should be excluded from a benefit to which the entire quotas of all other States were to be entitled.

It appears, from a resolve of Congress of March 29, 1781, that Captain Jordan was retained in service as a captain of artillery artificers.

The committee report a bill for the relief of Captain Jordan's legal representatives.

The Committee on Revolutionary Claims, to whom was referred the petition of Hugh M. Pettus, have considered the same, and report:

That the petitioner represents that he is the only child and heir of Samuel O. Pettus; that the said Samuel O. Pettus was a lieutenant of infantry in the Virginia line on continental establishment, and continued in service to the end of the revolutionary war. The petitioner prays to be allowed the commutation of five years' full pay, with interest, in lieu of the half pay for life granted by the resolutions of Congress to the officers of the continental line serving until the end of the war.

It appears, from a certificate of the auditor of Virginia, that the said Samuel O. Pettus received a certificate, issued on the 18th day of July, 1783, for the balance of his full pay as ensign and lieutenant to the 10th June, 1781. It also appears, from a copy of the records of the land office of Virginia, that the said Samuel O. Pettus received a warrant for the proportion of land allowed a lieutenant in the continental line, *for the war.*

The committee, being satisfied from the evidence in the case that the said Samuel O. Pettus was an officer in the continental army, and served to the end of the war, as stated in the petition, report a bill.

---

JANUARY 4, 1838.

The Committee on Revolutionary Claims, to whom the petition and papers of Nancy Haggard were referred, report:

That an act of Congress passed the 2d day of July, 1836, which directed the payment to Nancy Haggard, only daughter and sole heir of William Grymes, who was a captain in the army of the Revolution, and was slain in battle on the 1st of August, 1777, the principal sum due to her, for the seven years' half pay of a captain; which principal sum has been paid to her, and she now petitions for the interest due thereon at the time the principal was paid. The committee concur in the opinion that the interest claimed is justly due and ought to be paid, and report a bill.

---

JANUARY 4, 1838.

The Committee on Revolutionary Claims, to whom the resolution of the House of the 20th of December, 1836, was referred, report:

That it appears, by an act of Congress, the principal sum due to Lieut. Thornton Taylor, on account of his commutation pay, for his services to the end of the war of the Revolution, has been allowed to the heirs of the said Thornton Taylor; and that the said heirs now claim and petition for the payment of the interest which had accrued on the said principal sum till the same was paid. Your committee, under the influence of the uniform decision of Congress, with few exceptions, to allow interest on all commutation claims when the principal sum has been ascertained to be due, and believing the act of Congress of March, 1783, providing for commutation pay contains an express promise to pay interest thereon, concur in the opinion that interest should be allowed the petitioners in this case; and report a bill.

The Committee on Revolutionary Claims, to whom was referred the claim of the heirs and legal representatives of Francis Eppes, deceased, to seven years half pay, under the resolve of Congress of the 24th August, 1780, report:

That, by the journals of Congress, it appears that on the 18th of March, 1776, Francis Eppes, of the State of Virginia, was promoted from the grade of major to that lieutenant colonel in the first Virginia regiment; that by a letter from the Department of State, having reference to the papers of General Washington, and also by the testimony of witnesses, it is satisfactorily shown to the committee that the said Francis Eppes continued in the service, with the rank above mentioned, until his death, which happened about the close of the year 1776; and by the letter of the Third Auditor it appears that the seven years' half pay claimed on account of his services has not been paid. That at the time of his death Colonel Eppes left no widow, and only one child, Elizabeth Kell Eppes, who intermarried with Thomas Woodliff, by whom she had one child, Francis Eppes Woodliff; that upon the death of Elizabeth, her husband contracted a second marriage, and had issue a daughter, Martha Woodliff; that Francis Eppes Woodliff died without ever having married, and by will gave all his estate, real and personal, to his half-sister, Martha Woodliff, who married Robert Lancer; that she has since died, leaving her said husband and two children surviving.

By this summary notice of the history of the family, it is at once apparent that the husband, Robert Lancer, and his children, (on behalf of whom this application is made,) are not of the blood of Colonel Eppes, the officer. In construing, however, the effect and operation of this resolve of Congress, the committee feel justified upon principle, and on analogy to the practice and decisions of Congress under the resolutions giving half pay and commutation of half pay for revolutionary services, to regard the resolution of the 24th of August, 1780, as having vested a right to the seven years' half pay in the daughter of Colonel Eppes, which became as absolute and transmissible as the property in any other claim not actually reduced into possession, and that they are now entitled to the benefit of that resolution, who, though not of the blood of Colonel Eppes, shall happen to stand in relation of next of kin to Martha Woodliff, who, by will of the grandson, Francis Eppes Woodliff, became entitled to his entire property. The committee, however, according to a uniform rule which they have adopted, do not propose to determine by name the individual or individuals who are entitled to relief, but report a bill having reference to the terms of the resolution under which this claim arises.

---

The Committee on Revolutionary Claims, to which was referred the petition of Thomas Emory Sudler and Elizabeth A. Sudler, of Annapolis, in the State of Maryland, children, and a portion of the heirs at law of Emory Sudler and Elizabeth Sudler, on behalf of themselves and the other heirs at law of said Emory and Elizabeth Sudler, report:

That it is alleged that one William Wright, late of the State of Maryland, deceased, lost, by having the same *stolen*, with a large quantity of merchandise, from a warehouse in the city of Baltimore, in the year 1780, sundry loan-office certificates, issued from the loan office in the State of Maryland; that the said William Wright died in the year 1790, leaving Elizabeth, his widow, executrix of his will, and devisee of these certificates; and that the said Elizabeth afterwards intermarried with Emory Sudler.

The committee find that an act was passed by Congress, April 21, 1794, authorizing the renewal of loan-office and final settlement certificates which had been accidently destroyed, if presented on or before the 1st June, 1795; after which they were to be barred. Under this act it appears, from an official statement signed by the Auditor of the Treasury, dated March 8, 1802, and which is printed among the documents of Congress, that application was made, under that act, on the 20th May, 1795, (within the time limited in the act,) on behalf of the estate of William Wright, for renewal and payment of these certificates. The claim, it is stated by the accounting officers, was "not provided for by the act;" the act making provision for the renewal of certificates only which had been "*accidentally destroyed;*" whilst those of Mr. Wright were lost by robbery, and consequently could not be said to be "accidentally destroyed." The general act upon the subject not embracing their case, Emory Sudler, and Elizabeth his wife, late Elizabeth Wright, petitioned Congress in 1796, again in 1800, and Mrs. Sudler, after the death of her husband, again petitioned in 1810. The Committee of Claims made a report on the two first petitions, as well as on several other petitions, for lost or destroyed certificates, adverse to their renewal, on the ground that it was inexpedient at that time again to open the door of limitation.

A list of the numbers, dates, and other particulars of these certificates, is contained in an official certificate of the Register of the Treasury of the United States, dated December 15, 1836, and which accompanies this report; from which it appears that their specie value amounts to $1,504 42; that the fact of their loss and stoppage of payment was notified to the Treasury, and duly entered on the Treasury books; and that they still remain outstanding, and are unpaid by the United States.

In the statement of the Auditor of the Treasury, dated March 8, 1802, which has been referred to, are several other cases very similar to that of the petitioners. The committee find that most of these cases have been since settled under special acts of Congress; as also most of those mentioned in the report of the Committee of Claims, which stated that it was then inexpedient to open the act of limitation.

It is now upwards of fifty-five years since these certificates are said to have been stolen from their owner, and it is upwards of forty-one years since formal notice thereof was given to the proper authorities of the United States, and their payment stopped, should payment ever be claimed by any person other than the representatives of William Wright. No other person has ever claimed payment, nor have the certificates ever appeared at the Treasury; and as it is certified by the Register of the Treasury that they are still outstanding and unpaid, the committee do not hesitate to recommend that provision be made for their liquidation and payment to the legal representatives of William Wright; for which purpose a bill is herewith reported.

*List of certain loan-office certificates issued from the loan office in Maryland.*

| No. | Date. | In whose favor. | Nominal amount. | Specie value. |
|---|---|---|---|---|
| 1202 | May 20, 1779 | William Wright - | $600 | $46 42 |
| 1203 | do | do - | 600 | 46 42 |
| 1204 | do | do - | 600 | 46 42 |
| 1205 | do | do - | 600 | 46 42 |
| 1206 | do | do - | 600 | 46 42 |
| 1825 | do | do - | 500 | 38 65 |
| 1826 | do | do - | 500 | 38 65 |
| 1827 | do | do - | 500 | 38 65 |
| 1828 | do | do - | 500 | 38 65 |
| 1829 | do | do - | 500 | 38 65 |
| 1830 | do | do - | 500 | 38 65 |
| 1831 | do | do - | 500 | 38 65 |
| 1832 | do | do - | 500 | 38 65 |
| 1833 | do | do - | 500 | 38 65 |
| 1834 | do | do - | 500 | 38 65 |
| 1835 | do | do - | 500 | 38 65 |
| 1836 | do | do - | 500 | 38 65 |
| 1837 | do | do - | 500 | 38 65 |
| 1838 | do | do - | 500 | 38 65 |
| 1839 | do | do - | 500 | 38 65 |
| 1840 | do | do - | 500 | 38 65 |
| 1841 | do | do - | 500 | 38 65 |
| 1842 | do | do - | 500 | 38 65 |
| 2475 | do | do - | 1,000 | 77 40 |
| 2476 | do | do - | 1,000 | 77 40 |
| 2477 | do | do - | 1,000 | 77 40 |
| 2478 | do | do - | 1,000 | 77 40 |
| 2479 | do | do - | 1,000 | 77 40 |
| 2480 | do | do - | 1,000 | 77 40 |
| 2481 | do | do - | 1,000 | 77 40 |
| 1437 | Jan. 30, 1779 | Arell, Cooper, & Arell | 300 | 34 82 |

TREASURY DEPARTMENT,
*Register's Office, December* 15, 1836.

This is to certify that it appears, from the books of this office that the loan-office certificates mentioned and described in the within list are still outstanding and unpaid. And it further appears that a claim for payment thereof was presented at the Treasury Department, and notice given, under the act of the 24th April, 1794, that said certificates had been lost or stolen, and the payment thereof, should the same be hereafter presented, stopped.

T. L. SMITH, *Register.*

The Committee on Revolutionary Claims, to which was referred the petition of Vause Fox, administrator de bonis non of William Vause, deceased, have had the same under consideration, and report :

That the petitioner claims commutation pay in right of William Vause, deceased, who was a captain in the continental line of the army of the Revolution. In the opinion of the committee, the evidence referred with the petition well sustains the claim.

William Vause, agreeably to a letter of information obtained from the Third Auditor of the Treasury Department, appears upon the rolls of the 8th Virginia regiment to have been a captain from the 19th of February, 1777, the time of his appointment, to the 30th of November, 1779. The records of his office furnish no information of his services after this time ; but, to establish the continuance of his services beyond this period and beyond the time (21st of October, 1780) at which, to have become a supernumerary officer, was no divestiture of the right to commutation pay, the following evidence is believed to be sufficient.

The certificate of the auditor of public accounts, in the State of Virginia, shows that William Vause was paid, under the act of the November session, 1781, of that State, £565 19s. for his services in the continental line, as a captain, up to the 18th of February, 1781.

His heirs, too, were allowed a warrant for 666⅔ acres of land, his additional bounty of land for his seventh year's service. This information is supplied by the certificate of Frederick Keller, a clerk in the General Land Office.

The affidavit of Joseph Vanmeter, certified to be a man of unquestionable veracity, sets forth that he was well acquainted with Captain William Vause, of the 12th Virginia regiment on continental establishment during the revolutionary war ; that he knew said Vause from the time he entered the service until the day of his death, and served with him in the said regiment; that the said Vause returned home *just* before the close of the war, as a supernumerary officer, and never resigned his commission.

The affidavit of William Inskeep, an authenticated copy of which is filed with the petition, corroborates the statement that William Vause was in the continental service, and became a supernumerary officer at a late period of the war.

The committee report a bill allowing commutation pay to his legal representative.

----

JANUARY 4, 1838.

The Committee on Revolutionary Claims, to which was referred the petition of Israel White, legal representative of the late Captain Tarpley White, and of Lieutenant John White, have had the same under their consideration, and report :

That, by the deposition of Rowley White, and that of Samuel Tinsley, (the latter of whom was an officer of the army of the Revolution,) it appears that the said Tarpley White was a captain in the army of the Revolution.

The certificate of the register of the land office in Virginia shows that, on the 15th of July, 1783, a military land bounty warrant for four thousand acres; and on the 1st of June, 1805, two other such warrants for three hundred and thirty-three and one-third acres, each, were issued by the State of Virginia to Tarpley White, for seven years' services as a captain in the Virginia continental line.

The certificate of the auditor of public accounts in Virginia, also filed in the case, shows that, upon the settlement of accounts made in pursuance of the act of the General Assembly of Virginia, passed at its November session, in the year 1781, a certificate issued, on the 13th March, 1783, in the name of Tarpley White, as a captain of infantry, for £352 18s. 6d. for services continuing down to the 15th February, 1781.

In addition to this evidence, the certificate of General Robert Porterfield, who was a captain in the war of the Revolution, proves that Tarpley White served in that war, as a captain, in the campaigns of 1780 and 1781.

Under this view of the case, your committee cannot hesitate in the opinion that Tarpley White was a captain in the army of the Revolution on continental establishment; and, nothing appearing to induce a suspicion that he resigned, or otherwise divested himself of his title to his commutation pay, they have come to the conclusion that he was entitled to it; and accordingly report a bill.

As to the case of John White, your committee are fully satisfied that he was a lieutenant in the army of the Revolution. His commission, filed in the case, establishes the fact; but, under all the circumstances of the case, they are inclined to the belief that he received his commutation pay. The records of the War Department, according to a letter (filed) of the Third Auditor, show that an officer of the same name and grade did receive his commutation pay; and, although it is clear that there were two officers of the same name in the service, yet they think the John White in whose right the petitioner claims is the individual who received his commutation pay, because he (the latter) acted as a paymaster, and had a settlement of his accounts with the Government after the conclusion of the war. The presumption is natural that he did claim all that was due to him from the Government.

The committee have, therefore, come to the following resolution:

*Resolved*, That so much of the prayer of the petitioner as relates to the claim of commutation pay, on account of the services of John White, as a lieutenant in the army of the Revolution, be rejected.

---

JANUARY 4, 1838.

The Committee on Revolutionary Claims, to which was referred the petition of the heirs of Joel Hardaway, deceased, report:

That the petitioners claim commutation of five years' full pay, on account of the alleged revolutionary services of their ancestor, Joel Hardaway, deceased; and, also, payment of the specie value of a warrant for fifteen thousand pounds, said to have issued in his favor for advancements made to the Government in 1787. The letter of the Third Auditor states that the records of the Pension Office show that Joel Hardaway was a lieutenant in the 4th South Carolina regiment, in the war of the Revolution; but that they afford no evidence of the commencement or termination of his services. Various private memorandums are filed, purporting to show payments made by the said Hardaway, in the character of lieutenant during the revolutionary war, and coming down to 1782. No testimony is afforded to prove even the genuine character of these papers, which, at best, would afford but slight proof towards establishing the claim to commutation. The only foundation that is laid for the other branch of the claim consists of an alleged copy of a receipt, said to be signed by John Hopkins, assistant paymaster, with an endorsement by Nathaniel Lucas, stating that the original had been received by him in order to a final settlement; and a letter purporting to be written by one Isaac Hicks, having reference to the delivery of this warrant to Mr. Lucas. The committee are of opinion that the character and extent of the testimony submitted to them do not justify the granting of relief under either branch of the claim set forth by the petitioners: they therefore adopt the following resolution:

*Resolved,* That the prayer of the petitioners ought not to be granted.

---

JANUARY 4, 1838.

The Committee on Revolutionary Claims, to which was referred the petition of Elizabeth Burton, the widow and devisee of James Burton, report:

That the petitioner represents, that in the early part of the year 1776, James Burton was commissioned an ensign, and went to the North, where he remained in active service till the latter part of the year 1778, when he was sent on the recruiting service. In the spring of the year 1779 he was appointed a captain in the regiment of Colonel Francis Taylor, then stationed in Charlotteville, and continued in active service till that regiment was disbanded, in 1781, when he became supernumerary, as did the other officers, and remained so until the end of the war, but remained always ready and liable to be called into active service; and that he never received the five years' full pay in lieu of half pay promised to such officers of the revolutionary army as should serve to the end of the war; and the petitioner prays Congress to allow her the five years' full pay promised by the resolutions of the old Congress.

By the certificate of William Gordon, Esq., the clerk who has charge of the Bounty Land Office, it appears that an original commission, dated at Philadelphia, on the 8th of November, 1776, and signed by John Hancock, President of Congress, appointing James Burton an ensign in the army of the United States, is on file in that office; and that a warrant for 300 acres of land issued on the 8th of March, 1833, to the devisees of Captain James Burton, of the Virginia line.

By the certificate of the auditor of public accounts of the State of Virginia, it appears that, in pursuance of an act of Assembly, passed at the November session, 1781, a certificate issued on the 29th day of July, 1783, in the name of James Burton, as a lieutenant and adjutant of infantry, for £305 3s. 2d., and was given for services prior to the 1st of January, 1782; to wit: as lieutenant, in Colonel Taylor's regiment, from the 18th of January, 1779, to the 8th of October following; and as captain, from the 8th of October, 1779, to the 13th of December, 1780.

It further appears, by the certificate of Frederick Keller, a clerk in the General Land Office, that the records of that office show that a warrant, No. 6053, for 2,666⅔ acres, was granted by the State of Virginia to James Burton for his three years' services in the continental line as a lieutenant; and that another warrant, No. 7650, for 2,055 acres, was granted by the State of Virginia to Elizabeth Burton and others, devisees of said James Burton, for his services as a captain from March, 1776, to the end of the war.

In addition to the foregoing evidence, an authenticated copy of a certificate of John Roberts, who was a major of the regiment of guards to guard the "convention troops of Burgoyne's army," is filed in the case, which shows that James Burton, of Orange county, was first a lieutenant, and subsequently a captain, in the regiment that had under guard the "convention troops of Burgoyne's army," at the barracks, in Albemarle county, and that he continued in the service until that regiment was discharged, which was done about May, 1781.

James Burton seems to have remained a supernumerary from this time until the end of the war. The committee think the claim good, and therefore report a bill in favor of it.

----

JANUARY 4, 1838.

The Committee on Revolutionary Claims, to which was referred the petition of the heirs of Garland Burnley, deceased, report:

The petitioners, grandchildren of Captain Garland Burnley, deceased, state that their ancestor entered the army of the Revolution at the commencement of the war; that he first engaged in the "minute service" of Virginia, and was in a hard-fought action near the borough of Norfolk; that in the year 1776 he was appointed a lieutenant in Captain Spencer's company of regulars, raised in pursuance of an ordinance of the General Convention; that in 1778, he was appointed a captain in Colonel Francis Taylor's regiment, acknowledged by repeated acts of the Government to have been a continental regiment; and that he served until June, 1781, when the regiment was disbanded, and he became a supernumerary, without resigning his commission, and subject to orders until the close of of the war.

This statement of the petitioners is verified by the testimony submitted with the petition. From a report made by the Orange county committee, pursuant to an ordinance of the General Convention, and signed "Thomas Barbour, chairman," and "Benjamin Johnston, clerk," it appears that Lieutenant Burnley had been in the minute service, and was appointed a lieutenant in Spencer's company of regulars, to be raised in that county, and was engaged in enlisting men. From a certificate signed "Robert Taylor, jr.," it appears that, from an account-book kept in the handwriting of Colonel Francis Taylor, of the continental line, purporting to be an account of the moneys charged to the different officers and men in service with him, Garland Burnley is charged with different sums; and, also, "that the books and papers of the said Colonel Taylor prove that much confidence was reposed in Captain Burnley, and that the pay and muster-rolls of his company show that he, the said Burnley, was in actual service as late as the spring of 1781." By a certificate from the Auditor's office of Virginia, it appears that Garland Burnley was paid, for services as a captain in the Virginia continental line, to June 15, 1781; and by another certificate from the United States bounty land office, signed "William Gordon," it is shown that a land warrant for the quantity of acres to which a captain was entitled was issued to the heirs at law of Garland Burnley, and to which those only belonging to the continental line, and serving to the close of the war, or discharged by the order of Congress, were entitled.

From this testimony it is evident that Burnley was a captain in the Virginia line on continental establishment; that he served until after the new arrangement of the army, under the resolves of 1780, actually until June, 1781, when he became a retiring officer, without resigning his commission, and always holding himself ready to obey orders; that he thereby became entitled to the half pay for life promised by the resolves of October, 1780, and consequently to the five years' full pay, granted in lieu thereof, by the resolution of March, 1783. This being unpaid, according to the testimony of the Third Auditor, a bill is reported for the relief of the petitioners.

---

JANUARY 4, 1838.

The Committee on Revolutionary Claims, to which was referred the petition of Francis A. Thornton and Elizabeth P. Gwin, report :

That the petitioners are the children and legal representatives of Captain Presley Thornton, and, as such, claim the five years' full pay, in commutation of the half pay for life, promised by the resolves of Congress to such officers of the continental army as should serve to the close of the war ; which they assert he had never received before his death, which occurred in the year 1811.

They prove that their father, Captain Thornton, served in Colonel George Baylor's regiment of light dragoons until the close of the war, by the testimony of General James Wood, of the American revolutionary army, who expressly states that " Captain Presley Thornton, late of Baylor's regiment of cavalry, entered the service of the United States prior to the 10th of November, 1776, and continued in service until the conclusion of the war, in November, 1783;" upon which testimony Captain Thornton received bounty land from the State of Virginia for "his seventh year's service." As a further proof, they give the testimony of Benjamin Temple, late lieutenant colonel commanding second regiment of light dragoons, who certifies that, to his personal knowledge, Captain Presley Thornton, late of Colonel George Baylor's regiment of light dragoons in the United States army, was in actual service at the conclusion of the war in 1783. The Third Auditor of the Treasury certifies that there is nothing upon record in that office to show that the commutation now claimed has been heretofore paid.

The committee, believing the claim well founded and unpaid, report a bill for the relief of the petitioners.

48

The Committee on Revolutionary Claims, to whom was referred the petition of Edmund Christian and Nancy Hilliard, have had the same under consideration, and report :

That the petitioners represent that they are the only heirs of William H. Gregory, who was the son and only child of William Gregory, who was a captain in the Virginia continental line of the army of the Revolution, and that he died in that service ; and that the seven years' half pay to which the said William H. Gregory became entitled on account of the death of his father, has never been paid. They therefore pray Congress to pass an act directing the seven years' half pay, aforesaid, with interest, to be paid to them.

The evidence upon which the claim is grounded is as follows :

First : A certificate of the county court of Charles City county, in the State of Virginia, in the following words and figures, to wit : " At a court of monthly session, begun and held for Charles City county, at the courthouse, on Thursday, the 15th September, 1836, *Ordered*, That it be certified that it is proven to the satisfaction of the court that Captain William Gregory, of the war of the Revolution, died in the year 1776, leaving an only child, a son, William H. Gregory, to whom he bequeathed his estate ; that the said William H. Gregory died in the year 1829, without issue, and bequeathed his personal estate to his wife, Frances, and Edmund Christian, his half brother ; that Edmund Christian and Nancy Hilliard, who was Nancy Christian, of New Kent county, are the half brother and sister of the said William H. Gregory, deceased, and are the only heirs to any and all the property not specified in the will of the said William H. Gregory."

Second : Extracts from the journal of the committee of safety, in the State of Virginia, certified to be correctly copied by James E. Heath, auditor of public accounts ; which extracts are as follow, viz :

" *Friday, 8th March,* 1776.

" A warrant to Capt. Wm. Gregory, pd. £20 10*s.* for his recruiting expenses and balance of county money in Charles City county.

" *Ordered*, That the commanding officer at this place direct the march of Captain Gibson's rifle company, also of either Captain Gregory's company, from Charles City, or Capt. Ja. Johnston's, from Lunenberg, as upon a review shall appear to be best fitted to reinforce the troops stationed at Suffolk, as soon as possible."

" *Sunday, the* 10*th March,* 1776.

" Capt Gregory, and Lieutenants Dunn and Gregory, and Ensign Bell, of the sixth battalion, attended, received their commissions, took the oath prescribed by convention, and subscribed the articles of war."

Third : A letter from the Hon. John Forsyth, Secretary of State, in answer to one from Francis A. Dickins, Esq., of Washington city ; from which it appears that the name of William Gregory is upon a certified copy of a list of officers of the Virginia service among the papers of General Washington, on file in the State Department, as captain in the sixth Virginia regiment, with the words " Captain Gregory dead" written opposite to it.

Fourth : A certificate of the auditor of public accounts in the Commonwealth of Virginia shows that it does not appear from the records of his
office that William Gregory, a captain of the army of the Revolution in
the continental line, his heirs or representatives, ever received the seven
years' half pay allowed by act of Assembly, passed October, 1780, or under any other authority.

Fifth : By a letter of Peter Hagner, Third Auditor, it appears that
there is nothing on the records of his office to show that William Gregory
was a captain of the sixth Virginia regiment of the army of the Revolution, and, consequently, there is nothing to indicate the payment of the
seven years' half pay to his widow or any other person.

Upon the whole evidence, the committee decide that the seven years'
half pay is due from the Government, on account of the death of Captain
William Gregory in the continental service ; and accordingly, without deciding the question to whom payment should be made, they report a bill,
directing payment to be made to those who are entitled to receive it,
under the resolution of 24th August, 1780.

---

JANUARY 9, 1838.

The Committee on Revolutionary Claims, to whom was referred the
petition of John Thomas and Nathaniel Thomas, report :

That the petition states the petitioners are the only sons and surviving
children of John Thomas, a major general in the revolutionary war ; that
the said John Thomas, from the commencement of the said war until his
decease, was in actual service ; that, while in command of a large body
of troops in Canada, he was exposed to the contagion of the smallpox,
of which disease he died on the 2d day of June, 1776, at Chambly. The
petition prays that the same bounty awarded by Congress to major generals in the revolutionary army, who served to the end of the war, may
be granted to the petitioners.

The committee report against the petition, for the reasons that there is
no proof in support of the allegations contained in the petition, and that
the case, if admitted to be true as stated by the petitioners, does not fall
within any of the resolutions or laws of Congress on the subject.

---

JANUARY 9, 1838.

The Committee on Revolutionary Claims, to which was referred the
petition of John Wallace, the only heir at law of William Wallace, deceased, report :

The petition states that William Wallace, of Johnstown, county of
Montgomery, and State of New York, was the father of the petitioner ;
that he was a lieutenant, and served as such during the revolutionary war
between the kingdom of Great Britain and the United States of America,
in a regiment of infantry commanded by Colonel James Livingston, of the
New York line of infantry ; and that at no time did the said William Wallace receive from Government five years' full pay, or any part thereof, in

commutation of half pay for life, as lieutenant, provided by the resolutions of Congress of October, 1780; that the said William Wallace was ignorant of his claims in this respect upon Government until towards the close of his life; and that the said William Wallace departed this life in January, 1837, intestate, and leaving the petitioner sole and only heir at law of the said deceased.

The prayer of the petition is, that Congress will pass a law granting to the petitioner full pay for five years, in commutation of half pay for life, to which his ancestor, the said William Wallace, was entitled as lieutenant in said regiment.

The death of the said William Wallace at Johnstown, in the State of New York, on the 25th day of January, 1837, and that the said John Wallace is his sole heir at law, are satisfactorily established by proof.

It is proved by a document from the Third Auditor's office, in the Treasury Department, of the 5th day of January, 1838, that William Wallace was a lieutenant in Colonel James Livingston's regiment, and that he *resigned* on the 17th of August, 1779. It is certified by said document that this fact appears from a record of the New York line.

A letter from the War Department, Pension Office, dated January 6, 1838, to the committee, says, "that William Wallace, who was a lieutenant in Colonel James Livingston's regiment, entered the service on the 6th May, 1777, and resigned the 17th August, 1779. This clearly appears, not only from an affidavit on file in this office, but from the records also." The committee therefore decide and report against the prayer of the petitioner.

———

JANUARY 9, 1838.

The Committee on Revolutionary Claims, to which was referred the petition of Margaret White, widow of Colonel Anthony Walton White, report:

This case has been repeatedly examined, and favorable reports made thereon by different committees appointed on revolutionary claims, accompanied by bills of relief. It has again been re-examined; and a former report, detailing the facts of the case, and giving a part of the evidence, has been concurred in, adopted, and annexed to this, with a bill for the relief of the petitioner.

At the second session of the last Congress a bill for the relief of Mrs. White passed through a Committee of the Whole House, after a full debate, but was arrested on the question of engrossment, under the suggestion that Colonel White might not have settled with the State of Virginia, and that the United States might, in such a case, become liable to that State. In consequence, at the request of the committee, the bill was postponed, that time might be had to consult the authorities of Virginia on the subject. A reply to the inquiries made was not received until it had become too late to act again on the bill during that session.

The information obtained from Virginia, and other sources, in the opinion of the committee, clearly establishes the fact that Colonel White had settlements both with Virginia and the United States—with the former on the 30th day of January, 1787, and with the latter on the 12th of March,

1788, and 6th of March, 1789; in all of which settlements balances were found, *not against him*, but *due to him*, and that these balances were paid in final settlement certificates.

It is well known that Virginia did not issue final settlement certificates as long as a balance appeared against a claimant. It is equally well known that the United States acted on the same principle, and even withheld pensions until it was clearly shown that there was no balance due from the claimant to the United States. (Vide resolve of July 12, 1787.) It is also known that the United States issued no commutation certificates until the accounts of officers were adjusted, and a *certainty* existed that there was no balance due them from the officer. Yet Colonel White received a final settlement certificate from Virginia, as certified by the Auditor of that State; from the United States, as stated by Mr. Hagner, Third Auditor of the Treasury; and commutation certificates, as appears from the records of the War Department. How, under such circumstances, can it be supposed that his accounts were unsettled, and a balance existing against him?

That the $150,000, continental paper money, the value of which, according to the scale of depreciation then established, was $3,750, and now claimed, was never paid, appears distinctly from an *original* paper signed by John Pendleton, Auditor of Virginia, dated January 30, 1787, showing a settlement of Colonel White's *paper-money* account with Virginia, and containing a list of four receipts disallowed, and the reasons for their disallowance; among them, the identical charge of money advanced to Captain Belfield, and for which the present claim is made. This paper, in connexion with the explanatory certificate of Mr. Auditor Heath, (a copy of which as well as of the paper itself is hereto annexed,) conclusively proves that all the accounts of Colonel White with Virginia were settled at that time, as it expressly speaks of the *paper-money* account, and bears the same date as the final settlement certificate granted by Virginia to Colonel White for the balance of his pay, and which was forwarded by the Auditor of that State to the committee.

Upon reviewing the whole case, and all the testimony for and against, the committee are fully convinced that the claim is well founded; and trust that, after the many unfortunate and accidental delays which it has sustained, justice will at length be accorded to the widow of a most meritorious officer, who has strong claims upon the Government, not only for justice, but the most distinguished generosity. She asks only for strict justice.

Her own large fortune, and that of her husband, (one of the most wealthy men of the country at the commencement of the Revolution—their conjoint estates being a princely fortune,) was all absorbed in the vicissitudes of the revolutionary struggle, and in the scarcely equalled patriotism of her husband in the day and hour of his country's need. He descended in poverty to an untimely grave, writhing under a sense of national injustice; whilst she, bending to the earth under a weight of fourscore years, is lingering out existence dependent on the exertions of an only and widowed daughter, who supports herself, her own orphan children, and her aged mother, by teaching an academy: and all this whilst the Government, rich beyond the example of nations, is actually withholding money which the husband and father advanced to feed and clothe

the naked and starving soldiers of his country—soldiers whom he commanded, and often led, with unsurpassed bravery, to battle and to victory.

The aged widow still prays and hopes for justice, and speedy justice, from her country. Shall her hopes be again disappointed, and the feeble tenure upon which she holds life be broken by the shock?

*Copy of the original certificate of John Pendleton, Auditor of Virginia.*

AUDITOR'S OFFICE, *January* 30, 1787.

Receipts disallowed in the settlement of Lieutenant Colonel White's paper-money account:

|  |  |  |  | Paper pounds. |
|---|---|---|---|---|
| John Belfield, dated July 4, 1780 | · | - | - | £45,000 |
| James Gunn, dated June 26, 1780 | - | - |  | 6,900 |
| John Watts, dated March 7, 1781 | - | - |  | 4,134 |
| Alexander St. Clair, account | - | - | - | 357 |

The Auditor cannot admit these debts until it appears the money was actually expended in the public service; whenever that fact is ascertained, those sums will be allowed and reduced agreeably to law.

JOHN PENDLETON.

[The receipts of James Gunn and John Watts, as above, disallowed by the Auditor of Virginia, were allowed in his settlement with the United States.]

*Certificate of James E. Heath, present Auditor of Virginia, as to the identity of Mr. Pendleton's certificate, and as to Colonel White's settlement with Virginia.*

AUDITOR'S OFFICE,<br>
Virginia, June 2, 1837.

The agent for the heirs of Colonel Anthony W. White has shown to me an original paper, dated 30th January, 1787, which I know to be in the handwriting of John Pendleton, at that time auditor of public accounts of this Commonwealth; by which paper it appears that a settlement had been made of the *"paper-money account"* of Colonel White, in which description of account I presume would be included the within-mentioned charge of $150,000, that sum having been advanced to Colonel White on the 7th September, 1781, as appears from a copy of his receipt to Foster Webb, attested by said Webb, and as the charge of the same was made on the books of the Commonwealth against Colonel White several months anterior to the date of Mr. Pendleton's original paper showing that Colonel White's *"paper-money account"* had been settled. On the day of this settlement, to wit, the 30th January, 1787, a certificate issued to Colonel White for the balance of his full pay, (or depreciation,) and I should presume that that certificate would not have issued if Colonel White had been in arrears to the Commonwealth. It appears, moreover, that this item of $150,000 is credited to the Commonwealth in an account made out by Mr. Pierce,* and bearing the marks of antiquity; which has also been shown to me by the agent of Colonel White's heirs. Upon the whole, I think there is strong reason to believe that the sum of $150,000, within charged, must have been embraced in the settlement referred to in the paper signed by Mr. Pendleton. It is probable that the book containing that settlement, and the vouchers connected therewith, may have been delivered to the commissioners who adjusted the accounts between the United States and the several States; though of that I cannot, of course, speak with confidence. There are many such balances standing on the account-books of this office, which we take to be more *nominal* than real.

JAMES E. HEATH,
*Auditor of Virginia.*

---

*Certificate of the Auditor of Virginia that a final settlement certificate was granted to Colonel White on the 30th January, 1787, the same day that Mr. Pendleton certifies that he had settled his paper-money account.*

This is to certify that it appears, from a list in this office of such officers and soldiers of the Virginia continental line, during the revolutionary war, as settled their accounts, and received certificates for the balance of their full pay, according to an act of Assembly passed the November session, 1781, that a certificate issued on the thirtieth day of January, 1787, in the name of Anthony W. White, as lieutenant colonel of cavalry, for £597 16s. 1d.; which certificate appears to have been delivered to himself, and was given for services prior to the 1st of January, 1782 ; to wit: from the 1st August, 1780, to the 31st December, 1781.

Given under my hand at the Auditor's office, Richmond, this 7th day of January, 1837.

[No seal of office.]      JAMES E. HEATH,

*Auditor of Virginia.*

---

*Copy of the resolve of Congress of July 12, 1787.*

On the report of the Board of Treasury, it was

*Resolved,* That all officers of the line of the late army who may be entitled to pensions, in pursuance of the acts of Congress in that behalf made, shall, previous to the receipt of such pension, deposite with the proper officer appointed to discharge the same, in the State in which they reside, a certificate from the commissioner of army accounts, purporting that no balance is due from the claimant to the United States.

[It was after the adoption of this resolution, (*i. e.* on the 12th March, 1788, and 6th March, 1789,) that Colonel White received his final settlement certificates and commutation certificates from the United States.]

---

*The United States commissioner for settling the accounts of officers of the revolutionary army, and for issuing final settlement certificates. This officer prepared Colonel White's accounts for settlement with Virginia.

The Committee on Revolutionary Claims, to which was referred the petition of Margaret White, widow of Colonel Anthony Walton White, report:

That this case was examined, and a favorable report made thereon, accompanied by a bill for the relief of the petitioner, at the second session of the last Congress. The committee, on a re-examination, adopt the former report, and annex it to this. The bill which, owing to the pressure of other and prior business, could not receive the action of the House, is again reported.

The Committee on Revolutionary Claims, to which was referred the petition of Margaret White, widow of Colonel Anthony Walton White, report:

That Anthony Walton White, colonel of the first regiment of light dragoons in the revolutionary war, presented his petition in March, 1790, to the first Congress assembled under the present constitution, praying for the reimbursement of $150,000, advanced by him on the 4th of July, 1780, for the use of his regiment; the value of which sum, according to the scale of depreciation then established, was $3,750.

In the petition of 1790, Colonel White states that, on taking command of the cavalry in the South, he found all the quartermasters, foragemasters, and commissaries of that department, either captured, or destitute of resources for procuring the necessary supplies of provision and forage; which articles could only be obtained on the credit of himself and friends, or by plunder and the sword; and that a resort to the latter means being prohibited by both policy and humanity, he was obliged to raise on private loan $150,000, which he deposited in the hands of John Belfield, then a captain and paymaster in his regiment, for the use and benefit of his regiment; that the whole of said sum was in fact applied solely to that purpose, and the vouchers taken therefor placed by Belfield in the hands of staff officers for safe-keeping; but that the memorandum showing the names of the officers with whom they were deposited had been lost by Belfield, so that the petitioner was left without the means of obtaining and exhibiting the vouchers which would show the particular application of the money. He states that in 1788 he petitioned Congress for redress, but that body was dissolved before his case was finally acted on, and he prays to be reimbursed the money advanced. This petition appears to have been referred, with others, to the Secretary of War, who recommended the passage of a law authorizing the claims to be settled on equitable principles, and on the best evidence the nature of the case might admit. In May, 1792, a bill with this object passed the House, but was postponed in the Senate, in which body similar bills were introduced in 1793 and 1796, but not finally acted on. Since the death of Colonel White, his widow has presented two petitions, in the last of which she sets up an additional claim for the value of seven loan-office certificates. of $1,000 each, (the numbers of which are stated,) issued to Colonel White from the South Carolina loan office, and alleged to have been lost.

In support of the allegations of Colonel White's petition, the committee find in the papers the following testimony:

1st. The [original] receipt of Captain Belfield, dated July 4, 1780, for $150,000, placed in his hands for the use of the regiment, to be paid to them as he may please.

2d. The [original] certificate of Captain Belfield, dated the 2d of February, 1787, stating that the money had been applied exclusively to the use of the regiment, and accounted for by him to some of the staff; and that when the money was deposited with him by Colonel White, the regiment was in want, and distressed for many necessaries.

3d. The [orginal] certificate of Jonathan Burrall, commissioner for settling the accounts of the commissary and quartermaster's departments, dated September 2, 1788, stating that no charge appeared on the books of his office against John Belfield, captain and paymaster, by any commissary or quartermaster, for any disbursements by him for supplies to said regiment; but that few of the accounts of quartermasters in the Southern department had yet been rendered, and that, if any such charge should thereafter appear while he continued in office, they would be noticed and stoppages made. He continued in office at least as late as until May, 1789.

4th. The [original] affidavit of Colonel White himself, dated September 15, 1788, in which he verifies on oath the material facts that have been stated.

The petitioner also refers to the distressed situation of the Southern army, then, and now, notorious; and it is impossible not to take into consideration the general pecuniary embarrassments of the country and its Government; in consequence of which, in numerous instances, the support of the common cause was left to rest upon the advances and sacrifices to be made by individuals. These considerations do not, it is true, furnish of themselves any evidence to establish the fact of an advance in a particular instance; but they may be, and in this instance are, strongly corroborative of more direct testimony on the subject.

It is deemed proper, also, to refer to the following resolution of June the 19th, 1780, relating to this particular regiment, as showing at once the anxiety and the inability of Congress to provide for its proper equipment:

" *Resolved,* That it be earnestly recommended to the States of Virginia and North Carolina to use their utmost exertions to recruit, remount, and equip Baylor's and White's regiments of light dragoons, so as to complete them at least 150 rank and file in each regiment."*

* As further illustrative of the anxiety with which the proper equipment of Colonel White's regiment was viewed, when the British army was making such fearful progress through the Southern States, and also as showing the desperate state of the public finances at the very period when Colonel White so patriotically raised, upon his own private credit, and advanced for the support and equipment of his regiment, the money which forms the subject of the present claim, it is deemed proper to add the following resolution of the General Assembly of Virginia, dated July 14, 1780. By this resolution it will be perceived that Virginia, at the very time of Colonel White's advance of his own money for the support of his regiment, was unable to pay, even in depreciated paper money, for a single horse, but had to rely upon a purchase on credit:

"IN THE HOUSE OF DELEGATES, *July* 14, 1780.

" *Resolved,* That the Governor and Council be desired to appoint one or more purchasers, in such counties as they may think proper, to procure horses to remount the dragoons in Colonels White and Washington's corps, upon the best terms they can, granting certificates for the value

The committee are satisfied that Colonel White did, on the 4th day of July, advance to the paymaster of his regiment, and for its use, $150,000, of the value of $3,750 ; that the circumstances of the regiment were such as to call for this advance on his part, and render it proper ; and that the money so advanced was in fact disbursed for the use of the regiment. The liability of the United States for the repayment of the sum so advanced and disbursed, they consider unquestionable ; and on the principles of the resolution of the 3d of June, 1784, which directs that an interest of six per cent. per annum shall be allowed to all creditors of the United States for supplies furnished or services done from the time that the payment became due, as well as upon the grounds of common justice, they think interest should be allowed upon the sum advanced from the time it was placed in the hands of Belfield for the use of the regiment. But while it does not appear that there has been any failure of diligence in the presentation of this claim, by which any right of the claimant should be forfeited, no reason is perceived for placing it now upon better grounds than it would have occupied if it had been originally allowed, and the amount subscribed in the public funds under the act of August, 1790. A bill is therefore reported for the payment of $3,750, (the value of the sum advanced by Colonel White,) with interest, according to the provisions of the said act of August, 1790, to be computed from the 4th day of July, 1780.

With respect to the loan-office certificates, alleged to have been lost, the certificate of the Register of the Treasury, dated the 31st day of January, 1834, shows that the certificates described in the petition of Mrs. White, and also in the foregoing part of this report, are outstanding and unpaid, and, together with the great lapse of time, creates that strong presumption of their loss, on the ground of which Congress has, in numerous cases, directed payment to be made of their value. A provision is therefore inserted in the bill for the payment of $175, the value of said loan-office certificates, with interest thereon, at the rate of six per cent. per annum; that being the usual rate allowed in such cases.

-----

### *Appended to this report.*

1st. The original petition of Colonel White.
2d. The original receipt of John Belfield, dated July 4, 1780.
3d. The original certificate of John Belfield, dated 2d February, 1787.
4th. The original certificate of Jonathan Burrall, dated Sept. 2, 1788.
5th. The certificate of Michael Nourse, marked A.
6th. The original affidavit of Colonel White, dated September 15, 1788.
7th. The certificate of T. L. Smith, marked B.
8th. The certificate of T. L. Smith, marked C.

of the horses so purchased ; which certificates the General Assembly will, at their next session, make provision for the speedy payment of to the respective holders, together with an interest thereupon of *five per centum* from the time of purchase: *Provided,* That such purchases shall not exceed the number of three hundred horses, including those now belonging to the said corps, and those which may have been already purchased under any former resolution of Assembly."

"A copy. Test:

"JOHN BECKLEY, *C. H. D.*

"Agreed to by the Senate:

"WILLIAM DREW, *C. S.*"

## No. 1.

*To the Speaker and House of Representatives of the United States:*

The memorial of Anthony W. White, late colonel of the first regiment of dragoons in the service of the United States, most respectfully sheweth :

That your memorialist, on taking the command of the cavalry of the late army in the Southern department, found all the quartermasters, foragemasters, and commissaries of the said department, either captured by the British army in Charleston, or destitute of resources to render your memorialist any assistance in procuring supplies of provision and forage, &c., for the use of the men and horses under his command, which very necessary articles could only be obtained upon the credit of your memorialist and his friends, or by plunder and the sword : that humanity and policy forbade him to add so great a calamity to the unprotected and unfortunate inhabitants of the country, and therefore obliged your memorialist, during that period of general confusion and distress, to raise, on private loan, one hundred and fifty thousand dollars, for the purpose of procuring the articles necessary for the support and comfort of the troops committed to his care ; that your memorialist deposited the money so obtained in the hands of Major John Belfield, then a captain and paymaster of his regiment, as will appear by his receipt to your memorialist, which money was actually laid out for the use and benefit of the said men and horses, and no part of it applied for any private purpose whatsoever, which will also appear by the said paymaster's certificate ; that the said paymaster placed the vouchers for the expenditures of the said one hundred and fifty thousand dollars in the hands of staff officers, as he met with them, conceiving that they would be safer with their baggage, in the rear of an army, than with light troops generally on the lines ; that the said paymaster made a memorandum of the several quartermasters' and commissaries' names he put the said vouchers in the hands of, but unfortunately had mislaid the same, which leaves your memorialist destitute of relief, unless he obtains it from the justice of his country, as the said paymaster took charge of the said one hundred and fifty thousand dollars, not in his official line, but to oblige your memorialist, and to render, at the same time, a service to his suffering brother-soldiers ; that, to prevent the vouchers for the expenditures of the said one hundred and fifty thousand dollars (if not previously paid) being hereafter presented and paid, your memorialist did obtain from Mr. Jonathan Burrall, commissioner for the quartermaster and commissary's department, a certificate, setting forth that no charge in that office appeared against the said paymaster ; that no charge has been made by any commissary or quartermaster for any payments made to him, or for any disbursements by him, for supplies to the cavalry : and that if any appeared hereafter, in any of their accounts, it should be noticed, and stoppages made ; that your memorialist applied to the Congress of 1788 for redress, believing that the receipt and certificate of Major Belfield, whose integrity and honesty are well known to some of your members from the State of Virginia, would be thought equal, if not superior, to the vouchers for the expenditures of the said one hundred and fifty thousand dollars, and that Mr. Burrall's certificate would clear up any doubts of the said vouchers having been already paid, or the possibility of their being hereafter paid to any person but your memorialist; that the Congress of 1788 committed your memorialist's claim to three of their members, to be investigated, but broke up before their committee reported on the same, which obliges your memorialist to present his claim again to Congress. Your memorialist doubts not that many of the facts stated in this memorial have come within the knowledge of some of the members of Congress from the Southern States, and that all are but too well acquainted with the wretched situation of the American troops at the Southward during the year 1780. Your memorialist therefore prays, as he advanced his money to prevent the *citizen from plunder* and the *soldier from want,* that you will please to consider his claim, and render him that justice he may be found to merit.

ANTHONY W. WHITE.

---

### No. 2.

*Original receipt of Captain Belfield.*

HALIFAX, *July* 4, 1780.

Received of Colonel Anthony W. White, one hundred and fifty thousand dollars, for the use of his regiment, to be paid to them as he may please to direct.

J. BELFIELD, *Captain.*

---

### No. 3.

*Original certificate of Captain Belfield, that the money was expended for the regiment.*

RICHMOND, *February* 2, 1787.

I do certify that the one hundred and fifty thousand dollars put in my hands by Colonel White, and for which I gave my receipt, July 4, 1780, was applied to the use of his regiment, and accounted for by me to some of the staff departments. I further declare that no part of it was ever applied or made use of for him, or for any other private purposes whatever; and that the regiment was in want, and distressed for many necessaries, when Colonel White put the above-mentioned sum in my hands.

J. BELFIELD.

---

### No. 4.

*Certificate of Mr. Burrall, that no other person had obtained credit for the money.*

OFFICE OF ACCOUNTS FOR COM'Y & Q. M. DEPT.,
*New York, September* 2, 1788.

I certify that no charge appears against John Belfield, late a captain and paymaster of the 1st regiment of light dragoons, commanded by

Colonel Anthony W. White, in the books of this office ; neither has any charge been made by any commissary or quartermaster for any payments made to him, or for any disbursements by him, for supplies to said regiment. I must, however, observe, that very few of the accounts of the quartermasters in the Southern department are yet rendered ; but should any such charge hereafter appear in any of their accounts, while I am in office, it will be noticed, and stoppages made.

JON. BURRALL, Commissioner.

---

No. 5.

(A.)

Treasury Department,

Register's Office, January 22, 1834.

Sir : It appears from the records of accounts settled under the old Government, " that Jonathan Burrall, Esq., *late* commissioner for settling the accounts of the quartermaster and commissary departments," received his salary to " 8th May, 1789, inclusive." I presume, therefore, that he ceased to act as commissioner aforesaid on that day. Our records afford no other information on the subject.

Very respectfully,

MICHAEL NOURSE.

---

No. 6.

Original affidavit of Colonel White.

State of New York, *ss.*

Anthony W. White, of the city of New York, maketh oath, and saith, that on the 4th day of July, in the year of our Lord one thousand seven hundred and eighty, he, this deponent, placed in the hands of Captain John Belfield, the then paymaster of his regiment, the sum of one hundred and fifty thousand dollars, to be disposed of to and for the use of the said regiment ; and at the same time this deponent did direct and require the said John Belfield to take all the receipts for the several sums to be by him expended in the manner following, to wit : " Received of Captain John Belfield, of the 1st regiment of light dragoons, the sum of £———, in full for provision, forage, &c., sold and furnished by me for the use of the said regiment.—A. B." And this deponent doth further depose and say, that the said John Belfield did frequently afterwards show unto this deponent receipts by him taken from divers persons who had supplied the said regiment with necessaries ; and this deponent verily believes that he hath seen receipts, written in the manner aforesaid, for the whole of the moneys so as aforesaid delivered by this deponent to the said John Belfield, which was expended to and for the use of the said regiment. And this deponent further doth depose and say, that he was informed by the said John Belfield, that he, Belfield, had lodged the said receipts in the hands of the proper officers of the several staff departments, whenever he met with them, in order that they might be preserved for the satisfaction of this deponent, to whom alone they could be of any use ; and for the greater security, the said John Belfield informed this deponent that he had made a minute of the names of the several persons in whose hands he had deposited the said receipts, which he had unfortunately lost, with several other papers, while on command at the Southward. And this deponent doth further depose and say, that the said John Belfield hath given him, this deponent, the fullest satisfaction that the whole of the said one hundred and fifty thousand dollars was actually and *bona fide* laid out and expended to and for the use of the said regiment, in purchasing and procuring the necessary supplies of provision and forage for the men and horses of the said regiment. And this deponent doth further depose and say, that he did conceive and believe that the receipt of the said John Belfield for the said one hundred and fifty thousand dollars would have been a sufficient voucher for him, this deponent, to have produced, in order to entitle him to full compensation therefor; more especially as the motive which actuated him was generally known to be that of humanity, and a sincere desire to relieve, as much as in his power, the actual distresses of the troops committed to his care. And this deponent further doth depose and say, that no part of the said one hundred and fifty thousand dollars was ever applied by the said John Belfield, or by any other person, for any private purpose whatever, other than is hereinbefore particularly set forth, to the best of this deponent's knowledge and belief. And this deponent doth further depose and say, that he, this deponent, hath never received any of the said receipts from Captain Belfield, or from any other person, nor doth he know where to apply for the same; many of the persons to whom they were given by the said John Belfield, as aforesaid, being, in all probability, dead, or removed to a great distance, and out of the reach and knowledge of this deponent. And this deponent doth further depose and say, that he hath never received any payment of the said one hundred and fifty thousand dollars, or any part thereof, from the said Captain John Belfield, or from any other person whatever, or any security therefor.

And further this deponent saith not.

ANTHONY W. WHITE.

Sworn, this 15th day of September, 1788, before me,

W. POPHAM, *Notary Public.*

---

No. 7.

(B.)

TREASURY DEPARTMENT,

*Register's Office, February 5, 1834.*

SIR: In compliance with your request of the 3d instant, I have the honor to state that, in conformity with the resolution of Congress of the 28th of June, 1780, "continental paper money" was, on the 4th of July, 1780, received on loan at $40 for one ; and that accounts for money advanced on that day, and some time subsequently, were settled at the Treasury at that rate.

I have the honor to be, sir, your obedient servant,

T. L. SMITH, *Register.*

Hon. EBENEZER YOUNG.

---

No. 8.

(C.)

TREASURY DEPARTMENT,
*Register's Office, January* 31, 1834.

I certify that the following certificates, issued at the loan office in South Carolina, are outstanding and unpaid, viz :

| No. | Date. | To whom issued. | Amount. | |
|---|---|---|---|---|
| | | | Nominal. | Specie value. |
| 4388 | June 10, 1780 | Col. Anthony Walton White | $1,000 | $25 00 |
| 4396 | Do. | Do. | 1,000 | 25 00 |
| 4493 | Do. | Do. | 1,000 | 25 00 |
| 4494 | Do. | Do. | 1,000 | 25 00 |
| 4498 | Do. | Do. | 1,000 | 25 00 |
| 4520 | Do. | Do. | 1,000 | 25 00 |
| 4560 | Do. | Do. | 1,000 | 25 00 |
| | | | $7,000 | $175 00 |

T. L. SMITH, *Register.*

---

JANUARY 11, 1838.

The Committee on Revolutionary Claims, to which was referred the petition of the heirs of Leighton Yancy, report :

This case was examined by the Committee on Revolutionary Claims at the 1st session of the 24th Congress, and an unfavorable report made thereon. The committee believe that report to have been a proper one, and adopt it as part of this; believing that the relief asked ought not to be granted, for the reasons therein stated. This report may be found in the manuscript reports of the committee, page 89, 24th Congress, 2d session.

The Committee on Revolutionary Claims, to which was referred the petition of the widow and heirs of Leighton Yancy, report :

That they had this case under consideration at the last session of Congress, and made a report thereon; in the propriety of which they still concur, and which they adopt as their present report. It is as follows:

The Committee on Revolutionary Claims, to whom was referred the petition of the widow and heirs of Leighton Yancy, have had the same under their consideration, and report:

That the petitioners represent that Leighton Yancy was a captain in the continental line of the army of the Revolution, and, having served to the close of the war, was entitled to the commutation pay of an officer of that grade; that he was allowed and received the commutation pay of a lieutenant only; and pray that Congress will allow them the five years' full pay of a captain, deducting therefrom the five years' full pay of a lieutenant, formerly received by said Yancy.

In support of this claim, an act of the Virginia Legislature, passed the 12th of January, 1798, is relied on. The preamble of this act recites, "that during the late war Leighton Yancy served as a lieutenant in the first regiment of light dragoons, commanded by Colonel Theodore Bland, and that he afterwards became entitled to the rank of a captain; that, before he obtained a commission as such, the treaty of peace was concluded; in consequence of which, he has only received the bounty of land allowed a lieutenant; and it is reasonable he should be allowed a bounty proportionate to his services." The enacting part of the act then directs the register of the land office to issue to the said Leighton Yancy a warrant for one thousand three hundred and thirty-four acres and one-third of an acre of land, it being the difference between the bounty allowed a lieutenant and that of a captain. This is all the evidence filed in the case, except an extract from the records of the executive department of Virginia, showing that Leighton Yancy was entitled to the proportion of land allowed a captain of the continental line for six months' service over six years.

This being the state of the case, the committee entertain no doubt that Leighton Yancy was not entitled to the commutation pay of a captain. The act above recited shows clearly that, whatever his services might have been, he never, during the revolutionary war, bore the commission of captain, and, by consequence, cannot have been a captain in fact. No supposed title to the rank of a captain can, in the opinion of the committee, constitute a captaincy, without a commission.

The committee have therefore come to the following resolution:

*Resolved,* That the prayer of the petitioners be rejected.

----

**January 11, 1838.**

The Committee on Revolutionary Claims, to which was referred the petition of William Starke Jett, administrator and heir at law of Thomas Jett, deceased, have had that subject under consideration, and report:

That the petitioner represents that Thomas Jett, his father, during the war of the Revolution, loaned to the United States a sum of money, for which he obtained from the loan office for the State of Virginia thirteen loan-office certificates, dated on the 4th of March, 1779, and numbered from 443 to 445, (inclusive,) each for the nominal sum of six hundred dollars, and of the specie value of fifty-nine dollars and thirty-eight cents:

that soon after the termination of the war, his father died ; and, in consequence of the neglect of his executors, and their mismanagement of his
estate, letters of administration were granted to the petitioner, who has
made diligent search for the certificates aforesaid among his father's papers, without finding them.  He is satisfied they have been lost, and asks
the passage of an act to authorize the payment of the amount due on
them.

In support of the claim of the petitioner, a certificate of the Register
of the Treasury has been filed with his petition, by which it appears that
thirteen loan-office certificates of the description of those above set forth,
in the name of Thomas Jett, remain outstanding and unpaid.

The committee think the presumption reasonable that they were never
transferred, but were accidentally lost after the death of Thomas Jett ;
and therefore report a bill directing the amount due on them, with interest, to be paid to his legal representative, upon his entering into bond,
with security, to indemnify the Treasury against loss in case of their
future presentation for payment.

---

## January 11, 1838.

The Committee on Revolutionary Claims, to which was referred the
petition of the heirs of John Waters, report :

This case was before the committee at the 1st session of the 24th Congress, and also at the 2d session of the same Congress ; and in both cases
unfavorably reported on.  In these reports the committee concur, and
refer to—more particularly to the first report made ; being of opinion that
the relief asked ought not to be granted, for the reasons therein stated.

## June 15, 1836.

The petition of Lundy Waters, William Waters, John Waters, Elizabeth Sanders, and Susan Farrow, represents them as the holders of sundry
Virginia military land warrants, issued to them as heirs of John Waters,
deceased, in consideration of his services as a sergeant in Lee's legion,
and prays that Congress would pass a law authorizing the proper officers
to issue scrip to the petitioners in lieu of the warrants, because, as is
alleged, the petitioners were prevented by accident from depositing the
warrants with the Commissioner of the General Land Office previous
to the 1st day of September last, with a view to obtain scrip, as provided for by the act of the 3d March, 1835.  The original warrants are
filed with the petition, and bear date on the 7th August, 1835.  There
is no evidence of the existence of any accident which prevented the
filing of the warrants with the Commissioner of the General Land Office
in the time prescribed by the act of 3d March, 1835.  That allegation
rests on the assertion of the petitioners.  The committee perceive no
reason for special legislation in this case.  If the 650,000 acres appropriated by the act of the 3d March, 1835, have been exhausted, we are
of opinion that the warrants of the petitioners ought to remain, and ought
not to be satisfied, unless it shall please Congress to make provision for

all the Virginia military warrants now outstanding. Your committee therefore recommend the adoption of the following resolution :

*Resolved,* That the prayer of the petitioners ought not to be granted.

---

The Committee on Revolutionary Claims, to which was referred the memorial of Thomas Sumpter, report :

That the memorialist represents he is the son and heir-at-law of the late General Thomas Sumpter, who, during the war of the Revolution, loaned a considerable sum of money to the United States; and, as evidence thereof, he received thirty-two loan-office certificates of one thousand dollars each, current money, of the value, in specie, of twenty-five dollars each, equal to eight hundred dollars. That these certificates have been lost and remain unpaid; and the memorialist asks that the principal sum and interest thereon may be paid to him. On inquiry made of the Register of the Treasury, he reports that the thirty-two loan office certificates, a list of which he made and subscribed and is made part of this report, are entered on the books of the Treasury in the name of Thomas Sumpter, and are outstanding and unpaid. In pursuance of this information, the committee report a bill.

*List of loan-office certificates in the name of Thomas Sumpter, remaining outstanding and unpaid.*

| No. of certificate. | Date of certificate. | At what office issued. | Commencement of interest. | Nominal amount. | Specie value. |
|---|---|---|---|---|---|
| 4221 | June 1, 1780. | S. Carolina. | June 1, 1780. | $1,000 | $25 |
| 4231 | do | do | do | 1,000 | 25 |
| 4244 | do | do | do | 1,000 | 25 |
| 4257 | do | do | do | 1,000 | 25 |
| 4258 | do | do | do | 1,000 | 25 |
| 4259 | do | do | do | 1,000 | 25 |
| 4262 | do | do | do | 1,000 | 25 |
| 4263 | do | do | do | 1,000 | 25 |
| 4270 | do | do | do | 1,000 | 25 |
| 4271 | do | do | do | 1,000 | 25 |
| 4274 | do | do | do | 1,000 | 25 |
| 4277 | do | do | do | 1,000 | 25 |
| 4280 | do | do | do | 1,000 | 25 |
| 4282 | do | do | do | 1,000 | 25 |
| 4287 | do | do | do | 1,000 | 25 |
| 4290 | do | do | do | 1,000 | 25 |
| 4295 | do | do | do | 1,000 | 25 |
| 4306 | do | do | do | 1,000 | 25 |
| 4328 | do | do | do | 1,000 | 25 |

## LIST—Continued.

| No. of certificate. | Date of certificate. | At what office issued. | Commencement of interest. | Nominal amount. | Specie value. |
|---|---|---|---|---|---|
| 4990 | Oct. 17, 1780. | S. Carolina. | Oct. 17, 1780. | $1,000 | $25 |
| 4991 | do | do | do | 1,000 | 25 |
| 4993 | do | do | do | 1,000 | 25 |
| 5002 | do | do | do | 1,000 | 25 |
| 5003 | do | do | do | 1,000 | 25 |
| 5006 | do | do | do | 1,000 | 25 |
| 5007 | do | do | do | 1,000 | 25 |
| 5009 | do | do | do | 1,000 | 25 |
| 5013 | do | do | do | 1,000 | 25 |
| 5038 | do | do | do | 1,000 | 25 |
| 5042 | do | do | do | 1,000 | 25 |
| 5043 | do | do | do | 1,000 | 25 |
| 5108 | do | do | do | 1,000 | 25 |

TREASURY DEPARTMENT,
*Register's Office, November 27, 1837.*

T. L. SMITH, *Register.*

---

### JANUARY 11, 1838.

The Committee on Revolutionary Claims, to which was referred the petition of Simon Summers, of the District of Columbia, report:

That the petitioner represents that he entered into the service of the United States in the war of the Revolution, and was appointed adjutant of the sixth Virginia regiment on continental establishment, in which capacity he served from near the commencement to the entire close of that war, with the exception of a small portion of time during which he was on furlough on account of ill health. He further represents that, though his grade in the line of the army was that of a lieutenant, yet as, by a resolution of Congress, he was entitled to the pay and rations of a captain, he conceives himself entitled to the commutation pay due to the latter grade of officers; and prays that Congress will allow him five years' full pay in commutation of half pay for life, either as a captain or a lieutenant, as in their judgment may seem right.

The transcript of a record obtained by the committee from the Commissioner of Pensions, duly authenticated and filed in this case, shows that the petitioner, Simon Summers, of the county of Alexandria, in the District of Columbia, was, on the 9th day of February, 1829, admitted to the benefit of the act of Congress of the 15th of May, 1828. This is conclusive to prove that, in the opinion of the officer charged with the execution of this law, the said Summers either continued in active service to the end of the war, or, being a supernumerary officer, was included in provisions of the resolution of Congress of the 21st of October, 1780. In either event, the petitioner is entitled to a commutation pay ; and the committee, upon a review of the testimony contained in the transcript of the record aforesaid, think it sufficiently established the petitioner's claim to the benefits of the act of the 15th May, 1828 ; and, by consequence, his claim to five years' full pay in commutation of half pay for life. But the petitioner is entitled to such pay as a lieutenant, and not as a captain; of this, the resolution of Congress of the 11th of February, 1781, is decisive. The committee, therefore, report a bill allowing the said petitioner five years' full pay as a lieutenant.

---

### JANUARY 11, 1838.

The Committee on Revolutionary Claims, to which were referred the several memorials of the Marquise de la Goree, and the Comtesse D'Ambrugeac, grandchildren of Marshal Rochambeau, report :

The Committee on Revolutionary Claims have again had under consideration the memorial of the granddaughters of the Marshal Rochambeau. They are still of opinion, for the reasons assigned in the report made to the last Congress, (and which is hereto annexed,) that it is proper to make some provision for the family of the marshal.

The committee, on reconsideration, have adopted the bill heretofore reported, and again submit it for the consideration of Congress.

Your committee deem it courteous towards the memorialists to present, for the consideration of the Legislature, a translation of their observations upon the report of Mr. Beaumont, and the accompanying bill; observations so delicately made, as to place the granddaughters of the marshal in a position entitled to our affectionate regard, and which cannot fail to identify them with the grateful remembrance and admiration which the American people entertain for their illustrious ancestor.

The committee will close with this additional remark, that the case of General Lafayette ought not to govern as a precedent. He was a foreigner of uncommon merit, taken into our service, and commissioned by Congress in 1777. Marshal Rochambeau acted under his commission from the King of France; and, in point of strict right, could alone look to the King to reward his services. General Lafayette's claim was against the United States.

All which is respectfully submitted.

### FEBRUARY 10, 1836.

The Committee on Revolutionary Claims, to which were referred the several memorials of the Marquise de la Goree, and the Comtesse D'Ambrugeac, grandchildren of Marshal Rochambeau, report :

That this appeal to the magnanimity and generous sentiments of the people of the United States is predicated upon the eminent services rendered by Marshal Rochambeau, during our revolutionary struggle, in achieving our independence. It has been made under the auspices and by the advice of the illustrious Lafayette, whose name alone is a passport to the most generous feelings of the American people. Mr. Livingston, our late minister to France, in a despatch to the Secretary of State, dated Paris, October 22, 1833, bears the following testimony in behalf of the memorialists:

"I have been strongly urged by General Lafayette, and by the petitioners themselves, to call the attention of the President to the petitions of the heirs of Count Rochambeau, and of Messrs. Laumont and De Grammont, which were by him transmitted to Congress, but not acted upon." * * * * * "*The daughter of Count Rochambeau is in great poverty.* The essential services rendered in our Revolution by her father, and her destitute condition, create a claim on our gratitude and humanity."

In justification of the favorable action of Congress upon this application, the committee adduce the parallel case of the heirs of Count de Grasse. By the act of Congress of 27th February, 1795, it is declared, "That, in consideration of the extraordinary services of the Count de Grasse, rendered to the United States in the year 1781, on the special request of the commander-in-chief of their forces, the President of the United States be authorized to pay to each of his daughters one thousand dollars."

And by the act of January 15th, 1798, predicated upon the same consideration, it was directed that there should be paid annually, "during five years from the passage of said act, the sum of four hundred dollars to each of the four daughters of the late Count de Grasse, respectively."

The important services rendered to the United States by Marshal Rochambeau, as commander of the French forces, in aid of the cause of our independence, during the years 1780 and 1781, are too well known to require a recital in this report. His generous sacrifices, his ready support of all the measures, his cheerful compliance with and co-operation in all the views, of the illustrious Washington, and his delicate sympathy and respect for the feelings and sufferings of the American people amidst their severe trials, are above all commendation. It is true he was in the service of a foreign Government, and received his commission and pay from the unfortunate Louis XVI; but there is, nevertheless, a debt of gratitude justly due to him from the people of these States, which neither time nor circumstances can cancel. The names of Rochambeau, Lafayette, and De Grasse, are entwined with those of Washington, Knox, Lincoln, Muhlenberg, and Hamilton, in the wreath of unfading glory that adorns the American history, as associated in the crowning triumph of our Revolution in the surrender of Lord Cornwallis at Yorktown. The memorialists do not come forward to claim pay for the services of their ancestor, but, in obedience to his express advice towards the close of his life, "to cherish the most respectful regard towards the American people, as a family heritage; and if, after his death, misfortunes should overtake them, they should *appeal* to the generous sentiments of that people to whom he had rendered important services, with a certainty that such appeal would not be made in vain."

The present Count de Rochambeau, grandson and sole inheritor of the name of the marshal, in a letter addressed to Mr. Livingston, declines joining in the application for any pecuniary aid from our Government. He delicately adverts to the many distinguished testimonials of regard tendered by the American people, through their Government, to his illustrious ancestor, and particularly to the presentation, by General Washington, in pursuance of a resolution of Congress of 1781, of two pieces of cannon taken from the British army on the surrender at Yorktown, which were lost during the troubles in France in 1793.

That resolution was as follows :

"*Resolved*, That two pieces of the field ordnance taken from the British army under the capitulation of York, be presented by the commander-in-chief of the American army to Count de Rochambeau; and that there be engraved thereon a short memorandum, that Congress were induced to present them from considerations of the illustrious part which he bore in effecting that surrender."

The committee, viewing these trophies as mementoes of an important and glorious event, to which the Marshal Count Rochambeau had greatly contributed, and valuable only in that light, have deemed it suitable and proper that their loss should be supplied by some similar testimonial to his descendant.

The deeds of those glorious days of chivalry and patriotism awaken in the mind of every American emotions of the most lively gratitude. Their remembrance appeals to the noblest and most generous sympathies of our nature ; and the American Congress, which ought to be the true exemplar of American sentiment, has, on more than one occasion, manifested that sentiment by acts of becoming munificence.

The committee believe that some suitable allowance, in compliance with these memorials, is justified by the precedents adduced, as well as by considerations of national honor. They therefore report a bill.

---

*Translation of the note and observations, accompanying the letter of the granddaughters of Marshal Rochambeau to the President.*

NOTE.

The report presented on the 10th of February, 1836, by Mr. Beaumont, in the name of the Committee on Revolutionary Claims of the House of Representatives of the United States, respecting the petitions of the Marquise de la Goree and the Comtesse d'Ambrugeac, granddaughters of Marshal de Rochambeau, which had been submitted to Congress with the messages from the President of the United States in 1833, and on the 20th of June, 1834, is remarkable for the honorable expressions employed in it to establish the principle and show the justice of the grounds on which the said memorials were presented to Congress. It could not have spoken more positively than by the words, "a debt of gratitude is justly due to Marshal de Rochambeau from the people of these States, which neither time nor circumstances can cancel."

This report is also remarkable on account of the example which it affords of the respect of the United States for the great principles of public and international morals, by recalling with dignity, although during the existence of great and serious difficulties between France and the United States, the remembrance of deeds and times so honorable to France, and which, says the report, merit the eternal gratitude of the United States. What has been here stated, is amply justified by the following quotation from the report; which the granddaughters of Marshal de Rochambeau make with so much the more pleasure, as it coincides with the celebrated vote of thanks given to their grandfather on the 1st of January, 1783, by order of Congress, and by their President in person.

"The important services rendered to the United States by Marshal Rochambeau, as commander of the French forces, in aid of the cause of our independence, during the years 1780 and 1781, are too well known to require a recital in this report. His generous sacrifices, his ready support of all the measures, his cheerful compliance with and co-operation in all the views, of the illustrious Washington, and his delicate sympathy and respect for the feelings and sufferings of the American people amidst their severe trials, are above all commendation. It is true he was in the service of a foreign Government, and received his commission and pay from the unfortunate Louis XVI; but there is, nevertheless, a debt of gratitude justly due to him from the people of these States, which neither time nor circumstances can cancel.

"The names of Rochambeau, Lafayette, and De Grasse, are entwined with those of Washington, Knox, Lincoln, Muhlenberg, and Hamilton, in the wreath of unfading glory that adorns the American history, as associated in the crowning triumph of our Revolution in the surrender of Lord Cornwallis at Yorktown. The memorialists do not come forward to claim pay for the services of their ancestor, but, in obedience to his express advice towards the close of his life, 'to cherish the most respectful regard towards the American people as a family heritage; and if, after his death, misfortunes should overtake them, they should *appeal* to the generous sentiments of that people to whom he had rendered important services, with a certainty that such appeal would not be made in vain.'"

Certainly it would have been impossible to express more forcibly and more honorably the principles, the basis, and the motives on which the petition and the confidence of the granddaughters of Marshal de Rochambeau were founded; only, after the years 1780 and 1781, should have been added 1782 and 1783—an omission which doubtless arose from an error in printing.

While offering their sincere thanks to the committee, and to the gentleman who made the report, the granddaughters of Marshal de Rochambeau respectfully ask their permission to offer to them a few observations respecting the application of the principle which they have laid down; this is done with the utmost confidence in the honor of the committee. They also entreat them to interpret favorably their expressions and their intentions, as set forth in a dissertation on a subject so delicate, in which they will always bear in mind what they have heard of and for their venerable grandfather.

They know that they are addressing the representatives of a nation, powerful, celebrated, prosperous, and jealous of its rights and character.

## OBSERVATIONS.

Before examining the application, made by the committee, of the *principle* which they have so conscientiously and so decidedly established and supported, it will be proper first to quote the latter part of the report, and the resolution proposed by the committee.

"The deeds of those glorious days of chivalry and patriotism awaken in the mind of every American emotions of the most lively gratitude. Their remembrance appeals to the noblest and most generous sympathies of our nature ; and the American Congress, which ought to be the true exemplar of American sentiment, has, on more than one occasion, manifested that sentiment by acts of becoming munificence.

"The committee believe that some suitable allowance, in compliance with these memorials, is justified by the precedents adduced, as well as by considerations of national honor. They therefore report a bill."

The questions to be examined and determined, therefore, no longer relate to those declarations of generous and honorable feelings of gratitude, but entirely to the terms of the bill proposed by the committee, in application or in execution of a principle ; and of the assent to that principle, so eloquently and decidedly expressed by the committee.

The only precedent cited in the report is the assistance given, in 1795 and 1798, to the daughters of the Count de Grasse, in consideration of the services rendered by their father in the year 1781. This date is correctly given. Count de Grasse remained in the United States one month. It is also necessary to remark that, according to the report, the services of Marshal de Rochambeau, which began in 1780, ended at the same time with those of Count de Grasse. But it was not so ; for the marshal continued in service in the United States until peace had been made in Europe, and the complete independence of the United States had been acknowledged ; that is to say, until 1783. And since history has been cited in this case, it is also proper, while rendering justice to the services of Count de Grasse, to say, that the arrival of his fleet in Chesapeake bay, which afforded so much assistance to Generals Washington and Rochambeau in the reduction of Yorktown, was entirely due to the plan proposed by the marshal, and approved by General Washington ; and that Colonel Rochambeau, the father of the present petitioners, who had just arrived from France in the *Concorde*, with reinforcements and six millions of livres, which he had been sent to solicit, was the person despatched in the same frigate to look for Admiral de Grasse, who executed with promptitude and skill the celebrated plan of the two generals, mentioned by the marshal in his memoirs, written by himself, and published after his death.

But, without speaking further of the difference between the services rendered to the United States by Count de Grasse, and those of Marshal de Rochambeau, who was charged by France to require, if he should consider it necessary, the co-operation of that admiral ; and who, as the thanks of Congress, in 1783, show, possessed, in addition to his special claim on account of the taking of Yorktown, the general merit of his important services for four consecutive years ; the petitioners conceive themselves obliged, by respect for his memory, for the truth of history, and for the dignity of the American nation, the prosperity of which he aided in establishing, and foresaw, to point out to the committee the differences existing, as well in the natures as in the periods between the services on which their petition is based, and those of the only precedent cited in the report ; and, also, the difference between the circumstances, the power, and the prosperity of the United States in 1836 and in 1795 and 1798.

Is it not evident that the grant of one thousand dollars, and of four hundred dollars a year for five years, to the four daughters of Count de Grasse, in 1795, during the period of their emigration, was designed and intended to supply their wants during their temporary exile, to which they were subjected, like so many other French persons who received similar aid from other countries?

Is it not also evident that the United States could not, in 1795 and 1798, publicly declare that their annual revenues exceed their expense by two hundred millions of francs; that they are the only state without debts; and that they seek occasions to prove to France, their most intimate and oldest ally, their satisfaction at having at length received from her the twenty-five millions which have been so long in dispute?

The petitioners would consider themselves wanting in frankness towards the committee, and even in respect for the dignity of Congress, the memory of their grandfather, and that of General Lafayette, if they did not conclude their observations by what follows:

The report begins thus: " That this appeal to the magnanity and generous sentiments of the people of the United States is predicated upon the eminent services rendered by Marshal Rochambeau during our revolutionary struggle in achieving our independence. It has been made under the auspices, and by the advice of the illustrious Lafayette, whose name alone is a passport to the most generous feelings of the American people."

Here the granddaughters of the marshal call on the reporter and the members of the committee, as a jury chosen by the respectable representatives of the American people, to ask themselves a question. After having declared what is true, that the appeal was made under the auspices and advice of General Lafayette, does the committee suppose that General Lafayette could have been ignorant of the hopes and intentions of the granddaughters of the marshal, and could have confounded their case with that of the daughters of Count de Grasse? That he could have done so, who so often told them and other persons, " I have received $200,000 and about 50,000 acres of land from the Americans ; Congress will do for the descendants of the marshal what will be worthy of the magnanimity of the American people ; and I have, before my death, performed a duty which I have long been anxious to fulfil, that of establishing the fortune and the means of existence of the family of the marshal, my friend, my chief, and my model, who made much greater sacrifices than I have for the American cause."

The granddaughters of the marshal, after these words, which were repeated by the minister, Mr. Livingston, and others; and after the praises bestowed on the marshal in the report, have nothing more to say. They will await respectfully the result of the deliberations of the committee, and of Congress, which will not oppose to M. de Lafayette himself the argument that the marshal commanded a foreign armed force, which certainly deserved to be considered as forming, with that of the Americans, one army, and which might be termed the Franco-American army.

MARQUISE DA LA GOREE,<br>
COMTESSE D'AMBRUGEAC,<br>
*Granddaughters of Marshal de Rochambeau.*<br>
GENERAL COMTE D'AMBRUGEAC.

51

The Committee on Revolutionary Claims have been induced to report the accompanying bill, to prevent the necessity of special legislation and separate action on the several cases which fall within the operation of the principles of the bill. The committee deem it proper to give to the resolution of Congress, passed on the 16th September, 1776, promising lands to the officers and soldiers of the army, a retrospective operation, so as to provide for the heirs of those who were killed in the service before that date. The land, or its equivalent in scrip, is a poor boon in behalf of families whose ancestors sacrificed their lives in our struggle for independence.

The Committee on Revolutionary Claims, to which the subject was referred, report:

That they have deemed it proper, by the accompanying bill, to make a general provision in favor of all persons entitled to the half pay for seven years provided for by the resolution of Congress passed on the 24th of August, 1780. The object of the committee is, to save the trouble of special legislation in each particular case; and they apprehended the claims can be as well, if not better, examined into and adjusted by the Treasury Department, than they can be by the action of this committee in each case.

The Committee on Revolutionary Claims, to whom the petition of Hodijah Meade and Benjamin Meade was referred, report:

That the petitioners, as the heirs of Captain Everard Meade, who was an officer in the army of the Revolution, have been allowed the commutation pay, without interest, found to be due by the United States to the said Everard Meade, for his services as a captain of infantry in the Virginia continental line of the army to the end of the war.—(See the act of Congress passed the 30th day of June, 1834.)

They now petition for the interest due on the principal sum thus allowed them. The promise, on the part of the Government, to allow interest on commutation pay, is express and unequivocal; and the uniform practice of Congress was, both under the Confederation and Federal Government in a series of time, to allow interest, till within the last three or four years. The propriety of allowing interest on those claims has been questioned in one branch of Congress; in consequence of which, a few cases have been allowed without interest. This case is one of that number. The committee, nevertheless, feel bound, in conformity with the express engagement of the Government, to allow interest on commutation pay, and, with the almost uniform practice of Congress on the subject, to recommend the allowance of interest to the petitioners; and for that purpose a bill is reported.

The Committee on Revolutionary Claims, to whom was referred the petition of the heirs of Captain Robert Bealle, report:

That the petitioners claim commutation and interest for the services of Captain Robert Bealle, of the 13th Virginia regiment on continental establishment. By the depositions and other evidence filed with the petition, it is proved, in the most satisfactory manner, that Captain Robert Bealle was a captain in the 13th regiment Virginia line on the continental establishment, which regiment was afterwards called or reduced to the 7th; that he served as such until he retired as a supernumerary, in the year 1781. The testimony to this point will be found in the affidavits of sundry witnesses, and numbered from 5 to 10, inclusive; the certificate of General Wood, bearing date the 27th June, 1803; the certificate of the register of the land office of Virginia, and of Mr. Gordon, of the bounty land office, and the certificate of the Governor of Virginia; by which it appears additional bounty land was granted by that State to Captain Robert Bealle, and numbered 11 and 12. It appears by the evidence that there were two Captains Robert Bealle in the Virginia continental line; one of whom received his commutation, and is on the pension-list, under the act of May 15th, 1822, and now residing in Westmoreland county, Virginia. The same evidence proves, most conclusively, that Captain Robert Bealle, the grandfather of the petitioners, never received commutation.

The committee therefore believe that the petitioners are entitled to re-relief, and for that purpose report a bill.

---

No. 5.

LANCASTER, ss.

Presley Carr Lane, a member of the House of Representatives of the General Assembly of the State of Pennsylvania, from the county of Fayette, being duly sworn, deposeth and saith: That on the decease of Colonel Robert Bealle, (formerly a captain in the continental army,) this deponent, and widow of the said Colonel Robert Bealle, obtained letters of administration upon the estate of the deceased, in due form of law; that the said Colonel Robert Bealle left two children at the time of his death, who, he believes, are still living, to wit: Betsey Brooke Bealle, aged about seventeen or eighteen years, and Robert Bealle, aged about thirteen years. And this deponent further saith, that he agreed that warrants shall issue in favor of the said children, for any land that may belong to the said Colonel Robert Bealle by reason of his services in the army of the United States during the late war.

P. C. LANE.

Sworn to and subscribed this 4th day of March, 1800, before me, one of the justices of the peace for the county of Lancaster and Commonwealth of Pennsylvania.

A. HUBLEY.

I certify that the within is a true copy of a document one file in the office of the Department of War.

Given under my hand, at the War Office, this 17th day of September, 1808.

H. ROGERS.

---

No. 6.

I do hereby certify that I, the subscriber, was married to the late Captain Robert Bealle (now deceased) in the year 1781, and he then belonged to the United States army; and that he was the same Captain Robert Bealle alluded to in the certificates of Presley Carr Lane, Esq., General Jos. Winlock, and Doctor John Knight; and that the aforesaid Presley Carr Lane and myself did administer on the estate of the said Robert Bealle, in the year 1789, in Fayette county, Pennsylvania, all of which is of record in that office ; and I do furthermore certify that I had two children by him, which are both living, viz: Betsey Brooke Bealle, who has since intermarried with Adam Steele, and Robert Bealle.

Given under my hand, at Shelbyville, Kentucky, this 17th day of June, 1808.

ELIZABETH BEALLE.

COMMONWEALTH OF KENTUCKY, }
    *Shelby county,*    } *sct :*

This day Elizabeth Bealle, before me, a justice of the peace for said county, makes oath to the truth of the statements of facts contained in the above or foregoing certificate.

Given under my hand and seal, this 17th day of June, 1808.

JAMES BRADSHAW.

---

No. 7.

We, the subscribers, do certify that we were personally acquainted with the late Captain Robert Bealle, (now deceased;) that we both served with him in the same regiment in the United States army; that we were well informed that he married widow Elizabeth Stephenson; we were personally acquainted with them both after they were married, and until the death of the said Bealle, in the year 1789 ; that he had two children, viz: Betsey Brooke Bealle and Robert Bealle, which are both now living; and we have a full reference to the certificate of his wife, Elizabeth Bealle, of this date, which we know to be substantially correct,

Given under our hands, this 17th day of June, 1808.

JOSEPH WINLOCK,<br>
*Late lieutenant in the 7th Virginia regiment.*<br>
JNO. KNIGHT,<br>
*Late surgeon's mate, late 7th Virginia regiment.*

COMMONWEALTH OF KENTUCKY, ⎱ *sct :*
    *Shelby county,* ⎰

This day the before-named Joseph Winlock and John Knight came before me, a justice of the peace for said county, and made oath to the truth of the statements of facts contained in the above or foregoing certificate.

Given under my hand and seal, this 17th June, 1818.

JAMES BRADSHAW.

---

No. 8.

SHELBY COUNTY, STATE OF KENTUCKY,

June 17, 1808.

I do hereby certify that Robert Bealle entered into the service of the United States as a captain in the 13th Virginia regiment on continental establishment, at the commencement of the raising of said regiment, which was, some time after the battle of Genmantown, the 9th regiment, and at the close of the war was the 7th Virginia regiment; the said Robert Bealle served in the said regiment with myself until about the year 1781, when there was an arrangement took place in the army that turned out a number of officers as supernumeraries, of which the said Bealle was one ; and I have been well informed that the said Robert Bealle served one year previous to the raising of the 13th regiment, as a lieutenant under Captain John Stephenson, which, I believed, marched to the South about the year 1775 or 1776.

Given under my hand, the day and date above.

JOSEPH WINLOCK,<br>Late lieutenant in the 7th Virginia regiment.

COMMONWEALTH OF KENTUCKY, ⎱ *sct :*
    *Shelby county,* ⎰

This day Joseph Winlock before me, a justice of the peace for said county, and made oath to the truth of the statement of facts contained in the foregoing certificate.

Given under my hand and seal, this 17th June, 1808.

JAMES BRADSHAW.

---

No. 9.

SHELBY COUNTY, STATE OF KENTUCKY,

June 17, 1808.

I do certify that Robert Bealle was first captain in the 13th Virginia regiment ; that the regiment was afterwards the 9th Virginia regiment, and, last of all, before the expiration of the war, the same regiment was the 7th Virginia regiment. I think it was in the year 1781 that Captain Robert Bealle retired from the regiment, as supernumerary, by a law of Congress.

The said Robert Béalle was first lieutenant in Captain John Stephenson's company, under Colonel Muhlenberg, now General Muhlenberg, and was at the defending of Charleston, South Carolina, under General Lee, more than one year before the 13th Virginia regiment was raised.

Given under my hand, this day above.

JOHN KNIGHT,
*Late surgeon's mate, 7th Virginia regiment.*

COMMONWEALTH OF KENTUCKY, } *sct :*
    *Shelby county,*

This day John Knight, before me, a justice of the peace for said county, and made oath to the truth of the statement of facts contained in the foregoing certificate.

Given under my hand and seal, this 17th June, 1808.

JAMES BRADSHAW.

---

### No. 10.

JEFFERSON COUNTY, STATE OF KENTUCKY,

*March* 8, 1803.

I do hereby certify that Robert Bealle was first captain in the 13th Virginia regiment; that the regiment was afterwards the 9th Virginia regiment, and, last of all, or before the expiration of the war, the same regiment was the 7th Virginia regiment. I think it was in the year 1781 that Captain Robert Bealle retired from the regiment as supernumerary, by a law of Congress. The said Robert Bealle was first lieutenant in Captain John Stephenson's company, under Colonel Muhlenberg, now General Muhlenberg, and was at the defending of Charleston, South Carolina, under General Lee, more than one year before the 13th Virginia regiment was raised.

Given under my hand, the day and date above written.

JNO. HARRISON.

COMMONWEALTH OF KENTUCKY, } *sct :*
    *Jefferson county,*

This day Major John Harrison came before me, a justice of the peace for said county, and made oath to the truth of the statement of facts contained in the above certificate.

Given under my hand and seal, this 8th day of March, 1802.

JAMES TAYLOR, Jr., *J. P., J. C.*

---

### No. 11.

DEPARTMENT OF WAR,

*Bounty Land Office, January* 14, 1833.

I certify that the aforegoing, from page    to page   , inclusive, are true copies taken from the originals on file in this office, upon which a land warrant for 300 acres issued on the 16th September, 1808, to Betsey B. Steele and Robert Bealle, heirs at law of Robert Bealle, who was a captain in the Virginia continental line. I further certify that it appears by the records in this office, land warrant number 263, for 300 acres, issued on the 5th February, 1794, in the name of Robert Means, assignee of Robert Bealle, who was also a captain in the Virginia continental line.

WM. GORDON, *First Clerk.*

---

No. 12.

IN COUNCIL, *August* 6, 1808.

It is advised that Robert Bealle be allowed his additional bounty of land of seventeen months, for his services as captain in the continental army.

Extract from the journal.

DAN'L L. HYLTON,
*Clerk of the Council.*

VIRGINIA, *to wit :*

I do hereby certify that Dan'l L. Hylton, who signs the above order of Council, is clerk of the Council in this Commonwealth, and that full faith and credit ought to be given to all things certified by him as such.

Given under my hand as Governor, and under the seal of the Commonwealth, at Richmond, this 27th day of April, 1809.

JNO. TYLER.

---

JANUARY 17, 1838.

The Committee on Revolutionary Claims, to whom was referred certain documents, intended to make out a claim of commutation in favor of the heirs of Luke Cannon, deceased, who was ensign and lieutenant in the revolutionary war, report :

That the accompanying letter of the Third Auditor shows, to the satisfaction of the committee, there is no subsisting claim in this case, as the officer himself received commutation pay in his lifetime ; they are therefore of opinion that relief ought not to be granted.

TREASURY DEPARTMENT,
*Third Auditor's Office, January 12,* 1838.

SIR : I have the honor to state, in reply to your letter of the 10th instant, that it appears, from the revolutionary records, that Luke Cannon was, at the close of the war, a lieutenant in the Virginia line on continental establishment, and in that capacity he appears to have received his commutation of five years' full pay, in lieu of half pay for life.

With great respect,

PETER HAGNER, *Auditor.*

Hon. A. H. SHEPPERD,
*of the Committee on Revolutionary Claims,*
*House of Representatives, U. States.*

The Committee on Revolutionary Claims, to which was referred the petition of the representatives of Captain William Johnson, report:

That they have had the same under consideration, and find that it appears from the revolutionary records, on file in the Third Auditor's office, Treasury Department, that Captain William Johnson received his commutation of five years' full pay, in lieu of half pay for life, from Andrew Dunscomb, Esq., the United States agent, who settled with the Virginia continental line after the war. It so happens that the original papers on which Mr. Dunscomb's settlement with Captain Johnson was made have been preserved, and on comparing his signatures to said papers with a signature to a certain letter addressed to his mother, and dated July 10, 1779, submitted to the committee in support of the claim, there is not the shadow of a doubt that the officer, referred to in the petition referred to the committee, is the identical officer who received his commutation, as above stated, from Mr. Dunscomb.

JANUARY 18, 1838.

The Committee on Revolutionary Claims, to which was referred the petition of the heirs of Lieutenant Colonel William Fountain, report:

The case was examined at the 1st session of the 24th Congress, and favorably reported on, with a bill for the relief of the petitioners. That report the committee adopt, and ask that it may be considered as part of this. In accordance with it, a bill is again reported for the relief of the petitioners.

MAY 17, 1836.

The Committee on Revolutionary Claims, to which was referred the petition of the legal representatives of Lieutenant Colonel William Fountain, report:

It satisfactorily appears to the committee that William Fountain was the lieutenant colonel of the regiment of guards raised to guard the convention troops, and served as such until the regiment was disbanded, in May, 1781. This fact is established by the certificate of Major John Roberts, of that regiment. It also appears that said Fountain was in active service at an early period of the Revolution, before said regiment was raised. There is no evidence that he resigned his commission after the regiment was disbanded.

Commutation has been conceded to Colonel Taylor, the commandant of the regiment, by a favorable report from the committee during the present session, and we perceive no ground of difference between him and Lieutenant Colonel Fountain. We therefore report a bill for the relief of his legal representatives.

JANUARY 18, 1838.

The Committee on Revolutionary Claims, to which the subject was referred, made the following report:

Martha Jones, in behalf of herself and others, as heirs, claim commutation for the revolutionary services of Major William Langbourne. It appears from a resolution of Congress, dated October 6, 1783, (vol. 4, page 283,) that the services of the said Langbourne, from the commencement of the war, were recognised in a complimentary manner; and that it was resolved to confer upon him the brevet rank of lieutenant colonel. It further appears, from the statement of the Third Auditor, that an account was opened with said Langbourne, as major, the particulars of which cannot be fully ascertained, in consequence of the loss or destruction of the journal of accounts. It further appears that, in 1824, the heirs of said Langbourne obtained a land warrant for 6,224 acres, from the State of Virginia, for seven years' service as a major in the continental line. This warrant was issued upon various certificates being filed, copies of which are before the committee, and show satisfactorily the services of said Langbourne as late as 1781. The committee entertain no doubt but that said Langbourne was entitled to commutation as a major in the continental line, and therefore report a bill in favor of his legal representatives.

---

JANUARY 25, 1838.

The Committee on Revolutionary Claims, to whom was referred the petition of Sarah Mandeville, report:

That the claim set up in the petition is for the value of a dwelling-house and out-houses alleged to have been destroyed by the enemy during the revolutionary war, in consequence of their occupation by the American troops.

In support of this claim, a witness, named John Croft, swears that he resided in Peekskill, State of New York, in the year 1777, where John Mandeville, the late husband of the petitioner, owned a large frame dwelling-house, used by said Mandeville as an inn, together with a barn, carriage-house, and sheds; that, during that year, the American army, under General Putnam, encamped on said Mandeville's plantation, and took possession of and occupied the above-mentioned dwelling-house as head-quarters, and the barn, carriage-house, and sheds, for the reception of their baggage, ammunition, and provisions; that, during such possession, he frequently passed the premises, and always found sentinels placed around them both by day and night; that, while the houses were thus occupied by our troops, they were all burnt, about the 4th of October, 1777, by a part of the British forces which ascended the Hudson and landed at Peekskill. Witness says that, from an eminence a mile or two off, he actually saw the buildings burning, and that, after the enemy had retired, he approached and viewed the ruins, which were then still smoking. This witness is fully sustained by Henry Thomas, who adds that he was one of the men engaged in driving the British from Peekskill after the destruction of Mandeville's property. The petitioner, Sarah Mandeville, has also given testimony. Whilst her deposition confirms the foregoing statements, she goes farther, and gives the names of General Dougal, General Huntington, Colonel Burr, and Major Platt, who, under General Putnam, occupied her husband's house as headquarters. She says that one room of the house was used as the office of the paymaster, and that another was appropriated to the purpose of holding courts martial. It is stated to the committee, from a very respectable source, that Mrs. Mandeville and Mr. Croft are persons of fair character, and entitled to confidence. The truth of the foregoing statements, made by credible witnesses, is rendered still more probable from the well-ascertained historical fact that General Putnam and his forces did occupy a position at or near Peekskill, and retired to the heights upon the landing of the enemy on the 4th or 5th of October, 1777, the time at which Mandeville's property is alleged and proved to have been destroyed.

Your committee are of opinion that the prayer of the petition is reasonable, and ought to be granted ; and they accordingly report a bill.

---

JANUARY 25, 1838.

The Committee on Revolutionary Claims, to which was referred the petition of the heirs and legal representatives of Israel Honeywell, report:

The petitioners state that they are the heirs of Israel Honeywell, who served as an officer of militia during the revolutionary war, in Westchester county, New York ; that said Honeywell was the owner of a large and valuable real estate in said county of Westchester, at or near a place called Saw-mill river, on which were erected a valuable dwelling-house, barn, and cider-mill ; that said Honeywell, owing to his active partisan services. had become especially obnoxious to the British, who, in the fall of 1776, seized and carried away his four slaves, together with all his stock and moveable property. It is further alleged that, after the battle of White Plains, his house, barn, and cider-mill, were taken possession of by a portion of the American army, and occupied as an outpost until they were afterwards burned by the British troops. This petition is duly sworn to by Jemima Waten, the daughter and one of the heirs of said Israel Honeywell.

The material facts alleged in said petition are supported fully, in the opinion of the committee, by the depositions of Samuel Young, Jacob Odell, and Gilbert Underhill. These witnesses prove that the house was taken possession of as early as the winter of 1776, by the American troops, and occupied as an outpost until burned ; that before it was burned the family of said Honeywell removed from the premises to a place of greater security—leaving them in the possession of our troops, in whose possession they were in 1778, when the house, barn, and cider-mill were burned by Delancy's corps, a part of the British force stationed at the time at Morrisiana. It appears by the certificates of the persons before whom the depositions were taken, that the deponents are men of good character. From the proof adduced, the committee are of opinion that remuneration ought to be made for the value of the dwelling-house only, the proof not being explicit as to the possession of the other buildings by the American troops at the time they were destroyed ; therefore report a bill.

The Committee on Revolutionary Claims, to whom was referred the petition of the legal representatives of William Boyce, deceased, have had the same under consideration, and report:

That this case was considered by the Committee on Revolutionary Claims, at the last Congress, and the following report made thereon, viz:

MARCH 3, 1836.

The Committee on Revolutionary Claims, to which was recommitted the petition and accompanying papers of the personal representatives of William Boyce, deceased, report:

That they have reviewed the testimony in the case, and have come to the conclusion that the services of the said William Boyce, as a lieutenant in the war of the Revolution, were such as to entitle him to the five years' full pay, in lieu of half pay for life, promised by the resolution of 22d of March, 1783.

There exists no doubt that the said William Boyce was a first lieutenant in the fourth Virginia regiment on continental establishment; nor would the committee have hesitated to have reported in favor of allowing commutation pay, in the first instance, but for the statement of the First Auditor, that it appeared by the revolutionary records, on file in his office, that the said William Boyce became a supernumerary officer on the 30th of September, 1778. Since the recommitment of the petition evidence has been supplied convincing the committee that he was afterwards in active service, and continued so in the service as to have been entitled to commutation pay. The evidence on which this opinion is founded is contained in three depositions, that of James Martin, that of James Laffoon, and that of Vachel Faudre. In the first it is stated, expressly, that the said Boyce was engaged in the battle of Guilford courthouse, in 1781, and that he afterwards marched into the State of Virginia, with some troops. He acted as adjutant in the battle of Guilford.

In the deposition of Laffoon it is stated, while he (Laffoon) was lying at Hillsborough, in North Carolina, William Boyce, as adjutant, joined the regiment to which he belonged; that this regiment was at Camden when General Gates was defeated, and that said Boyce there commanded as adjutant. It is also stated, in the same deposition, that he acted as adjutant in the engagement of Guilford court-house.

In the deposition of Vachel Faudre, it is stated most expressly that William Boyce was engaged in the battle commonly known as Gates's defeat, in 1780. The deponent states that during the action the said Boyce was thrown from his horse, and that he and one Zachariah King assisted him in remounting his horse. After the "defeat," the American troops retreated in small detachments; that with which he (the deponent) fell in, went to Hillsborough, where he again found Adjutant Boyce. They were then separated, and he did not again see Boyce until the spring following, when he met him in Petersburg: that at a still later period than this, at Richmond, he found Adjutant Boyce in command, and saw him in a severe skirmish at Jamestown, where he acted with great bravery.

It is stated, in the same deposition, that William Boyce was in command, as adjutant, in the regiment to which the deponent belonged, at the siege of York, and until the surrender of Cornwallis, shortly after which event they were separated, and did not again see each other until about the 1st of December, 1811, near Lexington, in Kentucky.

If these depositions contain the truth, (and the committee have no reason to suspect they do not,) it is evident that William Boyce, though he was a supernumerary officer on the 30th of September, 1778, was again in active service, and, the presumption is, so continued until the close of the war.

The question may here be started, did he, after the time he was returned a supernumerary officer, in 1778, serve as a continental or as a militia officer? The committee feel authorized to draw the conclusion, presumptively at least, that his services were rendered in the capacity of a continental officer, from the fact, certified by the Secretary of the Commonwealth of Virginia, William H. Richardson, that William Boyce was allowed an *additional* bounty of land, as a lieutenant, for one year and nine months' service in the continental army. They, therefore, report a bill, allowing the legal representatives of said Boyce the commutation pay of a lieutenant.

The conclusion to which the committee come, in the foregoing report, seems to have been fully warranted by the evidence then before them; but this committee, believing that there might be some more satisfactory evidence obtained from the archives of the Revolution in Virginia, made application, through one of their members, to the auditor of public accounts of that State, for a certificate of the settlement which they presumed had been made with William Boyce, under the act of the Virginia Legislature, passed at the November session of 1781, and which certificate they have obtained. It shows, unfortunately for the petitioners, that Lieutenant William Boyce was settled with, for his services in the army, *only* up to the 30th of September, 1778; the very period at which he appears, by the old war rolls, on file in the War Department, to have become a supernumerary officer. This addition to the evidence obliges this committee to reverse the decision of the committee of the last Congress. If Lieutenant Boyce had served to a later period than the 30th of September, 1778, as a *continental* officer, the committee cannot conceive why a settlement, made in 1783, should have been for services *only* up to that time, when it is considered that the act, by authority of which the settlement was made, would have continued his full pay up to the 1st of January, 1782, if he had continued in the *continental* service to the close of the war, as is alleged.

It may be said that the parol testimony in the case proves service until after the surrender of Cornwallis. It is admitted that it does. But, was this service subsequent to the 30th of September, 1778, rendered in the continental line of the army? If it was, Boyce was entitled to commutation. If it was not, he was not entitled. The committee believe that Boyce, after he had become supernumerary, as to the continental line, went into the militia line of service, as did very many of the continental supernumerary officers, at different periods of the war. It was no strange thing for a continental officer, being supernumerary, to be found in the command of militia. On the contrary, they were generally selected by the authorities of the State of Virginia for that kind of service, in preference of the militia officers. This fact at once reconciles the parol with the record evidence in this case.

Again: it would seem a little strange that Lieutenant Boyce should have been recalled into the continental service proper, after being supernumerary, in view of the fact that there was a further reduction of the line of officers in 1779, (the next year after he had become supernumerary,) and another reduction in 1780. What reason could have existed for recalling the supernumerary officers into service, at a time when the corps of officers was so redundant as to make further reduction necessary?

*Resolved*, (as the opinion of this committee,) That the prayer of the petitioners be rejected.

----

JANUARY 25, 1838.

The Committee on Revolutionary Claims, to which was referred the petition of Jacob Greer, report:

The petitioner states that he found in a pocketbook belonging to his father-in-law, a soldier of the Revolution, "a fifty dollar bill of continental money," and asks that Congress may authorize the Treasurer to take in said bill and pay the money for it.

Neither the bill nor a description of it accompany the petition. What value was given for it is not known; neither can its value, at the time, be ascertained, under the circumstances stated.

The committee think the prayer unreasonable, for numerous reasons, not deemed necessary to detail. It believes the payment of all continental bills a question not proper to be even considered; a request which ought not, under any circumstances, to be granted. It is therefore

*Resolved*, That the prayer of the petitioner be rejected.

----

JANUARY 25, 1838.

The Committee on Revolutionary Claims, to which was referred the petition of the heirs of Captain Thomas Baytop, report:

This case was examined at the 1st session of the 24th Congress, and favorably reported on. Upon reviewing the case, and getting additional evidence from the authorities of Virginia, the committee has found reason for a change of opinion.

The petitioners state that their father, Thomas Baytop, entered the service of the United States in the early part of the Revolution, and served in the Virginia line on continental establishment to the close of the war. They therefore ask the commutation of half pay for life promised to such officers by the resolves of October, 1780, and March, 1783.

In support of this statement, several respectable witnesses (Henry Buchannan, B. Marnix, Almon Dunstan, and Alexander C. Shackleford) swear that they knew Captain Thomas Baytop during the war of the Revolution, and that he served to the close of the war in 1783. Dr. William Taliaferro, a highly respectable witness, swears that Captain Baytop resided at his father's house previous to his entering the service of the United States, and distinctly recollects that he returned from the service to that residence after the conclusion of the war, and not until then. From his own knowledge, and from the information and belief of others, he has no hesitation in saying that Captain Thomas Baytop entered the continental service at an early period of the revolutionary war, and served until its conclusion.

On the other hand, the name of Captain Thomas Baytop does not appear on any of the revolutionary records on file in the Third Auditor's office. He was settled with by the State of Virginia as an officer of the continental line, under the act of Assembly passed November, 1781. He received a certificate *himself* on the 22d of March, 1783, for the balance of his full pay for services prior to January 1, 1782, to wit : pay as captain lieutenant of artillery, from January 13, 1777, to February 5, 1778, and as captain, from 5th February, 1778, to December 11, 1779.

No parol evidence can contravene a record of this description. If Captain Baytop had served in the continental line longer than December, 1779, he would, when settling for the balance of his full pay in March, 1783, for services prior to January 1, 1782, have been paid for a longer period than December, 1779. This must be conclusive as to his not serving *in the continental line* to the conclusion of the war, or even to the spring of 1781, one or the other of which is necessary to entitle to the commutation of half pay. The probability is that he served in the continental line to December, 1779, and for the balance of the war either in the militia, volunteers, or State troops, and was, of consequence, not entitled to commutation. The committee, therefore, resolve that the prayer of the petitioners cannot be granted.

---

JANUARY 25, 1838.

The Committee on Revolutionary Claims, to which was referred the petition of the heirs of John Holcombe, deceased, have had the same under consideration, and report :

That the petitioners claim the commutation of five years' full pay, promised by the resolutions of the Continental Congress to such officers as should serve to the end of the war, or become supernumerary after the 21st of October, 1780.

The committee are opinion that John Holcombe was not entitled to commutation, because, as they understand the evidence, his services in the continental line terminated on the 25th of March, 1779. This conclusion is believed to be authorized by the certificate of the auditor of public accounts of the State of Virginia, which show that, on the 13th day of June, 1783, a certificate was issued in the name of John Holcombe, a captain of infantry, for £269 13s. 4d., as pay for his services as captain in the fourth Virginia regiment, from the 1st of January, 1777, to the 25th of March, 1779. If he had continued longer in the continental service, the committee think it unquestionable that he would have been paid, under the act of the November session of the Virginia Legislature, to a later period, even up to the 1st of January, 1782, if he had served to that time.

He appears, by the parol testimony in the case, to have been in service after 1779, but he was doubtless in the militia service. The supernumeraries of the continental line were generally, if not universally, employed by the State of Virginia to command her militia.

*Resolved*, As the opinion of this committee, that the prayer of the petitioners be rejected.

The Committee on Revolutionary Claims, to which was referred the petition of Susannah Hayne Pinckney, sole heir and representative of Captain Richard Shubrick, report:

The petitioner is the sole heir and only surviving daughter of Captain Richard Shubrick; she claims the seven years' half pay promised by the resolve of August 24, 1780, to the widow, or, in case of her death or intermarriage, to the children of such officers as have died, or shall hereafter die in the service.

It appears, from incontestable evidence, that Richard Shubrick was a captain of the 2d South Carolina regiment on continental establishment, (appointed November 15, 1776,) and that he died while in the public service, on the 8th day of November, 1777. Major General Moultre certified these facts in August, 1791.

It appears, also, that Captain Shubrick left a widow and two daughters; the widow intermarried some time after his decease; one of the daughters died, leaving no children, so that the petitioner, the only daughter, Susannah Hayne Pinckney, is now the sole heir and representative of Captain Richard Shubrick.

It appears, further, that this case was examined, under a reference made by the House, by the Secretary of War, General Knox, as early as November, 1791, and favorably reported on; upon which report there would, however, seem to have been no final action, at least as far as Captain Shubrick's heirs were concerned.

The committee believe the petitioner fully entitled to the seven years' half pay promised by the resolution of August 24, 1780; and as it appears never to have been paid, either by the United States or the State of South Carolina, a bill is reported for her relief.

---

The Committee on Revolutionary Claims, to which was referred the petition of Elias Hall and Alpheus Hall, report:

The petitioners represent themselves as the youngest sons and legal heirs of Captain John Hall, who was wounded and killed in the revolutionary war in the summer of 1777; and, after a recital of their own services and privations, not material to this examination, pray remuneration for personal property belonging to their father, destroyed by the enemy, and which, they themselves think, would have been valued, at the date of its destruction, at fourteen or fifteen hundred dollars.

The committee cannot respond favorably to the relief now prayed.

First. The spoliation occurred more than sixty years since, and is attested only by the frail and uncorroborated recollection of the petitioners themselves.

Secondly, and mainly. If the spoliation were proved by testimony the most explicit and disinterested, this Government repudiates the *principle* of awarding indemnity for property not pressed into public service, nor consumed in public use, but lost in the common desolation of war.

The Committee on Revolutionary Claims, to which was referred the petition of Theodore Middleton, have had the same under consideration, and report:

That the petitioner claims the commutation of five years' full pay in lieu of the half pay for life promised by the resolutions of the old Congress, in consideration of his services as lieutenant in the *extra* regiment of the Maryland continental line of the revolutionary army.

In support of the claim, the affidavit of Mountjoy Bailey, who was a captain in the said extra regiment, and the certificate of the register of the land office of Maryland, are adduced. Captain Bailey, in his affidavit, states positively that Theodore Middleton entered the service of the United States, as a lieutenant, in April, 1779, in the second Maryland extra regiment, and repaired immediately to Annapolis, the seat of Government; that he went from thence (the affiant being with him) to Philadelphia, and that, after leaving Philadelphia for a time, and returning again, he took shipping at the head of Elk river and came back to Annapolis, where he remained for a long time. Afterwards, he marched through the State of Virginia (Captain Bailey still being with him) into North Carolina, and was at the battle of Guilford, in March, 1781; after which time, to wit: in the month of October, 1781, he was returned by General Greene as a supernumerary officer.

The certificate of the register of the land office of Maryland states that it appears, by the army legers of the Revolution remaining in that office, that an account is opened against Theodore Middleton, a lieutenant (extra regiment) of the Maryland line, and that said accounts stand stated and settled on said legers, up to the 30th of March, 1781.

From the best information the committee have been able to obtain, they are of opinion that the extra regiment, to which the petitioner belonged, was of the continental establishment; and if so, the petitioner is unquestionably entitled to commutation, unless he forfeited his right by resigning his commission; and there is no circumstance known to the committee to justify the suspicion that he did resign.

The committee therefore report a bill allowing him commutation.

---

The Committee on Revolutionary Claims, to which was referred the petition of Susanna Shurley, having considered the same, report:

The petitioner represents that she is the widow of Bennett Shurley; that said Shurley was a regular soldier in the Maryland continental line, in the revolutionary war; that the certificate due her deceased husband, for 100 acres of bounty land, has been lost; and, to the end that she may use and enjoy said land, she prays the legislative authority to authorize and direct the renewal of said certificate.

William Warfield, a magistrate of Baltimore city, avouches the credit of Arthur McLean, who testifies that the petitioner is the widow of Bennett Shurley; that said Shurley was in the battles of Guilford, Camden, and Eutaw Springs, in the latter of which he was badly wounded. The letter of William Gordon, of the Bounty Land Office, dated October 12, 1836, bears evidence that land warrant No. 11706, for 100 acres, issued the 11th March, 1791, to Bennett Shurley, a private in the Maryland continental line; and that upon inquiry at the General Land Office, it is ascertained that no *patent* has ever issued in satisfaction of said numbered warrant. The committee, therefore, report a bill.

---

FEBRUARY 1, 1838.

The Committee on Revolutionary Claims, to which was referred the bill from the Senate (No. 46) for the relief of the legal representatives of Henry Morfit, report:

The committee report this bill, with an amendment allowing interest. They recommend the passage of this bill, upon the ground that the evidence convinces them that Lieutenant Morfit was transferred to the continental line of the regular army, and was entitled to the rank, pay, and emoluments, of a lieutenant in the line of the continental army, and that he was not an officer in the flying camp at the date of his second captivity.

---

FEBRUARY 1, 1838.

The Committee on Revolutionary Claims, to which was referred the petition of the heirs of John H. Overstreet, report:

That, from the certificates and letters accompanying the petition, it appears that John H. Overstreet served first as a cadet for a short time, and received a commission from the Governor of Virginia on the 28th of November, 1787, to serve under Robert Lawson, in the militia of that Commonwealth, on certain tours of duty; that in March, 1781, he received the appointment of captain of militia from Robert Lawson, brigadier general of militia, by the orders of General Green. It is further alleged, in said letters and certificates, that he was in the battles of Brandywine and Guilford, and was a brave and valuable soldier. All the services rendered by John H. Overstreet during the revolutionary war were in the militia, except the short time he served as a cadet in 1777. No evidence has been adduced by the petitioners that Captain Overstreet, under whom they claim as heirs, served on the continental establishment during the war, and, although he may have rendered the country valuable and meritorious services, as no provision has been made heretofore by Congress for similar services, the committee report that the prayer of the petitioners ought not to be granted.

---

FEBRUARY 6, 1838.

The Committee on Revolutionary Claims, to which was referred the petition of Jonas Bartlett, report:

The petitioner states that he is intermarried with Abigail Dale, who is the only daughter and heir of Jeremiah Dale, who was a non-commissioned officer in the army of the Revolution, and slain at Saratoga, in the year 1777.

He asks that his wife Abigail, sole heir and representative of said Jeremiah Dale, may have the benefit of the resolutions of May 15, 1778, and August 24, 1780, giving seven years' half pay to the widow or children of such officers of the army as may die in the service.

These resolutions, applying only to commissioned officers of the army, and not to non-commissioned officers or privates, the prayer of the petitioner cannot be granted, and the committee accordingly so resolve.

---

FEBRUARY 6, 1838.

The Committee on Revolutionary Claims, to which was referred the petition of the heirs of General James Hogan, report :

This case was examined at the first session of the twenty-fourth Congress, and an unfavorable report made thereon ; in which report the committee concur, and adopt it as part of this. It may be found in the manuscript reports of the Committee on Revolutionary Claims, vol. 3, p. 48.

General Hogan was a brigadier general in the army of the Revolution, and *died* in service during the war. His heirs have received the seven years' half pay to which the widow or children of officers dying in the service were entitled under the resolutions of August 24, 1780. They now ask for the bounty land to which an officer of General Hogan's rank was entitled. Congress promised a bounty in land only to those officers who served to the end of the war, or became supernumerary at some period thereof, and to the heirs of such as were " *slain by the enemy.*" The committee, therefore, again resolve that the prayer of the petitioners cannot be granted.

JUNE 15, 1836.

Certain individuals, in the character of heirs of General James Hogan, petition for bounty land for his military services in the war of the Revolution. It appears that General Hogan was taken prisoner by the enemy at the capture of Charleston, and died while in captivity. The resolutions promising bounty land to the officers of the revolutionary army do not embrace the case. It is insisted, however, that this ought to be an exception, and that Congress should grant the prayer of the petitioners, because the death of General Hogan was probably occasioned by his sufferings while in captivity, and hence it should be viewed in the same light as though he had been " slain by the enemy," which would have entitled his heirs to bounty land. The representatives of General Hogan received the seven years' half pay which they were entitled to under the resolutions of Congress, in consequence of his dying in the service, and the committee perceive no good reason for enlarging the provisions of those resolutions so as to provide for cases not embraced by them. They cannot foresee the extent to which the exception, if made, might carry us. Our attention has been called to two bills passed in 1825, one for the relief of Francis Wright's heirs, and the other for the relief of Thomas Williams. The first act only supplies the loss of a land warrant, and the last authorizes the issuing of a warrant to the soldier himself, and in neither can we find a precedent for favoring the petition in the present case.

The committee recommend the adoption of the following resolution :

*Resolved*, That the prayer of the petitioners ought not to be granted.

---

## FEBRUARY 17, 1838.

The Committee on Revolutionary Claims, to whom was referred the application of Charles Woodson, of Virginia, asking that commutation be granted him on account of the revolutionary services of his father, the late Tarlton Woodson, deceased, report :

That, as early as the year 1807, the said Tarlton Woodson presented his claim to Congress, setting forth an interesting detail of his services in the revolutionary war, which he alleges commenced as early as the year 1775, and stating, amongst other things, the fact of his being more than three years a prisoner to the enemy. After mentioning various military appointments conferred on him, the petitioner states, that in 1777 he was promoted to the command of major in Colonel Moses Hazen's independent continental regiment, enlisted and raised to serve during the war.

From the certificate of the Auditor of Virginia, it is shown that the said Tarlton Woodson received a certificate of pay as major on continental establishment up to the 31st of December, 1781, with the farther statement of that officer that there is no document in his office showing that said Woodson ever resigned. By inquiry at the office of the Third Auditor of the Treasury your committee learn that no evidence is there afforded of the said Woodson's having received or being entitled to commutation, but the records filed in the Pension Office show that he was a major in Colonel Hazen's corps, and taken prisoner on the 22d day of August, 1777.

Your committee feel fully justified, from the facts set forth, in coming to the conclusion that Tarlton Woodson became supernumerary under the reduction of the army, or remained in actual service up to the end of the war ; and that in either event he would, in his lifetime, have been entitled to five years' full pay as major, in lieu of half pay for life. That the said Woodson has died, leaving, as is clearly shown to your committee, Charles Woodson as his only child and legal representative ; in favor of whom your committee report a bill.

---

## FEBRUARY 17, 1838.

The Committee on Revolutionary Claims, to whom was referred the petition of Mary Sabor and Charles D. Coffin, report :

The petitioners represent themselves as among the heirs at law of James Fay, a soldier of the Revolution ; that said Fay enlisted for and during that war ; that he belonged to what was called the "Bay troops," or the "Massachusetts line ;" that he served under General Brooks a part of the time ; that he served until near the close of the war ; that he died in service, of putrid fever, at West Point. Therefore, the petitioners claim bounty land.

The committee have not thought it necessary to investigate the fact of the enlistment and service of James Fay; for the preliminary question occurs, admitting the allegations of the petition to be true, Are the heirs at law then entitled to the relief prayed ? The committee answer in the negative ; and do so with much reluctance, and with all the sympathy which a hard case naturally inspires. James Fay appears not to have been`slain by the enemy, but to have died of sickness in the service. It is not the province of the committee to vindicate the distinction between two such cases; the law performs that office, by providing for the one case in exclusion of the other. The law being imperative, and the committee being left without discretion, report unfavorably.

FEBRUARY 17, 1838.

The Committee on Revolutionary Claims, to whom the memorial of Thomas Triplett and the other heirs of Captain Thomas Triplett was referred, report :

That, by an act of Congress of the 2d of March, 1833, the commutation pay due by the United States to a captain in the continental line of the army at the end of the war of the Revolution was allowed to Captain Thomas Triplett, for his services as such. That accordingly, on the 5th of March, 1833, a Treasury warrant, number 62,467, for the sum of $7,245 45, was issued to H. Daniels, who received that amount at the Treasury of the United States, under and in pursuance of an authority given him by a certain Thomas Triplett, who claimed to be the legal representative of Captain Thomas Triplett aforesaid. That, though the testimonials of his heirship, produced by the said Thomas Triplett, were all in due form, and such as to afford no ground for the suspicion of a meditated fraud on the Treasury, it soon became manifest that a gross fraud had been perpetrated; that the $7,245 45 aforesaid had been paid to the said Thomas Triplett, upon evidence, subjecting him to the charges both of fraud and perjury ; that on these charges sundry criminal prosecutions, as well as a suit to recover the money erroneously paid as aforesaid, were instituted in behalf of the Government against the said Triplett ; that on one of the several indictments against the said Thomas Triplett, on the charges aforesaid, he was found guilty, and sentenced by the court to fine and imprisonment, in pursuance of which he was committed to jail, where he soon thereafter died ; that a judgment was obtained against him in behalf of the United States for the recovery of the money erroneously paid as aforesaid; but he being insolvent, a suit is now depending, in behalf of the Government, against H. Daniels, who, as the authorized agent of the said Thomas Triplett, received the money in question at the Treasury ; who still holds the money, and who is ready to refund it at any time he can do so, on the authority of a judgment against him in behalf of the United States. It is under the foregoing circumstances the memorialists, claiming to be the actual heirs of Captain Thomas Triplett, ask that the benefit of the aforesaid act, passed the 2d of March, 1833, may be extended to them ; and that such interest on the $7,245 45 as the Government may eventually recover and receive from the erroneous holders of that sum shall, when received into the Treasury, also be paid, by the Secretary of the Treasury, to the legal representatives of the said Captain Thomas Triplett. The committee concur in the opinion that the prayer of the memorialists is reasonable, and report a bill for their relief.

---

The Committee on Revolutionary Claims, to which was referred the petition of Nathaniel Bird, ask leave to report :

The petitioner states that he enlisted for three years in the army of the Revolution, in the Massachusetts line; that he entered service in the fore part of March, 1781, and served until the 31st of December, 1783, when he was honorably discharged, and that he has received but one month's pay for his service of two years and ten months. He therefore prays that a law may be passed providing for the payment of the wages due him. The petitioner further states that, " in about one year after his discharge, he sent to Henry Nelson, paymaster, but was not able to get any pay from him. In the spring of 1789 his brother, Amos Bird, took his discharge, and a power of attorney to call on said Nelson and get his pay. His brother Amos, when he received the discharge and power of attorney, was about starting on a journey to Kentucky; and if the pay was received, it was to be sent to the petitioner. In this situation the matter rested until the fall of 1819, when the petitioner visited his brother, then residing in the State of Missouri, and learnt, for the first time, that the papers and power of attorney were lost."

It appears that final-settlement certificates issued for the wages of the petitioner, and were placed in the hands of Henry Nelson for him. It also appears that these certificates have been settled and paid by the Government; so that, if the prayer of the petitioner be granted, the Government will have paid twice the amount of the petitioner's wages. The petitioner has insisted that Nelson was not his agent, and that he never received from Nelson the certificates placed in his hands, and that the Government is yet liable to him. Whether Nelson was the officer of the Government or the agent of the regiment in which the petitioner was a soldier, appointed by the troops, according to the opinion of the Third Auditor, the committee deem it unnecessary to decide; for, whether he acted in the one or the other capacity, the committee are of opinion the claim ought not to be paid a second time by the Government. There is no evidence before the committee to justify the opinion that Nelson embezzled the certificates placed in his hands for the soldiers. We ought not to presume that he acted fraudulently. The petition shows that the petitioner knew he was to apply to Nelson for his certificates or pay. It does not appear that the petitioner ever made a personal application. The certificates may have been delivered to the person sent to Nelson about a year after the discharge. There is as much ground to suppose a fraud in this messenger as on the part of Nelson. Amos Bird, the petitioner's brother, who also claims compensation for his revolutionary services, and which also seems to have been paid, states that he did not see Nelson when he was authorized to call on him by the petitioner. Under these circumstances, the committee cannot report favorably. The delay is not sufficiently accounted for.

The committee deem it proper to remark that this case was before the Committee on Revolutionary Claims, and a favorable report made thereon by Mr. Burges, on the 11th March, 1830; but it does not appear from the report that the committee was then apprized that the Government had paid the certificates which issued for the services of the petitioner and his brother Amos. Although the fact is mentioned that final-settlement certificates were issued, the report says nothing about their payment. The committee are of opinion that the prayer of the petitioner ought not to be granted.

FEBRUARY 20, 1838.

The Committee on Revolutionary Claims, to whom the memorial of the heirs of Thomas Wishart was referred, report:

That Sidney Wishart and the other heirs of Thomas Wishart claim the commutation pay due to the said Thomas Wishart for his services as a lieutenant in the army of the United States, in the war of the Revolution. It appears from the army records of that war, on file in the War Department, that the said Thomas Wishart was appointed, in November 1776, a lieutenant in the 15th Virginia regiment on the continental establishment of the army of the United States; that as such he received land bounty from the United States, and the pay of lieutenant to the —— day of September, 1778, at which time he became, as it is fair to presume, a supernumerary, under the arrangement of the army made about that time. His name is not on the list of officers retained in service, *nor on the list of those who became supernumerary* in pursuance of the reduction of the regiments in 1778; nor do any of the pay accounts now in existence show that he received pay subsequent to September, 1778. Upon this state of facts, and for the service aforesaid, Thomas Wishart had no claim on the United States for half pay or commutation; nor does it appear that Thomas Wishart in his lifetime, or his heirs since, set up a claim to commutation for that service. But it does appear (see manuscript reports of the Secretary of War) that in 1793 Thomas Wishart petitioned Congress for the commutation pay due him as a lieutenant in the continental service, and in support of his claim he adduced the following evidence, to prove his service as a continental officer, after he became supernumerary as aforesaid, in 1778, so as to entitle him to the benefit of the resolution of Congress of the 20th of October, 1780, which allowed half pay to all such officers as thereafter should become supernumerary, or retire for the want of service. The evidence referred to were the certificates of—

1st. Colonel David Mason, the colonel of the 15th Virginia regiment, certifying the petitioner (Lieutenant Thomas Wishart) was in service to the last of July, 1778, dated 11th of January, 1787.

2d. Of Colonel James Innes, that he understood petitioner was kept until some time in the year 1779, dated 16th of October, 1791.

3d. Of Colonel Josiah Parker, formerly of the Virginia line, stating his knowledge of the petitioner while with the northern army, and also in all the different invasions of Virginia, dated the 9th of December, 1791.

4th. Of Brigadier General Muhlenberg, who, in 1780, was senior continental officer in the southern department of the army. He certifies that he considered the petitioner as a continental officer, and employed him as such until April, 1781, when petitioner was surprised and taken prisoner; and that this is stated and certified from vouchers in his hands, and his personal knowledge, having received a satisfactory account in what manner the petitioner had been employed during the time he had been in Virginia.

Several of the foregoing certificates testify that the petitioner was a valuable officer. It was upon the foregoing evidence of service till April, 1781, in which month he was captured by the enemy, and detained a prisoner till the surrender of Yorktown on the 16th of the ensuing October, after which he was required to perform no further military duty. Petitioner, in 1793, claimed commutation; his petition was referred to the Secretary of War, who reported against the claim, on two grounds: first, that the petitioner was not returned by a board of officers as in service at the end of the war; secondly, that the claim was barred by the act of limitations. Upon these two grounds the claim was rejected in 1793, and very soon thereafter, it is said, the petitioner died.

In the month of December, 1833, the heirs of Thomas Wishart, seeing the act of limitations, as it affected such claims, was suspended, presented to Congress the memorial now under the consideration of this committee; and on the 11th of December of that year their memorial was referred to the Committee on Revolutionary Claims. On the 13th of January, 1834, that committee reported bill No. 613, allowing to the memorialist the commutation claimed. That bill was not acted on by the House before the adjournment of Congress, and on the 8th of December, 1834, that bill was again referred to the Committee on Revolutionary Claims, where it, and all other claims to commutation, remained unacted on by the committee during the whole of that Congress, by reason of the pendency of a bill reported from the same committee, intended to transfer to another tribunal the adjustment of the remaining claims to commutation. That bill failed to become a law, and on the 16th of December, 1835, the memorial in question was again presented to Congress, and referred to the Committee on Revolutionary Claims. No action on the case appears during that session; so that, on the 12th of December, 1836, it was once more referred to the same committee, and was assigned to the Hon. Joseph Crane for examination. His manuscript report in favor of the claim, accompanied by a bill, is on file with the memorial. The evidence in this case, above referred to, shows that Thomas Wishart entered the army of the United States as a lieutenant in the 15th Virginia regiment on continental establishment, and received pay as such till August, 1778, at which time, it is presumed, he became supernumerary; that he again entered into the service as a continental officer does not appear by any record now existing; to supply this, oral evidence of his service, obtained from officers of high character and rank in the army, is offered. The oral evidence referred to bears date almost contemporaneously with the service spoken of, and is given by officers of too much intelligence and experience to presume they misunderstood the matter about which they testified. The commissioners who made a list of the officers in service in 1782 were liable to mistakes, and did commit many errors, as has been familiarly demonstrated. While it is difficult, if not impossible, to imagine that Colonel Josiah Parker and General Muhlenberg could mistake as to what each of them testified on his own knowledge. Colonel Parker states his knowledge of Thomas Wishart in the northern army, and in all the different invasions of Virginia. General Muhlenberg, senior continental officer, says he considered Thomas Wishart a continental officer, and employed him as such until April, 1781, when he was taken prisoner ; and that this is stated and certified from vouchers in his hands, and his personal knowledge. Having received a satisfactory account in what manner Thomas Wishart had been employed in Virginia, this committee, without deciding whether Lieutenant Thomas Wishart became supernumerary in July, 1778, are of opinion, if he did, that *it* ought not to prejudice his claim to remuneration for *subsequent* services ; and be lieving, as the committee do, that he again entered the military service as a continental officer some time in 1779, and continued therein till the 16th of October, 1781, that he was entitled to commutation under the resolution of Congress of 20th October, 1780, allowing half pay for life to such officers of the army as might thereafter become supernumerary, or retire for the want of service. Lieutenant Wishart was captured by the enemy in April, 1781, and retaken on the surrender of Yorktown on the 16th of October ensuing. After that period there were no further active military operations, and many officers became supernumerary, or retired on leave. To one of these classes it is reasonable to presume Lieutenant Wishart belonged, and thereby became entitled to half pay or commutation.

The committee concur in the former reports made on this memorial, and report a bill.

----

FEBRUARY 20, 1838.

The Committee on Revolutionary Claims, to whom was referred the petition of Roger Stayner, have had the same under consideration, and report :

That the petitioner claims the five years' full pay, in commutation of the half pay for life, promised by the resolutions of the old Congress to certain officers of the continental line.

In the opinion of the committee, the evidence adduced well supports the petitioner's claim.

A certificate from the Bounty Land Office, given on the 5th day of November, 1828, and intended to be applied as evidence of the right of the said Stayner to a pension under the act of the 15th May, 1828, shows that a land warrant, No. 1245, issued to Roger Stayner, a captain in the Pennsylvania line, in the revolutionary war, for 300 acres of land, on the 6th day of June, 1827. It was further certified from the same office, and for the same purpose, that, by a list of officers returned as entitled to bounty land, it appears that Roger Stayner, a captain of the old second regiment of Pennsylvania, became supernumerary in consequence of being a prisoner.

By a certificate of the Auditor General of the State of Pennsylvania, given on the 16th day of December, 1828, it appears there is on file in his office a certificate of John Nicholson, bearing date September 20th, 1783, (the said Nicholson being at that time Auditor General of the State of Pennsylvania,) by which it appears that that Commonwealth was then indebted to Roger Stayner, late a captain of the second Pennsylvania regiment, in the sum of £393 16s. 11d. specie, with lawful interest from the 10th day of April, 1781, being the amount of the residue of the depreciation of his pay, pursuant to two acts of Assembly passed at Philadelphia the 18th of December, 1780, and the 10th of April, 1781.

It also appears, by a certificate of the secretary of the land office of the State of Pennsylvania, that Roger Stayner was returned as being entitled to a donation of land for his services as a captain in the Pennsylvania line, with this remark written in connexion with his name, "prisoner, included per resolution of January 1st, 1781."

The resolution of January 1st, 1781, referred to above, is in the following words:

"*Resolved*, That, in the new arrangement of the army, it is the sense of Congress that the officers of the continental line who have been exchanged since the said arrangement, or are now in captivity, ought to be considered and arranged according to their respective ranks, in the same manner with those who have not been prisoners."

From the evidence thus presented, the committee think it clear that Roger Stayner is entitled to *commutation*. He was a prisoner at the time of the new arrangement alluded to in the resolution of the 1st of January, 1781; and by this resolution the places in the army of those officers who were then in captivity are expressly preserved; and all who were officers of the continental line on and after the 21st of October, 1780, (not being supernumerary prior to that time,) and bore their commissions to the close of the war, were entitled to commutation. The committee report a bill for the relief of the petitioner.

---

FEBRUARY 23, 1838.

The Committee on Revolutionary Claims, to which the memorial of the heirs of Colonel William Nelson was referred, report:

That it appears, by the evidence on file with the memorial, that William Nelson entered into the military service of his country at the commencement of the war of the Revolution, as a private soldier; that he was soon thereafter promoted, and commissioned lieutenant colonel to the 7th Virginia regiment on continental establishment; that he served as such during the severe and trying campaigns to the North, in the years 1776 and 1777, in the course of which he was in the memorable battle of Brandywine, on the 11th of September, 1777, and that of Germantown, on the 25th of the ensuing October; that the gallantry and good conduct of Colonel Nelson, in both these bloody engagements, were conspicuous, and are recorded in the history of that period; that on the 25th of October, 1777, Colonel Nelson, on account of "ill health and the state of his affairs," tendered his resignation, which was accepted; (see the acceptance, signed George Washington, on file;) that, subsequently to his resignation, he became actively and very efficiently engaged in the military service of the State of Virginia, and, under the authority of that State, he commanded a regiment of militia during all the campaigns in Virginia—was in that capacity at the siege and surrender of Yorktown, after which it does not appear that he rendered any further military service; that, in consideration of the foregoing services, rendered by William Nelson to the United States, and to the State of Virginia, during a term

54

of three years in the aggregate, he was allowed the land bounty provided for *three years' service*, (see resolution of the Virginia Assembly, 21st of December, 1783;) that, in pursuance of said resolution, a warrant was issued to the said William Nelson for six thousand acres of land; (see the certificate of the register of the Virginia land office, dated 27th of December, 1783.) And it is upon the foregoing evidence of the military service of William Nelson his heirs now ask that he may be allowed the commutation pay promised by the several resolves of Congress to such officers as should continue in service to the *end of the war.* The resignation of William Nelson in 1777, as the memorialists admit, effectually barred his legal claim on the Government of the United States to commutation pay. But the memorialists appeal, on several considerations, to the equitable claim of William Nelson to the same remuneration accorded, by the act of Congress passed 1832, to certain supernumerary officers in the service of Virginia in the war of the Revolution. And in this view, it is particularly insisted that the allowance of land bounty to William Nelson, by Virginia, ought to be decisive in favor of their appeal. The committee do not perceive that the services of William Nelson, highly meritorious and distinguished as they appear to have been, created either a legal or equitable claim on Virginia for the half pay promised by that State to her officers who served to the end of the war, or who should become supernumerary; he therefore had no claim under the act of Congress of 1832, and referred to in the memorial. Nor does the allowance of land bounty by Virginia to William Nelson, for three years' service, in the view of the committee, at all strengthen the claim of William Nelson on the Congress of the United States to commutation pay. The entire Western domain was then (21st of December, 1783) the property of Virginia. In disposing of it, Virginia could not only, without responsibility to any one, satisfy all legal demands on the State for land, but voluntary donations could be made to meritorious individuals. Such seems to have been the case as respects William Nelson. The Virginia Assembly, before which the whole services of William Nelson were presented in December, 1783, and before which all his claims for those services were urged, only allowed him land bounty for *three* years. Why did not that Assembly allow him land bounty for service to the end of the war, or as a supernumerary? in virtue of which he also would have received from that State half pay for life. It seems evident that the utmost equity the State could accord in the case was land bounty for *three years' service.* The committee take that view of the case, and come to the conclusion that the prayer of the memorialists ought not to be allowed.

---

FEBRUARY 23, 1838.

The Committee on Revolutionary Claims, to whom was referred the petition of Captain Daniel Chapman, report:

That the petitioner, under a commission issued by Governor Trumbull, of Connecticut, in 1778, commanded a small craft cruising in Long Island sound against the enemy, in the revolutionary war; the crew consisted of seven men, who, in conjunction with the captain, owned, armed, and victualled the craft, called the "Success." In May, 1782, a Major Davis and a Captain Grennell, alleged to have been officers in the New York continental line of the revolutionary army, entered into a contract with Captain Chapman to guard and convey cloth from Long Island, to make clothes for the New York troops, and to land the same in the State of Connecticut; that these officers were acting as agents for the State of New York, in purchasing and procuring the clothing for the New York line, and entered into the contract, as agents of the State, with Captain Chapman. By the terms of the contract, a warrant or commission was to be procured for Captain Chapman to command the said craft, from the Governor of New York; and he was to receive five dollars per diem, and his men a fair compensation for the time they were employed in the said service. The commission or warrant was procured for Captain Chapman, signed by Governor Clinton, and the services performed from May to November, 1782. But no payment was ever received by him for the services rendered under the contract. In 1837 the House of Representatives of the State of New York passed an act authorizing remuneration to be made to Captain Chapman, which failed in the Senate because that body thought the claim was against the United States, instead of the State of New York. This State had various claims against the United States for moneys expended during the revolutionary war, which have long since been adjusted, settled, and paid; but whether this claim of Captain Chapman constituted an item in the account thus settled, cannot now be ascertained, in consequence of the destruction by fire of the papers and books, by the British, in 1814. It is, however, very evident that Captain Chapman had a fair and just claim against the State of New York. The evidence shows that Major Davis had, in 1781, become a supernumerary; and there is no evidence that, subsequent to that period, he ever re-entered the continental service. Nor is there any other evidence of Grennell being in the continental service than the statement of the claimant. All the witnesses to the application made by the petitioner to the New York Legislature, as well as Captain Chapman himself, concur in representing these officers as agents of the State. The contract was made with the authorized agents of the State, and the services rendered on the faith of the State: why should not the State, in good faith, fulfil her part of the contract? The warrant or commission under which Captain Chapman acted was delivered up by him to the State, in pursuance of a direction contained therein, after the services were performed. It is a fair inference that the State was informed of the nature of the contract, and of the sum due Captain Chapman by her agents: if so informed, a strong presumption arises that this claim constituted a part of the account presented by New York against the United States, and was, if just, allowed and liquidated in the settlement of the account. The committee cannot concur in opinion with the Senate of New York, and think the view taken by the House of Representatives of that State the accurate and just one; and

*Resolve*, That the prayer of the petitioner cannot be granted.

---

MARCH 1, 1838.

The Committee on Revolutionary Claims, to whom was referred the petition of the heirs of Abraham Tipton, deceased, report:

The petition represents that said Tipton was a captain in the continentai army of the Revolution, and as such died in the service of the country. The army-rolls in the office of the Third Auditor of the Treasury show that Abraham Tipton was appointed a captain in the Virginia line of the army, and that he commanded a company ; but said rolls do not conclusively show that he continued in service to the end of the war, nor that he died in service.

The testimony of Hugh McGavock, of Wythe county, Virginia, establishes the following facts : That he, himself, was an officer in the revolutionary war, and attached to Colonel Joseph Crockett's regiment of the Virginia State line ; that he has drawn half pay, and is now drawing a pension under the act of Congress of the 7th of June, 1832 ; that he was well acquainted with Abraham Tipton ; that he first made his acquaintance at the barracks in Albemarle county, Virginia, in 1780 ; that Tipton was then commanding a company in the same regiment; that Tipton continued in that service and capacity until his death, some time in 1781, when he was killed by the Indians near the falls of the Ohio river; that affiant was in company with Tipton, when, a short distance from the main body of the troops, he was shot down ; that, hastening away, and giving notice of the occurrence, he returned with a body of men and found Tipton dead, scalped, and almost divested of his clothing.

The heirs pray the allowance of commutation pay, in consideration of the services of their ancestor, commensurate with the grade of captain. The committee cheerfully admit that the proof in this case establishes the fact of the meritorious service rendered by Abraham Tipton : but at the same time insist that, under the circumstances and the law, that service constitutes no valid claim against this Government. The claim may be properly referrible to another tribunal.

The committee are constrained to render an unfavorable report.

---

MARCH 1, 1838.

The Committee on Revolutionary Claims, to whom was referred the petition of Joseph Richardson, of Caroline county, in the State of Maryland, have had the same under consideration, and report :

That the petitioner claims compensation for the services of his father, William Richardson, in the war of the Revolution.

From the evidence filed in the case, it appears that William Richardson served in the army of the Revolution, as a colonel, until the 22d day of October, 1779, when, owing to protracted indisposition, he resigned his commission. The committee are of opinion, upon this state of fact, that Colonel William Richardson was entitled to no compensation beyond his ordinary pay while in service. The half pay for life, and all similar provisions, were due only to those military officers who continued in service to the end of the war, and such supernumeraries as were embraced by the terms of the resolution of the 21st of October, 1780.

*Resolved, therefore, (as the opinion of this committee,)* That the prayer of the petitioner be rejected.

### March 1, 1838.

The Committee on Revolutionary Claims, to which was referred the petition of Andrew M. D. Jackson, in behalf of the heirs of Major William Jackson, report:

That the Committee on Pensions and Revolutionary Claims had this case, on the petition of William Jackson, the ancestor, under consideration in February, 1819, and were discharged from the further consideration of the same, with liberty to the petitioner to withdraw the same.

That, in February, 1820, the same was again, on the petition of Andrew M. D. Jackson, in behalf of the heirs of William Jackson, deceased, referred to the consideration of the Committee on Pensions and Revolutionary Claims; which committee, on the 23d day of that month and year, made an adverse report. (See record Reports, volume 1, page 308.) That in January, 1826, another adverse report was made by the Committee on Revolutionary Claims. The present committee ask that these previous reports may be taken and considered as a part of their report. Concurring in the views set forth in those reports, the committee are satisfied the prayer of the petitioner ought not to be granted.

It is proper to remark that document No. 12, under date of the 27th day of January, 1838, was presented by the petitioner to the committee. The committee do not think that it changes in any respect the aspect in which the case has hitherto been regarded.

---

### March 1, 1838.

The Committee on Revolutionary Claims, to which was referred the petition of Christiana Lowe and Richard Arell, the only children and devisees of the late David Arell, report:

That the petitioners in this case set forth that their father, David Arell, of Alexandria, now deceased, was commissioned a captain in the Virginia continental line in the war of the Revolution, some time after the commencement of the war, and served with fidelity till the close of the same, as they believe; and claim commutation of five years' full pay in lieu of half pay for life.

In support of the facts alleged in the petition, is, first, the letter of James L. Edwards, Pension office, February 28, 1834, certifying that, from a list of officers of the Virginia line on continental establishment, who have received certificates for the balance of their full pay, agreeably to an act of the Legislature of that State passed November session, 1781, it appears that David Arell, a captain of infantry, received, on the 17th of November, 1784, a certificate of £93 7s. 5d. Virginia currency; and that the records of that office afford no further information respecting the revolutionary services of Captain Arell.

The second piece of evidence is an authenticated copy of a resolution from the records of the land office, Virginia, 8th day of January, 1835, in the following words and figures:

"In the House of Delegates, *November* 26, 1785.

"*Resolved,* That the petition of David Arell, praying that he may be allowed the same proportion of land as is, by law, given to a captain serving three years, is reasonable.

"Test :            JOHN BECKLEY, *C. H. D.*
" 1784, December 4.   Agreed to by the Senate.
                  WILL. DREW, *C. S.*
   " A copy.   Test :       JOHN BECKLEY, *C. H. D.*
" A warrant for 4,000 acres issued to David Arell, April 12, 1785."

The third piece of evidence is the certificate of John C. Sowers, a justice of the peace of Augusta county, Virginia, dated the 13th day of June, 1835, certifying that Smith Thompson, a citizen of Staunton, in said county, personally appeared before him, and to him known as a worthy and truthful man, and made oath, in due form of law, that he was then in his 87th year; and that he was a regularly enlisted soldier, in the Virginia State line, in the war of the Revolution, and belonged to Colonel Grayson's regiment, which, after the appointment of Colonel Grayson to the board of war, was commanded by Colonel Nathaniel Gest ; and that he was in the within service till the winter of 1780 ; and after that period to the South, and was taken prisoner at Charleston, in May, 1780, but made his escape and joined the American army ; was at Guilford, and there saw Captain David Arell in command as an officer ; that he believes said Arell served till the war closed : has been told that said Arell settled in Alexandria.   Upon this certificate is endorsed the certificate, in due form, of Jefferson Renney, clerk of the county court of Augusta, in the State of Virginia, that John C. Sowers was a justice of the peace in and for said county; which certificate is dated the 4th day of January, 1836.

The good character and credibility of Smith Thompson, the witness, whose evidence is above set forth, is abundantly vouched for by B. G. Baldwin, John H. Peyton, of Staunton, Virginia, Alexander H. H. Stuart, James Points, Walter H. Tapp, clerk of the hustings courts of Staunton, Kenton Harper, mayor of the same place, D. W. Patterson, Thomas J. Michie, of the same place, and Nicholas C. Renney, clerk of the superior court of law and chancery of Augusta county, Virginia.   Several of these persons speak of the uncommon tenacity of memory which distinguishes this aged witness.

The committee, on inquiry at the Treasury Department, received for answer the following communication:

"TREASURY DEPARTMENT,
*Third Auditor's Office, January 18,* 1838.

" SIR : I have the honor to state, in reply to your letter of the 17th instant, that it appears, from the muster-rolls of the 3d regiment of the Virginia line on file in this office, that David Arell was appointed a captain on the 7th of October, 1776, and that he *resigned* on the 14th of February, 1778 ; of course, Captain Arell's services did not entitle him to commutation pay.

" With great respect,
" PETER HAGNER, *Auditor.*

" Hon. SAMUEL BIRDSALL,
    *of the Com. on Revolutionary Claims*
       *of the House of Representatives.*"

The committee submit, in addition to the preceding letter from Peter

Hagner, the following document, being a copy of the certificate of James E. Heath, auditor of Virginia, in answer to a communication from the committee in relation to the case of the heirs of Captain David Arell, addressed to him:

"This is to certify, that it appears from a list in this office of such officers and soldiers of the Virginia continental line, during the revolutionary war, as settled their accounts and received certificates for the balance of their full pay, according to an act of Assembly passed November session, 1781, that a certificate issued on the 17th day of November, 1784, in the name of *David Arell*, as captain of infantry, for £93 7s. 5d., which certificate appears to have been delivered to himself, and was given for services prior to the 1st January, 1782, to wit:

"Pay as captain from the 1st January, 1777, to 14th February, 1778.

"Given under my hand at the Auditor's office, Richmond, this 27th day of January, 1838.

"JAMES E. HEATH, Auditor."

From the evidence thus presented, it appears manifest to the committee that the prayer of the petitioners ought not to be granted.

---

MARCH 1, 1838.

The Committee on Revolutionary Claims, to which was referred the petition of William E. Pugh, Elizabeth A., Henry, Rebecca, and Nathaniel Pugh, heirs of the late William Pugh, of Nansemond county, Virginia, report as follows:

The petitioners state they are the only and sole heirs of the said William Pugh, deceased; and that the petitioner, William E. Pugh, is the executor of Henry Pugh, deceased, who was the only child and heir of William Pugh, deceased.

That the said William Pugh resided, during the revolutionary war, in Nansemond county, Virginia, and was an active partisan of the American cause; that, owing to his exertions and influence in the cause of liberty, he became obnoxious to the tories and British, and was, on that account, an especial object of their vengeance; that when the British, about the year 1779, marched from Norfolk to Suffolk, the then colonel of the regiment, *Willis Reddick*, for the better safety and security of the provisions and stores of his troops, removed them to *the farm* of the said William Pugh, some distance from Suffolk; that the enemy, on learning this, were conducted by the tories to *the farm* of the said Pugh; that they destroyed his property, burnt his houses, killed his stock, took away his negroes, and did many other acts of wanton violence to his property.

It is proved that Colonel Henry Pugh, late of North Carolina, now dead, was the son and only heir of William Pugh late of Nansemond county, Virginia; that the said Henry died in the year 1831, leaving him surviving William E. Pugh, Elizabeth A. Hunter, Henry R. Pugh, Rebecca C. Pugh, *Josiah M. Pugh*, and Nathaniel S. Pugh; *(Josiah M. Pugh* is, according to the proof, one more heir than is allowed to be by the petition;) and that the said Henry Pugh left a will, which was proved in Gates county court of pleas and quarter sessions, North Carolina, February term, 1833 ; and that William E. Pugh, son of the said Henry, is the executor named therein.

*William Faulk,* of Nansemond county Virginia, aged 74 years, states, in his affidavit, that he was well acquainted with William Pugh before and after the Revolution ; that he was an officer in the service and army of Virginia ; that his property was burnt and pillaged by the enemy to a large amount ; that his houses were burnt, and his other property taken and carried off ; that there were none who suffered in that struggle more severely than he : the amount of property actually lost and destroyed he cannot say; lest he should say too much, he would put his loss at about $2,000 ; that it might have been to a much larger amount ; that the said property lay in the county of Nansemond, and, as he believes, was sought out by the enemy for destruction.  This witness does not assign any reason for this destruction of property ; says nothing about the stores and provisions of the American troops, or of their being placed on the farm, or in the houses or out-houses of the said Pugh.

*John Harrell,* of the same county and State, states, in his affidavit, that he is in the 73d year of his age ; and that he was well acquainted with William Pugh during the revolutionary war ; and that he verily believes, had it not been for *his activity and vigilance in the cause of his country,* the enemy would not have had such an enmity against him as to have destroyed his property, as stated by William Faulk.

*Henry Skinner,* of the same county and State, states, in his affidavit, that he is in the 75th year of his age ; that he was well acquainted with William Pugh during the revolutionary war, and afterwards ; that he was an efficient man in the cause of freedom; that *his zeal caused the enemy to have a particular hatred towards him ;* that during the war, (and he believes in the year 1779,) the British burnt his houses and furniture, and injured him otherwise ; that his property lay in the county of Nansemond ; and that his houses burnt, at the lowest calculation, at the time of the destruction, must have been worth $2,000.

*Henry Harrison,* of the same place, states that he knew William Pugh during the revolutionary war ; that he was an active man, and knows that his houses were burnt by the English army in the year 1779 ; that he has seen the depositions of William Faulk and Henry Skinner, and that he believes those depositions to be true.

*Mathias Jones,* a justice of the peace of Nansemond county, Virginia, certifies that he is personally acquainted with William Faulk, John Harrell, Henry Skinner, and Henry Harrison ; and that they are honorable and reputable men.

*Abraham Reddick,* of Gates county, North Carolina, in his deposition, says he is 80 years of age, and was well acquainted with Captain William Pugh, of Nansemond county, Virginia, in the revolutionary war ; that the deponent at that time lived in that county, and was in the town of Suffolk when news arrived that the British were coming to that place; that at that time the stores and provisions for the American army were in said town ; that, for their better security, the colonel of the county (Willis Reddick) ordered them to be removed to the farm and houses of the said Willis Reddick and the said William Pugh, which were some miles apart, and in opposite directions from Suffolk ; that, while the British army was stationed in said county, they were conducted by or learned from the *tories* that those things were deposited in these houses for safe-keeping, (as he has always heard ;) that they went to said houses and burnt them, with every thing they contained, besides doing other large damages to their estates; that the houses destroyed, belonging to William Pugh, must have been worth at that time $3,000.

*Demesey Knight*, a justice of the peace of Gates county, North Carolina, certifies that he has long been acquainted with Abraham Reddick; that he stands unimpeachable for truth and veracity ; and that his testimony is, and ought to be, entitled to due faith and credit.

A paper in the words and figures following is found among the documents presented to the committee in this case :

" Nansemond county, August 23d, 1780: Received from William Pugh's division of militia, James Pearce, a deserter from the continental army, which, agreeably to an act of Assembly for speedily recruiting the quota of this State for the continental army, exempts the said division from a draught."

" WILLIS REDDICK."

Also a document in the following words:

### " In Council.

" It appearing that the property of William Pugh, of the county of Nansemond, hath been plundered by the enemy, he is hereby discharged from the payment of the tax laid by the act of Assembly, entitled ' An act for laying a tax payable in certain enumerated commodities.'

TH : JEFFERSON."

Although half a century has passed away since the burning of the houses mentioned in the petition, and the period of the application to Congress for relief, yet, if it clearly appeared that the British army committed this destruction of property at a time when the same was occupied by an order emanating from the proper quarter as a depot for the stores and provisions of the American troops, *and for that reason,* then the case would present a fair subject for indemnification on the part of the Government.

Do the facts present such a case ?

The petitioners do not allege that the stores and provisions of the American troops were deposited in the houses destroyed by the enemy, but that they were placed on the farm of William Pugh.

Colonel Henry Pugh, the only heir of William Pugh, died in the year 1831; and it is somewhat remarkable, if he regarded the claim now set up by his heirs as just, that he never made an effort to assert it.

The petitioners allege that William Pugh, from his exertions in the cause of his country, became an especial object of the vengeance of the enemy.

*John Harrell* and *Henry Skinner,* in their evidence, sustain this allegation of the petitioners; and the former swears that he believes that it was owing to the activity and vigilance of Pugh that the enemy destroyed his property. Neither of these witnesses proves that the stores and provisions for the American troops were placed on the farm of Pugh, or in the houses destroyed by the enemy.

*Henry Harrison* establishes one point only—that Pugh's houses were burnt by the English army in the year 1779.

These witnesses are all residents of the county of Nansemond, the place in which the property destroyed was situated ; yet neither of them says that the stores or provisions of the American troops were placed in the houses burnt by the enemy.

The deposition of Abraham Reddick, a witness aged 80 years, states that the houses were burnt by the British, and that the stores and provisions of the American troops were deposited in the houses thus destroyed, for safe-keeping, *as he has always heard.*

The committee are clearly of opinion that the proof is altogether insufficient to establish the claim set up, and that the prayer of the petition ought not to be entertained.

---

March 6, 1838.

The Committee on Revolutionary Claims, to whom was referred the petition of the legal representatives of Doctor Absalom Baird, have had the same under consideration, and report :

That on the 23d of June, 1836, an act was passed providing for the payment to the legal representatives of Doctor Absalom Baird, five years' full pay of a captain of infantry, being the commutation of half-pay for life, due said Baird, as a surgeon of the regiment of artificers, during the revolutionary war, but without interest. The committee are of opinion that interest ought to be allowed and paid on those claims; and to that end report a bill.

---

March 13, 1838.

The Committee on Revolutionary Claims, to whom was referred the petition of Robert McCready, beg leave to report :

That the petitioner sets forth a variety of services performed by him in the revolutionary war, both as a private soldier and officer of the militia of Pennsylvania. He has already been placed on the pension-roll, under the act of 1832, but complains of the low rate of his pension, and prays that he be paid as captain. This part of his prayer has been rejected by the Committee on Revolutionary Pensions, and your committee are now called on to decide upon so much of his claim as rests upon the allegation that, during most of his service, he received no pay or compensation. The petitioner offers no proof but the statement of one witness, who says he was with the petitioner during a campaign in 1778 ; that he (the witness) was not paid, nor does he believe the petitioner was.

Although the committee have stopped to notice the want of proof in this case, they must not be considered as intending to concede that, if the fullest proof had been made, they could admit even the propriety of now inquiring into the question whether payments should be made by the General Government for mere arrears of pay due the militia of the different States.

*Resolved,* That the prayer of the petitioner ought not to be granted.

The Committee on Revolutionary Claims, to whom was referred the petition of the heirs of James Broadus, deceased, report:

That, by the testimony of several witnesses, it is shown to the committee that James Broadus, the father of the petitioners, enlisted early in 1776, as a private soldier for and during the war of the Revolution; that during the progress of his service, he acted as sergeant, and was subsequently commissioned an ensign; that he continued actively engaged as a soldier and officer up to the fall of the year 1781, and was engaged in that year in the capture of the British forces at Yorktown. Some of those who testify to Ensign Broadus's services speak of their intimate acquaintance with him both before and after the war, and they confidently state that, though after the capture at Yorktown he returned home, they do not believe he ever resigned his commission, but continued ready to re-enter the service had the course of events rendered it necessary. As highly corroborative of this narration of the witnesses, the petitioners have produced the commission of said Broadus, showing that he was regularly appointed ensign in the 2d Virginia regiment, in the army of the United States, on the 7th day of January, 1780, to take effect from the 25th day of September, 1779; and, by application to the auditor of Virginia, it is shown that Ensign Broadus was paid as of the continental line, up to the 2d day of December, 1780. The letter of the Third Auditor of the Treasury confirms the general fact of his being in the continental service, but affords no evidence of his being entitled to, or having received, commutation.

The application of the petitioners was submitted to the last Congress, and an unfavorable report made thereon. By reference to this report, it will appear to have been mainly based on a doubt as to the statements of the witnesses. Since that decision, your committee have obtained the information from the auditor of Virginia already adverted to; by which it satisfactorily appears that Broadus was in the actual service as a continental officer down to the close of 1780, and after the resolution providing for half pay for life. They are of opinion that he continued in actual service to the close of the war, or became supernumerary upon the reduction of the army; and that, in either event, his representatives are entitled to five years' full pay in lieu of half-pay for life. They accordingly report a bill.

---

The Committee on Revolutionary Claims, to which was referred the resolution of the House of Representatives of the 14th of December, 1837, directing an inquiry to be made into the propriety of allowing to John Emmerson interest on his commutation pay, report:

That, by reference to the public records, it appears that John Emmerson was, on the 3d of August, 1829, admitted to the full benefit of the act of Congress of May, 1828, in consideration of his service as a lieutenant in the continental army to the end of the war of the Revolution; that for the same service he received land bounty from the United States; and that, in pursuance of an act of Congress passed in 1834, he was allowed, and received at the Treasury, the principal sum due to him for his commutation pay, without interest. He now asks the interest on the principal sum heretofore paid to him. The act of Congress establishing commutatation pay is as follows : " Officers shall be entitled to receive, at the end of the war, their five years' full pay, in lieu of half pay for life, in specie, or in securities on interest, as Congress should find most convenient."— (See resolution of Congress of 23d of March, 1783.) Congress, in *all cases*, redeemed this pledge by the issue of certificates bearing an interest of six per cent.

The committee consider the promise express, on the part of Congress, to pay commutation in money, or in bonds bearing interest. In all cases, therefore, where it appears that the principal sum is outstanding and unpaid, the committee think the interest accruing on such principal ought also to be paid. To do otherwise, would manifestly violate the obligation of Congress. It is therefore recommended that the interest claimed by John Emmerson be allowed; for which purpose a bill is reported.

---

## MARCH 13, 1838.

The Committee on Revolutionary Claims, to which was referred the petition of the heirs and legal representatives of Major John Campbell, deceased, an assistant deputy quartermaster general during the revolutionary war, report:

That, on the 10th day of June, 1833, the claims of the petitioners were adjusted and settled at the Treasury Department, in pursuance of an act of Congress for their relief, approved the 2d of March, 1833, on the same papers and vouchers furnished and presented by Major Campbell to the accounting officers of the Treasury in 1791 and 1792. The sum of six thousand six hundred ninety-five dollars and twenty-one cents was found to be due Major Campbell for services, commencing on the 25th December, 1776, and terminating on the 25th day of July, 1785. No allowance of interest was made, as appears from the report of Richard Harrison, dated on the 10th of June, 1833, because " the rules of settlement at the Treasury Department do not permit the allowance of interest, except in cases where it is specially provided for, in cases of contract, or expressly authorized by law." In June, 1833, the amount found due was paid by the Secretary of the Treasury to Peter Cooper, the attorney in fact of the parties entitled to receive it, who made the following reservation in his receipt, viz : " reserving to the said heirs and representatives the right to petition Congress for the payment of the interest on the said moneys since the same were due and payable to the said John Campbell." The account was almost exclusively composed of items of pay, subsistence, and travelling expenses. The allowance for pay, in conformity with the opinion of Colonel Pickering, was at the highest rate throughout the whole term of service ; and no complaint exists as to the principles on which the settlement was made, save the refusal, under the rules quoted, to allow interest on the balance due. The act of March 2, 1833, authorized and required the accounting officers " to audit and adjust, upon principles of equity and justice, the claims and accounts of the heirs and representatives of John Campbell," &c. ; and further provided "that the amount due, when ascertained, be paid." It did not expressly authorize the allowance of interest, yet a just construction of the broad and comprehensive expressions used would seem to have warranted the allowance. When a debt for services faithfully rendered has been long due, and withheld against the most energetic efforts of the claimant to obtain a settlement and liquidation, "the principles of equity and justice" require the allowance of interest on the balance due. Here, the services were performed previous to the month of July, 1785, and the debt was justly due at that period. The certificates of Generals Knox, Heath, McDougal, and many other distinguished military officers, who served with and knew John Campbell, bear strong evidence of his highly meritorious character, and faithful services at and during the whole period he was employed in the quartermaster general's department. Governor George Clinton, Chief Justice Jay, and Colonels Pickering and Hamilton, certify to the unblemished integrity and devoted patriotism of Major Campbell, as well as to the ability and fidelity with which every trust confided to him was performed. No doubt exists as to the performance of faithful services by the ancestor of the present claimants, or of the right he had to a just remuneration at the close of the war. Did the non-reception of this just claim arise from the negligence or default of the claimant; or was justice withheld and delayed by the negligence of the Government in the settlement of the claim? The letter of William Simmons, a clerk in the Treasury Department, dated September 17, 1792, shows that, immediately after the close of the revolutionary war, John Campbell applied for the settlement of his accounts. Mr. Simmons states: "In Mr. Denning's time, I recollect Mr. Campbell applying to him for a settlement of his accounts." The objection that existed to a final settlement was, that Mr. Campbell had delivered his accounts, from the commencement of his business to August, 1780, to Colonel Hughes, his principal, who refused to render his own accounts or those of his assistants." A Mr. Burrell succeeded Mr. Denning in the office of commissioner for the quartermaster department; and again Simmons states: "I recollect Mr. Campbell applying to him, also, for a settlement of his accounts; but the objection before assigned still existed. Ultimately, the accounts of Colonel Hughes, together with those of Mr. Campbell, from 1776, up to August, 1780, were destroyed by fire. As the charges for money advanced by Colonel Hughes to his assistant, (Campbell,) could not, in the opinion of the accounting officers, be ascertained with accuracy, from the default of Hughes, a final settlement could not be made with Major Campbell." To prevent the operation of the statute of limitations, Mr. Simmons further states: "He (Major Campbell) did not render them, [his accounts,] but lodged a claim, to save himself from being barred by the limitation." The accounts of Campbell were rightfully in the possession of his superior officer, (Colonel Hughes,) who was entitled to them and the vouchers, to enable him to settle with the accounting officers. No blame, therefore, attaches to Major Campbell for the difficulty that arose from the misconduct of his superior in withholding his accounts, or in their final destruction by fire, which precluded any settlement of the accounts from 1776 to 1780. In 1791, another application was made by Major Campbell for a settlement, and his papers, vouchers, and accounts were handed over to Mr. Simmons, chief clerk in the Auditor's office, for adjustment. The documentary evidence, from that period down to 1789, discloses the most urgent solicitations and earnest appeals to the Department for the adjustment and settlement of his accounts, by Major Campbell. In June, 1791, he writes to Colonel Pickering, at Philadelphia, requesting " a certificate to accompany his accounts to the Auditor." On the 8th of August, 1792, Colonel Pickering writes to Major Campbell " that he had seen Mr. Simmons, who had informed him that some of his best clerks had left the Auditor's office, which would further retard the settlement of his accounts." On the 29th August, 1792, Major Campbell again addresses Colonel Pickering, complaining of Government for withholding the settlement of his claims, and expressing the hope " that if the Government had taken leave of common justice and common honesty, Colonel Pickering had not." On the 11th September, 1792, Major Campbell addressed himself to Colonel Hamilton, stating "that in August, 1791, he had attended at the Auditor's office at considerable expense, to effect a settlement, but in vain ;" that in 1792, " he had again been to Philadelphia for the same purpose, but with no better success." On the 5th January, 1793, he addressed Richard Harrison, auditor, and emphatically asks, " Will you settle my accounts, and pay the balance to the time Colonel Pickering shall say I am entitled, from the 5th August, 1780 ? Will you pay the interest on such balance as shall appear to be due on such settlement?"

Almost the last act of Major Campbell's life was the prosecution of this claim, by giving letters of attorney on the 10th of February, 1798, to his friend William Degrove, authorizing him "to recover the claim from the United States." In 1799, the will of Major Campbell is offered for probate, and letters testamentary issued to Thomas Kirk, one of the executors in the will named. The evidence clearly establishes the most unwearied efforts and perseverance, on the part of this highly meritorious public officer, to obtain from the Government money justly due him, without success ; efforts and perseverance vainly employed to procure, in 1791, '92, and '93, the settlement of his accounts, upon the same papers and vouchers which, in 1833, were promptly received, recognised, and acted upon, by the accounting officers of the Treasury. He had spent eight years, the prime of his life, in actual service, to secure the rights and liberty of his country, and the residue in unavailing efforts to obtain the hard-earned pittance that was justly due him from that country ; and ultimately sunk into the grave, with the latter years of his life embittered, under the pressure of pecuniary embarrassments, by the withholding of the proper remuneration due him from the Government. If the principles of "equity and justice" ever required the allowance of interest, this case presents the strongest and most cogent claim to that allowance. The committee therefore report a bill for the relief of the petitioners.

----

MARCH 13, 1838.

The Committee on Revolutionary Claims, to whom the memorial of the heirs of Larkin Smith was referred, report :

That the memorialists claim the commutation pay due to the said Larkin Smith for his services as a captain of cavalry in the army of the United States to the end of the war of the Revolution ; and, in support of the claim, the following evidence, record and parol, is exhibited and relied on. The record, or documentary evidence, shows that as early as November, 1775, Larkin Smith was a private soldier in a Virginia minute company, commanded by Captain Oliver Towles. (See original muster-roll of that date, signed Oliver Towles, captain.) That in 1776 he is recognised, first as cadet, and then as ensign, in the company commanded by Captain Oliver Towles, and attached to the 6th battalion of Virginia forces on continental establishment. (See certificate of Auditor Heath, for pay as cadet; and the pay as ensign, on the pay and muster-roll of the company of Oliver Towles, signed Oliver Towles, captain 6th battalion of Virginia forces.) It is further shown, that pay was allowed to Larkin as captain of cavalry in the continental service to the 25th of November, 1782, and that a certificate for his two years' advanced pay was issued to him in pursuance of an act of the Virginia Assembly, directing that pay be allowed to such officers as have been in service prior to May, 1777, and still belong to the line of the army. (For both these payments see the certificates of Auditor Heath, and the act of the Virginia Assembly of November, 1781.) It also appears that the additional land bounty promised by Virginia to officers who served over six years and to the end of the war, has been allowed to Larkin Smith. (See journal of the Executive Council of Virginia, and certificate of the register of the Virginia land office.) The parol evidence of several respectable individuals, who each and all knew Larkin Smith intimately during the whole war, and for many years thereafter, represents that Larkin Smith was a highly patriotic and gallant officer; that he entered the military service at the commencement of the war of the Revolution, and continued in active service till late in the year 1783; about which time, the war being near its close, and no active operations going on, many officers became supernumerary, and retired on leave. Upon the foregoing evidence of service, Larkin Smith would, according to the uniform decisions of Congress in analogous cases, be entitled to the commutation pay claimed, unless there was evidence to show or sufficient reason to presume (as the Third Auditor does) that Larkin Smith died and resigned subsequent to the 25th of November, 1782, and before the 23d of November, 1783. In either of these events, his claim to commutation would have abated. The presumption of death is certainly erroneous, as Larkin Smith lived many years after the war closed; nor does the presumption that he resigned seem to be at all probable. None of the army records show that he resigned, and there is abundant record evidence of the resignation of many other officers. To presume that Larkin Smith resigned, under the foregoing circumstances, would reverse all the decisions of Congress in similar cases. The committee, therefore, report a bill providing for an allowance of the commutation claimed.

---

MARCH 20, 1838.

The Committee on Revolutionary Claims, to which was referred the petition of the heirs of William Piatt, made the following report:

The heirs of Captain William Piatt, of the revolutionary army, petition for commutation in lieu of half pay for life, which their ancestor was entitled to under the resolutions of the revolutionary Congress. It appears that he was paid in his lifetime the commutation now claimed. The petition states that Captain Piatt, after the Revolution, again entered the service of his country as a military officer, and was killed in St. Clair's defeat. There is no law allowing the heirs compensation on that account; and the committee are of opinion that no provision should be made for the heirs of one who lost his life in the Indian wars, without embracing all. To present a general bill on the subject would be foreign to the prescribed duties of the committee. They are therefore of opinion that the petitioners are entitled to no relief upon their petition.

------

TREASURY DEPARTMENT,
*Third Auditor's Office, March* 7, 1838.

SIR : I have the honor to state, in reply to your letter of this day's date, that it appears, from the revolutionary records on file in this office, that Captain William Piatt, of the New Jersey line, has received his commutation of five years' full pay, in lieu of half pay for life.

With great respect,
PETER HAGNER, *Auditor.*

Hon. J. R. UNDERWOOD,
*Of the Committee on Revolutionary Claims,*
*House of Representatives of the United States.*

------

MARCH 20, 1838.

The Committee on Revolutionary Claims, to whom was referred the petition of the heirs of John Barnes, have considered the same, and report :

In this case of John Barnes, Congress is asked to pass a law to allow the commutation of five years' full pay, with interest.

The evidence presented to establish the claim is as follows, viz :

1st. A certified copy of the settlement of the account, taken from the books of the Auditor of Virginia, at Richmond ; by which it appears that John Barnes's account was settled by the State of Virginia, as a lieutenant in the Virginia continental line, to the 31st of December, 1781—the latest period to which the State of Virginia settled the accounts of any of her continental officers.

2d. A certified copy of the evidence upon which the Executive of Virginia granted John Barnes bounty land ; from which it appears that John Barnes enlisted as a private in the Virginia continental line in 1776 ; was shortly afterwards promoted to the rank of ensign, and from that to lieutenant and quartermaster, and did not return home until after the surrender of Lord Cornwallis, and was paid by the State of Virginia for his services to the 31st of December, 1781.

3d. A letter from the Third Auditor, showing that the commutation has not been paid in this case, and that the records in his office furnish no evidence of the revolutionary services of John Barnes after November, 1779.

The committee, being satisfied that commutation is due, report a bill for the relief of the legal representatives of John Barnes.

The Committee on Revolutionary Claims, to whom a resolution was referred, directing an inquiry to be made into the expediency of allowing to the children and heirs of John Hopper, deceased, late of the county of Bergen, State of New Jersey, a reasonable compensation for a dwelling-house, and other property, burnt by the British troops in consequence of the military oceupancy of the said house by the troops of the United States at the time it was burnt, during the war of Revolution, report :

That the evidence before the committee shows that, while the dwelling-house and grist-mill of the said John Hopper were occupied by the troops of the United States, on or about the 16th day of April, 1780, under the command of Major Boyles, a detachment of the British from New York, commanded by Colonel Stewart and Colonel Buskirk, attacked the American troops stationed in said houses ; that, in the conflict which ensued, Major Boyles was mortally wounded in the house ; that the said John Hopper received about twenty wounds, but recovered ; that the troops of the United States, being overpowered, evacuated the said houses, which were immediately fired by the British, and wholly consumed, with a large amount of furniture and other effects contained in them. A list made out by John Hopper on the 16th of April 1780, and sworn to by him, and attested by two witnesses, is before the committee, and made a part of this report. The committee are satisfied that the dwelling-house and mill were destroyed as aforesaid, while they were in in the actual military occupancy of troops of the United States. The committee perceive in the past legislation of Congress that this is not a new case, and that the material questions involved in the expediency of now allowing such a claim have been settled by repeated acts both of the Continental and present Congress. For the acts of the present Congress, in such a case as that now under consideration, the committee refer to that allowing payment to the heirs of William Dewees, in the year 1817, for buildings and other property destroyed by the enemy at Valley Forge, in 1777 ; also to Willis Reddick, in 1834, for his houses burnt by the enemy in 1779 ; to Samuel Young, of West Chester, New York, in 1835, for houses destroyed by the enemy in February, 1780. There are other cases, but these involve and settle all the material questions, as to the principles and policy binding the Government to make remuneration to its citizens for such losses.

The allowance of this claim cannot furnish a precedent for other claims for destruction of property by the enemy. The danger of such a precedent, whatever it may be, has been incurred. The value of the buildings of John Hopper is stated at fourteen hundred and fifty dollars, which, from a description of the said buildings given by John Hopper, on oath, and by other witnesses, the committee consider a reasonable valuation, and for that sum report a bill. The committee make no allowance for the personal property alleged to have been lost by John Hopper in the houses destroyed, as aforesaid, by the enemy. To allow compensation for such a loss, would be contrary to the uniform usage of the Government. If otherwise, the evidence in this case is insufficient to sustain that portion of the claim.

MARCH 20, 1838.

The Committee on Revolutionary Claims, to which was referred the petition of the heirs of Thomas Boyles, report:

That the resolution of the 23d February directs the Committee on Revolutionary Claims to inquire into the expediency of awarding seven years' half pay to Martha Weathers, daughter and only heir of Major Thomas H. Boyles, late of the Pennsylvania continental line.

It appears by a letter from Mr. Gordon, of the Bounty Land Office, enclosing a copy of the papers upon which that office acted, that bounty land warrant No. 338, for 400 acres of land, issued on the 4th of March, 1807, to Sarah Weathers, daughter and only heir at law of Major Thomas H. Boyles, of the Pennsylvania continental line.

The copies enclosed in the letter above referred to are as follows, viz:

1st. A letter from Sarah Withers to the honorable Isaac Van Horne, then a member of Congress, dated Winchester, Virginia, 20th February, 1805, requesting him to procure the land warrant due on account of her late father's services.

2d. The affidavit of Evelina Jurde, dated 20th February, 1805, that she lived in the family of Jane Simpson, at the time of her intermarriage with Major Boyles, in the revolutionary war, and nursed Sarah Boyles, now Sarah Withers, his daughter, after his death, occasioned, as she believes, by the enemy, in 1779; and that the said Sarah Withers is the only heir of the said Major Boyles.

3d. The affidavit of Nicholas Orrick, taken 18th February, 1805, that Jane Simpson was lawfully married to Thomas Boyles, and that they had only one daughter, Sarah Boyles, now Sarah Withers.

4th. The certificate of J. Mentyes, late a lieutenant colonel in the Pennsylvania line, dated 5th February, 1805, that Major Thomas Boyles, of the Pennsylvania line, was mortally wounded at Peramus, in December, 1779, and died shortly after.

5th. The certificate of A. St. Clair, late a major general in the army of the Revolution, dated 9th February, 1805, that Thomas Boyles was a major in the Pennsylvania line, when he was mortally wounded, in the year 1779.

It also appears from these letters from the Third Auditor, that the name of Major Boyles does not appear on the records of his office after 1st of February, 1779, and that they do not show whether he was killed, or died, or how he left the service; and that the seven years' half pay, promised by the resolve of Congress of the 24th August, 1780, does not appear to have been paid, either by the United States or the State of Pennsylvania.

It further appears by a letter from the Register of the Treasury, that the seven years' half pay promised by the resolve of the 24th August, 1780, has not been paid by the United States.

From all which your committee are satisfied that Thomas H. Boyles was a major in the Pennsylvania continental line, and was mortally wounded in the year 1779, and died; that the seven years' half pay promised by the resolve of the 24th August, 1780, is yet due; they therefore report a bill to settle the claim.

The Committee on Revolutionary Claims, to which was referred the petition of John Smith, assignee of the devisee of Ballard Smith, deceased, report :

That the petitioner asks for commutation of five years' full pay, and interest, due to Lieutenant Ballard Smith, of Colonel Posey's regiment on continental establishment, and derives his claim thereto, by virtue of a deed of gift from Frances Smith, alias Sprangle, the mother and devisee of said Ballard Smith. The committee do not consider it necessary to decide on the legality of the claim of the petitioner, as it appears by a letter from the Third Auditor "that Lieutenant Ballard Smith, of Colonel Posey's detachment of the Virginia line, has received his commutation of five years' full pay in lieu of half pay for life." The committee, therefore, submit the following resolution :

*Resolved,* That the prayer of the petitioner ought not to be granted.

---

TREASURY DEPARTMENT,
*Third Auditor's Office, February,* 14, 1838.

SIR : I have the honor to state, in reply to your letter of the 13th instant, that it appears from the revolutionary records on file in this office, that Lieutenant Ballard Smith, of Colonel Posey's detachment of the Virginia line, has received his commutation of five years' full pay, in lieu of half pay for life.

With great respect,
PETER HAGNER,
*Auditor.*

Hon. ALEXANDER HARPER,
*of the Committee on Revolutionary Claims, H. of R.*

---

The Committee on Revolutionary Claims, to which was referred the case of Nathaniel Irish, made the following report :

In this case it is proved, by the Journals of the Revolutionary Congress, that Captain Nathaniel Irish was an officer of the regiment of artillery artificers commanded by Colonel Flower. His right to commutation, as such, is established, in the opinion of the committee, by the reasoning advanced in the report upon the case of Captain John Jordan, to which reference is made. The only difference between the cases of Captain Jordan and Captain Irish is this : In August, 1780, Captain Irish left his regiment, and was transferred to a command in the South, as commissary of military stores, and the question is, whether such transfer having occurred before the adoption of the resolution of the 21st October, 1780, deprives Captain Irish of his right to commutation, when it is clear that he served as commissary of military stores until 1785? It appears from the certificate of Richard Peters, Secretary of the Board of War, given in June, 1785, that at the time Captain Irish was ordered to the South, he objected to going on the service, " lest it should deprive him of the advantages he would reap by continuing with his regiment ;" to obviate which the " board agreed, so far as they had power so to do, that no prejudice should arise to Captain Irish from his going to the southward, as to promotion or compensation in the regiment, but his services on the southern business should be considered as a military duty in these respects." Under such circumstance, the committee are of opinion that Captain Irish was entitled to commutation, and therefore report a bill in favor of his legal representatives.

----

### MARCH 23, 1838.

The Committee on Revolutionary Claims, to which was referred the petition of the representatives of Daniel Williams, report :

That Joseph Williams, as executor of Daniel Williams, petitions for commutation alleged to be due his testator. It appears that Daniel Williams was a captain in the continental army of the Revolution, North Carolina line. He was paid as such, according to the certificate of the Secretary of State of North Carolina, for four years and two months, commencing, it would seem, on the 1st of April, 1777 ; for, on that day, he was commissioned captain, according to the Secretary. He must have continued, therefore, in service until June, 1781 ; and if he was not paid unless while in active service, if intervals while he was on furlough were not paid for, he may have continued in service until the end of the war. The Secretary certifies that he was omitted on the roll of the army in January, 1778, and mustered in January, 1779. The affidavits of respectable witnesses prove that he served until the end of the war. He obtained a pension under the act of 15th May, 1828. In his declaration for the purpose of getting a pension under that act, he states that he received certificates after the end of the war (called commutation certificates) for five years' full pay, instead of half pay for life. But the Third Auditor certifies that it does not appear, by the records in his office, that final-settlement certificates have been issued for the commutation of five years' full pay to Captain Williams. The petitioner states that Captain Williams did not swear to the declaration he made for the purpose of procuring the pension, and that the declaration only pursued a form prescribed by the War Department, and was not in Captain Williams's handwriting. It appears that the declaration does pursue the form in use in the War Department, as printed. The law does not require the declaration to be sworn to, and it does not appear that it was. There is no evidence in respect to the handwriting, by which the name of Captain Williams was subscribed to the declaration ; but the committee presume it to be genuine. It is very clear that Captain Williams served sufficiently long to be entitled to the benefits of the resolution of 21st October, 1780, allowing half pay for life. It is reasonable to presume that he continued to serve until the end of the war, or retired as a supernumerary, independent of the parol proof. In either case he would be entitled to commutation. The only doubt which the committee have entertained results from the statement made by Captain Williams himself, that he had received his commutation certificates ; which statement is made in his declaration, in order to obtain the benefits of the act of May, 1828. But when it is considered that such statement was not sworn to, that it pursued a prescribed form merely, and that the records contradict the fact stated, the committee are of opinion that commutation should be allowed; and to that end report a bill in favor of the legal representatives of Captain Williams.

---

The Committee on Revolutionary Claims, to whom was referred the petition of General William Madison, with the accompanying documents, present the following report:

The facts of the case, as exhibited, divide themselves into two parcels: first, those suggested by the petitioner; and, secondly, those sustained by the evidence of others. General Madison says, on oath, that he was first in the militia in 1778, whilst a student at Hampden Sidney college; that he was afterwards appointed a lieutenant, in the State legion of Virginia; that he was on the recruiting service in that capacity, and had but little success in this employment; and, on the invasion of the State, in 1781, he was a volunteer in the militia cavalry, and was from that service (still holding his commission in the legion) appointed a lieutenant in the regiment of artillery of the Virginia line on continental establishment, commanded by Colonel Harrison; that, after several months' service, and the surrender of Cornwallis, at Yorktown, in Virginia, the health of the petitioner suffered and languished in disease, and he was sent home on furlough, where he remained in a feeble state a great length of time, and was there visited by his captain, and ordered to hold himself in readiness for service, as soon as able to do so; and, finally, that he was willing to do so, and never did resign his commission.

The evidence of Robert Taylor, Esq., former Speaker of the Senate of Virginia, and recently member of the House of Representatives, and that of Mr. George Corvin, prove that General William Madison was in service as a lieutenant of artillery. Mr. Corvin says, on oath, that he was a lieutenant of artillery, in Harrison's regiment, and in actual service; that he knew the petitioner before and after the siege of Yorktown, and his family; and he speaks with confidence, from circumstances, of his (Madison's) service, and office as lieutenant in said regiment of artillery; and the court of Madison county certify its entire credence in the facts asserted. And, finally, the certificate of William Seldon, Esq., register of the land office of Virginia, bearing date the 8th January, 1838, showing that said Madison was " allowed bounty land, for his services as a lieutenant of artillery in the continental line, from September, 1781, to the end of the war." And your committee, believing the petitioner's claim to be just and valid, report a bill for his relief.

---

The Committee on Revolutionary Claims, to which was referred the petition of Priscilla Greer, of Pennsylvania, report:

That the application of the petitioner is to obtain the seven years' half pay alleged to be due on account of the revolutionary services of her father, John McClelland.

Several witnesses speak of their acquaintance with John McClelland, the father of the petitioner, during the early part of the revolutionary war. That they lived neighbors to him on the Juniatta, in the State of Pennsylvania ; and know that, in the summer of 1775, he joined the continental army, and was appointed first lieutenant in the company of Captain William Hendricks, belonging to the 1st Pennsylvania regiment. That in the fall of that year, and after he had enlisted several men for the service, and, among others a brother of one of the witnesses, Lieutenant McClelland marched, under his captain, to join the troops intended for the expedition against Quebec. They state that he never returned to his family and friends ; and that an account of his death was brought to the neighborhood by one of the very soldiers whom he had enlisted, and who stated that McClelland died on his march into Canada ; that he was present, and attended his funeral. As confirmatory of these statements, your committee perceive, on reference to the journals of Congress of that day, that amongst others, who are especially noticed as having fallen in the attack on Quebec, is Captain William Hendricks, under whom Lieutenant McClelland is said by the witnesses to have served. And in an interesting narrative of the peculiar sufferings incident to that campaign, written by the late Judge Henry, of Pennsylvania, who was himself engaged in that trying service, there is not only a particular notice of the death of McClelland, but a circumstantial account of his previous sickness and exposure. The writer speaks of his being attached to the command of Captain Hendricks, and mentions the section of Pennsylvania from which he came ; confirming in this, and all other important particulars, the narrative which the witnesses have given.

By an act of the Pennsylvania Legislature, approved the 27th of March, 1837, four hundred dollars is directed to be paid to the petitioner, in lieu of four hundred acres of donation-land " to which (in the language of the law) she is entitled for the services rendered by her father, Lieutenant John McClelland, in the war of the Revolution." This bounty of land, commuted in this instance for money, the committee are informed was intended only for those engaged in the continental service.

The evidence clearly shows that Lieutenant McClelland left an only child, the petitioner, and a widow, who afterwards married again, and has since died, leaving several other children by her last marriage.

The committee are of opinion that the evidence sufficiently establishes the claim to the seven years' half pay due on account of the revolutionary services of the said John McClelland, and have reported a bill for its payment, according to the intention of the resolution of Congress of the twenty-fourth of August, seventeen hundred and eighty.

---

MARCH 28, 1838.

The Committee on Revolutionary Claims, to whom was referred the petition of John Milling and Richard Nason, of South Carolina, report :

That the petitioners represent themselves as entitled to the commutation pay which they allege to be due on account of the revolutionary services of Hugh Milling, deceased. Hugh Milling was regularly appointed first lieutenant in the sixth continental regiment of South Carolina, on the 15th of September, 1778. On the 1st of November, 1779, J. R. Rutledge, at Charleston, South Carolina, certifies that Milling was a captain in said regiment, and mentions in his certificate that a regular appointment as captain was not granted him for the want of a blank commission.

Milling, in his lifetime, obtained the benefit of the act for the relief of certain surviving officers and soldiers of the Revolution, passed the 15th of May, 1828. In this application, he states that he received his commutation certificates for a sum equal to the amount of five years' full pay; but the Third Auditor of the Treasury states that the records of his office do not show that certificates were granted, as alleged by Milling, and that there is no evidence of his services on file. The petitioners would seem mainly to rely upon the fact that a warrant for military bounty land was granted by the United States to Hugh Milling, as captain in the South Carolina line. By reference, however, to the testimony on which said warrant was obtained, it is seen to have consisted of the affidavit of Milling himself, and two other witnesses, who merely confirm the truth of what he says. His own statement is, that in the month of February or March, 1780, he was a deranged officer, and thrown out of command; that his subsequent service was in the character of a volunteer. He was not, therefore, in actual service in the line of the army at the time that half pay for life was promised by the resolution of the 21st of October, 1780, or at any subsequent period, and consequently is not entitled to the commutation prayed for.

*Resolved,* That the prayer of the petition ought not to be granted.

---

### March 28, 1838.

The Committee on Revolutionary Claims, to which was referred the petition of Charles G. McHatton, administrator of the estate of the late Captain John McHatton, or McIlhatton, report:

That the petitioner asks the commutation and bounty land provided by the several resolves of Congress for the officers and soldiers of the revolutionary army on continental establishment. The committee find that the decedent, in his lifetime, applied to Congress for the same purpose, and that the Committee on Pensions and Revolutionary Claims of this House made an unfavorable report. There is no additional evidence produced by the present petitioner which, in the opinion of the committee, will justify a different conclusion at this time. That report was made on the 11th of January, 1822, and is numbered 567. The committee concur in that report, and make it a part of this report.

### Treasury Department,
#### *Third Auditor's Office, March 21, 1838.*

Sir: I have had the honor of receiving your letter of the 19th instant, requesting me to furnish you "with such information as may be in my power in relation to the services of Captain John McHatton, or McIlhatton, of the Pennsylvania line of the continental arm."

In reply, I have to state, that the only Captain John McIlhatton of whose services the records in this office furnish any information, belonged to the flying camp, a description of troops the officers of which were not entitled either to land or commutation from the United States.

You will find, on reference to page 803 of the volume in relation to Claims of the late publication of " American State Papers," that the case of Captain McHatton, or McIlhatton, has heretofore been before Congress. You will also find, appended to the report published in the volume referred to, a communication from this office, which contains all the information that the records enabled me to furnish in relation to Captain McIlhatton's services.

With great respect,

PETER HAGNER, *Auditor*.

Hon. ALEXANDER HARPER.

JANUARY 11, 1822.

The Committee on Pensions and Revolutionary Claims, to whom was referred, on the 12th of December, 1821, the petition, with accompanying papers, of John McHatton, have had the same under consideration, and report thereon:

That, heretofore, the petitioner had his said petition presented in the House of Representatives of the Congress of the United States, and, on the 4th day of January, 1821, it was referred to the Committee on Pensions and Revolutionary Claims, to consider and report thereon; and that, on the 17th of January, 1821, that committee made a report, which appears to be as follows:

" The Committee on Pensions and Revolutionary Claims, to whom was referred, on the 4th of January, 1821, the petition of John McHatton, have had the same under consideration, and report thereon:

" The petitioner states that he was, in July, 1776, by the State of Pennsylvania, appointed and commissioned a captain, to command a company of volunteers in the service of the United States; that he commanded said company two months, when he was appointed and commissioned, by the said State of Pennsylvania, a captain in the 'flying camp,' in the regiment commanded by Colonel Watts, belonging to the Pennsylvania line on continental establishment, as he states; that he commanded said company until he and his said company were made prisoners of war at Fort Washington; that, soon after he was made a prisoner of war, he was, by said State of Pennsylvania, commissioned a captain in the Pennsylvania continental line, and in the regiment commanded by Colonel McGaw; that he was retained a prisoner until about the time Lord Cornwallis surrendered at Yorktown, when he was exchanged, and returned to the army, and was soon after detached as a supernumerary officer, and sent home, and continued in service until the conclusion of the war in 1783. He states that he forwarded by mail two of his said commissions to the War office, but has understood they were not received, and that he has lost his other commission; and he now prays that the commutation of five years' full pay of a captain be granted to him, and likewise the bounty land he may, as a captain, be entitled to.

" The committee further report, that they have had recourse to the Department of the Treasury for information in this case of the petitioner, and the **Treasury Department** has sent to this committee a report from the Third Auditor in that Department, in which the Third Auditor states that he had reference to such parts of the records of the revolutionary army as have been preserved and are on file in that office ; and that he does not find any person by the name of the petitioner, but that he found Captain John McIlhatton, of the flying camp, of the Pennsylvania line, and that it appears that the State of Pennsylvania paid his depreciation, amounting to 142*l.* 8*s.*, and charged the same to the United States ; and that it also appears that he received from the United States the following sums in specie, whilst a prisoner, viz : of Elias Boudinot $174 79, of J. Beatty $101 51, making $276$\frac{40}{90}$ ; that the journal in which the particulars of these payments were stated being destroyed, it is impracticable to ascertain them, nor can it be ascertained how long the officer named continued in service ; that reference has been had to the register of final-settlement certificates issued to officers serving to the end of the war, which is complete, and also to the list of officers entitled to land, and the name of the officer is not to be found. Whether the petitioner is the same person with this one remarked on, the Third Auditor reports that he cannot state, but should presume, from some of the circumstances stated in the petition, and there being no record of any person of his name, that it is probable that such is the fact.

" The committee further report, that, on the 26th of January, 1784, Congress 'resolved, that half-pay cannot be allowed to any officer or to any class or denomination of officers to whom it has not heretofore been expressly promised.' It does not appear that the petitioner is included in any class or denomination of officers to whom half pay was expressly promised. In respect to the claim of the petitioner to bounty land, it does not appear that his name is included in the list of officers entitled to land, and therefore submit the following resolution :

"*Resolved,* That the prayer of the petitioner be not granted."

This committee further report, that the petitioner has again presented his said petition, with some accompanying papers, one of which is a statement, or exhibit, of the petitioner, in which he enumerates his services, stating that he was under command of General Braddock ; that he was with Colonel Dunbar, whose regiment had not come up ; that he was afterwards on General Stanwick's campaign, then on General Forbes's, then on General Monkton's, and then on Bouquett's campaign ; he states that he was first a soldier, then a corporal, then a sergeant, then an ensign, and continued in service until peace between the English and the French, and was then discharged. The petitioner then proceeds to state, in his said exhibit, as he does in his petition, his appointments and services in the time of the revolutionary war, viz : that he was appointed a captain in July, 1776, by the State of Pennsylvania, to command a company of volunteers of militia, and afterwards removed to command a company of flying camp, in Colonel Watt's regiment ; that he was taken a prisoner at the surrender of Fort Washington ; that he was immediately taken by the British to New York, thence to Long Island, and put on board the Jersey prison-ship ; and on Long Island, as he states, until exchanged just before the surrender of Lord Cornwallis. The petitioner then goes on to state, in his said exhibit, appearing to be of the 18th of October, 1821, that, while a prisoner of war, his friends sent him money from Pennsylvania, which supported him ; that he paid for his board, as he **states,** and never received; whilst a prisoner, any money from the United States, either as pay or to support him; and he further states that he did not receive any since he was made a prisoner, or for depreciation, or in any shape whatever, for or on account of his revolutionary services ; and he further sets forth, in his said exhibit, that, whilst he was a prisoner, he was sent to New York by Colonels Atly and Miles, who were American prisoners of war, to bring some money from the American commissioners for prisoners; that, with a permit, he went and received a certain sum (he does not remember how much) from, as near as he can recollect, a man of the name of Pintard; but whether he was a commissioner himself, or did business as a deputy for Boudinot, who, at that time, as the petitioner states, *kept an office in the city of New York,* [he does not know ;] that he was directed to deliver the said money to either of the said colonels, Atly or Miles, which he states he did ; but whether the money was sent them by their friends, or the public, he does not know ; and he states that he never received any of it, nor did he take a receipt when he delivered it ; that he does not think the commissary charged the money to him when he received it from his office; that he never had any part of it, and was nothing but an agent to convey it. The petitioner then goes on to state, in his said exhibit, that his father was a Scotchman, and spelt his name McIlhatton, and the name of his family, until after the Revolution, was spelt in that way; but since that time they had, as he states, spelt it McHatton, as it was shorter. That, in 1783, he removed to Kentucky, and has never been to the east of the Allegany mountains since.

This committee further report that the petitioner, in his said exhibit, states that his father spelt his name McIlhatton, and that the name of his family was spelt in that way until after the Revolution; and it appears, by the records in the Treasury Department, that John McIlhatton did receive from the State of Pennsylvania the sum of one hundred and forty-two pounds eight shillings for depreciation, which was charged to the United States; and that whilst he was a prisoner of war, he received, in two payments, the sum of two hundred and seventy-six dollars and some forty cents, as above mentioned. And the petitioner, in his said exhibit, declares that his friends sent him money from Pennsylvania, which supported him ; that he paid for his board; and that he never received, whilst a prisoner, any money from the United States, either as pay or to support him, and that he has not received any pay since he was a prisoner, or for depreciation, or in any shape whatever, for or on account of his revolutionary services.

This committee are humbly of opinion that the records in the Department of the Treasury are to be taken as conclusive evidence in this case, and in all similar cases; a contrary doctrine would go to destroy all evidence deducible from the records of that Department, and of every other department of this Government, and also the authenticity of the said records, and would produce consequences highly dangerous to the United States and to individuals citizens; and although the petitioner, as he states, did receive a sum of money from Pintard, he, notwithstanding that, must have received the several sums of money as stated in the report of the Third Auditor, which, from the long lapse of time, may have escaped the recollection of the petitioner.

This committee further report, that the petitioner states, as in this report above mentioned, that he was made a prisoner of war at Fort Washington; and that, soon after he was made a prisoner of war, he was, by the State of Pennsylvania, commissioned a captain in the Pennsylvania continental line, and in the regiment commanded by Colonel McGaw; that he was retained a prisoner until about the time that Lord Cornwallis surrendered at Yorktown, when he was exchanged and returned to the army, and was soon after detached as a supernumerary officer, and sent home, and continued in service until the conclusion of the war in 1783.

That, on the 24th of October, 1781, a letter of the 19th of that month, from General Washington, was read, informing the Congress of the Revolution of the reduction of the British army under the command of Earl Cornwallis, on the 19th instant, with a copy of the articles of capitulation. About that time the petitioner states that he was exchanged, and returned to the army ; and was soon after detached as a supernumerary officer, and sent home, and continued in service until the conclusion of the war in 1783. In what manner the petitioner could be at home and in the actual service of the United States until the conclusion of the war, in 1783, is not easily understood. " He prays that commutation of five years' full pay may be granted to him as a captain, and likewise grant him a land-warrant for the quantity of bounty land to which he may be entitled as a captain."

This committee further report, that reference has been had to the register of final-settlement certificates issued to officers serving to the end of the war, which is complete, and also to the list of officers entitled to land, and the name of the petitioner does not appear. Hence, it is inferred, that, if the petitioner was an officer at any time, in the line of the army on the continental establishment, he did not serve to the end of the war, and therefore is not entitled to commutation of five years' full pay in lieu of half pay for life, nor to any bounty land. The petitioner states that he was commissioned a captain in Colonel McGaw's regiment. This committee report, that, on the 15th day of May, 1778, Congress " resolved, unanimously, that all military officers commissioned by Congress, who now are, or hereafter may be, in the service of the United States, and shall continue therein during the war, shall, after the conclusion of the war, be entitled to receive annually, for the term of seven years, if they live so long, one-half of the present pay of such officers." Certain provisions are added to that resolution, which, it is presumed, do not relate to the petitioner. That Congress, on the 21st of October, 1780, " resolved, that the officers who shall continue in the service to the end of the war, shall also be entitled to half pay during life, to commence from the time of their reduction." And, on the 22d of March, 1783, Congress, on the report of a committee, " resolved, that such officers as are now in service, and shall continue therein to the end of the war, shall be entitled to receive the amount of five years' full pay, (as in that resolution is expressed,) instead of half pay promised by the resolution of the 21st of October, 1780." And, on the 31st of December, 1781, Congress, by resolutions, made provision relative to officers of the line of the army, considered as retiring from service on the 1st day of January, 1782, whose names were not returned as directed in one of said resolutions. That this case of the petitioner does not appear to be included within all or any one of the resolutions of Congress alluded to above in this report.

That, on the 24th of November, 1778, Congress "resolved, that all officers who have been in the service, and, having been prisoners with the enemy, now are, or hereafter may be, exchanged, or otherwise released, shall, if appointed by the authority of the State, be entitled, in case of vacancy, to enter into the service of their respective States, in such rank as they would have had if they had never been captured : *Provided, always,* That every such officer do, within one month after his exchange or release, signify to the authority of the State to which he belongs, his release, and his desire to enter again into the military service. That every officer so released and giving notice as aforesaid, shall, until entry into actual service, be allowed half pay of the commission to which, by the foregoing resolve, he stands entitled : *Provided, always,* That, in case of his receiving any civil office of profit, such half pay shall thenceforth cease." On the 22d of May, 1779, Congress "resolved, that all continental officers who are, or may be, exchanged, and not continued in service, be, after such exchange, considered as supernumerary officers, and entitled to the pay provided by a resolution of Congress of the 24th of November last."

That it does not appear to this committee that the petitioner was continued in service pursuant to the provisions of the said resolution of the 24th of November, 1778, and that, therefore, if a continental officer, he did, by the resolution of the 22d of May, 1779, become a supernumerary officer, which the petitioner states he was, and therefore is not, in that character, entitled to commutation of five years' full pay, instead of half pay for life. That the petitioner states he was an officer of the flying camp. On the 26th of May, 1781, Congress "resolved, that the officers of the flying camp, lately returned from captivity, be allowed depreciation by their respective States, in the same manner as officers of the line in such States." On the 3d of June, 1776, Congress "resolved, that a flying camp be immediately established in the middle colonies, and that it consist of ten thousand men ; that Pennsylvania be requested to furnish six thousand men of their militia; Maryland, of their militia, three thousand four hundred; Delaware Government, of their militia, six hundred ; that the militias be engaged to the first day of December next, unless sooner discharged by Congress." That the officers of the flying camp, being of the militia, are not entitled to the commutation of five years' full pay instead of half pay for life, is manifest ; that it appears, by the records of the Treasury Department, that the petitioner did receive a certain sum of money for depreciation from the State of Pennsylvania, which was charged to the United States; that that depreciation may be presumed to have been paid in pursuance of the said resolution of the 26th of May, 1781.

This committee further report, that the petitioner, in his said exhibit, sets forth a statement, in the words following; that is to say : " While a prisoner of war, my friends sent me money from Pennsylvania, which supported me. I paid for my board ; and I never received, whilst a prisoner, any money from the United States, either as pay or to support me ; nor have I received any pay since I was made a prisoner, or for depreciation, or in any shape whatever, for or on account of my revolutionary services."

In respect to this declaration of the petitioner, the committee observe, that, on the 3d of January, 1777, Congress "resolved, that General Washington be directed to propose and conclude with General Howe an agreement, whereby those who are or may be made prisoners by the enemy, may be supplied with provisions and other necessaries at the expense or on the credit of the United States." That, " on the 31st of July, 1778, Congress resumed the consideration of the report of the committee, to whom the petition from the prisoners of war on Long Island was referred; whereupon, resolved, that the commissioners of claims be directed to examine the estimate of the amount due for clothing and board for our prisoners of war in the hands of the enemy : resolved, that a sum of money, in specie, not exceeding twenty-six thousand six hundred and sixty-six dollars and sixty-six and two-thirds cents, be issued to Elias Boudinot, Esq., late commissary general of prisoners, for the discharge of such accounts for which he is to be accountable." And, on the 30th of July, 1778, " Congress ordered that a warrant issue on the Treasurer, in favor of Colonel E. Boudinot, late commissary of prisoners, for fifteen thousand dollars, to enable him to discharge some arrears of that department, the said Colonel Boudinot to be accountable :" that, on the 6th of June, 1777, Congress resolved, " that a commission be granted to Elias Boudinot, Esq., as commissary general of prisoners, the said commission to be dated the 15th day of May last." On the 9th of January, 1779, Congress resolved, " that the commissary general of prisoners be furnished with money, from time to time, by the Board of Treasury, for the purpose of subsisting the officers and soldiers of the United States, while in captivity and in the actual possession of the enemy, and to accommodate them with sufficient sums, on account, to defray their travelling expenses to their homes or regiments." On the 7th of June, 1779, Congress resolved, " that the commissary general of prisoners be authorized, from time to time, to pay, to the order of officers and soldiers in captivity, any sums not exceeding the amount of their pay and subsistence, in order to enable them to assist their families, and that he make monthly returns to the paymaster general of their accounts, respectively."

On the 25th of April, 1780, Congress passed resolutions for the benefit and accommodation of American prisoners of war with the enemy; among which Congress resolved, that " the sum of twelve thousand four hundred and sixty-three pounds like currency (New York currency) in specie, equal to thirty-one thousand one hundred and fifty-seven and a half dollars, be advanced to the commissary general of prisoners, which he be directed to distribute among all the officers in captivity ; and that the consideration of any further allowance or comparative preference be postponed to some future period." That, on the 23d of August, 1780, Congress passed a resolution appropriating large sums of money in specie for the use and accommodation of American prisoners of war with the enemy, those at New York inclusive. That, on the 8th of January, 1781, Congress, by resolution, " earnestly recommended to the several States, from New Hampshire to North Carolina inclusive, to procure and forward to the Treasurer of the United States, or to their commissary of prisoners appointed to reside at New York, by the first of March next, for the use of the officers in captivity at that place and on Long Island, and to be charged to the United States," large sums of money in specie or bills of exchange on New York, amounting to eighty thousand dollars. The resolutions above mentioned, with other resolutions that might be alluded to, are brought, at this late period, into remembrance, to show the care of, and attention to, American prisoners of war in captivity with the enemy, which was manifested by Congress, in order that they might be fully supported and provided for during their captivity, and also on their return from captivity. The petitioner states that he held the commission of a captain in time of his captivity, and, from that circumstance, as an officer, it may be presumed that he was not ignorant of the ample supplies of money in specie from time to time provided for, and actually remitted to, and put in the power of, the commissary of prisoners at and near New York, for the support of the American prisoners there; and it cannot be presumed that he did not partake and receive his portion of such ample provision for his support; and it may be presumed that a long lapse of years may have obliterated from his memory the bountiful support administered to him by the Congress of the Revolution, and therefore does not recollect to have received the several sums of money stated on the records of the Treasury Department by him to have been received.

This committee further report, that it does not appear that the petitioner was in the actual service of the United States (if he had even been an officer commissioned by Congress) after the time that he was exchanged and released from captivity; that it does not appear that the petitioner is included in any class or denomination of officers to whom half pay was expressly promised, and, therefore, half pay for life, or commutation thereof for five years' full pay, cannot be allowed to him; that no sufficient reason has been by him assigned why he permitted a claim of this magnitude to lie dormant from the time he ought to have claimed it, until in January, eighteen hundred and twenty-one, when his petition was first presented to Congress; that, if his said claim was just, it was honorable to demand it in due time, and to receive it: officers of the highest rank and honor in the line of the continental army, who were entitled to commutation, received it; it was an honorable provision for them, made by Congress for their noble and meritorious services in the prosecution of a just war, which delivered the United States from bondage, tyranny, and oppression: that the petitioner has not any just claim to commutation of five years' full pay instead of half pay for life; that he is not entitled to bounty land as provided for by resolutions of Congress; that if, by any most remote possibility, the petitioner could have or can have any claim in this case, it is long since barred by statutes of limitation. This committee, therefore, report the following resolution:

*Resolved*, That the prayer of the petitioner be rejected.

———

Treasury Department,
*Register's Office, January* 5, 1822.

Sir: I have the honor to transmit a copy of the report made by the Third Auditor of the Treasury on the memorial of John McHatton.

And am, with great respect, sir, your obedient, humble servant,

JOSEPH NOURSE.

Hon. John Rhea.

Treasury Department,
*Third Auditor's Office, January* 13, 1821.

Sir : I have the honor to state, in relation to the petition and accompanying documents of John McHatton, who claims to have been a captain in the Pennsylvania line during the revolutionary war, and asks commutation and land, that I have had reference to such part of the records of the revolutionary army as have been preserved and are on file in this office, and I do not find any person by the name of the petitioner, but find Captain John McIlhatton, an officer of the flying camp of the Pennsylvania line. It appears that the State of Pennsylvania paid his depreciation, amounting to 142*l.* 8*s.*, and charged the same to the United States ; and it also appears that he received from the United States the following sums in specie, whilst a prisoner, viz :

| | | | | | |
|---|---|---|---|---|---|
| Of E. Boudinot, | - | - | - | - | $174 79 |
| Of J. Beatty, | - | - | - | - | 101 51 |

$276 $\frac{40}{50}$

The journal in which the particulars of these payments were stated being destroyed, it is impracticable to ascertain them ; nor can it be ascertained how long the officer named continued in service. Reference has been had to the register of final-settlement certificates issued to officers serving to the end of the war, which is complete, and also to the list of officers entitled to land, and the name of the officer is not to be found. Whether the petitioner is the same person with the one remarked upon, I cannot state, but should presume, from some of the circumstances stated in the petition, and there being no record of any person of his name, that it is probable such is the fact.

The papers are returned.

With great respect, your obedient servant,
PETER HAGNER, *Auditor.*

The Hon. William H. Crawford,
*Secretary of the Treasury.*

---

March 29, 1838.

The Committee on Revolutionary Claims, to which was referred the petition of William Conner, report :

John Conner, representing himself as the only son and heir of William Conner, late an ensign in Colonel John Gibson's regiment of the Virginia continental line in the army of the Revolution, prays that commutation, or five years' full pay of ensign, may be allowed him. He admits, and it appears officially, that Ensign Conner resigned in January, 1782 ; consequently, he was not entitled to half pay for life, nor to five years' full pay as commutation of half pay for life. The petitioner, however, places his claim upon the ground that his father was compelled to resign from ill health, and that he died shortly thereafter. It is a sufficient answer to these allegations that they are not proved, and, if they had been, they could not be the foundation of a legal claim, and could only authorize a gratuity. The committee are of opinion that the petitioner is not entitled to any relief.

The Committee on Revolutionary Claims, to which was referred the petition of the heirs of George McCormick, beg leave to report:

The heirs of George McCormick, late a captain in the Virginia line of the continental army of the Revolution, petition for commutation pay. They are not entitled, because their ancestor resigned his commission in the fall of 1788. This fact excluded him from the provisions of the resolution of October, 1780, allowing half pay for life to the officers of the continental army, who might serve to the end of the war, or who retired as supernumeraries. The evidence of his resignation is his own oath, made in 1818, for the purpose of obtaining a pension under the act of March of that year. His statement is contained in the declaration filed in the Pension office, as the committee are informed by the Third Auditor. The committee are of opinion that the petitioners are entitled to no relief.

---

APRIL 13, 1838.

The Committee on Revolutionary Claims, to which was referred the petition of Mary Hopper, the widow of Captain John A. Hopper, late of Hopperstown, Bergen county, New Jersey, deceased, on behalf of the heirs and legal representatives of the said decedent, report:

That the evidence in this case clearly proves that in April, 1780, a Major Bills, of the continental army, with a garrison and soldiers, was quartered at Hopperstown, and occupied the dwelling-house and store-room of John A. Hopper, deceased, and had their arms, provisions, and ammunition stored therein. On the sixteenth day of April, 1780, at the dawn of day, a troop of British light-horse, from Staten island, surprised the American troops in garrison at Hopperstown, killing the commanding officer, and capturing a part of the garrison. Finding the buildings of Captain Hopper in the occupation of the American troops, and used as a depot, the commander of the enemy burnt the houses, together with the ammunition and stores of the garrison. All the personal property of Captain Hopper was consumed in the flames, leaving himself and family without even their wearing apparel. All who give evidence concur in the belief that the buildings of Captain Hopper were destroyed because they were occupied by the troops. As no other property in the town was destroyed by the enemy, except that of the father of Captain Hopper and his own, which was similarly occupied, it is strikingly corroborative of the belief expressed by the witnesses. The value of the real property destroyed is variously estimated by the witnesses, averaging from two thousand to four thousand five hundred dollars. The personal property consisted of seven thousand dollars in continental money, and five hundred dollars of personal property, as estimated by the widow. As the principle has been established by Congress, that personal property is not to be taken into the estimate, and paid for, when destroyed by the enemy, on high moral and political considerations, the estimate for it is excluded from consideration as to the amount which ought to be paid to the representatives of the decedent.

In the struggle for independence, Captain Hopper and his six brothers were active and efficient whigs; several of whom proved their devotion to the cause by the loss of life in the service. High-minded, and of a noble spirit, during his life Captain Hopper never applied for remuneration. His country was involved in debt, and burdened with difficulties; now, when it is free from claim, and abundantly able to pay, the heirs ask for remuneration for the loss of their ancestor. And the committee, satisfied of the justice of the claim, report a bill for the relief of the petitioners.

---

### APRIL 12, 1838.

The Committee on Revolutionary Claims, to which was referred the petition of John Christopher Colbey, for remuneration for bounty land, report:

That this claim is predicated on the enlistment, in 1778, of the petitioner as a soldier in the company of Captain Shaffner, of the revolutionary army, for the period of "during the war." At the defeat of the army under the command of General Gates, he received a severe wound; from which, after a long and protracted confinement, he partially recovered, and again joined his regiment, and continued in active service to near the close of the war; when, from hardships and exposure incident to the service, his old wound broke out anew, and rendered him unfit for actual service; on account of which he received his discharge. Immediately after his return home from the army, in 1783, his dwelling-house was consumed by fire, in which the papers and documents relating to his services in the army were destroyed. The petitioner receives a pension from the United States, but has never received any bounty land. The resolution of the 18th September, 1776, extended the grant of bounty land to all who were engaged or enlisted in the army of the United States during the war. In consequence of a wound received in the service, the petitioner was disabled and discharged before the termination of the war. A provision for a pension, instead of bounty land, was made by Congress for wounded soldiers. The grant of land, in express terms, by the resolutions of the Continental Congress, is confined to soldiers who served to the termination of the war. In no instance has a soldier who was discharged from the service prior to the close of the war, in 1783, for disability, or any other cause whatever, received bounty land under the resolves of Congress providing that bounty. The usage and practice of the Government has been uniform and unbroken; the committee, therefore, report against the prayer of the petitioner.

---

### APRIL 12, 1838.

The Committee on Revolutionary Claims, to which was referred the petition of Angelica Gilbert, a daughter of Captain Joseph Olney, late of Providence, Rhode Island, deceased, report:

That this claim is founded on the services of Captain Joseph Olney, deceased, who entered the naval service on board the Columbus, of Providence, Rhode Island, on the 20th of November, 1775, as a second lieutenant, and was subsequently promoted to the first lieutenancy of that vessel. On the 8th of December, 1776, he received from Congress a commission as a second lieutenant. On the 20th of August, 1777, he was appointed captain of the brig Cabot, and continued in service up to the 20th of August, 1783—as on that day he was, by the order of Congress, commissioned to command the sloop Peacock; but how much longer he continued in service remains unascertained. Captain Olney had a high reputation as a gentleman and intrepid officer, and aided in capturing many valuable prizes from the enemy. No specific claim is made or set forth by the petitioner, and no evidence is submitted to sustain any such claim. And as neither naval officers, seamen, nor marines, are embraced by the resolutions of the Continental Congress giving half pay or commutation, the committee report against the prayer of the petitioner.

---

APRIL 6, 1838.

The Committee on Revolutionary Claims, to whom the petition of Richard and Sarah C. Davis, late Sarah C. Dye, was referred, report:

That the petitioners claim the seven years' half pay promised the widows and children of such officers as should die in the military service of the United States, in the war of the Revolution; and they found their claim on the allegation that Lieutenant Jonathan Dye, under whom they claim, was killed in the battle of Brandywine. The claimants exhibit with their petition satisfactory evidence to show the following facts: That Jonathan Dye was a lieutenant in the Virginia continental line of the army aforesaid, and that he was killed in the battle of Brandywine; that at the time of his death he left a widow, Sarah Ann Dye, and one child only, Nancy Dye, who died in the lifetime of her said mother, intestate, unmarried, and without issue; that Sarah Ann Dye, widow of Lieutenant Jonathan, departed this life, leaving one child only, Sarah C. Dye, half sister to Nancy Dye, deceased, as aforesaid. It does not appear that Sarah Ann Dye, widow of Jonathan Dye, has received the seven years' half pay due to her under the resolution of Congress of the ―― day of ――――, as the widow of an officer in the continental line of the army who was killed in battle. And as it appears she lived till the 31st of December, 1813, leaving an only child, the petitioner Sarah C. Davis, who is proven to be the sole heir of her mother, and, as such, entitled to the seven years' half pay due to and not received by her mother, the committee consider the claim of the petitioners well founded, and report a bill for their relief.

---

APRIL 6, 1838.

The Committee on Revolutionary Claims, to whom was referred the petition of Solomon J. Lee, report:

That the petitioner states that he entered the service of the United States as a militiaman and teamster, in the year 1775; was draughted in the regiment commanded by Colonel Brown; was appointed an ensign; was principally employed in transporting provisions and munitions of war, and was mustered for military duty all the war. From the proof exhibited, it is probable that the petitioner performed the services stated by him in his application for relief; but if this be conceded, the committee are of opinion that the relief prayed for ought not to be granted, as it would be introducing a new principle in the action of this committee, which would open the door for the allowance of an innumerable class of claims, the settlement and payment of which was amply provided for shortly after the close of the revolutionary war, and which cannot now be investigated with any safety to the Government. Therefore,

*Resolved,* That the prayer of the petitioner be not granted.

---

APRIL 6, 1838.

The Committee on Revolutionary Claims, to whom the petition of Philip Lightfoot was referred, report:

That the petitioner claims, as only son and sole heir at law of Philip Lightfoot, deceased, the commutation pay due to his said father for his services as a lieutenant in the Virginia line on continental establishment in the army of the Revolution. Diligent inquiry has been made at all the Departments here and at Richmond, and no record evidence has been found to show that Philip Lightfoot was an officer. It does appear that, on the 11th of July, 1835, Governor Tazewell allowed land bounty to Philip Lightfoot as a lieutenant in the continental line, for three years' service. (See the certificate of the register of the land office at Richmond, Virginia.) This allowance was made by Governor Tazewell, on the evidence of two highly respectable and intelligent officers in the continental regiment of artillery commanded by Colonel Charles Harrison, to wit: Judge Francis T. Brooke and the late Colonel Edmund Brooke—both in service to the end of the war, and both have received commutation pay and land bounty from the United States. By the testimony of these officers, it is proven that Philip Lightfoot, father of the petitioner, was a lieutenant in Harrison's regiment of artillery on continental establishment; that he served in the campaign of 1781, in the army commanded by General Lafayette; that he was in actual service in July, 1781, and at the seige of York; that in the summer of 1781, about July, nearly all the regular soldiers attached to the portions of Harrison's regiment then in Virginia, were marched to the South, to join the army under General Greene; that nearly all the junior officers in Harrison's regiment were, by the foregoing detachment of the men, left in Virginia without regular command; that, to supply this, militia draughts and recruits were placed under their command, to aid in repelling the then invasion of Virginia; that after the siege of York, these militia draughts and recruits were discharged, and the officers were again without men to command, and so remained to the end of the war. Judge Brooke says he knew Philip Lightfoot well; that he was wealthy, and did not regard pay; that he never heard of his resignation; that he considered him in the condition of five-sixths of the officers of that regiment—at home, having no troops to command, virtually in service, though not actually in the field. (For the foregoing statement of the evidence in this case, see the affidavits of Francis T. Brooke and Edmund Brooke, and a certificate of John Taliaferro.) In acting on these cases, the committee receive with great caution parol evidence to show that the claimant was an officer in the continental service, and, as such, entitled to commutation pay. In all cases, record evidence, when attainable, is required to show—first, that the claimant was an officer; secondly, that his service was such as to entitle him to the pay claimed. There is no rule, however, so general in its application, as not to require necessary exceptions, in order to do justice. And it has generally been the practice to admit secondary evidence, when the best evidence is not in possession of, or attainable by, the party claiming. As to the present case, there are circumstances arising out of the history of the then and past times, sufficient to create a strong presumption that the records as to Harrison's regiment, from the time Lightfoot joined it to the close of the war, never were very perfect, owing to the reduced and scattered condition of its officers during that period; and that, imperfect as those records were, nearly all of them have been destroyed and lost. It is under these circumstances the petitioner offers secondary evidence to show that he was a lieutenant in Charles Harrison's regiment of artillery, and the evidence offered is that of the two officers of the same regiment above referred to. The committee, being satisfied, by the evidence in the case, that Philip Lightfoot was a lieutenant in the continental regiment of artillery commanded by Charles Harrison; that he was, as such, in actual service in the campaign of Virginia, to its close in 1781; and that subsequent to that time he became supernumerary to the close of the war, are of opinion that he was entitled to commutation pay, and report a bill.

---

### May 11, 1838.

The Committee on Private Land Claims, to which was referred the petition of James Maxwell, of Pennsylvania, report:

That it appears the petitioner enlisted and served in the eighth Pennsylvania regiment, during the war of the Revolution, and to the close thereof; that for said service he became entitled to a bounty land warrant for one hundred acres of land; that, without the knowledge of the petitioner, a warrant issued the 19th of March, 1799, for the quantity of land to which he was entitled, and afterwards, to wit, the 4th of January, 1810, a patent issued thereon in the name of Thomas Thompson, as assignee of the petitioner. The committee are satisfied, from the proof before them, that the alleged assignment to Thompson was made without the assent or knowledge of the petitioner, and that he has not received any benefit, directly or indirectly, for the same.

The committee are of opinion, therefore, that the petitioner is entitled to relief, and they report a bill accordingly.

---

### May 11, 1838.

The Committee on Revolutionary Claims report:

That it appears, by documentary evidence, that George Yates served as surgeon's mate, in the continental line of the army of the Revolution, to the end of the year 1782, up to which time he was paid. It does not appear that he ever received certificates for commutation pay. Upon this state of the facts, and for the reasons assigned by this committee in the report which accompanies the bill (No. 44) of the Senate for the relief of the legal representatives of Samuel Y. Keene, (to which the committee refer as part of this report,) they recommend the allowance of five years' full pay of a surgeon's mate to George Yates; and for that purpose a bill is herewith reported.

---

## MAY 11, 1838.

The Committee on Revolutionary Claims, to which was referred the claim of the legal representatives of John Towns, report:

That in this case commutation, with interest, is claimed. The evidence filed consists of the following, viz:

1. The affidavit of Reuben Long, an officer of the Revolution and a pensioner, that he was in the same regiment with John Towns, and left him in service on the 20th December, 1779.

2. The affidavits of Joseph Hopkinson and Hannah Ogle; the former of whom says that he boarded with Towns in 1791 and 1792, and frequently heard him relate anecdotes or occurrences which he said took place while he was in service; and the latter says she knows John Towns was an officer of the Virginia line, and she believes he served until the close of the war.

3. John Towns's oath of allegiance, made before Baron de Kalb 8th April, 1778.

4. A certified copy of the certificate of the Governor and Council of Virginia, allowing bounty lands.

5. The certificate of the Auditor of Virginia, showing that John Towns was a lieutenant in the Virginia continental line, and was paid as such for his services to the 31st of December, 1781.

6. Two letters from the Third Auditor: one, dated the 1st April, 1834, showing that Lieutenant John Towns was paid by the United States to the 12th March, 1782; and the other, dated 5th January, 1838, showing that he was paid to the 26th of March, 1782.

7. Copy of a part of the proceedings of a court-martial which tried John Towns, in January, 1781.

8. The affidavit of Captain John Towns, dated 3d February, 1781, showing that Lieutenant John Towns had his authority to go to Charleston in December, 1780, for which he appears to have been arrested.

9. A copy of a letter from General Greene to the Board of War, dated 24th May, 1781, transmitting a copy of the proceedings of the court-martial in the case of Lieutenant Towns, stating that he considered the court an illegal one.

From the foregoing evidence, the committee are satisfied that the services of John Towns were such as would have entitled him to commutation, and therefore report a bill for the relief of his legal representatives.

## MAY 11, 1838.

The Committee on Revolutionary Claims, to whom the bill of the Senate (No. 44) for the relief of the legal representatives of Samuel Y. Keene, was committed, report the same with an amendment.

That the petitioners claim the five years' full pay due to their deceased ancestor, Samuel Y. Keene, for his services as a surgeon's mate in the army of the United States, in the war of the Revolution; and they rest their claim on the promise made by Congress on the 21st of October, 1780, the 17th of January, 1781, and by the act of March, 1783; which promise was, to allow half pay for life, or five years' full pay in lieu thereof, to such officers of the army of the United States as should continue in service to the end of the war, or who should become supernumerary subsequent to the 21st of October, 1780. The record evidence in support of this claim shows that Samuel Y. Keene was appointed a surgeon's mate in the Maryland continental line of the army of the Revolution; that he acted as such two years and five months prior to January, 1783, in which month he became supernumerary, and was paid up to the 15th day of November, 1783. (See the statement of Peter Hagner, Third Auditor; the certificate of William Gordon, land-bounty agent; a letter of the register of the Maryland land office; also, the affidavits of Peter Brunback and John Jacobs.) By this evidence, it is shown beyond doubt that the service of Samuel Y. Keene was such as to entitle him to the benefit of the resolutions of Congress of the 21st of October, 1780, and of March, 1783. A construction, however, was given those resolutions in 1784, by the then Board of War, which excluded surgeon's mates from commutation pay; and that construction was sanctioned by the Continental Congress, so that this class of the officers of the army, and this only, has never received that pay. Within a few years past, the Senate of the United States has decided, it is believed unanimously, that surgeon's mates are entitled to commutation, and have passed many bills making that allowance. Under the act of 1828, to provide for the surviving officers of the army of the Revolution who served in the continental line to the end of the war, surgeon's mates have been admitted to the benefit of that act. They have, in all time, received full land bounty as officers of the army, and their widows have received the seven years' half pay promised by Congress to the widows of such officers of the army as should die in the service. Without adopting, as a binding precedent, the decision of the Continental Congress, or taking as their guide the more recent decisions on the subject, the committee assume that the claim of surgeon's mates to commutation pay must depend on the true exposition of the several acts of Congress which ended in a promise of that pay. The first act of Congress which bears on the question is that of the 15th of May, 1778, to wit: "*Resolved*, That all military officers commissioned by Congress, who now are, or hereafter may be, in the service of the United States, and shall continue therein during the war, shall, after the conclusion of the war, be entitled to receive, annually, for the term of seven years, if they live so long, one-half of the present pay of such officers."

Such is the language of a resolution designed to induce individuals to enter the military service, and to continue therein to the end of the war. It was under and in pursuance of this promise, surgeons offered to join the army; and surgeons, as well as mates, were commissioned by Congress in the same terms, manner, and form, as all other military officers were commissioned. They had the pay and corresponding rank of certain officers in the line of the army; it was required of them to appear in the uniform dress correspondent to their military rank; they were made subject to strict military law; and what gives confirmation to the fact that they were considered military officers by the authors of the aforesaid resolution of the 15th of May, 1778, is a contemporaneous resolution of Congress, expressly directing the Secretary of the Board of War to sign none other than military officers' commissions. It was under this express restriction the Secretary did sign the commissions of surgeon's mates, as military officers; and his authority to do so has never been disclaimed, or even questioned. If no subsequent legislation on this subject had been adopted, the question arises, would surgeon's mates, at the conclusion of the war, have been entitled to the seven years' half pay promised by the aforesaid resolution of the 15th of May, 1778? It is said, no; and the reason assigned in support of this negation, is, they were not military officers; that military officers mean officers combatant; that surgeon's mates are non-combatants, *ergo*, not military officers, and, therefore, not embraced in the resolution. In noticing this objection, the committee do not consider it necessary to enter on a critical examination of the abstract meaning of the term *military*, taken separately and unconnected; nor is it material to the actual merits of the question to insist on the impropriety of a resort to so rigid and technical an exposition of the term *military*, in order to exclude from a common benefit officers whose dangers, privations, duties, and services, were identical with those admitted by all to be embraced by the resolution; and to remark, that such an exposition of the term *military* would create a distinction, and a most invidious one, between officers of the same corps, never recognised in the annals of military practice. For a satisfactory meaning of the term *military officer*, the committee look to the associated words, the object, and the practical operations of the resolution, in which all military officers commissioned by Congress are mentioned. Taking this for their guide, the committee decide that surgeon's mates were, according to the language of, and practice under, the resolutions of Congress above referred to, military officers; and, as such, embraced in the promise contained in the resolution of the 15th of May, 1778. If any yet insist that the committee err in the view they have taken, it is respectfully asked—if surgeon's mates were not military officers, what were they? Surely, no one will say they were civil officers. Such an idea, if it exists, is at once refuted by the fact that the commissions of surgeon's mates were signed by the Secretary of the Board of War, which, by act of Congress, was restricted from signing any other than military commissions. (See resolution of Congress, 17th of October, 1777.)

The committee, having come to the conclusion that surgeon's mates are embraced in, and entitled to, the provisions of the resolution of Congress of the 15th of May, 1778, it remained for them to ascertain whether or not they became entitled to the half pay for life, or five years' full pay in lieu thereof, subsequently promised by Congress to such officers of the army as should serve to the end of the war, or who should become supernumerary subsequent to the 21st of October, 1780. It appears, from an examination of the journals of that period, that Congress, in pursuance

of the earnest recommendation of General Washington to increase the
seven years' half pay allowed the officers of the army by the resolution
of the 15th of May, 1778, to half pay for life, did adopt the following resolution on the 21st of October, 1780, to wit : " Congress resumed the consideration of the letter of General Washington, recommending half pay to
the officers of the army, for life, after the conclusion of the war; and, to
to provide for the organization of the several regiments of infantry requested from the respective States : *Resolved,* That the several regiments
of infantry requested from the respective States by a resolution of the 3d
instant, be augmented, and consist of one colonel, one lieutenant colonel,
one major where the full colonels are continued, or one lieutenant colonel
commandant and two majors where full colonels are not continued, nine
captains, twenty-two subalterns, one surgeon, one surgeon's mate, &c.
That the commander-in-chief, and commanding officer in the southern department, direct the officers of each State to meet and agree upon the officers for the regiments to be raised by their respective States, from those
who incline to continue in service ; and where it cannot be done by agreement, to be determined by seniority, and make return of those who are to
remain : which is to be transmitted to Congress, together with the names
of the officers to be reduced, who are to be allowed half pay for life. That
*the officers* who shall continue in service to the end of the war, shall also
be entitled to half pay for life, to commence from the time of their reduction." The committee consider the half pay promised the officers of the
army by the foregoing act a substitute for, and in lieu of, the seven years'
half pay allowed by the above-recited act of the 15th of May, 1778 ; and
as it has been shown that surgeon's mates, being military officers commissioned by Congress, were included in the act of 1778, it seems to result
that, as officers of the army, and components of an express military corps,
(see the organization of the regiments recited above,) they became entitled
to the half pay promised by the act of the 21st of October, 1780.    And if
all legislation on that subject had terminated here, the committee believe
no doubt ever would have existed as to the just claim of this class of officers, in common with others, to that pay.    But it seems there was subsequent legislation on the subject; and it remained for the committee to examine that legislation, and to ascertain whether, and to what extent, it
contravened all or any of the preceding legislation in relation to that matter.    After an assiduous investigation, the committee conclude that no
legislation subsequent to the 21st of October, 1780, could, or that by fair
construction did, contravene, or in any manner impair, the claim of the
officers of the army, or any class of such officers, to the half pay promised
them by the act of the 21st of October, 1780.    The half pay for life contracted by the act of 1780 to be paid to the officers of the army for certain
service to be performed by them, *instanter* became a vested right, of
which subsequent legislation, nor nothing whatever, could divest the officer, save a failure on his part to perform the prescribed service ; and it
would be a libel on the good sense and justice of the distinguished states-
men and patriots of that period to imagine even that any legislation, subsequent to the 21st of October, 1780, had for its object to impair the de-
liberate engagement made by that act to allow half pay for life to the officers of the army.    It is, however, insisted that the act of the 17th of January, 1781, excludes surgeon's mates from half pay ; and as it was in
pursuance of this act, as the committee believe, that the Secretary of the

Continental Board of War, in 1784, and in all time thereafter, refused to allow to surgeon's mates half pay claimed by them, and as the Congress of that period sustained this decision of the Secretary, the committee deemed it proper to examine, with great attention, that act, and its declared object. The committee did this, not because any provision in the act could, for the reasons stated above, deprive this class of officers of a right vested in them by a previous act; but to show that the act of the 17th of January, 1781, was intended for another and very distinct purpose. The circumstance which induced the act in question was, a doubt on the part of the officers of the hospital department of the army whether they were included in the half-pay provision of the act of the 21st of October, 1780. They addressed General Washington on the subject; and he addressed Congress in their behalf. In this movement, the surgeons and mates of the regiments took no part; they having no doubt as to their existing claim to half pay. Having this object only in view, " Congress, on the 17th of January, 1781, took into consideration the report of the committee on the letter of General Washington of the 5th of November last, enclosing a memorial from the officers of the hospital department; and thereupon came to the following resolutions: *Whereas*, by the plan for conducting the hospital department, passed in Congress the 30th day of September last, no proper establishment is provided for the officers of the medical staff, after their dismission from public service, which, considering the customs of other nations, and the late provision made for the army after the conclusion of the war, they appear to have a just claim to: for remedy whereof, and also for amending several parts of the abovementioned plan—*Resolved*, That all officers in the hospital department and medical staff, hereinafter mentioned, who shall continue in service to the end of the war, or be reduced before that time as supernumeraries, shall be entitled to, and receive, during life, in lieu of half pay, the following allowance, viz : The director of the hospital, equal to the half pay of a colonel, (that is, $30 per month ;) chief physicians and surgeons of the hospital and army, and hospital physicians and surgeons, purveyor, apothecary, and regimental surgeons, each equal to the half pay of a captain,'' (say $20 per month.) And it was because surgeon's mates, *eo nomine*, were not included in the foregoing enumeration, appended to a measure the express object of which was to provide for *all* the officers of the hospital department and medical staff, half pay has been refused to them.

A construction like that, so manifestly opposed to the avowed object of the act, is rendered more strikingly apparent by the fact that it excludes no other officer, while it includes the apothecary, an officer of inferior grade to the surgeon's mate, who is, as to similarity of duty, identical with the surgeon, and much more exposed to the hazards of war. Such a construction and execution of this act, as it respects surgeon's mates, is contrary to all the other provisions made by Congress for that indispensable class of officers in all military corps of an army. No pay or bounty was allowed the surgeon, or other officers of the army, by Congress, which was not extended, ratably, to the mate. Such has been the practice of other nations; and it was expressly in pursuance of the practice of other nations that Congress, in part, were influenced to adopt the resolution of the 17th of January, 1781. In deciding on this case, the Secretary of War and the Continental Congress must have been governed by the single circumstance that surgeon's mates, *eo nomine*, were not included in the list of officers. And taking this, as they probably did, to be the sole action of Congress on the subject; and, moreover, deeply influenced by the then pecuniary embarrassment of the Government, they came to a conclusion which this committee, with great deference and respect, think cannot be sustained by the previous acts of Congress, nor by a fair construction of the act of 17th of January, 1781. The committee are satisfied, by a connected view of the legislation on this subject, that the object of the act of 1781 was to fix the quantum of pay to be allowed all the officers of the hospital department and medical staff, at the conclusion of the war, in lieu of half the pay which was allowed those officers by the act of the 30th of September, 1780. And as there were other than commissioned officers attached to the hospital department and medical staff, in order to discriminate these, the words "officers hereinafter mentioned" are inserted. In making this enumeration in a very mixed and promiscuous order, a single commissioned officer (surgeon's mate) is omitted. The committee, being unable to discover, or even imagine, a reason for such omission, believe that it arose from inadvertence; and that if the claim in question rested solely on that omission, taken in connexion with all the objects of the act, it would be justly sustained, and ought to be allowed. If the omission to name an officer in an act, expressly designed to operate upon him, shall be so construed as not to affect him, how was it that the general officers of the army were allowed commutation pay? The act allowing commutation does not include the general officers, *eo nomine*, nor in terms even; yet, as it was the manifest object of Congress to allow that pay to all military officers commissioned by Congress, it was decided by Congress that such a construction should be given to the previous act as to include the general officers of the army. The committee consider the cases analogous; and that the decision as to the general officers ought to have been the decision as to surgeon's mates. Taking these views of the legislation of Congress, the committee are of opinion that surgeon's mates were included in the resolution of Congress of the 15th of May, 1778, allowing seven years' half pay to all military officers; that they were included in the resolution of the 21st of October, 1780, allowing certain officers of the army half pay for life, in lieu of the seven years' half pay aforesaid; that the half pay for life thus promised, became, *instanter*, a vested right, of which the officers could not be justly deprived by subsequent legislation; that the act of the 17th of January, 1781, was designed to benefit the officers of the hospital and medical staff, and ought not to be construed and executed so as, in any respect, to contravene that design; that, therefore, the construction heretofore given to that act, whereby surgeon's mates have been refused the half pay claimed by them, is incorrect, and ought to be reversed. It is therefore

*Resolved*, That surgeon's mates, who served in the army of the United States to the conclusion of the war of the Revolution, are entitled to commutation pay; and the bill of the Senate is reported for the relief of the petitioners, (the heirs of S. Y. Keene,) with an amendment.

### May 11, 1838.

The Committee on Revolutionary Claims, to which was referred the petition of the heirs of Henry D. Purcell, report:

That the petitioners ask commutation of five years' full pay, in lieu of half pay for life, in consideration of the services of said Henry D. Purcell, their ancestor, who served as a lieutenant of infantry in the Pennsylvania continental line to the end of the war. The petitioners refer the committee to the Third Auditor's office for evidence in support of their claim. The committee, on application to that office, find that said Henry D. Purcell did serve as a lieutenant in the Pennsylvania line on continental establishment to the end of the war, and in that capacity received his commutation afterwards. The letter of the Third Auditor to that effect, is hereby referred to, and made part of this report.

*Resolved,* That the prayer of the petitioners ought not to be granted.

---

Treasury Department,
*Third Auditor's Office, April* 19, 1838.

Sir: I have the honor to state, in reply to yours of the 18th instant, that it appears from the revolutionary records on file in this office that Henry D. Purcell served to the end of the war, as a lieutenant of infantry in the Pennsylvania continental line, and in that capacity he appears to have received his commutation of five years' full pay, in lieu of half pay for life.

With great respect,
PETER HAGNER, *Auditor.*

Hon. Alexander Harper,
*of the Committee on Revolutionary Claims, H. R.*

---

### May 11, 1838.

The Committee on Revolutionary Claims, to which the subject was referred, report:

That it appears to the satisfaction of the committee, by documentary and other evidence, that Joseph Savage was a surgeon's mate in the army of the Revolution; that he served in the continental line of the army, and was returned as in service at the end of the war, (see certificate of W. Gordon, land bounty agent.) Upon this state of facts, and for the reasons assigned by this committee in the report which accompanied Senate bill No. 44, for the relief of the legal representatives of Samuel Y. Keene, (to which the committee refer as part of this report,) they recommend the allowance to Joseph Savage of five years' full pay, allowed by the act of the 22d of March, 1783, to such officers of the continental line of the army as served to the end of the war. And a bill is reported.

Tne Committee on Revolutionary Claims, to which was referred the petition of the heirs of Abner Prior, report:

That, in this case, some of the heirs petition on behalf of themselves and the other heirs of Abner Prior, and ask Congress to pass a law to allow them commutation, with interest, in consequence of the services rendered by the said Prior as a surgeon's mate in the New York continental line. It appears by a letter from Mr. Hagner, that the records in his office show Abner Prior to have been a surgeon's mate in the New York continental line, and to have been paid for his services as such to the 4th November, 1783, and that he did not receive commutation. The committee therefore report a bill.

### MAY 11, 1838.

The Committee on Revolutionary Claims, to which was referred the petition of Eunice Burzette, report:

That the petitioner sets forth that she is the widow of Charles Burzette, who was a soldier during the revolutionary war, and that he served for the whole time the war continued, and that they were married in the year 1803, and he died in 1825, leaving no children.

The legal representatives of said Burzette are undoubtedly entitled to bounty land; but as the widow is not such, and as there are none known to the committee, they are of opinion that no action of Congress should be had on the subject of the petition.

### MAY 15, 1838.

The Committee on Revolutionary Claims, to which was referred the petition of John Bruno Hillary, on behalf of himself and his infant brother George Thomas Hillary, and Francis Killenberger, in right of his wife Mary Ellen, sister of said John and George Hillary, report:

That, by a record from the bounty land office, it is shown to the committee that, on the 20th of July, 1830, a warrant for two hundred acres of bounty land was issued by the Secretary of War to "Elizabeth Magruder, as daughter and only heir at law of Reynold Hillary, who was a lieutenant in the Maryland line." The heirship of the said Elizabeth was founded alone on her own affidavit, and that of one Fielder Magruder, in both of which she is stated to be the only heir at law of said Lieutenant Hillary; that, on the 25th of May, 1832, an act of Congress was approved, granting to the said Elizabeth Magruder, as the legal representative of the said Rignald, alias Reynold Hillary, five years' full pay, as the commutation of half pay for life due the said Lieutenant Hillary in his lifetime; by virtue of which said act the said Elizabeth received at the Treasury of the United States, on the 28th day of May, 1832, the sum of four thousand eight hundred and twenty-one dollars and forty-five cents for principal and interest. The petitioners allege that, in issuing this land warrant, and making the entire grant of commutation to the said Elizabeth Magruder, the Department of War and the Congress of the United States were deceived by her false representations; for, that their late father Rignald, alias Nick Hillary, was, as well as the said Elizabeth, the child and one of the lawful heirs of Lieutenant Reynold Hillary, and that they, as representing their parent, are entitled to a full moiety of what was due on account of the revolutionary services of their grandfather. That they were infants at the time of these transactions of which they complain; that shortly after the oldest of them arrived at lawful age, upon legal advice suits were instituted in Prince George's county, Maryland, and judgments obtained against the said Elizabeth Magruder for the one-half of the commutation pay wrongfully received by her; that executions have been sued out thereon, but the defendant has proved insolvent, and wholly unable to pay the same or any part thereof.

In support of their heirship, the petitioners have produced a number of depositions, from which the committee think it is unquestionably shown that Rignald, alias Nick Hillary, the father of the petitioners, was, as well as the said Elizabeth Magruder, the lawful child and heir of the said Lieutenant Hillary. On this subject the witnesses do not only establish the right of the petitioners by common hearsay or reputation, but most of them testify to their intimate acquaintance with Lieutenant Hillary and his family; that they knew Elizabeth Magruder and Nick, alias Rignald, to be his only children, and that no sort of suspicion ever attached to the birth of either. Even Fielder Magruder, whose affidavit was used to obtain the grant for the exclusive benefit of the said Elizabeth, now states, most unequivocally, that Elizabeth Magruder, and Nick, alias Rignald Hillary, were always said to be lawful brother and sister, and that they were the only children of Lieutenant Hillary.

It further appears to the committee, that Nick, alias Rignald Hillary, died in Georgetown, D. C., some twelve or fifteen years ago, leaving a widow and the petitioners, his children and heirs at law; that the oldest, John Bruno Hillary, was born July 12, 1811, and the youngest, George Thomas, March 22, 1822. From the statement of John Marbury, Esq., of Georgetown, it is shown that shortly after the passage of the act of May, 1832, in favor of Elizabeth Magruder, he was applied to by John B. Hillary for legal advice as to the best manner of proceeding in order to obtain redress for the injury done him and the other children by the said Elizabeth Magruder; that he advised suits to be brought against her in Prince George's county, Maryland; that, at his instance, John B. Brook, Esq., of that county, was employed to prosecute said suits. Mr. Marbury says that Mr. Brook is a diligent and faithful attorney, and doubts not that he has done all that could be done for his clients.

Mr. Brook, the gentleman above referred to, swears that he recovered judgments, in the names of John B. Hillary, and his sister Mary Ellen, for one-half of the amount of the commutation received by the said Elizabeth Magruder; that but two actions were brought, supposing that John B. and his sister were each entitled to one-fourth; he states that Mrs. Magruder appeared by counsel, and at November term 1835 confessed judgments for two thousand dollars each, to be severally released on payment of twelve hundred and five dollars and thirty cents, with interest from 29th May, 1832. That writs of *fieri facias* have been regularly issued to enforce satisfaction; that they have been levied on a small tract of poor land; but that, owing to the doubt of title in the defendant, the sheriff had, up to that time, been unable to effect a sale; that the defendant is in very reduced circumstances, and considers the chance of making any part of the debt as quite desperate. The sheriff of Prince George's county, Maryland, swears that the executions founded on the above-named judgments were levied on the right and interest of Elizabeth Magruder to a small parcel of poor land supposed to contain one hundred and five acres; that it was the only property, to the best of his knowledge, real, personal, or mixed, subject to these executions; has made repeated efforts to sell, but always without success, until the 13th of April, 1838, when, on offering it again, it was knocked off to the highest bidder for twenty dollars and two cents. He further swears that he believes Elizabeth Magruder, the defendant, is now utterly insolvent, and that no part of said judgments can be made by a renewal of the process thereon. To show still farther the want of all right on the part of Elizabeth Magruder to receive that portion of the commutation claimed by the petitioners, your committee state that, as early as 1786, it appears from the records of Prince George's county, Maryland, letters of administration on the estate of Lieutenant Hillary had been granted to his widow, Mary Hillary. It does not appear that upon her death, which happened many years ago, administration *de bonis non* was granted to the said Elizabeth Magruder, or any other person, or that she was in any other way authorized to collect and receive the dues and effects of her late father.

The committee are thoroughly satisfied that the petitioners are entitled to share in whatever bounty or debt may appear to have been earned by the revolutionary services of Lieutenant Hillary, and that their rights remain unimpaired by any thing that Elizabeth Magruder may, by false or partial statements, have induced Congress or either department of the Government to do; nor is their claim the less entitled to a favorable consideration on account of their having made a faithful but unavailing effort to obtain from her that indemnity which they now ask of Congress.

Before, however, granting the share of bounty land and commutation now proposed, the committee have, upon a re-examination of the evidence, satisfied themselves that Reynold Hillary was a lieutenant in the Maryland line on continental establishment, and that he continued in service to the close of the war. The deposition of Captain Joseph Cross, and the certificate from the pay-roll on file in the Treasury Department, they think, establish these facts: they are equally well convinced that neither bounty land nor commutation has been allowed or granted, except to the said Elizabeth Magruder, as herein set forth.

They report a bill for the relief of the petitioners.

----

## MAY 18, 1838.

The Committee on Revolutionary Claims have had under consideration a resolution of the House, instructing them to inquire into the expediency of so amending the act of the 5th of July, 1832, entitled " An act to provide for liquidating and paying certain claims of the State of Virginia," as to embrace officers entitled to five years' full pay in lieu of half pay for life; and to inquire into the expediency of providing for the payment of such judgments as have been or may hereafter be recovered against the State of Virginia, for half pay or commutation pay, under the act of the Legislature of Virginia, of May, 1779; and now report:

That the reasons which led to the passage of the act of July 5th, 1832, are fully and at large stated in the report of the select committee made on the 16th of January, 1832, by Mr. J. S. Barbour, and the documents thereto appended. (See House Reports and Documents of 1st session 22d Congress, No. 191.)

It is obvious from the report and documents referred to, that it was intended, by the passage of the act of 5th July, 1832, to relieve the State of Virginia from liabilities which she had incurred under her act of May, 1779. The committee are of opinion that it was perfectly just on the part of Congress to satisfy the claims of the officers and soldiers of the Virginia State and Continental lines, founded on the act of May, 1779. The liability of Virginia, to the extent of these claims, was incurred for the common benefit of the whole people of the United States in their revolutionary struggle, and, therefore, she should be indemnified by the nation. She has shown a sufficient excuse for the delay in the oscillating decisions of her judicial tribunals. But her courts have now settled the obligation which Virginia is under to certain classes of her officers under the act of May, 1779, which had been rejected; and, until recently, before the passage of the act of 5th July, 1832, Virginia had no reason to suppose that she would ever be burdened with these demands. The same reasons which required the passage of the act of 1832, equally apply in urging the propriety of passing an act for the indemnification of Virginia, to the full extent of her liabilities, under her act of May, 1779. The committee are informed that the act of 5th July, 1832, does not embrace and meet the full measure of the liability of Virginia under her act of 1779. To make a suitable provision where the act of 5th July, 1832, falls short, the committee report a bill.

The State of Virginia, on the 16th December, 1790, passed an act under which certain officers of the Virginia State line of her revolutionary army became entitled to commutation or five years' full pay, in lieu of half pay for life. Under the operations of this act, it is believed the representatives of certain Virginia State line officers have recovered commutation or five years' full pay from the State of Virginia, when the half pay for life allowed under the act of 5th July, 1832, did not equal the commutation or five years' full pay. In these cases, the half pay for life, allowed by the act of 1832, is credited in behalf of Virginia; but the amount over and above that, Virginia is required to pay. For such excesses, or for the difference between the half pay for life, settled and paid under the act of 5th July, 1832, and the commutation or five years' full pay settled under her act of 1790, Virginia desires now to be indemnified by the United States. Your committee are of opinion that there is no good ground upon which indemnification to this extent in behalf of Virginia can be allowed; because Virginia had no right to enlarge her liabilities for revolutionary services after the General Government had assumed the revolutionary debts of the several States, which was done prior to the passage of the Virginia act of 1790. The committee have, therefore, in the bill reported, distinctly rejected the idea of making provision for satisfying those claims against Virginia which depend upon the provisions of her act of 16th December, 1790.

All which is respectfully submitted.

MAY 18, 1838.

The Committee on Revolutionary Claims, to whom was referred the petition of Elisha Adair, report:

The petitioner prays Congress to pay him, as executor of his deceased father, the amount of certain bills of credit, or continental paper-money, which he alleges his father received in payment of supplies furnished the American army during the Revolution. If the correctness of the facts stated in the petition be conceded, the committee are of opinion that no relief should be granted. Up to the 29th day of November, 1779, inclusive, the Revolutionary Congress had authorized the issue of $200,000,000 in bills of credit, usually denominated continental paper-money. As early as the 18th day of March, 1780, it appears, from a resolve of Congress of that date, that these bills had depreciated until $40 of them were currently passed as of value equal to one specie dollar. In the transactions of that day, these bills were doubtless used in payments for property purchased at their current and not nominal value; and their current value was continually fluctuating and growing worse and worse. To redeem and pay the whole amount issued at its nominal value, especially if interest be added, would involve the nation in debt to the extent of many hundred millions of dollars. To redeem it at its depreciated market value at the times when it was received in payment for commodities, would be to adopt a rule dependent upon parol testimony, which would not be safely executed, owing to the great length of time elapsed since the date of the transactions. A redemption and payment of those bills in the hands of their present holders, by either rule, would still leave a very large number of persons who suffered from them, and whose losses would be unprovided for; to wit, those persons who received them in payment, and who parted from them at a greater rate of depreciation than when they were received. Such persons would have the same right to claim compensation for the amount of loss sustained by the depreciation of the bills while remaining in their hands, which the holders now have to any remuneration. To ascertain the extent of these losses would be utterly impossible.

In every view which the committee have been able to take, they perceive insurmountable difficulties in attempting at this day to remunerate the present holders of these bills of credit, or those who have suffered from their use as a currency. Millions of dollars have probably been destroyed in the expectation that no measure for its redemption would ever be adopted. The issuing of these bills was an act of necessity, forced upon the Revolutionary Congress by the circumstances in which they were placed. Their depreciation operated injuriously to all those engaged in the struggle for independence. Their circulation was so general, that the losses sustained operated as a tax upon the whole community. It is impossible now to ascertain who suffered most, or the extent of loss sustained by each individual. The few survivors of that period, and the descendants of those who are dead, are compensated for their losses in the free institutions which have been the result. It is the only compensation which they can at this late day receive, in the opinion of the committee: Therefore,

*Resolved,* That the prayer of the petitioner ought not to be granted.

MAY 18, 1838.

The Committee on Revolutionary Claims, to whom was referred the petition of Lucy Williamson, report :

That the petitioner, as the only child of the late Captain Rains Cook, sets up a claim for pay and commutation alleged to be due on account of the revolutionary services of her father. From the letter of Peter Hagner, Esq., Third Auditor of the Treasury, the committee are thoroughly satisfied that Rains Cook was a captain in the Georgia line, and that he served to the end of the war ; but from the same official source, they are informed that "he (Captain Cook) appears to have been settled with for his services to the end of the war, and also for his commutation of five years' full pay, in lieu of half pay for life. Nothing, therefore, appears to be due to Captain Cook on account of his revolutionary services." In two subsequent communications touching this claim, Mr. Hagner gives a circumstantial detail of the settlement, and amount paid, together with additional facts tending to show that there is nothing due the applicant from the United States. The committee annex copies of the Third Auditor's letters, and refer to them as affording, in their opinion, good grounds for the rejection of the prayer of the petition.

*Resolved,* That relief ought not to be granted in this case.

----

TREASURY DEPARTMENT,
*Third Auditor's Office, May* 17, 1836.

SIR : I have had the honor of receiving your letter of the 16th instant, accompanied by the honorable A. Huntsman's certificate in relation to Captain Rains Cook, of the revolutionary army; and in reply to your inquiries, I have to state, that it appears from the revolutionary records on file in this office that Rains Cook was, at the close of the war, a captain in the Georgia line on continental establishment, and, as such, he appears to have been settled with for his services to the end of the war, and also for his commutation of five years' full pay, in lieu of half pay for life. Nothing, therefore, appears to be due to Captain Cook on account of his revolutionary services.

With respect,

PETER HAGNER, *Auditor.*

Hon. WM. C. DUNLAP,
*House of Representatives, U. S.*

----

TREASURY DEPARTMENT,
*Third Auditor's Office, December* 28, 1836.

SIR : In reply to your letter of the 26th instant, I have the honor to state that it appears from the revolutionary records on file in this office, that Rains Cook was a captain in the Georgia line on continental establishment, and, as such, he appears to have served to the end of the war. The records do not show any thing to be due to him for pay or otherwise.

In regard to that part of your letter wherein you inquire if Captain Cook has received his commutation pay, where was it drawn, and to whom was it paid, I have to state that a final-settlement certificate appears to have been issued on the 17th of March, 1785, in his favor, for the sum of $972 16, on interest from the 15th of November, 1783, (the termination of the war;) and which certificate, with others issued at the same time to officers of the Georgia line for pay, commutation, &c., appears to have been placed in the hands of John Wereat, Esq., agent for distributing the final-settlement certificates of the officers of the Georgia line, and who appears to have had a settlement, and accounted for the certificates that were placed in his hands. As the certificate just mentioned is for a less sum than Captain Cook's commutation pay amounted to, it is proper to state that very few of the officers of the Georgia line had certificates issued to them for the precise amount of their commutation pay, (being charged on the settlement of the line with public moneys received by them on account;) but I have ascertained, from a careful examination of the settlement that was made with that line, that the whole amount allowed for commutation pay was equal to the commutation pay of all the officers of that line who were returned as being entitled to that grant.

With great respect,

PETER HAGNER, Auditor.

Hon. Robert Craig,
　　*of the Committee on Revolutionary Claims, H. R.*

---

Treasury Department,<br>
Third Auditor's Office, May 5, 1838.

Sir: I have had the honor of receiving your letter of the 3d instant, asking for information in regard to the settlement that was made with Captain Rains Cook, of the Georgia line of the revolutionary army, in addition to that embraced in my letter of the 28th of December, 1836, to the honorable Robert Craig. As you seem to think that, without further explanation, it may be contended that the final-settlement certificate mentioned in my letter to Mr. Craig was for pay alone, I will state that I am perfectly satisfied, from the examinations that I have made of the settlement that was made with the Georgia line, that the certificates issued to the officers, respectively, by the paymaster general and commissioner of army accounts, were for the balances found due them after bringing into view every thing that was due them for pay, rations, and commutation. This opinion is corroborated, and I may say established beyond doubt, by a report of the commissioner of army accounts, made on the 14th of October, 1785, wherein it is stated "that the accounts of this line (Georgia) being so fully discharged by the State, and so blended in each other, it became necessary for your commissioner to take up the settlement of the whole arrears due for pay, rations, and commutation, from the commencement to the end of the war. That your commissioner did accordingly, when the State had not made sufficient advances to cover the demand of the officer, issue his certificate for such balance as was found due to such officer."

The report from which the foregoing quotation is made, was made by John Pierce, Esq., who had himself repaired to Georgia, and attended personally to the settlement of the accounts of the line of that State.

With great respect,

PETER HAGNER, Auditor.

Hon. A. H. Shepperd,
　　*of the Committee on Revolutionary Claims, H. R.*

The Committee on Revolutionary Claims, to whom the petition on behalf of the heirs of James Hackley was referred, report:

That the petitioners claim the commutation pay due to James Hackley, for his service as a lieutenant in the continental army to the end of the war of the Revolution. It appears by an official statement of the evidence on which land bounty was allowed by the State of Virginia to James Hackley for his service as a lieutenant in the continental army to the end of the war, that said Hackley was in service in the years 1782 and 1783, as will appear by a certified return of John Wright, clerk in the office of commissioner of army accounts, and by Joseph Howell, jr., paymaster general of the continental army. (See paper A, as a part of this report.) It does not appear that this officer settled any account for pay with the auditor of Virginia, or with A. Dunscomb, the continental commissioner in Virginia; and his name is not on the army register of the continental line. This may be explained by the presumption that this officer rendered the whole of his services to the North, and that he settled his accounts with continental paymasters or commissioners where his services were performed. The committee consider the evidence referred to sufficient to sustain the claim of James Hackley to the commutation pay of a lieutenant, and report a bill.

---

A.

*To the Executive of Virginia :*

The undersigned, acting as the attorney in fact for Asa Winsett and Amos Winsett, the heirs of the late James Hackley, of Virginia, who was a lieutenant in the Virginia line on continental establishment in the revolutionary war, begs leave respectfully to present the claim of the said heirs for land due to the said Hackley, for his services to the end of the war; which fact, it is believed, does fully appear by the public records at Richmond, to which the Executive is respectfully referred. The undersigned prays that an examination may speedily take place, and the register of your land office be directed forthwith to issue the proper land warrant for whatever may be due to the heirs of the said James Hackley for his military services during the Revolution.

Respectfully,

JOHN METCALFE,
*Attorney in fact for Asa Winsett and Amos Winsett, heirs of James Hackley, deceased.*

---

CORPORATION OF FREDERICKSBURG, *to wit :*

Personally appeared before me, a justice of the peace for the corporation aforesaid, John Metcalfe, who made oath that, from information he has received, he verily believes that James Hackley, named in the within petition, was an officer in the revolutionary war, and served to the close of the war, and that he was a lieutenant when the war ended. And the said John Metcalfe, I further certify, is known personally to me as a gentleman of veracity and character. Given under my hand this 24th day of July, 1835.

JOHN H. WALLACE, *Recorder.*

*Report on the claim of the heirs of James Hackley, lieutenant of the continental line, for bounty land for his services.*

JULY 28, 1835.

SIR : This officer settled no account with State auditors, or with Mr. Dunscomb, the continental commissioner in Virginia, and his name is not on the army register of the continental line.

I, however, find his name on a "return of subsistence due sundry officers of the *Virginia line,* being balances of 1782 and 1783;" which document is now on file in my office. This return has been certified by John Wright, clerk in the office of commissioner of army accounts, and by Joseph Howell, jr., paymaster general of the continental army. I beg leave to remark that, probably, every officer whose name appears on this return (with the exception of James Hackley) has received his bounty land, and many of them have received their commutation of five years' full pay, in lieu of half pay for life. This officer, it is presumed, rendered the whole of his service in the Northern army, and settled his accounts with continental paymasters or commissioners.

On the evidence furnished by the aforesaid *return of subsistence, &c.,* I reported this claim good for a service to the end of the war, some time in the year 1833. I am still of the same opinion.

Respectfully submitted.

JOHN H. SMITH, *Commissioner, &c.*

To the GOVERNOR.

EXECUTIVE DEPARTMENT,
*Richmond, December* 28, 1836.

The foregoing are true copies of papers filed in this department.

WM. H. RICHARDSON,
*Secretary Com.*

MAY 18, 1838.

The Committee on Revolutionary Claims, to whom were referred a petition and resolution in favor of Captain James Moore, of New Jersey, report :

The petitioner sets up a claim for property destroyed by the enemy in the revolutionary war, and for the value of a wagon and team which he alleges to have been impressed into the public service during the retreat of our army through Princeton : he further alleges that he was a captain in the New Jersey militia, wss in several battles, and was charged with the custody of the British prisoners captured principally at the battle of Monmouth. This claim, made in mere general terms, without a specification of the property destroyed, seems first to have been presented to Congress in January, 1829. In its support, one S. Morford then made an affidavit, in which he merely states, generally, the truth of the allegations set forth in the petition, and the good character of the petitioner. On the 17th of November, 1831, this witness made a further deposition, in which he states that in 1776 Captain James Moore was the owner of an extensive tanyard in Princeton, and also carried on the business of a farmer and shoemaker; that, upon a near approach of the British and American forces to Princeton, in December of that year, Captain Moore, with a wagon and team, commenced removing his most valuable furniture, when Colonel Biddle, quartermaster general of the American army, caused the goods to be thrown out, and pressed the wagon and team into the public service, to aid in removing the baggage of our retreating forces; that Moore, with witness and others, joined the army, and retreated into Pennsylvania; that the enemy shortly after entered Princeton, and took away and destroyed the contents of the petitioner's tanyard, and all his hay and grain. Witness is not certain of the value of the property thus destroyed, but is of opinion that it is not less than twenty-five hundred dollars. His deposition goes on to narrate many instances of daring bravery and devotion to the American cause by the petitioner. Your committee doubt not the patriotism of the petitioner, and his suffering privations and sustaining losses in consequence of his devotion to the cause of his country; but they are unable to perceive in the circumstantial narration of his case, as given by the witness, any solid ground for relief. For the loss of houses and other property destroyed by the enemy in consequence of their occupation or use by the troops, relief has been granted in some cases, and is proposed in others: this important feature, however, does not appear in the present case. The claim for the wagon and team alleged to have been impressed into the public service is thought also to be untenable; for, in the absence of all proof on the subject, but the mere statement of the witness that he does not believe the property was returned or paid for, your committee do not think themselves justified in making the allowance, especially as it was usual for officers requiring such seizure of private property for public use to afford the owner a certificate of the fact and the value of the property taken. But, even if such evidence of an apparent claim were made out in this case, the committee would find great difficulty, and would apprehend much danger of imposition on the Government by making the allowance at this late day, especially as this description of claims was often passed on and allowed between individuals and the States and the General Government, without any means of establishing the same by evidence that could now be produced.

*Resolved,* That the prayer of the petitioner ought not to be granted.

---

MAY 18, 1838.

The Committee on Revolutionary Claims, to whom was referred the memorial of John B. White, praying that the commutation pay due to his father, Robert White, a captain in the army of the Revolution, may be paid to him, &c., report:

That Robert White was a lieutenant in the service of the United States in the Virginia line on continental establishment ; that he entered the service in the year 1775 as a private; that he was commissioned as a lieutenant in the eighth Virginia regiment in the army of the United States, to take rank as such from the first day of September, 1777; that the said Robert White was severely wounded in 1778, and, under the resolution of 1776, he was placed on the pension-list, for a partial pension, as an invalid, and continued to draw said pension until his death.  After he was wounded in 1778, it appears, from the evidence in the case, that he was promoted to a captaincy, and continued to render what service he could until the close of the war.  It is in evidence that he was a most vigilant and gallant officer.

A certificate is filed, bearing date November 15, 1799, from the register of the land office of Virginia, which clearly shows that Robert White was entitled to the land allowed a captain in the continental line, for the seventh and eighth years' service; and that warrant No. 4927 issued on said 15th November, 1799, to Robert White, a captain of the continental line, for 1,333⅓ acres of land.  There can be no doubt, then, of his service as a captain to the close of the war.

The committee cannot perceive that the resolution of Congress of the 7th of June, 1785, which, among other things, provides "that no officer who has accepted his commutation for half pay shall be entered on the list of invalids, unless he shall have first returned his commutation," ought in justice to embarrass this claim for commutation.  The evidence is very satisfactory that Robert White was placed on the pension-list for a disability received in 1778, while he was a lieutenant, and under the resolution of Congress of 1776 ; that he was immediately afterwards promoted to a captaincy, and in that capacity served to the close of the war; and upon no principle of justice can they withhold the commutation of five years' full pay in lieu of the half pay for life promised to him in October, 1780, which must have been after he had been placed on the pension-list as an invalid, and after his promotion to a captaincy, and, therefore, in the opinion of the committee, was a vested right.

They, therefore, report the accompanying bill.

---

### May 18, 1838.

The Committee on Revolutionary Claims, to which was referred the petition of the heirs of the late Captain George Rice, of Virginia, deceased, for commutation, report:

That, heretofore, reports have been made by committees against this claim, in which the committee concur.  George Rice, on the 18th day of January, 1776, was appointed a captain in the Virginia continental line, and became a supernumerary officer on the 30th day of September, 1778.  Under the resolutions of the Continental Congress, he was not entitled to the commutation of five years' full pay, in lieu of half pay for life.  The committee report against the claim.

The Committee on Revolutionary Claims, to which were referred the papers and documents relating to the claims of the heirs of George Rice, claiming commutation pay, report:

That the *paper*, purporting to be a memorial, *without any name subscribed*, represents that *their* ancestor, George Rice, served as a captain in the Virginia continental line to the close of the revolutionary war, &c., and thereby became entitled to commutation pay.

The proof adduced is the laconic affidavit of George Blackmore, who swears that George Rice "was a captain in the eleventh Virginia regiment on continental establishment; was a brave and meritorious officer, and served faithfully to the end of the war;" and a certificate given by Mr. Heath, auditor of public accounts at Richmond, Va., certifying that on the 18th day of June, 1783, a certificate issued to George Rice, as a captain of infantry, for £122 10*s.* 4*d.* delivered to himself, for services from the 1st to 17th January, 1777, as lieutenant, and from the 18th January, 1777, to 6th October, 1778, as captain.

Mr. Hagner, Third Auditor, states, under the date of 21st June, 1834, "that it appears" from "the revolutionary records in this office, that George Rice was appointed a captain in the Virginia continental line on the 18th January, 1777, and in that capacity became a supernumerary officer on the 30th September, 1778." He further states, "he was not entitled to commutation, and the resolution of Congress of the 10th December, 1778, directed that the year's pay allowed to supernumerary officers of the army by the resolution of the 24th November, 1778, should be made up in the pay-rolls of the regimental paymasters, and drawn from them by the said officers respectively."

From all which, the committee are led to the conclusion that there is nothing due to the heirs of Captain George Rice. The naked testimony of a witness who swears from mere recollection, after a lapse of more than fifty years, ought not to avail against the documentary evidence that goes directly to disprove the essential fact. Mr. Hagner shows that he, the said George Rice, became supernumerary in 1778; and the certificate of Mr. Heath, the auditor, corroborates the fact, by showing conclusively the settlement of his account, in 1783, for his services rendered previous and down to the 6th October, 1778; and as the year's pay due to supernumerary officers, in pursuance of the resolution of 24th November, 1778, was to be made up in the pay-rolls of the regimental paymasters, and drawn by the said officers, the committee deem the conclusion inevitable that there is nothing due on that account.

They therefore recommend the rejection of the claim.

---

The Committee on Revolutionary Claims, to which was referred the petition of Elias Burnham and wife, (the wife of the said Elias being the only daughter of Zophar Robinson, deceased,) report:

That Zophar Robinson, of Windham, in the State of Connecticut, deceased, enlisted in the army of the Revolution on the 4th day of April,

1777, for the full term of three years, and faithfully served during the whole period of his enlistment, which terminated on the 4th day of April, 1780, when he was honorably discharged. On the 25th day of February, 1781, he again enlisted in Colonel Durkee's regiment, in the Connecticut continental line, for a second term of three years, and continued in the service of his country until the 3d day of March, 1782, at which period he was "slain by the enemy," while on service as one of the picket guard. At his death he left surviving him a widow, (Charity, who is yet living, and has been for seven years last past in a state of insanity,) and one daughter, Chloe, who is intermarried with Elias Burnham, and are the petitioners in this case. That the said Charity has continued a widow from the death of her husband up to this period; and has been, and now is, supported, nursed, and maintain by Elias Burnham and his wife, who are themselves far from being in affluent circumstances. The destitute and insane widow of the gallant soldier, who fell in defence of the rights and liberties of his country, in the revolutionary war, appeals to the best sympathies of our nature; yet, when the case is examined in the character of a right or claim, its solution must depend on the resolutions, ordinances, and acts of Congress, and their due and proper construction. By the resolution of the 16th September, 1776, each non-commissioned officer and soldier who enlisted for the period of "during the war," and continued therein " to the close of the war," and the representatives of "such soldiers" (that is, those who enlisted for during the war) " as shall be slain by the enemy," were entitled to receive one hundred acres of bounty land. The evident object of the Continental Congress was to encourage enlistments "for during the war," so as to guard against the danger of frequent enlistment, and the consequent dispersing and weakening of the army by the expiration of the periods of enlistments. A three years' enlistment was not embraced by either the letter or spirit of the resolution, any subsequent acts or ordinances of Congress, although the right of the widow to a pension seems to be embraced in the pension laws.

The committee are, therefore, constrained to report against the relief prayed for by the petitioners.

---

MAY 29, 1838.

The Committee on Revolutionary Claims, to which the petition of the heirs of John Spotswood was referred, report :

That the petitioners claim the commutation pay due to John Spotswood for his services as a captain of infantry in the continental line of the army of the United States, to the end of the war of the Revolution. In support of this claim, record evidence, taken from the army accounts, shows that John Spotswood was in the military service as a captain in the continental line of the army, from the 1st day of January, 1777, to the 31st of December, 1781 ; up to which time he was paid. On the 10th of February, 1781, John Spotswood is officially returned as a captain in the continental line, then in service ; and Brigadier General George Weedon certified, on the 5th of April, 1783, that John Spotswood served in the Virginia continental line, from November, 1776, to that date, and that he was still in service.

Upon the foregoing evidence, it is clear that John Spotswood became entitled by service, to five years' full pay at the conclusion of the war; but upon his application for that pay it was refused, because he had been pensioned. Upon this point, it appears that John Spotswood was pensioned by the State of Virginia in the year 1786, under a law of that State of 1776, allowing pensions to such officers as should be disabled by wounds in the military service of that State, or in the continental line of that State. This pension was allowed in consequence of a severe wound received by Captain Spotswood in the battle of Germantown, and from the effects of which he many years after died, in the prime season of his usefulness to his family. It further appears that the pension allowed said Spotswood for partial disability was subsequently paid to him by the United States to the period of his death; but the commutation pay due to him for the service he performed to the end of the war has never been paid. The committee consider the pension for partial disability ought not to impair a claim to pay for service performed. Such was the opinion of Mr Madison, (see his letter on file.) Captain Spotswood applied soon after the war, to Andrew Dunscomb, army agent, for his commutation certificate, and was refused on account of his being a pensioner. From this refusal the petitioners appeal. The committee think the appeal ought to be sustained, and report a bill.

---

MAY 29, 1838.

The Committee on Revolutionary Claims, to whom the petition of the heirs of John P. Harrison was referred, report:

That the petitioners claim the five years' full pay due by the United States to John P. Harrison, for his services as a captain in the continental line of the army in the war of the Revolution, and who became supernumerary subsequent to the 21st of October, 1780. In support of this claim, the army records show that John P. Harrison was a captain in the continental line of the army, and that he was paid for his service as such to the 27th of October, 1780. (See the letter of Auditor Hagner and certificate of Auditor Heath, of Virginia.) It nowhere appears that the said Harrison resigned; and the just conclusion seems to be, he became supernumerary under the reduction of the army, in pursuance of the act of Congress of the 21st of October, 1780. By that act half pay for life was promised such officers as thereafter should become supernumerary. This half pay was, by the act of 1783, commuted into five years' full pay; to be paid in bonds, redeemable at the pleasure of the Government, with six per cent. interest thereon till paid. The committee find the evidence in the case satisfactory to show that John P. Harrison was entitled to the benefit of the acts above referred to, and report a bill.

---

MAY 29, 1838.

The Committee on Revolutionary Claims, to which was referred the Senate bill (No. 159) for the relief of Moses Van Campen, make the following report:

That the case of the petitioner has heretofore, on two several occasions, been before, and acted upon by, the Committee on Revolutionary Claims, viz : during the last and preceding sessions of Congress; and unfavorable reports were then made. The production of new and additional evidence has induced the committee to re-examine the case, which has resulted in a conviction that he is entitled to commutation, and that the bill passed by the Senate for his relief, and referred to the committee for investigation, ought to pass. The question that arises is one of fact, viz : Was there sufficient evidence adduced to satisfy the committee that the petitioner was an officer in the army of the United States on continental service, and did he serve to the close of the war? If he was, and did so serve, he is clearly entitled to relief. The additional evidence consists, first, of the affidavit of the applicant, dated on the 14th of May, 1838, in which he swears that, on the 8th day of April, 1780, he received a commission of ensign from Congress, and signed by the President thereof; that, in the month of February, 1781, he received the commission of a lieutenant from Congress, in the company of Captain Robinson; that the latter commission, on the 16th day of April, 1782, fell into the hands of the Indians, when the applicant was taken prisoner by them; that the commission of ensign was, in 1827, forwarded to Harrisburg, in Pennsylvania, and there lost by a member of the Legislature of that State.

The next piece of evidence is an extract from the comptroller general's office of Pennsylvania, duly certified on the 8th day of September, 1837, by the auditor general of that State, giving an abstract "of the account of Moses Van Campen against *the United States*," for his pay as ensign in Captain Robinson's company, from "April, 1780, to 10th February, 1781," and for his pay as a lieutenant from the "1Cth February, 1781, to the 4th November, 1783." This conclusively establishes the fact that the applicant was in the service of the United States, and so continued to the close of the war, and has received his pay as an officer in the Federal army. The letter of Peter Hagner, Esq., of the 18th day of May, 1838, addressed to William W. Potter, Esq., shows that Captain (afterwards Lieutenant Colonel) Robinson received his pay as a continental officer up to the 4th day of November, 1783, and "his commutation of five years' full pay, in lieu of half pay for life." On the 24th day of March, 1785, the General Assembly of Pennsylvania passed an act granting bounty lands to the officers and soldiers of that State in the continental service, of which the following is an extract from the 4th section : "That all officers or soldiers of the Pennsylvania regiments or of independent corps acknowledged by this State as of the *quota* of Pennsylvania in the *Federal army*, and officers being citizens of the State at the time of their entry into the service, not attached to the line of any other State, who have served therein to the end of the late war with Great Britain," &c. By this act, the grant of bounty lands was expressly confined to the officers and soldiers in the continental service. No officer who was in the service of the State, or whose commission was issued by or under the authority of the State, could, by any possibility, receive or be entitled to bounty land. Nor could any officer or soldier of the five companies of rangers, enlisted for nine months for the protection of the Western frontier, under the resolution of the 25th day of February, 1779, and who had served out the period of his enlistment or engagement, be embraced within the provisions of the act of 1785.

The next piece of evidence is an extract from the land office of Pennsylvania, duly certified by the secretary of the land office on the 24th day of May, 1838, proving that the comptroller general of Pennsylvania, whose duty it was under the act of 1785, returned and reported to the land office as follows : " Return of *the Pennsylvania line* entitled to donation land, reported by the late comptroller general—Van Campen, Moses, 1st lieutenant, Boyd's regiment, 400 acres, Nos. 834–849, 4th district." This is conclusive evidence that in 1785 the State of Pennsylvania recognised the applicant, and acknowledged him as an officer in the " *Pennsylvania line*" in the continental army. The loss of the commissions having been accounted for by the affidavit of the applicant, which was competent evidence for that purpose, the door was opened for the reception of secondary evidence. The additional evidence, connected with that on which the Senate reported the bill, carries conviction to the mind that Moses Van Campen was a continental officer, and served as such to the close of the revolutionary war ; and hence the committee recommend that the bill from the Senate for his relief be adopted.

---

### May 31, 1838.

The Committee on Revolutionary Claims, to whom the petition of the heirs of Lieutenant William Lewis was referred, report :

That the petitioners claim the seven years' half pay allowed the widow and children due to such officers of the army of the United States as died in the military service during the war of the Revolution.

It appears by the army records, that Lieutenant William Lewis was attached to the first Virginia regiment on continental establishment, and served in the company commanded by Captain John Fleming ; (see the letter of P. Hagner, and a certified reference to the journal of the Virginia convention of the 25th of June, 1776.) It also appears, by the evidence of Richard Spinner, a soldier, who was in service with said William Lewis, and by Lucy Marks, who at the time was his wife, that William Lewis died in service. There is some disagreement between these witnesses as to the precise time when the said William Lewis died : both state that his death occurred during the war ; but Lucy Marks, who it is presumed is most to be relied on, she being most affected by the event, says he died at Yorktown, while in service, on the 14th of November, 1779. (See affidavits of R. Spinner and Lucy Marks.)

As it appears from the certificate of Auditors Heath and Hagner that those entitled to the seven years' half pay now claimed have not received it, the committee decide that it ought to be paid to the claimants, and report a bill.

---

### May 31, 1838.

The Committee on Revolutionary Claims, to which was referred the memorial of Edward R. Laurens, administrator *de bonis non* of Thomas Rutledge, deceased, report :

That the said Rutledge loaned to the United States, in the month of February, 1780, a sum of money, for which he received certain loan-office certificates, which are alleged by the memorialist to have been lost, and that they have never been paid. It appears by the statement of the Register of the Treasury that the certificates were issued from the loan office, as is represented, and that they are still outstanding and unpaid.

The committee are satisfied of the justice of this claim, and therefore report a bill for the relief of the legal representatives of said Thomas Rutledge.

----

## MAY 31, 1838.

The Committee on Revolutionary Claims, to which had been referred the bill from the Senate (No. 164) for the relief of the heirs and legatees of Everard Meade, deceased, submitted the following report made to the Senate January 18, 1838, which the committee adopt:

" The Committee on Revolutionary Claims, to whom were referred the petition and papers of the heirs and legatees of Everard Meade, deceased, have had the same again under consideration, and ask leave to report:

" That heretofore, when this claim was before Congress, there was no satisfactory evidence that Everard Meade held an office of higher grade than that of captain during the revolutionary war; therefore an act was passed allowing to his heirs five years' full pay as a captain, which sum has been duly paid. Additional proof is now produced, which satisfies the committee that the said Everard was promoted to the rank of major, and that in that grade he continued to serve to the close of the revolutionary war, and that the petitioners are now entitled to receive such additional sum as will be equal to five years' full pay of a major; and for their relief, to this extent, they report a bill. The committee, for the reasons heretofore assigned, do not believe the petitioners are entitled to demand or receive interest either upon the sum heretofore paid, or that to which they are still entitled."

----

## JUNE 2, 1838.

The Committee on Revolutionary Claims, to which was referred the petition of John Conner, administrator of the estate of William B. Gould, report:

That David Gould was a senior hospital surgeon in the continental army, and died while in said service, on the 12th day of July, 1781, leaving an only child, William B. Gould, who became entitled to seven years' half pay by virtue of the resolution of Congress passed August 24, 1780.

William B. Gould was at the time of his father's death a minor, but made application when of age to Congress for the seven years' half pay; and a bill passed the House of Representatives for the allowance, but did not pass the Senate, in consequence of a doubt whether medical officers were included, which doubt has long since been removed.

William B. Gould applied to Congress several times from 1786 to 1794, and the claim remained until 1819, when he again petitioned; but no action was had prior to 1824, during which year he died.

The committee consider the petitioner entitled to relief, and report a bill.

The Committee on Revolutionary Claims, to whom was referred the petition of the heirs of Dr. Joseph Simon Pell, report :

The petitioners ask compensation for the services of their ancestor, Dr. Joseph Simon Pell, as surgeon in the State navy of Virginia during the revolutionary war, in pursuance of "the resolves of Congress granting in such cases half pay for life." The resolves of Congress under which the petitioners claim have not heretofore been construed to extend to the offcers of the navy ; and the committee deem it improper, at this time, to introduce a new principle in relation to claims for revolutionary services, which would open the door for the allowance of numerous claims equally meritorious, and which have not received the favorable consideration of Congress heretofore

*Resolved,* That the prayer of the petitioners ought not to be granted.

---

The Committee on Revolutionary Claims, to which was referred the petition of the heirs of Nathan Smith, report :

That Ann J. Smith, widow of Dr. Nathan Smith, petitions to be allowed commutation of five years' full pay, together with a balance of fourteen dollars and sixty-eight cents, which stands on the books of the Treasury as due on account of the revolutionary services of her late husband. It appears, by a letter from the Third Auditor, that Nathan Smith was a surgeon's mate in the Virginia continental line, and served until the 15th November, 1783. It also appears, by a certificate from the Register of the Treasury, that there is a balance of near fifteen dollars on the books of the Treasury due on account of the services of the said Nathan Smith. The committee, therefore, report a bill.

---

The Committee on Revolutionary Claims, to which was referred the petition of Isaac N. Piggott, asking pay for military services rendered by Captain James Piggott, deceased, report :

It appears, from the evidence submitted to the committee, that James Piggott, on the 6th day of April, 1776, was appointed captain of a company of foot, and commissioned by the General Assembly of the then province of Pennsylvania, in the second battalion of the military associators in the county of Westmoreland, for the protection of the then province against all hostile enterprises, and for the defence of American liberty ; that, on the 22d day of October, 1777, Captain Piggott resigned his commission, and the same was duly accepted by General Washington, as appears by document marked with the letter C.

It is alleged in the petition, that subsequent to the resignation of Captain Piggott, (but at what time it is not stated,) he raised a company of volunteers, and entered the regiment commanded by Colonel George Rogers

Clarke; that this regiment proceeded down the Ohio river, and, near a place then known as the Iron banks, on the Mississippi river, Captain Piggott, with the said regiment, was engaged in two battles with the Indians; that Captain Piggott from thence ascended that river to several points; that at Grand river his company erected a small place of defence, and known as "Piggott's block-house," now in St. Clair county, State of Illinois. It is further alleged in the petition that Captain Piggott was actively engaged in the service of his country in subduing the savages on the Western frontier, and defending it against their hostile invasions; and continued in such service until the cessation of hostilities on the part of the Indians. It does not appear at what time this service terminated.

Two depositions, taken before the Mayor of St. Louis, State of Missouri, have been submitted to the committee. The names of the affiants are *James McMeans* and *Jacob Swancy;* both of these persons swear that they were acquainted with Captain Piggott, in the years 1780, '81, or '82, and both swear they were members of Captain Piggott's company of volunteers, and that Captain Piggott was in actual service against the Indians on the Western frontier, and that his company was a part of the regiment of General George Rogers Clarke.

The committee report against the prayer of the petitioner.

----

### June 9, 1838.

The Committee on Revolutionary Claims, to which was referred the memorial of Catharine Telfair, daughter of Captain Isaiah Wool, of the New York line in the revolutionary war, praying bounty land, and other remuneration claimed to be due the said Catharine Telfair, on the ground of services of her said father in that war, report:

That the subject of this memorial has been examined by the committee, and they have come to the same conclusions as the former committee in reference to this case; and that, therefore, the prayer of the memorialist should not be granted.

The committee subjoin the report of the former committee, which is in these words:

### February 2, 1837.

The Committee on Revolutionary Claims, to which the petition of Catharine Telfair was referred, report:

The petitioner, daughter of Captain Isaiah Wool, of Colonel Lamb's corps of artillery in the revolutionary war, prays to be allowed bounty land, and other remuneration to which she considers herself and the other legal heirs of Captain Wool entitled, on account of her father's revolutionary services. It appears, by a letter from the Third Auditor, that the revolutionary records on file in his office show that Captain Wool was in service as early as 1776; and it further appears, from an original muster-roll of his company on file in the Pension office, which was sworn to on the 2d day of September, 1780, before Brigadier General Knox, of the artillery, that Captain Isaiah Wool *resigned* on the 21st day of August, 1780. His resignation at that time deprived him of any claim to bounty land, or to half pay for life, promised by the resolution of October 21, 1780, or the commutation thereof. The committee are therefore of opinion that the prayer of the petitioner ought not to be granted.

---

### June 13, 1838.

The Committee on Revolutionary Claims, to which was referred the bill for the relief of the heirs of Captain Robert Bealle, deceased, report:

That there were two Captains Robert Bealle in the Virginia line of the continental army—one of whom has received his five years' full pay. From the letter of the Third Auditor, of the 15th of February, 1838, and which is appended to this report, it appears that Captain Robert Bealle, last of "the 7th Virginia regiment, was mustered as having resigned on the 31st of December, 1780." This information was obtained by the committee after the first report was made in this case. This evidence is deemed conclusive by the committee.

*Resolved, therefore,* That said bill ought not to pass.

---

TREASURY DEPARTMENT,
*Third Auditor's Office, February* 15, 1838.

SIR : It appearing from the report which accompanied the bill reported by you on the 17th ultimo, "for the relief of the heirs and legal representatives of Captain Robert Bealle, deceased," that said Captain Bealle's last services were rendered in the 7th Virginia regiment, I deem it my duty to inform you that, on examining the rolls of that regiment, to-day, for information in relation to another officer's services, I discovered, accidentally, that Captain Robert Bealle, of that regiment, was mustered as having resigned on the 31st of December, 1780.

With great respect,
PETER HAGNER, *Auditor.*

Hon. ALEX. HARPER, *House of Reps.*

---

### June 27, 1838.

The Committee on Revolutionary Claims, to which was referred the petition of the heirs of Tristram Coffin, report:

That this claim has been before Congress for many years, and has been reported upon several times—in some instances favorably, in others unfavorably. It has been considered as a question of allowance for depreciation of continental paper, and on that ground has been rejected by committees. As this committee have adopted the rule that it is inexpedient to allow claims for depreciation, they report unfavorably on that point; but, in addition to that consideration, they are of opinion that the evidence adduced is insufficient to support the original claim.

The committee are of opinion the claim should not be allowed.

JUNE 27, 1838.

The Committee on Revolutionary Claims, to whom was referred a resolution instructing them to inquire into the expediency of allowing the claim of the heirs of Henry King, deceased, for services rendered, and money expended as assistant commissary of issues during the revolutionary war, report:

That there is an account against the United States in favor of Henry King, assistant commissary of issues, among the papers referred to them, in which said King charges, in substance, as follows:

| | £ | s. | d. |
|---|---|---|---|
| To my pay as quartermaster's sergeant in the 3d Maryland regiment, from the 30th of May to the 20th of October, 1778, at $10 per month - - - - - | 17 | 10 | 0 |
| To my pay as commissary's clerk at Fishkill landing, from the 21st of October to the 31st of December, 1778, at $35 per month - - - - - - | 30 | 12 | 6 |
| To one retained ration same time, at $10 - - - | 8 | 15 | 0 |
| To my pay as commissary's clerk at Fishkill landing, from the 1st of January, 1779, to the 19th of April, 1780, at $50 per month - - - - - - | 293 | 15 | 0 |
| To my pay as assistant commissary of issues in the Southern army, from the 10th of May, 1780, to the 10th of September, 1781, at $75 per month - - - | 511 | 17 | 6 |
| To one retained ration same time, at $10 per month - | 60 | 0 | 0 |

The item carried out originally at £450 has been changed to £511 17s. 6d., by charging at the rate of $90 per month for 6 months and 20 days of the time, and at the rate of $75 per month for the residue, and including another item for one retained ration, amounting to £33 15s.

On the credit side of the account, the United States are credited with £180 18s. 8½d., of which £162 18s. 6½d. are entered thus: "By the State of Maryland, as per account."

It appears that Henry King, as far back as 1794, petitioned Congress to pay the account from which the foregoing extracts are made; and mentioned other claims to which he said he was entitled, but for which no specific account was exhibited. The petition states that he served in the capacities and for the times charged in the account; but there is no evidence of the fact, except his own statement; and no evidence of the length of his service has yet been filed. In 1794 the claim was rejected upon the ground that such claims were barred by lapse of time. It does not appear why the claim had not been settled before it was thus barred. The claim has been presented to Congress, from time to time, since 1794; but at no time has the committee been able to perceive that any evidence of the length of the services of Henry King, either as commissary's clerk or assistant commissary, was furnished, except the statement made in the foregoing account. The committee cannot admit the principle, that an account presented against the Government, at this late period, for revolutionary services, should be proof of its own correctness. There is, therefore, no evidence before them on which they can report a bill in favor of the petitioners.

The Committee on Revolutionary Claims, to whom was referred the petition of Rebecca Stoddert, and others, children of the late Benjamin Stoddert, have had the same under consideration, and report:

That the petitioners claim four hundred and eighty-two dollars, which they allege was due to their father, Benjamin Stoddert, on account of the depreciation of his pay while he was in the service of the United States, as a captain of the continental army; and, also, the further sum of eight hundred and ninety-two dollars, a balance they allege to have been due to him, and never paid, on account of his salary as Secretary to the Board of War.

The foundation of the claim seems to be two letters written by the said Benjamin Stoddert, each addressed to the President of Congress. The first of these bears date 6th February, 1781, and sets up a claim against the Congress on account of the depreciation of his pay while a captain in the continental line. Enclosed in a copy of this letter, it is represented, was an account (found after his death) setting out the monthly depreciation of his pay, from September, 1777, to the 19th of April, 1779, and presenting a balance in his favor of $482. The other letter bears date March, 1781, and in this he claims $892 (specie) on account of his salary as Secretary to the Board of War, a resignation of which office was tendered by the letter first mentioned, and was accepted by Congress.

The committee find among the papers filed in the case a certificate in the following words, viz:

"LAND OFFICE,
"*Annapolis, January* 16, 1834.

" I certify that it appears by a depreciation pay-roll remaining in my office, that Benjamin Stoddert, a captain (Hartley's regiment) of the Maryland line, received £306 6s. 2d. depreciation money, issued to the Maryland quota of troops on continental establishment, on the 11th day of June, 1783.

"GEORGE G. BREWER,
"*Register Land Office, W. S. Md.*"

This certificate, the committee believe, fully shows an extinguishment of the claim for depreciation pay; and they believe the other branch of the claim has also been satisfied, for this reason: A certified copy of Benjamin Stoddert's account, as Secretary to the Board of War, obtained from the Register of the United States, shows that, on the 14th day of March, 1781, a warrant was drawn, by order of Congress, in favor of said Stoddert, on Thomas Smith, loan officer of the State of Pennsylvania, for eight hundred and seventy dollars. It is true this is not the precise sum Stoddert claimed in his letter, ($892,) but it is altogether probable that $870 was the true sum that was due to Mr. Stoddert, and that the warrant above mentioned was for the balance of his salary as Secretary to the Board of War. The proximity of the date of his application to Congress for this balance, and the date of the warrant, makes it all but a certainty. The committee, therefore, recommend the adoption of the following resolution:

*Resolved,* That the prayer of the petitioners be rejected.

The Committee on Revolutionary Claims, to whom was recommitted the petition of Theodore Middleton, together with the bill and other papers connected with it, have had the same under their consideration, and report:

That, having obtained further information in relation to the case, it is now their decided opinion that their first report was erroneous.

When the first report was made, the committee were under the belief that the extra regiment of Maryland, to which the petitioner was attached, constituted a part of the *quota* of the continental troops of that State. They have ascertained this opinion to have been founded in mistake. The extra regiment, aforesaid, was not of this description of troops, and, consequently, its officers cannot have been entitled to commutation.

The regiment aforesaid was raised by authority of the twelfth section of an act of the Legislature of Maryland, passed at the June session, 1780; and which act expressly directed the Executive of that State to commission its officers. (See 1st vol. Kilty's Revisal of the Laws of Maryland, chap. 10th.) The single fact that this regiment was commissioned by the State Executive is conclusive to show that it was not raised as a part of the continental line; for, as early as 1776, a resolution was adopted by the Congress that all commissions to the officers of the continental line of the army should emanate from Congress; and the subsequent practice of the Government was in strict conformity to this direction thus given, as far as the committee are informed. But, if any doubt could have existed as to the character of the troops directed to be raised by the aforesaid section of the act of the June session, 1780, that doubt was dispelled by a subsequent act of the Legislature of Maryland, passed 27th January, 1781. This latter act directed the non-commissioned officers and privates of the regiment extraordinary to be draughted into the battalions of the quota of that State; and that the commissioned officers should be recalled, with the exception of Colonel Alexander Lawson Smith, whom the Governor and Council were requested to recommend to the Board of War for the commission of a colonel in the continental line. (A copy of this last-mentioned act is filed in the case.)

The committee have reversed their first decision, and recommend the adoption of the following resolution:

*Resolved*, That the prayer of the petitioner be rejected.

----

The Committee on Revolutionary Claims, to which was referred the petition of the legal representatives of Captain Amasa Soper, deceased, report:

That Amasa Soper was a captain in Col. Marshall's regiment, in the Massachusetts line of the revolutionary army, from January 1, 1777, to October 30, 1780, at which time the records of the Third Auditor's department represent him as having resigned. The claimants represent that the remark on the roll should have been "relieved," not "resigned;" and in support of this, adduce a letter written by the Hon. Stephen Bradley to the Committee of Claims, in 1810, as follows:

WASHINGTON, *March* 27, 1810.

SIR : It is with reluctance I find myself obliged, at this distance of time, when I fear my recollection may, in some degree, be imperfect, to state certain facts in relation to the petition of Captain Soper, now pending before the Committee of Claims; the information, however, shall be as correct as it is in my power to make it.

I was not personally acquainted with Captain Soper in the revolutionary army ; but some time about the close of the war, Captain Soper moved with his family, consisting of a wife and several small children, into Vermont, and into the vicinity of the place in which I live, where he has resided ever since ; and I recollect, from that period to the commencement of the present constitution, to have heard him frequently speak of the commutation of half pay due to him from the United States. Some time in the fore part of the year 1791, (to the best of my recollection,) he called at my office with one David Quinton. for the purpose of giving the said Quinton a power of attorney to go to Philadelphia and obtain his commutation of half pay from the Secretary of War, or any other officer authorized to pay the same. On delivering the power of attorney, Captain Soper delivered to the said Quinton his commission, together with sundry other papers, among which was a permission from General Washington to Captain Soper to *retire* from the army, which I think was dated some time about the 1st of November, 1780. I cannot say positively that it was endorsed on the back of the commission, but am inclined to think it was; nor do I recollect the particular phraseology of the permission, or that it referred to any resolution of Congress, although that might have been the case. Said Quinton shortly after set out on his journey for Philadelphia, and in a few weeks information arrived that he had taken the smallpox and was dead. His family then lived within two or three miles of me, and I have no doubt the information of his having died with the smallpox was perfectly correct. I know that Captain Soper took great pains afterwards to obtain his commission and papers which he had delivered to the said Quinton, though I believe without effect. I remember, at his request, to have made inquiry at the War office, to find if the papers had not been left there, but could obtain no information respecting them. Some time, I think, in the latter part of the year 1793, I submitted his case to General Knox, then Secretary of War, with a power of attorney from Captain Soper to obtain for him his commutation of half pay; after examining into his case, General Knox informed me that unless he could find his commission, and General Washington's permission to retire from the army, he could not obtain the commutation of half pay, as he was not returned among the officers entitled to it. While Captain Soper was thus endeavoring to regain his papers, the act of limitation of February, 1793, ran against his claim.

I can further certify that Captain Soper has been, ever since my acquaintance with him, a hard-laboring, industrious, and good citizen, and is now very much reduced in point of property, and extremely embarrassed to get even the necessaries of life, which have very much increased of late by the death of his two sons, on whom he principally depended, and who have left several small children.

I have always understood by the officers of the army, and by other means, that Captain Soper was a brave, enterprising, and meritorious officer ; and it would give me pleasure to see him remunerated, if it can be done consistently with the known and established rules of Government.

I have the honor to be, very respectfully, sir, your obedient servant,

STEPHEN R. BRADLEY.

Hon. RICHARD M. JOHNSON,
*Chairman of the Committee of Claims.*

By a letter written to General Washington by Captain Soper, October 30, 1780, which has been recently found among the papers in the office of the Secretary of State, it appears to have been his intention to resign, as the subjoined extract shows:

[I] "therefore most humbly request your excellency to accept my resignation, and grant me a dismission from the army."

Under these circumstances, the whole record evidence in existence showing that he intended to resign, and actully did so, it is the opinion of the committee that the claim ought not to be allowed.

---

JUNE 27, 1838.

The Committee on Revolutionary Claims, to whom was referred the petition of the heirs of Morgan Alexander, have had the same under consideration, and report:

That the petitioners allege that their ancestor, Morgan Alexander, was, on account of his services as an officer in the war of the Revolution, entitled to *commutation or half pay* at the time of his death, which, they say, has never been paid ; and pray that an act may be passed, allowing them the commutation to which said Morgan Alexander was entitled.

The case is in substance as follows:

A letter from the Third Auditor shows that Morgan Alexander was a captain in the second Virginia regiment, very early in the war, and was charged with public money, and for which he was subsequently allowed a credit, as for money which had been received by him on account of the pay of his company.

An affidavit of George Blackman represents that he (Blackman) enlisted in the company commanded by Captain Morgan Alexander, on the 1st of January, 1777 ; and that the said company was marched, by said Alexander, to General Washington's army, then lying at Bound Brook, in the State of New Jersey, at which time and place he (Alexander) was promoted—but to what rank promoted, or to what corps he was attached, the affiant does not know ; his promotion having separated them. Marquis Calmis, afterwards a general, was commissioned captain to fill the vacancy in that grade occasioned by the promotion of Alexander. This affiant never heard that Alexander resigned. Marquis Calmis, of Woodford county, State of Kentucky, in his affidavit, states that Morgan Alexander was a captain in the second Virginia regiment, at that time commanded (as he believes) by Colonel Woodford ; and that he himself was a lieutenant in Captain Alexander's company. This affiant further states it as his belief that the said Alexander was commissioned a captain by a committee in the town of Winchester, in the month of September or October 1775; that he was afterwards promoted—but to what grade promoted, or to what corps attached, he does not know, but remembers to have seen him still in the service in October or November, 1777, shortly after the capture of Burgoyne's army: and that he (Alexander) informed him " that his health was so bad that he would have to go home, as he could not stand the cold climate, (being at Whitemarsh camp, above Germantown.")

John Smith, late of the county of Frederick, State of Virginia, states in his affidavit that he was a member of the committee for the said county of Frederick, in 1775, and that at his instance Morgan Alexander was recommended as a fit person to bear a captain's commission in one of the regiments, commanded, the one by Patrick Henry, the other by William Woodford; and that he was accordingly commissioned, and proceeded immediately to recruit his company; that he saw the company afterwards in Williamsburg, Virginia, and knows that it was stationed for some time afterwards at York.   The affiant further states that, in the year 1777, the said Alexander was promoted to the post of colonel.   During this year (1777) the affiant was a member of the Virginia Legislature, and the troops at Williamsburg passed in review before its members, and fired a *feu de joie* on account of Burgoyne's surrender ; Colonel Morgan Alexander was present on the occasion.   At the time of the battle of Monmouth (August, 1778) the affiant is sure Morgan Alexander was a colonel in the continental line.   The affiant further states that he distinctly recollects that Colonel Morgan Alexander was sent to suppress a collection of tories on the Eastern shore, (as near as he can recollect,) and for the manner in which he executed the undertaking received many high compliments. This expedition happened late in the war.

The affiant also states, that while he was a member of Congress, the representatives of Colonel Alexander requested his attention to this claim, which had been previously presented to Congress ; that he applied for information in regard to it at the proper department, and was told that the papers had been destroyed by the British in the last war.

It was never asserted, to the knowledge of the affiant, nor does he believe, that Colonel Alexander was ever in the militia service after the commencement of the Revolution.   He is confident that the commissions borne by him were commissions in the continental service, and not in the militia ; and that he never did resign to the best of his knowledge and belief, but continued in commission until some time in 1783, (precise period not recollected,) at which time he died still in commission, as he verily believes.

J. S. Davison states in his affidavit that on sundry occasions he had been applied to, as a justice of the peace in the county of Frederick, Virginia, to take the evidence of General John Smith, of said county, to prove the services of Morgan Alexander in the Revolution, and that he had written several affidavits for this purpose ; that on the occasion of making oath to the last one, the said General John Smith, when detailing the matters therein mentioned, made the following statement, (as near as the affiant can remember,) in substance : " That a portion of the officers of the continental army were sent home after the siege of York, and were permitted to remain there, subject, however, to an immediate call into service, and were, in consequence, denominated minute-men ; that Colonel Alexander, he believed, was of this number, and remained in this situation, attached to the army, as stated in former affidavits, until his death, some time during the year 1783 ;" that the foregoing lines, which are within quotations, contain substantially the communication made by the said General John Smith to the said J. S. Davison ; that they were omitted in the affidavit then written, under the supposition that they were entirely immaterial. The said J. S. Davison further states that, shortly after taking the deposition referred to above, General John Smith being far advanced in years, became indisposed, and his mind began gradually to sink away, and that at present (8th March, 1836) his memory is a perfect wreck.

It appears from the affidavit of Agnes Ross, of Loudoun county, Virginia, and the certificate of Lucy Balmain, of Frederick county, same State, that Morgan Alexander died (most probably) in the fall of the year 1783.

The foregoing details, in the opinion of the committee, present the case in its true aspect ; and while it is by no means clear that Morgan Alexander was not entitled to commutation, the evidence now adduced does not warrant a report in favor of the claim.

*Resolved,* That the prayer of the petitioner be rejected.

---

### June 27, 1838.

The Committee on Revolutionary Claims, to whom was referred the petition of the heirs of William Brinkley, report :

That the petitioners claim that commutation pay was due by the United States to William Brinkley, for his services as a captain in the North Carolina line of the army on continental establishment, in the war of the Revolution.

The evidence in this case shows that William Brinkley was a captain in the 3d regiment in the North Carolina line of the army ; but as there is no evidence of a satisfactory nature to show that the service of William Brinkley was such as to entitle him to commutation pay, the committee decide that the claim of the petitioners ought not to be allowed.

---

### June 27, 1838.

Mr. Shields, from the Committee on the Public Lands, laid before the House the following :

GENERAL LAND OFFICE, *April* 17, 1838.

Sir : The resolution of the House of Representatives, covered by your letter of the 12th instant, and which is in the following words, viz :

" *Resolved,* That the Committee on the Public Lands, who are already instructed to inquire into the expediency of granting certain appropriations of said lands to officers and soldiers of the Virginia State line in the revolutionary war, be, and they are hereby, also instructed to inquire into

the expediency of extending such appropriation to all other American officers, soldiers, seamen, and marines of that war, so as to equalize the bounty of each; and if any reason for discriminating in favor of the officers and soldiers of the Virginia line exist, that the same be reported to this House."—
is herewith returned, and in answer to your request, I have the honor to state that no legislation is required for satisfying warrants granted by the United States to the officers and soldiers who served in the continental army, which was composed of the several lines of the respective States, and which warrants, as soon as presented, are satisfied by the issue of scrip.

The quantity of land allowed as a bounty by the United States to the officers and soldiers of the continental army, provided they had served during the war, was as follows, viz:

| | |
|---|---|
| To a major general | 1,100 acres. |
| brigadier general | 850 do. |
| colonel | 500 do. |
| lieutenant colonel | 450 do. |
| major | 400 do. |
| surgeon | 400 do. |
| surgeon's mate | 300 do. |
| captain | 300 do. |
| lieutenant | 200 do. |
| ensign | 150 do |
| non-commissioned officer or private | 100 do. |

No bounty in land was allowed to officers, seamen, or marines of the United States navy.

The State of Virginia furnished to the continental army sixteen regiments, and for her own defence had in employ three regiments of State troops, besides a State navy. She also directed the enlistment of two regiments, to be commanded by General G. R. Clarke, for the special purpose of breaking up the posts of Vincennes and Kaskaskias; to all of whom a large bounty in land was awarded by acts of Assembly of 1779.

The quantity of land allowed under the laws was as follows, viz:

| | |
|---|---|
| To a major general, for six years' service | 15,000 acres. |
| brigadier general | 10,000 do. |
| colonel | 6,666⅔ do. |
| lieutenant colonel | 6,000 do. |
| chaplain | 6,000 do. |
| paymaster | 6,666⅔ do. |
| surgeon | 6,000 do. |
| surgeon's mate | 4,000 do. |
| major | 5,333⅓ do. |
| captain | 4,000 do. |
| lieutenant | 2,666⅔ do. |
| ensign | 2,666⅔ do. |
| sergeant | 400 do. |
| private | 200 do. |

If any officer served but *three* years, he received, notwithstanding, the same quantity of land, except the non-commissioned officers and privates, who received only one-half of the quantity allowed for six years.

The officers in her State navy received a still larger bounty in land, and, by what has come under my own observation, additional bounty in land has been allowed to almost every officer on the continental establishment.

The suggestion to equalize the bounty in land between the Virginia and the United States troops, would, in my opinion, if favorably entertained by Congress, require at least 30,000,000 acres of public lands, the Virginia claims alone having taken about 10,000,000 acres.

The appropriations made since 1830 for Virginia warrants was an act of liberality on the part of Congress, and not of absolute justice. The first appropriation by the act of 30th of May, 1830, was principally for the benefit of the Virginia *State* line, but in the subsequent acts no discrimination was made between the Continental and State lines, although the land reserved by Virginia between the Little Miami and Scioto, in Ohio, for the express purpose of satisfying the continental-line warrants, is not yet exhausted.

The great disparity in the quantity of land granted by Virginia and the United States to their respective officers, arose, no doubt, from the fact that the United States (in 1776, when Congress adopted the resolution promising a bounty in land) had, in fact, no territory out of which the promise could be redeemed. Virginia, on the contrary, claimed all the territory which now composes the States of Ohio, Indiana, Kentucky, and Illinois, and having such a large tract of waste land at disposal, induced her to hold out the prospect of so large a bounty to all who would enter her service.

I am, sir, with great respect, your obedient servant,

JAS. WHITCOMB,
*Commissioner.*

Hon. E. J. Shields,
*House of Representatives.*

---

July 2, 1838.

The Committee on Revolutionary Claims, to which was referred the petition of Philip Crapo, executor, &c. of Samuel Aborn, deceased, report:

That Samuel Aborn was a commissary at Pawtuxet, in the State of Rhode Island, during the revolutionary war, and, under the direction and at the request of the State of Rhode Island, rendered services and furnished supplies to the troops, from the 7th of December, 1776, to the 7th of February, 1777; that, at the time the said services were rendered and supplies furnished, they were, by the testator of the claimant, charged to the State of Rhode Island. On the 6th of September, 1790, George Olney, a commissioner appointed by the said State, settled the account of Colonel Samuel Aborn, and found a balance due to him, on the 1st of January, 1782, of four hundred and forty-one pounds twelve shillings and three pence. The whole account, including subsistence, supplies, and pay, amounted to one thousand and forty-five pounds and ten shillings, and closed on the 7th April, 1783. The various payments made by Rhode Island, on account, amounted to six hundred and three pounds seventeen shillings and nine pence; leaving the balance due, as above stated. On the 30th of June, 1791, the Lower House of Assembly resolved " that the above report be received, and that the sum of four hundred and forty-one pounds twelve shillings and three pence be paid the said Samuel Aborn out of the general treasury, in discharge of the above account." This vote was, in June, 1791, read in the Upper House of the Legislature of that State, who told Colonel Aborn "that they did not wish to put a non-concurrence on his account, nor could they concur with the Lower House; for that the time limited by Congress for the separate States to make any charge against the Union having expired, the State must pay out of its own treasury what ought to be paid by the Union," as appears by the certificate of Henry Ward, secretary. On this action of the Legislature of Rhode Island, Samuel Aborn, in January, 1794, preferred a petition to Congress for the allowance of his claim, which was referred to the Secretary of the Treasury, who, in 1795, returned the claims referred to him, including this one, with a report; when the petition, &c. were referred to the Committee of Claims, which, on the 2d March, 1796, reported unfavorable to the claim of the petitioner, Samuel Aborn; that no further proceedings were had during the lifetime of Samuel Aborn, who died in 1801. The committee can see no good reason why they should not adopt the report made in 1796, adverse to this claim. Certainly, the acquiescence of the petitioner's testator, in his lifetime, in the report, and the delay on the part of his legal representatives to re-present it for thirty-eight years, cannot add to its validity. The committee, therefore, report against the prayer of the petitioner.

---

JULY 2, 1838.

The Committee on Revolutionary Claims, to whom was referred the petition of Ann Levacher de Van Brun, report:

The petitioner states that she is the widow of John Levacher de Van Brun, of the Maryland line of the army of the United States; that he entered the service on the 10th of March, 1777; that on the 11th of June, 1782, he obtained a furlough from Congress; that he sailed for Europe on the 4th of August of that year, there to settle private business, intending to return after a short absence; that the ship in which he sailed and all on board were lost at sea.

G. G. Brewer, of the Maryland land office, under date of the 30th November, 1836, certifies that Lavacher de Van Brun was a lieutenant of the Maryland line on continental establishment; and that on the 7th June, 1781, he received an amount therein stated, depreciated money, issued to the Maryland quota of troops, as appears by the rolls of his office.

A certificate of the same officer, dated August 12, 1836, shows that Levacher de Van Brun's accounts on the army legers stand stated up to July, 1782; and that he received bounty land from Maryland for his revolutionary services.

The same officer, in a certificate dated 25th August, 1836, states that a paper on his files is endorsed in these words: "Arrangements of the five Maryland regiments, 1st January, 1783, with the promotions up to that period;" together with the further entry, " *Lieutenant* Levacher de Van Brun, *ensign* 10th March, 1777; date of *promotion* not known; gone to France."

The printed journals of the old Congress record the fact, that on the 11th June, 1782, that body granted Levacher a furlough to go to France. The committee report a bill.

---

The Committee on Revolutionary Claims, to which were referred sundry petitions praying Congress to make compensation to the survivors and to the descendants of those who were slain in the massacre of Wyoming for losses sustained, report:

That the claim of the petitioners is not based upon any resolution or act of the Congress of the Revolution, upon which any allowance or compensation can be made the sufferers or their descendants on the principle of discharging a contract. The application, therefore, rests upon the propriety of granting a gratuity under the peculiar circumstances of the case. The hardships and privations endured by the settlers in the Wyoming valley, and the devastations and murders perpetrated by their savage enemy, are well authenticated by history, and forcibly and feelingly presented in the document advocating the claims of the petitioners. It is therein shown that, in all probability, Connecticut would have made a suitable provision in behalf of the sufferers and their descendants, had that State retained jurisdiction over the country. The fact that the people of Wyoming were excluded, in consequence of the jurisdiction and claim of Pennsylvania, from the benefits of the legislation of Connecticut, which relieved other portions of her citizens who suffered during the Revolution, upon principles equally applicable to the Wyoming settlers, is not sufficient to give them a valid claim against the United States. We must test the validity of the claim independent of that circumstance. When that is done, it presents the single question whether the Government of the United States ought, at this day, to make provision for compensating the losses sustained by the inroads, devastations, and murders of a savage enemy during the Revolution. If it be proper to make such provision, the committee cannot perceive any sufficient reason for discriminating in favor of the Wyoming sufferers, so as to grant indemnity and relief to them, and withhold it from others. Why may not the families whose husbands and fathers were defeated and slain in the battle of the Bluelicks claim compensation? They marched to meet a savage enemy, to repel an invasion, to defend their firesides, and were slain. Why may not all those whose houses were burnt by savages, and whose childred, in the absence of their fathers, were often murdered, or carried off into captivity, during the Indian wars which prevailed at the period of the early settlements in Kentucky and Tennessee claim compensation, if the Government allows it in behalf of the Wyoming petitioners? The committee perceive no sufficient reason to discriminate, and are of opinion that all or none should be provided for. Ought any to be provided for? We think not. The principle upon which Governments are charged for damages done by a public enemy requires that the loss should be the consequence of the action of the Government. If (for illustration) the Government occupies the houses of the citizen for military purposes, and thereby induces the enemy to destroy them in order to dislodge or defeat an army, the suffering citizen my justly claim compensation. But where the enemy wantonly burns a city or town, or pillages a farm, or murders the head of a family, there is no just foundation to claim compensation. If the Government should acknowledge its responsibility in such cases, the consequences might be destructive to the patriotism of the country. The rule would tend to influence the citizen to abandon his property instead of defending it, and set up a claim against the Government for its loss, instead of protecting it by manly defence. The prayer of the petitioners for compensation on account of the burning of Charlestown, Massachusetts, during the Revolution, was rejected by the Committee on Revolutionary Claims of the 24th Congress, and we refer to the report in that case for principles applicable to this.

The committee are of opinion that the prayer of the petitioners ought not to be granted.

------

DECEMBER 22, 1837.

The Committee on Revolutionary Claims, to which the petition of the legal representatives of Doctor William Johonnot, deceased, was referred, report :

That this case was examined by the Committee on Revolutionary Claims at the first session of the twenty-third Congress, and a favorable report made thereon, accompanied by a bill for the relief of the petitioners. The Committee on Revolutionary Claims at the first session of the last Congress also had the claim under consideration, and reported favorably, by adopting the report of the preceding committee.

The committee at this session have again examined this case, and concur in the report made in January, 1834, which is referred to, and made part of this report ; and a bill is reported accordingly.

JANUARY 24, 1834.

The Committee on Revolutionary Claims, to which was referred the memorial of the heirs and representatives of Doctor William Johonnot, late of Boston, deceased, report :

The memorialists state that Doctor William Johonnot entered the service in the medical and hospital department in the earliest period of the revolutionary war ; and that, under the regulations of the 7th of April, 1777, he became chief apothecary of the hospitals in the eastern district ; (that he held this appointment, is proved by accounts accompanying the memorial ;) he continued in this highly responsible office till the 30th of September, 1780, when Congress, by the act of that day, placed the hospital and medical department under a new and different organization. By this latter arrangement, instead of a chief apothecary, with assistants in each district, it was provided that there should be *one* apothecary general, and *one* assistant apothecary general, for the whole hospital and medical department north of the Potomac river. It appears by the journals of Congress, to which the committee have referred, that Doctor William Johonnot was, on the 7th October, 1780, elected by ballot, by Congress, assistant apothecary general, under the regulations of the 30th of

September preceding. These same regulations also provided for the appointment of a purveyor general, and *one* assistant purveyor general. On the same day, it appears, from the journals of Congress, that Doctor Isaac Ledyard, who had been an officer of the hospital department under the old regulations, was elected by Congress assistant purveyor general.

Military operations having mostly ceased after the surrender of Lord Cornwallis, and the army being much reduced, and that portion which remained being either in garrison or inactive in the field, the extensive medical and hospital establishment which an active state of war had required became unnecessary.

Congress, therefore, on the 23d day of July, 1782, greatly reduced the hospital establishment; and, among other reductions, abolished the offices of assistant apothecary and assistant purveyor; and Doctor Johonnot and Doctor Ledyard retired, as they no doubt supposed, on half pay for life, as deranged officers. It is alleged that just at the close of the war, and as the final settlements were about to commence, Doctor Johonnot and his wife both died, and that no administration was taken out on his estate.

It will be seen in the proceedings in Doctor Ledyard's case, that when he applied for his "commutation" for half pay for life as assistant purveyor, it was refused him on the ground that the resolutions of Congress granting half pay to the officers of the hospital department made no mention of assistant purveyor or of assistant apothecary; the resolution merely mentioning "purveyor" and "apothecary," without any designation of *chief* or *assistant*. It can hardly be presumed that Congress, without specifying chief or assistant, meant to include or exclude one and not the other, of officers of so high a grade, and so few in number; and especially, as in the same resolution, which proceeded in the enumeration from a higher to a lower grade, officers of less pay and emolument followed in regular order after the general terms "apothecary and purveyor." Nor could it be presumed that either Congress, or these officers, who were then holding other offices entitling them to half pay for life, intended the relinquishment of it, by their appointment to places of higher pay, responsibility, and standing.

But a particular and able report was made in the case of Doctor Ledyard, to which the committee would refer, which was sanctioned by Congress, by the passage of a bill in favor of the heirs of Doctor Ledyard. And as the cases of Doctor Johonnot and Doctor Ledyard are alike in every feature, as to previous service, time of appointment, and time of derangement, and the amount of monthly pay, and, of course, standing in all essential respects on the same foundation, the committee conclude that a due regard to the merits of the case, as well as uniformity of decision, require that like relief should be granted.

As it regards that portion of the memorial which relates to a balance in favor of Doctor Johonnot, the committee find that a balance of $307 63 does stand to the credit of William Johonnot, on the books of the Third Auditor of the Treasury, but are not yet satisfied that this balance is actually due. The committee, therefore, report a bill for commutation only.

# 501

## December 22, 1837.

The Committee on Revolutionary Claims, to which was referred the petition of Apollos Cooper, report:

The heirs of Apollos Cooper petition Congress for such half pay, &c. as they are entitled to in consequence of their ancestor having been killed in the battle of Brandywine It appears that said Cooper was killed on the 11th of September, 1777, and that he was then a lieutenant in the Virginia continental line ; this satisfactorily appears from the letter of the Third Auditor. The affidavit of a witness proves that said Cooper was killed in the battle of Brandywine. It satisfactorily appears that said Cooper left a widow and three children ; the widow is dead, and one of the children. The committee are of opinion that the widow and children of said Cooper are entitled, under the resolution of Congress of the 24th day of August, 1780, to seven years' half pay, and they herewith report a bill authorizing its payment.

## December 22, 1837.

The Committee on Revolutionary Claims, who were instructed by a resolution of the House "to inquire into the expediency of issuing a duplicate military land warrant, heretofore issued to Crawford Johnston, a soldier of the Revolution, which has been lost," have had that subject under consideration, and report :

That, by a letter of Ethan A. Brown, Esq., late Commissioner of the General Land Office, under date the 26th of March, 1836, it appears a warrant, No. 1284, for one hundred acres of land, issued on the 2d of April, 1828, to Crawford Johnston, and that the same had not been presented at the General Land Office for the purpose of being satisfied.

By another letter, from D. Turner, Esq., late a member of the House of Representatives from the State of North Carolina, to the Hon. Mr. Hawkins of the present House of Representarives, it appears that he (Mr. Turner) had had in his possession a military land warrant issued in the name of Crawford Johnston, for his services in the Revolution, which issued during the session of 1827-'28. It was kept in his possession, at the request of the party interested, until by some means it was lost or mislaid, so that he had despaired of recovering it.

In addition to the foregoing statement, the committee have been informed, by a letter from the present Commissioner of the General Land Office, under date December 20, 1837, that up to this time the land warrant aforesaid had not been presented for the purpose of being satisfied. Upon this state of facts, the committee are of opinion that a duplicate military land warrant of that of No. 1284 ought to be issued to Crawford Johnston ; and for this purpose report a bill.

## February 16, 1838.

The Committee on Revolutionary Claims, to whom was referred the petition and papers of the heirs of William Bayley, a major in the army of the Revolution, have had the same under consideration, and submit the following report:

It appears from the proofs and documents before the committee, that the said William Bayley was a major during the war of the Revolution, in Colonel Swoop's regiment, called the flying camp; that, on the 13th day of July, 1792, the proper accounting officers adjusted his account, and the sum found to be due was fully paid to him. Upon the settlement, he neither *claimed*, nor was he *allowed*, the *commutation* of five years' full pay in lieu of half pay for life, or any part thereof, because he did not belong to a class of officers to which either half pay for life, or commutation of five years' full pay, had *been promised* by the resolutions of Congress on that subject. The committee recommend for adoption the following resolution:

*Resolved,* That the prayer of the petitioners ought not to be granted.

---

MARCH 6, 1838.

The Committee on Revolutionary Claims, to whom were referred the petition and papers of the heirs of Lieutenant Colonel John Cropper, deceased, have had the same under consideration, and ask leave to submit the following report:

It appears that Colonel Cropper entered the service as a captain, was afterwards promoted to the rank of major, and on the 20th day of March, 1779, was commissioned lieutenant colonel of the seventh Virginia regiment. He continued in active service from the commencement of the revolutionary war till on or about the 1st of September, 1779, when he expressed a wish to resign his commission and return home, on account of the distressed situation of his family, the enemy having taken and destroyed most of his property in his absence. Congress was unwilling that he should resign, as he was a valuable officer, and he was first allowed a limited, and then an unlimited furlough, which would enable him to join and remain with his family, until his services in the field might again be required, when he would be called to join his regiment. He was never afterwards called on to join his regiment, but continued in his own part of the country, in active service much if not all of his time, till the close of the war, under a commission from the State of Virginia.

It does not appear to the committee that Colonel Cropper ever resigned his commission, unless by accepting and acting under a commission from the State should be considered a virtual resignation. If he had retired to his home on the 1st of September, 1779, or at any subsequent period, with an unlimited furlough, never been again called into actual service, and never rendered any service whatever to the country, he would have been clearly entitled to his commutation of five years' full pay. It would, therefore, appear strange that continuing in active service in his own neighborhood, should place him in a worse situation than he would have been had he remained entirely inactive.

The committee do not believe the commission from the State ought to be considered a resignation of that held under the authority of Congress. Had the one exacted duties inconsistent with those required by the other, the acceptance of the last conferred might be considered a virtual resignation of the other. But this does not appear to be the case; the individual was left as much at liberty to join his regiment, if required, as he would have been had he received no commission from the State, and while actually doing duty under the last, he was aiding to carry into effect the object to be effected by the first.

The committee are satisfied that Colonel Cropper, and the officers of the army, believed he continued to hold his commission as lieutenant colonel to the close of the war, and that he was entitled to five years' full pay in lieu of half pay for life.

The committee have in all cases refused to allow interest upon such claims as this, unless the claimant could show that the payment of the principal sum had been demanded, and all proofs furnished, and vouchers offered, which would be necessary to justify the accounting officers in making the payment.

In this case it appears, that on the 1st day of January, 1785, Colonel Cropper did apply for the payment of the principal sum, which the committee believe was due to him, and which ought then to have been paid, and which has been unjustly withheld. They, therefore, report a bill for the relief of the petitioners.

---

MARCH 6, 1838.

The Committee on Revolutionary Claims, to whom the petition and papers of William W. Williams were referred, have had the same under consideration, and submit the following report :

It appears from the documents filed with the petition, that William Williams, the father of the petitioner, on or about the first day of April, 1778, was duly appointed and commissioned a captain, in the corps of invalids, in the army of the Revolution, and that he continued in the service of the United States to the close of the war.

The committee do not find any reason to believe that Captain Williams, or any person representing him, has ever received his commutation of five years' full pay, or anything in lieu thereof; on the contrary, they find that, in the year 1787, he made his last will and testament, in which he bequeathed the same to his wife, who appears to have survived him, and to have married a Mr. Williamson after his death.

The only doubt raised in this case is, whether Captain Williams may not have been placed on the roll of invalids in the State of Pennsylvania, prior to the year 1789, as he made a donation of one month's pay as a member of the Cincinnati Society of that State. Any doubt raised from that circumstance, the committee believe must be removed by the consideration that Captain Williams was *not* an officer of the Pennsylvania line, but a citizen of North Carolina, known and recognised as one of her officers who served to the end of the war, and to whom, in consideration of his services, she gave the usual quantity of land allotted by her laws to officers of his grade.

The proof is satisfactory, that the petitioner is the only son and heir of Captain Williams, but as it is in proof that the sum of money now claimed was given by will to Mrs. Williams, the mother of the petitioner, the committee believe it ought to be paid to the *personal representatives* of Captain Williams, who will be bound to dispose of it to whoever may be the true owner ; and they herewith report a bill.

---

### March 22, 1838.

The Committee on Revolutionary Claims have had under consideration the resolution of the Senate instructing them "to inquire into the propriety of granting a pension or other compensation to the Viscompte L'Eaumont, a French officer, wounded at the siege of Savannah."

There has been no evidence presented to the committee that, in their opinion, would warrant them in recommending the grant of a pension or other compensation to the Viscompte L'Eaumont. It is probable that he was engaged as a French officer in our revolutionary struggle, and as such, is entitled to a portion of our national gratitude. But no case is made out entitling him to any pension or compensation, under any resolution or act of Congress, nor to the extraordinary interposition of Congress.

The committee, therefore, move to be discharged from the further consideration of the subject.

---

### March 23, 1838.

The Committee on Revolutionary Claims have had under consideration certain documents referred to them, relating to the claim of the heirs of John S. Stubbs, on account of the alleged services of their ancestor as a lieutenant in the army of the Revolution, and respectfully report :

That the testimony does not show that the decedent, supposing him to have been in service as a lieutenant, either *continued* in the service to the *end* of the revolutionary war, or *died* in that service ; and therefore, in the opinion of the committee, his representatives are neither entitled to commutation pay, nor to seven years' half pay. They recommend the adoption of the following resolution :

*Resolved,* That the claim be rejected.

---

### May 15, 1838.

The Committee on Revolutionary Claims have, according to the order of the Senate, had under consideration the petition of the heirs of General Jacob Bayley, praying compensation for his services, losses, and sacrifices during the revolutionary war ; and they respectfully report :

That the only testimony adduced in this case is the deposition of Moody Bedel, and certain papers purporting to be copies of letters written during the revolutionary war, to and from said Bayley. Admitting that this testimony was sufficient to show his rank in the militia; his services and his zeal, it utterly fails to establish any pecuniary claim against the United States.

The committee, therefore, respectfully submit the following resolution :

*Resolved,* That the petition be rejected.

### MAY 15, 1838.

The Committee on Revolutionary Claims have, according to the order of the Senate, had under consideration the petition of the heirs of James Caldwell, praying indemnity for losses sustained by their ancestor during the revolutionary war, and respectfully report:

That, from the petition and accompanying documents, it appears that James Caldwell, the ancestor of the petitioners, a citizen of the State of New Jersey, was, during the war of the Revolution, engaged in the service of the United States, first as a chaplain to a regiment of militia, and afterwards as a commissary of supplies.

The British troops, in one of their incursions into that State, took possession of a place called Connecticut Farms, where James Caldwell then resided, and there perpetrated one of those outrages which too often marked their warfare in that contest. The wife of Caldwell was shot by a British soldier as she sat in her house in the midst of her children, and the place was given up to plunder and conflagration. The house of Caldwell, among others, was burned up; and for this loss the petitioners now seek an indemnification from the Government.

If the misfortunes of their ancestor, or his merits as a man and a patriot, could entitle the petitioners to the relief prayed for, their claim would perhaps be unquestionable : but the committee do not feel themselves warranted in awarding a pecuniary compensation on such grounds. The circumstances of this case show that the loss complained of was occasioned by a lawless, incendiary act of the common enemy, contrary to the rules of civilized warfare. In such cases this Government is not considered as being under any *obligation* to indemnify the sufferers, and on that ground the committee would feel itself constrained to decide against the petitioners, without entering into considerations of the impolicy of opening a door, at this late day, to such a class of claims.

The committee, therefore, respectfully submit the following resolution :

*Resolved*, That the petition be rejected.

### MAY 15, 1838.

The Committee on Revolutionary Claims, according to the order of the Senate, have had under consideration the petition of Patience Babcock, the widow of Phineas Babcock, praying payment for property taken from her husband during the revolutionary war, for the use of the troops of the United States, and respectfully report:

That the evidence produced in support of the claim is parol, and in some material respects, vague and uncertain. For this cause, and other general reasons, applicable to all such ancient claims, and which are too familiar to require repetition, the committee are of opinion that the prayer of the petitioner ought not to be granted, and they therefore recommend the adoption of the following resolution:

*Resolved*, That the prayer of the petitioner be rejected.

*Acts of Congress for the relief of the following-named persons, or their heirs and legal representatives, passed during the second session of the twenty-fifth Congress.*

Adams, Nathan, Peter, and William, heirs of, authorizing the issue of
   three duplicate land warrants, - - - - - approved April 20, 1838.
Ashe, John B., representatives of, allowed commutation, - - do. May 25, do.
Boyles, Thomas H., representatives of, allowed seven years' half pay, do. July 7, do.
Bunting, William B., representatives of, allowed seven years' half pay, do. July 7, do.
Campbell, Richard, representatives of, allowed seven years' half pay, do. July 7, do.
Carter, Thomas, Dr., heirs of, allowed additional half pay, - - do. May 25, do.
Chilton, John, heirs of, allowed seven years' half pay, - - do. July 7, do.
Cogswell, William, heirs of, allowed commutation, - - - do. June 12, do.
Duval, Daniel, representatives of, allowed commutation, - - do. June 13, do.
Fanning, Joshua, heirs of, allowed seven years' half pay, - - do. July 7, do.
Feely, Timothy, representatives of, allowed commutation, - - do. July 7, do.
Helphenstine, Peter, heirs of, allowed seven years' half pay, - do. June 12, do.
Irwin, Henry, heirs of, allowed seven years' half pay, - - do. July 7, do.
Johnson, Crawford, authorizing the issue of a duplicate land warrant, do. July 7, do.
Johonnot, William, representatives of, allowed commutation, - do. July 7, do.
McClelland, John, representatives of, allowed seven years' half pay, - do. July 7, do.
McGibboney, Patrick, representatives of, allowed commutation, - do. June 13, do.
Morfit, Henry, representatives of, allowed commutation, - - do. June 12, do.
Prescott, Joseph, allowed commutation, - - - - do. July 7, do.
Quarles, Wharton, administrator of, allowed the balance on a judg-
   ment obtained for half pay, - - - - - do. July 7, do.
Russwurm, William, heirs of, allowed commutation, - - do. June 12, do.
Smith, William Hooker, representatives of, allowed commutation, - do. July 7, do.
Snead, Charles, representatives of, allowed commutation, - - do. July 7, do.
Spitfathom, John, allowed commutation, - - - - do. June 12, do.
Van Campen, Moses, allowed commutation, - - - do. June 12, do.
Warren, Samuel, allowed commutation, - - - - do. June 12, do.
White, Anthony Walton, representatives of, allowing their claim, - do. July 7, do
Williams, Daniel, representatives of, allowed commutation, - - do. July 7, do
Witherell, James, allowed commutation, - - - - do. May 25, do.

# INDEX.

## A.

# F.

## H.

L.

M.